The passage from observation to generalization is no simple and assured matter. A deliberate method must be followed, setting up safeguards against unfair sampling and over-hasty generalizations. The required method is called "empirical" because it draws its data from publicly shared types of experience, which is what the ancient Greek word empeiria *connotated; and it maintains its public character at every step in that its findings can be checked by any competent observer. It is the method of science.*

—Philip Wheelright, philosopher

The Way of Philosophy

Before there could be science in the modern sense, it was necessary for [humans] to develop a lively curiosity about the world they lived in and to try to satisfy this curiosity by looking at the world rather than by peering into ancient tomes written by Aristotle or Galen or Augustine or Isidore of Seville. There had to be, in a word, a drastic change in the conception of authority, from that of the written word, especially the inspired word of God, to that of nature and empirical fact.

—W.T. Jones, historian

A History of Western Philosophy

It is fair to say that many of the foundations of social thought or sociological theories were laid down long before World War II, and that should be evident to everyone in the field. Indeed, it is quite striking, if one stops to think about it, that to this day, as we near the end of the century, the fundamental sociological theorists who are invoked by a very wide range of contemporary sociologists stand at the very early part of the century . . . . What has developed, I think, is a continuing specification of general ideas, and above all, a much more demanding form of empirical investigation than any of our founding fathers engaged in.

—Robert K. Merton, sociologist

Footnotes

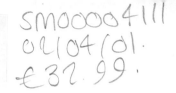

EMPIRICAL APPROACHES TO SOCIOLOGY

A COLLECTION OF CLASSIC AND CONTEMPORARY READINGS

THIRD EDITION

GREGG LEE CARTER

Bryant College

ALLYN AND BACON

Boston • London • Toronto • Sydney • Tokyo • Singapore

Series Editor: Jeff Lasser
Senior Editorial-Production Administrator: Joe Sweeney
Editorial-Production Service: Walsh & Associates, Inc.
Composition Buyer: Linda Cox
Manufacturing Buyer: Suzanne Lareau
Cover Administrator: Brian Gogolin

Internet: www.abacon.com

Library of Congress Cataloging-in-Publication Data

Carter, Gregg Lee
    Empirical approaches to sociology : a collection of classic and contemporary readings /
Gregg Lee Carter.—3rd ed.
        p.   cm.
    Includes bibliographical references.
    ISBN 0–205–30814–7
    1. Sociology.   I. Title.

HM585.C37   2000
301—dc21   00–028858

Printed in the United States of America

10 9 8 7 6 5 4 3 2 1   04 03 02 01 00

CONTENTS

PREFACE   xi

INTRODUCTION   1

PART 1
THE PROBLEM OF SOCIAL ORDER   7

CLASSIC

1. SOCIAL ORDER AND CONTROL VIA CLOSE SOCIAL TIES:
THE EXAMPLE OF SUICIDE   9
Émile Durkheim

2. SOCIAL ORDER AND CONTROL VIA FORCE: THE EXAMPLE OF THE
EXPROPRIATION OF THE ENGLISH AGRICULTURAL POPULATION FROM THE
LAND   15
Karl Marx

CONTEMPORARY

3. SUICIDE IN AMERICA: A TEST OF DURKHEIM'S THEORY OF RELIGIOUS AND
FAMILY INTEGRATION   21
K. D. Breault

4. CHANGING PATTERNS OF RACIAL DISCRIMINATION? THE CONTINUING
SIGNIFICANCE OF RACE: ANTIBLACK DISCRIMINATION IN
PUBLIC PLACES   30
Joe R. Feagin

PART 2
ISSUES IN SOCIOLOGICAL RESEARCH   49

CLASSIC

5. ATTITUDES VS. ACTIONS AND THE PITFALLS OF QUANTITATIVE
"SURVEY" RESEARCH   51
Richard T. LaPiere

CONTEMPORARY

6. THE MENTAL HOSPITAL FROM THE PATIENT'S POINT OF VIEW: THE PITFALLS
OF PARTICIPANT-OBSERVATION RESEARCH   58
Raymond M. Weinstein

7. THE IDEA OF CONTEXTUAL EFFECTS   74
Gregg Lee Carter

PART 3
CULTURAL EXPLANATIONS OF HUMAN BEHAVIOR   81

CLASSIC
8. ETHNOCENTRISM   83
William Graham Sumner

CONTEMPORARY
9. INDIA'S SACRED COW   86
Marvin Harris

PART 4
SOCIETY   93

CLASSIC
10. THE SMALL-WORLD PROBLEM: THE MYTH OF MASS SOCIETY   95
Stanley Milgram

CONTEMPORARY
11. THE INTERDEPENDENCE OF SOCIAL JUSTICE AND CIVIL SOCIETY   103
Caroline Hodges Persell

PART 5
SOCIALIZATION   119

CLASSIC
12. SOCIAL CLASS AND PARENTAL VALUES   123
Melvin L. Kohn

CONTEMPORARY
13. FAMILY SOCIALIZATION AND EATING DISORDERS IN COLLEGE-AGE WOMEN   136
Sharlene Hesse-Biber and Gregg Lee Carter

PART 6
GROUPS   147

CLASSIC
14. THE EFFECTS OF GROUP PRESSURE ON THE MODIFICATION AND DISTORTION OF JUDGMENTS   149
Solomon E. Asch

CONTEMPORARY
15. SOCIAL GROUPS AND PSYCHOLOGICAL DISTRESS   158
John Mirowsky and Catherine E. Ross

16. SOCIAL SUPPORT AS A MODERATOR OF LIFE STRESS   169
Sidney Cobb

PART 7
INTERACTION   183

CLASSIC
17. OBEDIENCE TO AUTHORITY   187
Stanley Milgram

CONTEMPORARY
18. INTERNET PARADOX: A SOCIAL TECHNOLOGY THAT REDUCES SOCIAL INVOLVEMENT AND PSYCHOLOGICAL WELL-BEING?   198
Robert Kraut, Michael Patterson, Vicki Lundmark, Sara Kiesler, Tridas Mukopadhyay, and William Scherlis

19. INTERACTION: THE WORK WOMEN DO   217
Pamela M. Fishman

20. PHYSICAL ATTRACTIVENESS IN SOCIAL INTERACTION   227
Harry T. Reis, John Nezlek, Ladd Wheeler

PART 8
CRIME, DEVIANCE, AND SOCIAL CONTROL   239

CLASSIC
21. CONTROL THEORY AND JUVENILE DELINQUENCY   243
Travis Hirschi

CONTEMPORARY
22. TRAJECTORIES OF CHANGE IN CRIMINAL OFFENDING: GOOD MARRIAGES AND THE DESISTANCE PROCESS   260
John H. Laub, Daniel S. Nagin, and Robert J. Sampson

23. ON BEING SANE IN INSANE PLACES   268
D. L. Rosenhan

PART 9
INEQUALITY   283

CLASSIC
24. UP AND DOWN OPPORTUNITY'S LADDER   289
James Davis

CONTEMPORARY
25. COGNITIVE SKILL AND ECONOMIC INEQUALITY: FINDINGS FROM THE NATIONAL ADULT LITERACY SURVEY   299
Stephen W. Radenbush and Rafa M. Kasim

26. SOCIAL CLASS AND LIFE CHANCES: CHARTERING AND BARTERING: ELITE EDUCATION AND SOCIAL REPRODUCTION   311
Caroline Hodges Persell and Peter W. Cookson, Jr.

27. SOCIAL CLASS AND POLITICAL PARTICIPATION   326
Leonard Beeghley

PART 10
RACE AND ETHNICITY   337

CLASSIC
28. OCCUPATIONAL BENEFITS TO WHITES FROM THE SUBORDINATION OF
AFRICAN AMERICANS   343
Norval D. Glenn

CONTEMPORARY
29. THE CONTINUING SIGNIFICANCE OF RACE REVISITED: A STUDY OF RACE,
CLASS, AND QUALITY OF LIFE IN AMERICA, 1972 TO 1996   347
Michael Hughes and Melvin E. Thomas

30. RACE, CULTURAL CAPITAL, AND SCHOOLING: AN ANALYSIS OF TRENDS IN
THE UNITED STATES   355
Matthijs Kalmijn and Gerbert Kraaykamp

31. BLACK GHETTOIZATION AND SOCIAL MOBILITY   363
Norman Fainstein

32. RACIAL PROGRESS   376
Abigail and Stephan Thernstrom

PART 11
GENDER   379

CLASSIC
33. SOCIALIZATION, GENETICS, AND GENDER ROLES   383
John Money and Anke A. Ehrhardt

CONTEMPORARY
34. MEN AS SUCCESS OBJECTS AND WOMEN AS SEX OBJECTS: A STUDY OF
PERSONAL ADVERTISEMENTS   391
Simon Davis

35. THE RELATIONSHIP BETWEEN WEIGHT AND CAREER PAYOFFS AMONG
WOMEN   397
Katherine M. Haskins and H. Edward Ransford

36. GENDER INEQUALITY AND SOCIALIZATION: THE INFLUENCES OF FAMILY,
SCHOOL, PEERS, AND THE MEDIA   409
Gregg Lee Carter and Sharlene Hesse-Biber

PART 12
SOCIAL CHANGE AND SOCIAL CONFLICT   429

CLASSIC
37. THE SUCCESS OF THE UNRULY   421
     William A. Gamson

CONTEMPORARY
38. A CROSS-CULTURAL THEORY OF POLITICAL CONFLICT
     AND VIOLENCE   448
     Marc Howard Ross

39. THE GREAT DISRUPTION: HUMAN NATURE AND RECONSTITUTION
     OF SOCIAL ORDER   460
     Francis Fukuyama

40. INSTRUMENTALISM AND THE SOCIAL CONSEQUENCES OF TECHNOLOGICAL
     CHOICE   478
     William Graves III

*Where is sociology's comparative advantage? To me it's obvious. Unlike our
academic competitors, we know things about contemporary reality. We get out
there, we talk to real people, we draw our conclusions from data, not from
novels about sensitive young intellectuals, artificial indoor experiments,
inscrutable thoughts of recherché European pundits, the memoirs of retired
diplomats or ideology . . . [However,] the feature of contemporary sociology that
is perhaps its greatest strength—its solid factual base—is under-represented in
introductory sociology textbooks and anthologies, whereas the features of
relative weakness—its concepts, propositions, and theory—are over-represented.*
—James A. Davis[1]

WHAT SETS THIS READER APART

Typical collections of readings in sociology are long
on "concepts" and short on data. Thus, they cannot
but disappoint those of us who believe, with James
A. Davis, that an appreciation of how data and theory fit together is crucial to every sociology course—
indeed, that it is part and parcel of thinking
sociologically and thinking critically. Every selection
in this volume, in contrast, is rich in data and demonstrates the interplay between sociological insight and
the relevant empirical observations.

I have sought out essays that address significant
sociological issues, contain high-quality data, and use
elementary analysis techniques. This has resulted in
many selections with historical and cross-cultural
leanings, to wit, about a quarter of the authors use
historical developments to assist their interpretations
of current sociological issues and data. Similarly, a
quarter of the selections contain cross-cultural references and comparisons.

Unlike other readers, *Empirical Approaches* provides students with a primer for critiquing articles.
At first glance, this primer may seem biased toward
quantitative thinking. A deeper look, however, reveals
that it will carry students not only through quantitative arguments, but through qualitative ones as well;
not only through sociology, but through any empirical
discipline (from history to physics). In short, critical
thinking is critical thinking. Its essentials are universal and are structured to assess proposed answers to
the question "Why?" and to suggest alternatives.
(Why does the world look the way it does and why do
things unfold the way they do? Why do earthquakes
happen? Why do people get cancer? Why are some
people poor? To what extent do the proposed explanations seem plausible?)

Empirical Approaches to Sociology thus contains a formula for success for all students. The work
world of the twenty-first century will make great
intellectual demands. Corporate leaders and professional people of all kinds will be flooded with more
quantitative, more historical, more cross-cultural,
and more unfiltered information than ever before.
Sorting through this deluge and doing something with

---

[1]"Comment on the 'Essential Wisdom of Sociology',"
Teaching Sociology 18:4, p. 531, October, 1990.

it will require more and better critical thinking and analytical writing; it will also require an appreciation of both the cultural diversities and the social regularities that abound in our world. *Empirical Approaches* lays a foundation for these requisite skills in thinking, writing, and sociological insight.

Finally, for those with the inclination and the resources, the readings for each subfield of sociology (e.g., inequality, socialization) are accompanied by a series of computer exercises that allow students to use real data to explore the sociological issues raised. These exercises are found in the workbook *Doing Sociology with Student CHIP: Data Happy 3rd Edition* (available from Allyn and Bacon) and will hold special interest for empirically oriented instructors. They will appeal to instructors trying to bridge the gap between what they do as researchers and what they teach in the classroom. The computer exercises are not a prerequisite for using this book, but are the "icing on the cake" for those who enjoy using computers in the classroom.

THEORETICAL ORIENTATIONS AND CRITERIA USED TO SELECT ESSAYS

Empirical Approaches is theoretically eclectic and is based on the premise that all of the major theoretical perspectives in sociology have explanatory value, depending upon the particular phenomenon under study. I have made no attempt to present a meticulous balance of perspectives. Rather, I have evaluated each potential selection according to the following criteria: Is an important sociological concept elucidated? Does the argument involve evidence? Is the analysis of data straightforward? Happily, the results of this search did, in fact, yield an anthology well balanced between micro and macro perspectives, as well as among major theoretical orientations (functionalist, conflict, and interactionist).

The selections presented in *Empirical Approaches* do not contain complex quantitative techniques (multiple regression, factor analysis, and so on). Instead, they rely on one or more of the following: a comparison of means or medians, elementary tabular analysis (including partial tables), bivariate correla-

tions, and qualitative approaches. For clarity, I have simplified tables and figures while remaining faithful to the data patterns actually reported. I took care, however, to ensure that the presented relationships between independent and dependent variables are resilient to multivariable controls and withstand more complex statistical analysis. In addition, if the data in the "contemporary essays" (see table of contents) are not current to within five years, I verified that the relationships among independent and dependent variables are not substantially different in more recent publications.

It was no small task to ferret out essays significant in the intellectual history of sociology and containing data analysis techniques that the typical introductory student could comprehend. Like all scientists, sociologists write and prepare research findings for each other, not for the public or the average college student. Nevertheless, I was able to assemble a set of readable essays that come very close to fulfilling what C. Wright Mills calls the "promise of sociology"—that is, they reveal "the intimate realities of ourselves in connection with larger social realities."[2] That they do so with evidence is so much the better; indeed, it is the bedrock idea motivating this book.

CLASSIC ESSAYS AND CONTEMPORARY OUTGROWTHS

Sociology, like all sciences, is cumulative. Current researchers and theorists do not work in an intellectual void. They build their research and thinking on the work of their predecessors. Advances in knowledge are incremental. "Quantum leaps" do not occur. Repeated or similar studies lead slowly to the acceptance of some ideas about how the social world operates and lead slowly to the rejection of others. The flavor of this cumulative process is brought out in *Empirical Approaches*: Each section contains at least one classic statement in the subfield, followed by at least one contemporary outgrowth. In some instances, the connections between the classic and the contem-

---

[2]C. Wright Mills, *The Sociological Imagination* (New York: Oxford University Press), 1959, p.15.

porary selections are straightforward. In Part 1, for example, Durkheim's theory of social integration and suicide is reformulated and retested in the contemporary selection by K. D. Breault. In other instances, however, the connections between the old and the new are less direct; contemporary researchers, using social forms unknown or uncommon in earlier eras (e.g., the dual-career family, homeless shelters), explore general sociological principles that originated with classic thinkers.

Contemporary sociologists tend to write better than their classical forerunners. Consider the assessment of Durkheim scholar George Catlin: "Durkheim's work, in common with . . . many other [classical] sociologists, too frequently lacks distinction of manner and lucidity of style. [Moreover,] it sometimes fails to avoid belabored platitudes."[3] I agree. Therefore, to spare the student the burden of perusing the difficult prose of the classical writers, I have kept their selections fewer in number and as short as possible—but without, I hope, giving their ideas short shrift.

Contemporary sociologists use more accurate and more comprehensive data and possess improved means for indicating or measuring the concepts under investigation. They also tend to have a fuller appreciation of the ways in which social structure and social situations influence individual thought and behavior. Given the cumulative nature of science, we should expect these improvements in data, measurement, and sociological insight. Nevertheless, contemporary researchers more commonly refine or extend classical thinking rather than refute it; for this reason it is important for students to read the early "masters" of sociological thought as a prelude to contemporary works.

ORGANIZATION OF THE BOOK

After the introductory chapter on the art of critical reading, *Empirical Approaches to Sociology* contains twelve major sections, each representing a major subfield in sociology. The order of the sections is that of most introductory sociology textbooks, beginning with social theory, research methods, and culture; continuing with society, socialization, groups, and interaction; and ending with crime/deviance/social control, inequality, race and ethnicity, gender, and social change and social conflict (new to this edition). Within each section, after my preliminary comments highlighting major concerns of the subfield and introducing key concepts, there are one or more classic articles, followed by one or more contemporary outgrowths.

Those instructors who emphasize institutions will quickly note that there are no individual chapters devoted to the major social institutions—family, economy, education, religion, and government. However, an examination of the table of contents reveals that essays focusing on each institution have been interwoven throughout the anthology. More specifically, the essays by Breault, Carter and Hesse-Biber (both selections), Cobb, Davis, Durkheim, Fishman, Fukuyama, Hirschi, Kohn, Laub *et al.*, Mirowsky and Ross, Money and Ehrhardt, and Persell deal, in part, with the family; Fainstein, Harris, Marx, and Persell have varying focuses on the economy; Carter, Davis, Hirschi, Kalmijn and Kraaykamp, Persell and Cookson, and Raudenbush and Kasim partly center on education; Breault, Carter, and Harris variously emphasize religion; and, finally, Beeghley, Gamson, Marx, and Persell selectively concentrate on government. Indeed, every selection can be used to illustrate the workings of at least one of the five key social institutions.

ACKNOWLEDGMENTS

I would like to thank the following individuals for their reviews of this new edition: Louis Anderson (Kankakee Community College), James Coverdill (University of Georgia), Cornelius Riordan (Providence College), and Ronit Shemtov (Sienna College). Earlier editions profited from the reviews of Professors Anderson, Coverdill, and Riordan, as well as from those of Diane Balduzy (North Adams State College), Walter Carroll (Bridgewater State College),

[3]George E. G. Catlin, "Introduction to the Translation." Pp. xi–xii in Émile Durkheim, *The Rules of Sociological Method* (New York: Free Press), 1938.

Michael Fraleigh (Bryant College), Karen Frederick (St. Anselm College), William Frey (State University of New York–Albany), Jack Harkins (*emeritus* College of DuPage), Lawrence Hazelrigg (Florida State University), Sharlene Hesse-Biber (Boston College), Guillermina Jasso (New York University), Robert Koegel (State University of New York, Farmingdale), Judith McDonnell (Bryant College), Debra Miller (Kent State University), Helen Raisz (Trinity College), John Patrick Smith (Clemson University), and J. Dennis Willigan (University of Utah).

The staff of Bryant College is cheery and always helpful: For this new edition, Elaine Lavallee and her student aides performed many valued support services, as did my assistant Michael Vieira. Bryant has a first-rate small college library, with a uniformly excellent staff: Colleen Anderson, Beth Ephraim, Gretchen McLaughlin, and Paul Roske helped me track down many references. Rachel Davis, of Ithaca, is a peerless copy editor.

At Allyn and Bacon, Karen Hanson (Executive Editor) and Jeff Lasser (Series Editor) were enthusiastic and encouraging for the creation of this new edition, as was Senior Publisher's Representative Mylan Jaixen.

Finally, for their love and forbearance, I am grateful to my wife, Lisa, and to my children, Travis, Kurtis, and Alexis.

A PRIMER ON CRITICAL READING

This introduction sets forth the intellectual steps for critiquing each of the articles you are about to read. Together these steps form a foundation for reading and thinking critically; they have nearly universal applicability. You can use them not only in sociology, but also in all courses that have empirical content (virtually all the natural, social, and business sciences), whether or not the subject matter is quantitative. Moreover, once these steps are incorporated into your thinking, they can help you critique studies reported in the popular media and the arguments presented to you in everyday discourse.

The fundamental strategy for explanation in all empirical disciplines, including sociology, is the following: To explain is to account for change in one phenomenon (variable, thing) with changes in another phenomenon or set of phenomena (variables, things). If you reflect for a moment, it should become apparent that this strategy is also fundamental in everyday explanations of life's events. For example, why are you sad at some times and happy at others? Most likely, your mood changes in reaction to changes in the events, people, and situations in which you are involved. To give a concrete example from my own life: A few years ago, I was unhappy because a foot injury halted my training for the Rhode Island Marathon. In sum, changes in my physical well-being created changes in my training that, in turn, changed my mood. When one thing is explained by another, we say that the first is *dependent* on the second. The second is *independent*. Accordingly, my foot injury was an *independent variable* that explained the halting of my training (a *dependent variable*). Whether a variable is independent or dependent hinges upon the slice of reality under investigation. Thus, as we continue along the pathway of causation, the halting of my training becomes the independent variable that explained the change in my mood.

Because the world is complex, we can quickly begin discussing many variables simultaneously. As such, it is often helpful to diagram the causal connections among variables. In its simplest form, such a diagram reads from left to right, with arrows imparting the causal order. For example, we would diagram the variables at hand as follows: foot injury→halting training→unhappiness. Social scientists use the term *model* to describe an interrelated set of variables that represent a slice of reality.

The most important models are those that are explanatory (recall that to explain is to account for change in one variable with changes in another variable or set of variables). Much of the research in sociology, as in all the sciences, is organized around developing and testing explanatory models. However, even when this is not a primary aim, virtually all non-fiction writing is organized around some sort of model of the world and how it operates. As a critical reader, you must develop the ability to discern the model at hand.

The first step in critiquing an article or argument is thus to identify the model. This involves identifying the dependent and independent variables and ascertaining the relationship between them. Let us illustrate using the following Associated Press newspaper article:

Poverty More Than Race Increases Risk of Cancer, Panel Concludes

BETHESDA, MD (AP). *A federal advisory panel yesterday focused new attention on poverty—far more than race—as one of the most powerful and underestimated risk factors for cancer in America.*

Both inadequate access to health care and unhealthy habits among the poor contribute to the problem, the President's Cancer Panel was told.

"Poor people are more focused on day-to-day survival—and I'm afraid that health care more often takes a back seat," Health and Human Services Secretary Louis Sullivan told the panel.

Added Dr. Samuel Broder, director of the National Cancer Institute: "It is difficult for an individual to say, 'I'll go for a mammogram today' when you are worried about how to pay for dinner."

He linked the higher cancer rates for poor people to what he called "poverty-driven lifestyles" that may include unhealthy diets, greater use of alcohol and tobacco, occupational risks, and less access to medical care.

People living below the federal poverty level have a death rate from cancer that is twice as high as that for the rest of the population. Black men, who outnumber whites in poverty three-to-one, have a 25 percent higher risk of contracting cancer.

Dr. Harold Freeman, a surgeon at Harlem Hospital in New York and the first black person to lead the panel, said, "Race in itself is not the cause of death. It is a circumstance in which people live, basically defined by poverty" (Providence Journal, *July 10, 1991, p. 4).*

STEP 1: WHAT IS THE MODEL?

In identifying the model, you must first determine the key dependent variable(s). A *dependent variable* is the phenomenon or event that the researcher or author is trying to explain. It's what is being caused. When sociologists think about individuals (as opposed to a collection of persons, such as a group or the residents of a city), the most important dependent variables they seek to explain involve behaviors and attitudes. (Why do some people drink heavily, while others abstain totally? Why do some whites hate blacks, while other whites are indifferent to skin color?) In the newspaper article quoted earlier, the key dependent variable is *cancer* (or the odds of dying from cancer).

Next, you must identify the key independent variable(s). An *independent variable* is the thing that explains, in part, the dependent variable. It is a reason for, or a cause of, the dependent variable. When trying to explain individual behaviors and attitudes, sociologists are drawn strongly to independent variables that indicate the groups and social networks to which people belong. In the newspaper article, the key independent variable is *poverty* (purportedly much more important than *race*, which once was considered another key determinant of cancer risk). Poverty is linked to cancer via the intervening variables (variables that are simultaneously independent and dependent) of unhealthy diets, use of alcohol and tobacco, occupational risks, and access to medical care. In sum, poverty partly determines this latter set of variables, which, in turn, partly determine the odds of dying from cancer.

Next, you must be able to recognize the *form of the relationship* between the independent and the dependent variables. The easiest functional forms to conceptualize and to identify are the straight-line or linear. If two variables are linearly positively related, then increases in one are associated with increases in the other. If two variables are linearly negatively related, then increases in one are associated with decreases in the other. In the above article, poverty is positively related with unhealthy diets, the use of alcohol and tobacco, and occupational risks, whereas it is negatively related to access to medical care.

Especially when our subject of empirical inquiry is people and their behavior, thoughts, and feelings, explanation (i.e., accounting for variation in a dependent variable with variation in one or more independent variables) is not the same thing as understanding. Understanding is deeper; it is that "aha, I see" experience within us. As a critical reader, you must understand why the independent variables are important. This understanding depends on your ability to empathize with the people under study. In other words, you must not only identify each key independent variable, but also recognize the interpretation showing why it has the effect that it does. This interpretation may or may not be explicit. In the Associated Press article, Dr. Broder's interpretative comments give us a deeper understanding of the relationship between poverty and access to health care when he states, "It is difficult for an individual to say 'I'll go for a mammogram today' when you are worried about how to pay for dinner."

A picture is worth a thousand words, and the model becomes clearer when we diagram it. The fundamental rule for diagramming a model is to begin on the left and follow the causal flow to the right until you've entered the final dependent variable; that is, the independent variable(s) on the left, the intervening variable(s) in the middle, and the dependent variable(s) on the right:

$$X1 \longrightarrow X2 \longrightarrow Y$$
(Independent)   (Intervening)   (Dependent)

If we follow this rule, our model diagram comes out like this:

STEP 2: HOW IS EACH VARIABLE MEASURED?

Variables are concepts. Theories clarify the causal links among concepts. To apply or test a theory, it is necessary to specify these concepts in terms of their manifestations in the concrete world. This process is called *measurement*. Scientific articles, such as those found in this book, are very good at alerting us to the difference between conceptual variables and their measurements. Popular media articles and everyday arguments are not so good at this. Regardless, as a critical reader you must have the ability to distinguish a concept from its measurement, realizing that they are not the same thing. Measurement answers in concrete empirical terms the question: "By X, what do you mean?" ("By 'educational quality' of a college, what do you mean? Do you mean the grade point average of the student body? Do you mean the per-

centage of faculty members with doctoral degrees?"). Models tested with different measurements will yield different results, though the results will not differ by much if both measurements are fairly valid—that is, if they are truly indicative of the phenomenon under study. And what if a researcher finds that a particular X and a particular Y are *not* related as hypothesized? Then one must ask, Did the research turn out this way because the model is wrong (i.e., does not truly represent reality)? Or perhaps the model is right, but simply was tested incorrectly (e.g., with poor measurements)?

In the newspaper article quoted previously, measurement issues are given short shrift (and this should raise the eyebrows of the critical reader). Poverty is measured as living below the federal poverty line; although this line is not given here, it is readily available from the U.S. Bureau of the Census (in 1997, the poverty line for a family of four was a cash income of approximately $16,000; this line is updated each year to reflect changes in the Consumer Price Index). Cancer is measured as a group death rate from the disease (e.g., number of blacks dying from cancer per 1,000 blacks); we must assume that all cancers are involved. We do not know the data source, but we could obtain it by contacting the presidential panel at the National Cancer Institute in Bethesda, Maryland. No measurements are given for any other variable. Thus, we cannot specifically answer the question "By X, what do you mean?" for unhealthy diets, occupational risks, or access to health care. Similarly, we are not really sure what constitutes a dangerous level of alcohol or tobacco use.

STEP 3: HOW WELL DO THE DATA FIT THE MODEL?

Critical thinkers realize that data rarely, if ever, fit a model perfectly. In sociology a perfect fit is even rarer because our measurements tend to be crude and because human affairs are so complex that any one data set is unlikely to contain the full range of needed independent variables. Thus, the fit between models and data is a matter of degree.

One standard that many scientists use to judge how well data fit models is statistical significance. A pattern in the data (say, a positive correlation between X and Y) is considered statistically significant if it is unlikely that it could have occurred by chance alone. For example, slightly more than a half million females and slightly less than a half million males live in Rhode Island. If it were simply a matter of chance who ended up in prison, then we would expect a little less than half of the state's prison population to be male and a little more than half to be female. But that is not the case. The prison population of Rhode Island (as in every state) is overwhelmingly male (95 percent or higher). Thus, the data contain a strong pattern that is unlikely to be due to chance and that would support this model: Sex (male)→Crime.

In several of the articles in this book, researchers report whether their findings are statistically significant. At this point in your intellectual career, you should conclude that the data fit the model well if statistically significant associations are reported. At the same time, however, you should be developing an internal set of standards and an intuitive sense of how well the findings fit the model. For example, in the previously cited newspaper article, few data are reported (and none for the intervening variables and cancer rates), but those that are convincingly support the following: (1) poverty is linked to dying of cancer ("People living below the federal poverty level have a death rate from cancer that is twice as high as that for the rest of the population"), and (2) race is linked to poverty and cancer ("Black men, who outnumber whites in poverty three to one, have a 25 percent higher risk of contracting cancer"). Imagine, however, that the article had reported that those below the poverty line had a 27.2 percent chance of suffering cancer, while those above the line had a 26.4 percent chance. Even though this difference might be statistically significant given a population of tens of millions of people both below and above the poverty line (all things equal, the larger the sample size, the greater the likelihood of finding statistical significance), substantively and intuitively we would not be persuaded that the Poverty→Cancer model has much

explanatory worth. Indeed, we would be prompted to seek out other potential predictors of cancer with which to construct more powerful models. Finally, you should be developing internal standards and an intuitive sense of how well data fit models because some scholarly essays and many journalistic articles do not contain quantitative information and therefore will not use tests of statistical significance.

STEP 4: PROPOSE AN ALTERNATIVE MODEL BASED ON YOUR ASSESSMENTS IN STEPS 1–3.

By definition, a model represents only a thin slice of reality. It can always be made more or less complex (say, by adding or deleting additional independent variables). Up to this point, in Steps 1–3, all the critical readers of an article should have made similar assessments (the various components of the model are either there or are not; the measurements are either presented or are not; the data are significant in total, in part, or not at all). At Step 4 you can make your unique contributions as a reader and a critic. If you are fairly well convinced by the model, its measurements, and the findings, then your contributions in Step 4 will be minimal (adding another independent variable, for example, along with your rationale). On the other hand, if you find the model unconvincing, either on theoretical grounds or because the data simply do not fit it very well (especially if you think the measurements of the variables seem adequate), then your Step 4 contribution may result in a complete reworking.

In the newspaper article previously cited, the theoretical model rings true to me. Further, the data presented, though scant, fit the model well. Thus, my "alternative model" is a tinkering of the original model, not a major overhaul. It would seem to me that getting cancer would increase the odds of working less or quitting one's job altogether; it would also seem likely that a person's expenses would rise, as any insurance one had, private or public, would unlikely cover all medical costs. Thus, it seems reasonable to argue that cancer feeds back into poverty;

in short, not only does poverty lead to cancer, but cancer leads to poverty. My alternative model can be sketched as follows:

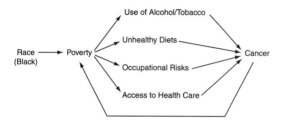

No matter what the model, you can always propose an alternative and produce a justification that appeals to intuition or collective common sense. (May your professor be generous in assessing your first efforts as a social theorist!)

Here, in summary form, are the steps we have been examining:

Steps Toward Critical Reading (and Thinking)
1. What is the model?
   a. What is the dependent variable(s)? (the phenomenon or the phenomena being explained)
   b. What are the independent variables? (the reasons for, or causes of, the dependent variable)
   c. How are the independent and the dependent variables functionally related? (e.g., as the independent changes, does the dependent variable increase or decrease?)
   d. Interpret the relationship between each independent and dependent variable. (What's happening in the world such that we would expect to find these two variables related?)
   e. Diagram the model.
2. How is each variable measured?
3. How well do the data fit the model?
4. Propose an alternative model based on your assessments in Steps 1-3.

A full appreciation of these steps takes practice. You must apply them again and again. However, even your initial use will sharpen your mind and reward you with insight.

A final comment: This brief primer on critical reading and thinking does not, of course, cover the full spectrum of analytic approaches to studying the world, in general, or the components of society, in particular. Instead, it lays a foundation upon which you can construct subtler and more sophisticated techniques of observation and analysis, whether the analysis involves reading, writing, researching, or just thinking. Indeed, such subtlety and sophistication will be apparent in many of the selections in this book.

PART 1

THE PROBLEM OF SOCIAL ORDER

The integration of society has always been a central concern of sociology. One may say that the root question of sociology is: how is social order possible?. . . It is hard to imagine how anyone could do sociology, even of a very limited sort, without implicitly dealing with this question.

—Peter L. Berger and Hansfried Kellne[1]

In the face of seemingly endless social change, what keeps society together and orderly? Major instigators of change include advances in technology, immigration, urbanization, industrialization, economic booms and busts, baby booms and busts, war, and civil unrest. Why do some societies, some groups, and some individuals thrive under shifting conditions, while others do not?

How individuals, groups, and societies achieve order in the face of social change was the central question that motivated classical sociology. We find some answers in the essays that follow.

French scholar Émile Durkheim (1858–1917) argued that order was rooted in the quality and quantity of social ties among individuals and groups. Along with Germans Karl Marx (1818–1883) and Max Weber (1864–1920), Durkheim was one of the most influential founders of modern sociology. All three had special interest in the political, social, and individual upheavals accompanying the industrialization of Europe in the eighteenth and nineteenth centuries. Durkheim was the first educator ever to hold the title of "professor of sociology." He spent his prolific academic career at the University of Bordeaux and at the Sorbonne. In his essay that follows, he examines one consequence of the weakening of social ties generated by industrialization—suicide.

Karl Marx viewed coercion and force as central to the maintenance of social order, with the lower classes being compelled to accept the dictates of the upper classes (more specifically, those who control the means of economic production). Unfortunately, many people only associate Marx with the *Communist Manifesto* and communism; however, he was also a dedicated and distinguished scholar. *Das Kapital*, his most rigorously researched work, was published in three volumes after his death by his colleagues Frederich Engels and Karl Kautsky. In the excerpt from *Das Kapital* published here, Marx demonstrates how the rich and powerful have used force and their control of the government to reshape society to meet their economic interests at the expense of the less affluent.

George Herbert Mead (1863–1931) held that social order was possible because individuals can learn—through social interaction—to empathize with one another, develop shared meanings of the world, and heed societal expectations of proper conduct. Because Mead did little empirical work, I have not excerpted his writings; however, his thinking has generated a host of sociological research and writing, which is represented here by Joe R. Feagin's contemporary essay (see below).

Contemporary sociologists answer the question of order by using essentially the same concepts: the quality and quantity of social ties, force and coercion, empathy, shared meanings, and societal expectations—as developed and enforced within the group and through social interaction—for proper conduct.

Kevin D. Breault, an associate professor of sociology at Austin Peay State University in Tennessee, confirms Durkheim's argument that weakened social ties can increase the likelihood of suicide. Durkheim and Breault demonstrate the fundamental precept of social science: that individual behavior can only be fully understood by examining social context, that is, the web of affiliations an individual has with other people.

The selection by Joe R. Feagin (University of Florida) serves a dual purpose. It not only supports Mead's claim that social order is negotiated and based on everyday interactions that are guided by socially enforced rules (or *norms*) of proper conduct, but also Marx's contention that those in power (in this case, white America) use force and coercion to repress weaker groups (in this case, black America) to maintain the existing social and economic hierarchy. More specifically, Feagin demonstrates that the generally weaker social and economic position of blacks in American society is reflected in the particulars of everyday interactions between whites and blacks, even middle-class blacks. He shows, for example, that blacks in public places (e.g., on the street) face insulting and discriminatory treatment that is much less frequently experienced by whites. Examples include avoidance actions, such as a white couple crossing the street when a black male approaches; rejection actions, such as poor service in restaurant and public accommodations; verbal attacks, such as shouting racial epithets in the street; physical threats and harassment by white police officers; and physical threats and attacks by other whites, such as attacks by white supremacists in the street.

NOTES _____

1. *Sociology Reinterpreted: An Essay on Method and Vocation* (New York: Anchor Books), 1981, p. 152.

CHAPTER 1

SOCIAL ORDER AND CONTROL
VIA CLOSE SOCIAL TIES:
THE EXAMPLE OF SUICIDE

ÉMILE DURKHEIM

We have thus successively set up the three following propositions:

- Suicide varies inversely with the degree of integration of religious society.
- Suicide varies inversely with the degree of integration of domestic society.
- Suicide varies inversely with the degree of integration of political society.

This grouping shows that whereas these different societies [i.e., social groups or social contexts] have a moderating influence upon suicide, this is due not to special characteristics of each but to a characteristic common to all. Religion does not owe its efficacy to the special nature of religious sentiments, since domestic and political societies both produce the same effects when strongly integrated. This, moreover, we have already proved when studying directly the manner of action of different religions upon suicide. [Similarly], it is not the special nature of the domestic or political tie which can explain the immunity they confer, since religious society has the same advantage. The cause can only be found in a single quality possessed by all these social groups, though perhaps to varying degrees. The only quality satisfying this condition is that they are all strongly integrat-

Reprinted with the permission of The Free Press, a division of Macmillan, Inc., from *Suicide: A Study in Sociology* (pp. 197–98, 208–10, 259–62, 271–72) by Émile Durkheim, translated by George Simpson. Copyright © 1951, 1979 by The Free Press. Original publication was in 1897.

ed social groups. So we reach the general conclusion: suicide varies inversely with the degree of integration of the social groups of which the individual forms a part.

But society cannot disintegrate without the individual simultaneously detaching himself from social life, without his own goals becoming preponderant over those of the community, in a word, without his personality tending to surmount the collective personality. The more weakened the groups to which he belongs, the less he depends upon them, the more he consequently depends only on himself and recognizes no other rules of conduct than what are founded on his private interests. If we agree to call this state egoism, in which the individual ego asserts itself to excess in the face of the social ego and at its expense, we may call egoistic the special type of suicide springing from excessive individualism.

But how can suicide have such an origin?

First of all, it can be said that, as collective force is one of the obstacles best calculated to restrain suicide, its weakening involves a development of suicide. When society is strongly integrated, it holds individuals under its control, considers them at its service and thus forbids them to dispose willfully of themselves. Accordingly it opposes their evading their duties to it through death. But how could society impose its supremacy upon them when they refuse to accept this subordination as legitimate? It no longer then possesses the requisite authority to retain them in their duty if they wish to desert; and conscious of its own weakness, it even recognizes their right to do freely what it can no longer prevent. So far as they are the admitted masters of their destinies, it is their privilege to end their lives. They, on their part, have no reason to endure life's suffering patiently. For they cling to life more resolutely when belonging to a group they love, so as not to betray interests they put before their own. The bond that unites them with the common cause attaches them to life and the lofty goal they envisage prevents their feeling personal troubles so deeply. There is, in short, in a cohesive and animated society a constant interchange of ideas and feelings from all to each and each to all, something like a mutual moral support, which instead of throwing the individual on his own resources, leads him to share in the collective energy and supports his own when exhausted.

MARITAL STATUS AND SUICIDE

[Table 1.1 supports the proposition for "domestic society" by showing] . . . that marriage has indeed a preservative effect of its own against suicide.[1]

[In short,] . . . the family is the essential factor in the immunity of married persons, that is, the family as the whole group of parents and children. . . .

TABLE 1.1   Influence of the Family on Suicide by Sex

MEN		
	SUICIDE RATE*	**COEFFICIENT OF PRESERVATION IN RELATION TO UNMARRIED MEN****
Unmarried men 45 years old	975	—
Husbands with children	336	2.9
Husbands without children	644	1.5
Unmarried men 60 years old	1,504	—
Widowers with children	937	1.6
Widowers without children	1,258	1.2
WOMEN		
	SUICIDE RATE*	**COEFFICIENT OF PRESERVATION IN RELATION TO UNMARRIED WOMEN*****
Unmarried women 42 years old	150	—
Wives with children	79	1.89
Wives without children	221	0.67
Unmarried women 60 years old	196	—
Widows with children	186	1.06
Widows without children	322	0.60

[*Per million inhabitants of France, 1889–1891]
[**Ratio of unmarried men to each category of marital status]
[***Ratio of unmarried women to each category of marital status]

DIVORCE AND SUICIDE

In the *Annales de demographie internationale* (September 1882), Bertillon published a remarkable study of divorce, in which he proved the following proposition: throughout Europe the number of suicides varies with that of divorces and separations.

If the different countries are compared from this twofold point of view, this parallelism is apparent (see Table 1.2). Not only is the relation between the averages evident, but the single irregular detail of any importance is that of Holland, where suicides are not as frequent as divorces.

The law may be yet more vigorously verified if we compare not different countries but different provinces of a single country. Notably, in Switzerland the agreement between the two series of phenomena is striking (see Table 1.3). The Protestant cantons have the most divorces and also the most suicides. The mixed cantons follow, from both points of view, and only then come the Catholic cantons. Within each group the same agreements appear. Among the Catholic cantons Solothurn and Inner Appenzell are marked by the high number of their suicides. Freiburg, although Catholic and French, has a considerable number of both divorces and suicides. Finally,

TABLE 1.2 Comparison of European States from the Point of View of Both Divorce and Suicide

	ANNUAL DIVORCES PER 1,000 MARRIAGES		SUICIDES PER MILLION INHABITANTS
Countries Where Divorce and Separation Are Rare			
Norway	0.54	(1875–80)	73
Russia	1.6	(1871–77)	30
England and Wales	1.3	(1871–79)	68
Scotland	2.1	(1871–81)	—
Italy	3.05	(1871–73)	31
Finland	3.9	(1875–79)	30.8
Averages	2.07		46.5
Countries Where Divorce and Separation Are of Average Frequency			
Bavaria	5.0	(1881)	90.5
Belgium	5.1	(1871–80)	68.5
Holland	6.0	(1871–80)	35.5
Sweden	6.4	(1871–80)	81
Baden	6.5	(1874–79)	156.6
France	7.5	(1871–79)	150
Wurttemberg	8.4	(1876–78)	162.4
Prussia	—		133
Averages	6.4		109.6
Countries Where Divorce and Separation Are Frequent			
Kingdom of Saxony	26.9	(1876–80)	299
Denmark	38	(1871–80)	258
Switzerland	47	(1876–80)	216
Averages	37.3		257

TABLE 1.3 Comparison of Swiss Cantons from the Point of View of Divorce and Suicide

	DIVORCES AND SEPARATIONS PER 1,000 MARRIAGES	SUICIDES PER MILLION		DIVORCES AND SEPARATIONS PER 1,000 MARRIAGES	SUICIDES PER MILLION
I. Catholic Cantons					
French and Italian					
Tessino	7.6	57	Freiburg	15.9	119
Valais	4.0	47			
Averages	5.8	50	Averages	15.9	119
German					
Uri	—	60	Solothurn	37.7	205
Upper Unterwalden	4.9	20	Inner Appenzell	18.9	158
Lower Unterwalden	5.2	1	Zug	14.8	87
Schwyz	5.6	70	Luzern	13.0	100
Averages	3.9	37.7	Averages	21.1	137.5
II. Protestant Cantons					
French					
Neufchatel	42.4	560	Vaud	43.5	352
German					
Bern	47.2	229	Schaffhausen	106.0	602
Basel (city)	34.5	323	Outer Appenzell	100.7	213
Basel (country)	33.0	288	Glaris	83.1	127
			Zurich	80.0	288
Averages	38.2	280	Averages	92.4	307
III. Cantons Mixed as to Religion					
Argau	40.4	195	Geneva	70.5	360
Grisons	30.9	116	Saint Gall	57.6	179
Averages	36.9	155	Averages	64.0	269

the mixed cantons, with the one exception of Argau, are classed in exactly the same way in both respects.

The same comparison, if made between French departments, gives the same result. Having classified them in eight categories according to the importance of their suicidal mortality, we discovered that the groups thus formed were arranged in the same order as with reference to divorces and separations [see Table 1.4].

One must seek the cause of this remarkable relation, not in the organic predispositions of people but in the intrinsic nature of divorce. As our first proposition here we may assert: in all countries for which we have the necessary data, suicides of divorced people are immensely more numerous than those of other portions of the population [see Table 1.5].

Thus, divorced persons of both sexes kill themselves between three and four times as often as mar-

TABLE 1.4   Suicide and the Prevalence of Divorce and Separation in French Departments

	SUICIDES PER MILLION	AVERAGE OF DIVORCES AND SEPARATIONS PER 1,000 MARRIAGES
1st group (5 departments)	< 50	2.6
2nd group (18 departments)	51–75	2.9
3rd group (15 departments)	76–100	5.0
4th group (19 departments)	101–150	5.4
5th group (10 departments)	151–200	7.5
6th group (9 departments)	201–250	8.2
7th group (4 departments)	251–300	10.0
8th group (5 departments)	> 300	12.4

ried persons, although younger (40 years in France as against 46 years), and considerably more often than widowed persons in spite of the aggravation resulting from the latter from their advanced age. What is the explanation? . . .

Now divorce implies a weakening of matrimonial regulation. Where it exists, and especially where law and custom permit its excessive practice, marriage is nothing but a weakened [shadow] of itself; it is an inferior form of marriage. It cannot produce its useful effects to the same degree. Its restraint upon desire is weakened; since it is more easily disturbed

and superseded, it controls passion less and passion tends to rebel. It consents less readily to its assigned limit. The moral calmness and tranquility which were the husband's strength are less; they are replaced to some extent by an uneasiness which keeps a man from being satisfied with what he has. Besides, he is the less inclined to become attached to his present state as his enjoyment of it is not completely sure: the future is less certain. One cannot be strongly restrained by a chain which may be broken on one side at any moment. One cannot help looking beyond one's own position when the ground underfoot does

TABLE 1.5   Suicides in a Million

		UNMARRIED ABOVE 15 YEARS		MARRIED		WIDOWED		DIVORCED	
		MEN	WOMEN	MEN	WOMEN	MEN	WOMEN	MEN	WOMEN
Prussia	(1887–1889)*	360	120	430	90	1,471	215	1,875	290
Prussia	(1883–1890)*	388	129	498	100	1,552	194	1,952	328
Baden	(1885–1893)	458	93	460	85	1,172	171	1,328	—
Saxony	(1847–1858)	—	—	481	120	1,242	240	3,102	312
Saxony	(1876)	555.18[†]		821	146	—	—	3,252	389
Wurttemberg	(1846–1860)	—	—	226	52	530	97	1,298	281
Wurttemberg	(1873–1892)	251	—	218[†]		405[†]		796[†]	

*There appears to be some error in the figures for Prussia here.—Ed.
[†]Men and women combined.—Ed.

not feel secure. Hence, in the countries where marriage is strongly tempered by divorce, the immunity of the married man is inevitably less. As he resembles the unmarried under his regime, he inevitably loses some of his own advantages. Consequently, the total number of suicides rises.[2]

NOTES

1. M. Bertillon . . . had already given the suicide-rate for the different categories of marital status with and without children. He found the following results:

Husbands w. children	205
Widowers w. children	526
Husbands w. no children	478
Widowers w. no children	1,004
Wives w. children	45
Widows w. children	104
Wives w. no children	158
Widows w. no children	238

These figures refer to [suicides per million and] the years 1861–68. Given the general increase in suicides, they confirm our own figures. . . [Ed. note: Only substantive footnotes are included in this selection.]

2. It will be objected that where marriage is not tempered by divorce the rigid obligation of monogamy may result in disgust. This result will of course follow if the moral character of the obligation is no longer felt. What actually matters in fact is not only that the regulation should exist, but that it should be accepted by the conscience. Otherwise, since this regulation no longer has moral authority and continues only through the force of inertia, it can no longer play any useful role. It chafes without accomplishing much.

_____CHAPTER 2_____

SOCIAL ORDER AND CONTROL VIA FORCE: THE EXAMPLE OF THE EXPROPRIATION OF THE ENGLISH AGRICULTURAL POPULATION FROM THE LAND

KARL MARX

In England, serfdom had disappeared in practice by the last part of the fourteenth century. The immense majority of the population[1] consisted then, and to a still larger extent in the fifteenth century, of free peasant proprietors, however much the feudal trappings might disguise their absolute ownership. In the larger seigniorial domains, the old bailiff, himself a serf, was displaced by the free farmer. The wage-laborers of agriculture were partly peasants, who made use of their leisure time by working on the large estates, and partly an independent, special class of wage-laborer, relatively and absolutely few in numbers. The latter were also in practice peasants, farming independently for themselves, since, in addition to their wages, they were provided with arable land to the extent of four or more acres, together with their cottages. Moreover, like the other peasants, they enjoyed the right to exploit the common land, which gave pasture to their cattle, and furnished them with timber, fire-wood, turf, etc.[2] In all countries of Europe, feudal production is characterized by division of the soil amongst the greatest possible number of sub-feudatories. The might of the feudal lord, like that of the sovereign, depended not on the length of his rent-roll, but on the number of his subjects, and the latter depended on the number of peasant proprietors. Thus although the

soil of England, after the Norman conquest, was divided up into gigantic baronies, one of which often included some 900 of the old Anglo-Saxon lordships, it was strewn with small peasant properties, only interspersed here and there with great seigniorial domains. Such conditions, together with the urban prosperity so characteristic of the fifteenth century, permitted the development of . . . popular wealth . . . [but not] in the form of capital.

The prelude to the revolution that laid the foundation of the capitalist mode of production was played out in the last third of the fifteenth century and the first few decades of the sixteenth. A mass of "free" and unattached proletarians was hurled onto the labour-market by the dissolution of the bands of feudal retainers, who, as Sir James correctly remarked, "everywhere uselessly filled house and castle." Although the royal power, itself a product of bourgeois development, forcibly hastened the dissolution of these bands of retainers in its striving for absolute sovereignty, it was by no means the sole cause of it. It was rather that the great feudal lords, in their defiant opposition to the king and Parliament, created an incomparably larger proletariat by forcibly driving the peasantry from the land, to which the latter had the same feudal title as the lords themselves, and by usurpation of the common lands. The rapid expansion of wool manufacture in Flanders and the corresponding rise in the price of wool in England

From *Capital, Vol. I* (New York: Vintage Books, 1977 [1867]), ch. 27, pp. 877–895.

provided the direct impulse for the evictions. The old nobility had been devoured by the great feudal wars. The new nobility was the child of its time, for which money was the power of all powers. Transformation of arable land into sheep-walks was therefore its slogan. . . .

The process of forcible expropriation of the people received a new and terrible impulse in the sixteenth century from the Reformation, and the consequent colossal spoliation of church property. The Catholic church was, at the time of the Reformation, the feudal proprietor of a great part of the soil of England. The dissolution of the monasteries, etc., hurled their inmates into the proletariat. The estates of the church were to a large extent given away to rapacious royal favourites, or sold at a nominal price to speculating farmers and townsmen, who drove out the old-established hereditary sub-tenants in great numbers, and threw their holdings together. The legally guaranteed property of the poorer folk in a part of the church's tithes was quietly confiscated. . . .

Even in the last few decades of the seventeenth century, the yeomanry, the class of independent peasants, were more numerous than the class of farmers. [However] . . . by about 1750 the yeomanry had disappeared, and so, by the last decade of the eighteenth century, had the last trace of the common land of the agricultural labourer. We leave on one side here the purely economic driving forces behind the agricultural revolution. We deal only with the violent means employed.

After the restoration of the Stuarts, the landed proprietors carried out, by legal means, an act of usurpation which was effected everywhere on the Continent without any legal formality. They abolished the feudal tenure of land, i.e. they got rid of all its obligations to the state, "indemnified" the state by imposing taxes on the peasantry and the rest of the people, established for themselves the rights of modern private property in estates to which they had only a feudal title, and, finally, passed those laws of settlement which had the same effect on the English agricultural labourer, *mutatis mutandis,* as the edict of the Tartar Boris Godunov had on the Russian peasantry [this was the Edict of 1857, by which peasants who

had fled from their lords could be pursued for five years and forcibly returned to them when caught].

The "Glorious Revolution" brought into power, along with William of Orange, the landed and capitalist profit-grubbers. They inaugurated the new era of practicing on a colossal scale the thefts of state lands which had hitherto been managed more modestly. These estates were given away, sold at ridiculous prices or even annexed to private estates by direct seizure. All of this happened without the slightest observance of legal etiquette. The Crown lands thus fraudulently appropriated, together with stolen Church estates, in so far as these were not lost again during the republican revolution, form the basis of the present princely domains of the English oligarchy. The bourgeois capitalists favoured the operation, with the intention, among other things, of converting the land into a merely commercial commodity, extending the area of large-scale agricultural production, and increasing the supply of free and rightless proletarians driven from their land. Apart from this, the new landed aristocracy was the natural ally of the new bankocracy, of newly hatched high finance, and of the large manufacturers, at that time dependent on protective duties. The English bourgeoisie acted quite as wisely in its own interest as the Swedish burghers, who did the opposite: hand in hand with the bulwark of their economic strength, the peasantry, they helped the kings in their forcible resumption of crown lands from the oligarchy, in the years after 1604 and later on under Charles X and Charles XI.

Communal property—which is entirely distinct from the state property we have just been considering—was an old Teutonic institution which lived on under the cover of feudalism. We have seen how its forcible usurpation, generally accompanied by the turning of arable into pasture land, begins at the end of the fifteenth century and extends into the sixteenth. But at that time the process was carried on by means of individual acts of violence against which legislation, for a hundred and fifty years, fought in vain. The advance made by the eighteenth century shows itself in this, that the law itself now becomes the instrument by which the people's land is stolen, although the big farmers made use of their little independent methods as well.[3] The Parliamentary form of the robbery is that of "Bills for Inclosure of Commons," in other words decrees by which the landowners themselves grant themselves the people's land as private property, decrees of expropriation of the people. Sir F. M. Eden refutes his own crafty special pleading, in which he tries to represent communal property as the private property of the great landlords who have taken the place of the feudal lords, when he himself demands a "general Act of Parliament for the enclosure of Commons" (thereby admitting that a parliamentary *coup d'état* is necessary for their transformation into private property), and moreover calls on the legislature to indemnify the expropriated poor.

While the place of the independent yeoman was taken by tenants at will, small farmers on yearly leases, a servile rabble dependent on the arbitrary will of the landlords, the systematic theft of communal property was of great assistance, alongside the theft of the state domains, in swelling those large farms which were called in the eighteenth century capital farms, or merchant farms, and in "setting free" the agricultural population as a proletariat for the needs of industry.

The eighteenth century, however, did not yet recognize as fully as the nineteenth the identity between the wealth of the nation and the poverty of the people. Hence the very vigorous polemic, in the economic literature of that time, on the "enclosure of commons." From the mass of material that lies before me, I give a few extracts chosen for the strong light they throw on the circumstances of the time. "In several parishes of Hertfordshire," writes one indignant person, "twenty-four farms, numbering on the average 50 to 150 acres, have been melted up into three farms."[4] "In Northamptonshire and Leicestershire the enclosure of common lands has taken place on a very large scale, and most of the new lordships, resulting from the enclosure, have been turned into pasturage, in consequence of which many lordships have not now 50 acres ploughed yearly, in which 1,500 were ploughed formerly. The ruins of former dwelling-houses, barns, stables, etc." are the sole traces of the former inhabitants. "An hundred houses and families have in some open field villages ...

dwindled to eight or ten ... The landholders in most parishes that have been enclosed only fifteen or twenty years, are very few in comparison of the numbers who occupied them in their open-field state. It is no uncommon thing for four or five wealthy grazers to engross a large enclosed lordship which was before in the hands of twenty or thirty farmers, and as many smaller tenants and proprietors. All these are hereby thrown out of their livings with their families and many other families who were chiefly employed and supported by them."[5] It was not only land that lay waste, but often also land that was still under cultivation, being cultivated either in common or held under a definite rent paid to the community, that was annexed by the neighbouring landowners under pretext of enclosure. "I have here in view enclosures of open fields and lands already improved. It is acknowledged by even the writers in defence of enclosures that these diminished villages increase the monopolies of farms, raise the prices of provisions, and produce depopulation ... and even the enclosure of waste lands (as now carried on) bears hard on the poor, by depriving them of a part of their subsistence, and only goes towards increasing farms already too large."[6] "When," says Dr Price, "this land gets into the hands of a few great farmers, the consequence must be that the little farmers" (previously described by him as "a multitude of little proprietors and tenants, who maintain themselves and families by the produce of the ground they occupy by sheep kept on a common, by poultry, hogs, etc., and who therefore have little occasion to purchase any of the means of subsistence") "will be converted into a body of men who earn their subsistence by working for others, and who will be under a necessity of going to market for all they want. ... There will, perhaps, be more labour, because there will be more compulsion to it. ... Towns and manufactures will increase, because more will be driven to them in quest of places and employment. This is the way in which the engrossing of farms actually operates. And this is the way in which, for many years, it has been actually operating in this kingdom."[7] He sums up the effect of the enclosures in this way: "Upon the whole, the circumstances of the lower ranks of men are altered in almost every respect for the worse. From little occupiers of land, they are reduced to the state of day-labourers and hirelings; and, at the same time, their subsistence in that state has become more difficult."[8] In fact, the usurpation of the common lands and the accompanying revolution in agriculture had such an acute effect on the agricultural labourers that, even according to Eden, their wages began to fall below the minimum between 1765 and 1780, and to be supplemented by official Poor Law relief. Their wages, he says, "were not more than enough for the absolute necessaries of life." . . .

By the nineteenth century, the very memory of the connection between the agricultural labourer and communal property had, of course, vanished. To say nothing of more recent times—have the agricultural population received a farthing's compensation for the 3,511,770 acres of common land which between 1801 and 1831 were stolen from them and presented to the landlords by the landlords, through the agency of Parliament?

The last great process of expropriation of the agricultural population from the soil is, finally, the so called "clearing of estates," i.e. the sweeping of human beings off them. All the English methods hitherto considered culminated in "clearing." As we saw in the description of modern conditions given in a previous chapter, when there are no more independent peasants to get rid of, the "clearing" of cottages begins; so that the agricultural labourers no longer find on the soil they cultivate even the necessary space for their own housing. But what "clearing of estates" really and properly signifies, we learn only in the Highlands of Scotland, the promised land of modern romantic novels. There the process is distinguished by its systematic character, by the magnitude of the scale on which it is carried out at one blow (in Ireland landlords have gone as far as sweeping away several villages at once; but in the Highlands areas as large as German principalities are dealt with), and finally by the peculiar form of property under which the embezzled lands were held.

The Highland Celts were organized in clans, each of which was the owner of the land on which it was settled. The representative of the clan, its chief or "great man," was only the titular owner of this property, just as the Queen of England is the titular owner of all the national soil. When the English government succeeded in suppressing the [internecine] wars of these "great men," and their constant incursions into the Lowland plains, the chiefs of the clans by no means gave up their time-honoured trade as robbers; they merely changed its form. On their own authority, they transformed their nominal right to the land into a right of private property, and as this came up against resistance on the part of their clansmen, they resolved to drive them out openly and by force. "A king of England might as well claim to drive his subjects into the sea," says Professor Newman . . . In the eighteenth century the Gaels were both driven from the land and forbidden to emigrate, with a view to driving them forcibly to Glasgow and other manufacturing towns.[9] As an example of the method used in the nineteenth century . . . the "clearings" made by the Duchess of Sutherland will suffice here. This person, who had been well instructed in economics, resolved, when she succeeded to the headship of the clan, to undertake a radical economic cure, and to turn the whole county of Sutherland, the population of which had already been reduced to 15,000 by similar processes, into a sheep-walk. Between 1814 and 1820 these 15,000 inhabitants, about 3,000 families, were systematically hunted and rooted out. All their villages were destroyed and burnt, all their fields turned into pasturage. British soldiers enforced this mass of evictions, and came to blows with the inhabitants. One old woman was burnt to death in the flames of the hut she refused to leave. It was in this manner that this fine lady appropriated 794,000 acres of land which had belonged to the clan from time immemorial. She assigned to the expelled inhabitants some 6,000 acres on the seashore—2 acres per family. The 6,000 acres had until this time lain waste, and brought in no income to their owners. The Duchess, in the nobility of her heart, actually went so far as to let these waste lands at an average rent of 2s. 6d. per acre to the clansmen, who for centuries had shed their blood for her family. She divided the whole of the stolen land of the clan into twenty-nine huge sheep farms, each inhabited by a single family, for the most part imported English farm-servants. By 1825 the 15,000 Gaels had already been replaced by 131,000 sheep. The remnant of the original inhabitants, who had been flung onto the seashore, tried to live by catching fish. They became amphibious, and lived, as an English writer says, half on land and half on water, and [therewith] only half on both.[10]

But the splendid Gaels had now to suffer still more bitterly for their romantic mountain idolization of the "great men" of the clan. The smell of their fish rose to the noses of the great men. They scented some profit in it, and let the seashore to the big London fishmongers. For the second time the Gaels were driven out.

Finally, however, part of the sheep-walks were turned into deer preserves. Everyone knows that there are no true forests in England. The deer in the parks of the great are demure domestic cattle, as fat as London aldermen. Scotland is therefore the last refuge of the "noble passion." "In the Highlands," reports Somers in 1848, "new forests are springing up like mushrooms. Here, on one side of Gaick, you have the new forest of Glenfeshie; and there on the other you have the new forest of Ardverikie. In the same line you have the Black Mount, an immense waste also recently erected. From east to west—from the neighbourhood of Aberdeen to the crags of Oban—you have now a continuous line of forests; while in other parts of the Highlands there are the new forests of Loch Archaig, Glengarry, Glenmoriston, etc. Sheep were introduced into glens which had been the seats of communities of small farmers; and the latter were driven to seek subsistence on coarser and more sterile tracts of soil. Now deer are supplanting sheep; and these are once more dispossessing the small tenants, who will necessarily be driven down upon still coarser land and to more grinding penury. Deer-

forests[11] and the people cannot coexist. One or other of the two must yield. Let the forests be increased in number and extent during the next quarter of a century, as they have been in the last, and the Gaels will perish from their native soil. . . . This movement among the Highland proprietors is with some a matter of ambition . . . with some love of sport . . . while others, of a more practical cast, follow the trade in deer with an eye solely to profit. For it is a fact, that a mountain range laid out in forest is, in many cases, more profitable to the proprietor than when let as a sheep-walk. . . . The huntsman who wants a deer-forest limits his offers by no other calculation than the extent of his purse. . . . Sufferings have been inflicted in the Highlands scarcely less severe than those occasioned by the policy of the Norman kings. Deer have received extended ranges, while men have been hunted within a narrower and still narrower circle. . . . One after one the liberties of the people have been cloven down. . . . And the oppressions are daily on the increase. . . . The clearance and dispersion of the people is pursued by the proprietors as a settled principle, as an agricultural necessity, just as trees and brushwood are cleared from the wastes of America or Australia; and the operation goes on in a quiet, business-like way, etc."[12]

[In sum], the spoliation of the Church's property, the fraudulent alienation of the state domains, the theft of the common lands, the feudal and clan property and its transformation into modern private property under circumstances of ruthless terrorism, all these things were just so many idyllic methods of primitive accumulation. They conquered the field for capitalist agriculture, incorporated the soil into capital, and for the urban industries the necessary supplies of free and rightless proletarians.

NOTES _____

1. The petty proprietors who cultivated their own fields with their own hands, and enjoyed a modest competence ... then formed a much more important part of the nation than at present. If we may trust the best statistical writers of that

age, not less than 160,000 proprietors who, with their families, must have made up more than a seventh of the whole population, derived their subsistence from little freehold estates. The average income of these small landlords ...

was estimated at between £60 and £70 a year. It was computed that the number of persons who tilled their own land was greater than the number of those who farmed the land of others' (Macaulay, *History of England,* 10th ed., London, 1854, Vol. 1, pp. 333, 334). Even in the last third of the seventeenth century, four-fifths of the English people were agriculturalists (loc. cit., p. 413). I quote Macaulay, because as a systematic falsifier of history he minimizes facts of this kind as much as possible. [Ed. note: Marx has a tendency to write very long and discursive footnotes, most of which are deleted from this chapter.]

2. We must never forget that even the serf was not only the owner of the piece of land attached to his house, although admittedly he was merely a tribute-paying owner, but also a co-proprietor of the common land. . . .

3. "[Big] farmers forbid cottagers to keep any living creatures besides themselves and children, under the pretence that if they keep any beasts or poultry, they will steal from the farmers' barns for their support; they also say, keep the cottagers poor and you will keep them industrious, etc., but the real fact, I believe, is that the farmers may have the whole right of common to themselves" (*A Political Inquiry into the Consequences of Enclosing Waste Lands,* London, 1785, p. 75).

4. Thomas Wright, *A Short Address to the Public on the Monopoly of Large Farms,* 1779, pp. 2, 3.

5. Rev. Addington, *Inquiry into the Reasons for or against Inclosing Open Fields,* London, 1772, pp. 37–43 passim.

6. Dr. R. Price, op. cit., Vol. 2, pp. 155–56. Forster, Addington, Kent, Price and James Anderson should be read and compared with the miserable prattle of the sycophantic MacCulloch, in his catalogue *The Literature of Political Economy,* London, 1845.

7. Price, op. cit., p. 147. . . .

8. Price, op. cit., p. 159. . . .

9. In 1860 some of the people who had been expropriated by force were exported to Canada under false pretenses. Others fled to the mountains and neighbouring islands. They were followed by the police, came to blows with them and escaped.

10. When the present Duchess of Sutherland entertained Mrs. Beecher Stowe, authoress of *Uncle Tom's Cabin,* with great magnificence in London to show her sympathy for the Negro slaves of the American republic—a sympathy she prudently forgot, along with her fellow aristocrats, during the Civil War, when every "noble" English heart beat for the slave-owners—I gave the facts about the Sutherland slaves in the *New York Tribune* ["The Duchess of Sutherland and Slavery," *New York Daily Tribune,* February 9, 1983]. . . .

11. The deer-forests of Scotland do not contain a single tree. The sheep are driven from, and then the deer driven to, the naked hills, and this is then called a deer-forest. Not even timber-planting and real forest culture.

12. Robert Somers, *Letters from the Highlands; or the Famine of 1847,* London, 1848, pp. 12–28 passim. . . . The English economists of course explained the famine of the Gaels in 1847 by referring to over-population. . . .

_____CHAPTER 3_____

SUICIDE IN AMERICA:
A TEST OF DURKHEIM'S THEORY OF
RELIGIOUS AND FAMILY INTEGRATION

K. D. BREAULT

Recently, [great] attention has been given to Durkheim's social integration theory of egoistic suicide. For egoistic suicide, Durkheim argues that suicide rates increase as religious, family, and political integration decrease . . .

In this paper, two parts of Durkheim's theory of egoistic suicide—religious and family integration—are tested with corrected and reliable U.S. church membership rates reliable and comparable divorce rates for the 50 states for six years between 1933 and 1980 and for 216 counties with populations of 200,000 or more in 1980. In addition, these same counties are analyzed for the year 1970. Moreover, the paper tests for a variety of control variables that have been related to suicide in previous research, that is, population change, income, urbanity, unemployment, and female labor-force participation . . .

Durkheim argues that religion provides protection from suicide because it promotes shared values, intense interaction, and strong social bonds. Religion, the family, politics, and the workplace are all social contexts or "societies" in which people are physically, emotionally, and psychologically bonded . . .

Durkheim argues that the larger the family one has and the greater the interaction there is in family life, the less likelihood there is of suicide. In order to test this thesis, Durkheim argues that married persons are more integrated than single, widowed, or divorced

From the *American Journal of Sociology*, 92 (1986), pp. 629, 632, 634–656. Reprinted by permission of the University of Chicago Press.

persons; widowed or divorced persons are more integrated than single persons; and married persons with children are more integrated than married persons without children.

CONTROL VARIABLES

In addition to religious and family integration, I analyze a set of variables that have been associated with suicide in previous research. The first of these, population change (i.e., percentage of population growth and percentage of different-county migrants, a measure of turnover) is a general indicator of social integration that was associated with U.S. suicide rates in the recent paper by Stark et al. (1983). Communities that have a stable membership are probably more highly integrated than those that are made up of newcomers and temporary residents. In fact, high rates of population change are related to the weakening of many kinds of voluntary organizations, including churches (Stark et al. 1983). To the extent that high rates of population change and turnover are related to impermanent interpersonal relationships and the lack of close attachments, population change would be expected to be related to suicide.

Per-capita income, urbanity, unemployment, and female labor-force participation are tested as additional controls. Breed (1963), Hamermesh and Soss (1974), and Powell (1958) have pointed to personal income and its correlates, including occupational status, in determining the likelihood of suicide. For example, using an economic approach, Hamermesh and Soss (1974) found a negative relationship between level of income and suicide. Their study, however, ignored the relevant social variables and urbanity and female labor-force participation, as well as some obvious facts about suicide, for example, the high suicide rates of young people. The main sample analyzed was also very small.

In addition, urbanity, long associated with the industrialization and modernization tradition in the suicide literature, has often been related to suicide and anomie (Morselli 1903; Halbwachs 1930; Krohn 1978; Stack 1978). Following some earlier work, Krohn's cross-national study suggests that urbanity is related to anomie and perhaps, therefore, to anomic suicide.

The fourth control variable is unemployment, which has been used in a large number of studies of suicide (e.g., Boor 1980; Henry and Short 1954; Pierce 1967; Platt 1984; Sholders 1981; Stack 1983b). Unemployment is often considered to be a measure of Durkheim's anomic suicide, but certain interpretive difficulties may be involved here. In his discussion of anomic suicide, Durkheim is talking mainly about economic crises and not about long-standing economic disturbances such as chronic unemployment. But it should be noted that Durkheim incorrectly considered economic crises to be endemic in the "transitional" period, a time of social and economic maladjustment between what he had earlier called mechanical and organic solidarity. Unemployment during the Great Depression would be a more appropriate indicator for Durkheim's theory. Nevertheless, chronic unemployment has been related to suicide in the literature, although usually it only slightly attenuates other, more important suicide correlates.

Female labor-force participation, a variable associated with the status integration tradition of Gibbs and Martin (1964; and see Gibbs 1969), has been related to suicide in some recent papers (e.g., Newman, Whittemore and Newman 1973; Stack 1978). According to status integration theory, suicide should vary to the extent that people occupy incompatible statuses. For women, it is argued that the greater the conflict between working inside and outside the home, the higher the susceptibility to suicide. New-

man et al. (1973) found a strong positive relationship between female labor-force participation and suicide in a study of 75 community areas in Chicago and 112 census tracts in Fulton County, Georgia. In a recent paper based on 1970 census data, Stafford and Gibbs (1985) found no support for status integration theory.

To summarize, there is a relatively small, generally supportive body of recent literature on Durkheim's social integration theory of egoistic suicide . . .

DATA AND METHODS

Bivariate and multiple-regression analysis was performed on the data. Suicide was the dependent variable; church membership, divorce, percentage of population change, percentage of different-county migrants, per-capita income, percentage of unemployment, and percentage of female labor-force participation were the independent variables. At the state level, the years for the analysis were 1933, 1940, 1950, 1960, 1970, and 1980. Data for all variables were available from 1950 to 1980. Some of the variables were not available for 1933 and 1940 (see below). From 1933 to 1950 the sample included 48 states for each year; from 1960 to 1980 the 50 states were included. At the county level, 216 counties with a population of 200,000 or more were analyzed for 1970 and 1980. County data for all variables were available for these years. The population cutoff of 200,000 (relaxed somewhat for 1970) was chosen because, on a year-to-year basis, suicide rates vary considerably in smaller population bases . . .

The data on suicide rates (per 100,000 population) come from the U.S. National Center for Health Statistics (*Vital Statistics of the United States*, 1933–80). Table 3.1 selectively presents the raw suicide and social integration data for the 35 highest- and lowest-ranking counties in suicide for 1980. Critics have reservations about officially reported data on suicide (e.g, Douglas 1967), but a growing body of literature suggests that although suicides are unreported in some local areas, systematic downward bias in suicide reporting is not of a magnitude to distort research findings significantly (Stack 1983b, p. 244). In particular, the empirical work of Pescosoli-

TABLE 3.1   Suicide and Social Integration Indicators for the 35 Counties Ranking Highest and Lowest in Suicide, 1980

COUNTY, STATE	SUICIDE	CHURCH MEMBERSHIP	DIVORCE	MIGRATION
San Francisco; California.	29.1	30.7	5.1	26.1
Denver, Colorado.	25.1	43.5	7.2	29.7
Clark, Nevada	23.9	29.7	18.1	42.4
Lee, Florida	20.9	41.9	7.9	37.1
Marin, California	20.8	27.0	6.5	30.2
Broward, Florida	20.7	41.3	6.1	32.6
Bernalillo, New Mexico	20.2	53.3	10.2	26.2
Dade, Florida.	20.0	44.3	7.0	22.1
Pinellas, Florida.	20.0	42.7	6.6	30.1
Jefferson, Colorado	19.7	28.8	6.8	39.1
Maricopa, Arizona	19.4	38.1	7.4	30.0
Sarasota, Florida.	19.1	42.0	6.9	35.4
Oklahoma, Oklahoma	18.9	61.2	8.1	22.3
Sonoma, California	18.7	28.9	6.8	29.3
Lucas, Ohio.	18.1	53.1	5.7	11.8
Multnomah, Oregon.	17.9	41.0	8.3	24.7
Riverside, California	17.9	29.8	6.1	35.9
Pima, Arizona	17.8	38.3	8.2	30.7
Polk, Florida	17.8	49.6	8.5	26.1
San Mateo, California	17.8	33.0	5.6	26.5
San Joaquin, California.	17.7	39.8	6.1	21.9
Arapahoe, Colorado	17.6	31.1	5.9	50.4
Palm Beach, California	17.4	45.6	6.4	32.5
Sacramento, California	17.3	30.7	7.2	25.0
Kern, California	17.2	40.3	6.8	23.0
New York, New York.	16.8	44.6	6.7	23.7
Richmond, Virginia	16.8	. . .*	5.5	22.9
Duval, Florida	16.7	47.8	9.9	20.2
Volusia, Florida	16.6	41.9	6.4	32.5
Adams, Colorado.	16.5	29.0	5.5	40.0
El Paso, Colorado	16.5	34.8	7.7	41.2
Lane, Oregon	16.5	29.5	7.8	30.3
Solano, California	16.5	29.8	7.1	30.2
Alameda, California.	16.4	35.6	6.0	22.7
San Diego, California.	16.2	29.8	5.6	31.4
Bronx, New York	8.8	55.6	4.2	13.2
Westmoreland, Pennsylvania	8.8	69.8	2.5	12.3
Will, Illinois.	8.8	59.9	3.6	25.5
Cumberland, North Carolina	8.7	39.7	5.3	37.4
Middlesex, Massachusetts	8.7	74.7	3.0	15.9
Norfolk, Massachusetts.	8.7	61.7	2.4	20.1
Ramsey, Minnesota.	8.7	62.1	4.1	19.1
Onondaga, New York.	8.6	62.3	3.8	15.3

(continued)

TABLE 3.1 Continued

COUNTY, STATE	SUICIDE	CHURCH MEMBERSHIP	DIVORCE	MIGRATION
Albany, New York	8.5	64.2	3.7	18.7
New London, Connecticut	8.5	46.2	5.6	32.4
Queens, New York	8.5	47.0	2.5	17.8
Douglas, Nebraska	8.4	58.7	5.2	17.5
Essex, Massachusetts	8.4	56.8	3.2	12.1
Monmouth, New Jersey	8.3	53.4	3.9	20.0
New Haven, Connecticut	8.3	64.8	4.3	13.6
Plymouth, Massachusetts	8.2	52.6	3.3	18.5
Bergen, New Jersey	8.1	75.8	3.3	16.0
Cook, Illinois	8.1	64.5	3.7	9.3
Erie, New York	8.1	75.8	3.6	7.3
Hartford, Connecticut	8.1	67.6	4.4	14.1
Nassau, New York	8.1	61.8	2.6	14.6
Burlington, New Jersey	8.0	48.8	4.4	27.6
Lancaster, Pennsylvania	8.0	55.9	3.1	13.5
Mercer, New Jersey	7.9	57.3	4.4	17.0
Cameron, Texas	7.8	78.1	3.5	17.6
Morris, New Jersey	7.6	53.7	3.6	23.5
Middlesex, New Jersey	7.3	65.1	4.4	19.9
Essex, New Jersey	7.1	59.7	3.1	11.8
Camden, New Jersey	6.9	59.1	4.1	17.2
Richmond, New York	6.9	64.8	2.7	18.3
Suffolk, New York	6.9	56.8	3.3	14.9
Union, New Jersey	6.8	74.9	3.2	15.2
Hidalgo, Texas	6.6	72.7	.6	16.8
Kings, New York	6.5	45.4	2.7	11.2
Hudson, New Jersey	6.3	72.9	3.3	14.7
Passaic, New Jersey	6.0	54.3	3.5	14.8
Rockland, New York	5.1	55.0	2.2	18.8

Note: Suicide rates averaged over three years. For the purposes of this table, ties were broken alphabetically. $N = 216$.
*Published data are apparently unreliable.

do and Mendelsohn (1986) suggests that the biases that official rates may include are often the result of competing cross-pressures on officials, the resulting official rates closely approximating the actual incidence of suicide. Still, not all suicide data are created equal. It is most likely that U.S. data are much more reliable than those in cross-national studies in which a variety of countries with different reporting and data-gathering methodologies are involved.[1] Finally, note that the present variables are neither age nor sex

specific because much of the relevant data are both dependent and independent variables is lacking. The reader should be aware that some sex and age groups are unusually susceptible to suicide: men and old and young people.

The indicator of religious integration is church membership. At the outset, it should be understood that church membership is not a perfect measure of Durkheim's religious integration variable. I suggest that an ideal measure would include not only affiliation or membership, as the one used here does, but a more complete measure of the degree of religiosity and the extent of involvement in and commitment to church and church-related activities. Unfortunately, such data do not exist. Church membership, therefore, is the next best choice, a category that covers much but not all of Durkheim's notion of religious integration . . .

My interpretation is that Durkheim's concept of social integration refers to the magnitude and intensity of people's ties or connections to one another (shared values being an important element in this). If this interpretation is correct (space limitations do not permit an extended discussion), then the more that people associate in religious societies or denominations (church membership), the higher the social integration is. Group association or membership is accordingly the key to Durkheim's theory of social integration.

Several studies have attempted the mammoth task of compiling church membership by state and county (National Council of the Church of Christ 1954; Johnson, Picard, and Quinn 1974; Quinn et al. 1982). As good as they are, however, these studies seriously underreport church membership rates, and they are of little value for ecologically sensitive research purposes (Stark 1987). In particular, members of many black denominations, Jews, and members of nonmainstream religious groups have not been counted. For example, the failure to include black denominations in the 1974 study resulted in the following church membership rates for these southern states: Louisiana, 59.8%, ranked eleventh; South Carolina, 52.4%, ranked twentieth; Mississippi, 51.5%, ranked twenty-third. Among the states that ranked higher than these southern states in the 1974 study were Massachusetts and Connecticut. When these rates were corrected for black denominations, Louisiana ranked second, Mississippi fifth, and South Carolina sixth, with 81.4%, 76.2%, and 71.9%, respectively. Needless to say, Massachusetts and Connecticut ranked lower. The 1982 study, which is an improvement over the earlier work, nevertheless undercounts church membership by more than 10% nationally and by 15%–25% for some southern states.

I use Stark's (1980, 1987) corrected church membership rates for 1971 and 1980, extend his correction procedures to the 1950 rates, and interpolate church membership rates for 1960. Because of the high degree of stability in church membership rates over time, interpolation is justified in this case. As a measure of the stability of church membership rates, Spearman's rank-order correlation coefficient for church membership by state for the two years 1950 and 1970 is r's = .89 (Pearson's r = .90). For 1933 and 1940, comparable data on church membership are lacking. In short, the new data on church membership I use may constitute the most reliable measure of religious integration extant.[2]

The indicator of family integration is divorce rate (per 1,000 population). Arguably, divorce is the most appropriate indicator of Durkheim's family integration variable. In previous studies, divorce is the most commonly used indicator of Durkheim's family integration and has the virtue of being one of his original indicators. More important, throughout his life, Durkheim considered divorce to be the main factor responsible for what he argued was the modern trend toward ever diminishing family integration (e.g., Lukes 1973, pp. 530–34). Other theoretically less satisfactory indicators of family integration, such as percentage of single people, behave in a manner similar to that obtained here and are highly correlated with divorce. An important paper by Gove and Hughes (1980) demonstrated strong effects of percentage living alone on suicide (see also Hughes and Gove 1981).

The divorce data come from the U.S. National Center for Health Statistics (*Vital Statistics of the United States*, 1933–80). Across states and counties, divorce rates are highly reliable and comparable. In their indicator of divorce. Breault and Barkey (1982) control for marriage. For cross-national studies this may be suitable, but for the U.S. the rate of first marriage would be the only reasonable control and it is not available.

The state-level population-change variable (*County and City Data Book*, 1950–80; *Statistical Abstract of the United States*, 1933–80). While this measure has been previously used as an indicator of social integration (Stark et al. 1983), it is not one of Durkheim's original variables. For Durkheim, societywide social integration is mainly mediated through social groups, for example, the family and religious groups. I note this difference because in my opinion the literature has not paid enough attention to the differences between Durkheim's theory and the various tests of his theory, including his own.

For the county-level analysis a more integration-sensitive population-change variable is employed—percentage of different-county migrants, that is, intercounty migration or turnover (*County and City Data Book*, 1950–80). Some counties that enjoy stability in population size nevertheless have extremely high turnover. The county-level operationalization of population change measures population turnover, unlike the cruder measure of population growth used at the state level.

Per-capita income data come from the U.S. Bureau of Economic Analysis (*Survey of Current Business*, 1933–80), percentage urban from the U.S. Bureau of the Census (*County and City Data Book*, 1950–80; *Statistical Abstract of the United States*, 1933–80), and unemployment and female labor-force participation rates from the U.S. Bureau of Labor Statistics (*Geographic Profile of Employment and Unemployment*, 1960–80) and the National Labor

Library. For 1933, reliable and comparable unemployment data are not available by state, and for that year and 1940 good data on female labor-force participation are also unavailable.

ANALYSIS AND RESULTS

Tables 3.2 and 3.3 present the matrices of correlation coefficients for the state-level analysis, 1950–80, and for the 216 counties in 1970 and 1980. The bivariate analysis shows that, in every year for which data are available, the social integration indicators—church membership, divorce, and population change—are strongly associated with suicide. In no year and at neither level of analysis are urbanity and female labor-force participation significantly related to suicide. In 1960, at the state level, income is significantly related to suicide in the positive direction, and unemployment is significantly related to suicide in four (1940, 1950, 1960, and 1970) of the five years for which data for the variable are available. In two of those years, 1940 and 1950, unemployment is strongly associated with suicide. At the county level, income is unrelated to suicide, but unemployment is moderately related to suicide in 1970.

As expected, church membership, divorce, and population change are all significantly related to one

TABLE 3.2 Matrix of Correlation Coefficients for State-Level Data, 1970 and 1980

	S	C	D	P	I	UR	UN	F
S	1.0	—.605*	.847*	.798*	.201	.018	.151	—.065
C	—.490*	1.0	—.588*	—.490*	—.450*	—.008	—.289*	.215
D	.705*	—.436*	1.0	.788*	.178	—.026	.106	—.116
P	.520*	—.424*	.712*	1.0	.069	—.073	.100	—.008
I	.063	—.355*	.098	.490*	1.0	.415*	.212	—.156
Ur.....	.116	.073	.156	.438*	.480*	1.0	.209	.036
Un	.350*	—.384*	.342*	.170	—.014	.113	1.0	—.046
F.....	—.193	.220	—.104	.207	.212	.232*	—.256*	1.0

Note: 1980 figures are found above the $r = 1.0$ diagonal, 1970 figures below. All coefficients represent linear relationships. S = suicide rate, 1970 and 1980. I = per-capita income, 1970 and 1980. C = church membership, 1971 and 1980. Ur = percentage urban, 1970 and 1980. D = divorce rate, 1970 and 1980. Un = unemployment, 1970 and 1980. P = population change, 1961–70 and 1971–80. F = female labor-force participation, 1970 and 1980.
*Correlations are significant at the. 05 level or better.

TABLE 3.3   Matrix of Correlation Coefficients for County-Level Data, 1970 and 1980

	S	*C*	*D*	*M*	*I*	*UR*	*UN*	*F*
S	1.0	−.542*	.505*	.281*	−.103	.052	.051	.087
C	−.524*	1.0	−.434*	−.588*	−.090	−.030	−.083	−.131
D	.569*	−.488*	1.0	.434*	.125	−.084	.017	−.018
M	.350*	−.386*	.469*	1.0	.171*	−.007	.051	.033
I	−.034	.026	−.217*	.165*	1.0	.192*	−.110	−.105
Ur	.108	−.058	.149*	.119	.134*	1.0	.113	.093
Un	.240*	−.365*	.334*	.049	−.321*	−.048	1.0	−.129
F	−.055	.082	−.062	.090	.026	.110	−.123	1.0

Note: 1980 figures are above the *r* = 1.0 diagonal, 1970 figures below. All coefficients represent linear relationships. *S* = suicide rate, 1970 and 1980. *I* = per-capita income, 1970 and 1980. *C* = church membership, 1971 and 1980. *UR* = percentage urban, 1970 and 1980. *D* = divorce rate, 1970 and 1980. *UN* = unemployment, 1970 and 1980. *M* = percentage different-county migrants, 1965–70 and 1975–80. *F* = female labor-force participation, 1970 and 1980.
*Correlations are significant at the .05 level or better.

another. Typically, at the state level, population change and divorce are more highly interrelated than the other variables, although that is not true at the county level. The reader is reminded that at the county level a different population-change variable (migrants/turnover) is being used. In 1970 and 1980, at the state level, population change and divorce are very highly intercorrelated, but for the same years at the county level more moderate intercorrelations between migrants and divorce obtain. In all, despite some dramatic shifts in unemployment and population patterns over the years of the study, the bivariate correlations are remarkably stable. Finally, I found no significant nonlinear results in the bivariate analysis . . .

[In] the multiple-regression analysis church membership and divorce are among the most important factors explaining suicide . . .

SUMMARY AND DISCUSSION

This paper provides support for Durkheim's social integration variables and his theory of egoistic suicide. At six years (1933, 1940, 1950, 1960, 1970, and 1980) and at two levels of analysis (county and state) church membership and divorce are among the strongest determinants of suicide rates in a set of variables that included economic and social change indicators. The consistency of these results over the 47 years of the study is all the more impressive when it is noted that suicide, divorce, and church membership have all undergone significant change. After the Great Depression, suicide rates fell, only to increase in recent decades. Divorce rates have also gone up dramatically, while church membership rates have fallen. The results of the county-level analysis represent a downward internal replication of the state-level results . . .

Population change, an indicator connected to Durkheim's overall conception of social integration, but not one of his original variables, did not work as well as church membership and divorce. In every year studied but 1980, population change was not related to suicide after controlling for the other indicators. In 1970 and 1980, at the county level, the migration indicator is less strongly related to suicide than is either church membership or divorce . . .[3]

I cannot fail to comment on the striking lack of social integration (as measured here) in the western part of the United States (Table 3.1). This is true not only for California and Nevada but also for such disparate states as Alaska and Arizona, Oregon and Colorado, and New Mexico and Montana, and this pattern varies little during the 47 years encompassed by the study. The West is consistently high in suicide, divorce, population growth, and turnover and consistently low in church membership. Decreasing rates of social integration for the South were also found, and in the future the South should approach the West in suicide rates. Today suicide rates are rising faster in the South than in any other part of the country (see Miller 1980). Between 1960 and 1980, suicide rates for all states increased an average of 26%. This is no small increase, but during the same period in nine Southern states suicide rates increased over 40%. Leading the way were South Carolina (70.8%), Texas (56.6%), Louisiana (51.8%), Georgia (47.9%), and Oklahoma (47.1%).

Most of the economic and social change indicators I used were found to be unrelated to suicide after controlling for the social integration indicators. This does not mean definitively that these variables are not important in suicide, but rather that in this study they are of little importance. It should be strongly stressed that future research should continue to explore economic and social change variables but in conjunction with social integration variables . . .

NOTES

1. There is a variety of reasons why cross-national studies of suicide are methodologically flawed. Suicide rates, measures of religious integration, divorce rates, as well as modernization indicators (deriving from the modernization-biased set of nations for which data are available) are all suspect cross-nationally. The same can be said of control variables such as unemployment and female labor-force participation, both of which are not strictly comparable across any large number of nations. Obviously, this criticism is very damaging to Durkheim's own empirical study, *Suicide*.

2. Stark's correction procedures can be applied to the county level only with great difficulty. In the present study, 1980 county-level data were left as is, without correction. For the less reliable 1970 data, I used the following correction procedure. Only counties in states known to have undercounted church members significantly were considered for correction. In addition, in these mostly southern states, the 1980 church membership rate was substituted if the 1970 county figure was 15 percentage points lower than the 1980 figure. Only about 8% of the sample was so corrected. This procedure allowed the largest undercounting errors to be dealt with in a conservative manner. The result of the correction was to increase support slightly for the theory being tested.

3. *Author's postscript:* Research since 1986 gives us a better understanding of Durkheim's theory and suicide. A study I published in 1988 (*American Journal of Sociology*, v. 93, pp. 1479–86) showed that with the full set of counties, divorce remains a very important suicide correlate. One of my recent studies—conducted with one of my former students (*Social Forces*, 1995, v. 74, pp. 1479–86)— of *individuals* as opposed to aggregates like counties or states, found mixed results for Durkheim's social integration-suicide hypothesis. While divorced or separated men have significantly higher risks of suicide, single and widowed men are not at increased risk when socioeconomic status is controlled. More generally, researches have been slow to incorporate psychological variables, and because factors such as depression and alcohol abuse are important in psychological research, we will not know if Durkheim was right until social integration and psychological factors are simultaneously controlled.

REFERENCES

Boor, Myron. 1980. "Relationships between Unemployment Rates and Suicide Rates in Eight Countries, 1962–76." *Psychological Reports* 47:1095–1101.

Breault, K. D., and Karen Barkey. 1982. "A Comparative Analysis of Durkheim's Theory of Egoistic Suicide." *Sociological Quarterly* 23:321–31.

Breed, Warren. 1963. "Occupational Mobility and Suicide." *American Sociological Review* 28:179–88.

Douglas, Jack. 1967. *The Social Meanings of Suicide.* Princeton, N.J.: Princeton University Press.

Gibbs, Jack P. 1969. "Marital Status and Suicide in the United States: A Special Test of the Status Integration Theory." *American Journal of Sociology* 74:521–33.

Gibbs, Jack P., and Walter P. Martin. 1964. *Status Integration and Suicide.* Eugene: University of Oregon Press.

Gove, Walter R., and Michael Hughes. 1980. "Reexamining the Ecological Fallacy: A Study in which Aggregate Data Are Critical in Investigating the Pathological Effects of Living Alone." *Social Forces* 58:1157–77.

Halbwachs, Maurice. (1930) 1978. *The Causes of Suicide.* London: Routledge & Kegan Paul.

Hamermesh, Daniel, and Neal M. Soss. 1974. "An Economic Theory of Suicide." *Journal of Political Economy* 82:83–98.

Henry, Andrew F., and James F. Short, Jr. 1954. "Living Alone, Social Integration, and Mental Health." *American Journal of Sociology* 87:48–74.

Hughes, Michael, and Walter R. Gove. (1981). "Living Alone, Social Integration, and Mental Health." *American Journal of Sociology* 87: 48–74.

Johnson, Douglas W., Paul R. Picard, and Bernard Quinn. 1974. *Churches and Church Membership in the U.S.* Atlanta: Glenmary Research Center.

Krohn, Marvin D. 1978. "A Durkheimian Analysis of International Crime Rates." *Social Forces* 57:654–70.

Lukes, Steven. 1973. *Emile Durkheim.* New York: Harper & Row.

Miller, Marv. 1980. "The Geography of Suicide." *Psychological Reports* 47:699–702.

Morselli, Enrico A. 1903. *Suicide: An Essay on Comparative Moral Statistics.* New York: Free Press.

National Council of the Church of Christ. 1954. *Churches and Church Membership in the U.S.* New York: National Council of the Church of Christ, U.S.A.

Newman, John, Kenneth R. Whittemore, and Helen G. Newman. 1973. "Women in the Labor Force and Suicide." *Social Problems* 21:220–30.

Pescosolido, Bernice A., and Robert Mendelsohn. (1986). "Social Causation or Social Construction of Suicide? An Investigation into the Social Organization of Official Rates." *American Sociological Review* 51:81–101.

Pierce, Albert. 1967. "The Economic Cycle and the Social Suicide Rate." *American Sociological Review* 32:457–62.

Platt, Stephen. 1984. "Unemployment and Suicidal Behavior: A Review of the Literature." *Social Science and Medicine* 19:93–115.

Powell, Elwin. 1958. "Occupation, Status and Suicide: Toward a Redefinition of Anomie." *American Sociological Review* 23:131–39.

Quinn, Bernard, Herman Anderson, Martin Bradley, Paul Goetling, and Peggy Shrine. 1982. *Churches and Church Membership in the U.S.* Atlanta, Glenmary Research Center.

Sholders, Mary Alice. 1981. "Suicide in Indianapolis, 1976–80." *Sociological Focus* 14:221–31.

Simon, Julian L. 1968. "The Effect of Income on the Suicide Rate." *American Journal of Sociology* 74:302–3.

Stack, Steven. 1978. "Suicide: A Comparative Analysis." *Social Forces* 57:644–53.

———. 1983b. "The Effect of the Decline in Institutionalized Religion on Suicide." *Journal for the Scientific Study of Religion* 22:239–52.

Stafford, Mark C., and Jack P. Gibbs. (1985). "A Major Problem with the Theory of Status Integration and Suicide." *Social Forces* 63:643–60.

Stark, Rodney. 1980. "Estimating Church Membership Rates for Ecological Areas." Funded by the National Institute of Juvenile Justice and Delinquency Prevention, Law Enforcement Assistance Administration, U.S. Department of Justice. Washington, D.C.: Government Printing Office.

Stark, Rodney. (1987). "Correcting Church Membership Rates: 1971 and 1980." *Review of Religious Research* 29:69–77.

Stark, Rodney, Daniel F. Doyle, and Jesse Rushing. 1983. "Beyond Durkheim: Religion and Suicide." *Journal for the Scientific Study of Religion* 22:120–31.

U.S. Bureau of the Census. 1933–80. *Statistical Abstract of the United States,* Washington, D.C.: Government Printing Office.

U.S. Bureau of the Census. 1950–80. *County and City Data Book.* Washington, D.C.: Government Printing Office.

U.S. Bureau of Economic Analysis. 1933–80. *Survey of Current Business.* Washington, D.C.: Government Printing Office.

U.S. Bureau of Labor Statistics. 1960–80. *Geographic Profile of Employment and Unemployment.* Washington, D.C.: Government Printing Office.

U.S. National Center for Health Statistics. 1933–80. *Vital Statistics of the United States,* Washington, D.C.: Government Printing Office.

CHAPTER 4

CHANGING PATTERNS OF RACIAL DISCRIMINATION?
THE CONTINUING SIGNIFICANCE OF RACE: ANTIBLACK DISCRIMINATION IN PUBLIC PLACES

JOE R. FEAGIN

Title II of the 1964 Civil Rights Act stipulates that "all persons shall be entitled to the full and equal enjoyment of the goods, services, facilities, privileges, advantages, and accommodations of any place of public accommodation . . . without discrimination or segregation on the ground of race, color, religion, or national origin." The public places emphasized in the act are restaurants, hotels, and motels, although racial discrimination occurs in many other public places. Those black Americans who would make the greatest use of these public accommodations and certain other public places would be middle-class, i.e., those with the requisite resources.

White public opinion and many scholars have accented the great progress against traditional discrimination recently made by the black middle class. A National Research Council report on black Americans noted that by the mid-1970s many Americans "believed that . . . the Civil Rights Act of 1964 had led to broad-scale elimination of discrimination against blacks in public accommodations" (Jaynes and Williams 1989, p. 84). In interviews with whites in the late 1970s and early 1980s, Blauner (1989, 197)

found that all but one viewed the 1970s as an era of great racial progress for American race relations. With some exceptions (see Collins 1983; Landry 1987; Willie 1983), much recent analysis of middle-class blacks by social scientists has emphasized the massive progress made since 1964 in areas where there had been substantial barriers, including public accommodations. Racial discrimination as a continuing and major problem for middle-class blacks has been downplayed as analysts have turned to the various problems of the "underclass." For example, Wilson (1978, 110–111) has argued that the growth of the black middle class since the 1960s is the result of improving economic conditions and of government civil rights laws, which virtually eliminated overt discrimination in the workplace and public accommodations. According to Wilson, the major problem of the 1964 Civil Rights Act is its failure to meet the problems of the black underclass (Wilson 1987, 146–7).

Here I treat these assertions as problematic. Do middle-class black Americans still face hostile treatment in public accommodations and other public places? If so, what form does this discrimination take? Who are the perpetrators of this discrimination? What is the impact of the discrimination on its middle-class victims? How do middle-class blacks cope with such discrimination?

From *American Sociological Review*. 1991, Vol. 56 (February): 101–116. Copyright © 1991 American Sociological Association. Reprinted by permission.

ASPECTS OF DISCRIMINATION

Discrimination can be defined in social-contextual terms as "actions or practices carried out by members of dominant racial or ethnic groups that have a differential and negative impact on members of subordinate racial and ethnic groups" (Feagin and Eckberg 1980, 1–2). This differential treatment ranges from the blatant to the subtle (Feagin and Feagin 1986). Here I focus primarily on blatant discrimination by white Americans targeting middle-class blacks. Historically, discrimination against blacks has been one of the most serious forms of racial/ethnic discrimination in the United States and one of the most difficult to overcome, in part because of the institutionalized character of color coding. I focus on three important aspects of discrimination: (1) the variation in sites of discrimination; (2) the range of discriminatory actions; and (3) the range of responses by blacks to discrimination.

Sites of Discrimination

There is a spatial dimension to discrimination. The probability of experiencing racial hostility varies from the most private to the most public sites. If a black person is in a relatively protected site, such as with friends at home, the probability of experiencing hostility and discrimination is low. The probability increases as one moves from friendship settings to such outside sites as the workplace, where a black person typically has contacts with both acquaintances and strangers, providing an interactive context with greater potential for discrimination.

In most workplaces, middle-class status and its organizational resources provide some protection against certain categories of discrimination. This protection probably weakens as a black person moves from those work and school settings where he or she is well-known into public accommodations such as large stores and city restaurants where contacts are mainly with white strangers. On public streets blacks have the greatest public exposure to strangers and the least protection against overt discriminatory behavior,

including violence. A key feature of these more public settings is that they often involve contacts with white strangers who react primarily on the basis of one ascribed characteristic. The study of the micro-life of interaction between strangers in public was pioneered by Goffman (1963; 1971) and his students, but few of their analyses have treated hostile discriminatory interaction in public places. A rare exception is the research by Gardner (1980; see also Gardner 1988), who documented the character and danger of passing remarks by men directed against women in unprotected public places. Gardner writes of women (and blacks) as "open persons," i.e., particularly vulnerable targets for harassment that violates the rules of public courtesy.

The Range of Discriminatory Actions

In his classic study, *The Nature of Prejudice*, Allport (1958, 14–15) noted that prejudice can be expressed in a series of progressively more serious actions, ranging from antilocution to avoidance, exclusion, physical attack, and extermination. Allport's work suggests a continuum of actions from avoidance, to exclusion or rejection, to attack. In his travels in the South in the 1950s a white journalist who changed his skin color to black encountered discrimination in each of these categories (Griffin 1961). In my data, discrimination against middle-class blacks still ranges across this continuum: (1) avoidance actions, such as a white couple crossing the street when a black male approaches; (2) rejection actions, such as poor service in public accommodations; (3) verbal attacks, such as shouting racial epithets in the street; (4) physical threats and harassment by white police officers; and (5) physical threats and attacks by other whites, such as attacks by white supremacists in the street. Changing relations between blacks and whites in recent decades have expanded the repertoire of discrimination to include more subtle forms and to encompass discrimination in arenas from which blacks were formerly excluded, such as formerly all-white public accommodations.

Black Responses to Discrimination

Prior to societal desegregation in the 1960s, much traditional discrimination, especially in the South, took the form of an asymmetrical "deference ritual" in which blacks were typically expected to respond to discriminating whites with great deference. According to Goffman (1956, 477) a deference ritual "functions as a symbolic means by which appreciation is regularly conveyed to a recipient." Such rituals can be seen in the obsequious words and gestures—the etiquette of race relations—that many blacks, including middle-class blacks, were forced to utilize to survive the rigors of segregation (Doyle 1937). However, not all responses in this period were deferential. From the late 1800s to the 1950s, numerous lynchings and other violence targeted blacks whose behavior was defined as too aggressive (Raper 1933). Blauner's (1989) respondents reported acquaintances reacting aggressively to discrimination prior to the 1960s.

Deference rituals can still be found today between some lower-income blacks and their white employers. In her northeastern study Rollins (1985, 157) found black maids regularly deferring to white employers. Today, most discriminatory interaction no longer involves much asymmetrical deference, at least for middle-class blacks. Even where whites expect substantial deference, most middle-class blacks do not oblige. For middle-class blacks contemporary discrimination has evolved beyond the asymmetrical deference rituals and "No Negroes served" type of exclusion to patterns of black-contested discrimination. Discussing race and gender discrimination in Great Britain, Brittan and Maynard (1984) have suggested that today "the terms of oppression are not only dictated by history, culture, and the sexual and social division of labor. They are also profoundly shaped at the site of the oppression, and by the way in which oppressors and oppressed continuously have to renegotiate, reconstruct, and re-establish their relative positions in respect to benefits and power" (7). Similarly, white mistreatment of black Americans today frequently encounters new

coping strategies by blacks in the ongoing process of reconstructing patterns of racial interaction.

Middle-class strategies for coping with discrimination range from careful assessment to withdrawal, resigned acceptance, verbal confrontation, or physical confrontation. Later action might include a court suit. Assessing the situation is a first step. Some white observers have suggested that many middle-class blacks are paranoid about white discrimination and rush too quickly to charges of racism (Wieseltier 1989, June 5; for male views of female "paranoia" see Gardner 1988). But the daily reality may be just the opposite, as middle-class black Americans often evaluate a situation carefully before judging it discriminatory and taking additional action. This careful evaluation, based on past experiences (real or vicarious), not only prevents jumping to conclusions, but also reflects the hope that white behavior is not based on race, because an act not based on race is easier to endure. After evaluation one strategy is to leave the site of discrimination rather than to create a disturbance. Another is to ignore the discrimination and continue with the interaction, a "blocking" strategy similar to that Gardner (1980, 345) reported for women dealing with street remarks. In many situations resigned acceptance is the only realistic response. More confrontational responses to white actions include verbal reprimands and sarcasm, physical counterattacks, and filing lawsuits. Several strategies may be tried in any given discriminatory situation. In crafting these strategies middle-class blacks, in comparison with less privileged blacks, may draw on middle-class resources to fight discrimination.

THE RESEARCH STUDY

To examine discrimination, I draw primarily on 37 in-depth interviews from a larger study of 135 middle-class black Americans in Boston, Buffalo, Baltimore, Washington, D.C., Detroit, Houston, Dallas, Austin, San Antonio, Marshall, Las Vegas, and Los Angeles. The interviewing was done in 1988–1990; black interviewers were used. I began with respondents known as members of the black middle class to knowledgeable consultants in key cities. Snowball sampling from these multiple starting points was used to maximize diversity.

The questions in the research instrument were primarily designed to elicit detailed information on the general situations of the respondents and on the barriers encountered and managed in employment, education, and housing. There were no specific questions in the interview schedule on public accommodations or other public-place discrimination; the discussions of that discrimination were volunteered in answer to general questions about barriers to personal goals and coping strategies or in digressions in answers to specific questions on employment, education, and housing. These volunteered responses signal the importance of such events. While I report below mainly on the responses of the 37 respondents who detailed specific incidents of public discrimination, in interpreting the character and meaning of modern discrimination I also draw on some discussions in the larger sample of 135 interviews and in five supplementary and follow-up interviews of middle-class blacks conducted by the author and two black consultants.

"Middle class" was defined broadly as those holding a white-collar job (including those in professional, managerial, and clerical jobs), college students preparing for white-collar jobs, and owners of successful businesses. This definition is consistent with recent analyses of the black middle class (Landry 1987). The subsample of 37 middle-class blacks reporting public discrimination is fairly representative of the demographic character of the larger sample. The subsample's occupational distribution is broadly similar to the larger sample and includes nine corporate managers and executives, nine health care or other professionals, eight government officials, four college students, three journalists or broadcasters, two clerical or sales workers, one entrepreneur, and one retired person. The subsample is somewhat larger than the overall sample, with 35 percent under age 35 vs. 25 percent in the larger sample, 52 percent in the 35–50 bracket vs. 57 percent, and 11 percent

over 50 years of age vs. 18 percent. The subsample is broadly comparable to the larger sample in income: 14 had incomes under $36,000, seven in the $36,000–$55,000 range, and 16 in the $56,000 or more range. All respondents had at least a high school degree, and more than 90 percent had some college work. The subsample has a somewhat lower percentage of people with graduate work: 39 percent vs. 50 percent for the larger sample. Both samples have roughly equal proportions of men and women, and more than sixty percent of both samples reported residing in cities in the South or Southwest—37 percent of the overall sample and 34 percent of the subsample resided in the North or West.

DESCRIPTIVE PATTERNS

Among the 37 people in the subsample reporting specific instances of public-place discrimination, 24 reported 25 incidents involving public accommodations discrimination, and 15 reported 27 incidents involving street discrimination. Some incidents included more than one important discriminatory action; the 52 incidents consisted of 62 distinguishable actions. The distribution of these 62 actions by broad type is shown in Table 4.1.

Although all types of mistreatment are reported, there is a strong relationship between type of discrimination and site, with rejection/poor-service discrimination being most common in public accommodations and verbal or physical threat discrimination by white citizens or police officers most likely in the street.

The reaction of these middle-class blacks reflect the site and type of discrimination. The important steps taken beyond careful assessments of the situation are shown in Table 4.2. (A dual response is recorded for one accommodations incident.)

The most common black responses to racial hostility in the street are withdrawal or a verbal reply. In most avoidance situations (e.g., a white couple crossing a street to avoid walking past a black college student) or attack situations (e.g., whites throwing

TABLE 4.1 Percentage Distribution of Discriminatory Actions by Type and Site: Middle-class Blacks in Selected Cities, 1988–1990

	SITE OF DISCRIMINATORY ACTION	
TYPE OF DISCRIMINATORY ACTION	PUBLIC ACCOMMODATIONS	STREET
Avoidance	3	7
Rejection/poor service	79	4
Verbal epithets	12	25
Police threats/harassment	3	46
Other threats/harassment	3	18
Total	100	100
Number of actions	34	28

TABLE 4.2 Percentage Distribution of Primary Responses to Discriminatory Incidents by Type and Site: Middle-class Blacks in Selected Cities, 1988–1990

	SITE OF DISCRIMINATORY ACTION	
RESPONSE TO DISCRIMINATORY INCIDENT	PUBLIC ACCOMMODATIONS	STREET
Withdrawal/exit	4	22
Resigned acceptance	23	7
Verbal response	69	59
Physical counterattack	4	7
Response unclear	—	4
Total	100	99
Number of responses	26	27

beer cans from a passing car), a verbal response is difficult because of the danger or the fleeting character of the hostility. A black victim often withdraws, endures this treatment with resigned acceptance, or replies with a quick verbal retort. In the case of police harassment, the response is limited by the danger, and resigned acceptance or mild verbal protests are likely responses. Rejection (poor service) in public accommodations provides an opportunity to fight back verbally—the most common responses to public accommodations discrimination are verbal coun-

terattacks or resigned acceptance. Some black victims correct whites quietly, while others respond aggressively and lecture the assailant about the discrimination or threaten court action. A few retaliate physically. Examining materials in these 37 interviews and those in the larger sample, we will see that the depth and complexity of contemporary black middle-class responses to white discrimination accents the changing character of white-black interaction and the necessity of continual negotiation of the terms of that interaction.

RESPONSES TO DISCRIMINATION: PUBLIC ACCOMMODATIONS

Two Fundamental Strategies: Verbal Confrontation and Withdrawal

In the following account, a black news director at a major television station shows the interwoven character of discriminatory action and black response. The discrimination took the form of poor restaurant service, and the responses included both suggested withdrawal and verbal counterattack.

> He [her boyfriend[was waiting to be seated. . . . He said, "You go to the bathroom and I'll get the table. . . ." He was standing there when I came back; he continued to stand there. The restaurant was almost empty. There were waiters, waitresses, and no one seated. And when I got back to him, he was ready to leave, and said, "Let's go." I said, "What happened to our table?" He wasn't seated. So I said, "No, we're not leaving, please." And he said, "No. I'm leaving." So we went outside, and we talked about it. And what I said to him was, you have to be aware of the possibilities that this is not the first time that this has happened at this restaurant or at other restaurants, but this is the first time it has happened to a black news director here or someone who could make an issue of it, or someone who is prepared to make an issue of it.
>
> So we went back inside after I talked him into it and, to make a long story short, I had the manager come. I made most of the people who were there (while conducting myself professionally the whole time) aware that I was incensed at being treated this way. . . . I said, "Why do you think we weren't seated?" And the manager said, "Well, I don't really know." And I said, "Guess." He said, "Well I don't know, because you're black?" I said, "Bingo. Now isn't it funny that you didn't guess that I didn't have any money (and I opened up my purse) and I said, "because I certainly have money. And isn't it odd that you didn't guess that it's because I couldn't pay for it because I've got two American Express cards and a Master Card right here. I think it's just funny that you would have assumed that it's because I'm black." . . . And then I took out my card and gave it to him and said, "If this happens again, or if I hear of this happening again, I will bring the full wrath of an entire news department down on this restaurant." And he

> just kind of looked at me. "Not [just] because I am personally offended. I am. But because you have no right to do what you did, and as a people we have lived a long time with having our rights abridged. . . ." There were probably three or four sets of diners in the restaurant and maybe five waiters/waitresses. They watched him standing there waiting to be seated. His reaction to it was that he wanted to leave. I understood why he would have reacted that way, because he felt that he was in no condition to be civil. He was ready to take the place apart and . . . sometimes it's appropriate to behave that way. We hadn't gone the first step before going on to the next step. He didn't feel that he could comfortably and calmly take the first step, and I did. So I just asked him to please get back in the restaurant with me, and then you don't have to say a word, and let me handle it from there. It took some convincing, but I had to appeal to his sense of, this is not just you, this is not just for you. We are finally in a position as black people where there are some of us who can genuinely get their attention. And if they don't want to do this because it's right for them to do it, then they'd better do it because they're afraid to do otherwise. If it's fear, then fine, instill fear.

This example provides insight into the character of modern discrimination. The discrimination was not the "No Negroes" exclusion of the recent past, but rejection in the form of poor service by restaurant personnel. The black response indicates the change in black-white interaction since the 1950s and 1960s, for discrimination is handled with vigorous confrontation rather than deference. The aggressive black response and the white backtracking underscore Brittan and Maynard's (1984, 7) point that black-white interaction today is being renegotiated. It is possible that the white personnel defined the couple as "poor blacks" because of their jeans, although the jeans were fashionable and white patrons wear jeans. In comments not quoted here the news director rejects such an explanation. She forcefully articulates a theory of rights—a response that signals the critical impact of civil rights laws on the thinking of middle-class blacks. The news director articulates the American dream: she has worked hard, earned the money and credit cards, developed the appropriate middle-class behavior, and thus has under the law a *right* to be served. There is defensiveness in her actions too, for she feels a need to legitimate her status by showing her purse and credit cards. One important factor that enabled her to take such assertive action was her power to bring a TV news team to the restaurant. This power marks a change from a few decades ago when very few black Americans had the social or economic resources to fight back successfully.

This example underscores the complexity of the interaction in such situations, with two levels of negotiation evident. The negotiation between the respondent and her boyfriend on withdrawal vs. confrontation highlights the process of negotiating responses to discrimination and the difficulty in crafting such responses. Not only is there a process of dickering with whites within the discriminatory scene but also a negotiation between the blacks involved.

The confrontation strategy can be taken beyond immediate verbal confrontation to a more public confrontation. The president of a financial institution in a Middle Atlantic city brought unfavorable publicity to a restaurant with a pattern of poor service to blacks:

> *I took the staff here to a restaurant that had recently opened in the prestigious section of the city, and we waited while other people got waited on. And decided that after about a half hour that these people don't want to wait on us. I happened to have been in the same restaurant a couple of evenings earlier, and it took them about forty-five minutes before they came to wait on me and my guest. So, on the second incident, I said, this is not an isolated incident, this is a pattern, because I had spoken with some other people who had been warmly received in the restaurant. So, I wrote a letter to the owners. I researched and found out who the owners were, wrote a letter to the owners and sent copies to the city papers. That's my way of expressing myself, and letting the world know. You have to let people, other than you and the owner, know. You have to let others know you're expressing your dismay at the discrimination, or the barrier that's presented to you. I met with the owners. Of course, they wanted to meet with their attorneys with me, because they wanted to sue me. I told them*

> *they're welcome to do so. I don't have a thing, but fine they can do it. It just happens that I knew their white attorney. And he more or less vouched that if I had some concern that it must have been legitimate in some form. When the principals came in—one of the people who didn't wait on me was one of the owners, who happened to be waiting on everybody else—we resolved the issue by them inviting me to come again. And if I was fairly treated, or if I would come on several occasions and if I was fairly treated I would write a statement of retraction. I told them I would not write a retraction. I would write a statement with regard to how I was treated. Which I ultimately did. And I still go there today, and they speak to me, and I think the pattern is changed to a great degree.*

This example also demonstrates the resources available to many middle-class black Americans. As a bank executive with connections in the white community, including the legal community, this respondent used his resources not only to bring discrimination to public attention but also to pressure a major change in behavior. He had the means to proceed beyond the local management to both the restaurant owners and the local newspapers. The detailed account provides additional insight into the black–white bargaining process. At first the white managers and owners, probably accustomed to acquiescence or withdrawal, vigorously resisted ending the blatant discrimination. But the verbal and other resources available to the respondent forced them to capitulate and participate in a negotiation process. The cost to the victor was substantial. As in the first incident, we see the time-consuming and energy-consuming nature of grappling with poor-service discrimination. Compared to whites entering the same places, black Americans face an extra burden when going into public accommodations putatively made hospitable by three decades of civil rights law protection.

The confrontation response is generally so costly in terms of time and energy that acquiescence or withdrawal are common options. An example of the exit response was provided by a utility company executive in an east coast city:

I can remember one time my husband had picked up our son . . . from camp; and he'd stopped at a little store in the neighborhood near the camp. It was hot, and he was going to buy him a snowball. And the proprietor of the store—this was a very old, white neighborhood, and it was just a little sundry store. But the proprietor said he had the little window where people could come up and order things. Well, my husband and son had gone into the store. And he told them, "Well, I can't give it to you here, but if you go outside to the window, I'll give it to you." And there were other [white] people in the store who'd been served [inside]. So, they just left and didn't buy anything.

Here the act seems a throwback to the South of the 1950s, where blacks were required to use the back or side of a store. This differential treatment in an older white neighborhood is also suggestive of the territorial character of racial relations in many cities. The black response to degradation here was not to confront the white person or to acquiesce abjectly, but rather to reject the poor service and leave. Unlike the previous examples, the impact on the white proprietor was negligible because there was no forced negotiation. This site differed from the two previous examples in that the service was probably not of long-term importance to the black family passing through the area. In the previous sites the possibility of returning to the restaurants, for business or pleasure, may have contributed to the choice of a confrontational response. The importance of the service is a likely variable affecting black responses to discrimination in public accommodations.

Discrimination in public accommodations can occur in many different settings. A school board member in a northern city commented on her experiences in retail stores:

[I have faced] harassment in stores, being followed around, being questioned about what are you going to purchase here. . . . I was in an elite department store just this past Saturday and felt that I was being observed while I was window shopping. I in fact actually ended up purchasing something, but felt the entire time I was there—I was in blue jeans and sneakers, that's how I dress on a Saturday—I felt that I was

being watched in the store as I was walking through the store, what business did I have there, what was I going to purchase, that kind of thing. . . . There are a few of those white people that won't put change in your hand, touch your skin—that doesn't need to go on. [Do you tell them that?] Oh, I do, I do. That is just so obvious. I usually [speak to them] if they're rude in the manner in which they deal with people. [What do they say about that?] Oh, stuff like, "Oh, excuse me." And some are really unconscious about it, say "Excuse me," and put the change in your hand, that's happened. But I've watched other people be rude, and I've been told to mind my own business. . . . [But you still do it?] Oh, sure, because for the most part I think that people do have to learn to think for themselves, and demand respect for themselves. . . . I find my best weapon of defense is to educate them, whether it's in the store, in a line at the bank, any situation, I teach them. And you take them by surprise because you tell them and show them what they should be doing, and what they should be saying and how they should be thinking. And they look at you because they don't know how to process you. They can't process it because you've just shown them how they should be living, and the fact that they are cheating themselves, really, because the racism is from fear. The racism is from lack of education.

This excessive surveillance of blacks' shopping was reported by several respondents in our study and in recent newspaper accounts (see Jaynes and Williams 1989, 140). Several white stereotypes seem to underlie the rejection discrimination in this instance—blacks are seen as shoplifters, as unclean, as disreputable poor. The excessive policing of black shoppers and the discourtesy of clerks illustrate the extra burden of being black in public places. No matter how affluent and influential, a black person cannot escape the stigma of being black, even while relaxing or shopping. There is the recurring strain of having to craft strategies for a broad range of discriminatory situations. Tailoring her confrontation to fit the particular discrimination, this respondent interrupted the normal flow of the interaction to call the whites to intersubjective account and make a one-way experience into a two-way experience. Forced into new situations, offending whites frequently do not know how "to process" such an aggressive response. Again we see how middle-class blacks can force a reconstruction of traditional responses by whites to blacks. The intensity of her discussion suggests that the attempt to "educate" whites comes with a heavy personal cost, for it is stressful to "psych" oneself up for such incidents.

The problem of burdensome visibility and the inescapable racial stereotyping by whites was underscored in the reply of a physician in an east coast city to a question about whether she had encountered barriers:

> Yes. All the time. I hate it when you go places and [white] people . . . think that we work in housekeeping. Or they naturally assume that we came from a very poor background. . . . A lot of white people think that blacks are just here to serve them, and [that] we have not risen above the servant position.

Here the discriminatory treatment comes from the white traveller staying in a hotel. This incident exemplifies the omnipresence of the stigma of being black—a well-dressed physician staying in an expensive hotel cannot escape. Here and elsewhere in the interview her anger suggests a confrontational response to such situations.

Middle-class black parents often attempt to protect their children from racial hostility in public places, but they cannot always be successful. A manager at an electronics firm in the Southwest gave an account of his daughter's first encounter with a racial epithet. After describing racist graffiti on a neighborhood fence in the elite white suburb where he lives, he described an incident at a swimming pool:

> I'm talking over two hundred kids in this pool; not one black. I don't think you can go anywhere in the world during the summertime and not find some black kids in the swimming pool. . . . Now what's the worst thing that can happen to a ten-year-old girl in a swimming pool with all white kids? What's the worst thing that could happen? It happened. This little white guy called her a "nigger." Then called her a "motherfucker" and told her to "get out of the god-damn pool." . . . And what initiated that, they had these lit-

> tle inner tubes, they had about fifteen of them, and the pool owns them. So you just use them if they are vacant. So there was a tube setting up on the bank, she got it, jumped in and started playing in it. . . . And this little white guy decided he wanted it. But, he's supposed to get it, right? And he meant to get it, and she wouldn't give it to him, so out came all these racial slurs. So my action was first with the little boy. "You know you're not supposed to do that. Apologize right now. Okay, good. Now, Mr. Lifeguard, I want him out of this pool, and you're going to have to do better. You're going to have to do better, but he has to leave out of this pool and let his parents know, okay?"

Taking his daughter back the next day, he observed from behind a fence to make certain the lifeguard protected her. For many decades black adults and children were excluded from public pools in the South and Southwest, and many pools were closed during the early desegregation period. These accommodations have special significance for middle-class black Americans, and this may be one reason the father's reaction was so decisive. Perhaps the major reason for his swift action was because this was the first time that his daughter had been the victim of racial slurs. She was the victim of cutting racist epithets that for this black father, as doubtless for most black Americans, connote segregated institutions and violence against blacks. Children also face hostility in public accommodations and may never shake this kind of experience. At a rather early point, many black parents find it necessary to teach their children how to handle discriminatory incidents.

The verbal responses of middle-class blacks to stigmatization can take more subtle forms. An 80-year-old retired schoolteacher in a southern city recounted her response to a recent experience at a drapery shop:

> The last time I had some draperies done and asked about them at the drapery shop, a young man at that shop—when they called [to him], he asked, and I heard him—he said, "The job for that nigger woman." And I said to the person who was serving me, "Oh my goodness, I feel so sorry for that young man. I didn't know people were still using that sort of language and saying those sorts of things." And that's the way I deal

with it. I don't know what you call that. Is that sarcasm? Sarcasm is pretty good. . . . Well I've done that several times. This being 1989 . . . I'm surprised that I find it in this day and time.

One white clerk translated the schoolteacher's color in a hostile way while the other apparently listened. Suggested here is the way many whites are content to watch overt racist behavior without intervening. The retired teacher's response contrasts with the more confrontational reactions of the previous examples, for she used what might be called "strategic indirection." With composure she directed a pointedly sarcastic remark to the clerk serving her. Mockery is a more subtle tactic blacks can use to contend with antilocution, and this tactic may be more common among older blacks. Later in her interview this angry woman characterizes such recurring racial incidents as the "little murders" that daily have made her life difficult.

Careful Situation Assessments

We have seen in the previous incidents some tendency for blacks to assess discriminatory incidents before they act. Among several respondents who discussed discrimination at retail stores, the manager of a career development organization in the Southwest indicated that a clear assessment of a situation usually precedes confrontations and is part of a repertoire of concatenated responses:

If you're in a store—and let's say the person behind the counter is white—and you walk up to the counter, and a white person walks up to the counter, and you know you were there before the white customer, the person behind the counter knows you were there first, and it never fails, they always go, "Who's next." Ok. And what I've done, if they go ahead and serve the white person first, then I will immediately say, "Excuse me, I was here first, and we both know I was here first," . . . If they get away with it once, they're going to get away with it more than once, and then it's going to become something else. And you have to, you want to make sure that folks know that you're not being naive, that you really see through what's happening. Or if it's a job opportunity or something like

that, too, [we should do the] same thing. You first try to get a clear assessment of what's really going on and sift through that information, and then . . . go from there.

The executive's coping process typically begins with a sifting of information before deciding on further action. She usually opts for immediate action so that whites face the reality of their actions in a decisive way. Like the account of the school board member who noted that whites would sometimes not put money directly in her hand, this account illustrates another aspect of discrimination in public accommodations: For many whites racial hostility is embedded in everyday actions, and there is a deep, perhaps subconscious, recoil response to black color and persona.

The complex process of evaluation and response is described by a college dean, who commented generally on hotel and restaurant discrimination encountered as he travels across the United States:

When you're in a restaurant and . . . you notice that blacks get seated near the kitchen. You notice that if it's a hotel, your room is near the elevator, or your room is always way down in a corner somewhere. You find that you are getting the undesirable rooms. And you come there early in the day and you don't see very many cars on the lot and they'll tell you that this is all we've got. Or you get the room that's got a bad television set. You know that you're being discriminated against. And of course you have to act accordingly. You have to tell them, "Okay, the room is fine, [but] this television set has got to go. Bring me another television set." So in my personal experience, I simply cannot sit and let them get away with it [discrimination] and not let them know that I know that that's what they are doing. . . .

When I face discrimination, first I take a long look at myself and try to determine whether or not I am seeing what I think I'm seeing in 1989, and if it's something that I have an option [about]. In other words, if I'm at a store making a purchase, I'll simply walk away from it. If it's at a restaurant where I'm not getting good service, I first of all let the people know that I'm not getting good service, then I [may] walk away from it. But the thing that I have to do is to let people know that I know that I'm being singled out for a separate treatment. And then I might react in any number of ways—depending on where I am and how badly I want whatever it is that I'm there for.

This commentary adds another dimension to our understanding of public discrimination, its cumulative aspect. Blacks confront not just isolated incidents—such as a bad room in a luxury hotel once every few years—but a lifelong series of such incidents. Here again the omnipresence of careful assessments is underscored. The dean's interview highlights a major difficulty in being black—one must be constantly prepared to assess accurately and then decide on the appropriate response. This long-look approach may indicate that some middle-class blacks are so sensitive to white charges of hypersensitivity and paranoia that they err in the opposite direction and fail to see discrimination when it occurs. In addition, as one black graduate student at a leading white university in the Southeast put it: "I think that sometimes timely and appropriate responses to racially motivated acts and comments are lost due to the processing of the input." The "long look" can result in missed opportunities to respond to discrimination.

Using Middle-Class Resources for Protection

One advantage that middle-class blacks have over poorer blacks is the use of the resources of middle-class occupations. A professor at a major white university commented on the varying protection her middle-class status gives her at certain sites:

If I'm in those areas that are fairly protected, within gatherings of my own group, other African Americans, or if I'm in the university where my status as a professor mediates against the way I might be perceived, mediates against the hostile perception, then it's fairly comfortable. . . . When I divide my life into encounters with the outside world, and of course that's ninety percent of my life, it's fairly consistently unpleasant at those sites where there's nothing that mediates between my race and what I have to do. For example, if I'm in a grocery store, if I'm in my car, which is a 1970 Chevrolet, a real old ugly car, all those things—being in a grocery store in casual clothes, or being in the car—sort of advertises some-

thing that doesn't have anything to do with my status as far as people I run into are concerned.

Because I'm a large black woman, and I don't wear whatever class status I have, or whatever professional status [I have] in my appearance when I'm in the grocery store, I'm part of the mass of large black women shopping. For most whites, and even for some blacks, that translates into negative status. That means that they are free to treat me the way they treat most poor black people, because they can't tell by looking at me that I differ from that.

This professor notes the variation in discrimination in the sites through which she travels, from the most private to the most public. At home with friends she faces no problems, and at the university her professional status gives her some protection from discrimination. The increase in unpleasant encounters as she moves into public accommodations sites such as grocery stores is attributed to the absence of mediating factors such as clear symbols of middle-class status—displaying the middle-class symbols may provide some protection against discrimination in public places.

An east coast news anchorperson reported a common middle-class experience of good service from retailers over the phone:

And if I was seeking out a service, like renting a car, or buying something, I could get a wonderful, enthusiastic reaction to what I was doing. I would work that up to such a point that this person would probably shower me with roses once they got to see me. And then when I would show up, and they're surprised to see that I'm black, I sort of remind them in conversation how welcome my service was, to put the embarrassment on them, and I go through with my dealings. In fact, once my sister criticized me for putting [what] she calls my "white-on-white voice" on to get a rental car. But I needed a rental car and I knew that I could get it. I knew if I could get this guy to think that he was talking to some blonde, rather than, you know, so, but that's what he has to deal with. I don't have to deal with that. I want to get the car.

Being middle-class often means that you, as many blacks say, "sound white" over the phone. Over the phone middle-class blacks find they get fair treatment because the white person assumes the caller is white, while they receive poorer (or no) service in person. Race is the only added variable in such inter-personal contact situations. Moreover, some middle-class blacks intentionally use this phone-voice resource to secure their needs.

RESPONSES TO DISCRIMINATION: THE STREET

Reacting to White Strangers

As we move away from public accommodations set-tings to the usually less protected street sites, racial hostility can become more fleeting and severer, and thus black responses are often restricted. The most serious form of street discrimination is violence. Often the reasonable black response to street discrim-ination is withdrawal, resigned acceptance, or a quick verbal retort. The difficulty of responding to vio-lence is seen in this report by a man working for a media surveying firm in a southern industrial city:

> I was parked in front of this guy's house. . . . This guy puts his hands on the window and says, "Get out of the car, nigger." . . . So, I got out, and I thought, "Oh, this is what's going to happen here." And I'm talking fast. And they're, "What are you doing here?" And I'm, "This is who I am. I work with these people. This is the man we want to put in the survey." And I point-ed to the house. And the guy said, "Well you have an out-of-state license tag, right?" "Yea." And he said, "If something happened to you, your people at home wouldn't know for a long time, would they?" . . . I said, "Look, I deal with a company that deals with television. [If] something happens to me, it's going to be a national thing." . . . So, they grab me by the lapel of my coat, and put me in front of my car. They put the blade on my zipper. And now I'm thinking about this guy that's in the truck [behind me], because now I'm thinking that I'm going to have to run somewhere. Where am I going to run? Go to the police? [laughs] So, after a while they bash up my headlight. And I drove [away].

Stigmatized and physically attacked solely because of his color, this man faced verbal hostility and threats of death with courage. Cautiously drawing on his middle-class resources, he told the attackers his death would bring television crews to the town. This resource utilization is similar to that of the news director in the restaurant incident. Beyond this ver-bal threat his response had to be one of caution. For most whites threatened on the street, the police are a sought-after source of protection, but for black men this is often not the case.

At the other end of the street continuum is non-verbal harassment such as the "hate stare" that so traumatized Griffin (1961). In her research on street remarks, Gardner (1980) considered women and blacks particularly vulnerable targets for harassment. For the segregation years Henley (1978) has docu-mented the ways in which many blacks regularly deferred to whites in public-place communications. Today obsequious deference is no longer a common response to harassment. A middle-class student with dark skin reported that on her way to university class-es she had stopped at a bakery in a white residential area where very few blacks live or shop. A white couple in front of the store stared intently and hate-fully at her as she crossed the sidewalk and entered and left the bakery. She reported that she had experi-enced this hate stare many times. The incident angered her for some days thereafter, in part because she had been unable to respond more actively to it.

In between the hate stare and violence are many other hostile actions. Most happen so fast that with-drawal, resigned acceptance, or an immediate verbal retort are the reasonable responses. The female pro-fessor quoted earlier described the fleeting character of harassment:

> I was driving. This has [happened] so many times, but one night it was especially repugnant. I think it had to, with my son being in the car. It was about 9:30 at night, and as I've said, my car is old and very ugly, and I have been told by people shouting at intersec-tions that it's the kind of car that people think of as a low-rider car, so they associate it with Mexican Americans, especially poor Mexican Americans. Well, we were sitting at an intersection waiting to make a turn, and a group of middle-class looking white boys drive up in a car. And they start shouting things at us

in a real fake-sounding Mexican American accent, and I realized that they thought we were Mexican Americans. And I turned to look at them, and they started making obscene gestures and laughing at the car. And then one of them realized that I was black, and said, "Oh, it's just a nigger." And [they] drove away.

This incident illustrates the seldom-noted problem of "cross discrimination"—a black person may suffer from discrimination aimed at other people of color by whites unable to distinguish. The white hostility was guided by certain signals—an old car and dark skin—of minority-group status. The nighttime setting, by assuring anonymity, facilitated the hurling of racist epithets and heightened the negative impact on this woman, who found the harassment especially dangerous and repulsive because she was with her son. She drove away without replying. Later in the interview she notes angrily that in such incidents her ascribed characteristic of "blackness" takes precedence over her achieved middle-class characteristics and that the grouped thinking of racism obscures anything about her that is individual and unique.

For young middle-class blacks street harassment can generate shock and disbelief, as in the case of this college student who recounted a street encounter near her university in the Southwest:

I don't remember in high school being called a "nigger" before, and I can remember here being called a "nigger." [When was this?] In my freshman year, at a university student parade. There was a group of us, standing there, not knowing that this was not an event that a lot of black people went to! [laughs] You know, our dorm was going, and this was something we were going to go to because we were students too! And we were standing out there and [there was] a group of white fraternity boys—I remember the southern flag—and a group of us, five or six of us, and they went past by us, before the parade had actually gotten under way. And one of them pointed and said, "Look at that bunch of niggers!" I remember thinking, "Surely he's not talking to us!" We didn't even use the word "nigger" in my house. . . . [How did you feel?] I think I wanted to cry. And my friends—they were from a southwestern city—they were ready to curse them, and I was just standing there with my mouth open. I think I wanted to cry. I could not believe it, because you got

here and you think you're in an educated environment and you're dealing with educated people. And all of this backward country stuff . . . you think that kind of stuff is not going on, but it is.

The respondent's first coping response was to think the assailants were not speaking to her and her friends. Again we see the tendency for middle-class blacks to assess situations carefully and to give whites the benefit of the doubt. Her subsequent response was tearful acquiescence, but her friends were ready to react in a more aggressive way. The discriminators may have moved on before a considered response was possible. This episode points up the impact of destructive racial coding on young people and hints at the difficulty black parents face in socializing children for coping with white hostility. When I discussed these street incidents involving younger blacks with two older black respondents, one a southern civil rights activist and the other an Ivy-League professor, both noted the problem created for some middle-class black children by their well-intentional parents trying to shelter them from racism.

It seems likely that for middle-class blacks the street is the site of recurring encounters with various types of white malevolence. A vivid example of the cumulative character and impact of this discrimination was given by another black student at a white university, who recounted his experiences walking home at night from a campus job to his apartment in a predominantly white residential area:

So, even if you wanted to, it's difficult just to live a life where you don't come into conflict with others. Because every day you walk the streets, it's not even like once a week, once a month. It's every day you walk the streets. Every day that you live as a black person you're reminded how you're perceived in society. You walk the streets at night; white people cross the streets. I've seen white couples and individuals dart in front of cars to not be on the same side of the street. Just the other day, I was walking down the street, and this white female with a child, I saw her pass a young white male about 20 yards ahead. When she saw me, she quickly dragged the child and herself across the busy street. What is so funny is that this area has had an unknown white rapist in the area for about four years. [When I pass] white men tighten their grip on their women. I've seen people turn around and seem like they're going to take blows from me. The police constantly make circles around me as I walk home, you know, for blocks. I'll walk, and they'll turn a block. And they'll come around me just to make sure, to find out where I'm going. So, every day you realize [you're black]. Even though you're not doing anything wrong; you're just existing. You're just a person. But you're a black person perceived in an unblack world. (This quote includes a clarification sentence from a follow-up interview.)

In a subsequent comment this respondent mentioned that he also endured white men hurling beer cans and epithets at him as he walked home. Again the cumulation of incidents is evident. Everyday street travel for young black middle-class males does not mean one isolated incident every few years.

Unable to "see" his middle-class symbols of college dress and books, white couples (as well as individuals) have crossed the street in front of cars to avoid walking near this modest-build black student, in a predominantly white neighborhood. Couples moving into defensive postures are doubtless reacting to the stigma of "black maleness." The student perceives such avoidance as racist, however, not because he is paranoid, but because he has previously encountered numerous examples of whites taking such defensive measures. Many whites view typical "street" criminals as black or minority males and probably see young black males as potentially dangerous (Graber 1980, 55). This would seem to be the motivation for some hostile treatment black males experience in public places. Some scholars have discussed white perceptions of black males as threatening and the justifiability of that perception (Warr 1990), but to my knowledge there has been no discussion in the literature of the negative impact of such perceptions on black males. This student reports that being treated as a pariah (in his words, a "criminal and a rapist") has caused him severe psychological problems. When I discussed this student's experiences with a prominent black journalist in a northeastern city, he reported that whites sometimes stop talking—and white women grab their purses—on downtown office-building elevators when he enters. These two men had somewhat different responses to

such discrimination, one relatively passive and the other aggressive. In a follow-up interview the student reported that he rarely responded aggressively to the street encounters, apart from the occasional quick curse, because they happened too quickly. Echoing the black graduate student's comments about processing input and missed opportunities, he added: "I was basically analyzing and thinking too much about the incident." However, the journalist reacts more assertively; he described how he turns to whites in elevators and informs them, often with a smile, that they can continue talking or that he is not interested in their purses.

On occasion, black middle-class responses to street hostility from white strangers are even more aggressive. A woman who now runs her own successful business in a southwestern city described a car incident in front of a grocery store:

We had a new car . . . and we stopped a 7-11 [store]. We were going to go out that night, and we were taking my son to a babysitter. . . . And we pulled up, and my husband was inside at the time. And this person, this Anglo couple, drove up, and they hit our car. It was a brand new car. So my husband came out. And the first thing they told us was that we got our car on welfare. Here we are able-bodied. He was a corporate executive. I had a decent job, it was a professional job, but it wasn't paying anything. But they looked at the car we were driving, and they made the assumption that we got it from welfare. I completely snapped; I physically abused that lady. I did. And I was trying to keep my husband from arguing with her husband until the police could come. . . . And when the police came they interrogated them; they didn't arrest us, because there was an off-duty cop who had seen the whole incident and said she provoked it.

Here we see how some whites perceive blacks, including middle-class blacks, in interracial situations. The verbal attack by the whites was laced with the stereotype about blacks as welfare chiselers. This brought forth an angry response from the black couple, which probably came as a surprise to the whites. This is another example of Brittan and Maynard's (1984, p. 7) point that discriminatory interaction is shaped today by the way in which oppressors and oppressed mediate their relative positions. Note too the role of the off-duty police officer. The respondent does not say whether the officer was white or black, but this detail suggests that certain contexts of discrimination have changed—in the past a (white) police officer would have sided with the whites. This respondent also underscores her and her husband's occupational achievements, highlighting her view that she has attained the American middle-class ideal. She is incensed that her obvious middle-class symbols did not protect her from verbal abuse.

The importance of middle-class resources in street encounters was dramatized in the comments of a parole officer in a major West Coast city. He recounted how he dealt with a racial epithet:

> 'I've been called "nigger" before, out in the streets when I was doing my job, and the individual went to jail. . . . [Ok, if he didn't call you a "nigger," would he have still gone to jail?] Probably not. [. . . Was the person white?] Yes, he was. And he had a partner with him, and his partner didn't say anything, and his partner jaywalked with him. However, since he uttered the racial slur, I stopped him and quizzed him about the laws. And jaywalking's against the law, so he went to jail.

On occasion, middle-class blacks have the ability to respond not only aggressively but authoritatively to street discrimination. This unusual response to an epithet was possible because the black man, unknown to his assailant, had police authority. This incident also illustrates a point made in the policing literature about the street-level discretion of police officers (Perry and Sornoff 1973). Jaywalking is normally a winked-at violation, as in the case of the assailant's companion. Yet this respondent was able to exercise his discretionary authority to punish a racial epithet.

Responses to Discrimination by White Police Officers

Most middle-class blacks do not have such governmental authority as their personal protection. In fact, white police officers are a major problem. Encounters with the police can be life-threatening and thus limit the range of responses. A television commenta-

tor recounted two cases of police harassment when he was working for a survey firm in the mid-1980s. In one of the incidents, which took place in a southern metropolis, he was stopped by several white officers:

> "What are you doing here?" I tell them what I'm doing here. . . . And so me spread on top of my car. [What had you done?] Because I was in the neighborhood. I left this note on these peoples' house: "Here's who I am. You weren't here, and I will come back in thirty minutes." [Why were they searching you?] They don't know. To me, they're searching, I remember at that particular moment when this all was going down, there was a lot of reports about police crime on civilians. . . . It took four cops to shake me down, two police cars, so they had me up there spread out. I had a friend of mine with me who was making the call with me, because we were going to have dinner together, and he was black, and they had me up, and they had him outside. . . . They said, "Well, let's check you out. . . . And I'm talking to myself, and I'm not thinking about being at attention, with my arms spread on my Ford [a company car], and I'm sitting there talking to myself, "Man, this is crazy, this is crazy."
>
> [How are you feeling inside?] Scared, I mean real scared. [What did you think was going to happen to you?] I was going to go to jail. . . . Just because they picked me. Why would they stop me? It's like, if they can stop me, why wouldn't I go to jail, and I could sit in there for ten days before the judge sees me. I'm thinking all this crazy stuff. . . . Again, I'm talking to myself. And the guy takes his stick. And he doesn't whack me hard, but he does it with enough authority to let me know they mean business. "I told you stand still; now put your arms back out." And I've got this suit on, and the car's wet. And my friend's hysterical. He's outside the car. And they're checking him out. And he's like, "Man, just be cool, man." And he had tears in his eyes. And I'm like, oh, man, this is a nightmare. This is not supposed to happen to me. This is not my style! And so finally, this other cop comes up and says, "What have we got here Charlie?" "Oh, we've got a guy here. He's running through the neighborhood, and he doesn't want to do what we tell him. We might have to run him in." [You're "running through" the neighborhood?] Yeah, exactly, in a suit in the rain?! After they got through doing their thing and harassing me, I just said, "Man this has been a hell of a week."

And I had tears in my eyes, but it wasn't tears of upset. It was tears of anger; it was tears of wanting to lash back. . . . What I thought to myself was, man, blacks have it real hard down here. I don't care if they're a broadcaster; I don't care if they're a businessman or a banker. . . . They don't have it any easier than the persons on skid row who get harassed by the police on a Friday or Saturday night.

It seems likely that most black men—including middle-class black men—see white police officers as a major source of danger and death (See Louis Harris and Associates 1989; "Mood of Ghetto America" 1980, June 2, 32–34; Roddy 1990, August 26). Scattered evidence suggests that by the time they are in their twenties, most black males, regardless of socioeconomic status, have been stopped by the police because "blackness" is considered a sign of possible criminality by police officers (Moss 1990; Roddy 1990, August 26). This treatment probably marks a dramatic contrast with the experiences of young white middle-class males. In the incident above the respondent and a friend experienced severe police maltreatment—detention for a lengthy period, threat of arrest, and the reality of physical violence. The coping response of the respondent was resigned acceptance somewhat similar to the deference rituals highlighted by Goffman. The middle-class suits and obvious corporate credentials (for example, survey questionnaires and company car) did not protect the two black men. The final comment suggests a disappointment that middle-class status brought no reprieve from police stigmatization and harassment.

Black women can also be the targets of police harassment. A professor at a major white university in the Southwest describes her encounters with the police:

When the cops pull me over because my car is old and ugly, they assume I've just robbed a convenience store. Or that's the excuse they give: "This car looks like a car used to rob a 7-11 [store]." And I've been pulled over six or seven times since I've been in this city—and I've been here two years now. Then I do what most black folks do. I try not to make any sudden moves so I'm not accidentally shot. Then I give them my identification. And I show them my university I.D. so they

won't think that I'm someone that constitutes a threat, however they define it, so that I don't get arrested.

She adds:

[One problem with] being black in America is that you have to spend so much time thinking about stuff that most white people just don't even have to think about. I worry when I get pulled over by a cop. I worry because the person that I live with is a black male, and I have a teen-aged son. I worry what some white cop is going to think when he walks over to our car, because he's holding on to a gun. And I'm very aware of how many black folks accidentally get shot by cops. I worry when I walk into a store, that someone's going to think I'm in there shoplifting. And I have to worry about that because I'm not free to ignore it. And so, that thing that's supposed to be guaranteed to all Americans, the freedom to just be yourself is a fallacious idea. And I get resentful that I have to think about things that a lot of people, even my very close white friends whose politics are similarly to mine, simply don't have to worry about.

This commentary about a number of encounters underscores the pyramiding character of discrimination. This prominent scholar has faced excessive surveillance by white police officers, who presumably view blacks as likely criminals. As in the previous example, there is great fear of white officers, but her response is somewhat different: She draws on her middle-class resources for protection; she cautiously interposes her middle-class status by pulling out a university I.D. card. In the verbal exchange her articulateness as a professor probably helps protect her. This assertive use of middle-class credentials in dealing with police marks a difference from the old asymmetrical deference rituals, in which highlighting middle-class status would be considered arrogant by white officers and increase the danger. Note, too, the explicit theory of rights that she, like many other middle-class blacks, holds as part of her American dream.

CONCLUSION

I have examined the sites of discrimination, the types of discriminatory acts, and the responses of the victims and have found the color stigma still to be very important in the public lives of affluent black Americans. The sites of racial discrimination range from relatively protected home sites, to less protected workplace and educational sites, to even less protected public places. The 1964 Civil Rights Act guarantees that black Americans are "entitled to the full and equal enjoyment of the goods, services, facilities, privileges, advantages, and accommodations" in public accommodations. Yet the interviews indicate that deprivation of full enjoyment of public facilities is not a relic of the past; deprivation and discrimination in public accommodations persist. Middle-class black Americans remain vulnerable targets in public places. Prejudice-generated aggression in public places is, of course, not limited to black men and women—gay men and white women are also targets of street harassment (Benokraitis and Feagin 1986). Nonetheless, black women and men face an unusually broad range of discrimination on the street and in public accommodations.

The interviews highlight two significant aspects of the additive discrimination faced by black Americans in public places and elsewhere: (1) the cumulative character of an *individual's* experiences with discrimination; and (2) the *group's* accumulated historical experiences as perceived by the individual. A retired psychology professor who has worked in the Midwest and Southwest commented on the pyramiding of incidents:

> I don't think white people, generally, understand the full meaning of racist discriminatory behaviors directed toward Americans of African descent. They seem to see each act of discrimination or any act of violence as an "isolated" event. As a result, most white Americans cannot understand the strong reaction manifested by blacks when such events occur. They feel that blacks tend to "over-react." They forget that in most cases, we live lives of quiet desperation generated by a litany of daily large and small events that whether or not by design, remind us of our "place" in American society.

Particular instances of discrimination may seem minor to outside white observers when considered in isolation. But when blatant acts of avoidance, verbal harassment, and physical attack combine with subtle and covert slights, and these accumulate over months, years, and lifetimes, the impact on a black person is far more than the sum of the individual instances.

The historical context of contemporary discrimination was described by the retired psychologist, who argued that average white Americans

> . . . ignore the personal context of the stimulus. That is, they deny the historical impact that a negative act may have on an individual. "Nigger" to a white may simply be an epithet that should be ignored. To most blacks, the term brings into sharp and current focus all kinds of acts of racism—murder, rape, torture, denial of constitutional rights, insults, limited opportunity structure, economic problems, unequal justice under the law and a myriad of . . . other racist and discriminatory acts that occur daily in the lives of most *Americans of African descent—including professional blacks.*

Particular acts, even antilocution that might seem minor to white observers, are freighted not only with one's past experience of discrimination but also with centuries of racial discrimination directed at the entire group, vicarious oppression that still includes racially translated violence and denial of access to the American dream. Anti-black discrimination is a matter of racial-power inequality institutionalized in a variety of economic and social institutions over a long period of time. The microlevel events of public accommodations and public streets are not just rare and isolated encounters by individuals; they are recurring events reflecting an invasion of the microworld by the macroworld of historical racial subordination.

The cumulative impact of racial discrimination accounts for the special way that blacks have of looking at and evaluating interracial incidents. One respondent, a clerical employee at an adoption agency, described the "second eye" she uses:

> I think that it causes you to have to look at things from two different perspectives. You have to decide whether things that are done or slights that are made are made because you are black or they are made because the person is just rude, or unconcerned and uncaring. So it's kind of a situation where you're

always kind of looking to see with a second eye or a second antenna just what's going on.

The language of "second eye" suggests that blacks look at white-black interaction through a lens colored by personal and group experience with cross-institutional and cross-generational discrimination. This sensitivity is not new, but is a current adaptation transcending, yet reminiscent of, the black sensitivity to the etiquette of racial relations in the old South (Doyle 1937). What many whites see as black "paranoia" (e.g., Wieseltier 1989, June 5) is simply a realistic sensitivity to white-black interaction created and constantly reinforced by the two types of cumulative discrimination cited above.

Blacks must be constantly aware of the repertoire of possible responses to chronic and burdensome discrimination. One older respondent spoke of having to put on her "shield" just before she leaves the house each morning. When quizzed, she said that for more than six decades, as she leaves her home, she has tried to be prepared for insults and discrimination in public places, even if nothing happens that day. This extraordinary burden of discrimination, evident in most of the 135 interviews in the larger sample, was eloquently described by the female professor who resented having to worry about life-threatening incidents that her "very close white friends . . . sim-

ply don't have to worry about." Another respondent was articulate on this point:

> *. . . if you can think of the mind as having one hundred ergs of energy, and the average man uses fifty percent of his energy dealing with the everyday problems of the world—just general kinds of things—then he has fifty percent more to do creative kinds of things that he wants to do. Now that's a white person. Now a black person also has one hundred ergs; he uses fifty percent the same way a white man does, dealing with what the white man has [to deal with], so he has fifty percent left. But he uses twenty-five percent fighting being black, [with] all the problems being black and what it means. Which means he really only has twenty-five percent to do what the white man has fifty percent to do, and he's expected to do just as much as the white man with that twenty-five percent. . . . So, that's kind of what happens. You just don't have as much energy left to do as much as you know you really could if you were free, [if] your mind were free.*

The individual cost of coping with racial discrimination is great, and, as he says, you cannot accomplish as much as you could if you retained the energy wasted on discrimination. This is perhaps the most tragic cost of persisting discrimination in the United States. In spite of decades of civil rights legislation, black Americans have yet to attain the full promise of the American dream.

REFERENCES

Allport, Gordon. 1958. *The Nature of Prejudice.* Abridged. New York: Doubleday Anchor Books.

Benokraitis, Nijole and Joe R. Feagin. 1986. *Modern Sexism: Blatant, Subtle and Covert Discrimination.* Englewood Cliffs: Prentice-Hall.

Blauner, Bob. 1989. *Black Lives, White Lives.* Berkeley: University of California Press.

Brittan, Arthur and Mary Maynard. 1984. *Sexism, Racism and Oppression.* Oxford: Basil Blackwell.

Collins, Sheila M. 1983. "The Making of the Black Middle Class." *Social Problems* 30:369–81.

Doyle, Betram W. 1937. *The Etiquette of Race Relations in the South.* Port Washington, NY: Kennikat Press.

Feagin, Joe R. and Douglas Eckberg. 1980. "Prejudice and Discrimination." *Annual Review of Sociology* 6:1–20.

Feagin, Joe R. and Clairece Booher Feagin. 1986. *Discrimination American Style* (rev. ed). Melbourne, FL: Krieger Publishing Co.

Gardner, Carol Brooks. 1980. "Passing By: Street Remarks, Address Rights, and the Urban Female," *Sociological Inquiry* 50:328–56.

———. 1988. "Access Information: Public Lies and Private Peril." *Social Problems* 35:384–97.

Goffman, Erving. 1956. "The Nature of Deference and Demeanor." *American Anthropologist* 58:473–502.

———. 1963. *Behavior in Public Places.* New York: Free Press.

———. 1971. *Relations in Public.* New York: Basic Books.

Graber, Doris A. 1980. *Crime News and the Public.* New York: Praeger.

Griffin, John Howard. 1961. *Black Like Me.* Boston: Houghton Mifflin.

Henley, Nancy M. 1978. *Body Politics.* Englewood Cliffs, N.J.: Prentice-Hall.

Jaynes, Gerald D. and Robin Williams, Jr. (eds.). 1989. *A Common Destiny: Blacks and American Society.* Washington, D.C.: National Academy Press.

Landry, Bart. 1987. *The New Black Middle-Class.* Berkeley: University of California Press.

Louis Harris and Associates. 1989. *The Unfinished Agenda on Race in America.* New York: NAACP Legal Defense and Educational Fund.

"Mood of Ghetto America." 1980, June 2, *Newsweek:* 32–4.

Moss, E. Yvonne. 1990. "African Americans and the Administration of Justice." *Assessment of the Status of African-Americans,* edited by Wornie L. Reed. Boston: University of Massachusetts, William Monroe Trotter Institute: 79–86.

Perry, David C. and Paula A. Sornoff. 1973. *Politics at the Street Level.* Beverly Hills: Sage.

Raper, Arthur F. 1933. *The Tragedy of Lynching.* Chapel Hill: University of North Carolina Press.

Roddy, Dennis B. 1990, August 26. "Perceptions Still Segregate Police, Black Community." *The Pittsburgh Press,* B1.

Rollins, Judith. 1985. *Between Women.* Philadelphia: Temple University Press.

Warr, Mark. 1990. "Dangerous Situation: Social Context and Fear of Victimization." *Social Forces* 68:891–907.

Wieseltier, Leon. 1989. June 5. "Scar Tissue." *New Republic:* 19–20.

Willie, Charles. 1983. *Race,. Ethnicity, and Socioeconomic Status.* Bayside: General Hall.

Wilson, William J. 1978. *The Declining Significance of Race.* Chicago: University of Chicago Press.

———. 1987. *The Truly Disadvantaged: The Inner City, the Underclass, and Public Policy.* Chicago: University of Chicago Press.

PART 2

ISSUES IN SOCIOLOGICAL RESEARCH

Considering that Durkheim, Weber, Simmel, and the American scene, e.g., George Mead, are systematically treated as the major source of contemporary ideas, that says very much about the developments of sociology earlier this century. What has developed, I think, is a continuing specification of general ideas, and above all, a much more demanding form of empirical investigation than any of our founding fathers engaged in.

—Robert K. Merton[1]

For some, the "great divide" in the sociological perspective is both a cause and a consequence of the two basic research orientations in the discipline. The orientations can be variously described: qualitative versus quantitative, subjective versus objective, observing and empathizing versus counting and measuring.

Richard T. LaPiere spent his entire academic career, both as student and professor, at Stanford University. His classic study of discrimination supports the qualitative-subjective-empathizing orientation. Quantitative studies on discrimination reveal an image of the world that is very different from the image qualitative research offers us. In the former, people fill out questionnaires—that is, answer *survey* questions—to indicate what they do or think, while in the latter the sociologist actually observes their behaviors and has discussions with them to uncover their thoughts. LaPiere's research also highlights a very important caveat to keep in mind when conducting or evaluating sociological

---

[1]Knowledge Transcends National Boundaries: An Interview with Robert K. Merton," *Footnotes* 19:8, p. 4, October, 1991.

research: There is a gap, sometimes a very large one, between people's attitudes and their behaviors—what they say they do or will do versus what they actually do.

Raymond M. Weinstein is a professor of sociology at the University of South Carolina in Aiken. His analysis of qualitative versus quantitative sociological studies of patients in mental hospitals demonstrates how the two research orientations can generate very different portrayals of the same social situation. But unlike LaPiere, who also showed how quantitative and qualitative studies of the same issue can produce divergent findings, Weinstein argues that the limitations of qualitative methods can bias our understanding of social life. Among these limitations is the fact that qualitative observations typically cannot be appraised for accuracy because two or more observers with different backgrounds are usually not used (yet all qualitative sociologists would agree that individuals with different backgrounds will often interpret the same situation differently). Further, people interviewed and observed in qualitative studies do not comprise representative samples. Moreover, those most willing to talk with and cooperate with a researcher may very well be atypical of the group to which they belong; many are disgruntled or on the fringes of the group.

Part 2 ends with one of my own essays. I try to show how quantitative methods can reveal a core concept in sociology: that individuals with the same personal characteristics behave and think differently when exposed to different social situations. The essay also demonstrates how quantitative sociologists try to incorporate the subjective orientation into their research.

_____ CHAPTER 5 _____

ATTITUDE VS. ACTIONS AND THE PITFALLS OF QUANTITATIVE "SURVEY" RESEARCH

RICHARD T. LAPIERE

By definition, a social attitude is a behaviour pattern, anticipatory set or tendency, predisposition to specific adjustment to designated social situations, or, more simply, a conditioned response to social stimuli.[1] Terminological usage differs, but students who have concerned themselves with attitudes apparently agree that they are acquired out of social experience and provide the individual organism with some degree of preparation to adjust, in a well-defined way, to certain types of social situations if and when these situations arise. It would seem, therefore, that the totality of the social attitudes of a single individual would include all his socially acquired personality—which is involved in the making of adjustments to other human beings.

But by derivation social attitudes are seldom more than a verbal response to a symbolic situation. For the conventional method of measuring social attitudes is to ask questions (usually in writing) that demand a verbal adjustment to an entirely symbolic situation. Because it is easy, cheap, and mechanical, the attitudinal questionnaire is rapidly becoming a major method of sociological and socio-psychological investigation. The technique is simple. Thus from a hundred or a thousand responses to the question

"Would you get up to give an Armenian woman your seat in a street car?" the investigator derives the "attitude" of non-Armenian males towards Armenian females. Now the question may be constructed with elaborate skill and hidden with consummate cunning in a maze of supplementary or even irrelevant questions yet all that has been obtained is a symbolic response to a symbolic situation. The words "Armenian woman" do not constitute an Armenian woman of flesh and blood, who might be tall or squat, fat or thin, old or young, well or poorly dressed—who might, in fact, be a goddess or just another old and dirty hag. And the questionnaire response, whether it be "yes" or "no," is but a verbal reaction and this does not involve rising from the seat or stolidly avoiding the hurt eyes of the hypothetical woman and the derogatory stares of other street-car occupants. Yet, ignoring these limitations, the diligent investigator will jump briskly from his factual evidence to the unwarranted conclusion that he has measured the "anticipatory behavior patterns" of non-Armenian males towards Armenian females encountered on street cars. Usually he does not stop here, but proceeds to deduce certain general conclusions regarding the social relationships between Armenians and non-Armenians. Most of us have applied the questionnaire technique with greater caution, but not I fear with any greater certainty of success.

Some years ago I endeavored to obtain comparative data on the degree of French and English antipathy towards dark-skinned peoples.[2] The informal questionnaire technique was used, but, although the responses so obtained were exceedingly consistent, I supplemented them with what I then considered an index to overt behavior. The hypothesis as then stated *seemed* entirely logical. "Whatever our attitude on the validity of 'verbalization' may be, it must be recognized that any study of attitudes through direct questioning is open to serious objection, both because of the limitations of the sampling method and because in classifying attitudes the inaccuracy of human judgment is an inevitable variable. In this study however, there is corroborating evidence on these attitudes in the policies adopted by hotel proprietors. Nothing could be used as a more accurate index of color prejudice than the admission or non-admission of colored people to hotels. For the proprietor must reflect the group attitude in his policy regardless of his own feelings in the matter. Since he determines what the group attitude is towards African Americans through the expression of that attitude in overt behavior and over a long period of actual experience, the results will be exceptionally free from those disturbing factors which inevitably affect the effort to study attitudes by direct questioning."

But at that time I overlooked the fact that what I was obtaining from the hotel proprietors was still a "verbalized" reaction to a symbolic situation. The response to an African American's request for lodgings might have been an excellent index of the attitude of hotel patrons living in the same hotel as an African American. Yet to ask the proprietor "Do you permit members of the African American race to stay here?" does not, it appears, measure his potential response to an actual African American.

All measurement of attitudes by the questionnaire technique proceeds on the assumption that there is a mechanical relationship between symbolic and nonsymbolic behavior. It is simple enough to prove that there is no *necessary* correlation between speech and action, between response to words and to realities they symbolize. A parrot can be taught to swear, a child to sing "Frankie and Johnny" in the Mae West manner.[3] The words will have no meaning to either child or parrot. But to prove that there is no *necessary* relationship does not prove that such a relationship may not exist. There need be no relationship between what the hotel proprietor says he will do and what he actually does when confronted with a colored patron. Yet there may be. Certainly we are justified in assuming that the verbal response of the hotel proprietor would be more likely to indicate what he would actually do than would the verbal response of people whose personal feelings are less subordinated to economic expediency. However, the following study indicates that the reliability of even such responses is very small indeed.

Beginning in 1930 and continuing for two years thereafter, I had the good fortune to travel rather extensively with a young Chinese student and his wife.[4] Both were personable, charming, and quick to win the admiration and respect of those they had the opportunity to become intimate with. But they were foreign-born Chinese, a fact that could not be disguised. Knowing the general "attitude" of Americans towards the Chinese as indicated by the "social distance" studies that have been made, it was with considerable trepidation that I first approached a hotel clerk in their company. Perhaps that clerk's eyebrows lifted slightly: but he accommodated us without a show of hesitation. And this in the "best" hotel in a small town noted for its narrow and bigoted "attitude" towards Orientals. Two months later I passed that way again, phoned the hotel and asked if they would accommodate "an important Chinese gentleman." The reply was an unequivocal "No." That aroused my curiosity and led to this study.

In something like ten thousand miles of motor travel, twice across the United States, up and down the Pacific Coast, we met definite rejection from those asked to serve us just once. We were received at 66 hotels, auto camps, and Tourist Homes, refused at one. We were served at 184 restaurants and cafes scattered throughout the country and treated with what I judged to be more than ordinary consideration in 72 of them. Accurate and detailed records were kept of all these instances. An effort, necessarily subjective, was made to evaluate the overt response of hotel clerks, bell boys, elevator operators, and waitresses to the presence of my Chinese friends. The factors entering into the situations were varied as far and as of often as possible. Control was not, of course, as exacting as that required by laboratory experimentation. But it was as rigid as is humanly possible in human situations. For example, I did not take the "test" subjects into my confidence fearing that their behavior might become self-conscious and thus abnormally affect the response of others towards them. Whenever possible I let my Chinese friend negotiate for accommodations (while I concerned myself with the car or luggage) or sent them into a restaurant ahead of me. In this way I attempted to "factor" myself out. We sometimes patronized high-class establishments after a hard and dusty day on the road and stopped at inferior auto camps when in our most presentable condition.

In the end I was forced to conclude that those factors that most influenced the behavior of others towards the Chinese had nothing at all to do with race. Quality and condition of clothing, appearance of baggage (by which, it seems, hotel clerks are prone to base their quick evaluations), cleanliness and neatness were far more significant for person to person reaction in the situations I was studying than skin pigmentation, straight black hair, slanting eyes, and flat noses. And yet an air of self-confidence might entirely offset the "unfavorable" impression made by dusty clothes and the usual disorder to appearance consequent upon some hundred miles of motor travel. A supercilious desk clerk in a hotel of noble aspirations could not refuse his master's hospitality to people who appeared to take their request as a perfectly normal and conventional thing, though they might look like tin-can tourists and two of them belong to the racial category "Oriental." On the other hand, I became rather adept at approaching hotel clerks with that peculiar crab-wise manner that is so effective in provoking a somewhat scornful disregard. And then a bland smile would serve to reverse the entire situation. Indeed, it appeared that a genial smile was the most effective password to acceptance. My Chinese friends were skillful smilers, which may account, in part, for the fact that we received but one rebuff in all our experience. Finally, I was impressed with the

fact that even where some tension developed due to the strangeness of the Chinese it would evaporate immediately when they spoke in unaccented English.

The one instance in which we were refused accommodations is worth recording here. The place was a small California town, a rather inferior auto-camp into which we drove in a very dilapidated car piled with camp equipment. It was early evening, the light so dim that the proprietor found it somewhat difficult to decide the genus *voyageur* to which we belonged. I left the car and spoke to him. He hesitated, wavered, said he was not sure that he had two cabins, meanwhile edging towards our car. The realization that the two occupants were Orientals turned the balance or, more likely, gave him the excuse he was looking for. "No," he said, "I don't take Japs!" In a more pretentious establishment we secured accommodations, and with an extra flourish of hospitality.

To offset this one flat refusal were the many instances in which the physical peculiarities of the Chinese served to heighten curiosity. With few exceptions this curiosity was considerably hidden behind an exceptional interest in serving us. Of course, outside of the Pacific Coast region, New York, and Chicago, the Chinese physiognomy attracts attention. It is different, hence noticeable. But the principal effect this curiosity has upon the behavior of those who cater to the traveler's needs is to make them more attentive, more responsive, more reliable. A Chinese companion is to be recommended to the white traveling in his native land. Strange features when combined with "human" speech and action seems, at times, to heighten sympathetic response, perhaps on the same principle that makes us uncommonly sympathetic towards the dog that has a "human" expression in his face.

What I am trying to say is that in only one out of 251 instances in which we purchased goods or services necessitating intimate human relationships did the fact that my companions were Chinese adversely affect us. Factors entirely unassociated with race were, in the main, the determinant of significant variations in our reception. It would appear reasonable to conclude that the "attitude" of the American people, as reflected in the behavior of those who are for pecuniary reasons presumably most sensitive to the antipathies of their white clientele, is anything but negative towards the Chinese. In terms of "social distance" we might conclude that native Caucasians are not averse to residing in the same hotels, auto-camps, and "Tourist Homes" as Chinese and will with complacency accept the presence of Chinese at an adjoining table in restaurant or cafe. It does not follow that there is revealed a distinctly "positive" attitude towards the Chinese, that whites prefer the Chinese to other whites. But the facts as gathered certainly preclude the conclusion that there is an intense prejudice towards the Chinese.

Yet the existence of this prejudice, very intense, is proven by a conventional "attitude" study. To provide a comparison of symbolic reaction to symbolic social situations with actual reaction to real social situations, I "questionnaired" the establishments which we patronized during the two year period. Six months were permitted to lapse between the time I obtained the overt reaction and the symbolic. It was hoped that the effects of the actual experience with Chinese guests, adverse or otherwise, would have faded during the intervening time. To the hotel or restaurant a questionnaire was mailed with an accompanying letter purporting to be a special and personal plea for response. The questionnaires all asked the same question, "Will you accept members of the Chinese race as guests in your establishment?" (see Table 5.1). Two types of questionnaire were used. In one this question was inserted among similar queries concerning Germans, French, Japanese, Russians, Armenians, Jews, Negroes, Italians, and Indians. In the other the pertinent question was unencumbered. With persistence, completed replies were obtained from 128 of the establishments we had visited; 81 restaurants and 47 hotels, auto-camps and "Tourist Hotels." In response to the relevant question 92 percent of the latter replied "No." The remainder replied "Uncertain; depend upon circumstances." From the woman proprietor of a small auto-camp I received the only "Yes," accompanied by a chatty letter describing the nice visit she had had with a Chinese gentleman and his sweet wife during the previous summer.

A rather unflattering interpretation might be put upon the fact that those establishments who had provided for our needs so graciously were, some months later, verbally antagonistic towards hypothetical Chinese. To factor this experience out responses were

TABLE 5.1 Distribution of Results from Questionnaire Study of Establishment "Policy" Regarding Acceptance of Chinese as Guests

Replies are to the question: "Will you accept members of the Chinese race as guests in your establishment?"

	HOTELS, ETC., VISITED		HOTELS, ETC., NOT VISITED		RESTAURANTS, ETC., VISITED		RESTAURANTS ETC., NOT VISITED	
Total	47		32		81		96	
	1*	2*	1	2	1	2	1	2
Number replying	22	25	20	12	43	38	51	45
No	20	23	19	11	40	35	47	41
Undecided: depend upon circumstances	1	2	1	1	3	3	4	3
Yes	1	0	0	0	0	0	0	1

*Column (1) indicates in each case those responses to questionnaires which concerned Chinese only. The figures in columns (2) are from the questionnaires in which the above was inserted among questions regarding Germans, French, Japanese, etc.

secured from 37 hotels and 96 restaurants located in approximately the same regions, but uninfluenced by this particular experience with Oriental clients. In this, as in the former case, both types of questionnaires were used. The results indicate that neither the type of questionnaire nor the fact of previous experience had important bearing upon the symbolic response to symbolic social situations.

It is impossible to make direct comparison between the reactions secured through questionnaires and from actual experience (see Table 5.2). On the basis of [Table 5.1's] data it would appear foolhardy for a Chinese to attempt to travel in the United States. And yet, as I have shown, actual experience indicates that the American people, as represented by the personnel of hotels, restaurants, etc., are not at all averse to fraternizing with Chinese within the limitations that apply to social relationships between Americans themselves. The evaluations that follow are undoubtedly subject to the criticism that any human judgment must withstand. But the fact is that, although they began their travels in this country with considerable trepidation, my Chinese friends soon lost all fear that they might receive a rebuff. At first somewhat timid and considerably dependent upon me for guidance and support, they came in time to feel fully self-reliant and would approach new social situations without the slightest hesitation.

The conventional questionnaire undoubtedly has significant value for the measurement of "political attitudes." The presidential polls conducted by the Literary Digest have proven that. But a "political attitude" is exactly what the questionnaire can be justly held to measure: a verbal response to a symbolic situation. Few citizens are ever faced with the necessity of adjusting themselves to the presence of the political leaders whom, periodically, they must vote for— or against. Especially is this true with regard to the president, and it is in relation to political attitudes towards presidential candidates that we have our best evidence. But while the questionnaire may indicate what the voter will do when he goes to vote, it does not and cannot reveal what he will do when he meets Candidate Jones on the street, in his office, at his club, on the golf course, or wherever two men may meet and adjust in some way one to the other.

The questionnaire is probably our only means of determining "religious attitudes." An honest answer to the question "Do you believe in God?" reveals all there is to be measured. "God" is a symbol; "belief" a verbal expression. So here, too, the questionnaire is efficacious. But if we would know the emotional responsiveness of a person to the spoken or written word "God" some other method of investigation must be used. And if we would know the extent to which that responsiveness restrains his behavior it is to his behavior that we must look, not to his questionnaire response. Ethical precepts are, I judge, something more than verbal professions. There would seem little to be gained from asking a man if his religious faith prevents him from committing sin. Of course it does appear—on paper. But "moral attitudes" must have a significance in the adjustment to actual situations or they are not worth the studying. Sitting at my desk in California I can predict with a high degree of certainty what an "average" business man in an average Mid-Western city will reply to the question "Would you engage in sexual intercourse with a prostitute in a Paris brothel?" Yet no one, least of all the man himself, can predict what he would actually do should he by some misfortune find himself face to face with the situation in question. His moral "attitudes" are no doubt already stamped into his personality. But just what those habits are which will be invoked to provide him with some sort of adjustment to this situation is quite indeterminate.

It is highly probable that when the "Southern Gentleman" says he will not permit African Americans to reside in his neighborhood we have a verbal response to a symbolic situation that reflects the "attitudes" which would become operative in an actual situation. But there is no need to ask such a question of the true "Southern Gentleman." We knew it all the time. I am inclined to think that in most instances where the questionnaire does reveal nonsymbolic attitudes the case is much the same. It is only when we cannot easily observe what people do in certain types of situations that the questionnaire is

TABLE 5.2 Distribution of Results Obtained from Actual Experience in the Situation Symbolized in the Questionnaire Study

CONDITIONS	HOTELS, ETC.		RESTAURANTS, ETC.	
	ACCOMPANIED BY INVESTIGATOR	CHINESE NOT SO ACCOMPANIED AT INCEPTION OF SITUATION	ACCOMPANIED BY INVESTIGATOR	CHINESE NOT SO ACCOMPANIED AT INCEPTION OF SITUATION
Total	55	12	165	19
Reception very much better than investigator would expect to have received had he been alone, but under otherwise similar circumstances	19	6	63	9
Reception different only to extent of heightened curiosity, such as investigator might have incurred were he alone but dressed in manner unconventional to region yet not incongruous	22	3	76	6
Reception "normal"	9	2	21	3
Reception perceptibly hesitant and not to be explained on other than "racial" grounds	3	1	4	1
Reception definitely, though temporarily, embarrassing	1	0	1	0
Not accepted	1	0	0	0

Note: When the investigator was not present at the inception of the situation the judgments were based upon what transpired after he joined the Chinese. Since intimately acquainted with them it is probable that errors in judgment were no more frequent under these conditions than when he was able to witness the inception as well as results of the situation.

resorted to. But it is just here that the danger in the questionnaire technique arises. If Mr. A adjusts himself to Mr. B in a specified way we can deduce from his behavior that he has a certain "attitude" towards Mr. B and, perhaps, all of Mr. B's class. But if no such overt adjustment is made it is impossible to discover what A's adjustment would be should the situation arise. A questionnaire will reveal what Mr. A writes or says when confronted with a certain combination of words. But not what he will do when he meets Mr. B. Mr. B is a great deal more than a series of words. He is a man and he acts. His action is not necessarily what Mr. A. "imagines" it will be when he reacts verbally to the symbol "Mr. B."

No doubt a considerable part of the data that the social scientist deals with can be obtained by the questionnaire method. The census reports are based upon verbal questionnaires and I do not doubt their basic integrity. If we wish to know how many children a man has, his income, the size of his home, his age, and the condition of his parents, we can reasonably ask him. These things he has frequently and conventionally converted into verbal responses. He is competent to report upon them, and will do so accurately, unless indeed he wishes to do otherwise. A careful investigator could no doubt even find out by verbal means whether the man fights with his wife (frequently, infrequently, or not at all), though the neighbors would be a more reliable source. But we should not expect to obtain by the questionnaire method his "anticipatory set or tendency" to action

should his wife pack up and go home to Mother, should Elder Son get into trouble with the neighbor's daughter, the President assume the status of a dictator, the Japanese take over the rest of China, or a Chinese gentleman come to pay a social call.

Only a verbal reaction to an entirely symbolic situation can be secured by the questionnaire. It may indicate what the responder would actually do when confronted with the situation symbolized in the question, but there is no assurance that it will. And so to call the response a reflection of a "social attitude" is to entirely disregard the definition commonly given the phrase "attitude." If social attitudes are to be conceptualized as partially integrated habit sets that will become operative under specific circumstances and lead to a particular pattern of adjustment they must, in the main, be derived from a study of humans behaving in actual social situations. They must not be imputed on the basis of questionnaire data.

The questionnaire is cheap, easy, and mechanical. The study of human behavior is time consuming, intellectually fatiguing, and depends for its success upon the ability of the investigator. The former method gives quantitative results, the latter mainly qualitative. Quantitative measurements are quantitatively accurate; qualitative evaluations are always subject to the errors of human judgment. Yet it would seem far more worth while to make a shrewd guess regarding that which is essential than to accurately measure that which is likely to prove quite irrelevant.

NOTES

1. See Daniel D. Droba, "Topical Summaries of Current Literature," *The American Journal of Sociology*, 1934, p. 513.
2. "Race Prejudice: France and England," *Social Forces*, September 1928, pp. 102–111.

3. Mae West was a robust, sultry, sardonic movie star of the 1920s and 1930s.
4. The results of this study have been withheld until the present time out of consideration for their feelings.

CHAPTER 6

THE MENTAL HOSPITAL FROM THE PATIENT'S POINT OF VIEW: THE PITFALLS OF PARTICIPANT-OBSERVATION RESEARCH

RAYMOND M. WEINSTEIN

The mental hospital and the patients confined there have been the objects of intensive study by social scientists. Since the early 1950s a number of studies have appeared dealing with those characteristics of the hospital (such as formal structure, informal relations, staff behavior and ideology, and ward environment) that impinge upon mental patients and affect the course of their illness. Typically, portraits of the mental hospital from the patient's view have been painted with *qualitative* data, by scientists observing, interviewing, or masquerading as patients. Presented in Table 6.1 are examples of such studies, together with the attitudes toward or perceptions of hospitalization, staff, and treatment that were ascribed to patients.

Overwhelmingly, qualitative researchers have criticized the mental hospital or charged that it has a deleterious effect upon patients. Hospitalization is generally pictured in an authoritarian context, whereby patients are forced to define themselves as mentally ill, change their thinking and behavior, suffer humiliations, accept restrictions, and adjust to institutional life. Hospital staff are characterized, at best, as

insensitive to patients' needs or unconcerned about their recovery, and, at worst, as physically abusive to patients or unjustly controlling their lives. Psychiatric treatments are described as unnecessary, emotionally threatening, and unsuccessful for many patients, while therapist-patient relationships are seen as strained and impersonal. In short, in the studies listed in Table 6.1, it is concluded that mental patients have negative views of hospitalization, staff, and treatment.

Not surprisingly, these conclusions drawn by the qualitative researchers, mainly sociologists, coincide with the societal reaction or "labelling theory" approach to mental illness and hospitalization. According to this approach persons who have been committed have been publicly labelled as "mentally ill" and become members of a deviant group (Gove, 1970). Because of society's adverse reaction to patients, they develop an ignominious self-image. Societal reaction theorists contend that institutionalization, rather than curing persons of their psychopathology, only serves to create a relatively permanent population of deviants (Roman, 1971). It is assumed that anything to do with mental hospitals is viewed negatively by patients and their relatives. Indeed, in recent years ex–mental patients have joined the ranks of the politically active, demanding improvements in the quality of institutional care and freedom from forced medication and shock treatments (Anspach, 1979).

From *Deviance and Mental Illness* (1982), edited by Walter R. Gove, pp. 121–143. © Sage Publications, Inc. Reprinted by permission of Sage Publications, Inc. The reader should contrast the findings on mental hospitals in this essay with the findings reported by D. L. Rosenhan in Part 8.

TABLE 6.1 Qualitative Studies of Mental Hospitals from the Patient's View

		PATIENTS' ATTITUDES TOWARD OR PERCEPTIONS OF		
STUDY	TYPE OF HOSPITAL	HOSPITALIZATION	STAFF	TREATMENT
Caudill et al. (1952)	Private	Patients feel "pressured" in the hospital to give up their defenses and relinquish normal social roles.	Patients believe doctors withhold information from them, feel compelled to counterpose staff.	Patients think psychotherapy is "endless one-way talk," are apprehensive about the lack of specific therapeutic goals.
Dunham and Weinberg (1960)	State	Patients deny being mentally ill, feel stigmatized, resent conforming to hospital norms	Patients feel neglected by the doctors, feel coerced and abused by the attendants.	Patients dislike ECT because of its unpleasantness and adverse effects, resist psychotherapy because therapists try to change their ideas.
Goffman (1961)	State	Patients see hospital as an authoritarian structure and suffer restrictions on liberties, depersonalization, and loss of self-esteem.	Patients have a keen sense of staff insensitivity and abuse via staff's avoidance of relationships, discreditations, and placement of derogatory information into the files.	Patients hate and fight psychiatrists in the course of psychotherapeutic relations; they follow a "psychiatric line" in order to be judged as no longer in need of treatment.
Pine and Levinson (1961)	State	Patients see hospitalization as a "problem"; they must develop a new new self-image, accept patient role, become reconciled to loss of freedom.	Patients feel powerless in the hands of doctors, fear the authority of the staff and retaliations by them.	Patients think talking about life difficulties threatening; pressures to engage in psychotherapy conflict with their values, defenses, and character traits.
Rosenhan (1973)	12 different hospitals	Patients sense they have no legal rights, restricted freedoms, a loss of credibility, and lack of privacy in the hospital.	Patients believe staff are indifferent and avoid contact with them, dislike staff criticism in front of others.	Patients feel depersonalized by treatment due to the relatively short time spent in psychotherapy and the heavy reliance on psychotropic medication.
Scheff (1966)	State	Patients feel hospitalization forces them into a deviant social role and conform to the stereotyped behavior expected of them.	Patients resent the careless and hurried manner in which psychiatrists examine them, think psychiatrists hospitalize patients arbitrarily.	Patients become extremely indignant and angry when they are forcibly treated; treatment convinces patients they are "sick" and prolongs what may otherwise have been a transitory episode.
Stanton and Schwartz (1954)	Private	Patients feel removed from society, experience loneliness and anxiety, and must conform to the informal organization of the hospital.	Patients believe no one in the hospital understands them, fear the power of the staff, and feel they act in contradictory manners.	Patients do not understand the purpose of psychotherapy, do not believe they benefit from it, and think there is an impersonal barrier in the therapeutic relationship.

Surprisingly, the traditional psychiatric perspective (generally the polar opposite of labelling theory) supports the idea that many patients harbor unfavorable attitudes toward hospitalization, staff, and treatment. Psychiatrists are well aware that patients frequently do not benefit from treatment and are released from mental hospitals without being "cured" (Clarke, 1979). Since treatment goals are often scaled down to limited resources, overburdened staff, and inadequate facilities, patients may return to the community less than satisfied with the outcome of their hospitalization. A basic tenet in psychiatry is that the patient need not like the doctor or believe in therapy, and open expressions of hostility are welcomed (Eaton and Peterson, 1969: 401). Therapists are often confronted with patients who manifest the "negative therapeutic reaction," Freud's formulation of a patient's sense of guilt, need for punishment, and moral masochism (Olinick, 1964). With this syndrome of negativism, patients vocalize defiant attitudes toward therapists because any improvement or temporary suspension of symptoms produces an exacerbation of their mental illness.

Some social scientists, however, have challenged the conclusions drawn from the qualitative studies and/or defended the mental hospital. Linn (1968) contends that observational data give us a one-sided and homogeneous conception of patienthood, and that a majority of patients in fact have positive attitudes because hospitalization helps them cope with their emotional and environmental problems. Gove and Fain (1973) claim that the mental hospital has a beneficial or benign effect, as most ex-patients show improvements in interpersonal relationships and community participation. To Townsend (1976) the impressionistic approach of the researchers in Table 6.1 has resulted in questionable interpretations of mental hospitalization, since empirical investigations of patients have consistently failed to reveal changes in their self-conceptions. A sociologist-patient confesses that before being committed he had feared hospitalization, anticipated abuse by staff, and envisioned such evils as ice baths, shock treatments, and straitjackets (Killian and Bloomberg, 1975). After discharge, by contrast, he felt that hospital treatment

had facilitated rather than retarded his recovery and believed the experience had been a pleasant one.

The techniques employed in the qualitative studies have also been questioned. Descriptions of the mental hospital from the patient's perspective may be insightful and thought-provoking, but there are inherent limitations to the data. Reznikoff et al. (1959) point out that the accuracy of the observations cannot be appraised. The objectivity of the inferences reported is suspect since two or more observers with different backgrounds and training were not used. Moreover, Reznikoff et al. argue that subjective and experiential data are almost impossible to quantify for individual or group comparisons and perforce have limited applicability. Linn (1968) maintains that the patients interviewed or observed in the qualitative studies did not constitute representative samples. How typical the anecdotes and incidents cited were of the total hospital population remains a mystery. Linn is also critical of these researchers because they viewed patients as passive or powerless participants in the hospital system rather than as informants with useful opinions on the treatment process.

Studies of the kind listed in Table 6.1 tend to eclipse the relatively few *quantitative* reports in the literature dealing with the attitudes of hospitalized mental patients. Social scientists have seldom taken representative samples of patients, questioned them directly about the hospital or their illness, utilized objective tests or validated scales, and presented the findings in statistical format. Weinstein (1972) believes this neglect or lack of interest in patients' views is due to a "bias" among researchers, a tacit acceptance of the medical model of mental illness. Since the mentally ill (by definition) possess some kind of psychopathology, their opinions of themselves or their situation are assumed to be symptomatic of their illness and thus unreliable. Similarly, Sonn (1977) claims that patients' statements are deemed by psychiatrists to be unconscious distortions of reality and not to be taken at face value. In psychiatry patients are seen as objects of study rather than coinvestigators in the treatment process, and their views are discounted because of an incongruence with existing styles of therapy or research.

The handful of quantitative works concerning patients' views of mental hospitals does not constitute a unified body of knowledge. The few dozen studies are, for the most part, disjointed. Different scientists and investigative teams have largely focused on a specific patient attitude and have not used the same or similar methodological techniques. The purpose of this chapter, therefore, is to review these quantitative studies of patient attitudes toward the mental hospital, to draw together the diverse methodologies, findings, and conclusions. The degree of patients' positiveness or favorableness is the theoretical focus around which the quantitative data are organized. Of key importance is the overall level of favorableness, that is, the number of studies in which patients perceived hospitalization, staff, and treatment favorably. Such a review, it is hoped, will complement the wealth of qualitative data already familiar to social scientists and shed light on the controversy between the critics and defenders of mental hospitals.

QUANTITATIVE STUDIES

The quantitative studies of interest to us (Table 6.2) cover a wide range of topics. These researchers tested various attitudes of patients toward hospitalization, staff, and treatment in general (for example, conceptions of a hospital's authoritarian control, staff roles, and therapeutic effectiveness) as well as specific opinions of their own institutions (evaluations of the benefits of hospitalization, helpfulness of staff, usefulness of treatment modalities). To measure these different attitudes, a wide variety of methodological techniques was utilized. Certain researchers favored objective tests with a small number of questions or statements, whereas others constructed questionnaire scales from scores or even hundreds of items. For each study, the different measures of patients' attitudes toward hospitalization, staff, and treatment were identified. These measures were based on patient responses to individual questions or statements, or the scaling of test items together.

For each measure of patients' attitudes in each study listed in Table 6.2, it was determined if hospitalization, staff, or treatment was viewed, either favorably or unfavorably. In some studies, the measurement criteria listed were simply used. Researchers utilizing open-ended questions categorized the replies not only by content but purposefully to reflect a positive, neutral, or negative attitude. Researchers using multiple-choice questions gave patients choices that signified the degree to which they were helped in the hospital, while those choosing rating scales or ranking procedures had the quality of favorableness built in to the different points. In the majority of studies, however, patients' attitudes were not analyzed in terms of favorableness and the data had to be interpreted in this context. Thus, on the agreement-disagreement scales the statements were dichotomized in terms of positive or negative descriptions of hospitalization, staff, or treatment. With the semantic differential technique, the adjectives rated suggested positions of approval or disapproval. On the factor-analytic and interval scales, favorableness was determined by the difference between the midpoint of the subscales and the patients' mean scores; subscale scores indicated the degree of endorsement of particular attitudes, the content of which denoted a favorable or unfavorable view.

It is important to comment on the data accuracy and sample representativeness of the quantitative studies, since some researchers have criticized the qualitative studies largely on these grounds. For almost all methods of measurement used in the studies in Table 6.2, the validity of the data (extent to which differences in test scores reflect true differences in patients' attitudes) was either demonstrated or presumed. Rating scales, rank orderings, agreement-disagreement scales, multiple-choice questions, and open-ended questions all have "face validity," are measures based directly on the attitude in question, and do not purport to measure any other attitude. The developers of the semantic differential demonstrated the validity of this technique. On the factor-analytic and interval scales, which purport to measure various abstractions, validational data were gathered. The reliability of these measurements (extent to which test scores do not resect chance or random errors) was checked in most cases, via the consistency or stability of patient responses or scores.

TABLE 6.2 Quantitative Studies of Mental Patients' Attitudes

STUDY	TYPE OF HOSPITAL	PATIENT SAMPLE	MEASUREMENT TECHNIQUES	NUMBER OF ATTITUDE MEASURES FAVORABLE (F) OR UNFAVORABLE (U) TOWARD					
				HOSPITALIZATION		STAFF		TREATMENT	
				F	U	F	U	F	U
Allen and Barton (1976)	University	95	Open-ended questions	1	—	—	3	2	2
Almond et al. (1968)	University	66	Agreement-disagreement scales					11	4
Backner and Kissinger (1963)	Veterans	30	Semantic differential			3	—		
Barton and Scheer (1975)	University	19	Agreement-disagreement scales					10	6
Chastko et al. (1971)	University	47	Open-ended questions, rating scale					2	—
Dowds and Fontana (1977)	Veterans	54	Rating scales					13	1
Ellsworth and Maroney (1972); Ellsworth et al. (1971)	Veterans	1,141	Factor-analytic scales	3	—	2	—		
Freeman and Kendell (1980)	Public	166	Multiple-choice questions					11	2
Fryling and Fryling (1960)	State	48	Open-ended questions	3	1			2	1
Giovannoni and Ullmann (1963)	Veterans	35	Semantic differential			1	—		
Goldman (1965)	Veterans	139	Multiple-choice questions	—	1				
Goldstein et al. (1972)	University	346	Rating scales	5	1	7	—	7	1
Gordon and Groth (1961)	Veterans	60	Semantic differential	5	—	2	—		
Gould and Glick (1976)	University	44	Rank orderings					15	5
Gove and Fain (1973)	State	429	Multiple-choice questions	1	—			1	—
Gynther et al. (1963)	City	121	Multiple-choice questions	1	—	1	—	1	—
Hamister (1955)	Veterans	99	Rank orderings			*			
Handler and Perlman (1973)	State	80	Rating scales			*			
Hillard and Folger (1977)	State	32	Multiple-choice questions					5	2
	State	21	Semantic differential					1	6
Linn (1968)	State	185	Open-ended questions	7	5				
Lowenkopf and Greenstein (1972)	Private	100	Open-ended questions					3	—

Study	Setting	N	Instrument						
Luft et al. (1978)	City	183	Multiple-choice questions	7	2	4	2	2	—
Mayer and Rosenblatt (1974)	State	220	Agreement-disagreement scales, rank orderings		2	4		4	1
Mayo et al. (1971)	Veterans	18	Agreement-disagreement scales	1	1	—	1	4	1
Moos (1974)	State	1,231	Interval scales	2		—	3	4	1
	Veterans	1,687		1	1	1	2	3	2
	University	391		1	1	2	1	3	2
Morrow (1973)	State	64	Rating scales	3				2	—
Pettit (1971)	Provincial	50	Semantic differential			1		1	3
Pierce et al. (1972)	General	17	Interval scales	1	3	2	1	2	3
Polak (1970)	City	11	Open-ended questions					—	1
	Provincial	7						1	
Reznikoff and Toomey (1960)	Private	142	Picture test, incomplete statements, multiple-choice questions, interval scale	3	1	3	1	3	1
Roback and Snyder (1965)	State	101	Interval scale	1	—				
	Veterans	119		1	—				
Skodol et al. (1980)	City	30	Agreement-disagreement scales					16	12
I. F. Small et al. (1965); J. G. Small et al. (1965)	City	154	Open-ended questions	1	1			—	5
Souelem (1955)	State	103	Interval scale	1	—				
Spencer (1977)	State	50	Rating scale, multiple-choice questions					11	9
Spiegel and Younger (1972)	Veterans	254	Factor-analytic scales	1	1	1	—		
Townsend (1975)	State	110	Semantic differential	1	1	1	—		
Verinis and Flaherty (1978)	Veterans	27	Interval scales	1	1	3	—	4	1
Wing (1962)	Public	256	Open-ended question	—	1	1			
Wolfensberger (1958)	State	95	Interval scale	1	—				
Zaslove et al. (1966, 1968)	University	93	Open-ended questions	1	—		2	1	3

*Data for the total sample were not reported or could not be calculated. However, in these studies patient and staff attitudes toward staff in terms of favorableness were compared.

In the vast majority of quantitative studies, representative samples were taken. Some researchers selected all admissions over several weeks or months, others selected all discharges during a given time frame. Cross sections of a hospital's population were also obtained by random samples of patients or wards.

More detailed information on the validity, reliability, sample representativeness, and measures of favorableness of the studies in Table 6.2 can be found in earlier reports (Weinstein, 1979, 1981a, 1981b).

FAVORABLENESS OF PATIENTS' ATTITUDES

The overall favorableness of patients' attitudes was determined by counting the number of different hospital *samples,* separately for each of the three types of attitudes, that had findings "in a favorable direction"—more measures on the favorable than the unfavorable column. For each sample judged to be attitudinally favorable, this meant that either (a) more than half the mental patients viewed hospitalization, staff, or treatment positively, or the total sample received a mean score on the better side of the midpoint, when a single scoring technique was used by researchers, or (b) there was a majority of positive responses or mean scores on the better side of the midpoint when multiple questions, tests, or subscales were used. These criteria appear to be the best means of assessing the issue of attitudinal favorableness across the various studies, given the fact that multiple measures were often used and patients sometimes tested at different institutions. In each sample, findings in a favorable direction imply that the patients exhibit a tendency, and not a unanimity, to view hospitalization, staff, or treatment positively.

All Table 6.2 study samples were included in the overall determination of favorableness except 2 (Hamister, 1955; Handler and Perlman, 1973). Of the 39 Table 6.2 studies that tested patients' perceptions of hospitalization, 27, or 69 percent, had findings in a favorable direction. Patients were unfavorable or ambivalent toward the mental hospital in the other 12 samples (Goldman, 1965; Keith-Spiegel et al., 1970; Kish, 1971; Klass et al., 1977; Levinson and Gallagher, 1964:75–79; Moos, 1974: 60 state and

university hospitals; Pierce et al., 1972; I. F. Small et al., 1965; Spiegel and Younger, 1972; Verinis and Flaherty, 1978; Wing, 1962). Concerning patients' attitudes toward staff, 20 of the 27 hospital samples (74 percent) were positive, the rest either neutral or negative (Allen and Barton, 1976; Jansen and Aldrich, 1973; Klass et al., 1977; Mayo et al., 1971; Moos, 1974:60 state and veterans hospitals; Zaslove et al., 1968). Of the 44 different studies in Table 6.2 dealing with treatment, patients espoused favorable views on 35, or 80 percent, of them. Here a majority of patients in 9 samples were not on the positive side (Allen and Barton, 1976; Hillard and Folger, 1917; Jansen, 1973; Lee, 1979; Pierce et al., 1972; Polak, 1970—both hospitals; I. F. Small et al., 1965; Zaslove et al., 1966). . . .

An important issue is whether or not patients' opinions of the mental hospital *change* as a consequence of their commitment. Unfortunately, only a few of the researchers listed in Table 6.2 tested patients at 2 or more time periods, so this issue cannot be given the attention it deserves. Nevertheless, the data do suggest that patients' attitudes improve, or at least do not worsen, between admission and discharge. Of the 6 studies that measured attitudes toward hospitalization, 3 found that patients became more favorable over time (Allen and Barton, 1976; Pierce et al., 1972; I. F. Small et al., 1965) and 3 reported no changes (Gynther et al., 1963; Reznikoff and Toomey, 1960). Both studies concerned with staff discovered that patients registered positive changes (Pierce et al., 1972; Reznikoff and Toomey, 1960). Of the 8 studies looking at treatment, patients' attitudes improved in 5 (Allen and Barton, 1976; Gynther et al., 1963; Pierce et al., 1972; Reznikoff and Toomey, 1960; Verinis and Flaherty, 1978) and remained the same in 3 (Dowds and Fontana, 1977; I. F. Small et al., 1965). Follow-up interviews 3–18 months after discharge revealed that patients espoused either the same (J. G. Small et al., 1965) or less favorable (Allen and Barton, 1976) attitudes toward both hospitalization and treatment. . . .

Each study in Table 6.2 with data for the total sample contains one or more measures of attitudinal favorableness. The measures may be examined individually in terms of content to determine the particular characteristic or aspect of hospitalization, staff, or treatment that patients perceive either positively or negatively. The patient samples contain 116, 90, and 279 questions, tests, or subscales for the 3 types of attitudes, respectively. Each of these measures was thus content analyzed and placed into different categories. The favorableness of these measures, by category, was then tabulated for all study samples combined (Tables 6.3, 6.4, and 6.5).

From Table 6.3 it is clear that patients view most aspects of mental hospitalization quite favorably. A good proportion of the questions, tests, and subscales

in almost all content categories were endorsed by various samples. Patients especially feel that the hospital is organized well and has a salutary atmosphere, and that institutionalization is beneficial, is not very restrictive, has a good effect on patients, and seldom stigmatizes patients. The data in Table 6.4 reveal that patients are rather pleased with the accessibility, receptivity, and support of staff (in general), and give high marks to psychiatrists and nurses. However, patients have negative opinions more often than positive toward staff's permissiveness and dominance and are ambivalent about the helpfulness of attendants. As Table 6.5 depicts, not all characteris-

TABLE 6.3   Favorableness of Patient Sample Responses or Mean Scores to Questions, Tests, and Subscales Dealing with Attitudes toward Hospitalization, by Content

| | QUESTIONS, TESTS, AND SUBSCALES | | | |
| | FAVORABLE | | UNFAVORABLE | |
CONTENT OF ATTITUDES	*N*	*%*	*N*	*%*
Benefits of hospitalization[a]	26	84	5	16
Restrictiveness of hospitalization[b]	14	82	3	18
Organization of the hospitalization[c]	7	70	3	10
Amenities of the hospital[d]	5	56	4	44
Hospital's effect on patients[e]	19	70	8	30
Atmosphere of the hospital[f]	7	78	2	22
Stigma of hospitalization[g]	5	71	2	29
Expectations of hospitalization[h]	4	67	2	33
Total	87	75	29	25

[a] Helpfulness of hospitalization, quality of patient care, general orientation toward mental hospitals.

[b] Arbitrariness of restrictions, limitations imposed on patients, hospital's rules and regulations, difficulties in getting released, authoritarian character of the hospital.

[c] Satisfaction with ward, orderliness of ward, cleanliness of ward, building safety, activities on ward.

[d] Comforts of the hospital, meals, relaxation, escape from pressures, being alone at the hospital.

[e] Hospital provides for patients' dependency needs, gives patients insight into problems, gets patients involved with other patients.

[f] Hospital is entertaining, has programs to keep patients busy, raises patients' morale.

[g] Hospital changes patients' reputation at home, family and friends betray patient to get him/her into the hospital; people reject ex-patients.

[h] Acceptance of hospitalization, fears of commitment, motivation to go to the hospital.

TABLE 6.4   Favorableness of Patient Sample Responses or Mean Scores to Questions, Tests, and Subscales Dealing with Attitudes toward Staff, by Content

| | QUESTIONS, TESTS, AND SUBSCALES | | | |
| | FAVORABLE | | UNFAVORABLE | |
CONTENT OF ATTITUDES	*N*	%	*N*	%
Accessibility of staff[a]	6	86	1	14
Receptivity of staff[b]	10	77	3	23
Permissiveness of staff[c]	4	44	5	56
Dominance of staff[d]	4	44	5	56
Support of staff[e]	5	71	2	29
Helpfulness of				
Psychiatrists	17	89	2	11
Nurses	9	82	2	18
Attendants	2	50	2	50
Other staff groups	7	64	4	36
Total	64	71	26	29

[a] Staff's attentiveness to patients, availability for consultation, activity with patients.

[b] Staff's understanding of patients' problems, ability to communicate with the mentally ill, respect or concern for patients, expressions of kindness, acceptance of patients.

[c] Staff's encouragement of patient-staff arguments, tolerance of patients' anger or aggressive behavior.

[d] Staff's control over patients, enforcement of rules and regulations.

[e] Staff's helpfulness to patients, encouragement to get well, therapeutic effectiveness.

tics of psychiatric treatment in general or specific therapies are viewed equally favorably by hospitalized patients. Patients are strongly positive in their orientations toward the hospital's therapeutic value, assistance with medical problems, restrictions, and environment, are ambivalent about its patient freedoms and responsibilities, and are negative toward its staff-patient relations. Individual and milieu therapies are perceived quite positively by patients, while occupational, medication, activity, and electroconvulsive therapies are looked at somewhat positively. Patients are equally divided in their beliefs about the beneficial effects of group therapy.

DISCUSSION

The findings presented in this report lead us to conclude that the pictures of hospitalization, staff, and treatment drawn by patients bear little resemblance to the ones sketched by the critics of mental hospitals. Social scientists who have gathered qualitative data—by observing or interviewing patients informally or assuming the role of pseudopatient—have largely argued that patients are unfavorable in attitude because of their fear of commitment, loss of freedom, social stigma, abuse by staff, sense of powerlessness, anxiety about treatment, poor relationships with therapists, problems in adjusting to institutional life, and lack of apparent "cures" for patients at the time of discharge. However, patients responding to formal interviews and questionnaires repeatedly stress the bright, not the dark, side of the mental hospital. This review of quantitative data for numerous samples representative of different types of hospital populations has revealed that a rather large majority of patients voice favorable attitudes

TABLE 6.5 Favorableness of Patient Sample Responses or Mean Scores to Questions, Tests, and Subscales Dealing with Attitudes toward Treatment, by Content

| | QUESTIONS, TESTS, AND SUBSCALES | | | |
| | FAVORABLE | | UNFAVORABLE | |
CONTENT OF ATTITUDES	N	%	N	%
Treatment in general				
Therapeutic value[a]	22	79	6	21
Medical assistance[b]	10	100	—	—
Patient freedoms and responsibilities[c]	21	51	20	49
Staff-patient relations[d]	3	33	6	67
Ward restrictions[e]	10	91	1	9
Ward environment[f]	24	83	5	17
Specific therapies				
Individual	13	81	3	19
Group	7	50	7	50
Occupational	10	59	7	41
Milieu	17	89	2	11
Medication	6	60	4	40
Activity	18	69	8	31
ECT	29	59	20	41
Total	190	68	89	32

[a] Treatment is helpful, patients get well as a result of treatment.

[b] Hospital provides medical treatment, helps with hearing aids and false teeth.

[c] Treatment encourages patients to express themselves, act spontaneously, help care for other patients, seek out activities, cope with personal problems, become autonomous, help make decisions about ward activities and patient behavior.

[d] Staff explain treatment to patients, act on patients' suggestions, communicate freely with patients, are friendly, are sociable.

[e] Hospital pressures patients to conform, fails to discharge them on time, does not make ward rules known, has unclear program goals.

[f] Hospital provides work programs, recreational activities, small group meetings, contacts with community agencies and family members, order and organization on the ward, practical assistance to patients.

toward mental hospitals in general as well as their own institutions. Patients often claim that they (or other patients) benefit from hospitalization, are not bothered by restrictions, sense no stigma, are helped by psychiatrists and nurses, are accepted by staff, get well as a result of treatment, are satisfied with ward conditions, and value different therapies. The evidence indicates that the defenders of mental hospi-

tals have more accurately portrayed the views of patients than have the critics.

That Table 6.1 researchers' descriptions of the meaning of hospitalization, staff, and treatment for patients deviate so markedly from the meanings patients themselves ascribe to their hospital experiences is due, in part, to certain methodological biases inherent in such qualitative studies. The role of observer in the hospital, for example, can lead researchers to misinterpret the patient's point of view. Linn (1968) notes that when he observed patients on the ward he wondered how they could tolerate such "deplorable conditions," but when he later formally interviewed these same patients he began to understand their social situation; patients' favorableness toward the hospital seemed justified in light of the poverty, isolation, and disability from which many had come. The role of pseudopatient is not a satisfactory method of data collection either. Since the researchers are not mentally ill and are therefore not in a position to benefit from treatment, they cannot possibly perceive their experiences in the same manner as do bona fide patients. Caudill et al. (1952) openly state that the use of pseudopatients involves a subjectivity bias and discuss some of the disadvantages of this procedure. Similarly, Rosenhan (1973) [see Part 8] admits that he and the earlier pseudopatients had distinctly "negative reactions" and do not pretend to describe the experiences of true patients. A third problem with the qualitative data on mental hospitals is the lack of representatives. Informal interviews do not test attitudes in a systematic way, but instead are usually limited to topics that patients mention spontaneously, those most problematic to them at the time (Sonn, 1977). Such unstructured data tend to be collected via a nonprobability sampling of patients and are not interpreted within the context of a total hospital experience.

Qualitative researchers' theoretical biases also help to explain why the negative aspects of hospitalization, staff, and treatment have been exaggerated in their reports. It is clear that these scientists were not neutral toward patients or completely objective in their orientations. Goffman (1961:x) contends that his view of the mental hospital "is probably too much that of a middle-class male," that perhaps he "suffered vicariously about conditions that lower-class patients handle with little pain," and that unlike some patients he "came to the hospital with no great respect for the discipline of psychiatry." Qualitative researchers tended to identify with the disadvantaged patients, and were deeply concerned with their welfare although

they had no direct responsibility toward them. These scientists were "outsiders" whose central aim was to analyze the mental hospital as a life setting for patients, as Levinson and Gallagher (1964:9) put it, "with emphasis upon its pathogenic, ego-wounding, corrosive qualities." Another fault of the qualitative studies, according to Linn (1968), is the conceptual error of assuming that patients in mental hospitals have a homogeneous definition of their situation, that is, that they all view their institutionalization with embitterment, distrust, and hostility. He believes that in any mental hospital there are at least as many patients with favorable as unfavorable viewpoints, who see their treatment as a retreat from poor environmental conditions and a chance to begin a new life.

Findings from hospital studies other than those reviewed here offer clues as to why patients are so favorably disposed toward mental hospitals. Hudgens (1963) found that at the time of admission the patients' key motivations for entering treatment were to be protected or cared for permissively, to escape from the pressures of everyday life, to improve interpersonal relationships, and to establish control over feelings and behavior. Martin et al. (1977) observed that a very small minority of patients viewed their recovery as beyond their control and remained passive in treatment; most adopted an active role and endeavored to better their adjustment to the hospital. Gove and Fain (1977) contend that there is nothing intrinsic in the commitment process that is seriously debilitating; a follow-up study of committed and voluntary patients indicated that the situation and behavior (via employment, marriage, or relationships) of both groups improved after discharge. Studies of recidivism show that most patients return to the hospital voluntarily—because of poverty, deprivation, inactivity, or the lack of alternatives open to them (Rosenblatt and Mayer, 1974).

The assumptions of the labelling theory approach to mental illness and hospitalization vis-à-vis the attitudes of patients seem to apply to only a small proportion of them. We observed that a minority of patients in approximately three-fourths of the quantitative studies reviewed, and a majority in one fourth, expressed negative or ambivalent opinions of hospitalization, staff, and treatment. These patients were especially critical of staff-patient relations, staff permissiveness, and staff control. These results underscore the fact that a good many patients still sense the coerciveness of mental hospitals, exactly as the qualitative researchers beginning in the 1950s so aptly described. Affirmative changes in hospital administration and growth of adieu therapy during the past two decades have apparently not completely assuaged the negative impressions of patients. Since the attitudes of the vast majority of patients in the Table 6.2 samples were positive, our observations are thus consistent with a growing number of studies in recent years that have found labelling theory to be a less than adequate framework for interpreting psychiatric phenomena (see Greenley, 1979; Quadagno and Antonio, 1976).

The traditional psychiatric perspective likewise does not adequately account for the attitudes of the majority of hospitalized patients. There is reason to presume that many patients would harbor negative feelings, since mental illness involves psychic pain, distress, and anxiety, and patients are sufficiently distraught by the time they reach the hospital. However, this potential for negativism is never realized for most patients. It may be that unfavorable attitudes are only characteristic of higher-class patients or those from environments that are more attractive than the hospital, a small percentage of the total psychiatric population at any given moment. Or perhaps the bulk of patients in institutions, regardless of class status or social situation, are favorably disposed to the hospital because it offers them the opportunity to relieve symptoms, learn to cope with little difficulties, overcome personal inadequacies, or correct behavioral problems. Whatever the reason, it seems that psychiatrists and other mental health professionals have misjudged how patients might feel about their illness, hospitalization, or treatment. This conclusion is substantiated by studies that have reported that staff often failed to accurately estimate patient attitudes (Kahn et al., 1979; Zaslove et al., 1966).

The patients and personnel of mental hospitals have been found, in various studies, to differ significantly in their perceptions of mental illness (Weinstein, 1977:13). Patients have less general knowledge of psychiatry, adhere more to custodial ideology, and believe more in physical causation than do professional or treatment staff. It was anticipated, therefore, that patients would be less favorable toward hospitalization, staff, or treatment than hospital personnel, but this was borne out in only 19 of the 47 cases summarized that compared both groups. In the remaining cases patients were more favorable than staff slightly more often than they were similar to them. Thus, although in any mental hospital there are sharp differences between its patients and personnel in social status, role expectations, and personal experiences, such differences are not always manifested in terms of attitude.

Qualitative methods in social research are important means of obtaining data on human behavior and cultural patterns. Participant observations and informal interviews are especially useful for uncovering people's interpretations of social events and their own or someone else's behavior. One of the most important functions of qualitative methods is to stimulate or "set the stage" for later data collection via quantitative methods, and this is exactly what happened with studies of the mental hospital from the patient's view. Several Table 6.2 researchers (Levinson and Gallagher, 1964:8-11; Linn, 1968; Reznikoff et al., 1959) reviewed the earlier qualitative studies and stated categorically that these works formed the backdrop for their quantitative studies of patients' attitudes. However, the data generated from the two types of methods differ greatly because by and large qualitative researchers failed to consider the positive experiences patients often encounter in the hospital. Studies of the kind given in Table 6.1 have overlooked the fact that the hospital provides various social and psychological opportunities for patients, the potential for rehabilitation, and at times a more protective environment than that enjoyed on the outside (Killian and Bloomberg, 1975). Much of this research has disregarded the restitutive processes that can occur inadvertently with mental hospitalization (such as for personal stability or family reintegration) and has instead focused on the debilitating processes (Gove, 1970). Unfortunately, it is the qualitative report of the mental hospital—with interesting, though one-sided, anecdotes and descriptions—that is more often read, quoted, and cited by mental health professionals.

The key observation of this study, that patients in about 75 percent of the hospital samples reviewed espoused favorable attitudes, was frankly quite surprising to us. We had anticipated that patients in per-haps 20 to 30 percent of the Table 6.2 studies would be positive, as we, too, pictured the mental hospital as a "total institution" with all the concomitant detriments the term implies. We can thus join ranks with other mental health researchers who have recently reported results that run counter to popular beliefs (Frank et al., 1978; Pearlin and Schooler, 1979). The facts concerning patients' degree of favorableness toward mental hospitals do not coincide with the myth about patients' attitudes.

REFERENCES

Allen, J. C., and G. M. Barton. (1976). "Patient comments about hospitalization: Implications for change." *Comprehensive Psychiatry* 17:631–640.

Almond, R., K. Keniston, and S. Boltax. (1968), "The value system of a milieu therapy unit." *Archives of General Psychiatry* 19:545–561.

Anspach, R. R. (1979). "From stigma to identity politics: Political activism among the physically disabled and former mental patients." *Social Science and Medicine* 13A:765–773.

Backner, B. L., and R. D. Kissinger. (1963). "Hospitalized patients' attitudes toward mental health professionals and mental patients." *Journal of Nervous and Mental Disease* 136:72–75.

Barton, G. M., and N. Scheer. (1975). "A measurement of attitudes about an activity program." *American Journal of Occupational Therapy* 29:284–287.

Caudill, W., F. C. Redlich, H. R. Gilmore, and E. B. Brody. (1952). "Social structure and interaction processes on a psychiatric ward." *American Journal of Orthopsychiatry* 22:314–334.

Chastko, H. E., I. D. Glick, E. Gould, and W. A. Hargreaves. (1971). "Patients' post hospital evaluations of psychiatric nursing treatment." *Nursing Research* 20:333–338.

Clarke, G. J. (1979) "In defense of deinstitutionalization." *Milbank Memorial Fund Quarterly* 57:461–469.

Dowds, B. N., and K. F. Fontana. (1977). "Patients' and therapists' expectations and evaluations of hospital treatment: Satisfactions and disappointments." *Comprehensive Psychiatry* 18:295–300.

Dunham, H. W., and S. K. Weinberg. (1960). *The Culture of the State Mental Hospital*. Detroit: Wayne State University.

Eaton, M. T., and M. H. Peterson. (1969). *Psychiatry*. Flushing, NY: Medical Examination.

Ellsworth, R., W. Klett, H. Gordon, and R. Gunn. (1971). "Milieu characteristics of successful psychiatric treatment programs." *American Journal of Orthopsychiatry* 41:427–441.

Ellsworth, R., and R. Maroney. (1972). "Characteristics of psychiatric programs and their effects on patients' adjustment." *Journal of Consulting and Clinical Psychology* 39:436–447.

Frank, A., S. Eisenthal, and A. Lazare. (1978). "Are there social class differences in patients' treatment conceptions? Myths and facts." *Archives of General Psychiatry* 35:61–69.

Freeman, C. P. L., and R. E. Kendell. (1980). "ECT: I. Patients' experiences and attitudes." *British Journal of Psychiatry* 137:8–16.

Fryling, V. B., and A. G. Fryling. (1960). "Patients' attitudes toward sociotherapy." *Psychiatric Quarterly* (Supplement) 34:97–115.

Giovannoni, J. M., and L. P. Ullmann. (1963). "Conceptions of mental health held by psychiatric patients." *Journal of Clinical Psychology* 19:398–400.

Goffman, E. (1961). *Asylums*. Garden City, NY: Doubleday.

Goldman, A. R. (1965). "Wanting to leave or stay in a mental hospital: Incidence and correlates." *Journal of Clinical Psychology* 21:317–322.

Goldstein, R. H., J. Racy, D. M. Dressier, R. A. Ciottone, and J. R. Willis. (1972). "What benefits patients? An inquiry into the opinions of psychiatric inpatients and their residents." *Psychiatric Quarterly* 46:49–80.

Gordon, H. L., and C. Groth. (1961). "Mental patients wanting to stay in the hospital." *Archives of General Psychiatry* 4:124–130.

Gould, E., and I. D. Glick. (1976). "Patient-staff judgments of treatment program helpfulness of a psychiatric ward." *British Journal of Medical Psychology* 49:23–33.

Gove, W. R. (1970). "Societal reaction as an explanation of mental illness: An evaluation." *American Sociological Review* 35:873–884.

Gove, W. R., and T. Fain. (1973). "The stigma of mental hospitalization: An attempt to evaluate its consequences." *Archives of General Psychiatry* 28:494–500.

Gove, W. R., and T. Fain. (1977). "A comparison of voluntary and committed psychiatric patients." *Archives of General Psychiatry* 34:669–676.

Greenley, J. I. (1979). "Familial expectations, posthospital adjustment, and the societal reaction perspective on mental illness." *Journal of Health and Social Behavior* 20:217–227.

Gynther, M. D., M. Reznikoff, and M. Fishman. (1963). "Attitudes of psychiatric patients toward treatment, psychiatrists and mental hospitals." *Journal of Nervous and Mental Disease* 136:68–71.

Hamister, R. (1955). "An investigation of patient and staff opinions concerning the effectiveness of neuropsychiatric staff members." *Journal of Social Psychology* 41:115–137.

Handler, L., and G. Perlman. (1973). "The attitudes of patients and aides toward the role of the psychiatric aide." *American Journal of Psychiatry* 130:322–325.

Hillard, J. R., and R. Folger. (1977). "Patients' attitudes and attributions to electroconvulsive shock therapy." *Journal of Clinical Psychology* 33:855–861.

Hudgens, R. W. (1963). "Psychiatric inpatients at a teaching hospital: An inquiry into reasons for admission and factors promoting clinical change." *Archives of General Psychiatry* 9:384–389.

Jansen, D. J. (1973). "What state hospital psychiatric patients want more of and less of in treatment." *Journal of Consulting and Clinical Psychology* 41:3–17.

Jansen, D. J., and M. W. Aldrich. (1973). "State hospital psychiatric patients evaluate their treatment teams." *Hospital and Community Psychiatry* 24:768–770.

Kahn, M. A., L. Obstfeld, and S. Heiman. (1979). "Staff conceptions of patients' attitudes toward mental disorder and hospitalization as compared to patients' and staff's actual attitudes." *Journal of Clinical Psychology* 35:415–420.

Keith-Spiegel, P., H. M. Grayson, and D. Spiegel. (1970). "Using the discharge interview to evaluate a psychiatric hospital." *Mental Hygiene* 54:298–300.

Killian, L. M., and S. Bloomberg. (1975). "Rebirth in a therapeutic community: A case study." *Psychiatry* 38:39–54.

Kish, G. B. (1971). "Evaluation of ward atmosphere." *Hospital and Community Psychiatry* 22:159–161.

Klass, D. B., G. A. Growe, and M. Strizich. (1977). "Ward treatment milieu and posthospital functioning." *Archives of General Psychiatry* 34:1047–1052.

Lee, H. S. (1979). "Patients' comments on psychiatric inpatient treatment experiences: Patient-therapist relationships and their implications for treatment outcome." *Psychiatric Quarterly* 51:39–54.

Levinson, D. J., and E. B. Gallagher. (1964). *Patienthood in the Mental Hospital.* Boston: Houghton Mifflin.

Linn, L. S. (1968). "The mental hospital from the patient perspective." *Psychiatry* 31:213–223.

Lowenkopf, E. and M. Greenstein. (1972). "How state hospital patients view their illness." *Diseases of the Nervous System* 33:679–683.

Luft, L. L., K. Smith, and M. Kace. (1978). "Therapists', patients, and inpatient staff's views of treatment modes and outcomes." *Hospital and Community Psychiatry* 29:505–511.

Martin, P. J., M. H. Friedmeyer, J. E. Moore, and R. A. Claveaux. (1977). "Patients' expectancies and improvement in treatment: The shape of the link." *Journal of Clinical Psychology* 33:827–833.

Mayer, J. E., and A. Rosenblatt. (1974). "Clash in perspective between mental patients and staff." *American Journal of Orthopsychiatry* 44:432–441.

Mayo, C., R. G. Havelock, and D. L. Simpson. (1971) "Attitudes toward mental illness among psychiatric patients and their wives." *Journal of Clinical Psychology* 27:128–132.

Moos, R. H. (1974). *Evaluating Treatment Environments: A Social Ecological Approach.* New York: John Wiley.

Morrow, W. I. (1973). "Effects of a nursing home visit on state hospital patients' attitudes toward nursing home placement." *Journal of Geriatric Psychiatry* 6:122–133.

Olinick, S. L (1964). "The negative therapeutic reaction." *International Journal of Psychoanalysis* 45:540–548.

Pearlin, L. I., and C. Schooler. (1979). "Some extensions of the structure of coping." *Journal of Health and Social Behavior* 20:202–205.

Pettit, D. E. (1971). "Patients' attitudes toward ECT—not the 'shocker' we think?" *Canadian Psychiatric Association Journal* 16:365–366.

Pierce, W. D., E. J. Trickett, and R. H. Moos. (1972). "Changing ward atmosphere through staff discussion of the perceived ward environment." *Archives of General Psychiatry* 26:35–41.

Pine, F., and E. J. Levinson. (1961). "A sociopsychological conception of patienthood." *International Journal of Social Psychiatry* 7:106–123.

Polak, P. (1970). "Patterns of discord: Goals of patients, therapists, and community members." *Archives of General Psychiatry* 23:277–283.

Quadagno, J. S., and R. J. Antonio. (1976). "Labeling theory as an oversocialized conception of man: The case of mental illness." *Sociology and Social Research* 60:33–45.

Reznikoff, M., J. P. Brady, and W. W. Zeller. (1959). "The psychiatric attitudes battery: A procedure for assessing attitudes toward psychiatric treatment and hospitals." *Journal of Clinical Psychology* 15:260–265.

Reznikoff, M., and L. C. Toomey. (1960). "Attitudinal change in hospitalized psychiatric patients." *Journal of Clinical and Experimental Psychopathology* 21:309–314.

Roback, H., and W. U. Snyder. (1965). "A comparison of hospitalized mental patients' adjustment with their attitudes toward psychiatric hospitals." *Journal of Clinical Psychology* 21:228–230.

Roman, P. M. (1971). "Labeling theory and community psychiatry: The impact of psychiatric sociology on ideology and practice in American psychiatry." *Psychiatry* 34:378–390.

Rosenblatt, A., and J. E. Mayer. (1974). "The recidivism of mental patients: A review of past studies." *American Journal of Orthopsychiatry* 44:697–706.

Rosenhan, D. L. (1973). "On being sane in insane places." *Science* 179:250–258.

Scheff, T. J. (1966). *Being Mentally Ill: A Sociological Theory.* Chicago: Aldine.

Skodol, A. E., R. Plutchik, and T. B. Karasu. (1980). "Expectations of hospital treatment: Connecting views of patients and staff." *Journal of Nervous and Mental Disease* 168:70–74.

Small, I. F., J. G. Small, and R. Gonzalez. (1965). "The clinical correlates of attitudinal change during psychiatric treatment." *American Journal of Psychotherapy* 19:66–74.

Small, J. G., I. F. Small, and M. P. Hayden. (1965). "Prognosis and change in attitude: The importance of shifts of opinion in psychiatric patients." *Journal of Nervous and Mental Disease* 140:215–217.

Sonn, M. (1977). "Patients' subjective experiences of psychiatric hospitalization." Pp. 245–264 in T. C. Manschreck and A. M Kleinman (eds.), *Renewal in Psychiatry.* New York: John Wiley.

Souelem, O. (1955). "Mental patients' attitudes toward mental hospitals." *Journal of Clinical Psychology* 11:181–185.

Spencer, J. (1977). "Psychiatry and convulsant therapy." *Medical Journal of Australia* 1:844–847.

Spiegel, D., and J. B. Younger. (1972). "Ward climate and community stay of psychiatric patients." *Journal of Consulting and Clinical Psychology* 39:62–69.

Stanton, A. H., and M. S. Schwartz. (1954). *The Mental Hospital.* New York: Basic Books.

Toomey, L. C., M. Reznikoff, J. P. Brady, and D. W. Schumann. (1961). "Attitudes of nursing students toward psychiatric treatment and hospitals." *Mental Hygiene* 45:589–602.

Townsend, J. M. (1975). "Cultural conceptions and mental illness: A controlled comparison of Germany and America." *Journal of Nervous and Mental Disease* 160:409–421.

Townsend, J. M. (1976). "Self-concept and the institutionalization of mental patients: An overview and critique." *Journal of Health and Social Behavior* 17:263–271.

Verinis, J. S., and J. A. Flaherty. (1978). "Using the Ward Atmosphere Scale to help change the treatment environment." *Hospital and Community Psychiatry* 29:238–240.

Weinstein, R. M. (1972). "Patients' perceptions of mental illness: Paradigms for analysis." *Journal of Health and Social Behavior* 13:38–47.

Weinstein, R. M. (1977). "Patient attitudes toward mental illness and the mentally ill." *Current Concepts in Psychiatry* 3:7–13.

Weinstein, R. M. (1979). "Patient attitudes toward mental hospitalization: A review of quantitative research." *Journal of Health and Social Behavior* 20:237–258.

Weinstein, R. M. (1981a). "Mental patients' attitudes toward hospital staff: A review of quantitative research." *Archives of General Psychiatry* 38:483–489.

Weinstein, R. M. (1981b). "Attitudes toward psychiatric treatment among hospitalized patients: A review of quantitative research." *Social Science and Medicine* 15E:301–314.

Wing, J. K. (1962). "Institutionalism in mental hospitals." *British Journal of Social and Clinical Psychology* 1:38–51.

Wolfensberger, W. P. (1958). "Attitudes of alcoholics toward mental hospitals." *Quarterly Journal of Studies of Alcohol* 19:447–451.

Zaslove, M. O., J. T. Ungerleider, and M. C. Fuller. (1966). "How psychiatric hospitalization helps: Patient views vs. staff views." *Journal of Nervous and Mental Disease* 142:568–576.

Zaslove, M. O., J. T. Ungerleider, and M. C. Fuller. (1968). "The importance of the psychiatric nurse: Views of physicians, patients, and nurses." *American Journal of Psychiatry* 125:482–486.

CHAPTER 7

THE IDEA OF CONTEXTUAL EFFECTS

GREGG LEE CARTER

A major insight of sociology is that individuals with similar characteristics act and think differently when exposed to different situations. An important part of sociological inquiry is to ask what situations encourage people to behave, think, or feel in particular ways—perhaps even in ways that might seem peculiar if only individual traits are considered.

In the technical literature, this insight is called "contextual effects." The idea has a long scholarly tradition, from Durkheim's discovery that Protestants are less likely to commit suicide in Catholic countries than in Protestant countries, to Coleman's finding that poor children tend to do better when sent to schools with middle-class children than to schools with other poor children. . . .

Analyses combining individual and contextual (social structural or situational) variables bridge the micro and macro levels of analysis. That is, they provide a concrete means for connecting an individual's attitudes, sentiments, and behavior, on the one hand, with the influences of social settings and groups on such attitudes, sentiments, and behavior, on the other.

Because of its prominence in sociological inquiry, all [students of sociology should be exposed to] . . . a rich assortment of examples of "contextual effects." [The examples provided here combine] . . . noteworthy data with elementary analysis techniques.

. . .

From "Teaching the Idea of Contextual Effects," *Teaching Sociology* 19(4), pp. 526–531, October 1991. © American Sociological Association. Used by permission.

ILLUSTRATION 1: THE IMPORTANCE OF ORGANIZATIONAL CONTEXT IN PREDICTING THE STRENGTH OF THE RELATIONSHIP BETWEEN SOCIAL CLASS AND ACADEMIC PERFORMANCE

Tables 7.1 to 7.3 provide a first illustration of the idea of combining individual and contextual variables. The data are of the highest quality; they are taken from the National Center for Education Statistics' (NCES) *National Longitudinal Study of the High School Class of 1972*. Table 7.1 reveals a sharp difference between the academic achievement of high school students from poor family backgrounds and those from middle-class backgrounds.

Yet, when we introduce the control variable of whether poorer students attend public or Catholic schools, we see a drastic reduction in the strength of the relationship in parochial schools and a slight strengthening in public schools (see Tables 7.2 and 7.3). The important issue, of course, is not religion per se, but the assumption that Catholic schools are more likely to be socially organized in ways that encourage academic achievement—regardless of a student's social class origins. This assumption is empirically testable; indeed, Tables 7.4 and 7.5 reveal that NCES data support it (note that these data come from NCES's *High School and Beyond* study). In short, we find Catholic schools much more likely to maintain order and discipline and somewhat more likely to offer college preparatory curricula. Thus, school type—Catholic versus public—is a proxy variable for the context variables of level of discipline and of the educational tracking to which students are exposed. In short, poorer adolescents respond differently in different educational environments. When

TABLE 7.1   Social Class and Cognitive Achievement

COGNITIVE ACHIEVEMENT (%)	SOCIAL CLASS ORIGINS		
	POOR	MIDDLE CLASS	
High	27.1	79.9	% difference between social classes on low level of achievement
	(622)	(2,090)	
Low	72.9	20.1	52.8
	(1,677)	(526)	
(Column Sum)	(2,229)	(2,616)	Total $N = 4,915$

SOURCE: *National Longitudinal Study of the High School Class of 1972* (National Center for Education Statistics); adapted from Riordan and Mazur (1988, p. 75; Data Set NLS72B, using only their "high" and "low" categories for SES and SENTEST).

TABLE 7.2   Social Class and Cognitive Achievement for Students Attending Public Schools

COGNITIVE ACHIEVEMENT (%)	SOCIAL CLASS ORIGINS		
	POOR	MIDDLE CLASS	
High	24.9	79.1	% difference between social classes on low level of achievement
	(548)	(1,883)	
Low	75.1	20.9	54.2
	(1,653)	(499)	
(Column Sum)	(2,201)	(2,382)	Total $N = 4,583$

SOURCE: *National Longitudinal Study of the High School Class of 1972* (National Center for Education Statistics); adapted from Riordan and Mazur (1988, p. 75, Data Set NLS72B, using only their "high" and "low" categories for SES and SENTEST).

TABLE 7.3   Social Class and Cognitive Achievement for Students Attending
Catholic Schools

COGNITIVE ACHIEVEMENT (%)	SOCIAL CLASS ORIGINS		
	POOR	MIDDLE CLASS	
High	75.5	88.5	% difference between
	(74)	(207)	social classes on low
			level of achievement
Low	24.5	11.5	13.0
	(24)	(27)	
(Column Sum)	(98)	(234)	Total $N = 332$

SOURCE: *National Longitudinal Study of the High School Class of 1972* (National Center for Education Statistics); adapted from Riordan and Mazur (1988, p. 75, Data Set NLS72B, using only their "high" and "low" categories for SES and SENTEST).

TABLE 7.4   School Type and Level of Discipline

LEVEL OF DISCIPLINE (%)	SCHOOL TYPE		
	PUBLIC	CATHOLIC	
High	23.5	91.7	% difference between
	(3,457)	(1,709)	school types on
			level of discipline
Low	76.5	8.3	68.2
	(11,249)	(154)	
(Column Sum)	(14,706)	(1,863)	Total $N = 16,569$

SOURCE: *High School and Beyond Study* (class of 1982; National Center for Education Statistics); adapted from Riordan and Mazur (1988, p. 82, Data Set HSB82D, using their variables SCHOOL and ORDER).

TABLE 7.5   School Type and Curricular Emphasis

	SCHOOL TYPE		
CURRICULAR EMPHASIS (%)	**PUBLIC**	**CATHOLIC**	
Pre-College	33.2	63.1	% difference between
	(4,884)	(1,175)	types of school on
			vocational/general
			curriculum
Vocational/General	66.8	36.9	68.2
	(9,822)	(688)	
(Column Sum)	(14,706)	(1,863)	Total N = 16,569

SOURCE: *High School and Beyond Study* (class of 1982; National Center for Education Statistics); adapted from Riordan and Mazur (1988, p. 82, Data Set HSB82D, using their variables SCHOOL and TRACK).

they are exposed to college-oriented, disciplined academic environments, their family backgrounds become less important in determining their academic achievements.

ILLUSTRATION 2: THE IMPORTANCE OF RELIGION PREVALENCE IN PREDICTING THE STRENGTH OF THE RELATIONSHIP BETWEEN PROTESTANTISM AND SUICIDE

Data presented in Durkheim's *Suicide* offer a second illustration of the effects of a social context variable on individual behavior. Durkheim argues that Protestantism places great emphasis on the directness of an individual's relationship with God and on one's freedom of inquiry in understanding this relationship. Thus when a Protestant sins, he or she feels God's eyes directly upon him or her, feels excessively guilty, and becomes prone to suicide. Catholics, on the other hand, have social buffers between themselves and God, provided by the Church's hierarchy and by more complex social organization. Sinful Catholics have strong traditions that they may follow to alleviate guilt. For example, they may confess to a priest, who gives them a chance for moral atonement (through penance) and who can offer social support; thus suicide becomes less likely. Indeed, Durkheim's data support his interpretation: in the late nineteenth century, the Protestant states of Prussia, Saxony, and Denmark averaged 190 suicides per million inhabitants, while the average suicide rate for the Catholic states of Spain, Portugal, and Italy was 96 per million (see Durkheim 1951, p. 152).

When Protestants found themselves living among a large number of Catholics, however, the Catholic mind-set seemed to rub off—presumably through social interaction between Catholics and Protestants, as well as through the role models the former provided the latter. In short, when the contextual variable of the salience of Catholicism is introduced, Protestant suicide rates drop significantly. In nineteenth-century Prussia, for example, where Catholics constituted about one-third of the total population, the Protestant suicide rate was 196 per million; in Austria, however, where Catholics accounted for 90 percent of the population, the Protestant rate dropped to 80 per million (see Durkheim 1951, p. 154).

ILLUSTRATION 3: THE IMPORTANCE OF SOCIAL STRUCTURE IN PREDICTING THE STRENGTH OF THE RELATIONSHIP BETWEEN RELIGIOUS AFFILIATION AND ADOLESCENTS' SELF-ESTEEM

A third example of contextual analysis is taken from Rosenberg's classic work on adolescents' self-esteem. Rosenberg (1986) argues that adolescents raised in contexts in which they are "sociologically deviant"— that is, have social characteristics unlike those of most others around them—are more likely to find themselves flawed when social comparisons are made. The upshot is that such individuals are more likely than others to suffer from low self-esteem. Rosenberg's data support his thesis for religious affiliation; that is, where an individual's own religion differs from the religion of most others in his or her neighborhood, that person has an increased chance of suffering low self-esteem. In a probability sample of New York high students, for example, Rosenberg found 29 percent of the Catholic students who were raised in predominantly Catholic neighborhoods suffering from low self-esteem; this proportion increased to 41 percent, however, for Catholic students raised in neighborhoods where the predominant religion was Judaic or Protestant. The findings were consistent for all religious groups; that is, Jewish students raised in Jewish neighborhoods had higher self-esteem than their counterparts raised in non-Jewish neighborhoods; the same was true for Protestant students (see Rosenberg 1986, p. 102).

ILLUSTRATION 4: THE IMPORTANCE OF SOCIAL STRUCTURE IN PREDICTING THE STRENGTH OF THE RELATIONSHIP BETWEEN RELIGIOSITY AND DELINQUENCY

A fourth example of the power of contextual analysis is revealed in Rodney Stark's explication of the relationship between religiosity and juvenile delinquency. Studies done at the individual level of analysis sometimes reveal a relationship between these two variables (Albrecht, Chadwick, and Alcorn 1977;

Higgins and Albrecht 1977) and sometimes do not (Burkett and White 1974; Hirschi and Stark 1969). Stark's recounting of how he arrived at his final interpretation is an excellent illustration of contextual-effects thinking:

Does religion inhibit delinquency or not? ... One day the light dawned. I had been thinking only about individuals, about how the beliefs of the individual were supposed to shape behavior. But I should have been thinking about groups and about how religious culture is sustained through interaction. Put another way, I began to see that religion is not primarily an individual characteristic, a set of beliefs and practices of particular persons, but that it is first and foremost a social structure. What counts is not only whether a person is religious but also the proportion of religious people in their environment.

Teenagers form and sustain their interpretations of norms in day-to-day interaction with their friends. If most of a young person's friends are not actively religious, then religious considerations will rarely enter into the process by which norms are accepted or justified. Even if the religious teenager does bring up religious considerations, these will not strike a responsive chord in most of the others. This is not to suggest that nonreligious teenagers don't believe in the norms or discuss right and wrong, but that they will do so without recourse to religious justifications. In such a situation, the effect of the religiousness of some individuals will be smothered by group indifference to religion, and religion will tend to become a very compartmentalized component of the individual's life— something that surfaces only in specific situations such as Sunday school and church. In contrast, when the majority of a teenager's friends are religious, then religion enters freely into everyday interactions and becomes a valid part of the normative system.

[In short,] religious individuals [are] less likely than others to break the norms, but only in communities where the majority of people are actively religious. . . . [Indeed,] surveys done in communities and other social settings where most people belong to a church . . . find that teenagers active in religion are less delinquent than others. In contrast, studies done where most people do not belong to a church . . . find no correlation between religion and delinquency. (p. 96)

. . . . Put another way, a religion gains the power to alter behavior when it is supported by attachments to

others who accept the authority of the moral beliefs that religion teaches. (Stark 1990, p. 190)

ILLUSTRATION 5: THE IMPORTANCE OF THE PRESTIGE OF THE WORK CONTEXT IN PREDICTING THE STRENGTH OF THE RELATIONSHIP BETWEEN EDUCATION AND JOB SATISFACTION

[As a final example of contextual-effects consider the] . . . 1985 General Social Survey data, [which] reveal a positive relationship between education and self-reported job satisfaction: respondents with at least some college report the highest levels of job satisfaction, while those with less than a high school education report the least; high school graduates—those with exactly 12 years of education—fall in between. However, as shown in column 1 of Table 7.6, the relationship is reversed when we introduce the control variable of "job prestige" set at the "lower prestige" level. More specifically, when highly educated individuals find themselves working in low prestige jobs—presumably, jobs that they and their co-workers regard as beneath a person with college education—they report dramatically lower levels of job satisfaction. On the other hand, the original positive relationship between education and job satisfaction is strengthened significantly when the control variable is set at the "higher prestige" level (see column 2 of Table 7.6). Again, the change in the original relationship is due primarily to changes in the reports of the more highly educated individuals; that is, these individuals declare much higher levels of job satisfaction (presumably because they are working in jobs that they and their co-workers think demand at least some education at the college level). In short, the relationship between the individual characteristics of education and job satisfaction is modified—in readily interpretable directions—by the work context in which it is found.

SUMMARY COMMENTS

. . . Perhaps because nowadays it is most often explicitly discussed and defined only in methodologically arcane articles, the idea of contextual effects is not introduced formally in any of the 40 or so most prominent introductory sociology texts.

The problem is *not* that many contextual arguments are not made repeatedly in these texts (although invariably they are made without displaying the kind of data contained in the present note). The problem is that without being introduced formally to the idea of contextual effects, students lack the conceptual framework—and the associated vocabulary—with which to recognize the common ground underlying these arguments. [Students taking sociology courses are being socialized] . . . into the sociological perspective. Essential to any socializing process is the acquisition of a vocabulary to help order

TABLE 7.6   Percentage of GSS Respondents Reporting "High" Job Satisfaction by Education and Occupational Prestige

EDUCATION	OCCUPATIONAL PRESTIGE (%)	
	LOWER	HIGHER
Less than high school (0–11 years)	67.4 (31)	60.0 (9)
High school graduate (12 years)	62.5 (25)	85.4 (35)
At least some college (13+ years)	41.7 (5)	87.2 (41)

SOURCE: *General Social Survey, 1985* (National Opinion Research Center, University of Chicago, 1985); adapted from Savage (1988), using only his "very satisfied" and "not very satisfied" categories for JOB SATISFACTION and only his "low" and "medium" categories for OCCUPATIONAL PRESTIGE.

and construct reality. The rubric "contextual effects" encourages students to think sociologically. It evokes the very essence of our discipline. Indeed, it captures C. Wright Mills's contention that the promise of sociology is "understanding the intimate realities of ourselves in connection with larger social realities" (1959, p. 15).

REFERENCES

Albrecht, S. L., B. A. Chadwick, and D. S. Alcorn. 1977. "Religiosity and Deviance: Application of an Attitude-Behavior Contingent Consistency Model." *Journal for the Scientific Study of Religion* 16:263–74.

Burkett, S. R., and M. White. 1974. "Hellfire and Delinquency: Another Look." *Journal for the Scientific Study of Religion* 13:455–62.

Durkheim, E. 1951 (orig. 1897). *Suicide*. New York: Free Press.

Higgins, P. C., and G. L. Albrecht. 1977. "Hellfire and Delinquency Revisited." *Social Forces* 55:952–58.

Hirschi, T., and R. Stark. 1969. "Hellfire and Delinquency." *Social Problems* 17:202–13.

Mills, C. W. 1959. *The Sociological Imagination*. New York: Oxford University Press.

Riordan, C., and A. Mazur. 1988. *Introductory Sociology Workbook (with CHIP Software)*. New York: Harper and Row.

Rosenberg, M. 1986. *Conceiving the Self*. Malabar, FL: Krieger.

Savage, D. 1988. *A User's Guide to Social Scene and Social Trend*. New York: Holt, Rinehart and Winston.

Stark, R. 1990. *Sociology*. 3rd ed. Belmont, CA: Wadsworth.

PART 3

CULTURAL EXPLANATIONS OF HUMAN BEHAVIOR

Why do the Chinese dislike milk and milk products? Why would the Japanese die willingly in a Banzai charge that seemed senseless to Americans? Why do some nations trace descent through the father, others through the mother, still others through both parents? Not because different peoples have different instincts, not because they were destined by God or Fate to different habits, not because the weather is different in China and Japan and the United States. Sometimes shrewd common sense has an answer that is close to that of the anthropologist: "because they were brought up that way." By "culture" . . . [we mean] the total life way of a people, the social legacy the individual acquires from his group. Or culture can be regarded as that part of the environment that is the creation of man.

—Clyde Kluckhohn[1]

To explain different patterns of culture we have to begin by assuming that human life is not merely random or capricious. Without this assumption, the temptation to give up when confronted with a stubbornly inscrutable custom or institution soon proves irresistible. Over the years I have discovered that lifestyles which others claimed were totally inscrutable actually had definite and readily intelligible causes. . . . Even the most bizarre-seeming beliefs and practices turn out on closer inspection to be based on ordinary, banal, one might say "vulgar" conditions, needs, and activities.

—Marvin Harris[2]

---

[1]*Mirror for Man* (New York: Whittlesey House), 1949, p. 17.
[2]*Cows, Pigs, Wars, and Witches: The Riddles of Culture* (New York: Random House), 1974, pp. 4–5.

The description and explanation of different human cultures are among the most fascinating aspects of sociology. The essays in Part 3 describe cultures that differ greatly from that of the United States.

The above quotes by Kluckhohn and Harris represent the two basic parts of cultural explanation. The first is to know where someone comes from and some of the cultural traits of that society. For example, suppose we meet two women from India, Indira and Mitra, and are struck by the fact that they abstain from eating beef (they go to McDonald's and order *salads*, can you imagine?!). Why? If we know a little about India and its culture, we can answer this question: The dominant religion is *Hinduism* (espoused by 80% or so of the population); further, this religion considers it a sacrilege to kill or consume cattle. Thus, the first part of our cultural explanation of behavior is straightforward and relatively easy: Indira and Mitra don't eat beef because they're from India, where most of the people don't eat beef—indeed, where cows are revered. The women are simply following the rules of behavior by which they were reared.

The second part of cultural explanation is harder to develop and can run intellectually deep. It addresses the question "Why does any particular aspect of a culture arise and then persist?" Sociologists usually seek the answer in one of two basic realms: (1) the way in which the aspect or trait is *functional* for the well-being and survival of the society and its members; or (2) the way in which the aspect or trait serves the needs of the rich and powerful—those who control the economy and the government (compare Karl Marx's essay in Part 1).

William Graham Sumner (1840–1910) developed the first "sociology" course taught in the United States (1875) and wrote the first American sociology textbook, *Folkways* (1906). Able to read in thirteen languages, Sumner perused everything he could about as many societies as possible. He used his 150,000 pages of notes to develop the cultural concepts in *Folkways*. The excerpt reprinted here develops the idea of *ethnocentrism* (the tendency for every group to think that its ways of doing things are the best), showing its many faces and the many ways in which it structures our thinking about ourselves and others.

Marvin Harris of the University of Florida is a master of cultural explanation. Here he uses economic data and deft reasoning to demonstrate how not eating cows makes Indians healthier and richer than if they were to do so. When I was growing up in Nevada in the 1960s, our image of India was that of a nation overflowing with skinny people—people who were really foolish for not devouring the millions of cows that were free to roam the streets and fields. What an eye-opener Harris's analysis would have been for us back then. It may well be this for you now.

CHAPTER 8

ETHNOCENTRISM

WILLIAM GRAHAM SUMNER

Ethnocentrism is the technical name for this view of things in which one's own group is the center of everything, and all others are scaled and rated with reference to it. Folkways[1] correspond to it to cover both the inner and the outer relation. Each group nourishes its own pride and vanity, boasts itself superior, exalts its own divinities, and looks with contempt on outsiders. Each group thinks its own folkways the only right ones, and if it observes that other groups have folkways, these excite its scorn. Opprobrious epithets are derived from these differences. "Pig-eater," "cow-eater," "uncircumcised," "jabberers" are epithets of contempt and abomination. The Tupis called the Portuguese by a derisive epithet descriptive of birds which have feathers around their feet, on account of trousers. For our present purpose the most important fact is that ethnocentrism leads a people to exaggerate and intensify everything in their own folkways which is peculiar and which differentiates them from others. It therefore strengthens the folkways.

ILLUSTRATIONS OF ETHNOCENTRISM

The Papuans on New Guinea are broken up into village units which are kept separate by hostility, cannibalism, head hunting, and divergences of language and religion. Each village is integrated by its own language, religion, and interests. A group of villages is sometimes united into a limited unity by connubium.[2] A wife taken inside of this group unit has full status; one taken outside of it has not. The petty group units are peace groups within and are hostile to all outsiders. The Mbayas of South America believe that their deity has bidden them live by making war on others, taking their wives and property, and killing their men.

When Caribs were asked whence they came, they answered, "We alone are people." The meaning of the name Kiowa is "real or principal people." The Lapps call themselves "men," or "human beings." The Greenland Eskimo think that Europeans have been sent to Greenland to learn virtue and good manners from the Greenlanders. Their highest form of praise for a European is that he is, or soon will be, as good as the Greenlander. The Tunguses call themselves "men." As a rule it is found that nature peoples call themselves men. Others are something else—perhaps not defined—but not real men. In myths the origin of their own tribe is that of the real human race. They do not account for the others. The Ainos [natives of Japan] derive their name from that of the first man, whom they worship as a god. Evidently the name of the god is derived from the tribe name. The Ovambo name is a corruption of the name of the tribe for themselves, which means "the wealthy." Amongst the most remarkable people in the world for ethnocentrism are the Seri of Lower California. They observe an attitude of suspicion and hostility to all outsiders, and strictly forbid marriage with outsiders.

The Jews divided all mankind into themselves and Gentiles. They were the "chosen people." The Greeks and Romans called the outsiders "barbarians."

From *Folkways: A Study in the Sociological Importance of Usages, Manners, Customs, Mores, and Morals* (New York: Ginn and Company, 1906), pp. 13–15, 111. Sumner cites fourteen data sources and references in this essay in support of his depictions of various cultural practices; these citations have been deleted here.

In Euripides' tragedy of *Iphigenia in Aulis* Iphigenia says that it is fitting that Greeks should rule over barbarians, but not contrariwise, because Greeks are free, and barbarians are slaves. The Arabs regarded themselves as the noblest nation and all others as more or less barbarous. In 1896, the Chinese minister of education and his counselors edited a manual in which this statement occurs: "How grand and glorious is the Empire of China, the middle kingdom! She is the largest and richest in the world. The grandest men in the world have all come from the middle empire." In all the literature of all the states equivalent statements occur, although they are not so naively expressed. In Russian books and newspapers the civilizing mission of Russia is talked about, just as, in the books and journals of France, Germany, and the United States, the civilizing mission of those countries is assumed and referred to as well understood. Each state now regards itself as the leader of civilization, the best, the freest, and the wisest, and all others as inferior. Within a few years our own man-on-the-curbstone has learned to class all foreigners of the Latin peoples as "dagos," and "dago" has become an epithet of contempt. These are all cases of ethnocentrism.

PATRIOTISM

Patriotism is a sentiment which belongs to modern states. It stands in antithesis to the medieval notion of catholicity. Patriotism is loyalty to the civic group to which one belongs by birth or other group bond. It is a sentiment of fellowship and cooperation in all the hopes, work, and suffering of the group. Medieval catholicity would have made all Christians an in-group and would have set them in hostility to all Mohammedans and other non-Christians. It never could be realized. When the great modern states took form and assumed control of social interests, group sentiment was produced in connection with those states. Men responded willingly to a demand for support and help from an institution which could and did serve interests. The state drew to itself the loyalty which had been given to men (lords), and it became the object of that group vanity and antagonism which

had been ethnocentric. For the modern man patriotism has become one of the first of duties and one of the noblest of sentiments. It is what he owes to the state for what the state does for him, and the state is, for the modern man, a cluster of civic institutions from which he draws security and conditions of welfare. The masses are always patriotic. For them the old ethnocentric jealousy, vanity, truculency, and ambition are the strongest elements in patriotism. Such sentiments are easily awakened in a crowd. They are sure to be popular. Wider knowledge always proves that they are not based on facts. That we are good and others are bad is never true. By history, literature, travel, and science men are made cosmopolitan. The selected classes of all states become associated; they intermarry. The differentiation by states loses importance. All states give the same security and conditions of welfare to all. The standards of civic institutions are the same, or tend to become such, and it is a matter of pride in each state to offer civic status and opportunities equal to the best. Every group of any kind whatsoever demands that each of its members shall help defend group interests. Every group stigmatizes any one who fails in zeal, labor, and sacrifices for group interests. Thus the sentiment of loyalty to the group, or the group head, which was so strong in the Middle Ages, is kept up, as far as possible, in regard to modern states and governments. The group force is also employed to enforce obligations of devotion to group interests. It follows that judgments are precluded and criticism is silenced.

CHAUVINISM

That patriotism may degenerate into a vice is shown by invention of the name for the vice: chauvinism. It is a name for boastful and truculent group self-assertion. It overrules personal judgment and character, and puts the whole group at the mercy of the clique which is ruling at the moment. It produces the dominance of watchwords and phrases which take the place of reason and conscience in determining conduct. The patriotic bias is a recognized perversion of thought and judgment against which our education should guard us. . . .

MISSIONS AND MORES

The contrasts and antagonisms of the mores of different groups are the stumbling-blocks in the way of all missionary enterprise, and they explain many of the phenomena which missions present. We think that our "ways" are the best, and that their superiority is so obvious that all heathen, Mohammedans, Buddhists, etc., will, as soon as they learn what our ways are, eagerly embrace them. Nothing could be further from the truth. It is difficult to an untraveled Englishman, who has not had an opportunity of throwing himself into the spirit of the East, to credit the disgust and detestation that numerous everyday acts, which appear perfectly harmless to his countrymen, excite in many Orientals. If our women are shocked at polygamy and the harem, Mohammedan women are equally shocked at the ball and dinner dresses of our ladies, at our dances, and at the manners of social intercourse between the sexes. Negroes in East Africa are as much disgusted to see white men eat fowl or eggs as we are at any of their messes. Missions always offer something from above downwards. They contain an assumption of superiority and beneficence. Half-civilized people never admit their assumption. They meet it just as we would meet a mission of Mohammedans or Buddhists to us. Savages and barbarians dismiss "white man's ways" with indifference. The virtues and arts of civilization are almost as disastrous to the uncivilized as its vices. It is really the great tragedy of civilization that the contact of lower and higher is disastrous to the former, no matter what may be the point of contact, or how little the civilized may desire to do harm.

NOTES

1. *Folkways* constitute the multitude of rules and customs of a society that govern the behavior of its members. The violation of a folkway results in milder penalties than the violation of a *more;* mores represent a society's most serious rules. Mores are discussed later in this essay. An example of a modern folkway is "one's socks should match." An example of a more is "Thou shalt not kill."
2. A marriage system in which men are restricted to a particular group in choosing their mates.

_____CHAPTER 9_____

INDIA'S SACRED COW

MARVIN HARRIS

News photographs that came out of India during the famine of the late 1960s showed starving people stretching out bony hands to beg for food while sacred cattle strolled behind undisturbed. The Hindu, it seems, would rather starve to death than eat his cow or even deprive it of food. The cattle appear to browse unhindered through urban markets eating an orange here, a mango there, competing with people for meager supplies of food.

By Western standards, spiritual values seem more important to Indians than life itself. Specialists in food habits around the world like Fred Simoons at the University of California at Davis consider Hinduism an irrational idealogy that compels people to overlook abundant, nutritious foods for scarcer, less healthful foods.

What seems to be an absurd devotion to the mother cow pervades Indian life. Indian wall calendars portray beautiful young women with bodies of fat white cows, often with milk jetting from their teats into sacred shrines.

Cow worship even carries over into politics. In 1966 a crowd of 120,000 people, led by holy men, demonstrated in front of the Indian House of Parliament in support of the All-Party Cow Protection Campaign Committee. In Nepal, the only contemporary Hindu kingdom, cow slaughter is severely punished. As one story goes, the car driven by an official of a United States agency struck and killed a cow. In order to avoid the international incident that would have occurred when the official was arrested for murder,

the Nepalese magistrate concluded that the cow had committed suicide.

Many Indians agree with Western assessments of the Hindu reverence for their cattle, the zebu, or *Bos indicus,* a large-humped species prevalent in Asia and Africa. M. N. Srinivas, an Indian anthropologist, states: "Orthodox Hindu opinion regards the killing of cattle with abhorrence, even though the refusal to kill vast number of useless cattle which exist in India today is detrimental to the nation." Even the Indian Ministry of Information formerly maintained that "the large animal population is more a liability than an asset in view of our land resources." Accounts from many different sources point to the same conclusion: India, one of the world's great civilizations, is being strangled by its love for the cow.

The easy explanation for India's devotion to the cow, the one most Westerners and Indians would offer, is that cow worship is an integral part of Hinduism. Religion is somehow good for the soul, even if it sometimes fails the body. Religion orders the cosmos and explains our place in the universe. Religious beliefs, many would claim, have existed for thousands of years and have a life of their own. They are not understandable in scientific terms.

But all this ignores history. There is more to be said for cow worship than is immediately apparent. The earliest Vedas, the Hindu sacred texts from the second millennium B.C., do not prohibit the slaughter of cattle. Instead, they ordain it as part of sacrificial rites. The early Hindus did not avoid the flesh of cows and bulls; they ate it at ceremonial feasts presided over by Brahman priests. Cow worship is a relatively recent development in India; it evolved as the Hindu religion developed and changed.

From *Human Nature Magazine* 1(2), pp. 28, 30–36, February 1978. Copyright © 1978 by Human Nature, Inc.; reprinted by permission of the publisher.

This evolution is recorded in royal edicts and religious texts written during the last 3,000 years of Indian history. The Vedas from the first millennium B.C. contain contradictory passages, some referring to ritual slaughter and others to a strict taboo on beef consumption. A. N. Bose, in *Social and Rural Economy of Northern India, 600 B.C.–200 A.D.,* concludes that many of the sacred-cow passages were incorporated into the texts by priests of a later period.

By 200 A.D. the status of Indian cattle had undergone a spiritual transformation. The Brahman priesthood exhorted the population to venerate the cow and forbade them to abuse it or to feed on it. Religious feasts involving the ritual slaughter and consumption of livestock were eliminated and meat eating was restricted to the nobility.

By 1000 A.D., all Hindus were forbidden to eat beef. Ahimsa, the Hindu belief in the unity of all life, was the spiritual justification for this restriction. But it is difficult to ascertain exactly when this change occurred. An important event that helped to shape the modern complex was the Islamic invasion, which took place in the eighth century A.D. Hindus may have found it politically expedient to set themselves off from the invaders, who were beefeaters, by emphasizing the need to prevent the slaughter of their sacred animals. Thereafter, the cow taboo assumed its modern form and began to function much as it does today.

The place of the cow in modern India is every place—on posters, in the movies, in brass figures, in stone and wood carvings, on the streets, in the fields. The cow is a symbol of health and abundance. It provides the milk that Indians consume in the form of yogurt and ghee (clarified butter), which contribute subtle flavors to much spicy Indian food.

This, perhaps, is the practical role of the cow, but cows provide less than half the milk produced in India. Most cows in India are not dairy breeds. In most regions, when an Indian farmer wants a steady, high-quality source of milk he usually invests in a female water buffalo. In India the water buffalo is the specialized dairy breed because its milk has a higher butterfat content than zebu milk. Although the farmer milks his zebu cows, the milk is merely a by-product.

More vital than zebu milk to South Asian farmers are zebu calves. Male calves are especially valued because from bulls come oxen, which are the mainstay of the Indian agricultural system.

Small, fast oxen drag wooden plows through late-spring fields when monsoons have dampened the dry, cracked earth. After harvest, the oxen break the grain from the stalk by stomping through mounds of cut wheat and rice. For rice cultivation in irrigated fields, the male water buffalo is preferred (it pulls better in deep mud), but for most other crops, including rainfall rice, wheat, sorghum, and millet, and for transporting goods and people to and from town, a team of oxen is preferred. The ox is the Indian peasant's tractor, thresher, and family car combined; the cow is the factory that produces the ox.

If draft animals instead of cows are counted, India appears to have too few domesticated ruminants, not too many. Since each of the 70 million farms in India requires a draft team, it follows that Indian peasants should use 140 million animals in the fields. But there are only 83 million oxen and male water buffalo on the subcontinent, a shortage of 30 million draft teams.

In other regions of the world, joint ownership of draft animals might overcome a shortage, but Indian agriculture is closely tied to the monsoon rains of late spring and summer. Field preparation and planting must coincide with the rain, and a farmer must have his animals ready to plow when the weather is right. When the farmer without a draft team needs bullocks most, his neighbors are all using theirs. Any delay in turning the soil drastically lowers production.

Because of this dependence on draft animals, loss of the family oxen is devastating. If a beast dies, the farmer must borrow money to buy or rent an ox at interest rates so high that he ultimately loses his land. Every year foreclosures force thousands of poverty-stricken peasants to abandon the countryside for the overcrowded cities.

If a family is fortunate enough to own a fertile cow, it will be able to rear replacements for a lost team and thus survive until life returns to normal. If, as sometimes happens, famine leads a family to sell its cow and ox team, all ties to agriculture are cut. Even if the family survives, it has no way to farm the land, no oxen to work the land, and no cows to produce oxen.

The prohibition against eating meat applies to the flesh of cows, bulls, and oxen, but the cow is the most sacred because it can produce the other two. The peasant whose cow dies is not only crying over a spiritual loss but over the loss of his farm as well.

Religious laws that forbid the slaughter of cattle promote the recovery of the agricultural system from the dry Indian winter and from periods of drought. The monsoon, on which all agriculture depends, is erratic. Sometimes, it arrives early, sometimes late, sometimes not at all. Drought has struck large portions of India time and again in this century, and Indian farmers and the zebus are accustomed to these natural disasters. Zebus can pass weeks on end with little or no food and water. Like camels, they store both in their humps and recuperate quickly with only a little nourishment.

During droughts the cows often stop lactating and become barren. In some cases the condition is permanent but often it is only temporary. If barren animals were summarily eliminated, as Western experts in animal husbandry have suggested, cows capable of recovery would be lost along with those entirely debilitated. By keeping alive the cows that can later produce oxen, religious laws against cow slaughter assure the recovery of the agricultural system from the greatest challenge it faces—the failure of the monsoon.

The local Indian governments aid the process of recovery by maintaining homes for barren cows. Farmers reclaim any animal that calves or begins to lactate. One police station in Madras collects strays and pastures them in a field adjacent to the station. After a small fine is paid, a cow is returned to its rightful owner when the owner thinks the cow shows signs of being able to reproduce.

During the hot, dry spring months most of India is like a desert. Indian farmers often complain they cannot feed their livestock during this period. They maintain the cattle by letting them scavenge on the sparse grass along the roads. In the cities the cattle are encouraged to scavenge near food stalls to supple-

ment their scant diet. These are the wandering cattle tourists report seeing throughout India.

Westerners expect shopkeepers to respond to these intrusions with the deference due a sacred animal; instead, their response is a string of curses and the crack of a long bamboo pole across the beast's back or a poke at its genitals. Mahatma Gandhi was well aware of the treatment sacred cows (and bulls and oxen) received in India. "How we bleed her to take the last drop of milk from her. How we starve her to emaciation, how we ill-treat the calves, how we deprive them of their portion of milk, how cruelly we treat the oxen, how we castrate them, how we beat them, how we overload them" [Gandhi, 1954].

Oxen generally receive better treatment than cows. When food is in short supply, thrifty Indian peasants feed their working bullocks and ignore their cows, but rarely do they abandon the cows to die. When cows are sick, farmers worry over them as they would over members of the family and nurse them as if they were children. When the rains return and when the fields are harvested, the farmers again feed their cows regularly and reclaim their abandoned animals. The prohibition against beef consumption is a form of disaster insurance for all India.

Western agronomists and economists are quick to protest that all the functions of the zebu cattle can be improved with organized breeding programs, cultivated pastures, and silage. Because stronger oxen would pull the plow faster, they could work multiple plots of land, allowing farmers to share their animals. Fewer healthy, well-fed cows could provide Indians with more milk. But pastures and silage require arable land, land needed to produce wheat and rice.

A look at Western cattle farming makes plain the cost of adopting advanced technology in Indian agriculture. In a study of livestock production in the United States, David Pimentel of the College of Agriculture and Life Sciences at Cornell University, found that 91 percent of the cereal, legume, and vegetable protein suitable for human consumption is consumed by livestock. Approximately three-quarters of the arable land in the United States is devoted to growing food for livestock. In the production of meat and milk, American ranchers use enough fossil fuel to equal more than 82 million barrels of oil annually.

Indian cattle do not drain the system in the same way. In a 1971 study of livestock in West Bengal, Stewart Odend'hal [1972] of the University of Missouri found that Bengalese cattle ate only the inedible remains of subsistence crops—rice straw, rice hulls, the tops of sugar cane, and mustard-oil cake. Cattle graze in the fields after harvest and eat the remains of crops left on the ground; they forage for grass and weeds on the roadsides. The food for zebu cattle costs the human population virtually nothing. "Basically," Odend'hal says, "the cattle convert items of little direct human value into products of immediate utility."

In addition to plowing the fields and producing milk, the zebus produce dung, which fires the hearths and fertilizes the fields of India. Much of the estimated 800 million tons of manure produced annually is collected by the farmers' children as they follow the family cows and bullocks from place to place. And when the children see the droppings of another farmer's cattle along the road, they pick those up also. Odend'hal reports that the system operates with such high efficiency that the children of West Bengal recover nearly 100 percent of the dung produced by their livestock.

From 40 to 70 percent of all manure produced by Indian cattle is used as fuel for cooking; the rest is returned to the fields as fertilizer. Dried dung burns slowly, cleanly, and with low heat—characteristics that satisfy the household needs of Indian women. Staples like curry and rice can simmer for hours. While the meal slowly cooks over an unattended fire, the women of the household can do other chores. Cow chips, unlike firewood, do not scorch as they burn.

It is estimated that the dung used for cooking fuel provides the energy-equivalent of 43 million tons of coal. At current prices, it would cost India an extra 1.5 billion dollars in foreign exchange to replace the dung with coal. And if the 350 million tons of manure that are being used as fertilizer were replaced with commercial fertilizers, the expense would be even greater. Roger Revelle of the University of California at San Diego has calculated that 89 percent of the

energy used in Indian agriculture (the equivalent of about 140 million tons of coal) is provided by local sources. Even if foreign loans were to provide the money, the capital outlay necessary to replace the Indian cow with tractors and fertilizers for the fields, coal for the fires, and transportation for the family would probably warp international financial institutions for years.

Instead of asking the Indians to learn from the American model of industrial agriculture, American farmers might learn energy conservation from the Indians. Every step in an energy cycle results in a loss of energy to the system. Like a pendulum that slows a bit with each swing, each transfer of energy from sun to plants, plants to animals, and animals to human beings involves energy losses. Some systems are more efficient than others; they provide a higher percentage of the energy inputs in a final, useful form. Seventeen percent of all energy zebus consume is returned in the form of milk, traction, and dung. American cattle raised on Western rangeland return only 4 percent of the energy they consume.

But the American system is improving. Based on techniques pioneered by Indian scientists, at least one commercial firm in the United States is reported to be building plants that will turn manure from cattle feedlots into combustible gas. When organic matter is broken down by anaerobic bacteria, methane gas and carbon dioxide are produced. After the methane is cleansed of the carbon dioxide, it is available for the same purposes as natural gas—cooking, heating, electric generation. The company constructing the biogasification plant plans to sell its product to a gas-supply company, to be piped through the existing distribution system. Schemes similar to this one could make cattle ranches almost independent of utility and gasoline companies, for methane can be used to run trucks, tractors, and cars as well as to supply heat and electricity. The relative energy self-sufficiency that the Indian peasant has achieved is a goal American farmers and industry are now striving for.

Studies like Odend'hal's understate the efficiency of the Indian cow, because dead cows are used for purposes that Hindus prefer not to acknowledge. When a cow dies, an Untouchable, a member of one of the lowest ranking castes in India, is summoned to haul away the carcass. Higher castes consider the body of the dead cow polluting; if they handle it, they must go through a rite of purification.

Untouchables first skin the dead animal and either tan the skin themselves or sell it to a leather factory. In the privacy of their homes, contrary to the teachings of Hinduism, untouchable castes cook the meat and eat it. Indians of all castes rarely acknowledge the existence of these practices to non-Hindus, but most are aware that beefeating takes place. The prohibition against beefeating restricts consumption by the higher castes and helps distribute animal protein to the poorest sectors of the population that otherwise would have no source of these vital nutrients.

Untouchables are not the only Indians who consume beef. Indian Muslims and Christians are under no restriction that forbids them beef, and its consumption is legal in many places. The Indian ban on cow slaughter is state, not national, law and not all states restrict it. In many cities, such as New Delhi, Calcutta, and Bombay, legal slaughterhouses sell beef to retail customers and to restaurants that serve steak.

If the caloric value of beef and the energy costs involved in the manufacture of synthetic leather were included in the estimate of energy, the calculated efficiency of Indian livestock would rise considerably. As well as the system works, experts often claim that its efficiency can be further improved. Alan Heston [et al., 1971], an economist at the University of Pennsylvania, believes that Indians suffer from an overabundance of cows simply because they refuse to slaughter the excess cattle. India could produce at least the same number of oxen and the same quantities of milk and manure with 30 million fewer cows. Heston calculates that only 40 cows are necessary to maintain a population of 100 bulls and oxen. Since India averages 70 cows for every 100 bullocks, the difference, 30 million cows, is expendable.

What Heston fails to note is that sex ratios among cattle in different regions of India vary tremendously, indicating that adjustments in the cow population do take place. Along the Ganges River, one of the holiest shrines of Hinduism, the ratio drops to 47 cows for every 100 male animals. This ratio reflects the preference for dairy buffalo in the irrigated sectors of the Gangetic Plains. In nearby Pakistan, in contrast, where cow slaughter is permitted, the sex ratio is 60 cows to 100 oxen.

Since the sex ratios among cattle differ greatly from region to region and do not even approximate the balance that would be expected if no females were killed, we can assume that some culling of herds does take place; Indians do adjust their religious restrictions to accommodate ecological realities.

They cannot kill a cow but they can tether an old or unhealthy animal until it has starved to death. They cannot slaughter a calf but they can yoke it with a large wooden triangle so that when it nurses it irritates the mother's udder and gets kicked to death. They cannot ship their animals to the slaughterhouse but they can sell them to Muslims, closing their eyes to the fact that the Muslims will take the cattle to the slaughterhouse.

These violations of the prohibition against cattle slaughter strengthen the premise that cow worship is a vital part of Indian culture. The practice arose to prevent the population from consuming the animal on which Indian agriculture depends. During the first millennium B.C., the Ganges Valley became one of the most densely populated regions of the world.

Where previously there had been only scattered villages, many towns and cities arose and peasants farmed every available acre of land. Kingsley Davis, a population expert at the University of California at Berkeley, estimates that by 300 B.C. between 50 million and 100 million people were living in India. The forested Ganges Valley became a windswept semidesert and signs of ecological collapse appeared; droughts and floods became commonplace, erosion took away the rich topsoil, farms shrank as population increased, and domesticated animals became harder and harder to maintain.

It is probable that the elimination of meat eating came about in a slow, practical manner. The farmers who decided not to eat their cows, who saved them for procreation to produce oxen, were the ones who survived the natural disasters. Those who ate beef lost the tools with which to farm. Over a period of centuries, more and more farmers probably avoided beef until an unwritten taboo came into existence.

Only later was the practice codified by the priesthood. While Indian peasants were probably aware of the role of cattle in their society, strong sanctions were necessary to protect zebus from a population faced with starvation. To remove temptation, the flesh of cattle became taboo and the cow became sacred.

The sacredness of the cow is not just an ignorant belief that stands in the way of progress. Like all concepts of the sacred and the profane, this one affects the physical world; it defines the relationships that are important for the maintenance of Indian society.

Indians have the sacred cow, we have the "sacred" car and the "sacred" dog. It would not occur to us to propose the elimination of automobiles and dogs from our society without carefully considering the consequences, and we should not propose the elimination of zebu cattle without first understanding their place in the social order of India.

Human society is neither random nor capricious. The regularities of thought and behavior called culture are the principal mechanisms by which we human beings adapt to the world around us. Practices and beliefs can be rational or irrational, but a society that fails to adapt to its environment is doomed to extinction. Only those societies that draw the necessities of life from their surroundings without destroying those surroundings inherit the earth. The West has much to learn from the great antiquity of Indian civilization, and the sacred cow is an important part of that lesson.

REFERENCES

Gandhi, Mohandas K. 1954. *How to Serve the Cow*. Bombay: Navajivan Publishing House.

Heston, Alan, et al. 1971. "An Approach to the Sacred Cow of India." *Current Anthropology* 12, 191–209.

Odend'hal, Stewart. 1972. "Gross Energetic Efficiency of Indian Cattle in Their Environment." *Journal of Human Ecology* 1, 1–27.

PART 4

SOCIETY

The most grievous mistake in the social sciences is to read the character of a society through a single overriding concept, whether it be capitalism *or* totalitarianism, *and to mislead one as to the complex (overlapping and even contradictory) features of any modern society, or to assume that there are "laws of social development" in which one social system succeeds another by some inexorable necessity. Any society, since it mingles different kinds of economic, technological, political, and cultural systems (some features of which are common to all, some of which are historical and idiosyncratic), has to be analyzed from different vantage points, depending on the question one has in mind. . . .*

A pre-industrial [society] is primarily extractive, *its economy based on agriculture, mining, fishing, timber and other resources such as natural gas or oil. An industrial [society] is primarily* fabricating, *using energy and machine technology, for the manufacture of goods. A post-industrial [society] is one of* processing *in which telecommunications and computers are strategic for the exchange of information and technology. . . .*

The post-industrial society, as I have implied, does not displace *the industrial society, just as an industrial society has not done away with the agrarian sectors of the economy. Like palimpsests, the new developments overlie the previous layers, erasing some features and thickening the texture of society as a whole.*

—Daniel Bell[1]

---

[1]*The Coming of Post-Industrial Society: A Venture in Social Forecasting* (New York: Basic Books), 1976, pp. xii–xiv.

"Societies" are typically the largest units that sociologists study. Quite often, a particular society is coterminous with a nation-state. For example, sociologists and other academics will speak of, say, *French society* or *Japanese society* or *American society*. However, as the breakup of the Soviet Union and of Yugoslavia demonstrated in the early 1990s, this is not always the case. What many Americans had once thought was *Soviet* society turned out to be really *Russian* society. What they learned was that the former Soviet Union had been comprised of a multitude of societies—for example, *Georgian, Armenian, Uzbekian*.

As Daniel Bell observes in the quotation above, all societies have some elements in common, as well as many differences. For example, all societies develop *institutions* to solve common problems of survival: how to produce and distribute goods and services (solved via the *economy*), how to control sexual relations and procreation (the *family*), how to fix certain rules that everyone must follow and to regulate human interactions (the *polity* or *government*), how to train individuals to fulfill work and other important social roles (*education*), and how to answer the metaphysical questions that beset the human mind (*religion*).

As societies have become larger, more urbanized, and more complex, the belief of many observers, and perhaps the fear of even more, is that people have become lost in a sea of strangers. When individuals are cut off from one another, social problems rooted in loneliness and isolation—suicide, alcoholism, drug addiction, and crime—seem bound to increase and become difficult to control. However, Stanley Milgram (1933–1984) ingeniously demonstrated how, even in very large and very complex societies, human beings are not isolated, but rather are linked to one another through interconnecting social networks. Indeed, he demonstrated that we live in a small world. For example, it is likely that you are interpersonally connected to me. That is, you probably know someone, who knows someone, who knows someone that knows me—even though I live in Rhode Island and you may live thousands of miles away. Sound incredible? Read Milgram.

Caroline Hodges Persell of New York University describes how American society, which is typical of most modern industrial democracies (most of Europe, Japan, Canada, Australia, New Zealand), has experienced a decline of "civil society" (the social groups and relationships in which we are embedded, e.g., families, schools, neighborhoods, communities); for example, throughout the 1960s, 1970s, 1980s, and early 1990s, out-of-wedlock births and single-parent families increased, as did the prevalence of drug use and crime. All of this was followed by declining levels of "social capital," for example, trust in others and confidence in government and the educational system. ("*Social capital* can be defined simply as a set of informal values or norms shared among members of a group that permits cooperation among them. If members of the group come to expect that others will behave reliably and honestly, then they will come to trust one another. Trust is like a lubricant that makes the running of any group or organization more efficient."[2]) Persell marshals a great deal of data in support of her argument that the decline in civil society has been a function of economic distress—due to the loss of high-paying manufacturing jobs, corporate downsizing, and growing inequality (e.g., the ratio of top executive salaries to average worker salaries catapulted from 40:1 in 1974 to 211:1 in 1995). Further, she traces the effects of a declining civil society—for example, the fundamental transforming of the social order from its basis on voluntary compliance and informal community social controls to formal coercion (police, jails, capital punishment). To wit, the state of California now spends more on its prisons than it does on its universities.

---

[2]Francis Fukuyama, *The Great Disruption: Human Nature and the Reconstitution of Social Order* (New York: The Free Press, 1999), p. 16. Also, see Fukuyama's essay in Part 12.

_____CHAPTER 10_____

THE SMALL-WORLD PROBLEM:
THE MYTH OF MASS SOCIETY

STANLEY MILGRAM

Almost all of us have had the experience of encountering someone far from home, who, to our surprise, turns out to share a mutual acquaintance with us. This kind of experience occurs with sufficient frequency so that our language even provides a cliche to be uttered at the appropriate moment of recognizing mutual acquaintances.

We say, "My it's a small world."

The simplest way of formulating the small-world problem is: Starting with any two people in the world, what is the probability that they will know each other? A somewhat more sophisticated formulation, however, takes account of the fact that while persons X and Z may not know each other directly, they may share a mutual acquaintance—that is, a person who knows both of them. One can then think of an acquaintance chain with X knowing Y and Y knowing Z. Moreover, one can imagine circumstances in which X is linked to Z not by a single link, but by a series of links, X-a-b-c-d . . .y-Z. That is to say, person X knows person *a* who in turn knows person *b*, who knows *c* . . . who knows *y*, who knows Z.

Therefore, another question one may ask is: Given any two people in the world, person X and person Z, how many intermediate acquaintance links are needed before X and Z are connected?

Concern with the small-world problem is not new, nor is it limited to social psychologists like myself. Historians, political scientists, and commu-

nication specialists share an interest in the problem. Jane Jacobs, who is concerned with city planning, describes an acquaintance chain in terms of a children's game:

> When my sister and I first came to New York from a small city, we used to amuse ourselves with a game we called Messages. I suppose we were trying, in a dim way, to get a grip on the great, bewildering world into which we had come from our cocoon. The idea was to pick two wildly dissimilar individuals—say a head hunter in the Solomon Islands and a cobbler in Rock Island, Illinois—and assume that one had to get a message to the other by word of mouth; then we would each silently figure out a plausible, or at least possible, chain of persons through which the message could go. The one who could make the shortest plausible chain of messengers won. The head hunter would speak to the head man of his village, who would speak to the trader who came to buy copra, who would speak to the Australian patrol officer when he came through, who would tell the man who was next slated to go to Melbourne on leave, etc. Down at the other end, the cobbler would hear from his priest, who got it from the mayor, who got it from a state senator, who got it from the governor, etc. We soon had these close-to-home messengers down to a routine for almost everybody we could conjure up . . .

The importance of the problem does not lie in these entertaining aspects, but in the fact that it brings under discussion a certain mathematical structure in society, a structure that often plays a part, whether recognized or not, in many discussions of history, sociology, and other disciplines. For example, Henri Pirenne and George Duby, important historians, make

Reprinted with permission from *Psychology Today* Magazine, 1(1), pp. 61–67, May 1967. Copyright © 1967 (Sussex Publishers, Inc.).

the point that in the Dark Ages communication broke down between cities of western Europe. They became isolated and simply did not have contact with each other. The network of acquaintances of individuals became constricted. The disintegration of society was expressed in the growing isolation of communities, and the infrequent contact with those living outside a person's immediate place of residence.

There are two general philosophical views of the small-world problem. One view holds that any two people in the world, no matter how remote from each other, can be linked in terms of intermediate acquaintances, and that the number of such intermediate links is relatively small. This view sees acquaintances in terms of an infinitely intersecting arrangement that permits movement from any social group to another through a series of connecting links.

The second view holds that there are unbridgeable gaps between various groups and that therefore, given any two people in the world, they will never link up because people have circles of acquaintances which do not necessarily intersect. A message will circulate in a particular group of acquaintances, but may never be able to make the jump to another circle. This view sees the world in terms of concentric circles of acquaintances, each within its own orbit.

THE UNDERLYING STRUCTURE

Sometimes it is useful to visualize the abstract properties of a scientific problem before studying it in detail; that is, we construct a model of the main features of the phenomenon as we understand them. Let us represent all the people in the United States by a number of blue points. Each point represents a person, while lines connecting two points show that the two persons are acquainted. [Illustrations have been deleted.] Each person has a certain number of first-hand acquaintances, which we shall represent by the letters $a, b, c, \ldots n$. Each acquaintance in turn has his own acquaintances, connected to still other points. The exact number of lines radiating from any point depends on the size of a person's circle of acquaintances. The entire structure takes on the form of a complex network of 200 million points, with complicated connections

between them. . . . One way of restating the small-world problem in these terms is this: Given any two of these points chosen at random from this universe of 200 million points, through how many intermediate points would we pass before the chosen points could be connected by the shortest possible path?

RESEARCH AT M.I.T.

There are many ways to go about the study of the small-world problem, and I shall soon present my own approach to it. But first, let us consider the important contributions of a group of workers at The Massachusetts Institute of Technology, under the leadership of Ithiel de Sola Pool. Working closely with Manfred Kochen of IBM, Pool decided to build a theoretical model of the small-world, a model which closely parallels the idea of points and lines [developed earlier]. However, unlike my own model, which is purely pictorial, Pool and Kochen translate their thinking into strict mathematical terms.

To build such a model they needed certain information. First, they had to know how many acquaintances the average man has. Surprisingly, though this is a very basic question, no reliable answers could be found in the social science literature. So the information had to be obtained, a task which Michael Gurevitch, then a graduate student at M.I.T, undertook. Gurevitch asked a variety of men and women to keep a record of all the persons they came in contact with in the course of 100 days. It turned out that on the average, these people recorded names of roughly 500 persons, so that this figure could be used as the basis of the theoretical model. Now, if every person knows 500 other people, what are the chances that any two people will know each other? Making a set of rather simple assumptions, it turns out that there is only about one chance in 200,000 that any two Americans chosen at random will know each other. However, when you ask the chances of their having a mutual acquaintance, the odds drop sharply. And quite amazingly, there is better than a 50-50 chance that any two people can be linked up with two intermediate acquaintances. Or at least, that is what the Pool-Kochen theory indicates.

Of course, the investigators were aware that even if a man has 500 acquaintances, there may be a lot of inbreeding. That is, many of the 500 friends of my friend may be actually among the people I know anyway, so that they do not really contribute to a widening net of acquaintances; the acquaintances of X simply feed back into his own circle and fail to bring any new contacts into it. . . . It is a fairly straightforward job to check up on the amount of inbreeding if one uses only one or two circles of acquaintances, but it becomes almost impossible when the acquaintance chain stretches far and wide. So many people are involved that a count just isn't practical.

So the big obstacle one runs up against is the problem of social structure. Though poor people always have acquaintances, it would probably turn out that they tend to be among other poor people, and that the rich speak mostly to the rich. It is exceedingly difficult to assess the impact of social structure on a model of this sort. If you could think of the American population as simply 200 million points, each with 500 random connections, the model would work. But the contours of social structure make this a perilous assumption, for society is not built on random connections among persons but tends to be fragmented into social classes and cliques.

A HARVARD APPROACH

The Pool and Kochen mathematical model was interesting from a theoretical standpoint, but I wondered whether the problem might not be solved by a more direct experimental approach. The Laboratory of Social Relations at Harvard gave me $680 to prove that it could. I set out to find an experimental method whereby it would be possible to trace a line of acquaintances linking any two persons chosen at random.

Let us assume for the moment that the actual process of establishing the linkages between two persons runs only one way: from person A to person Z. Let us call person A the *starting* person, since he will initiate the process, and person Z the *target* person, since he is the person to be reached. All that would be necessary, therefore, would be to choose a starting person at random from the 200 million people who live in the United States, and then randomly choose a target person.

This is how the study was carried out. The general idea was to obtain a sample of men and women from all walks of life. Each of these persons would be given the name and address of the same target person, a person chosen at random, who lives somewhere in the United States. Each of the participants would be asked to move a message toward the target person, using only a chain of friends and acquaintances. Each person would be asked to transmit the message to the friend or acquaintance who he thought would be most likely to know the target person. Messages could move only to persons who knew each other on a first-name basis.

As a crude beginning, we thought it best to draw our starting persons from a distant city, so we chose Wichita, Kansas for our first study and Omaha, Nebraska for our second. (From Cambridge, these cities seem vaguely "out there," on the Great Plains or somewhere.) To obtain our sample, letters of solicitation were sent to residents in these cities asking them to participate in a study of social contact in American society. The target person in our first study lived in Cambridge and was the wife of a divinity school student. In the second study, carried out in collaboration with Jeffrey Travers, the target person was a stockbroker who worked in Boston and lived in Sharon, Massachusetts. To keep matters straight, I will refer to the first study as the Kansas Study, and the second as the Nebraska Study. These terms indicate merely where the starting persons were drawn from.

Each person who volunteered to serve as a starting person was sent a folder containing a document, which served as the main tool of the investigation. Briefly, the document contains:

1. The name of the target person as well as certain information about him. This orients the participants toward a specific individual.
2. A set of rules for reaching the target person. Perhaps the most important rule is: "*If you do not know the target person on a personal basis, do*

not try to contact him directly. Instead, mail this folder . . . to a personal acquaintance who is more likely than you to know the target person . . . it must be someone you know on a first-name basis." This rule sets the document into motion, moving it from one participant to the next, until it is sent to someone who knows the target person.

3. A roster on which each person in the chain writes his name. This tells the person who receives the folder exactly who sent it to him. The roster also has another practical effect; it prevents endless looping of the folder through participants who have already served as links in the chain, because each participant can see exactly what sequence of persons has led up to his own participation.

In addition to the document, the folder contains a stack of 15 business reply, or "tracer," cards. Each person receiving the folder takes out a card, fills it in, returns it to us, and sends the remaining cards along with the document to the next link.

Several other features of the procedure need to be emphasized. First, each participant is supposed to send the folder on to one other person only. Thus the efficiency with which the chain is completed depends in part on the wisdom of his choice in this matter. Second, by means of the tracer card, we have continuous feedback on the progress of each chain. The cards are coded so we know which chain it comes from and which link in the chain has been completed. The card also provides us with relevant sociological characteristics of the senders of the cards. Thus, we know the characteristics of completed, as well as incompleted, chains. Third, the procedure permits experimental variation at many points.

In short, the device possesses some of the features of a chain letter, though it does not pyramid in any way; moreover it is oriented toward a specific target, zeroes in on the target through the cooperation of a sequence of participants, and contains a tracer that allows us to keep track of its progress at all times.

WOULD IT WORK?

The question that plagued us most in undertaking this study was simply: Would the procedure work? Would any of the chains started in Kansas actually reach our target person in Massachusetts? Part of the excitement of experimental social psychology is that it is all so new we often have no way of knowing whether our techniques will work or simply turn out to be wispy pipe dreams.

The answer came fairly quickly. It will be recalled that our first target person was the wife of a student living in Cambridge. Four days after the folders were sent to a group of starting persons in Kansas, an instructor at the Episcopal Theological Seminary approached our target person on the street. "Alice," he said, thrusting a brown folder toward her, "this is for you." At first she thought he was simply returning a folder that had gone astray and had never gotten out of Cambridge, but when we looked at the roster, we found to our pleased surprise that the document had started with a wheat farmer in Kansas. He had passed it on to an Episcopalian minister in his home town, who sent it to the minister who taught in Cambridge, who gave it to the target person. Altogether the number of intermediate links between starting person and target person amounted to *two!*

HOW MANY INTERMEDIARIES?

As it turned out, this was one of the shortest chains we were ever to receive, for as more tracers and folders came in, we learned that chains varied from two to 10 intermediate acquaintances, with the median at five (see Figure 10.1). A median of five intermediate persons is, in certain ways, impressive, considering the distances traversed. Recently, when I asked an intelligent friend of mine how many steps he thought it would take, he estimated that it would require 100 intermediate persons or more to move from Nebraska to Sharon. Many people make somewhat similar estimates, and are surprised to learn that only five intermediates will—on the average—suffice. Somehow it does not accord with intuition. Later, I shall try to explain the basis of the discrepancy between intuition and fact.

On a purely theoretical basis, it is reasonable to assume that even fewer links are essential to complete the chains. First, since our participants can send the

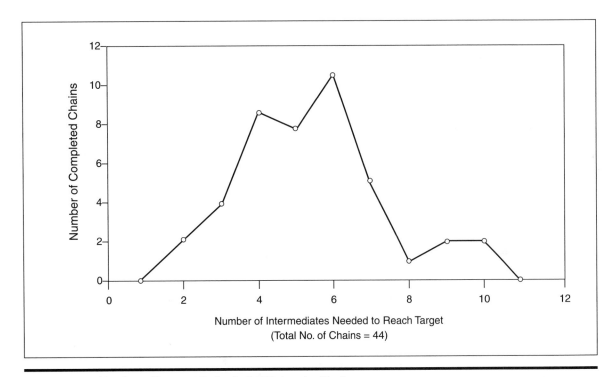

FIGURE 10.1   Number of Intermediaries in the Nebraska Study

folder to only one of their 500 possible contacts, it is unlikely that even through careful selections, they will necessarily and at all times select the contact best able to advance the chain to the target. On the whole they probably make pretty good guesses but surely, from time to time, they overlook some possibilities for short cuts. Thus, the chains obtained in our empirical study are less efficient than those generated theoretically.

Second, by working on a highly rational basis, each intermediary moves the folder toward the target person. That is, a certain amount of information about the target person—his place of employment, place of residence, schooling, and so forth—is given to the starting subject, and it is on the basis of this information alone that he selects the next recipient of the folder. Yet, in real life, we sometimes know a person because we chance to meet him on an ocean liner, or we spend a summer in camp together as teenagers, yet

these haphazard bases of acquaintanceship cannot be fully exploited by the participants.

There is one factor, however, that could conceivably have worked in the opposite direction in our experiments, giving us the illusion that the chains are shorter than they really are. There is a certain decay in the number of active chains over each remove, even when they do not drop out because they reach the target person. Of 160 chains that started in Nebraska, 44 were completed and 126 dropped out. These chains die before completion because on each remove a certain proportion of participants simply do not cooperate and fail to send on the folder. Thus, the results we obtained on the distribution of chain lengths occurred within the general drift of a decay curve. It is possible that some of the incompleted chains would have been longer than those that were completed. To account for this possibility, Harrison White of Harvard has constructed a mathematical model to show what the distribution of chain lengths would look like if all chains went through to completion. In terms of this model, there is a transformation of the data, yielding slightly longer chains.

EXAMINING THE CHAINS

Several features of the chains are worth examining, for they tell us something about the pattern of contact in American society. Consider, for example, the very pronounced tendency in our Kansas Study for females to send the folder on to females, and males to send it on to males. Of the 145 participants involved in the study, we find:

Female	→	*Female*	*56*
Male	→	*Male*	*58*
Female	→	*Male*	*18*
Male	→	*Female*	*13*

Thus participants were three times as likely to send the folder on to someone of the same sex as to someone of the opposite sex. Exactly why this is so is not easy to determine, but it suggests that certain kinds of communication are strongly conditioned by sex roles.

Participants indicated on the reply cards whether they were sending the folder on to a friend, a relative, or an acquaintance. In the Kansas Study, 123 sent the folder to friends and acquaintances, while only 22 sent it to relatives. Cross-cultural comparison would seem useful here. It is quite likely that in societies which possess extended kinship systems, relatives will be more heavily represented in the communication network than is true in the United States. In American society, where extended kinship links are not maintained, acquaintance and friendship links provide the preponderant basis for reaching the target person. I would guess, further, that within certain ethnic groups in the United States, a higher proportion of familial lines would be found in the data. Probably, for example, if the study were limited to persons of Italian extraction, one would get a higher proportion of relatives in the chain. This illustrates, I hope, how the small-world technique may usefully be used to illuminate varied aspects of social structure. . . .

COMMON PATHWAYS

Each of us is embedded in a small-world structure. It is not true, however, that each of our acquaintances constitutes an equally important basis of contact with the larger social world. It is obvious that some of our acquaintances are more important than others in establishing contacts with broader social realms; some friends are relatively isolated, while others possess a wide circle of acquaintances, and contact with them brings us into a far-ranging network of additional persons.

Referring to our Nebraska Study, let us consider in detail the pattern of convergence crystallizing around the target person—the stockbroker living in Sharon, Massachusetts, and working in Boston. . . . A total of 64 chains reached him (44 chains originated in Nebraska and 20 chains, from an auxiliary study, originated in the Boston area). Twenty-four of the chains reached him at his place of residence in the small town outside of Boston. Within Sharon, 16 were given to him by Mr. Jacobs, a clothing merchant in town. Thus, the clothing merchant served as the principal point of mediation between the broker and a larger world, a fact which came as a considerable surprise, and even something of a shock for the broker. At his place of work, in a Boston brokerage house, 10 of the chains passed through Mr. Jones and five through Mr. Brown. Indeed 48 percent of the chains to reach the broker were moved on to him by three persons: Jacobs, Jones, and Brown. Between Jacobs and Jones there is an interesting division of labor. Jacobs mediates the chains advancing to the broker by virtue of his residence. Jones performs a similar function in the occupational domain, and moves 10 chains enmeshed in the investment brokerage network to the target person.

More detail thus fills in the picture of the small world. First we learn that the target person is not surrounded by acquaintance points, each of which is equally likely to feed into an outside contact; rather, there appear to be highly popular channels for the transmission of the chain. Second, there is differentiation among these commonly used channels, so that certain of them provide the chief points of transmission in regard to residential contact, while others have specialized contact possibilities in the occupational domain. For each possible realm of activity in which the target person is involved, there is likely to emerge a sociometric star with specialized contact possibilities.

GEOGRAPHIC AND SOCIAL MOVEMENT

The geographic movement of the folder from Nebraska to Massachusetts is striking. There is a progressive closing in on the target area as each new person is added to the chain. . . . In some cases, however, a chain moves all the way from Nebraska to the very neighborhood in which the target person resides, but then goes round and round, never quite making the necessary contact to complete the chain. Some chains died only a few hundred feet from the target person's house, after a successful journey of 1000 miles. Thus we see that social communication is sometimes restricted less by physical distance than by social distance. . . .

INTUITION AND FACT

As we saw above, many people were surprised to learn that only five intermediaries will, on the average, suffice to link any two randomly chosen individuals, no matter where they happen to live in the United States. We ought to try to explain the discrepancy between intuition and fact.

The first point to remember is that although we deal directly with only five intermediaries, behind each of them stands a much larger group of from 500 to 2500 persons. That is, each participant has an acquaintance pool of 500 to 2500 persons from which he selects the person who, he thinks, is best able to advance the chain. Thus we are dealing only with the end product of a radical screening procedure.

The second thing to remember is that geometric progression is implicit in the search procedure, but nothing is more alien to mathematically untutored intuition than this form of thinking. As youngsters, many of us were asked the question: If you earned a

penny a day and the sum were doubled each day, how much would you have earned by the end of a 30 day working period? Most frequently people give answers on the order of $1.87 or $6.45, when in fact the sum is more than $10 million for one 30-day working period, the last day alone yielding $5,368,700.12. Elements of geometric progression with an increase rate far more powerful than mere doubling underlie the small-world search procedures and thus with only a few removes, the search extends to an enormous number of persons.

Finally, when we state there are only five intermediate acquaintances, this connotes a closeness between the position of the starting person and the target person. But this is in large measure misleading, a confusion of two entirely different frames of reference. If two persons are five removes apart, they are far apart indeed. Almost anyone in the United States is but a few removes from the President, or from Nelson Rockefeller, but this is true only in terms of a particular mathematical viewpoint and does not, in any practical sense, integrate our lives with that of Nelson Rockefeller. Thus, when we speak of five intermediaries, we are talking about an enormous psychological distance between the starting and target points, a distance which seems small only because we customarily regard "five" as a small manageable quantity. We should think of the two points as being not five persons apart, but "five circles of acquaintances" apart—five "structures" apart. This helps to set it in its proper perspective.

There is a very interesting theorem based on the model of the small-world. It states that if two persons from two different populations cannot make contact, then no one within the entire population in which each is embedded can make contact with any person in the other population. In other words, if a particular person, *a*, embedded in population A (which consists of his circle of acquaintances), cannot make contact with a particular person, *b*, embedded in population B, then:

1. No other person in A can make contact with *b*.
2. No other person in A can make contact with any other person in B.

3. In other words, the two sub-populations are completely isolated from each other.

Conceivably, this could happen if one of the populations were on an island never visited by the outside world. In principle, any person in the United States can be contacted by any other in relatively few steps, unless one of them is a complete and total hermit, and then he could not be contacted at all.

In sum, perhaps the most important accomplishment of the research described here is this: Although people have talked about the small-world problem, and have even theorized about it, this study achieved, as far as I know, the first empirically created chains between persons chosen at random from a major national population.

Although the study started with a specific set of questions arising from the small-world problem, the procedure illuminates a far wider set of topics. It reveals a potential communication structure whose sociological characteristics have yet to be exposed [e.g., how well would chains of acquaintances cross racial lines]. When we understand the structure of this potential communication net, we shall understand a good deal more about the integration of society in general. While many studies in social science show how the individual is alienated and cut off from the rest of society, this study demonstrates that, in some sense, we are all bound together in a tightly knit social fabric.

_____CHAPTER 11_____

THE INTERDEPENDENCE OF SOCIAL JUSTICE AND CIVIL SOCIETY

CAROLINE HODGES PERSELL

INTRODUCTION

I consider three issues in this paper: First, is civil society declining? Second, if it is, why is this happening, and here I will propose an alternative explanation to the "values," "big government," and "generational" explanations that have been offered by others. Third, I will suggest some consequences of these trends.

DEFINITIONS

First, a couple of definitions. Civil society has both institutional and qualitative dimensions. Institutionally, it consists of all the social groups and social relationships in which we are embedded: families, communities, religious organizations, social movements, ethnic identity groups, schools, neighborhoods, sports leagues, labor unions, PTAs and other voluntary associations, professional or occupational associations, clubs, support groups, coffee shops, barber shops, bridge groups, and so forth. The term *civil society* also refers to the quality of our social life, including safety, mortality, civility, respect for diversity, and social order. Social order and civil society are not fully coterminous, however. Social order maintained by police or military states or single, monolithic political parties do not comprise most people's ideal civil society because that ideal values

From *Sociological Forum* 12(2), pp. 149–172, Spring 1997. Reprinted by permission of the author and Plenum Publishing Corporation. Some footnotes have been deleted or incorporated into the main text.

civil liberties as well as civil social relations. Civil society, then, is much more than simply social order at any price. It is also a broader concept than the idea of social economy or the third sector, used by Rifkin (1995), because it includes informal social relationships and networks as well as formal ones, the family as well as institutions in the nonprofit sector, and it includes trust, anomia, tolerance, and other social attitudes.

Civil society and social justice are interdependent. One reason is because the three major arenas in modern societies—economy, state, and especially civil society—offer somewhat distinct conceptions of social justice or normative orders, based on their dominant values.

Modern industrial capitalism is not without its ultimate values and commensurate metric of justice. Its ultimate value is simply *more*—greater productivity and greater efficiency—more goods and services at lower economic cost. Noneconomic costs are considered exogenous and irrelevant. From the standpoint of this ultimate value, the just distribution of rewards might be said to depend on merit or performance, including for example "a fair day's wage for a fair day's work." Those who add the most value—whether in productivity, efficiency, or both—should get the most rewards. This view resembles the functionalist view of social stratification. Moreover, in such a metric of social justice, inequalities are not necessarily considered bad because they offer incentives for people to work hard and make themselves more valuable in the market.

In the political sphere, justice is, ideally, derived from somewhat different ultimate values, such as universalism, equality before the law, and equal rights, perhaps within a protective constitutional framework that applies to all citizens. Considerable attention is paid to rights, opportunities, and procedures but less to outcomes. Finally, civil society provides fertile seedbeds for still other ultimate values, such as commitment, responsibility, trust, solidarity, caring, love, intimacy, companionship, protection, and extra help when needed. While civil society offers multiple conceptions of social justice, in general, these ideas are more particularistic than those found in the economy or polity. They may, for example, be focused more on need than on contribution and on outcomes as well as opportunities.

Consider the practices of families that often contain conceptions of justice from all three realms. Most families espouse universalism and favor treating all their children equally, at least most of the time. If the supply is limited, they do not usually give one child a tall glass of milk and another child none. If there is an inheritance, most parents leave equal amounts to each child, regardless of whether one earns more than another. At Christmas or Hanukkah, parents usually strive for relative equality of gifts for all their children. They also give more gifts at such holidays than at birthdays, as my colleague Guillermina Jasso (1993) has noted, perhaps to reduce the strain on family cohesiveness of unequal distributions. But, families also respond to particular needs. If one child has a medical or other problem needing expensive treatment (glasses, braces, or something more serious), families do not usually deny that treatment on the grounds that it would constitute "unequal treatment." Finally, families sometimes apply market metrics. If one child does well in school, a family may provide more education for that child than for another who does not thrive in school, especially if resources are scarce.

I suggest that when all three arenas—economy, state, and civil society—are strong, then their various conceptions of social justice also will be alive and well and continually will be competing, forcing trade-offs between different ultimate values and contending frames of justice. No single conception of justice will prevail to the exclusion of others. If one or more

spheres are weak, social justice may not be debated or even considered, and relative advantage or sheer power will dominate the actions taken. However, power without moral legitimacy is neither as authoritative nor as effective as legitimate power.

Others have commented on the decline of civil society. These commentators have ranged across the political spectrum, including William Bennett, Dan Quayle, Ben Wattenburg, Senator Daniel Patrick Moynihan, Senator William Bradley, and Robert Putnam.

As indicators of decline, some focus most heavily on growing numbers of out-of-wedlock births and single-parent families, drug use, and crime rates. Others document declining associational memberships, reduced socializing with friends and neighbors, plummeting rates of voting, the erosion of trust in others, and sinking confidence in societal institutions such as government, education, and science. To these indicators we might add soaring rates of teen suicide (suicide rates among 15–24 year-olds jumped from 5.2 per 100,000 in 1960 to 13.2 in 1990), relatively low life expectancy in the U.S.,[1] growing numbers and percentages of people, especially children (40%), in poverty (the highest rate since 1962), and rapidly rising rates of incarceration, among others.

Observers also deplore the rising incidence of scapegoating and ethnic hate crimes, the erosion of civility in universities and on the highways (people being shot over arguments in traffic), the growing use of streets as public toilets (and not just by homeless people but suburban visitors as well, whom we in New York fondly refer to as "the bridge and tunnel crowd"), the rise in illegal dumping of trash, including toxic waste, and I could go on and on.

Why have these changes in civil society occurred? Some, for example, William Bennett, Dan Quayle, and Ben Wattenberg (1995), stress the "loss of values" as the cause. Their proposed solutions make many people uneasy—for example, requiring prayer in the schools or making abortion illegal.

The "Contract with America" (or "*On* America" as Frances Fox Piven said last year at the ESS meetings) blames big government, wasteful spending, and high taxes, a story that appears to have been accepted by many of those who voted in the 1994 congressional elections.

Robert Putnam has taken a rigorous, scholarly approach to explaining the decline of one aspect of civil society, namely social capital. Social capital includes membership in civic associations, trusting others, and voting. In their study of civil traditions in modern Italy, Putnam *et al.* discovered how the "norms and networks of civic engagement have fostered economic growth" and how civic associational membership is powerfully related to effective public institutions (1995a:176).

The General Social Survey (GSS) and other data Putnam (1995a, 1995b, 1996) cites for the United States show declines in social capital, beginning in the late 1940s and accelerating in the 1980s. He rejects several possible explanations (the growth of working women, less leisure, mobility and suburbanization, the shrinking percentage of married persons, racial hostility by whites, and the rise of the welfare state), and he provisionally offers a generational explanation. He suggests that television is a plausible culprit, because its expansion correlates very well with the maturation of the baby boomers and Generation Xers who differ so dramatically from their elders with respect to civic memberships, trust, and participation.

However, I propose an *alternative explanation, or at least a supplemental one*, for the decline in civil society. Another factor also varies for America's postwar generations besides television, *and that suspect is the structural economic transformation in the U.S. and how it has been managed*. The percent of the U.S. labor force in manufacturing has declined steadily since its peak in 1950 when it was about one third of all workers. "Today less than 17% of the workforce is in manufacturing," and Peter Drucker estimates it will drop below 12% in the next decade (Rifkin, 1995:8). *The End of Work* is the attention-grabbing description Jeremy Rifkin gives to these changes in his book of that title. The *New York Times* ran a special series in 1996 entitled "the Downsizing of America," reporting the poignant stories of people who have lost their jobs, their job security, and who have little or no prospect of ever again getting as good a job as they once had, because of corporate restruc-

turing. Altogether, 2.5 million Americans lost their jobs to corporate restructuring just between 1990 and 1995, and since 1979, more than 43 million jobs have been extinguished in the United States.[2] This total equals one-third of all jobs in the country today.

If, as these structural changes occurred, all three spheres were producing strong contending conceptions of justice, universalism might argue for the pain to be shared, for example, be reducing the work week to 30 hours as Volkswagen has done in Germany: particularism might direct attention to the special needs of persons most severely affected by the process—women and children, especially those of color; while the market performance metric might suggest that all who responded successfully to competitive pressures should share fairly in the gains. *Instead, however, we witness a disdain for social justice according to ANY of these metrics of justice, including the market's own.*

CHANGES IN THE DISTRIBUTION OF INCOME AND WEALTH

In the United States, economic restructuring has been accompanied by the social creation of vast changes in the distribution of income and wealth. The socially created nature of these consequences is evident when we consider Japan. The head of one of Japan's major trading companies said, "We would be outcasts if we did what many American firms do" (Sanger and Lohr, 1996:13). When Nippon Steel closed a blast furnace in Kamaishi, they set up a factory making artificial meat out of soybeans. The sole purpose was to create jobs, whether or not it was profitable, and it never has been (Sanger and Lohr, 1996:13).

While familiar to many of you, let me review what has happened to the distribution of income and wealth in the U.S. since World War II. The 1947–1973 post-World War II era experienced broad-based prosperity, with real productivity gains averaging 2.5% per year. These gains were shared pretty evenly across all five income quintiles in the work force. The rising tide raised all boats. From 1973 to 1979 there was much slower growth, and twice as much of the gain went to the top quintile as to the bottom quintile. In 1979–1989 there was generally slow growth, and the bottom quintile of earners experienced a *net decline* in the share of earnings they received, while *70% of the rise in average family income went to the top 1% and 97% of the gains went to the richest 20% of households* (Krugman, 1992; Mishel, 1995; Wolff, 1995a).

Another way to consider this dramatic change in income distribution is to examine the *range* of pay inequality. In 1974 in the U.S., the ratio of the earnings of top executives to the average worker was 40:1. By 1995 that ratio had soared to 211:1. In 1990 the ratio in Japan was 16:1, and in Germany it was 21:1. (Last I looked, those two countries were our biggest global economic competitors.) Not only has the economic tide risen more slowly since 1973, it has raised the level of the yachts very rapidly, while the rowboats remain mired in the mud.

Now, what about the distribution of wealth in the United States? Here I draw on the work of my colleague in the Economics Department at New York University, Edward Wolff, who noted that in 1989, wealth inequality in the United States was at a 60-year high, with the top 1% of wealth holders controlling 39% of total households wealth.[3]

From 1983 to 1989, "the top 1% of wealth holders received 62% of the total gain in marketable wealth. . . . The next 19% received 37%," *while the bottom 80% saw their wealth increase by only 1%.* "This pattern represents a distinct turnaround from the 1962-83 period, when every group enjoyed some share of the overall wealth growth and the gains were roughly in proportion to the share of wealth held by each in 1962" (Wolff, 1995b:12–13).[4] Of course, the intersection of class, race, and gender produces even more enormous inequalities.

Comparisons with other countries provide some perspective on the United States. In the U.S. in 1989, the top 1% held 39% of household wealth; in France in 1986, it was 26%; in Canada in 1984, it was 25%; in Great Britain 18%, and in Sweden in 1986, 16% (Wolff, 1995a).

A liberal might find the simple grossness of inequalities within the economic realm and their rapid increase to be unjust, prima facie. Alan Ryan, writing

in the *New York Review of Books*, offers an additional perspective when he says,

> *The misery of the world of "eat or be eaten" is not to be measured in income statistics. It is a moral disaster. The United States has always been built around a work ethic. We do not go to work only to earn an income, but to find meaning in our lives. What we do is a large part of who we are. To see ourselves as nothing more than a means to profits reaped by others is a blow to our self-respect. To be thrown out of work after twenty years with the same firm, as if we were of no more value than a piece of worn-out machinery, is, indeed, to feel like a piece of junk. (1996:11)*

He captures how economic dislocation denies out other social roles and identities and dismisses nonmarket normative standards.

Ryan's view is consistent with Michael Walzer's argument (1983, 1991) that economic inequalities become unjust when they invade other spheres of life. Walzer sees the relative dominance of the market over other realms of distributive justice as much more important than relative equality or inequality within the market itself. Therefore, to be a serious injustice, inequality not only would need to be increasing within the economic realm, but would need to affect other realms of social life.[5]

I suggest that growing economic injustice is undermining civil society. To support this, we need several kinds of evidence. First, do people perceive a change in their economic situations through time? I can share with you the preliminary results of research I am doing with Adam Green and Liena Gurevich, two of our most outstanding graduate students at New York University (Persell *et al.*, 1996). I would like to thank them for their excellent efforts on this project this year.[6]

We find that people perceive their economic distress to be increasing since 1972. Indicators of economic distress include measures of whether they think they are likely to lose their jobs, whether they have ever been unemployed, their perception of their relative financial position, their real incomes, and their sense that their financial situation has changed for the worse in the last few years.

Second, are their perceptions of economic distress related to their attitudes? In the GSS, we can see that people have become more likely to agree that "the lot of the average man[7] is getting worse" (anomia5 in the GSS, Figure 11.1). The percent agreeing that the condition is getting worse has moved, although not in a straight line, from 56% in 1973 to 69% in 1994 (a difference of 13 percentage points).

If people feel there is something unjust about this change, we would expect that anomia7 might also increase (anomia7 is measured by the percentage who agree that "officials are not interested in the lot of the average man"). Anomia7 has increased from 60% agreeing in 1973 to 76% in 1994 (a difference of 16 percentage points, Figure 11.2).

It is even more instructive, however, to examine the difference between blacks and whites on anomia7 over time (Figure 11.3). African Americans in 1973 were much more likely than whites to agree that offi-

cials are not interested in the "lot of the average man." As a result, they couldn't rise too much (a ceiling effect may have been operating). They move from 76% agreeing in 1973 to 81% in 1994, an increase of only 5 percentage points. The views of whites, however, can and do rise dramatically (from 57% in 1973 to 75% in 1994, *an increase of 18 percentage points) as they come to resemble blacks' views much more closely over time*. This trend is consistent with an argument that the economic situation of whites (more unequal, uncertain, and unjust) has come to resemble that of blacks more than it did in the past, while whites have also come to resemble blacks more in their views of officials' interest.

EFFECTS ON CIVIL SOCIETY

Is economic distress related to trust and associational memberships, as well as to rising anomia? If so,

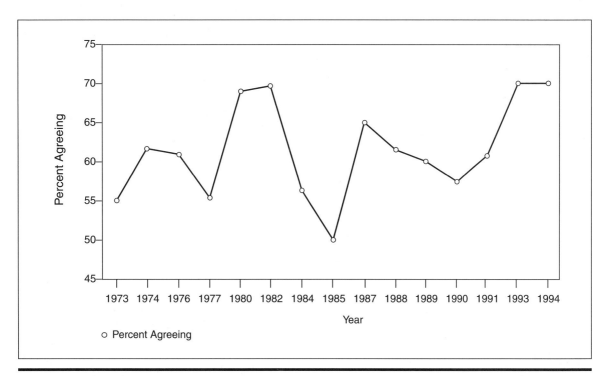

FIGURE 11.1   GSS Survey Anomia5 by Year. Percent Agreeing Lot of Average Man Is Getting Worse

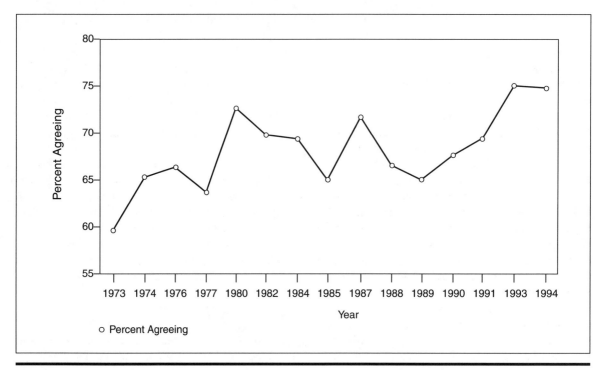

FIGURE 11.2　GSS Survey Anomia7 by Year. Percent Agreeing Officials Not Interested in Average Man

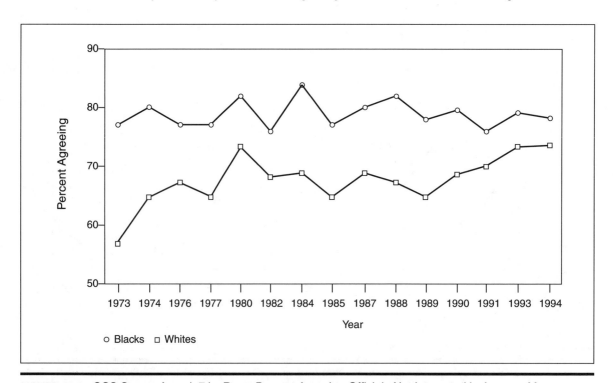

FIGURE 11.3　GSS Survey Anomia7 by Race. Percent Agreeing Officials Not Interested in Average Man

then economic distress might be a plausible alternative explanation to television for observed declines in social capital and civil society. Based on our [multivariable] analyses, we find that people who have experienced economic distress are *less* likely than people who have not to belong to one or more associations and to trust others. They also express more anomia (Figure 11.4).[8]

These results are consistent with Mark Granovetter's observation that trust is generated and malfeasance discouraged when agreements are "embedded" within a larger structure of personal relations and social networks (1985). This provides empirical evidence that economic distress is negatively related to social capital. It is no surprise to sociologists who know William Julius Wilson's work (1987), which documents how the economic backbone developed osteoporosis when major manufacturing jobs left the inner city, and then community institutions began

crumbling as well. When the number of jobs paying "family wages" declined, marriage rates declined as well, and out-of-wedlock birth rates soared.[9] Elijah Anderson's work (1989, 1990) shows the importance of family-sustaining jobs for forming economically self-reliant families and how the lack of job prospects may lead to sexual prowess (and fatherhood), rather than the capacity to support a family as a marker of manhood.[10]

EFFECTS ON OTHER ASPECTS OF CIVIL SOCIETY

Besides associational memberships and trust, civil society includes acceptance of diversity and public safety. The first can be measured with indices of espoused racial and gay tolerance, using GSS data.[11] Economic distress is both directly and indirectly related to espoused racial tolerance (Figure 11.5).

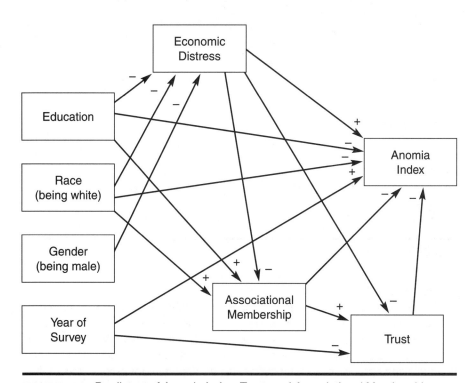

FIGURE 11.4 Predictors of Anomia Index, Trust, and Associational Membership

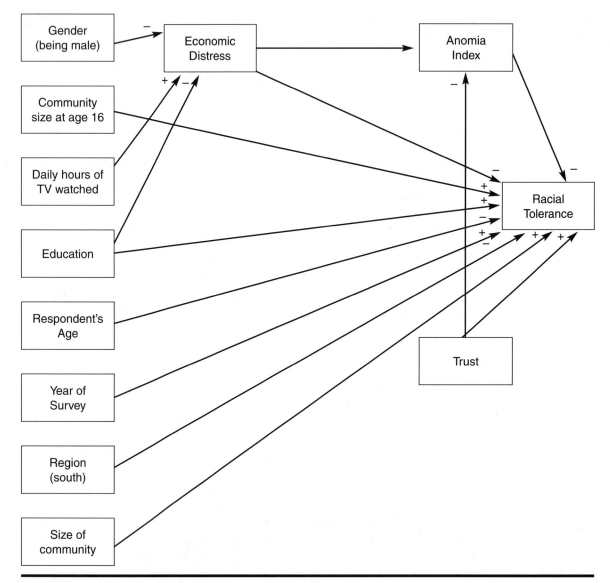

FIGURE 11.5   Predictors of Racial Tolerance for Whites

Trusters, people who feel less anomic, and people who experience less economic distress are more likely to espouse racial tolerance. Education, age, year of survey, non-Southern residence, size of community where respondent lived at age 16, and current community size also are importantly related to espoused racial tolerance.

Trust and higher real incomes are related to greater espoused tolerance of gays, while anomia is related to less gay tolerance. Age, year of survey, residence outside the South, community size at age 16, current community size, female gender, and education are independently important for espoused gay tolerance as well (Figure 11.6). These results are consis-

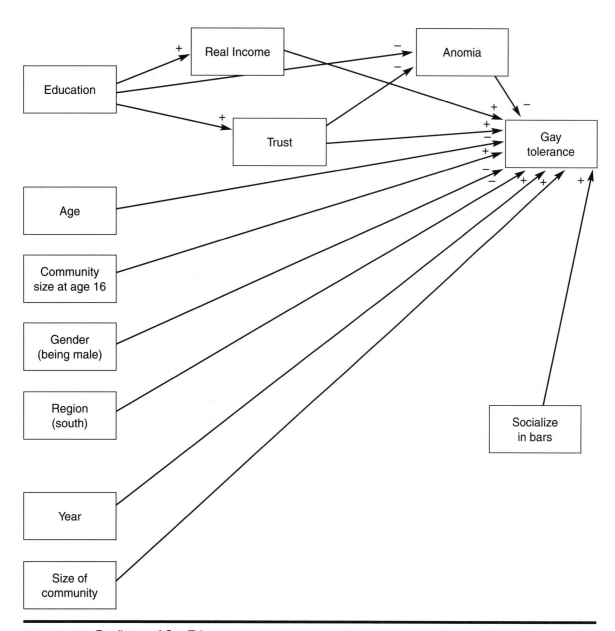

FIGURE 11.6   Predictors of Gay Tolerance

tent with the argument that economic distress affects other aspects of civil society, in this case, espoused tolerance.

With respect to crime and public safety, criminologists have documented how friendship networks and associational memberships mediate the relationships between economic conditions and delinquent behavior. Communities where residents have lower socioeconomic status, where there is more residential mobility, greater ethnic and racial heterogeneity, and more urbanization have lower rates of participation in community associations and fewer friendship networks than do communities with higher SES residents, less mobility, more homogeneity, and less urbanization, according to Sampson and Groves (1989). When there are more friendship networks and more participation in community organizations, adults exercise more control over the activities of youths. When there are fewer social networks, adults exercise less control over youths, and deviant peer groups are more likely to develop and promote negative social learning, leading to an increase in delinquent behavior and predatory crimes.

Sampson and Laub (1990) analyze whether the social bonds developed in adulthood can offset the effects of early childhood delinquency. They report that marital cohesiveness, emotional closeness and compatibility with one's spouse, and job stability are strong predictors of law-abiding behavior among adults, *even when their childhood delinquency is controlled*. (One of the ironies of longer and mandatory sentences for youthful offenders is that it virtually assures that they will not establish successful marital and job attachments, making it more likely that they will continue their criminal behavior throughout adulthood, as my colleague, David Greenberg, mentioned to me.)

Not only criminal behavior, but the economic and educational achievement of young people in communities is affected. Cohesive, well-organized communities with more social capital on both the family and community level contribute positively to educational achievement, according to Furstenberg and Hughes (1994).[12] These and other research studies underscore the importance of economic security and strong family and community networks for human development and crime reduction. Civil society plays an essential role, *but civil society cannot flourish without economic sustenance*.

This story has been told again and again with respect to African Americans, and at the public policy level, it has largely been ignored. Will the story fall on more receptive ears as it increasingly affects white Americans, or will more and more white families and communities also be sacrificed on the alter

of the "market God" (Baker, 1996), leading to higher crime rates in suburbia, the further growth of white militia groups perhaps, and higher levels of social disorder? Will the criminal justice system respond in the same way it has in the past? If so, the jail and prison population will soar far above the more than 1.5 million people it hit last year (Bureau of Justice Statistics, 1996).

When perceptions of social justice and civil society erode, that rot transforms the foundation of social order, from one based more upon voluntary compliance buttressed by informal community social controls, toward one based increasingly on formal coercion—resting much more heavily upon police, jails, and capital punishment. This is consistent with the startling fact that the state of California now spends more on its prison system than it does on its famous system of higher education (Baker, 1996).

EFFECTS ON POLITICAL LIFE

Economic distress appears to depress social networks, trust, and tolerance, while elevating anomia and crime. Democratic political life is also affected. Associational membership and trust are strongly related to political interest as are education, year of survey, male gender, social contact with friends, job security, and age (Figure 11.7). Associational membership and trust are also related to voting in 1988, as is education and age (Figure 11.8). These results suggest that enervating social capital and civil society also eviscerates political society. A strong civil society is related to a strong political arena. This is very consistent with Ernest Gellner's views (1994) of the interdependence of civil society and political life, as well as with Putnam *et al.'s* observations (1995) that civic associations are powerfully associated with effective public institutions.

EFFECTS ON ECONOMIC LIFE

Finally, over time, lacerating civil society depresses economic prosperity. A commitment to "market efficiency" unrestrained by nonmarket norms of justice becomes a drag on itself, surely the final irony. This

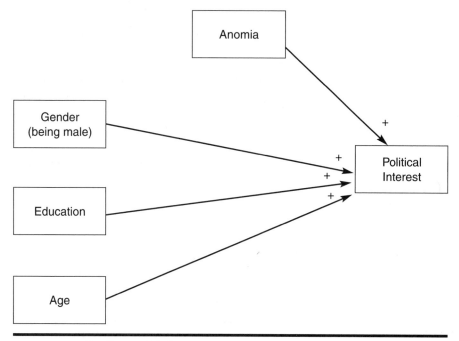

FIGURE 11.7   Predictors of Political Interest

happens because economic injustice and eroding civil society create cultural and structural changes that inhibit economic productivity.

Cultural changes include the decline in trust, growing hedonism in consumption, and rising disdain for work. Structural changes include lower aggregate demand and growing financialization of the economy. Cultural and structural changes lead to growing polarization in the population and greater separation between social classes. These changes in turn undermine a shared moral purpose, and with the deterioration in civil society and rising crime, they contribute

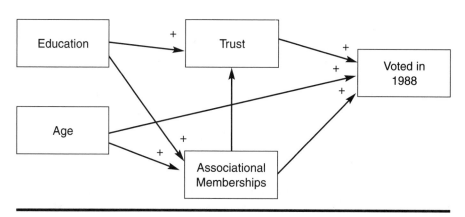

FIGURE 11.8   Predictors of Voting in 1988

to higher security costs, declining investment in productivity, and lower productivity.

CULTURAL CHANGES

Trust is essential for sustainable economic activity. In his comparison of economic growth in northern vs. southern Italy, Robert Putnam and his associates found that regions with more associations and less hierarchy grew faster than regions with fewer associations and more hierarchy, controlling for their level of development in 1970 (Putnam *et al.,* 1995:176). Charles Kadushin's recent paper (1995) in the *American Sociological Review* suggests that the concept of "enforceable trust," a key factor in high finance, explains the importance of friendship in the operation of the French financial elite.

Several times in history, great empires that became very unequal also experienced cultural shifts. By the end of the 16th century, the Spanish elites disdained to earn their income from commerce (Elliott, 1964: 204, 313, 194–195). Similarly, in the 18th century, the Dutch moved from a nation of manufacturers and merchants toward a more unequal economy. As Braudel notes (1992:197), the preoccupation of the rich with their luxurious gardens and country houses led to great prejudice toward business and trade and was accompanied by a growing interest in fine imported wines, elaborated culinary tastes, and a preference for French rather than Dutch paintings.

As economic inequalities are translated into cultural distinctions, increasing polarization occurs between classes. The very rich in Holland more and more cut themselves off from the rest of society (Braudel, 1992:197). In his posthumous book, *The Revolt of the Elites*, Christopher Lasch (1995) describes the loss of commitment to place and community within the upper class, no doubt related to the growing importance of multinational rather than family firms (observed by Michael Useem, 1984) and the increase in offshore investments. Robert Reich (1991) has described the retreat of the well-to-do from public institutions and spaces into private schools, clubs, and gated communities. Andrew Beveridge's (1996)

census analysis reveals extensive geographical economic concentrations. While Paul DiMaggio (1996) reports little evidence for growing cultural polarizations on many attitudinal indicators, he did find two exceptions—namely abortion and attitudes toward the poor—where Americans do appear to be moving further apart through time.

Although Daniel Bell did not stress the polarizing consequences of capitalism, he did note a more general cultural contradiction of capitalism in the way it fuels hedonism and how, "in the hedonistic life, there is a loss of will and fortitude. More importantly, men become competitive with one another for luxuries, and they lose the ability to share and sacrifice. . . . They also lose the sense of solidarity which makes men feel as brothers to one another . . . [and] some moral purpose, a *telos,* which provides the moral justifications for the society" (Bell, 1976: 83). The loss of moral purpose is well described by John Kenneth Galbraith (1992) in *The Culture of Contentment.* In their study of Italy, Putnam *et al.* note that the social contract that sustains collaboration in the civic community is not legal but moral (1995:183).

When shared social networks that cut across social cleavages and a shared moral compass[13] are lost, economic rationality, which is a means, can become an end. This can lead to human beings being treated as discardable objects, no different from an old machine. The problem is, this tendency is cumulative and forms a vicious cycle.[14]

STRUCTURAL CHANGES

Growing economic inequality not only undermines civil society, but it changes economic demand and investment, and the growing concentration of wealth can cause recessions. According to Keynes, the rich save more, leading to a decline in a aggregate demand (Keynes, 1936). Growing inequality weakens the buying power of the middle and working classes, who are increasingly unable to buy the goods and services produced by the economy—whether cars,[15] refrigerators, clothing, dental care, insurance, or whatever.

There is only so much a small affluent class can buy and use, even within the remarkably elastic parameters of conspicuous consumption.

Recession can turn into depression if the financial system collapses. Financialization, speculation, and panics contribute to collapse. When markets become "financialized," assets and goods are purchased only for resale and not for productive purposes (Galbraith, 1955; Kindleberger, 1978).

Both economic inequality and financialization fuel speculation, partly because of the very different ways the middle class and the upper class invest their savings. The middle class generally wants security, and hence uses bank accounts, CDs, and increasingly, mutual funds, as we learn from Paul Starr (1996). The upper class wants, and can afford to take risk to try to get, a bigger return. They are more likely to be involved with derivatives, hedge funds, takeovers, arbitrage activity, initial public offerings (IPOs), and other more speculative enterprises. Most of these are not funded by middle-income people (except in the Orange County California government).

Speculative bubbles eventually burst and create panics. Fernand Braudel (1992: 200–201, 245–275), criticizing the "perversion of capital," noted that Holland's small financial elite in the late 18th century had so much to invest, even as ordinary Dutchmen faced highly regressive taxes, they made increasingly risky loans, creating bubbles and panics.

As Ed Wolff notes, "The increase in wealth inequality recorded over the 1983–89 period in the United States is almost unprecedented. The only other period in the twentieth century during which concentration of household wealth rose comparably was from 1922 to 1929. Then inequality was buoyed primarily by the excessive increase in stock values, which eventually crashed in 1929, leading to the Great Depression of the 1930s" (1995b:13).

The 1920s were also notable for the way they drew in larger numbers of middle- and working-class investors, who were among the hardest hit by the crash. Financier Bernard Baruch is reputed to have decided to exit the stock market when the man shining his shoes gave him a market tip.

CONSEQUENCES FOR ECONOMIC PRODUCTIVITY

Financialization may also reduce investments in productivity. "A survey of 1,000 companies by the American Management Association found that fewer than half the companies laying off people managed to increase their operating profits after workers were shed" (Sanger and Lohr, 1996:12). Without changes in strategies or investments in their human or physical capital, companies may strive to improve their stock price but not their actual productivity.

Productivity is also depressed by crime and by soaring costs of nonproductive expenditures for security and the criminal justice system. The number of security guards rose from 602,000 in 1985 to 803,000 in 1992 and is projected to grow 50% to 1.2 million by 2005, making it the fourth fastest growing occupation in the U.S. (U.S. Bureau of Labor Statistics, 1993). The total costs of the criminal justice system for all governments have skyrocketed from $10.5 billion in 1987 to $74.3 billion in 1990 (U.S. Department of Commerce, 1990, 1994).[16] This is paid for with tax dollars that could otherwise be enhancing rather than containing human lives.

Structured social inequality has contributed to declines in productivity in previous historical eras. The social anthropologist Vernon Childe (1964) noted how the era of agrarian revolution—which began with a number of highly significant innovations including the plow, the wheel, money, and writing—was followed, almost paradoxically, by a rather stagnant period in human affairs because rulers lost touch with the technology of their times, in part because of their scorn for physical labor. The producers, who had the knowledge to make innovations, knew that the benefits would be enjoyed mainly by the rulers. Therefore, they had little motivation to improve their work processes.

CONCLUSIONS

In conclusion, I suggest that civil society is declining as a direct result of economic injustice and distress. This drop has many negative consequences for tolerance, for the next generation, for crime and a just social order, for political democracy, and for a healthy economy. The real challenge before all of us, whether in the U.S., Eastern Europe, Western Europe, or developing nations is how to nurture, sustain, and enhance various conceptions of social justice, and strong political and civil societies while experiencing sustainable gains in economic productivity.

NOTES

1. While life expectancy has generally increased across the world in recent years, the low relative ranking of U.S. life expectancy among economically developed countries has persisted.

In 1990–1991, middle-aged U.S. men ranked 23rd in an international comparison of death rates. Longitudinal data "shows a causal connection between income [distribution] and mortality for individuals in economically developed countries." A cross-national study reveals that as the level of income received by those at the bottom of the income distribution increases, national mortality rates decrease markedly (Dulceep, 1995:39).

2. The first year data were available, based on the analysis by the *New York Times* of data compiled by the Labor Department's Bureau of Labor Statistics (Uchitelle and Kleinfield, 1996:27).

3. As this paper was being written, it was reported that between 1989 and 1992, the top 1% lost share somewhat, while the next 9% gained. According to a survey for the Federal Reserve and the IRS, "the portion of the wealth in the hands of the richest 1% declined to 30.4% from 37.1% from 1989 to 1992," while "the next richest 9% saw their share of the wealth grow to 36.8% from 31.2%" (Stevenson, 1996:D1, D7).

4. In this earlier period, the top 1% received 34% of the wealth gains, the next 19% claimed 48%, and the bottom 80% got 18% (Wolff, 1995b:12–13). Gini coefficients are an indicator commonly used to summarize data on the degree of inequality of income, wealth, or anything else of value. Gini ranges from 0 (exact equality) to 1 (one person owns everything); a high Gini coefficient, therefore, means greater inequality. "This measure, like the others reviewed here, points to an increase in inequality: between 1983 and 1989 the Gini coefficient increased from 0.80 to 0.84" (Wolff, 1995b:13).

5. The first response of conservation economists was to deny that any increase in inequality has occurred (Mishel, 1995). The vigor with which they rushed to do this suggests that they too may see such an increase as potentially problematic.

6. We would also like to thank Dean Savage of Queens College for making the GSS and his Extract program available on the Queens College Sociology Department World Wide Web page. The address is http://www.soc.qc.edu.

7. We have to remember that the GSS began in 1972.

8. Here the measure of anomia is a combined one, consisting of both anomia5 and anomia7.

9. The rate of out-of-wedlock births to white mothers is rising much faster than is the rate for black mothers.

10. Jay MacLeod's ethnography done in the Boston area shows the devastating immediate effects of spare economic opportunities for the white Hallway Hangers, as well as their longer-term effects on the black brothers (1995).

11. The index of racial tolerance was created using the following four variables: RACPUSH: "(Negroes/Blacks) shouldn't push themselves where they're not wanted." RACSEG: "White people have a right to keep (Negroes/Blacks) out of their neighborhoods if they want to."

12. They also conclude that social capital operates through the direct supervision of young people by both families and communities.

13. Or what sociologists would call a normative framework.

14. As Putnam *et al.* note, "Stocks of social capital, such as trust, norms, and networks, tend to be self-reinforcing and cumulative. Virtuous circles result in social equilibria with high levels of cooperation, trust, reciprocity civic engagement, and collective well-being. . . . Conversely, the absence of these traits in the *un*civic community is also self-reinforcing. Defection, distrust, shirking, exploitation, isolation, disorder, and stagnation intensify one another in a suffocating miasma of vicious circles" (1995:177).

15. Witness the rise and demand for second-hand cars, also known as "previously owned."

16. Not adjusted for inflation.

REFERENCES

Anderson, Elijah. 1989. "Sex codes and family life among poor inner-city youths." *Annals AAPSS* 501 (January):59–78.

———— 1990. *Streetwise*. Chicago: University of Chicago Press.

Baker, Russell. 1996. "The market god." *New York Times* (March 23):21.

Bell, Daniel. 1976. *The Cultural Contradictions of Capitalism*. New York: Basic Books.

Beveridge, Andrew. 1996. "Increasing inequality: New evidence from old data." Paper presented at the 66th Eastern Sociological Society annual meeting, Boston, MA, March 29.

Braudel, Fernand. 1992. *The Perspective of the World, Civilization and Capitalization 15th–18th Centuries.* Volume III. (1979) Berkeley, CA: University of California Press.

Childe, Vernon. 1964. *What Happened in History*. Baltimore, MD: Penguin.

DiMaggio, Paul. 1996. "Have Americans' social attitudes become more polarized?" Robin M. Williams, Jr., lecture presented at the 66th Eastern Sociological Society annual meeting, Boston, MA, March 30.

Duleep, Harriet-Orcutt. 1995. "Mortality and income inequality among economically developed countries." *Social Security Bulletin* (Summer: 34–50).

Elliott, J. H. 1964. *Imperial Spain 1469–1716*. New York: St. Martin's Press.

Furstenberg, Frank F., Jr. and Mary Elizabeth Hughes. 1994. "The influence of neighborhoods on children's development: A theoretical perspective and a research agenda." Unpublished paper prepared for the conference Indicators of Children's Well-Being, Bethesda, MD (November 17–18).

Galbraith, John Kenneth. 1955. *The Great Crash, 1929.* Boston: Houghton Mifflin.

————. 1992. The Culture of Contentment. Boston: Houghton Mifflin.

Gellner, Ernest. 1994. *Conditions of Liberty: Civil Society and Its Rivals*. New York: Allen Lane/Penguin Press.

Granovetter, Mark. 1985. "Economic action and social-structure: The problem of embeddedness." *American Journal of Sociology* 91(3):481–510.

Jasso, Guillermina. 1993. "Analyzing conflict severity: Predictions of distributive justice theory for the two-subgroup case." *Social Justice Research* 6:357–382.

Kadushin, Charles. 1995. "Friendship among the French financial elite." *American Sociological Review* 60:202–221.

Keynes, John Maynard. 1936. *The General Theory of Employment, Interest and Money*. London: Macmillan and Co., Limited.

Kindleberger, Charles, P. 1978. *Manias, Panics, and Crashes*. New York: Basic Books.

Krugman, Paul. 1992. "The rich, the right, and the facts." *The American Prospect* 11 (Fall):19–31. (http://epn.org/prospect/11/11krug.html).

Lasch, Christopher. 1995. *The Revolt of the Elites*. New York: W. W. Norton.

MacLeod, Jay. 1995. *Ain't No Makin' It*. Second Edition. Boulder, CO: Westview.

Mishel, Lawrence. 1995. "Rising tides, sinking wages." *The American Prospect* 23 (Fall):60–64 (http://epn.org/prospect/23/23mish.html).

Persell, Caroline Hodges, Adam Green, and Liena Gurevich. 1996. "Exploring relationships between material conditions, social capital, and intolerance." [tentative title]. Unpublished manuscript in progress, New York University.

Putnam, Robert D. 1995a. "Bowling alone: Democracy in America at the end of the twentieth century." Nobel Symposium, Uppsala, Sweden, August 27–30, 1994.

————. 1995b. "Tuning in, tuning out: The strange disappearance of social capital in America." *PS: Political Science & Politics*, (December):664–683.

————. 1996. "The strange disappearance of civic America." *The American Prospect* 24 (Winter) (http://epn.org/prospect/24/24putn.html).

Putnam, Robert D. with Robert Leonardi and Raffaela Y. Nanetti. 1995. *Making Democracy Work: Civic Traditions in Modern Italy*. Princeton, NJ: Princeton University Press.

Relch, Robert. 1991. The Work of Nations: Preparing Ourselves for 21st-Century Capitalism. New York: Knopf.

Rifkin, Jeremy. 1995. *The End of Work*. New York: Putnam.

Rimer, Sara. 1996. "A hometown feels less like home." *New York Times* (March 6):A1, A16–A18.

Ryan, Alan. 1996. "Too nice to win? A review of Bill Bradley, *Time Present, Time Past: A Memoir*." *New York Review of Books* (March 21):8–12.

Sampson, Robert J. and W. Byron Groves. 1989. "Community structure and crime: Testing social-disorganization theory." *American Journal of Sociology* 94 (January):774–802.

Sampson, Robert J. and John H. Laub. 1990. "Crime and deviance over the life course: The salience of adult social bonds." *American Sociological Review* 55 (October):609–627.

Sanger, David E. and Steve Lohr. 1996. "A search for answers to avoid lay-offs." *New York Times* (March 9):1, 12–13.

Starr, Paul. 1996. "The new inequality and popular capitalism." Paper presented at the 66th Eastern Sociological Society annual meeting, Boston, MA, March 29.

Stevenson, Richard W. 1996. "The rich are getting richer, but not the very rich." *New York Times* (March 13):D1, D7.

Uchitelle, Louis and N. R. Kleinfield. 1996. "On the battlefields of business, millions of casualties." *New York Times* (March 3):1, 26–29.

U.S. Bureau of Labor Statistics, Office of Employment Projections. 1993. "Occupations with the largest job growth, 1992–2005" (http://stats.bls.gov:80/emptab2.htm).

U.S. Department of Commerce, U.S. Bureau of the Census. 1990. *Statistical Abstract of the United States: 1990*. 110th Edition. Washington, DC: U.S. Government Printing Office.

U.S. Department of Commerce, U.S. Bureau of the Census. 1994. *Statistical Abstract of the United States: 1994*. 114th Edition. Washington, DC: U.S. Government Printing Office.

U. S. Department of Justice, Bureau of Justice Statistics. 1996. *Corrections Statistics*. (http://www.ojp.usdoj.gov/bjs/correct.htm)

Useem, Michael. 1984. *The Inner Circle: Large Corporations and the Rise of Business Political Activity in the U.S. and U.K.* New York: Oxford University Press.

Walzer, Michael. 1983. *Spheres of Justice: A Defense of Pluralism and Equality*. New York: Basic Books.

———. 1991. "The idea of civil society: A path to social reconstruction." *Dissent* (Spring):293–304.

Wattenberg, Ben J. 1995. *Values Matter Most*. New York: Free Press.

Wilson, William Julius. 1987. *The Truly Disadvantaged: The Inner City, the Underclass, and Public Policy*. Chicago: University of Chicago Press.

Wolfe, Alan. 1989. *Whose Keeper? Social Science and Moral Obligation*. Berkeley: University of California Press.

Wolff, Edward N. 1995a. "How the pie is sliced: America's growing concentration of wealth." *The American Prospect* 22 (Summer):58–64 (http://epn.org/prospect/22/22wolf.html).

———. 1995b. *Top Heavy: A Study of the Increasing Inequality of Wealth in America*. New York: The Twentieth Century Fund Press.

PART 5

SOCIALIZATION

*S*ocialization is the process of learning how to act in particular situations and in particular roles; it is also the process of learning how to think about oneself, other people, and reality in general. The process starts at birth and continues throughout life. Everything we do and think "properly" (according to the standards of our culture) must be learned. Moreover, most of this learning occurs through social interaction. Social interaction involves several processes that encourage us to act or think in particular ways (the "correct" ways) as opposed to other ways (the "wrong" ways).

Through observing others as they play life's roles (parent, child, sibling, teacher, student, friend, and so on), we may come to *model* our behavior and thinking after these individuals. *Role models* may be either positive or negative. A positive role model is one we wish to emulate; we see reward in being like this. For example, many children grow up to be hard workers because they saw their parents work hard and profit from it. A negative role model is one we want *not* to be like. For example, an adolescent may have a parent who will not discuss intimate matters (e.g., sex, falling in love, friends that use drugs). This may leave the adolescent feeling unsatisfied with the parent-child relationship, feeling that the relationship is a lot less than it could or should be. Later, as an adult and parent in turn, he or she may use that parent as a negative role model; that is, the once-dissatisfied adolescent may take pains to be intimate with his or her child, the exact opposite of the situation in which he or she had been raised.

During social interaction, individuals also shape one another's behavior and thinking through *sanctions*—either negative (punishments) or positive (rewards). When there is a great power differential between those interacting (e.g., for example, parent and child, teacher and pupil), the dominant actor's views will tend to rule. Dominant actors such as the parent or the teacher (or their associated institutions, e.g., the family, school) are called *agents of socialization*. For example, a quiet, respectful demeanor is one of the behavioral goals that most teachers want a student to acquire. "Talking back" (the teacher says "Quiet down," to which the student retorts, "YOU quiet down!") warrants reprimand or punishment from the teacher ("Sit in the corner"; "Go to the principal's office"). On the other hand, raising one's hand before speaking is rewarded with a smile or some other approving reaction that sends the message to the student that "this is the way to be."

The sociological perspective on socialization emphasizes social interaction. This perspective traces its roots to Charles Horton Cooley (1864–1929) and George Herbert Mead (1863–1931). Cooley and Mead emphasized the social interactional roots of our self-conception. From where else could we arrive at conceptions of ourselves as being, say, "pretty," "handsome," "smart," or "stupid" except from our interactions with others and the messages they send us during those interactions?

Cooley's concept of the *looking-glass self* (the idea that we see ourselves as we think others see us) was tested empirically, and largely confirmed, by the research of Miyamoto and Dornbusch.[1]

Some psychologists have emphasized processes other than social interaction as the root causes of how we come to act and think in particular ways while in particular situations and while playing particular roles. To wit, Sigmund Freud (1856–1939) saw the development of our self-conceptions as dependent upon the intimate, traumatic, and sexually tinted biological experiences (e.g., toilet-training, nursing) during the first six years of life. For example, he argued that unrestrained thumb-sucking could lead some children to "develop into kissing epicures with a tendency to perverse kissing, or as men, [to] . . . a strong desire for drinking and smoking."[2]

However, Freud did little systematic, empirical testing of his theories. With regard to his argument that very early childhood experiences determine our self-conceptions and personalities (if you think about it, a very depressing notion, as it offers us little hope of change), William Sewell was one of the first and most creative scholars to develop an empirical test. Thank goodness he found no confirmation.[3] Of course, Sewell's research was oriented toward what might be called "normal" ranges of intimate or sexually tinted biological experiences in early childhood (e.g., some babies are breast-fed while others are bottle-fed; some kids are toilet-trained at the age of 1, others at 2, others not until 3). The long-term effects on personality and self-conception of extremely "deviant" early childhood experiences—for example, incest—are well-documented.[4]

Cognitive development theory is another psychological approach to socialization that downplays social interaction; it is associated with the voluminous writings and research of Jean Piaget. He emphasizes that a child's conceptions of self and others and of reality are closely linked to biological development, almost to the exclusion of social factors. Thus, for example, irrespective of sex, race, or social class, all six-year-olds regard dark colors as unpleasant and light colors as pleasant.[5] Psychologist Jerome Kagan captures the flavor of the cognitive development approach when he states:

The course of a life, like the cycle of the seasons, consists of a set of inevitable, genetically determined phenomena which, depending on time and place, are exhibited in a local script whose surface details can take on remarkable variety. The Eskimo infant living near Hudson Bay remains physically close to its mother for most of the first year; the infant born on an Israeli kibbutz is cared for by a hired caregiver; the Mayan infant of northwest Guatemala, wrapped in tattered pieces of woven cloth, spends much of the first year sleeping in a hammock hung from the roof of the house. But—despite the differences in affectivity, alertness, and maturity of motor coordination produced by these varied rearing conditions—by three years of age, children from these three cultures share the capacity to recognize the past, to become fright-

---

[1]S. Frank Miyamoto and Sanford M. Dornbusch, "A Test of Interaction Hypotheses of Self Conception: The Looking-Glass Self Revisited," *American Journal of Sociology* 61:5 (March 1956), pp. 399–403.

[2]*The Basic Writings of Sigmund Freud*, edited by A. A. Brill (New York: Modern Library), 1938, p. 586.

[3]William Sewell, "Infant Training and the Personality of the Child," *American Journal of Sociology* 58 (September 1952), pp. 150–159.

[4]See Mary de Young, *The Sexual Victimization of Children* (London: McFarland), 1982; Derek Jehu, *Beyond Sexual Abuse: Therapy with Women Who Were Childhood Victims* (New York: John Wiley), 1988; and Patricia Beezley Mrazek and C. Henry Kempe (eds.), *Sexually Abused Children and Their Families* (New York: Pergamon), 1981.

[5]E. V. Demos, *Children's Understanding and Use of Affect Terms* (Cambridge, MA: Harvard University, Ph.D. dissertation), 1974; as cited in Jerome Kagan, *The Nature of the Child* (New York: Basic Books), 1984, p. 213.

ened by the unusual, and to understand the significance of an adult prohibition—a trio of talents that emerge in that order.[6]

Even though many of the ideas of cognitive development theory are intuitively pleasing and are supported by substantial scientific research,[7] sociologists still emphasize social interaction processes as essential to socialization and the development of self-conception and personality. For example, Marvin Harris's selection in Part 3 emphasizes how the different cultural traditions of India and the western nations like the United States lead to very different propensities to eat beef. Part 5 begins with a similarly oriented essay by Melvin L. Kohn of Johns Hopkins University. Kohn establishes that social class influences the value orientations parents instill in their children. His findings reveal that, independent of religion and national background, middle-class parents are more likely to raise children to be *self-directed*, whereas working-class parents are more likely to raise children to *conform to external authority*. Phrased differently, middle-class parents are more likely to emphasize that a child *thinks for him/herself*, while working-class parents are more like to emphasize that a child obeys. Why does this particular relationship exist between social class and values exist? The short answer is that economic success for working-class parents depends upon their following their bosses' orders, while success for middle-class individuals more often depends upon their creativity in problem solving (e.g., factory floor work is usually much more delimited than, say, the diagnostic work of a physician or the lesson planning of a teacher).

Kohn's essay is followed by the more recent research of Sharlene Hesse-Biber, of Boston College, and myself. Hesse-Biber and I demonstrate that the nature of social interaction within a family critically influences the odds of a young woman developing an eating disorder such as anorexia or bulimia. We show, for example, that daughters who were regularly criticized by one or both of their parents regarding weight and physical appearance are much more likely to develop an eating disorder during adolescence and young adulthood. However, the importance of this criticism is greatly dependent upon whether the parent is overweight. What is your own guess? That is, do you think having a critical parent who is overweight would have a greater or smaller impact on the odds of a daughter developing an eating disorder? Think about it, make your guess, then go read our essay.

---

[6]Kagan, *op. cit.,* p. 75.

[7]Thomas Likona (ed.), *Moral Development and Behavior: Theory, Research, and Social Issues* (New York: Holt, Rinehart and Winston), 1976.

_____Chapter 12_____

SOCIAL CLASS AND PARENTAL VALUES

MELVIN L. KOHN

It is a commonplace thought among social scientists that, no matter what the subject of study, we should always measure people's social class positions, for class is nearly always significantly involved. Remarkable though it seems, one aspect of social structure, hierarchical position, is related to almost everything about men's lives—their political party preferences, their sexual behavior, their church membership, even their rates of ill health and death. Moreover, the correlations are not trivial; class is substantially related to all these phenomena.

These facts are abundant and beyond dispute. What is not at all clear, though, is why class has such widespread ramifications. How do these impressive and massive regularities come about? What, specifically, is it about "class" that makes it important for so much of human behavior?

This question is too broad to be answered in a single empirically based [essay]. We therefore focus on the relationship of class to one strategic realm of human experience, values and orientation. The heart of our work is an exploration of class and parental values for children. We describe the impact of class on parental values, trace the consequences for parental behavior of class differences in values, and then attempt to interpret why class matters for values. . . .

A REFORMULATION

Understanding the nature of the ties between social class and parent-child relationships is part of the more general problem of understanding the effects of social structure upon behavior. We believe that social class has proved to be so useful a concept because it embodies more than simply one or another of the items used to index it—such as education or occupational position—and more than any of the large number of social, cultural, and psychological variables with which it is correlated. The concept, "class," captures the reality that the intricate interplay of all these variables creates different basic conditions of life at different levels of the social order. Members of different social classes, by virtue of enjoying (or suffering) different conditions of life, come to see the world differently—to develop different conceptions of social reality, different aspirations and hopes and fears, different "conceptions of the desirable."

The last is particularly important for present purposes, for from people's conceptions of the desirable—especially of what characteristics are desirable in children—we can discern their objectives in child rearing. Thus, conceptions of the desirable—that is, *values*—become the key concept for this analysis, the bridge between position in the larger social structure and the behavior of the individual. The intent of the analysis is to trace the effects of social class position on values and the effects of values on behavior.

In doing this, we follow an old tradition in sociological inquiry, but apply it to a subject matter where it has not much been used, with methods often thought foreign. The tradition is the "sociology of knowledge," the effort to trace the underpinnings of belief, value, and ideology to men's positions in the social structure. It is based on the works of the giants—Marx, Weber, Durkheim, Veblen, Tawney, and Mannheim.

The subject matter, parent-child relationships, is customarily approached from a psychodynamic perspective. We mean our perspective to be, not antithetical to that, but complementary. We do not underestimate the consequences for children of class differences in parent-child relationships, but our focus is explicating why there are class differences.

The methods are those of survey research, with all the statistical trimmings. Sociological classicists may shudder at the thought of despoiling a classical tradition of inquiry with statistical significance levels, correlation coefficients, and the like, but we think these modern methods are appropriate to the old, important problems. . . .

THE STUDIES

The Washington study, conducted in 1956–57, is based on interviews with 339 mothers, from families broadly representative of the white middle and working classes, but deliberately not representative of the city of Washington. All the mothers had a child in the fifth grade of a local public or parochial school. In a random sample of 82 families, the father and the fifth grade child were interviewed, too, using interview schedules comparable to that used for the mothers. The interviews focused on parental values, disciplinary practices, and the major dimensions of parent-child relationships.

The Turin study, conducted by Leonard Pearlin in 1962–63 was designed to be comparable to the Washington study. Thus it, too, is based on samples broadly representative of the middle and working classes, but deliberately not representative of the city of Turin. It is limited to families having children equivalent in school grade (and age) to those in the Washington study. The children themselves were not interviewed in this study, but there is a much larger sample of fathers (341) and a larger sample of mothers (520). The interviews covered the same subjects as did those in Washington, with some important

additions—notably, questions asked of fathers about their occupational circumstances. . . .

SOCIAL CLASS

In this [essay], we use a multidimensional index of class, based on the two dimensions of stratification that appear to be the most important in contemporary American society—occupational position and education. We also index two other dimensions of social stratification—income and subjective class identification. . . .

Implicit in the foregoing are the ideas that class is an abstraction from a complex reality, that in all probability power, privilege, and prestige are continuously distributed in society, and that it is an oversimplification to speak of any given number of social classes. It is often useful, nevertheless, to deal in oversimplifications. . . . For convenience, we temporarily adopt an oversimplified model, one implicit in most research on social class and family relationships in the United States. This model conceives of society as divided into four relatively discrete classes: a "lower class" of unskilled manual workers, a "working class" of manual workers in semiskilled and skilled occupations, a "middle class" of white-collar workers and professionals, and an "elite," differentiated from the middle class not so much in terms of occupation as of wealth and lineage. The middle class can be thought of as comprising two distinguishable segments: an upper-middle class of professionals, proprietors, and managers, who generally have at least some college training, and a lower-middle class of small shopkeepers, clerks, and salespersons, generally with less education.

The sampling methods of the Washington and Turin studies require that we use some such model. Since we do not have data for the entire range of social classes, we must have descriptive terms for part of the range—the working and middle classes. . . .

INDICES OF CLASS

In [the American study], social class position has been indexed by Hollingshead's two-factor "Index of Social Position," a weighted combination of occupational position and education.[1] In the Italian study, Hollingshead's classification of occupational position was used alone, for occupational levels in Italy are quite comparable to those in the United States, but educational levels are not. . . .

In the Washington study, our sampling methods were designed to exclude the highest and lowest socioeconomic strata. . . . Thus, most of the families fall naturally into the second, third, and fourth of the five socioeconomic levels into which Hollingshead divides the population. In analyzing these data, we consider the first three of Hollingshead's levels to be middle class and the remaining two to be working class. (Dividing the Washington sample into the middle and the working class by this procedure results in virtually the same dichotomization of the sample as if we used the U.S. Census classification of occupations—treating professionals, proprietors, clerks, and salesmen as middle class; foremen, skilled, semiskilled, and unskilled workers as working class.)

It must be emphasized that the working-class sample is composed preponderantly of stable working class rather than of lower class families—in the sense that the men have steady jobs, and that their education, income, and skill levels are above those of the lowest socioeconomic stratum.

Since the Turin study was designed to be comparable to the Washington study, it too excludes the highest and lowest socioeconomic strata. Thus, a similar dichotomization of the sample into a working class and a middle class is appropriate, with the dividing line falling between blue- and white-collar workers. . . .

SOCIAL CLASS AND PARENTAL VALUES: THE WASHINGTON STUDY

Despite its importance to social policies and to sociological theory, there has been relatively little empirical study of values, even less on the relationship of social stratification to values, and almost none on the relationship of class to parental values.

Prior to the present research, only two studies (of which we know) had dealt explicitly with the relationship of social class to parental values. The Lynds, in their now-classic community study, *Middletown,* asked mothers to "score a list of fifteen habits according to their emphases upon them in training their children" and discovered that working-class mothers put greater emphasis on obedience than do mothers of higher social class position (1929:143). Some 17 years later, Duvall (1946) characterized working-class (and lower middle-class) mothers' values as "traditional"—these mothers want their children to be neat and clean, to obey and respect adults, to please adults. In contrast to this emphasis on how the child comports himself, middle-class mothers' values are more "developmental"—they want their children to be eager to learn, to love and confide in the parents, to be happy, to share and cooperate, to be healthy and well. Duvall's traditional-developmental dichotomy does not describe the difference between middle- and working-class parental values quite exactly, but it does point to the essence of the difference, a concern with external conformity or with internal process.

It is our purpose to pursue the problem posed by the Lynds and Duvall—to study the relationship of social class to parental values—and then to see what implications class differences in parental values might have for child-rearing practices. But before we can carry out such studies it is necessary to have an adequate index of parental values. This, in turn, requires that we be clear about what we mean by the concept, "value."

DEFINING AND INDEXING PARENTAL VALUES

We conceive of values as standards of desirability criteria of preference. . . . By parental values we mean the values that parents would most like to see embodied in their children's behavior—the characteristics they consider most desirable to inculcate in their children.

How does one measure parental values? No approach is completely satisfactory. To ask people to tell us their values is obviously subject to the risk that they may not really know or at any rate may not be able to formulate them in terms that we shall understand; moreover, they may not wish to be altogether frank. But inferring values from observed behavior may not be satisfactory either,[2] for we cannot be certain that we are correctly distinguishing the normative from other components of action. Actions may deceive as well as words, one often misinterprets people's intent.

Our solution, in the Washington study, was to take the most straightforwardly naive course—to *ask* parents what they value—and then to subject their assertions to critical examination. Instead of simply assuming that their stated values matter for their behavior, we shall go on to see whether or not these values bear a meaningful relationship to how they act.

From the preceding discussion, it is clear that a central manifestation of value is to be found in *choice*. It tells us little to know merely that a parent values honesty for his child; the critical question is whether he values honesty more or less than self-control, or obedience, or some other valued characteristic. It is also clear that if we are to make valid comparisons of middle- to working-class parental values, the index of values must put no premium upon articulateness or imagination, which may be primarily reflective of formal education.

Both considerations can be satisfied by the device of presenting all parents with a list of characteristics known to be generally valued and asking them to choose those few that they value most of all. This we did. The list was compiled from the suggestions made by parents interviewed during the development and pretesting of the interview schedule. In those interviews we searched for any and all characteristics the parents thought desirable for their 10- or 11-year-old children. The 17 that seemed most generally valued by parents having children of this age were:

> That he is honest.
> That he is happy.
> That he is considerate of others.
> That he obeys his parents well.
> That he is dependable.
> That he has good manners.
> That he has self-control.
> That he is popular with other children.

> That he acts in a serious way.
> That he is a good student.
> That he is neat and clean.
> That he is curious about things.
> That he is ambitious.
> That he is able to defend himself.
> That he is affectionate.
> That he is liked by adults.
> That he is able to play by himself.

From this list, the parents were asked to choose the three characteristics that they considered to be the most important in a boy or girl of their fifth-grader's age. (Here, as throughout the interview, parents were asked the questions with reference to a specific child, the fifth-grader. If that child was a boy, we asked about the characteristics most desirable for a boy of his age; if a girl, we asked about the characteristics most desirable for a girl of her age.)

This, then, is the index of parental values: the choice of 3 of these characteristics as more desirable than the other 14 for a 10- or 11-year-old boy or girl. . . . Let us see what it yields. Do middle- and working-class parents assert different values for their children? We turn to the data of the Washington study for an answer.

CLASS AND VALUES

Middle- and working-class mothers share a common, but by no means identical, set of values (Table 12.1). There is considerable agreement in what is highly valued in the two social classes. In both classes, happiness and such standards of conduct as honesty, consideration, obedience, dependability, manners, and self-control are most highly ranked for both boys and girls of this age. Standards of conduct outrank all other requisites except happiness.

Although there is agreement on this broad level, middle-class mothers differ from working-class mothers in which of these values they emphasize. Middle-class mothers give higher priority to values that reflect *internal dynamics*—the child's own and his empathic concern for other people's. Specifically, they are significantly[3] more likely than are working-class mothers

TABLE 12.1   Mothers' Values, by Social Class and Sex of Child

	FOR BOYS		FOR GIRLS		COMBINED	
	MIDDLE CLASS	WORKING CLASS	MIDDLE CLASS	WORKING CLASS	MIDDLE CLASS	WORKING CLASS
[Percentage][a] who value						
That he is honest	44	57	44	48	44	53
That he is happy	44*	27*	48	45	46*	36*
That he is considerate of others	40	30	38*	24*	39*	27*
That he obeys his parents well	18*	37*	23	30	20*	33*
That he is dependable	27	27	20	14	24	21
That he has good manners	16	17	23	32	19	24
That he has self-control	24	14	20	13	22*	13*
That he is popular with other children	13	15	17	20	15	18
That he is a good student	17	23	13	11	15	17
That he is neat and clean	7	13	15*	28*	11*	20*
That he is curious about things	20*	6*	15	7	18*	6*
That he is ambitious	9	18	6	8	7	13
That he is able to defend himself	13	5	6	8	10	6
That he is affectionate	3	5	7	4	5	4
That he is liked by adults	3	5	7	4	5	4
That he is able to play by himself	1	2	0	3	1	2
That he acts in a serious way	0	1	0	0	0	1
Number of cases	(90)	(85)	(84)	(80)	(174)	(165)

*Social class differences statistically significant, $p < 0.05$, using the t test for the difference between two proportions.

[[a]Kohn originally presented *proportions;* these have been multiplied by 100 to transform them into *percentages.*—Ed.]

to value happiness (in particular, for sons), consideration, self-control, and curiosity. Working-class mothers, by contrast, give higher priority to values that reflect *behavioral conformity*—obedience and neatness.

It must be repeated that the class differences are variations on a common theme, most of the highest rated values reflecting respect for the rights of others. The middle-class variant focuses on the internal processes of self-direction and empathic understanding, while the working-class variant focuses on conformity to externally defined standards.

The difference between the classes is illustrated anew by the sex distinctions mothers do or do not make. Middle-class mothers conceptions of the desirable are much the same for boys and for girls. But working-class mothers distinguish between the sexes:

They are more likely to regard dependability, school performance, and ambition as important for boys, and to regard happiness, neatness and cleanliness, and good manners as important for girls. We think this difference in mothers making or not making a sex distinction reflects the differential emphasis on self-direction and behavioral conformity. If the focus is internal dynamics, the same values should apply to boys and to girls. But if the focus is externally imposed standards, then what is appropriate for boys is different from what is appropriate for girls. Working-class mothers draw precise distinctions between what is behaviorally proper for boys and for girls; these distinctions are irrelevant to middle-class mothers.

As for fathers: Judging from our small sample of 82 fathers, their values are similar to those of mothers (Table 12.2). Essentially the same rank order of choices holds for fathers as for mothers, with one exception—fathers rank daughters' happiness lower than do mothers. Moreover, among fathers, too, consideration and self-control are more highly valued in the middle class, and obedience is more highly valued in the working class. There are two additional class differences for fathers: Dependability is more highly regarded in the middle class, and the ability to defend oneself, in the working class.

The question of whether or not working-class fathers make the same sex distinctions that mothers do must be answered equivocally, for our sample of working-class fathers of girls is very small. There are no statistically significant differences, but with so small a sample, that is hardly definitive.

In any event, the class differences in fathers' values are consistent with those in mothers' values. We take this to indicate that middle-class parents (fathers as well as mothers) are more likely to ascribe predominant importance to children's acting on the basis of internal standards of conduct, while working-class parents ascribe greater importance to compliance with parental authority.

But what does it mean to say that parents ascribe predominant importance to one value over another? We have found, for example, that working-class parents value neatness and cleanliness more highly than do middle-class parents. Offhand, this seems strange, for neatness and cleanliness are such stereotypically middle-class values. Perhaps middle-class parents simply take them for granted.

TABLE 12.2 Fathers' Values, by Social Class and Sex of Child

	FOR BOYS		FOR GIRLS		COMBINED	
	MIDDLE CLASS	WORKING CLASS	MIDDLE CLASS	WORKING CLASS	MIDDLE CLASS	WORKING CLASS
[Percentage][a] who value						
That he is honest	60	60	43	55	52	58
That he is happy	48	24	24	18	37	22
That he is considerate of others	32	16	38	9	35*	14*
That he obeys his parents well	12*	40*	14	36	13*	39*
That he is dependable	36*	12*	29	0	33*	8*
That he has good manners	24	28	24	18	24	25
That he has self-control	20	8	19	0	20*	6*
That he is popular with other children	8	16	24	45	15	25
That he is a good student	4	12	10	36	7	19
That he is neat and clean	16	20	14	9	15	17
That he is curious about things	16	12	10	0	13	8
That he is ambitious	20	12	14	0	17	8
That he is able to defend himself	4	16	0	18	2*	17*
That he is affectionate	0	4	5	18	2	8
That he is liked by adults	0	8	0	9	0	8
That he is able to play by himself	0	8	5	0	2	6
That he acts in a serious way	0	4	0	0	0	3
Number of cases	(25)	(25)	(21)	(11)	(46)	(36)

*Social class differences statistically significant, $p < 0.05$, using the *t* test for the difference between two proportions. . . .

[[a]Kohn originally presented *proportions;* these have been multiplied by 100 to transform them into *percentages.*—Ed.]

The issue is central to any effort at measuring values. In essence, the argument is that middle-class parents think neatness and cleanliness are important, but not as problematic as some other values. In the circumstances of middle-class life, neatness and cleanliness are easily enough attained to be of less immediate concern than are other values. (Conversely, working-class mothers may be less likely than middle-class mothers to value happiness for their sons, not because they think it less important that their sons be happy, but because other concerns are more pressing.) Parents rate values, not only in terms of intrinsic desirability, but also in terms of how problematic is their realization.

To put the matter more generally, we believe that there are two main elements in people's ratings of values. One element is their judgment of *intrinsic importance*—which essentially means their judgment of where any given value would rank in a hierarchy of values if all other relevant considerations were equal. Second is their judgment of the *probability of realization* of the value—if it is 100 percent certain of attainment, it will be rated down in comparison to values whose attainment is problematic.

Parents are most likely to accord high priority to those values that seem important, in that failure to achieve them would affect the children's futures adversely, and problematic, in that they are difficult to achieve. Our index of parental values measures

conceptions of the *important, but problematic*. In judging what is important but problematic, middle-class parents give higher priority to children's acting on the basis of internal standards of conduct, while working-class parents give higher priority to their conforming to parental authority. . . .

CLASS: ITS COMPONENTS AND ITS CORRELATES

In discussing the relationships of social class to values we have talked as if American society were composed of two relatively homogeneous groupings, manual and white-collar workers, together with their families. Yet it is likely that there is considerable variation in values, associated with other bases of social differentiation, within each class. If so, it should be possible to differentiate the classes in such a way as to specify more precisely the relationships of social class to values. . . .

Religious background is particularly appropriate as a criterion for distinguishing relatively distinct groups within the social classes. It is not so highly related to values that Protestant mothers differ significantly from Catholic mothers of the same social class (Table 12.3). (Even when the comparison is restricted to Catholic mothers whose children attend Catholic school versus Protestant mothers of the same social class, there are no significant differences.)

TABLE 12.3   Mothers' Values, by Social Class and Religious Background

	MIDDLE-CLASS PROTESTANT	MIDDLE-CLASS CATHOLIC	WORKING-CLASS PROTESTANT	WORKING-CLASS CATHOLIC
[Percentage][a] of mothers who value				
Obedience	17	25	33	36
Neatness, cleanliness	8	15	17	27
Consideration	36	38	26	29
Curiosity	24	12	7	5
Self-control	28	15	15	9
Happiness	47	42	38	30
Number of cases	(88)	(52)	(107)	(56)

[[a]Kohn originally presented *proportions;* these have been multiplied by 100 to transform them into *percentages.*—Ed.]

But the combination of class and religious background does enable us to isolate groups that are more homogeneous in their values than are the social classes *in toto*. There is an ordering, reasonably consistent for all class-related values, proceeding from middle-class Protestant mothers, to middle-class Catholic, to working-class Protestant, to working-class Catholic. (Jewish mothers—almost all middle class—are very similar to middle-class Protestant mothers in their values.) Middle-class Protestants and working-class Catholics constitute the two extremes whose values are most dissimilar.

Another relevant social distinction is between urban and rural background [we classified as having a rural background all mothers who, prior to age 15, had lived on a farm for some time other than simply summer vacations]. As with religious background, we can arrange mothers into four groups delineated on the basis of class and rural-urban background in an order that is reasonably consistent for all class-related values. The order is: middle-class urban, middle-class rural, working-class urban, working-class rural. The extremes are middle-class mothers raised in the city and working-class mothers raised on farms.

It would be valuable to examine the effects of a number of other major lines of social demarcation upon parental values, but the Washington sample does not permit this. We cannot, for example, compare whites to blacks, people of one region of the country to those of another, small-town residents to large-city residents. We cannot take adequate account of national background, because the sample is too small to permit comparisons among the various national backgrounds—although we do find that mothers who are at least second-generation American-born do not differ appreciably in their values from mothers who are not.

For now, we tentatively conclude that it is possible to specify the relationship between social class and values more precisely by subdividing the social classes on the basis of other lines of social demarcation—but that social class seems to provide the single most potent line of demarcation.

Correlates of Class

There are a large number of other variables, each of them correlated with social class, that might possibly account for the class-values relationships. We have reexamined the relationship of class to values, controlling each of a large number of possibly relevant correlates of social class. *None* of them differentiates mothers of the same social class into groups having decidedly different values or affects the relationship of class to values. These variables include the size of the family, the mother's age, the ordinal position of the child in the family, the length of time the family has lived in the neighborhood, the social class composition of the neighborhood, whether or not the mother has been socially mobile (from the status of her childhood family), and her class identification. It should be especially noted that class differences in mothers' values do not result from the relatively large proportion of families of government workers included in the sample. Wives of government employees do not differ from other mothers of the same social class in their values.

In sum, we find that these correlates of social class do *not* explain the relationship of class to values. . . .

Conclusions to This Point

The first conclusion must be that parents, whatever their social class, deem it very important indeed that their children be honest, happy, considerate, obedient, and dependable. Middle- and working-class parents share values that emphasize, in addition to children's happiness, their acting in a way that shows a decent respect for the rights of others. All class differences in parental values are variations on this common theme.

Middle-class parents, however, are more likely to emphasize children's *self-direction,* and working-class parents to emphasize their *conformity to external authority*. This basic tendency is apparent in the greater propensity of middle-class parents to choose consideration and self-control, and of working-class parents to choose obedience and neatness, as highly desirable. It is apparent, too, in the differential meanings that seem to be attributed to honesty and in the generally different patterns of association in choice of values. It is even discernible in middle-class mothers valuing the same characteristics for boys and for girls, while working-class mothers—more attuned to the manifestly appropriate and less to children's intent—value more masculine characteristics for boys, more feminine characteristics for girls.

On the Meaning of Self-Direction and Conformity

We conclude that middle-class parents are more likely to value self-direction; working-class parents are more likely to value conformity to external authority. . . . Since the terms self-direction and conformity have many connotations, some of which we do not intend, we must make clear precisely what we mean by them. . . .

The essential difference between the terms, as we use them, is that self-direction focuses on *internal* standards for behavior; conformity focuses on *externally* imposed rules. (One important corollary is that the former is concerned with intent, the latter only with consequences.) Self-direction does not imply rigidity, isolation, or insensitivity to others; on the contrary, it implies that one is attuned to internal dynamics—one's own, and other people's. Conformity does not imply sensitivity to one's peers, but rather obedience to the dictates of authority. . . . [Thus], it should be clear that our use of the term conformity differs also from the meaning it has in most experimental studies, where the conformity studied is acquiescence to majority opinion of a small group in face-to-face contact (cf. Asch, 1952;[4] Jahoda, 1959). Rather, we mean *conformity to authority*, often a distant and sometimes a diffuse authority. A face-to-face group may take on the reality of authority, but that is a special case, and not the focus of this study. . . .

The class difference in parental valuation of self-direction and conformity is potentially important—both for helping us understand class differences in how parents raise children, and as an indication of the broader relationship of class to values and orientation.

But is the difference in parental values a general fact, or is it somehow peculiar to the time and social circumstances of the Washington study? To answer that, we turn to the Turin study.

A CROSS-NATIONAL COMPARISON: THE TURIN STUDY

The central problem for this [section] is whether the relationship of social class to parental values is specific to the historical, cultural, and economic circumstances of Washington, D.C., in the late 1950s, or is a more general phenomenon. Is high valuation of conformity by working-class parents a response peculiar to the affluence and economic security of that place and time? If so, we must confine our interpretation to those limited circumstances; if not, it will be more appropriate to interpret the relationship of class to values in terms of conditions that are generally characteristic of industrial societies.

In the absence of definitive evidence about the "typicality" of the Washington findings, two alternative interpretations seem plausible. The first assumes that the relationship of class to values was especially pronounced under the conditions of affluence that were obtained when the Washington study was conducted. It emphasizes that, with the end of mass immigration, there has emerged in the United States a stable working class, largely derived from the manpower of rural areas, uninterested in mobility into the middle class, but very much interested in security, respectability, and a decent standard of living (cf. Miller and Riessman, 1961). This working class has come to enjoy a standard of living formerly reserved for the middle class, but has not chosen a middle-class style of life. In effect, the working class has striven for, and partially achieved, an American dream distinctly different from the dream of success and achievement. In an affluent society, it is possible for the worker to be the traditionalist—politically, economically, and, most relevant here, in his values for his children. Working-class parents may want their children to conform to external authority because the parents themselves accept the status quo: they are willing to defer to authority, in return for security and respectability.

The alternative interpretation of the relationship of class to values assumes its generality. From this perspective, what needs to be explained is not so much that working-class parents value conformity as that middle-class parents value self-direction. In all modern societies, middle-class parents can—and must—instill in their children a degree of self-direction that would be less appropriate to the conditions of life of the working class. Although there is substantial truth in the characterization of the middle-class way of life as one of great conformity, it is nevertheless true that, relative to the working class, middle-class conditions of life require more independent action. Furthermore, the higher levels of education enjoyed by the middle class make possible a degree of internal scrutiny difficult to achieve without the skills in dealing with the abstract that formal education can provide. Finally, the economic security of many middle-class occupations, the level of income these occupations provide, and the status they confer, permit their incumbents to focus on the subjective and the ideational. Middle-class conditions of life both allow and demand a greater degree of self-direction than do those of the working class.

Which is it? Do the Washington findings indicate what happens to a working class when it becomes affluent, or do they reflect differences in conditions of life that are built into the social structure of other, perhaps all, industrial societies? There is little in the research literature to help us answer this question. We cannot assess whether or not the relationship of class to values has been stable over time, for all directly pertinent data are of fairly recent vintage. Even the Lynds' (1929) study goes back only to the late 1920's. As for stability from place to place, there is one limited but important piece of information: From public opinion polls in a number of different countries, Inkeles (1960) ingeniously gleaned data showing that working-class parents consistently place greater emphasis on obedience than do middle-class parents. The implication is that class differences in parental values are not a phenomenon specific to

Washington, D.C., or even to the United States. But these data are hardly definitive.

A more certain basis for choosing between the two interpretations requires at least one study comparable to that done in Washington in a place that offers a different cultural and historic context, less affluence, and less economic security. Turin, Italy was chosen to be that place.

NATION, CLASS, AND VALUES

No single comparative study can tell us whether the relationship of class to values is universal. But even one study that demonstrates a similar relationship of class to parental values in a sufficiently dissimilar context would have significance for establishing the generality of the relationship. Turin seemed a good place to conduct such a study, especially because there we could be confident not only of cultural dissimilarity and much less affluent economic conditions, but also of a politically more radical working-class tradition.

The question then becomes: Is social class related to parental values in Turin, Italy in much the same way as in Washington, D.C.—despite the great differences in history, culture, and material conditions of life? Is working-class parents' high valuation of obedience a result of circumstances peculiar to the United States? Or is the necessity of conforming to external authority so built into the conditions of working-class life that even in a markedly dissimilar political, economic, and social context, working-class parents would have their children learn to conform to external standards?

To answer these questions requires an examination of the relationship of both nationality and class to parental values (Table 12.4). Italian and American parents of the same social class differ more in their value priorities than do middle- and working-class parents of either country. One indication of this is that the rank order of value-choices differs much more from country to country than from class to class in either country.[5] Another indication is that the percentage differences[6] associated with nationality

TABLE 12.4 Parental Values, by Social Class and Sex of Parent—Turin, Italy, Compared to Washington, D.C.

| | ITALY | | | | UNITED STATES | | | |
| | FATHERS | | MOTHERS | | FATHERS | | MOTHERS | |
[Percentage][a] who value	MIDDLE CLASS	WORKING CLASS	MIDDLE CLASS	WORKING CLASS	MIDDLE CLASS	WORKING CLASS	MIDDLE CLASS	WORKING CLASS
That he is honest	54	54	55	55	52	58	44	53
That he has good manners	32*	44*	44	51	24	25	19	24
That he obeys his parents	31*	45*	36*	48*	13*	39*	20*	33*
That he acts in a serious way	25	18	18	20	0	3	0	1
That he has self-control	23*	11*	16*	8*	20*	6*	22*	13*
That he is dependable	23*	13*	21*	10*	33*	8*	24	21
That he is able to defend himself	21	14	17*	8*	2*	17*	10	6
That he is ambitious	19	17	21	19	17	8	7	13
That he is happy	14*	7*	16	14	37	22	46*	36*
That he be considerate of others	11	9	10*	3*	35*	14*	39*	27
That he is affectionate	10	12	13	12	2	8	5	4
That he is neat and clean	9	14	7*	14*	15	17	11*	20*
That he is popular with other children	9	7	6	4	15	25	15	18
That he is a good student	8*	24*	13*	24*	7	19	15	17
That he is liked by adults	4	9	5	9	0	8	5	4
That he is curious about things	3	1	2	1	13	8	18*	6*
That he is able to play by himself	1	2	0	1	2	6	1	2
Number of cases	(160)	(148)	(263)	(205)	(46)	(36)	(174)	(165)

Note: Italian parents who did not answer the question completely have been excluded from this table.

*Social class differences statistically significant, $p < 0.05$, using the t test for the difference between two proportions.

[[a]Kohn originally presented *proportions*; these have been multiplied by 100 to transform them into *percentages*.—Ed.]

are greater than those associated with class. In either social class, American parents are more likely to value happiness, popularity, and consideration; Italian parents are more likely to value manners, obedience, and seriousness. American parental values seem to be focused more on the child *qua* child, Italian parental values more on the child as proto-adult.[7]

Despite the differences between Italian and American parental values, almost all the class relationships noted in the United States are found in Italy, too. Of the eight characteristics significantly related to social class in Washington, six are significant in Turin, too—obedience and neatness being more highly valued by the working class in both places, self-control, dependability, happiness, and consideration by the middle class in both places. (The two that are not related to class in Turin as they are in Washington are curiosity and the ability to defend oneself; we suspect imprecisions of translation.[8]) In addition, there are two class differences in Turin that were not significant in Washington: Italian working-class parents value manners more than do middle-class parents—which is obviously consistent with other indications of their higher valuation of conformity. They also value children's being good students more highly than do middle-class parents. This fact is at first puzzling—until we remember that "good student" implies conformity to school requirements, in contrast to the intellectuality implied in "curiosity."

The preceding discussion assumes that the index of parental values is as exhaustive of the range of parental values for Italians as for Americans. Fortunately, the pretest interviews indicated that it is. This was confirmed by the survey itself: When parents were asked if there were any characteristics not on this list that they considered important, nothing substantively different was suggested.

Taking all the evidence together, we conclude that in both Italy and the United States, middle-class parents are more likely to value characteristics that bespeak self-direction; working-class parents are more likely to value characteristics that bespeak conformity to external standards.

It must be stressed that few of the differences in proportions of middle- and working-class parents who value any given characteristic are large. What is impressive is that the relationship of social class to parental values is consistent in the two countries—despite the cultural differences.

One thing is especially clear: A high valuation of obedience is not something peculiar to the American working class. On the contrary, obedience is more highly valued by working- than by middle-class parents in either country, and by Italians more than by Americans in either social class. The cumulative effect of nationality and class is that obedience is valued more highly by Italian working-class parents than by any of the other groups.

NOTES

1. Hollingshead classifies occupational positions into seven categories, education into another set of seven categories, then weights the occupational scores by seven and the educational scores by four, adds the two, and finally divides the resulting composite scores into five socioeconomic levels. The major occupational categories are: (1) Higher executives, proprietors of large concerns, and major professionals. (2) Business managers, proprietors of medium-sized businesses, and lesser professionals. (3) Administrative personnel, proprietors of small independent businesses, and minor professionals. (4) Clerical and sales workers, technicians, and owners of little businesses. (5) Skilled manual employ-ees. (6) Machine operators and semiskilled employees. (7) Unskilled employees. The educational categories are: (1) Professionally trained. (2) College graduate. (3) Some college. (4) High school graduate. (5) 10–11 years of school, some high school. (6) 7–9 years of school, approximately grade school graduate. (7) Less than 7 years of school, approximately some grade school . . . [See] Hollingshead and Redlich, 1958:387–397.

2. Compare LaPiere's essay in Part 2.—Ed.

3. For the sake of those readers who have no special interest in methods of statistical analysis, we shall wherever possible relegate information about statistical procedures,

levels of confidence, and the like to footnotes, where they can be ignored by the uninterested and read by the concerned. Except where explicitly indicated, all findings discussed in this essay are statistically significant at the 0.05 level of confidence or better. Of course, the fact that a finding is statistically significant does not necessarily make it socially important; in the National study, with its large sample, many trivial findings are statistically significant at levels of confidence much more impressive than 0.05. That a finding is not statistically significant, on the other hand, does not make it unimportant. We take the conservative position, though, that when a finding is not significant at the 0.05 level or better, one is well advised to treat it with extreme caution, no matter how well it fits one's preconceptions. The tests of statistical significance used in this chapter are chi-squared (and its equivalent, the t test for the difference between two proportions) and, where there are few cases in a comparison, Fisher's exact test.

4. See Asch's essay in Part 6.—Ed.

5. The rank order correlations for the value-choices of Italian and American parents are: (1) among middle-class mothers: 0.37; (2) among working-class mothers: 0.43; (3) among middle-class fathers: 0.44; and (4) among working-class fathers: 0.43. The rank order correlations for the value-choices of middle- and working-class parents are: (1) among Italian mothers: 0.79; (2) among American mothers: 0.88; (3) among Italian fathers: 0.73; and (4) among American fathers: 0.47. (The last of these is based on too few cases to be taken literally).

6. The statistical tests employed in this [section] are the t test for the difference between two proportions and chi-squared.

7. One other difference between the two countries is not shown in Table 12.4. Italian mothers make virtually no distinction between what is desirable for boys and for girls. In fact, the sex of the child makes no difference for any of the analyses of the Turin data presented [here]. Thus, for simplicity of presentation, the data will not be presented separately for boys and for girls.

8. In the case of curiosity, we could find no Italian equivalent that was as free of the connotation of voyeurism. As for ability to defend oneself, we think that to working-class American fathers it connoted protecting oneself in physical combat, but to Italian fathers it connoted looking out for oneself in a potentially hostile world.

REFERENCES

Asch, Solomon E. 1952. *Social Psychology*. New York: Prentice-Hall.

Duvall, Evelyn M. 1946. Conceptions of parenthood. *American Journal of Sociology* 52 (November): 193–203.

Hollingshead, August B. and Frederick C. Redlich. 1958. *Social Class and Mental Illness: A Community Study*. New York: Wiley.

Inkeles, Alex. 1960. Industrial man: The relation of status to experience, perception, and value. *American Journal of Sociology* 66 (July): 1–31.

Jahoda, Marie. 1959. Conformity and independence: A psychological analysis. *Human Relations* 12: 99–120.

Lynd, Robert S. and Helen Merrell Lynd. 1929. *Middletown: A Study in Contemporary American Culture*. New York: Harcourt, Brace and Company.

Miller, S. M. and Frank Riessman. 1961. The working class subculture: A new view. *Social Problems* 9 (Summer): 86–97.

CHAPTER 13

FAMILY SOCIALIZATION AND EATING DISORDERS IN COLLEGE-AGE WOMEN

SHARLENE HESSE-BIBER AND GREGG LEE CARTER

Past research has consistently found that between 4 and 9 percent of female college students meet the clinical criteria for the eating disorders of anorexia nervosa and bulimia (Drewnowski *et al*. 1988; Pope *et al*. 1984; Pyle *et al*. 1991). Further, studies indicate that between 60 and 80 percent of college women engage in regular binge eating and other abnormal behaviors. Many college women of normal weight continue to express a strong desire to be thinner and to hold beliefs about food and body image that are similar to those of women who have actual eating disorders (Gray and Ford 1985; Hesse-Biber 1989, 1996; Zuckerman *et al., 1984*).

Given the prevalence of disordered eating among college women, researchers have sought to specify factors that place women at risk for the development of eating disorders. An extensive literature suggests that the family plays a significant role (Pike and Rodin 1991; Strober and Humphrey 1987; Strober *et al*. 1990). Women raised in families that are hypercritical of weight issues are at a greater risk of experiencing disordered eating patterns (Keel *et al*. 1997; Moreno and Thelen 1993; Pike and Rodin 1991). Furthermore, teasing about weight and body image during early childhood has been shown to have a detrimental impact on an individual's body image in later life (Fabian and Thompson 1989).

We here explore first-hand accounts of the impact of family attitudes concerning weight and body image and how this influences the lives of college-age

women (or young alumnae). We buttress our explorations with a quantitative analysis of our qualitative data.

METHODOLOGY

This study consists of data collected from 55 young women two years post-college. The sample was drawn from an original population of 144 women who participated in a longitudinal study of eating patterns at a private New England college (Hesse-Biber 1989). Potential subjects were identified by matching their code numbers to the original list of names obtained in the initial study. Letters asking for volunteers to continue a project on eating patterns of alumnae were sent out to potential subjects. They were told that they would be contacted by telephone by the primary investigator. Potential subjects were asked to be involved in a confidential, personal interview followed by a questionnaire. The 55 women who participated in the study showed considerable homogeneity in terms of demographic data and early family history. They were all white, middle-class, and of Christian religious background. A majority of their parents were married. Their fathers worked full-time outside the home. The majority of the mothers did not work outside the home until their children were at least school-age, and even then, most maintained part-time jobs or jobs that observed school-day hours.

The interviews were open-ended, covering a wide range of psychological, environmental, developmental, and sociocultural issues. They were conducted using an interview guide and took between two and three hours.

Original chapter written for this volume; some passages have been excerpted from Sharline Hesse-Biber, *Am I Thin Enough Yet?* (New York: Oxford University Press, 1966).

THE FAMILY AND THE THINNESS MESSAGE: MOTHERS, FATHERS, AND SIBLINGS

Growing up in American society, we are of course taught to value what our society values. We learn to see ourselves as others see us. Self-image develops through social interaction. Our significant others, such as family, are the mirrors that reflect us. What others value in us provides the basic building blocks of selfhood. As noted by George Herbert Mead (1934, p. 135): "The self has a character which is different from that of the physiological organism with a development all its own. The self is not even present at birth but arises later in the process of social experience and activity." As part of membership in our society, young women have to learn how "to be a body." And, to no small degree, what a woman observes in the mirror is what she uses as a measure of her worth as a human being.

Women's bodily focus arises from discussions with their friends, interactions with family and social groups, and messages they receive from outside this intimate circle. The family is a child's first interpreter of the larger world. Some families mimic the cultural values of thinness, while others modify that message. In general, the women in our study commented on the great importance that family opinion had on how they perceived themselves.

In some cases, mothers and fathers can serve to modulate cultural norms of thinness and alleviate some of the pressures young girls may feel. Joanna's mother was accepting of her regardless of her weight. Joanna, who is not overweight, described her mother's attitude:

My mother, all she wants is that I'm happy. I can weigh 500 pounds as long as I'm happy. Her focus was always on my health, not so much with my appearance. So her comments were more towards always that positive support. Very rarely do I remember her giving like negative comments about how I looked. It was mostly encouraging. My mother would stay stuff like "You have a beautiful face, you have beautiful hands." She'd focus on individual qualities about me.

On the other hand, a number of the women who were struggling with eating issues describe their families exhibiting an overemphasis on physical appearance. Examples of the tension sparked by the emphasis on physical appearance include the following:

Joan: My brothers and sisters would go around and make pig noises. . . . My dad would say, "You need to lose weight." And I'd try and I'd be successful.

Becky: My brothers would mention to my mother, and she would say, "Rob thinks you are getting fat," and then she'd say, "Maybe you should stop eating so much." He [father] commented a lot. Never bad. Always good. He'd say, "You look good, you lost weight." He was always commenting on pretty young girls. So I knew it was important to him that I look good too. I wanted him to see that I could be as pretty as all the girls he was commenting on. I wanted him to be proud of me for that, and I knew he was.

Eliza: She [mother] was very critical. I was always the fat one and she was the thin one. She always made sarcastic remarks. You know, just something like, "You better watch what you eat. You're going to get fat. You look chunky there." She said, "thin down" all my life. . . . That I have the fattest thighs in the world. I'm the fat one. I'm her fat daughter.

Florence: I was sitting at the table and he [father] would just turn to one of the girls . . . and he would say, "You're getting a little fat belly."

Mary: My dad used to call me fat. I wouldn't have noticed on my own. . . . I was three years old when my dad was calling me fat.

Relatively little is known about how young women experience their parents' attitudes toward their bodies while growing up and how these attitudes affect their subsequent feelings about their weight and their perception of their problems with weight, body image, and eating disorders. Through such first-person accounts, we can explore this.

MOTHERS AND DAUGHTERS

Early on, parents or significant others are important "guides" in the process of body watching. Perhaps the earliest memories respondents have regarding their bodies and food involve family conversations. Mothers play a big role in sending messages regarding dieting. Often they express fears about their daughters becoming overweight. Elena notes how her mother was always watching her weight since she was young:

> *My mother wanted me to have everything she never had. She wanted me to have a college education. She wanted me to have more than she did. But she was critical of my body image. If she didn't like what I was wearing, she'd tell me right off the bat: "Don't you know how to dress!" Last year she called me a moose, and that hurt. Sometimes I think I need that, like just to make me aware so that I do something about my weight. I can see all her pushing me. It's gotten me what I am. At my house we get on the scale every day. And my mother will ask : "What do you weigh?" It's a big thing.*
>
> *When I'm home I drop weight like that, because my mother is always on my back saying "C'mon, c'mon." When we go out to eat, she tells me what I should order. When I look fine, my mother says nothing about my body, not even a compliment. But when I start gaining weight, the criticism begins.*

Becky and Susan echo Elena's sentiments:

> *Becky: One time I went on a camping trip, and I gained like four pounds and my mom said: "You've got to lose weight." I mean, she watched what I ate. Like if I was going to get a piece of cake she would be like, "Don't eat that."*
>
> *Susan: My mother was very critical of my appearance. I was always the fat one and she was the thin one. She would say that I have the fattest thighs in the world, and that I'd better watch what I'm eating. She would always make sarcastic remarks. She would say, "If you want to diet, I'll help you. I'll make special meals for you. I'll do anything I can for you." She was good in that aspect, but in the back of my mind I knew she was always going to say something about when I picked up that Twinkie!*

Mothers are crucial brokers of the wider cultural norms. Some research studies note that a mother's attitude about her own body image and eating behavior is very important in influencing her daughter's attitudes. Having a mother who is obsessed with being thin and who diets regularly is an important risk factor for the development of problem eating in her adolescent daughter (Attie and Brooks-Gunn

1992). Cathleen notes, for example, that her own mother was careful about her weight and was constantly on a diet. She took Cathleen to the doctor when she was not getting rid of her baby fat. Her mother put a high premium on looking good for herself and her daughter. Cathleen notes:

> *You know, my mother thought I was fat. I was eleven years old at the time. She put me on extensive diets, and I didn't like that. She gave me these amino tablets and she'd like search around and make sure I didn't take cookies with me to school. She watched me. She took me to her weight doctor. My mother said: "Well, you know you've got to get rid of that baby fat." I actually remember the moment when I got shame. I guess you call it that. I was undressing, and all of a sudden, I jumped away from the window. I was eleven when I suddenly realized I should cover myself up.*

BODY COMPARISONS

Snow White's stepmother, the Queen in the Grimms' fairy tale, prided herself on being the fairest in the land. She consulted her magic talking mirror for reassurance every day. But when Snow White grew up to be more beautiful, as confirmed by the mirror, the wicked Queen ordered her killed. In the end, of course, the King's son rescued Snow White, and the cruel, jealous Queen met a grisly end.

Many women perceive others as more attractive than themselves and, like the stepmother, feel envy, rage, and even violence toward them. Good-looking women, regardless of their other attributes, are just more competition for the few Princes out there. Our interview subjects reported that they constantly compared themselves to their sisters, mothers, and girlfriends. When they felt they didn't measure up, their resentment and anger often rivaled those of that wicked Queen.

Sometimes the competition hits close to home, as when mothers, daughters, and siblings compare their bodies (Attie and Brooks-Gunn 1992). "My mother was a model," Lucy told us. "She was always Little Miss Beauty Queen. And there was pressure for me to follow in her footsteps. But my mother was jealous of me. I could feel that tension between us.

She would often say, 'Well, you look a little scruffy today.'"

Irene was competitive with both her mother and her sister:

> When I was in high school, my mom dyed her hair blonde, and was skinnier than I, and I was incredibly jealous. It drove me crazy. I didn't want guys I liked to meet her. I didn't really tell her, but on the beach she'd wear bikinis, and I hated it. I thought my mother was trying to be a teenager when she was older, and I was really jealous of her. I like being with my father alone rather than with my mother, because I guess I feel that I'm still competing with her.

Betty's Story

Betty's story provides us with an extreme example of how a mother's physical characteristics and dieting behavior led her daughter to take a very dim view of her own body image:

> My mom would always tell me that I was very chunky. She's 5' 1" and weighs about 100 pounds, so she always fits into size two and four clothes. And here I am, I can't fit a piece of her clothing on my elbow. I'm the fat one, her fat daughter. I don't want to be near her. She always looks good, has to have the nicest clothes. I just feel very obese next to her.

Through her chronic dieting, Betty's mother conveyed an important message to her daughter when she was growing up. Later on, in college, Betty recapitulated her mother's attitudes about weight and eating issues in her own way, by becoming bulimic:

> My mom considers herself overweight. She always dieted, trying all those new, different diets, and I'd go on them with her. She tried diet books and the new rotation diet. She'll fluctuate, losing some but then she'll gain it back. Right now she's at a point where she says, "I'd like to be thinner, but your dad and I like to eat." And they go out to eat often and it's hard to stay on a diet. So she's coming to accept it, but I think she'd still like to lose weight.

Betty described how her mother always prepared big meals. "My brothers and father liked to eat. We always had a lot of food on the table and we usually had seconds. My grandfather would reward us for cleaning our plates. Even now I feel like I have to eat everything on my plate, even if I'm not hungry."

Not surprisingly, Betty was always very conscious of her weight and body image. "I have this little chart that I try to follow. It has your height and your build, if you're medium or small boned. It has how many calories are in anything you eat. My mom put it in my stocking at Christmas."

When she was a college freshman, she gained enough weight to prompt her father's remark that she was getting a "little chubby." Her bulimia started during her sophomore year, after a Christmas party:

> I made myself throw up. I had been drinking at the party, and I just ate out of control. I couldn't believe that I had eaten all that stuff. It was cookies mainly. I never thought I could throw up, and then I tried and it worked. I tried so hard to keep my weight down, and I was 115 and that's where I wanted to stay. And then I'd creep back up. To get all the food out of my stomach, especially that high calorie food, I threw up.
>
> I didn't have time to join a fitness club and I tried to run, but I didn't feel like I was exercising. I could just feel myself gaining weight and that made me nervous and I felt like if I didn't have time to exercise, then throwing up was kind of the answer. I tried dieting and I wouldn't eat for awhile, and then I would eat a lot. I can't go a whole day without eating. I think that's a major reason why I throw up too. Because I like to eat.

Trapped by two conflicting messages, "Be Thin" and "Eat," Betty used bulimia as a solution.

FATHER'S ATTITUDE TOWARD DAUGHTER'S PHYSICAL APPEARANCE

Mothers are often viewed as more involved with their daughters' physical appearance (Smetana 1988; Spitzack 1990). Research suggests that while both parents appear to influence their children's physical appearance and eating, they differ in style: "Mother criticizes, father compliments" (Spitzack 1990, p. 83). Few research studies, however, have examined the impact of fathers' attitudes toward daughters' physical appearance.

Jessica's father typifies the "silent" father: "I can't recall my father saying much about my appearance. Like if I put on a skirt on he'd say: 'Oh, you do have legs' and he joked about it. Never anything negative." Helen's father was also quiet. On special occasions he might say a word or two:

It was one of those things where if you bought a new dress for a prom, and you tried it on for him he'd say, "Oh, that looks great" or "very nice" or whatever. But as far as day to day, he'd never say anything. To tell you the truth I don't think he would even know what to say because that's not the type of question that he'd answer. He'd think, "What kind of a question is that, 'how do I look?'"

Reviewing the literature on family and personality factors in the development of eating disorders, Stephen Wonderlich (1992, pp. 103–126) cites three specific types of families that are at high risk for daughters' development of bulimia: (1) the perfect, (2) the overprotective, and (3) the chaotic. All three family types have stressed the importance of weight and body image. All three types are characterized by "extreme levels of paternal (versus maternal) power" (p. 105). All three family types "reflect the difficulty that the family experiences negotiating the affected children's transition from adolescence to young adulthood." Barbara's family appears to be an example of the "perfect" family. And her story gives us an extreme example of how fathers can amplify the message that to be beautiful is to be loved. This message dominated Barbara's outlook on life, and led to the development of a full-blown eating disorder.

Barbara's Story

Barbara was about to turn 20 when she was interviewed for this study. From appearances, she seemed a happy, well-adjusted college co-ed. She was not overweight, but she did want to lose a few pounds and spent considerable time working out at the college gym. But she had a hidden history of being anorexic, starting in seventh grade. Her bulimic symptoms began in the ninth grade and continued throughout her high school and college years.

Barbara's parents had had serious marital problems for a long time. Her father, toward whom she felt a great deal of ambivalence, had very high standards of feminine beauty. She grew up observing how difficult it was for her mother to live up to her father's expectations of the ideal woman:

For my father, a woman has to look perfect. She has no brains. My mother has to go to my dad's functions and she has to just sit there with a smile on her face and look great at parties. My father loves it that his wife looks so much younger than everybody else . . . I don't think they were ever friends. They were just kind of physically attracted to each other. She does everything to please my father. She would go on a diet for my father. She colors her hair for my father. She got fake contacts for my father. She lies out in the sun all summer. That's all my dad wants to do, be as tan as he can, and she wants to be as tan as she can for him. . . . And, oh my god, my father would get in fights, would not even talk to my mother for like a week, because her toenails weren't painted and she was wearing open-toed shoes!

Barbara did not escape her father's criticism of her own body. As a preadolescent she was taller than the other girls in her class, and this made her feel "big": "When I was little my dad always used to make fun of me. I was never fat, just tall, but he used to pinch my stomach and say 'Barbie, you got a little rubber tire in there.'" So she stopped eating in the seventh grade:

I lost so much weight they were going to send me to a hospital, because I refused to eat. I wanted to be thin and I loved it. I ate the minimum, a little bowl of cereal for breakfast. I wouldn't eat a dessert. I remember my father forcing me to eat a bowl of ice cream. I was crying and he said, "You're going to eat this, you know," which was funny because he always used to call me fat. I used to lie down every night on my bed and loved to see how my hipbones would stick out so much.

When my father said, "You're even skinner than your sister," I was so happy inside. It was like an accomplishment; finally for once in my life I was thinner than my sister. I remember going shopping with her to get jeans. I tried on size zero and they fell off. It was the best feeling I'd ever had in my entire life. I went back to school weighing under 90 pounds and I was about five feet six inches. I loved competitive sports, so when I couldn't play tennis anymore because I was fainting, I started eating. I started noticing that I could eat so much and get on the scale and I wouldn't even gain any weight because I was playing so much tennis. My eating was normal during that period, the 8th grade. But I wouldn't eat in front of anyone.

Then she started bingeing:

I threw up in school a couple of times. It was awful. It was the worst feeling. You know you are about to throw up but you have to get the last bite in. I don't understand how, when you are going to throw up, you're walking right to the bathroom and you're still shoving food in. My bingeing would only happen when I was alone, because my mother would come home about 5 p.m. and my dad would come home later.

Barbara's eating problems continued into her college years. She described a typical binge:

I still binge and I always do the exact same thing. I put on my backpack and go to the local food store. I don't want to talk to anybody. I always get cookies, cake, and ice cream because it's easy to throw up. Chipwiches, brownies, sundaes. Once I stole from the cafeteria because I was too embarrassed to buy it. The minute I get back to my room, I lock the door and turn on the music. I can't throw up in my bathroom because other girls will hear so I turn on the music and throw up in my room. I'll get a garbage bag from downstairs first. It's so gross. After I throw up I feel awful—it can be so exhausting all you do is fall asleep.

For Barbara, there was no escaping the pressure to be thin and attractive, "because that's what my father thinks and likes. I guess I want to live up to his standard." Yet she knew how devastating this has been for her mother and how rocky a relationship her parents had:

I always said to my mom that I'd never want to marry someone like Dad. I don't want what happened to my mom to happen to me. He just wants my mother to look young for the rest of her life. He doesn't want her to go gray. The big joke in my house now is that my

mother's going through menopause and she just cries all the time. And my dad is like: "You're so old." And my mother is just devastated. She looks a lot younger, but my dad always tells her she looks old. She doesn't look old. A lot of people ask if she's my sister. And I mean, she has to wear bikinis. She doesn't want to. She always has to wear full-face makeup on the beach, because you can't show like any blemishes, or anything. You have to look perfect. It always drove my father crazy that my sister and I don't wear makeup.

My father is definitely there when we go shopping. He always looks through women's fashion magazines, cuts out photos for us. "I think you should get this outfit." I mean we have piles of these stupid pictures. When my mom and dad came up to visit me at college, I had to change to go out to dinner, because I wasn't wearing a skirt. I thought I looked fine, but he was embarrassed.

I get angry, but then again, it's the way I've always been brought up. My dad would say, "Yeah, we might be kind of crazy, but look how much we've given you." I was always angry at my mom for never saying anything. She always knew I was right, but she would never say anything. She was always such a wimp.

My dad has never seen divorce as an alternative. He thinks, you get married, it's for life. I know inside he loves my mother more than anybody, all of us. It's weird. He can't show it, but I know he does. When I was growing up I remember always listening to them fight. When my mother would be crying, I would say, "Why don't you just leave him?" and my mother's reason was, "I like my financial life style. I like going to Europe every year. I like having a summerhouse. I like having my summers off. If I get divorced I can't have any of that."

Barbara's response to these pressures was bulimia. She used compulsive eating to numb her anxiety and anger, and purging to relieve her dread of being fat and unloved.

She had also begun to develop some of the psychological symptoms that are classic for women with eating problems, like maturity fears. In many ways Barbara was afraid of growing up and facing what her mother experienced as an adult married woman. Instead, she loved playing the kid role. Barbara loved making up fantasy tales and swinging very high on the swings in the playground. As she puts it:

I was always the goofball. You know, like I never grew up. The night before I left for college my mother said I didn't have to go. She was like, "You're my baby, I don't care if you don't go to college."

SIBLINGS

The role of siblings and boyfriends as mediators of cultural values has little documentation. It is clear, however, that older siblings can be an important influence on how young girls think about their bodies. For example, Judith's older sister made fun of her weight:

My older sister teased me because I was larger than all my siblings. I was three or four inches taller than even my older sister. And I think I was also bigger. I started developing earlier. She used to say, "You're a fatso." It used to get me mad, but then when I looked at myself, I would think, "But, I'm not fat!"

Katy reported:

My five brothers and sisters would go around and make pig noises. At the time it really hurt my feelings because I'm a very sensitive person. I really was upset but my parents really didn't know I was. It bothered me that they never really said "Katy may be heavy, but she's a person, she's your sister, don't talk to her like that." They never said that to me and I think I resent it to this day.

It was typical in Katy's family to label each other according to certain body features, and hers was her weight:

One of my brothers was little, and we called him Little Bit. Jeffry had buckteeth, Judy had freckles. My sister had a funny nose. My older sister we called the Prima Donna because she's always putting everything on and looks so nice. Everyone had a label.

LINKING QUALITATIVE AND QUANTITATIVE ANALYSIS

To aid in identifying the key patterns in these 55 interviews, we coded them with a qualitative data analysis software package (HyperRESEARCH 1999). For example, Katy's reporting that her "five brothers and sisters would go around and make pig noises" was

given the code "Parents-or-peers-or-siblings critical" (PPSC). Whenever we found an instance of this in any of the 55 interviews, we gave it the PPSC code. In all, we developed 230 different codes. We then used CrossTab_Preparer (see Carter, Hesse-Biber, and MacDonald 1999) to convert many of these codes into quantitative variables. For example, 16 of our interviewees reported a parent, peer, or sibling as critical of their eating habits and bodies; the relevant parts of their interviews were given the PPSC code. CrossTab_Preparer created the "variable" PPSC by giving these 16 interviews the value of "yes" and the other 39 a value of "no."

The following tables present quantitative summaries of a key relationship identified in our presentation. More specifically, Table 13.1 shows a clear relationship between PPSC and an interviewee's odds of having developed an eating disorder (EATDIS) such as bulimia or anorexia. In a manner that would have been otherwise difficult to uncover, Tables 13.2 and 13.3 show a clear interaction between PPSC and having an overweight parent (or not) in determining the likelihood of an interviewee developing an eating disorder. More specifically, we find that PPSC only really matters in the context of a family where the parents are *not* overweight. In sum, having a critical parent who is at the same time overweight seems to have little impact on a daughter developing an eating disorder, whereas a daughter with parents who are both "thinnish" and *critical* has a strong likelihood of developing bulimia or anorexia. (More extensive analyses linking our qualitative data to quantitative analysis are forthcoming in Hesse-Biber 2002).

FURTHER DISCUSSION

The link between the macrocosm (the wider cultural norms of thinness) and the microcosm (the individual) is initially mediated by the family, which translates and embellishes upon society's pressures on women to be thin. The family is an important mirror that reflects us. What they value in us provides the basic building blocks of selfhood. Unlike personality, tastes, and social values, our physical appearance is always visible to others. It is a critical factor in the

TABLE 13.1   The Relationship Between Having an Eating Disorder (EATDIS) and Growing up with Parents, Peers, or Siblings Being "Critical" of One's Body and Eating Habits (PPSC)

		PPSC		
		No	*Yes*	
EATDIS	Yes	12.8	56.3	
		(5)	(9)	
	No	87.2	43.8	
		(34)	(7)	
		100%	100%	
		(39)	(16)	N=55

TABLE 13.2   The Relationship Between Having an Eating Disorder (EATDIS) and Growing up with Parents, Peers, or Siblings Being "Critical" of One's Body and Eating Habits (PPSC) for Those Interviewees Having An Overweight Parent

		PPSC		
		No	*Yes*	
EATDIS	Yes	27.3	25.0	
		(3)	(1)	
	No	72.7	75.0	
		(3)	(8)	
		100%	100%	
		(11)	(4)	N=15

TABLE 13.3   The Relationship Between Having an Eating Disorder (EATDIS) and Growing up with Parents, Peers, or Siblings Being "Critical" of One's Body and Eating Habits (PPSC) for Those Interviewees *Not* Having An Overweight Parent

		PPSC		
		No	*Yes*	
EATDIS	Yes	7.1	66.7	
		(2)	(8)	
	No	92.9	33.3	
		(26)	(4)	
		100%	100%	
		(28)	(12)	N=40

development of self-concept for women, especially during adolescence and young adulthood. Weight is an important aspect of appearance, affecting young women's sense of social and psychological well-being. As we have observed, a young woman's sense of her body arises from a range of interactions within her family.

What can be done within the family unit to enhance positive body esteem and healthier attitudes toward weight and body image? We interviewed a group of women ranging from their thirties to sixties and asked them what advice or solutions they might offer to help promote social change around women's problems with body image. They agreed that changing society would most likely happen in small increments. It was not going to happen quickly or on a massive scale, but on a small group and peer group level, in the words of one woman in her forties, with our "significant others." She viewed the family as an important locus for social change:

> A person's life extends out, like an embrace. I know I can work on myself, but I also know the impact that I have with my stepchildren and my siblings and friends. And they have an influence on me. I think we all have that sphere of influence to work on. It's all of our sisters and daughters that we need to make aware of the issues of body image. I think demonstrating some of my changed ways of being and my changed attitudes toward my body have made a difference to my stepdaughter, my younger sisters, my best friend. They've watched me gain weight and not freak out about it too much. I mean, not get crazed as I would have in my 20s, where two pounds was cause for terrible alarm and self-abuse. I think by just living the way I'm living and calling their attention to it enough, it's made an impression on them.

Ellen, a writer, noted how she has tried to influence her extended family by asking them to not pay so much attention to her 8-year-old daughter's looks:

> My relatives can never greet one another without saying "Hi, you lost weight! Don't you look good!" That's hello, the first thing. One time my Aunt Mary came to see us and she said "Ellen . . . !" then she stopped and didn't know what to say, because I'd gained a little weight. I looked at her and felt sorry for her, she was

so over-dyed, over-made-up, over-dressed. Because she's so afraid of who she is under it. I'm not terribly assertive with my family, but they know they can't pull that around my daughter. They can't talk about her future, or what she's eating. I won't let them comment on her appearance. They can't do that, because to me, it takes her away from her childhood.

To change the wider society it's important to begin at home. Maybe change happens when a mother stops dieting to demonstrate to her daughters that she is breaking free of the cultural demands for thinness. Maybe it's in a family's attitudes at the dinner table. As Miranda, one of the students we interviewed, reported: "My parents never used food as a temptation or a weapon, like 'you won't get dessert if you do something.'" These personal gestures are important examples of how social change can start with our own close family circle. The authors of *The Mother-Daughter Revolution: From Betrayal to Power* (Debold, Wilson, and Malavé 1993) believe that mothers' influence is of primary importance in shaping their daughters' future lives. But they need to recover their own lost selves—the ones that went underground at adolescence in the face of patriarchal culture. By finding and reintegrating their truthful, assertive childhood voices, mothers can help prevent the same thing from happening to their vulnerable daughters. They can initiate a process of validation for young girls. The authors claim: "Not only does an authorizing mother validate her daughter's reality, but she adds her authority as a mother, as a woman who has experience in this culture, to amplify and harmonize with her daughter"(p. 129). The ultimate goal—the hopeful vision—is to have a community alliance of mothers and daughters and discerning males who, together, would resist the devaluation of women's selfhood.

REFERENCES

Attie, Ilana, and Jeanne Brooks-Gunn. 1992. "Developmental issues in the study of eating problems and disorders." In Janis H. Crowther, D. L. Tennenbaum, S. E. Hobfall, and M.A.P. Stephens (eds.), *The Etiology of Bulimia Nervosa: The Individual and Familial Context* (pp. 35–38). Washington, DC: Hemisphere Publishing Corporation.

Carter, Gregg Lee, Sharlene Hesse-Biber, and Laurie MacDonald. 1999. "Using CrossTab_Preparer—Enhancing Qualitative Data Analysis with Quantitative Techniques." Paper presented at the 94th Annual Meeting of the American Sociological Association. August. Chicago, Illinois.

Debold, Elizabeth, Marie Wilson, and Idelisse Malavé. 1993. *Mother-Daughter Revolution: From Betrayal to Power*. New York: Addison-Wesley.

Drewnowski, A., D. Yee, and D. D. Krahn. 1988. "Bulimia in college women: Incidence and recovery." *American Journal of Psychology* 145:753–55.

Fabian, L. J., and J. K. Thompson. 1989. "Body image and eating disturbance in young females." *International Journal of Eating Disorders* 8:63–74.

Gray, James J., and Kathryn Ford. 1985. "The incidence of bulimia in a college sample." *International Journal of Eating Disorders* 4:201–10.

Hesse-Biber, Sharlene. 1989. "Eating patterns and disorders in a college population: Are college women's eating problems a new phenomenon?" *Sex Roles* 20:71–89.

_____. 1996. *Am I Thin Enough Yet?* New York: Oxford University Press.

_____. 2002. *The Cult of Thinness*. Forthcoming.

HyperRESEARCH. 1999. http://www.researchware.com/.

Keel, P. T., J. Harnden, J. Heatherton, and C. Hornig. 1997. "Mothers, fathers, and daughters: Dieting and disordered eating." *Eating Disorders* 5: 216–228.

Mead, George Herbert. 1934. *Mind, Self, and Society*. Chicago: University of Chicago Press.

Moreno, A., and M. H. Thelen. 1993. "Parental factors related to bulimia nervosa." *Addictive Behaviors* 18:681–89.

Pike, Kathleen. M., and Judith Rodin. 1991. "Mothers, daughters, and disordered eating." *Journal of Abnormal Psychology* 100:198–204.

Pope, Harrison J, James J. Hudson, D. Yurglen-Todd, and M. Hudson. 1984. "Prevalence of anorexia and bulimia in three student populations." *International Journal of Eating Disorders* 3:2–52.

Pyle, Richard, Patricia A. Newman, Patricia A. Halvorson, and James E. Mitchell. 1991. "An ongoing cross-sectional study of the prevalence of eating disorders in freshman college students." *International Journal of Eating Disorders* 10: 667–77.

Smetana, J. G. 1988. "Concepts of self and social convention: Adolescents' and parents' reasoning about hypothetical and actual family conflicts." In M. R. Gunnar and W. A. Collins (eds.), *Development During the Transition to Adolescence* (pp. 79–122). Hillsdale, NJ: Lawrence Erlbaum.

Spitzack, C. 1990. *Confessing Excess.* Albany: State University of New York.

Strober, M., and L. L. Humphrey. 1987. "Familial contributions to the etiology and course of anorexia nervosa and bulimia." *Journal of Consultative Psychology* 55:654–59.

Strober, M., C. Lampert, W. Morrell, J. Burroughs, and C. Jacobs. 1990. "A controlled family of anorexia nervosa: Evidence of familial aggregation and lack of shared transmission with affective disorders." *International Journal of Eating Disorders* 9:239–253.

Wonderlich, Stephen. 1992. "Relationship of family and personality factors in bulimia. In J. H Crowther, D. L. Tennenbaum, S. E. Hobfoll, and M.A.P. Stephens (eds.), *The Etiology of Bulimia Nervosa: The Individual and Familial Context* (pp. 103–126). Washington: Hemisphere Publishing Corporation.

Zuckerman, Diana M., Anne Colby, and Norma C. Ware. 1984. *The Prevalence of Bulimia Among College Students.* Cambridge, MA: Henry A. Murray Research Center, Radcliffe College.

PART 6

GROUPS

No concept is more fundamental to sociology—or to the life of an individual—than that of the social "group." We are born into groups, play in groups, learn in groups, and work in groups. Interactions within groups contribute to our self-images, lead us to health or disease, and influence, if not define, our basic understanding of the world: how it looks and what are the right and wrong ways to act in and to think about it.

Groups can be differentiated in many ways, only a few of which will be discussed here. For example, some, called *primary groups*, involve our most intimate interactions, for example, the family or our closest circle of friends. Other groups involve our more "businesslike" interactions, for example, our work groups or school; sociologists call these *secondary groups*. Many of you will likely end up working in large bureaucratic organizations, for big companies or for the government. Quite often, people give their allegiance to large organizations (one kind of secondary group) by way of their allegiance to primary groups within the organizations. For example, high school can appear to be a boring, amorphous, even scary place. But many students do not ever consider dropping out because of their close ties to small groups within the school—sports teams, clubs, friendship cliques, and so on. Similarly, many jobs are boring and make one feel simply like a "cog" in a giant and impersonal wheel of production. However, many employees holding such jobs rarely miss work and do not ever think of looking for another job. Why? Because they have close ties to people at work. They may have close friends whom they enjoy both on and off the job, or they may play on the company bowling team or have some similar primary group involvement.

Another key differentiating feature of groups is their *size*. Group size is positively associated with conformity. Thus, for example, in the smallest group (the *dyad*) you may "act up" to get your way with, say, your best friend or your girlfriend. However, as you find more and more eyes looking upon you—that is, as the group becomes larger—you will find it much harder to get your own way, and indeed more generally to "listen to your own drummer." Solomon E. Asch (professor emeritus, Swarthmore College) supports this assertion with scientific evidence in his classic study, appearing here as the first essay in Part 6.

An important aspect of groups is the manner in which they channel an individual's perception and definition of particular situations. In other words, how an individual views the world is partly influenced by his or her particular mix of group memberships. For example, many sociological studies of the workplace reveal that what constitutes a "good day's work" is determined by one's fellow workers; those who exceed the group norm have to suffer epithets like "rate-buster" or "speed king," while those who work too little must endure the stigma of being called a "chiseler." The contemporary essays in Part 6 expand on the idea that different group memberships generate different perceptions, behaviors, and states of health. Professors John Mirowsky and Catherine E. Ross, both of Ohio State University, show how psychological distress depends upon the groups to which individuals belong. For example, they demonstrate that married individuals are less likely to suffer distress compared to their unmarried counterparts (the divorced, widowed, or those never married). They argue that married individuals are more likely to feel loved, cared for, esteemed, and valued—all of which offer benefit in handling the ups and downs of everyday living. Similarly, Sidney Cobb (professor emeritus, Brown University) demonstrates that individuals with close primary group ties survive illness and personal crisis better than those without such ties.

_____CHAPTER 14_____

THE EFFECTS OF GROUP PRESSURE
ON THE MODIFICATION AND DISTORTION
OF JUDGMENTS

SOLOMON E. ASCH

We shall here describe in summary form the conception and first findings of a program of investigation into the conditions of independence and submission to group pressure. This program is based on a series of earlier studies conducted by the writer while a Fellow of the John Simon Guggenheim Memorial Foundation. . . . Our immediate object was to study the social and personal conditions that induce individuals to resist or to yield to group pressures when the latter are perceived to be *contrary to fact.* The issues which this problem raises are of obvious consequence for society; it can be of decisive importance whether or not a group will, under certain conditions, submit to existing pressures. Equally direct are the consequences for individuals and our understanding of them, since it is a decisive fact about a person whether he possesses the freedom to act independently, or whether he characteristically submits to group pressures.

The problem under investigation requires the direct observation of certain basic processes in the interaction between individuals, and between individuals and groups. To clarify these seems necessary if we are to make fundamental advances in the understanding of the formation and reorganization of attitudes, of the functioning of public opinion, and of the operation of propaganda. Today we do not possess an adequate theory of these central psycho-social processes. Empirical investigation has been predominantly controlled by general propositions concerning group influence which have as a rule been assumed but not tested. With few exceptions investigation has relied upon descriptive formulations concerning the operation of suggestion and prestige, the inadequacy of which is becoming increasingly obvious, and upon schematic applications of stimulus-response theory.

The Bibliography articles are representative of the current theoretical empirical situation. Basic to the current approach has been the axiom that group pressures characteristically induce psychological changes *arbitrarily,* in far-reaching disregard of the material properties of the given conditions. This mode of thinking has almost exclusively stressed the slavish submission of individuals to group forces, has neglected to inquire into their possibilities for independence and for productive relations with the human environment, and has virtually denied the capacity of men under certain conditions to rise above group passion and prejudice. It was our aim to contribute to a clarification of these questions, important both for theory and for their human implications, by means of direct observation of the effects of groups upon the decisions and evaluations of individuals.

THE EXPERIMENT AND FIRST RESULTS

To this end we developed an experimental technique which has served as the basis for the present series of studies. We employed the procedure of placing an individual in a relation of radical conflict with all the other members of a group, of measuring its effect upon him in quantitative terms, and of describing its psychological consequences. A group of eight individuals was instructed to judge a series of simple, clearly structured perceptual relations—to match the length of a given line with one of three unequal lines. Each member of the group announced his judgments publicly. In the midst of this monotonous "test" one individual found himself suddenly contradicted by the entire group, and this contradiction was repeated again and again in the course of the experiment. The group in question had, with the exception of one member, previously met with the experimenter and received instructions to respond at certain points with wrong—and unanimous—judgments. The errors of the majority were large (ranging between $\frac{1}{2}''$ and $1\frac{3}{4}''$) and of an order not encountered under control conditions. The outstanding person—the critical subject—(whom we had placed in the position of a *minority of one* in the midst of a *unanimous majority*) was the object of investigation. He faced, possibly for the first time in his life, a situation in which a group unanimously contradicted the evidence of his senses.

This procedure was the starting point of the investigation and the point of departure for the study of further problems. Its main features were the following: (1) The critical subject was submitted to two contradictory and irreconcilable forces—the evidence of his own experience of an utterly clear perceptual fact and the unanimous evidence of a group of equals. (2) Both forces were part of the immediate situation; the majority was concretely present, surrounding the subject physically. (3) The critical subject, who was requested together with all others to state his judgments publicly, was obliged to declare himself and to take a definite stand vis-à-vis the group. (4) The situation possessed a self-contained character. The critical subject could not avoid or evade the dilemma by

reference to conditions external to the experimental situation. (It may be mentioned at this point that the forces generated by the given conditions acted so quickly upon the critical subjects that instances of suspicion were rare.)

The technique employed permitted a simple quantitative measure of the "majority effect" in terms of the frequency of errors in the direction of the distorted estimates of the majority. At the same time we were concerned from the start to obtain evidence of the ways in which the subjects perceived the group, to establish whether they became doubtful, whether they were tempted to join the majority. Most important, it was our object to establish the grounds of the subject's independence or yielding—whether, for example, the yielding subject was aware of the effect of the majority upon him, whether he abandoned his judgment deliberately or compulsively. To this end we constructed a comprehensive set of questions which served as the basis of an individual interview immediately following the experimental period. Toward the conclusion of the interview each subject was informed fully of the purpose of the experiment, of his role and of that of the majority. The reactions to the disclosure of the purpose of the experiment became in fact an integral part of the procedure. We may state here that the information derived from the interview became an indispensable source of evidence and insight into the psychological structure of the experimental situation, and in particular, of the nature of the individual differences. Also, it is not justified or advisable to allow the subject to leave without giving him a full explanation of the experimental conditions. The experimenter has a responsibility to the subject to clarify his doubts and to state the reasons for placing him in the experimental situation. When this is done most subjects react with interest and many express gratification at having lived through a striking situation which has some bearing on wider human issues.

Both the members of the majority and the critical subjects were male college students. We shall report the results for a total of fifty critical subjects in this experiment. In Table 14.1 we summarize the successive comparison trials and the majority estimates.

TABLE 14.1   Lengths of Standard and Comparison Lines

TRIALS	LENGTH OF STANDARD LINE (IN INCHES)	COMPARISON LINES (IN INCHES)			CORRECT RESPONSE	GROUP RESPONSE	MAJORITY ERROR (IN INCHES)
		1	2	3			
1	10	8.75	10	8	2	2	—
2	2	2	1	1.50	1	1	—
3	3	3.75	4.25	3	3	1*	+0.75
4	5	5	4	6.50	1	2*	−1.00
5	4	3	5	4	3	3	—
6	3	3.75	4.25	3	3	2*	+1.25
7	8	6.25	8	6.75	2	3*	−1.25
8	5	5	4	6.50	1	3*	+1.50
9	8	6.25	8	6.75	2	1*	−1.75
10	10	8.75	10	8	2	2	—
11	2	2	1	1.50	1	1	—
12	3	3.75	4.25	3	3	1*	+0.75
13	5	5	4	6.50	1	2*	−1.00
14	4	3	5	4	3	3	—
15	3	3.75	4.25	3	3	2*	+1.25
16	8	6.25	8	6.75	2	3*	−1.25
17	5	5	4	6.50	1	3*	+1.50
18	8	6.25	8	6.75	2	1*	−1.75

*Starred figures designate the erroneous estimates by the majority.

The quantitative results are clear and unambiguous:

1. There was a marked movement toward the majority. One-third of all the estimates in the critical group were errors identical with or in the direction of the distorted estimates of the majority. The significance of this finding becomes clear in the light of the virtual absence of errors in control groups, the members of which recorded their estimates in writing. The relevant data of the critical and control groups are summarized in Table 14.2.

2. At the same time the effect of the majority was far from complete. The preponderance of estimates in the critical group (68 percent) was correct despite the pressure of the majority.

3. We found evidence of extreme individual differences. There were in the critical group subjects who remained independent without exception, and there were those who went nearly all the time with the majority. (The maximum possible number of errors was 12, while the actual range of errors was 0–11.) One-fourth of the critical subjects were completely independent; at the other extreme, one-third of the group displaced the estimates toward the majority in one-half or more of the trials.

The differences between the critical subjects in their reactions to the given conditions were equally striking. There were subjects who remained completely confident throughout. At the other extreme were those who became disoriented, doubt-ridden, and experienced a powerful impulse not to appear different from the majority.

For purposes of illustration we include a brief description of one independent and one yielding subject.

TABLE 14.2   Distribution of Errors in Experimental and Control Groups

NUMBER OF CRITICAL ERRORS	CRITICAL GROUP* FREQUENCY (NO. OF TRIALS = 50)	CONTROL GROUP FREQUENCY (NO. OF TRIALS = 37)
0	13	35
1	4	1
2	5	1
3	6	
4	3	
5	4	
6	1	
7	2	
8	5	
9	3	
10	3	
11	1	
12	0	
Total	50	37
Mean	3.84	0.08

*All errors in the critical group were in the direction of the majority estimates.

Independent

After a few trials he appeared puzzled, hesitant. He announced all disagreeing answers in the form of "Three, sir; two, sir"; not so with the unanimous answers. At trial 4 he answered immediately after the first member of the group, shook his head, blinked, and whispered to his neighbor: "Can't help it, that's one." His later answers came in a whispered voice, accompanied by a deprecating smile. At one point he grinned embarrassedly, and whispered explosively to his neighbor: "I always disagree—darn it!" During the questioning, this subject's constant refrain was: "I called them as I saw them, sir." He insisted that his estimates were right without, however, committing himself as to whether the others were wrong, remarking that "that's the way I see them and that's the way they see them." If he had to make a practical decision under similar circumstances, he declared, "I would follow my own view, though part of my reason would tell me that I might be wrong." Immediately following the experiment the majority engaged this subject in a brief discussion. When they pressed him to say whether the entire group was wrong and he alone right, he turned upon them defiantly, exclaiming: "You're *probably* right, but you may be wrong!" To the disclosure of the experiment this subject reacted with the statement that he felt "exultant and relieved," adding, "I do not deny that at times I had the feeling: 'to heck with it, I'll go along with the rest.'"

Yielding

This subject went with the majority in 11 out of 12 trials. He appeared nervous and somewhat confused, but he did not attempt to evade discussion; on the contrary, he was helpful and tried to answer to the best of his ability. He opened the discussion with the statement: "If I'd been the first I probably would have responded differently"; this was his way of stating that he had adopted the majority estimates. The primary factor in his case was loss of confidence. He perceived the majority as a decided group, acting without hesitation: "If they had been doubtful I probably would have changed, but they answered with such confidence." Certain of his errors, he explained, were due to the doubtful nature of the comparisons; in such instances he went with the majority. When the object of the experiment was explained, the subject volunteered: "I suspected about the middle—but tried to push it out of my mind." It is of interest that his suspicion was not able to restore his confidence and diminish the power of the majority. Equally striking is his report that he assumed the experiment to involve an "illusion" to which the others, but not he, were subject. This assumption too did not help to free him; on the contrary, he acted as if his divergence from the majority was a sign of defect. The principal impression this subject produced was of one so caught up by immediate difficulties that he lost clear reasons for his actions, and could make no reasonable decisions.

A FIRST ANALYSIS OF INDIVIDUAL DIFFERENCES

On the basis of the interview data described earlier, we undertook to differentiate and describe the major forms of reaction to the experimental situation, which we shall now briefly summarize.

Among the *independent* subjects we distinguished the following main categories:

1. Independence based on *confidence* in one's perception and experience. The most striking characteristic of these subjects is the vigor with which they withstand the group opposition. Though they are sensitive to the group, and experience the conflict, they show a resilience in coping with it, which is expressed in their continuing reassurance on their perception and the effectiveness with which they shake off the oppressive group opposition.

2. Quite different are those subjects who are independent and *withdrawn*. These do not react in a spontaneously emotional way, but rather on the basis of explicit principles concerning the necessity of being an individual.

3. A third group of independent subjects manifest considerable tension and *doubt,* but adhere to their judgments on the basis of a felt necessity to deal adequately with the task.

The following were the main categories of reaction among the *yielding* subjects, or those who went with the majority during one-half or more of the trials.

1. *Distortion of perception* under the stress of group pressure. In this category belong a very few subjects who yield completely, but are not aware that their estimates have been displaced or distorted by the majority. These subjects report that they came to perceive the majority estimates as correct.

2. *Distortion of judgment.* Most submitting subjects belong to this category. The factor of greatest importance in this group is a decision the subjects reach that their perceptions are inaccurate, and that those of the majority are correct. These subjects suffer from primary doubt and lack of confidence; on this basis they feel a strong tendency to join the majority.

3. *Distortion of action.* The subjects in this group do not suffer a modification of perception nor do they conclude that they are wrong. They yield because of an overmastering need not to appear different from or inferior to others, because of an inability to tolerate the appearance of defectiveness in the eyes of the group. These subjects suppress their observations and voice the majority position with awareness of what they are doing.

The results are sufficient to establish that independence and yielding are not psychologically homogeneous, that submission to group pressure (and freedom from pressure) can be the result of different psychological conditions. It should also be noted that the categories described [previously], being based exclusively on the subjects' reactions to the experimental conditions, are descriptive, not presuming to explain why a given individual responded in one way rather than another. The further exploration of the basis for the individual differences is a separate task upon which we are now at work.

EXPERIMENTAL VARIATIONS

The results described are clearly a joint function of two broadly different sets of conditions. They are determined first by the specific external conditions, by the particular character of the relation between social evidence and one's own experience. Second, the presence of pronounced individual differences points to the important role of personal factors, of factors connected with the individual's character structure. We reasoned that there are group conditions which would produce independence in all subjects, and that there probably are group conditions which would induce intensified yielding in many, though not in all. Accordingly we followed the procedure of *experimental variation,* systematically altering the quality of social evidence by means of systematic variation of group conditions. Secondly, we deemed it reasonable to assume that behavior under the experimental social pressure is significantly related to certain basic, relatively permanent characteristics of the individual. The investigation has moved in both of these directions. Because the study of the character-qualities which may be functionally connected with independence and yielding is still in progress, we shall limit the present account to a sketch of the representative experimental variations.

THE EFFECT OF NON-UNANIMOUS MAJORITIES

Evidence obtained from the basic experiment suggested that the condition of being exposed *alone* to the opposition of a "compact majority" may have played a decisive role in determining the course and strength of the effects observed. Accordingly we undertook to investigate in a series of successive variations the effects of *non-unanimous* majorities. The technical problem of altering the uniformity of a majority is, in terms of our procedure, relatively simple. In most instances we merely directed one or more members of the instructed group to deviate from the majority in prescribed ways. It is obvious that we cannot hope to compare the performance of the same individual in two situations on the assumption that they remain independent of one another. At best we can investigate the effect of an earlier upon a later experimental condition. The comparison of different experimental situations therefore requires the use of different but comparable groups of critical subjects. This is the procedure we have followed. In the variations to be described we have maintained the conditions of the basic experiment (e.g., the sex of the subjects, the size of the majority, the content of the task, and so on) save for the specific factor that was varied. The following were some of the variations we studied:

1. *The presence of a "true partner."* (a) In the midst of the majority were two naive, critical subjects. The subjects were separated spatially, being seated in the fourth and eighth positions, respectively. Each therefore heard his judgment confirmed by one other person (provided the other person remained independent), one prior to, the other subsequently to announcing his own judgment. In addition, each experienced a break in the unanimity of the majority. There were six pairs of critical subjects. (b) In a further variation the "partner" to the critical subject was a member of the group who had been instructed to respond correctly throughout. This procedure permits the exact control of the partner's responses. The partner was always seated in the fourth position; he therefore announced his estimates in each case before the critical subject.

The results clearly demonstrate that a disturbance of the unanimity of the majority markedly increased the independence of the critical subjects. The frequency of pro-majority errors dropped to 10.4 percent of the total number of estimates in variation (a), and to 5.5 percent in variation (b). These results are to be compared with the frequency of yielding to the unanimous majorities in the basic experiment, which was 32 percent of the total number of estimates. It is clear that the presence in the field of *one other* individual who responded correctly was sufficient to deplete the power of the majority, and in some cases to destroy it. This finding is all the more striking in the light of other variations which demonstrate the effect of even small minorities provided they are unanimous. Indeed, we have been able to show that a unanimous majority of three is, under the given conditions, far more effective than a majority of eight containing one dissenter. That critical subjects will under these conditions free themselves of a majority of seven and join forces with one other person in the minority is, we believe, a result significant for theory. It points to a fundamental psychological difference between the condition of being alone and having a minimum of human support. It further demonstrates that the effects obtained are not the result of a summation of influences proceeding from each member of the group; it is necessary to conceive the results as being relationally determined.

2. *Withdrawal of a "true partner."* What will be the effect of providing the critical subject with a partner who responds correctly and then withdrawing him? The critical subject started with a partner who responded correctly. The partner was a member of the majority who had been instructed to respond correctly and to "desert" to the majority in the middle of the experiment. This procedure permits the observation of the same subject in the course of transition from one condition to another. The withdrawal of the partner produced a powerful and unexpected result. We had assumed that the critical subject, having gone through the experience of opposing the majority with a minimum of support, would maintain his independence when alone. Contrary to this expectation, we found that the experience of having had and then lost a partner restored the majority effect to its full force, the proportion of errors rising to 28.5 percent of all judgments, in contrast to the preceding level of 5.5 percent. Further experimentation is needed to establish whether the critical subjects were responding to the sheer fact of being alone, or to the fact that the partner abandoned them.

3. *Late arrival of a "true partner."* The critical subject started as a minority of one in the midst of a unanimous majority. Toward the conclusion of the experiment one member of the majority "broke" away and began announcing correct estimates. This procedure, which reverses the order of conditions of the preceding experiment, permits the observation of the transition from being alone to being a member of a pair against a majority. It is obvious that those critical subjects who were independent when alone would continue to be so when joined by another partner. The variation is therefore of significance primarily for those subjects who yielded during the first phase of the experiment. The appearance of the late partner exerts a freeing effect, reducing the level to 8.7 percent. Those who had previously yielded also became markedly more independent, but not completely so, continuing to yield more than previously independent subjects. The reports of the subjects do not cast much light on the factors responsible for the result. It is our impression that having once committed himself to yielding, the individual finds it difficult and painful to change his direction. To do so is tantamount to a public admission that he has not acted rightly. He therefore follows the precarious course he has already chosen in order to maintain an outward semblance of consistency and conviction.

4. *The presence of a "compromise partner."* The majority was consistently extremist, always matching the standard with the most unequal line. One instructed subject (who, as in the other variations, preceded the critical subject) also responded incorrectly, but his estimates were always intermediate between the truth and the majority position. The critical subject therefore faced an extremist majority whose unanimity was broken by one more moderately erring person. Under these conditions the frequency of errors was reduced but not significantly. However, the lack of unanimity determined in a strikingly consistent way the *direction* of the errors. The preponderance of the errors, 75.7 percent of the total, was moderate, whereas in a parallel experiment in which the majority was unanimously extremist (i.e., with the "compromise" partner excluded), the incidence of moderate errors was reduced to 42 percent of the total. As might be expected, in a unanimously

moderate majority, the errors of the critical subjects were without exception moderate.

THE ROLE OF MAJORITY SIZE

To gain further understanding of the majority effect, we varied the size of the majority in several different variations. The majorities, which were in each case unanimous, consisted of sixteen, eight, four, three, and two persons, respectively. In addition, we studied the limiting case in which the critical subject was opposed by one instructed subject. Table 14.3 contains the means and the range of errors under each condition.

With the opposition reduced to one, the majority effect all but disappeared. When the opposition proceeded from a group of two, it produced a measurable though small distortion, the errors being 12.8 percent of the total number of estimates. The effect appeared in full force with a majority of three. Larger majorities of four, eight, and sixteen did not produce effects greater than a majority of three.

The effect of a majority is often silent, revealing little of its operation to the subject, and often hiding it from the experimenter. To examine the range of effects it is capable of inducing, decisive variations of conditions are necessary. An indication of one effect is furnished by the following variation in which the conditions of the basic experiment were simply reversed. Here the majority, consisting of a group of sixteen, was naive; in the midst of it we placed a single individual who responded wrongly according to instructions. Under these conditions the members of the naive majority reacted to the lone dissenter with amusement and disdain. Contagious laughter spread through the group at the droll minority of one. Of significance is the fact that the members lack awareness that they draw their strength from the majority, and that their reactions would change radically if they faced the dissenter individually. In fact, the attitude of derision in the majority turns to seriousness and increased respect as soon as the minority is increased to three. These observations demonstrate the role of social support as a source of power and stability, in contrast to the preceding investigations which stressed the effects of withdrawal of social support, or to be more exact, the effects of social opposition. Both aspects must be explicitly considered in a unified formulation of the effects of group conditions on the formation and change of judgments. . . .

SUMMARY

We have investigated the effects upon individuals of majority opinions when the latter were seen to be in a direction contrary to fact. By means of a simple technique we produced a radical divergence between a majority and a minority, and observed the ways in which individuals coped with the resulting difficulty. Despite the stress of the given conditions, a substantial proportion of individuals retained their independence throughout. At the same time a substantial minority yielded, modifying their judgments in accordance with the majority. Independence and yielding are a joint function of the following major factors:

1. *The character of the stimulus situation.* Variations in structural clarity have a decisive effect:

TABLE 14.3   Errors of Critical Subjects with Unanimous Majorities of Different Size

		SIZE OF MAJORITY					
	CONTROL	1	2	3	4	8	16
Number of trials	37	10	15	10	10	50	12
Mean number of errors	0.08	0.33	1.53	4.0	4.2	3.84	3.75
Range of errors	0–2	0–1	0–5	1–12	0–11	0–11	0–10

with diminishing clarity of the stimulus-conditions the majority effect increases.

2. *The character of the group forces.* Individuals are highly sensitive to the structural qualities of group opposition. In particular, we demonstrated the great importance of the factor of unanimity. Also, the majority effect is a function of the size of group opposition.

3. *The character of the individual.* There were wide, and indeed, striking differences among individuals within the same experimental situation. The hypothesis was proposed that these are functionally dependent on relatively enduring character differences, in particular those pertaining to the person's social relations.

BIBLIOGRAPHY

Asch, S. E. Studies in the principles of judgments and attitudes: II. Determination of judgments by group and by ego-standards. *Journal of Social Psychology,* 1940, 12, 433–465.

Asch, S. E. The doctrine of suggestion, prestige and imitation in social psychology. *Psychological Review,* 1948, 55, 250–276.

Asch, S. E., Block, H., and Hertzman, M. Studies in the principles of judgments and attitudes. I. Two basic principles of judgment. *Journal of Psychology,* 1938, 5, 219–251.

Coffin, E. E. Some conditions of suggestion and suggestibility: A study of certain attitudinal and situational factors influencing the process of suggestion. *Psychological Monographs,* 1941, 53, No. 4.

Lewis, H. B. Studies in the principles of judgments and attitudes: IV. The operation of prestige suggestion. *Journal of Social Psychology,* 1941, 14, 229–256.

Lorge, I. Prestige, suggestion, and attitudes. *Journal of Social Psychology,* 1936, 7, 386–402.

Miller, N. E., and Dollard, J. *Social Learning and Imitation.* New Haven: Yale University Press, 1941.

Moore, H. T. The comparative influence of majority and expert opinion. *American Journal of Psychology,* 1921, 32, 16–20.

Sherif, M. A study of some social factors in perception. *Archives of Psychology, N.Y.,* 1935, No. 187.

Thorndike, E. L. *The Psychology of Wants, Interests, and Attitudes.* New York: D. Appleton-Century Company, Inc., 1935.

CHAPTER 15

SOCIAL GROUPS AND PSYCHOLOGICAL DISTRESS

JOHN MIROWSKY AND CATHERINE E. ROSS

COMMUNITY MENTAL HEALTH SURVEYS

Before the 1960s little was known about social patterns of emotional well-being and distress. Mental health studies looked at people in psychiatric treatment or in institutions such as the Army or mental hospitals. Ideas about social stress were based on clinical interviews with small numbers of patients or on records of groups in unusual circumstances. The first representative community surveys uncovered several unexpected findings.

All the findings we discuss are based on community surveys of mental health. Large, representative samples of people in the community are interviewed either in person or by telephone. This avoids the biases of basing conclusions on people who have sought help; people with the time, money, or inclination to do so. Everyone has an equal chance of being interviewed: those who sought help and those who did not, the middle class and the poor, men and women, those for whom visiting a psychiatrist is shameful and those for whom it is acceptable, those with access to care and those without it.

The research we discuss uses multiple regression or some form of multivariate analysis to statistically control for confounding factors (Tufte, 1974). This allows researchers to draw conclusions about the effect of one factor (e.g., marital status) independent of others (e.g., age or education).

Four basic social patterns of distress were revealed in early community surveys done in the 1960s and in many surveys conducted since: (1) women are more distressed than men; (2) married persons are less distressed than unmarried persons; (3) the greater the number of *undesirable* changes in a person's life the greater his or her level of distress; (4) the higher a person's socioeconomic status (defined by education, job, and income) the lower that person's level of distress. These findings are now well established and thus may seem obvious, but they were not common knowledge thirty years ago.

Before community surveys, many theorists believed that responsibility, commitment to work, and upward mobility were stressful, whereas dependency, protection, and freedom from responsibility were not. Three decades ago women had little economic responsibility. Men had to go out and beat the world or be beaten by it, daily braving the rigors of commuter traffic and workplace tension. Women could stay home contentedly (so it was assumed) ministering to the needs of the family, kept safe by protecting males. Many were surprised to learn that women have higher levels of depression, anxiety, and malaise than men. Some people thought that married people, especially married men, faced burdensome responsibilities whereas singles led a free and happy life. In fact, married people have lower levels of distress than singles, especially married men. Similarly, many assumed that executives and others at the top of the status hierarchy were made tense and anxious by heavy responsibilities (a view reinforced by the heart disease literature on "type A personality"), while those at the bottom were relatively carefree and content. Harried executives, rushing to the next meeting, might envy laborers with few responsibilities; but in fact, power, responsibility, and control were found to reduce distress.

Average (Mean) Levels of Depression of Four Key Social Groups

Mean depression levels in different categories of sex, marital status, education, and family income, based on 2000 adults in the United States from the Women and Work Study are presented in Figure 15.1. Depression levels are measured by a ten-item depression scale.

These findings at first stood as fascinating new discoveries, then as core facts in the growing body of research. After it became clear that these are robust and replicable findings, the focus of research switched from *demonstrating* the facts to *explaining* them. Just as astronomers were once driven by the desire to explain the recorded motions of the sun, moon, and planets, research on psychological distress is currently based on the desire to explain the recorded association with gender, marriage, events, and status. In this chapter we describe the established social patterns of distress.

First we need to clarify the nature of the facts. To begin with, they are probabilistic. When we say that women are more distressed than men we do not mean that all women are more distressed than all men. We mean that, on average, women are more distressed than men, and that a randomly chosen woman is more likely to be distressed than a randomly chosen man. Second, social facts are hard facts, but not eternal ones. The facts about distress can change as society changes. In particular, the difference in distress between men and women could disappear if certain trends continue. The reasons social differences in distress exist are also reasons the differences might disappear.

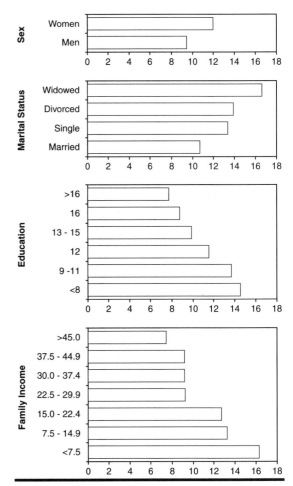

FIGURE 15.1   Average Levels of Depression by Sex, Marital Status, Education, and Family Income

THE FOUR BASIC PATTERNS

Gender

Gove and his colleagues were among the first sociologists to examine why women are more distressed than men. While biologists might think to scrutinize hormones or patterns of sex-typed behavior among primates, sociologists have a different perspective. For heuristic purposes they think of people as essentially interchangeable at birth. It is clear that by adulthood there are many important differences in the things people prefer, value, believe, and do. Many of these differences are shaped by individual situations and personal histories; perhaps the same is true of differences in emotions. Perhaps women are more distressed than men because of differences in the lives that men and women live. Fifteen years ago the majority of adult women were exclusively housewives and men were the breadwinners and job holders. Gove reasoned that if women are more distressed than men because of something different in their lives, then women who are employed will be less distressed than women who are exclusively housewives. This is exactly what he found in his sample of 2248 respondents (chosen by stratified random sampling) throughout the United States. A number of follow-up studies replicated the finding (Gove and Geerken, 1977b; Gove and Tudor, 1973; Kessler and McRae, 1982; Richman, 1979; Rosenfield, 1980; Ross, Mirowsky, and Ulbrich, 1983). It was an important discovery. Freud argued that women are born to be housewives and mothers and cannot be happy in the competitive world outside the home. Parsons (1949), an influential social theorist of the 1950s and 1960s, argued that society and the people in it function most smoothly when women specialize in the loving, nurturing family realm and men specialize in the competitive, acquisitive job-holding realm. The discovery that women with jobs are less distressed than women without them overturned a century of armchair theorizing.

Gove's research shook certain preconceptions about women, but did not explain everything. Although employed women are less distressed than housewives, employed women are *more* distressed than employed men. Having a job is not the whole story. What explains the difference in distress between employed men and women? A clue turned up in a study by Kessler and McRae (1982), using data from 2440 randomly sampled American adults interviewed in 1976. They found that employment is associated with less distress among women whose husbands help with housework and child care, but that there is little advantage to employment among women whose husbands do not help. Surprisingly, they also found that the housework and child care contributed by husbands of employed women does not increase the husband's distress. Researchers had been comparing different types of women; perhaps it was time to compare different types of couples.

American marriages are changing, from arrangements in which the husband has a job and the wife stays home caring for the children and doing housework to arrangements in which the husband and wife both have jobs and share the housework and child care (Oppenheimer, 1982). Although many today may believe this a positive change, not many would have thought so in 1900. The change did not happen because of preferences and values, but because the logic of social arrangements in 1900 undermined itself as the economy grew and changed from one based on manufacturing to one based on services.

At the beginning of the century, women only took jobs in the period between graduating school and getting married. A married woman worked outside the home only if her husband could not support the family. Women could be paid much less than men with equivalent education and skills because the women's jobs were temporary or supplemental. Many jobs quickly became "women's work," particularly services such as waiting on tables, operating telephone switchboards, elementary schoolteaching, nursing, and secretarial work. The economic incentive for employers to hire women, combined with economic growth and the shift from manufacturing to services, increased the demand for female employees. Eventually there were not enough unmarried or childless women to fill the demand, and employers began reducing the barriers to employment for married women and encouraging those whose children were grown to return to work. Still, the demand for labor in female occupations continued to grow faster than the supply of women in accepted social categories, and by the 1950s' growth in female employment reached the sanctum sanctorum—married women with young children (Oppenheimer, 1973). Throughout the century individual women were drawn into the labor force by contingencies: economic need, the availability of work, and the freedom to work (Waite, 1976). Despite the low pay and limited opportunities, many women came to prefer working and earning money, and many husbands began to realize the benefits of two paychecks instead of one. But who was taking care of the house and children? This brings us back to the question of why employed women are more distressed than employed men.

DEPRESSION IN FOUR TYPES OF FAMILIES

Depression levels of wife and husband in four types of marriages are presented in Figure 15.2. Data are from 680 couples in the Women and Work Study. Depression levels are measured by a ten-item depression scale. Marriage types are based on the wife's employment status, preferences for her employment, and the household division of labor. The results are shown adjusting for income, education, age, religion, and race.

In 1978, Huber surveyed a national probability sample of 680 married couples (Huber and Spitze, 1983). Respondents, chosen by random digit dialing, were interviewed by telephone. If the respondent was married, his or her spouse was also interviewed,

making it one of the first surveys of a large, representative sample of married persons throughout the United States to interview both the husband and wife in each couple. With Huber, we compared the husband's and wife's distress in four types of marriages. (Ross, Mirowsky, and Huber, 1983). Distress was measured by a modified form of the Center for Epidemiological Studies' depression scale.

In the first type of marriage the wife does not have a job, she and her husband believe her place is in the home, and she does all the housework and child care. This is the traditional marriage and in 1978 accounted for roughly 44% of all couples. Because this type of marriage is internally consistent— preferences match behavior—it may be psychologically beneficial, but more so for the husband. He is head of the household and has the power and prestige associated with economic resources. The wife, on the other hand, is typically dependent and subordinate. We found that the wife in this type of marriage has a higher level of depression than her husband.

In the second type of marriage the wife has a job but neither she nor her husband want her to, and she does all the housework and child care. This accounted for roughly 19% of the couples. Both of them believe that he should provide for the family while she cares for the home and children, but she has taken a job because they need the money. Psychologically, this is the worst type of marriage for both partners, and their distress is greater than in any other marriage type. The wife may feel that it is not right that she has to work, that her choice of husband was a poor one, that she cannot do all the things a "good" mother should; and she carries a double burden of paid and unpaid work. To the extent that the husband has internalized the role of breadwinner, he may feel that his wife's employment reflects unfavorably on him, indicating that he is not able to support his family. He may feel guilty and ashamed that she has a job, worry about his loss of authority, and suffer self-doubt and low self-esteem. This is the only type of marriage in which the husband is more distressed than his wife.

Although adjustment may come slowly, people do not long sustain tension between the way they live

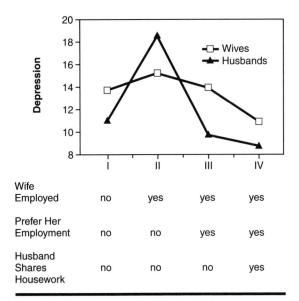

FIGURE 15.2 Depression Levels of Wife and Husband in Four Types of Marriages

and the way they think they should live. As economic, demographic, and historical changes nudge lives into new patterns, husbands and wives come to view her employment more positively, particularly as more of their friends and neighbors become two paycheck families. Thus, in the third type of marriage the wife has a job and she and her husband favor her employment, but she remains responsible for the home. About 27% of all couples fell into this category. The husband is better off than ever before. He has adjusted psychologically, his standard of living is higher, and the flow of family income is more secure. He has even lower distress than men in the first type of marriage. However, things are not quite as good for his wife. She is better off than in the second type of marriage, but still carries a double burden. In a system in which the wife stays home and the husband goes out to work it makes sense for her to do the most time-consuming household chores. When she also works outside the home, and particularly when she stops thinking of her job as temporary, it becomes clear to her that the traditional division of the chores is no longer sensible or fair. Typically, she assigns tasks to the children, mechanizes tasks like dishwashing, uses frozen foods and eats out more often, cuts down on optional events like dinner parties, and does not clean as often. Even so, the demands on her time are likely to be much greater than those on her husband's (Robinson, 1980). The wife's level of distress in this type of marriage is about the same as in the first type, and the gap between her distress and her husband's is greater than in any other type of marriage.

Once the wife accepts the permanence of her new role as employed worker, she may begin pressing for greater equality in the division of household labor. Although the husband may initially resist, once he has grown accustomed to the economic benefits of two paychecks, he is likely to be open to negotiation. If his wife presses the issue, he often makes concessions rather than lose her earnings. In the fourth type of marriage the wife has a job, she and her husband approve of her employment, and they share housework and child care *equally*. This accounted for about 11% of the couples. Both the husband and the wife are less distressed in this type of marriage than in any

other, and the gap between them is smaller than in any other type of marriage.

The gap that remains is probably due to two things: First, the large majority of wives in type IV marriages still earn less than their husbands. Second, the category contains a small minority of wives who are very distressed because they are employed mothers of young children and have difficulty arranging child care.

In adapting to the wife's employment, the central problem for husbands seems to be one of self-esteem—of overcoming any embarrassment, guilt, or apprehension associated with the wife's employment. For wives the central problem is getting the husband to share the housework.

We began with the unexpected discovery that women are more distressed than men, and housewives are more distressed than women with jobs. We conclude that couples who share both the economic responsibilities and the household responsibilities also share much the same level of psychological well-being, and are less distressed than other couples. The difference in distress between men and women does not appear to be innate. The difference is there because men and women lead different lives, and as their lives converge the difference begins to disappear.

About 20% of the employed wives surveyed were in marriages in which the husband shares the housework and child care. An analysis of the factors that increase the husband's share of the housework shows that husbands with higher levels of education do more. Husbands also do more the higher the wife's earnings, and they do *less* the more their own earnings exceed the wife's. Thus, equality in the division of labor at home, which provides psychological benefits to both husband and wife, depends on their economic equality in the workplace.

MARRIAGE

We now come to the second major social pattern of psychological distress: Married people are less distressed than unmarried ones. Most of us are not surprised that widowed, divorced, and separated peoples are more distressed than married people, but it is surprising to find that adults who are single are almost as distressed as those who are divorced or separated.

What is it about marriage that improves emotional well-being? At first researchers thought it might be simply the presence of another adult in the household. A person who lives alone may be isolated from an important network of social and economic ties: the privileges and obligations centered on the home and family. These ties help create a stabilizing sense of security, belonging, and direction. Without them a person may feel lonely, adrift, and unprotected. Since unmarried people often live alone but married people almost always live together (often with children), this might explain why unmarried people are more distressed. Hughes and Gove subdivided three types of unmarried persons (never married, divorced or separated, widowed) according to whether they lived alone (1981). Contrary to what they expected, Hughes and Gove found that unmarried people are not more distressed if they live alone. The big difference is between married people and others, not between people who live alone and others.

One fact about marriages is that some are better than others. Is it better to be in a bad marriage than to be unmarried? Gove and his colleagues surveyed married people about happiness with marriage (Gove, Hughes, and Style, 1983). The 62% who report being very happy with their marriage are less distressed than unmarrieds, but the 34% who only say they are pretty happy with their marriage are no less distressed than the unmarrieds, and the 4% who say they are not too happy or not at all happy with their marriage are *more* distressed than unmarrieds of all types.

A good marriage provides something very important: the sense of being cared for, loved, esteemed, and valued as a person. Pearlin interviewed a representative sample of 2300 Chicago-area adults in 1972, and interviewed the same people again in 1976. He asked them if they could talk to their wives (or husbands) about things they felt were important to them, and count on their spouses for understanding and advice. Those who said "yes" were much less distressed by job disruptions such as being laid off, fired, or sick than those who said "no" (Pearlin *et al.*, 1981). A close, confiding relationship actually

protected the men and women against these stressful events. On the other hand, in situations when a spouse expects more than he or she is willing to give back, acts like the only important person in the family, and cannot be counted on for esteem and advice, men and women feel demoralized, tense, worried, neglected, unhappy, and frustrated (Pearlin, 1975a, b). Thus, it is not enough merely to have someone around. It is better to live alone than in a marriage characterized by a lack of consideration, caring, and equity.

It is easy to imagine that the victim of an unfair marriage is distressed by the situation, but what about the exploiter? Does a person gain or lose psychologically by taking unfair advantage of a spouse? The cynical view is that spouses are less depressed the more they get things their own way. Because one partner's dominance depends upon the other's submission, it follows that one partner's well-being results in the other's depression. The optimistic view is that exploiters, as well as victims, are more distressed than they would be in an equitable relationship. According to equity theory, exploiters face the disapproval of others, worry about retaliation and punishment, feel guilty, and must live with the obstruction and hostility of the victim (Mirowsky, 1985). In their hearts the husband and wife both know what is fair; if they do what is right they will both lead happier and more productive lives (Walster, Walster, and Berscheid, 1978).

Using the data on 680 married couples described earlier, we found one truth in both the cynical and the optimistic views (Mirowsky, 1985). The respondents were asked who decides what house or apartment to live in, where to go on vacation, whether the wife should have a job, and whether to move if the husband gets a job offer in another city. The responses ranged from the wife deciding to sharing the decisions equally to the husband deciding. Mapping the average levels of depression across this range revealed U-shaped patterns for wives and for husbands. Each spouse is least depressed if, to some extent, decisions are shared. However, the balance of influence associated with the lowest average depression is different for husbands and wives: each is least depressed having somewhat more influence than the other. The actual influence in these major decisions is typically closer to the balance that would minimize the husband's depression than it is to the balance that would minimize his wife's depression. This is one reason wives tend to be more depressed than their husbands. In one out of ten marriages, the wives are so far from their ideal balance of influence they are about 50% more depressed than would otherwise be the case.

We know why some marriages are worse than others or worse than no marriage at all, but the question of why unmarried persons are more distressed than marrieds is still not completely answered. The hypothesis is that unmarried persons are less likely to have a close, confiding relationship—someone they talk to about personal things and count on for understanding, help, and advice. If this explanation is correct, future research should find that unmarried persons with high levels of social support have levels of psychological well-being comparable to those of married persons.

UNDESIRABLE LIFE EVENTS

So far we have been discussing the amount of distress people feel in different ongoing situations, such as being married, divorced, or widowed. Distress may also be associated with *changing* from one situation to another. The third major fact revealed in community surveys is that undesirable changes are distressing. At first, researchers believed that all major changes, good and bad, are distressing. As research progressed it became clear that only undesirable life events produce distress.

In the 1960s medical researchers noticed that major changes in a person's life seemed to increase susceptibility to disease. How could changes have this effect? Reasoning from laboratory experiments on regulatory mechanisms, the researchers concluded that every person's behavior tends to settle into an optimal pattern that minimizes the energy and resources expended to meet daily needs. Habits are easy, efficient solutions to everyday problems. Big changes in a person's life (such as getting married or

taking a new job) disrupt habits and force the person to use mental and physical energy to adapt—that is, to develop a new set of habits that are optimal in the new situation.

To study the impact of change, Holmes and Rahe asked a group of people to judge the amount of change produced by each of a number of events (1967). Each event was assigned a value, called a life-change unit. The researchers then asked another group to name the changes that had happened in their lives in the past year, counted up the life-change units for each person, and found that people with more units of change suffered more illness and psychological distress. This finding initiated a wave of research that spilled across scientific and national boundaries. Researchers around the world began counting life-change units and correlating them with all kinds of physical and mental problems. Wherever they looked, they seemed to find a devastating effect of change.

Although it was never the intent of the researchers involved, an image of the healthy, happy life emerged: a placid existence of undisturbed routines. Should we each withdraw to an asylum of our own making? The studies correlating change with sickness and distress seemed to say we should. In fact, the change theory of distress was so well-accepted that for years researchers never examined the impact of negative and positive events separately. When they did the evidence was clear: study after study found that undesirable events—not desirable ones—cause distress (Gersten *et al.*, 1974; Mueller, Edwards, and Yarvis, 1977; Myers, Lindenthal, and Pepper, 1971; Ross and Mirowsky, 1979; Vinokur and Selzer, 1975; Williams, Ware, and Donald, 1981).

We analyzed data from the New Haven Study headed by J. K. Myers (Ross and Mirowsky, 1979). The project collected information on life events and distress of 720 randomly chosen adults in New Haven, Connecticut, interviewed in 1967 and again in 1969 (Myers, Lindenthal, and Pepper, 1971, 1974). We found that the more negative events people experienced the greater their distress. Positive events did *not* increase distress—change per se is not distressing. Subsequent research further refined this conclusion. Undesirable events over which a person has no control are most detrimental to psychological well-being (McFarlane *et al.*, 1983). Controllable events—those in which the person has played some part and shared some responsibility—are less distressing. Some people had speculated that uncontrollable negative events are less distressing than controllable ones because fate, rather than oneself, can be blamed. Events outside the person's control suggest less personal inadequacy and thus protect self-esteem. This argument, while plausible, is not supported by research. Negative events over which a person has no control are more distressing than ones in which the person has played a part. Uncontrollable negative events increase feelings of helplessness and powerlessness. They leave people with the demoralizing sense that they are at the mercy of the environment; that no action will be effective in preventing bad things from happening in the future; and that they are not in control of their lives.

There is a postscript to this research. Not only is positive change not distressing, but people who view change as a challenge, who are instrumental, who set new goals and struggle to achieve them, have *low* levels of psychological distress (Kobassa, Maddi, and Courington, 1981). Change is not a useful explanation for the social patterns of distress, while feelings of instrumentalism and control (as opposed to powerlessness and lack of control) are.

SOCIOECONOMIC STATUS

Events are brief periods that mark a transition. If undesirable events take their toll, ongoing situations are worse. If you lose your job, the event itself is distressing. Being unemployed for a prolonged period of time is more distressing. The problems that are always there can wear at the nerves and demoralize the spirit.

Some people have more problems and fewer resources with which to solve them. They are the poor and uneducated, working at menial jobs or living on welfare in rundown neighborhoods where crime is a constant threat. Others have fewer problems and more resources to help them cope. They are the well-to-do and educated, working at challenging and fulfilling jobs, and living in pleasant neighborhoods. The difference between these two groups is remarkable. It dwarfs the difference between men and women or between the married and unmarried, bringing us to the fourth fact: High socioeconomic status improves psychological well-being and low status increases psychological distress.

Although the impact of social status and achievement on distress seems obvious, there is a cultural myth of the successful person as driven by a sense of inadequacy, loneliness, or neurotic anxiety. This myth is not accurate. In fact, the typical successful person is active, inquisitive, open, and self-assured. If ever there was a formula for psychological well-being, this is it. How do some people get there, and others find themselves so far away?

The reasons for the vast difference in distress between the upper and lower ranks of society are intimately linked to the reasons those ranks exist. It is a self-amplifying process. Some people begin with fewer advantages, resources, and opportunities; this makes them less able to achieve and more likely to fail. Failure in the face of effort increases cognitive and motivational deficits, which, in turn, produce more failure and distress. These forces have been examined by Kohn and his colleagues (Kohn, 1972; Kohn and Schooler, 1982), Pearlin and his colleagues (Pearlin and Schooler, 1978; Pearlin *et al.*, 1981), Wheaton (1980, 1983), and by us (Mirowsky and Ross, 1983, 1984).

There are two things that combine to produce psychological distress: one is a problem, the other is the inability to cope with the problem. A person who can solve his or her problems is, in the long run, happier than a person with no problems at all. There are two crucial characteristics of people who cope with problems successfully. The first is *instrumentalism*, which is the belief that you control your own life, that outcomes depend on your own choices and actions, and that you are not at the mercy of powerful people, luck, fate, or chance. When a problem arises, the instrumental person takes action. He or she does not ignore the problem or passively wait for it to go away. Furthermore, he or she takes action before problems occur, shaping the environment to his or her advantage. A second crucial characteristic is cognitive *flexibility*. The flexible person can imagine complex and/or multiple solutions to a problem and sees many sides to an issue. He or she does not cling to habit and tradition. When necessary, the flexible person can negotiate and innovate. Instrumentalism and flexibility together eliminate the impact of undesirable events and of chronic stressful situations on distress (Wheaton, 1983).

These characteristics are needed most where they are found least. Instrumentalism is learned through a long history of success in solving increasingly difficult problems, and flexibility is learned in solving complex problems. Instrumentalism and flexibility are mostly learned in college and on the job, but only jobs that are complex, unsupervised, and not routine have the desired effect (Kohn and Schooler, 1982). Kohn and his colleagues interviewed a representative sample of 3101 employed men in the United States in 1964 and again in 1974. They found that jobs that are simple, closely supervised, and routine reduce cognitive flexibility.

The people at the bottom of society are the most burdened with chronic hardship, barriers to achievement, inequity, victimization, and exploitation. Their instrumentalism is reduced by demoralizing personal histories. Their cognitive flexibility is reduced by limited horizons and constraining jobs in which they are told what to do rather than allowed to make their own decisions. Wheaton noted the important distinction between coping ability and coping effort: Low flexibility reduces the *ability* to cope with problems (1980). Low instrumentalism reduces the *motivation* to use whatever energy and resources are available. Without the will or ability to cope with the overwhelming stressors present at the bottom of the social hierarchy, the unsolved problems of the poor and poorly educated accumulate. This combination of more problems and fewer resources to cope with them increases the psychological distress of the disadvantaged.

A NOTE ON RACE

In the United States, blacks are disproportionately disadvantaged. On average, blacks have lower levels of education and income than whites, in large part due to a long history of discrimination. Thus, blacks have higher levels of psychological distress than whites because they tend to have low socioeconomic status (Mirowsky and Ross, 1980). Even at the same income level, blacks may be worse off than whites: recent evidence indicates that poor blacks have higher levels of distress than poor whites (Kessler and Neighbors, 1986). This may be because discrimination and blocked opportunity interfere with the upward mobility of this group. Perceptions of blocked goals are especially likely to make a person feel helpless, powerless, and unable to control life.

DISCUSSION

Patterns of psychological distress tell us about the quality of life in various social positions. Misery is an inherently meaningful yardstick in social research, serving much the same function as mortality in medical research. Although community surveys of the social patterns of distress only began in the 1960s, they have already corrected some erroneous preconceptions. In particular, the observed patterns of distress challenge the idea that emotional well-being results from a placid life of dependency, protection, and freedom from responsibility. Instead, the surveys show that responsibility, commitment, achievement, and a sense of control in one's own life, and reciprocity, consideration, and equity in personal relationships, are the sources of well-being.

The United States is in the middle of far-reaching historical changes. As forms of production become outmoded, the skills associated with them become obsolete. As families get smaller and more women are employed, traditional household arrangements also become obsolete. In the aggregate, people make these changes. As individuals, people are made over by them. They adapt in one of two ways. Individuals can be overwhelmed, demoralized, discouraged, and distressed or they can be creative, curious, openminded, active, and distressed.

REFERENCES

Gersten, Joanne C., Thomas S. Langer, Jeanne G. Eisenberg, and Lida Orzek. "Child Behavior and Life Events: Undesirable Change or Change Per Se?" In *Stressful Life Events*, Barbara S. Dohrenwend and Bruce P. Dohrenwend, eds., pp. 159–170. New York: Wiley, 1974.

Gove, Walter R., and Michael R. Geerken. "The Effect of Children and Employment on the Mental Health of Married Men and Women." *Social Forces* 56:66–76, 1977b.

Gove, Walter R., and Jeannette F. Tudor. "Adult Sex Roles and Mental Illness." *American Journal of Sociology* 78:812–835, 1973.

Gove, Water R., Michael M. Hughes, and Carolyn B. Style. "Does Marriage Have Positive Effects on the Psychological Well-Being of the Individual?" *Journal of Health and Social Behavior* 24:122–131, 1983.

Holmes, Thomas H., and Richard H. Rahe. "The Social Readjustment Rating Scale." *Journal of Psychosomatic Research* 11:213–218, 1967.

Huber, Joan, and Glenna Spitze. *Sex Stratification: Children, Housework, and Jobs*. New York: Academic Press, 1983.

Hughes, Michael M., and Walter R. Gove. "Living Alone, Social Integration, and Mental Health." *American Journal of Sociology* 87:48–74, 1981.

Kessler, Ronald C., and James A. McRae. "The Effect of Wives' Employment on the Mental Health of Married Men and Women." *American Sociological Review* 47:216–227, 1982.

Kessler, Ronald C., and Harold W. Neighbors. "A New Perspective on the Relationships Among Race, Social Class, and Psychological Distress." *Journal of Health and Social Behavior* 27:107–115, 1986.

Kobassa, Suzanne C., Salvatore R. Maddi, and Sheila Courington. "Personality and Constitution as Mediators in the Stress-Illness Relationship." *Journal of Health and Social Behavior* 22:368–378, 1981.

Kohn, Melvin. "Class, Family, and Schizophrenia." *Social Forces* 50:295–302, 1972.

Kohn, Melvin, and Carmi Schooler. "Job Conditions and Personality: A Longitudinal Assessment of Their Reciprocal Effects." *American Journal of Sociology* 87:1257–1286, 1982.

McFarlane, Allan H., Geoffrey R. Norman, David L. Streiner, and Ranjan G. Roy. "The Process of Social Stress: Stable, Reciprocal, and Mediating Relationships." *Journal of Health and Social Behavior* 24:160–173, 1983.

Mirowsky, John. "Depression and Marital Power: An Equity Model." *American Journal of Sociology* 91:557–592, 1985.

Mirowsky, John, and Catherine E. Ross. "Minority Status, Ethnic Culture, and Distress: A Comparison of Blacks, Whites, Mexicans, and Mexican-Americans." *American Journal of Sociology* 86:479–495, 1980.

Mirowsky, John, and Catherine E. Ross. "Paranoia and the Structure of Powerlessness." *American Sociological Review* 48:228–239, 1983.

Mirowsky, John, and Catherine E. Ross. "Mexican Culture and Its Emotional Contradictions." *Journal of Health and Social Behavior* 25:2–13, 1984.

Mueller, D. D., W. Edwards, and R. M. Yarvis. "Stressful Life Events and Psychiatric Symptomatology: Change or Undesirability?" *Journal of Health and Social Behavior* 1:307–316, 1977.

Myers, Jerome K., Jacob J. Lindenthal, and Max P. Pepper. "Life Events and Psychiatric Impairment." *Journal of Nervous and Mental Disease* 52:149–157, 1971.

Oppenheimer, Valerie Kincade. "Demographic Influence on Female Employment and the Status of Women." In *Changing Women in a Changing Society*, Joan Huber, ed., pp. 184–199. Chicago: University of Chicago Press, 1973.

Oppenheimer, Valerie Kincade. *Work and Family: A Study in Social Demography*. New York: Academic Press, 1982.

Parsons, Talcott. "The Social Structure of the Family." In *The Family: Its Function and Destiny*, Ruth Anshen, ed., pp. 173–201. New York: Harper, 1949.

Pearlin, Leonard I. "Sex Roles and Depression." In *Life Span Developmental Psychology: Normative Life Crisis*, Nancy Datan and Leon H. Ginsberg, eds., pp. 191–208. New York: Academic Press, 1975a.

Pearlin, Leonard I. "Status Inequality and Stress in Marriage." *American Sociological Review* 40:344–357, 1975b.

Pearlin, Leonard I., and Carmi Schooler. "The Structure of Coping." *Journal of Health and Social Behavior* 19:2–21, 1978.

Pearlin, Leonard I., Morton A. Liberman, Elizabeth G. Menaghan, and Joseph T. Mulan. "The Stress Process." *Journal of Health and Social Behavior* 22:337–356, 1981.

Richman, Judith. Women's Changing Work Roles and Psychological-Psycho-Physiological Distress. Presented at the American Sociological Association annual meeting. Boston, 1979.

Robinson, John P. "Housework Technology and Household Work." In *Women and Household Labor,* Sarah Fenstermaker Berk, ed., pp. 53–67. Beverly Hills, CA: Sage, 1980.

Rosenfield, Sarah. "Sex Differences in Depression: Do Women Always Have Higher Rates?" *Journal of Health and Social Behavior* 21:22–42, 1980.

Ross, Catherine E., and John Mirowsky. "A Comparison of Live Event Weighting Schemes: Change, Undesirability, and Effect-Proportional Indices." *Journal of Health and Social Behavior* 20:166–177, 1979.

Ross, Catherine E., John Mirowsky, and Joan Huber. "Dividing Work, Sharing Work, and In-Between: Marriage Patterns and Depression." *American Sociological Review* 48:809–823, 1983.

Ross, Catherine E., John Mirowsky, and Patricia Ulbrich. "Distress and the Traditional Female Role: A Comparison of Mexicans and Anglos." *American Journal of Sociology* 89:670–682, 1983.

Tufte, Edward R. *Data Analysis for Politics and Policy*. Englewood Cliffs, NJ: Prentice Hall, 1974.

Vinokur, A., and M. Selzer. "Desirable versus Undesirable Life Events: Their Relationship to Stress and Mental Distress." *Journal of Personality and Social Psychology* 32:329–337, 1975.

Waite, Linda J. "Working Wives: 1940–1960." *American Sociological Review* 41:65–80, 1976.

Walster, Elaine, G. William Walster, and Ellen Berscheid. *Equity: Theory and Research*. Boston, MA: Allyn and Bacon, 1978.

Wheaton, Blair. "The Sociogenesis of Psychological Disorder: An Attributional Theory." *Journal of Health and Social Behavior* 21:100–124, 1980.

Wheaton, Blair. "Stress, Personal Coping Resources, and Psychiatric Symptoms: An Investigation of Interactive Models." *Journal of Health and Social Behavior* 24:208–229, 1983.

Williams, Ann W., John E. Ware, and Cathy A. Donald. "A Model of Mental Health, Life Events, and Social Supports Applicable to General Populations." *Journal of Health and Social Behavior* 22:324–336, 1981.

CHAPTER 16

SOCIAL SUPPORT AS A MODERATOR OF LIFE STRESS

SIDNEY COBB

*I assure you it is much wholesomer to be a complaisant, good humored,
contented Courtier, than a Grumbletonian Patriot, always whining and snarling.*

—John Adams to his wife Abigail, The Hague, July 1, 1782

Everybody talks about health, but nobody does much about it. The issue was stated clearly by Stephen Smith (1874), the first president of the American Public Health Association. He said, "[T]he customs of society must be so changed that the physician is employed to prevent rather than cure disease." Only recently has this concept begun to be implemented in the United States as a part of the Health Maintenance Organization movement (MacLeod and Pressin, 1973). It is, therefore, timely to address ourselves to preventive issues. As the title suggests, this essay will focus on social support. It will examine some of the areas in which social support has been demonstrated to have dramatic health-related effects and identify some in which it seems to have had no effects. It will not attempt to review all the diverse literature on this subject, for exhaustive bibliographies are available (Gore, 1973; Kaplan, Cassel, and Gore, 1973; Pinneau, 1975). Rather, it will emphasize the

way that social support acts to prevent the unfortunate consequences of crisis and change.

Before proceeding, we must come to some mutual understanding of the concept of social support. For the present discussion, social support is conceived to be information belonging to one or more of the following three classes:

1. Information leading the subject to believe that he is cared for and loved.
2. Information leading the subject to believe that he is esteemed and valued.
3. Information leading the subject to believe that he belongs to a network of communication and mutual obligation.

Let us examine each in turn.

Information that one is cared for and loved or, as the Greeks might say, information about *agapé,* is transmitted in intimate situations involving mutual trust. In a dyadic relationship, this information meets Murray et al.'s (1938) need succorance for one person, need nurturance for the other, and need affiliation for both. It is often called emotional support.

From *Psychosomatic Medicine* 38:5 (Sept.–Oct. 1976), pp. 300–314. Copyright © American Psychosomatic Society. Reprinted by permission.

Information that one is valued and esteemed is most effectively proclaimed in public. It leads the individual to esteem himself and reaffirms his sense of personal worth, it may be called esteem support.

Information that one belongs to a network of mutual obligation must be common and shared. It must be common in the sense that everyone in the network has the information and shared in the sense that each member is aware that every other member knows. The relevant information is of three kinds. The first answers the questions: What is going on and how did it begin? What is the relationship between us? How and when did we get here? These questions are the essence of history. The second pertains to goods and services that are available to any member on demand and includes information about the accessibility of services that are only occasionally needed, e.g., equipment, specialized skills, technical information. The third contains information that is common and shared with respect to the dangers of life and the procedures for mutual defense. In this last sense, the knowledge that a competently staffed hospital is available in case of need is socially supportive.

The present meaning of social support does not include the activities of the hospital in repairing a broken leg. Those activities are material services and are not of themselves information of any of the major classes mentioned [earlier]. This does not mean that the deferential manner of the intern may not provide esteem support or that the tender care of the nurses may not communicate emotional support. It is only to say that the services do not in themselves constitute such support because social support, being information, cannot be measured as mass or energy. This distinction is important, for goods and services may foster dependency, while the classes of information listed [previously] do not. In fact, they tend to encourage independent behavior.

This set of dimensions is hardly new. Angyal (1965), Antonovsky (1974), Fromm (1955), Leighton (1959), Weiss (1969), and many others have illustrated and illuminated them. Perhaps the most notable illumination is the novel *Come Near* by Alexander Leighton (1971). Gerald Caplan (1974) and his colleagues have taught the importance of these concepts in community mental health. But let's face it, these notions have been expressed over the millennia in the writings of most of the world's religious leaders. I have only added some precision and emphasized that it is information rather than goods or services that is central to the concept.

The first group, emotional support, was initially expressed in the need terms of Murray (1938). The second can similarly be expressed as need recognition from the Murray lexicon. The third is clearly akin to at least two of Leighton's (1959) essential striving sentiments: "Orientation in terms of one's place in society . . ." and "The securing and maintaining of membership in a definite human group." This means that the whole concept can be expressed in person-environment fit terms (French, Rodgers, and Cobb, 1974; Moos and Insel, 1974) or as the extent to which the relevant needs are met.

Social support begins *in utero,* is best recognized at the maternal breast, and is communicated in a variety of ways, but especially in the way the baby is held (supported). As life progresses, support is derived increasingly from other members of the family, then from peers at work and in the community, and perhaps, in case of special need, from a member of the helping professions. As life's end approaches, social support, in our culture, but not in all cultures, is again derived mostly from members of the family.

As will be seen in the section on the mechanism of this effect, it is my current opinion that social support facilitates coping with crisis and adaptation to change. Therefore, one should not expect dramatic main effects from social support. There are of course some main effects simply because life is full of changes and crises. The theory says that it is in moderating the effects of the major transitions in life and of the unexpected crises that the effects should be found. This theory is supported by the work of Pinneau (1975), who found few effects in cross-sectional studies.

With this background, it is time to turn to a careful examination of the extent to which this social support protects an individual as he passes through the various transitions and crises of the life cycle. We will begin with the infant *in utero* and end with death.

PREGNANCY, BIRTH, AND EARLY LIFE

The elegant study of Nuckolls et al. (1972) is a good place to start this review. This was a study of 170 army wives [who] delivered at a large military hospital. Data on life change scores before and during pregnancy and on psychosocial assets were collected. The measure of psychosocial assets (TAPPS) covers all three of the areas described [earlier] as the main components of social support in a subjective way and relatively little else except for some assessment of affect, which we know from other studies to be associated with support.

A recalculation of the data of Nuckolls et al. (1972) is presented in Table 16.1. Those women who are designated as having high life change scores are those who were above the median both before and during pregnancy. All other women have been included in the low category. The measure of social support (TAPPS) is split at the median. As can readily be seen, the proportion of women having complications is excessive (91%) only in the high life change/low social support cell. However, the upper left-hand cell (high life change and high support) is the really interesting one, for here 15 women were exposed to the same high frequency of life changes but had no increase in complications, presumably because of some protective effect exerted by the high level of social support. One useful point about this study is

that, if the association is causal, the direction is clear, for the complications cannot have influenced the TAPPS score, which was measured at the first visit, or the life changes, almost all of which occurred well before the complications. This kind of moderating effect will appear again and again as this review progresses.

Another approach to social support in pregnancy is reported by Morris et al. in 1973. The data come from a study of "wantedness" of babies in 60 major hospitals in 17 cities. A simplified presentation of their findings is to be seen in Table 16.2. It is clear that, at least for women who have completed high school, the reporting that a baby was wanted at the time it was conceived is associated with a significant decrease in the frequency of low birth weight. This is true for both blacks and whites. Over against this, one must set a Swedish study that did not find a difference in birth weight between babies for whom abortion was requested but refused and other babies (Hultin and Ottosson, 1971). However, education was not used as a control variable in this study. It is not reasonable to suppose that "wantedness" is information that is transmitted from mother to fetus and influences growth rate. Rather, it seems likely that the most common reason that a woman rejects her baby is that she herself feels inadequately socially supported. The societal reaction to illegitimate pregnancy is a case in point. In this instance, the causal

TABLE 16.1   Percentage of Women with Complications of Pregnancy by Life Change Score and Social Support (TAPPS)

	SOCIAL SUPPORT			
LIFE CHANGE SCORE	**HIGH**	**LOW**	**t**	**P**
High[a]	33% (15)[b]	91% (11)	3.87	<0.001
Low	39% (72)	49% (72)		NS*

SOURCE: Recalculated from data of Nuckolls et al. (1972).

Interaction $t = 2.24$, $P < 0.05$.

[a]High both before and during pregnancy.

[b]Numbers in parentheses are the numbers of women in the respective cells.

[*NS = not significant.]

TABLE 16.2   Percentage of Babies with Birth Weight <2,500 g by Education, Race, and Wantedness

	WANTED OR DID NOT MATTER		TIMING ERROR OR UNWANTED		
	N	PERCENTAGE	*N*	PERCENTAGE	*P*
Less than 12 years education					
Black	867	10.7	1,657	11.5	NS*
White	2,118	4.9	1,434	6.1	NS*
12 or more years education					
Black	227	3.1	257	10.5	<0.001
White	875	2.4	359	6.4	<0.010

SOURCE: Recalculated from data of Morris et al. (42).

[*NS = not significant.]

direction is not so clear, for the inquiry was made the day after delivery and it is possible that babies known to be small were less likely to be declared to have been wanted than those known to be large.

Moving on to the first major social demand that the child faces, namely, achievement of sphincter control, Stein and Susser (1967) tell us that control of bladder function at night was significantly delayed for those children whose mothers went out to work while the children were in the second six months of life. This was not true if the mother went to work earlier or later in the child's life nor was it true of the small number of children who had a substantial parental separation. These data are open to a variety of possible interpretations, so further study is indicated, but it seems at least possible that social support given by the mother during the time when toilet training is beginning is important to the early acquisition of sphincter control.

When we get to the important area of later social development, there are two studies. Forssman and Thuwe (1966) have shown that wanted children adapt to and/or cope with the stresses of growing up better than those who started out with a parental request for abortion that was denied, in a study that followed a matched series of 120 cases and 120 controls until age 21. The cases fared worse with respect to juvenile delinquency and need for psychiatric treatment. Particularly striking was the distribution with respect to

educational achievement. This is presented in Table 16.3. It is of special interest that the authors point out that the negative effects were essentially wiped out for those cases that were reared by their two natural parents together. The force of simple economic factors in this situation cannot be neglected.

The more recent study by Dytrych et al. (1975) of the children of Czech mothers who had been twice refused abortion for the relevant pregnancy has an appropriately matched control group but is subject to the criticism, on the material so far presented, that the number of significant findings does not seem to exceed the number to be expected by chance. However, the findings in the area of socialization in a school are quite suggestive because, of the 15 performance and behavioral items presented, all are in the predicted direction and two are significant. We will all look forward to the full report with interest. The possibility that social support increases the efficiency of socialization in school must be kept in the forefront of our minds.

TRANSITIONS TO ADULTHOOD

There seems to be little information about the effects on the transitions to college, to first job, and to marriage. This is an area in which the literature must be more thoroughly combed and in which specific research is indicated.

TABLE 16.3 The Educational Achievement of Unwanted Children Compared with That of Controls

	UNWANTED	CONTROLS	TOTAL
Advanced study	17 (14%)*	40 (33%)	57
Completed required schooling	90 (75%)	74 (62%)	164
Retarded	13 (11%)	6 (5%)	19
Total	120	120	240

SOURCE: Data of Forssman and Thuwe (1966).

[*Percentages have been added to this table; they are calculated by columns and, therefore, should be compared by rows.—Ed.]

$X^2 = 13.4$, $p < 0.005$.

HOSPITALIZATION

The effects of social support on an individual in relation to hospitalization for mental and physical illness are widespread, but much of the evidence is inferential. That is to say, the several studies in question imply differences in social support without measurement. The social breakdown syndrome, which is so intimately intertwined with admission to a mental hospital, can be largely prevented (Gruenberg, Snow, and Bennett, 1969). This prevention is accomplished by a community-oriented service providing continuing care from the same team with hospitalization held to the minimum. Surely, that which is provided is mostly social support, although some specific services are included.

Moving on to hospitalization of children for tonsillectomy, there is a considerable volume of clinical literature. Much of this was summarized by Jessner and her colleagues back in 1952 (Jessner, Blom, and Waldfogel, 1952). It indicates that supportive behavior on the part of parents and staff is helpful in preventing post-hospital psychological reactions. Recalculation of Jessner's own data indicates that the simple provision, by the parents, of adequate information about the anticipated hospitalization has a significant effect in preventing postoperative reactions.

In concluding this section, we should take note of the evidence that treating patients with myocardial infarcts at home carries no greater, and perhaps less, risk of death than treating them in the hospital intensive care unit. This is despite all the intensive care and fancy equipment that is available in the hospital. Mather and his colleagues (Mather, 1974; Mather et al., 1971) deserve congratulations for their foresight and courage in setting up this field experiment. The mechanism by which staying at home exerts protective effect was presumably identified by Leigh et al. in 1972, when they pointed to the association of cardiac arrhythmias with high separation anxiety and the direction of hostility inward rather than outward. Both of these psychological sets are presumably reduced in the supportive atmosphere of the home. Obviously, network support is particularly at issue. However, Engel (1976) suggests that the effect may be due simply to protection from environmental insults.

RECOVERY FROM ILLNESS

This section shows the importance of the supportive physician in recovery from congestive heart failure and from surgical procedures and the importance of psychosocial assets in the recovery from psychosomatic illness, especially tuberculosis and asthma. Then the evidence that social support keeps the patient in treatment and promotes compliance with prescribed regimens will be reviewed.

In 1953, Chambers and Reiser (1953) described the association of emotionally significant events with the onset of episodes of cardiac failure. In addition, they demonstrated the extraordinarily beneficial effects that emotional support from the physician could have on the course of the disease. A related finding is reported by Egbert et al. (1964). They took two comparable groups of surgical patients. One group was given special supportive care by the anesthetist and the other served as a control. The surgeons managing the patients did not know which patient was in which group. The patients in the special care group needed substantially less medication for pain and were discharged on the average 2.7 days earlier than the control group. Both findings were statistically highly significant.

This same kind of effect must be demonstrable for a variety of other conditions involving fragile equilibrium. It points to the fact that social support is an important component of the therapeutic process. As Francis Peabody (1927) stated in his essay *The Care of the Patient,* "One of the essential qualities of the clinician is interest in humanity, for the care of the patient is in caring for the patient." More recently, Lambert (1973) and Caplan (1974) have emphasized the importance of social support in the psychiatric management of life crises.

Some years ago, Berle, working with Harold Wolf and others (Berle, Pinsky, Wolf, and Wolf, 1952), developed an index of social and psychological characteristics of the patient, which had substantial prognostic value with regard to recovery from psychosomatic illness. Over half of the score on this index is easily codable to the categories of social support enumerated [earlier]. Holmes et al. (1961) showed that this scale was highly predictive of the outcome of sanatorium treatment for tuberculosis, in that all the treatment failures were in the lowest third of the scores on this index. This is consonant with the evidence reviewed by Chen and Cobb (1960), suggesting that tuberculosis is a disease of social isolation, i.e., low social support.

More recently, de Araujo and van Arsdel, working with Holmes and Dudley (1973) in Seattle, used this Berle Index to show a remarkable interaction of social support with life change with respect to the need for steroid therapy in adult asthmatics. Table 16.4 summarizes their data. The figures in the cells are average daily doses of steroids (prednisone or

TABLE 16.4   Average Daily Steroid Dosage in Milligrams per Day for Patients with Asthma by Life Change Score and Social Support (Berle Index)

LIFE CHANGE SCORE	BERLE INDEX	
	HIGH	LOW
High	5.6 (12)[a]	19.6 (11)[b]
Low	5.0 (10)	6.7 (4)

SOURCE: de Araujo et al. (1973).
[a]Number of cases.
[b]This cell is significantly different from each of the other cells (*p* < 0.01).

equivalent). It is clear that those with low life change scores needed only small doses of steroids and that those with a lot of life changes and a low Berle Index needed three to four times as much. The important point about this table is that those with a high Berle Index were protected from the need for high doses of steroids that presumably would be generated by a high life change score. It is this interaction between life change and support, in a way that suggests a protective effect of support, that is the focus of this review.

There are a lot of pathways to the [aforementioned] effects. They fall into two major classes. The first is a direct effect through neuroendocrine pathways. This is the one that we in psychosomatic medicine are most apt to emphasize. The second is through promoting compliant behavior on the part of the patient. There is a large quantity of very consistent evidence pointing to the fact that those patients who are not socially isolated and are well supported are, in our casual lingo, good patients, in that they stay in treatment and follow our recommendations. The evidence on dropping out of treatment is summarized by Baekeland and Lundwall (1975), who state, "The importance of social isolation and/or lack of affiliation was indicated in 19 out of 19 studies (100%) that considered them." In a review of compliance with therapeutic regimens that does not overlap with the above, Haynes and Sackett (1974) indicate that only one of 22 articles in which social-support-relevant variables were measured gave evidence contrary to the hypothesis that social support is positively associated with compliance. Six of the 22 articles found no evidence either way. As data on such matters go, this association of cooperative patient behavior with various components of the social support complex is one of the best established facts about the social aspects of medical practice.

LIFE STRESS

Here data will be presented on the dangers of stopping drinking without social support and the way in which social support protects against depression in the face of extensive life changes. After that, we will go on to two particular life changes: job loss and bereavement.

Joan Jackson, in a chapter in Sparer's book *Personality, Stress and Tuberculosis* (1954), presented some truly remarkable data, the significance of which did not receive adequate recognition at the time. I have recalculated her data in Table 16.5. She compared the men sent to the police farm for alcoholism with the alcoholics admitted to the tuberculosis sanatorium with respect to the frequency of men attempting to stop drinking in the preceding year with and without the support of an institutionally based program and/or Alcoholics Anonymous. As you can see, the frequency distributions are highly significantly

different ($p < 0.005$). The relative risk calculation says in essence that men who tried to stop drinking on their own, i.e., without the support of an organized program, had 20 times the likelihood of being admitted to the tuberculosis sanatorium as their peers who did not try to stop or who tried with support. In fact, the numbers suggest that the risk of tuberculosis is reduced for those who try with support, but they are too small to be convincing. This is an impressive difference and deserves attention from those who work with alcoholics. Again, the social support dimension emerges as especially important for tuberculosis.

Turning to the work of George Brown and his collaborators (Brown, Bhrolchain, and Harris, 1975), one finds another striking datum. In Table 16.6 is shown the percent of a random sample of women classified as having a severe affective [emotional] disorder. They are divided by whether or not they had a confidant. A confidant was defined as a person, usually male, with whom the woman had "a close intimate and confiding relationship." The table makes it clear that those women who had severe events and lacked a confidant were roughly 10 times more likely to be depressed than those in any of the other three cells. If one assumes that the events had some causal relationship here, one is forced to the conclusion that the intimate relationship is somehow protective. Although one must be cautious about interpreting the effect of life events on depression because depressed

TABLE 16.5 The Risk of Tuberculosis to Men Stopping Drinking in the Preceding 12 Months without Social Support

	ALCOHOLIC ADMISSIONS TO	
	POLICE FARM	TB SANATORIUM
Stopped drinking during past 12 months		
Without support	1	18
With support	5	2
Did not stop drinking	28	27
Total	34	47

$X^2 = 14.8$, $p < 0.005$; relative risk = $(18 \times 33)/(1 \times 29) = 20$.

SOURCE: Recalculated from data of Jackson (1954).

TABLE 16.6 Percentage of a Random Sample Who Had a Recent Onset of Affective Disorder by Life Stress and Social Support

	SOCIAL SUPPORT	
LIFE STRESS	CONFIDANT	NO CONFIDANT
Severe event or major difficulty	4% (2/45)	38%[a] (17/45)
Neither	1% (1/82)	3% (1/34)

SOURCE: Brown et al. (1975).
[a]Significantly different from each of the other cells ($p < 0.001$).
Interaction: $t = 3.60$, $p < 0.001$.

people over-report unpleasant events, I have seen no evidence that depressed people tend to deny their confidants.

Alcoholism is related to depression, so it is not surprising that Quinn (1973) found that escapist drinking, but not other forms of drinking, is significantly elevated only among those who have high job stress and are not supported by their supervisors. These data come from the National Quality of Employment Survey, 1972–73 (Quinn, 1973).

EMPLOYMENT TERMINATION

This is a major life crisis for most [working adults], particularly if they have dependents and have been stably employed for some years. My colleagues and I have a special study of this matter. The doctoral dissertation of Susan Gore (1973) was specifically focused on the moderating effect of social support on a selected set of outcome variables. Our total study examined a wide variety of economic, social, psychological, and medical variables in 100 men whose jobs were abolished and 74 men whose employment was stable. The men were visited by public health nurses before the termination, soon after the termination, and then at 6, 12, and 24 months after the plant closings. The men were all married blue-collar workers with about 19 years of seniority. In this study, the measure focused almost entirely on network support, although there was one item on subjective emotional support. This measure had moderating effects on some physiological variables and some indicators of

illness, but not with regard to others. Cholesterol and uric acid levels in the serum were higher during the weeks surrounding the termination for those with little support than for those with adequate support. No such differences were observed with respect to norepinephrine in the urine or creatinine in the serum, although important changes over time were noted with respect to each and both were modified by the level of psychological defense (Cobb, 1974). The changes in level of complaints noted on a symptom check list was significantly moderated by high social support, but no effect was noted on hypertension or, surprisingly enough in view of the findings of Cobb et al. (1969), on peptic ulcer. At the other end of the social support scale, the finding that marital hostility is associated with ulcer disease was replicated.

When it came to arthritis, the data presented in Table 16.7 emerged. Here it can be seen that there was a 10-fold increase in the proportion of men found to have two or more joints swollen as one went from the highest to the lowest quartile of the social support dimension. This was not predicted in advance, so the matter was examined with some care and the finding stands up no matter how you look at it.

BEREAVEMENT

Everyone acts as though social support were important to those who are bereaved and many authors suggest that this should be appropriate behavior, but hard evidence on the subject seems difficult to come by. Parkes (1972) presents some suggestive evidence

TABLE 16.7 The Effect of Social Support in Preventing Joint Swelling in Relation to Job Loss

	SOCIAL SUPPORT			
	HIGH	**MED**	**LOW**	**TOTAL**
Two or more joints with observed swelling	1 (4%)*	5 (12%)	12 (41%)	18
Other	27 (96%)	36 (88%)	17 (59%)	80
Total	28	41	29	98[a]
Percentage with two or more joints swollen	4	12	41	

[*Percentages have been added to this table; they are calculated by columns and, therefore, should be compared by rows.—Ed.]

[a] Two cases have missing data.

Gamma = 0.732; $p < 0.0003$.

that opportunities for affiliation and affiliative behavior correlate positively with good psychological state 13 months after bereavement. The most striking data are provided by Burch (1972). Recalculating her data, it is possible to conclude that a married man who lost his mother had no increased probability of suicide. However, if he were single or his marriage had been terminated, his risk of suicide was increased ninefold by the death of his mother. Dr. Burch also showed that those men who had less contact with relatives had a greater probability of suicide than those with more contact. Considering the importance of the question and the potential of the study design, the analyses presented by Gerber et al. (1975) are disappointing. One wishes that the data were more fully presented and more appropriately analyzed. However, on four of the six health dimensions presented, the bereaved subjects who had received professional support were better off during the period 5–8 months after bereavement. Further research in this area is clearly indicated.

AGING AND RETIREMENT

In this area, as in hospitalization of children, there are a lot of strong impressions about the importance of social support in protecting people from the consequences of the stress of growing old and infirm. The best data that have come to hand are those of Blau (1973). She supports the view that being married or

being employed or having substantial social activity ("participation") is protective against the development of low morale. Similarly, Lowenthal and Haven (1968) find in a sample of 280 persons aged 63 and older that 85% of those with low social interaction were depressed, whereas only 42% of those with high social interaction were depressed.

THREAT OF DEATH

Life threats are most striking in battle and as life's end approaches. These two situations will be examined in turn. There are many studies of the effects of morale, which is presumably a derivative of social support on the frequency of neuropsychiatric disorders. Rose's (1956) rather clean study illustrates the point. He compared two battalions from the same regiment with respect to morale and neuropsychiatric casualties. These battalions were otherwise quite similar. The battalion with high morale had roughly half as high a rate of psychiatric casualties as the battalion with low morale. To the extent that high morale involves high self-esteem and group cohesiveness, mutual esteem support and network support are central to the maintenance of morale.

In a similar vein, Swank (1949) found that every soldier in the Normandy campaign who had lost 75% or more of his buddies developed combat exhaustion. Reid (1947) reports almost identical findings for bomber crews in the Royal Air Force. Just to clinch the matter firmly, I quote from the military experience of two distinguished psychiatrists. Francis Braceland (1947) said, "It became obvious early in the course of the war that the most important prophylactics against psychiatric casualties in the military forces were proper individual motivation and high morale. . . ." William Menninger (1947) added, "We seemed to learn anew the importance of group ties in the maintenance of mental health."

It would be improper to close this review without drawing attention to the life sparing effects of anticipated ceremonial occasions. Phillips and Feldman (1973) in a truly remarkable paper showed in five different populations that deaths are reduced in the 6 months preceding birthdays and increased in the succeeding 6 months. A summary of their data is presented in Figure 16.1. They went on to hypothesize that, if this were a social support effect, it should be more striking for the most distinguished. This they found to be dramatically confirmed.

DISCUSSION

We have seen strong and often quite hard evidence, repeated over a variety of transitions in the life cycle from birth to death, that social support is protective. The very great diversity of the studies in terms of criteria of support, nature of sample, and method of data collection is further convincing that we are dealing with a common phenomenon. We have however, seen enough negative findings to make it clear that social support is not a panacea.

The conclusion that supportive interactions among people are important is hardly new. What is new is the assembling of hard evidence that adequate social support can protect people in crisis from a wide variety of pathological states: from low birth weight to death, from arthritis through tuberculosis to depression, alcoholism, and other psychiatric illness. Furthermore, social support can reduce the amount of medication required and accelerate recov-

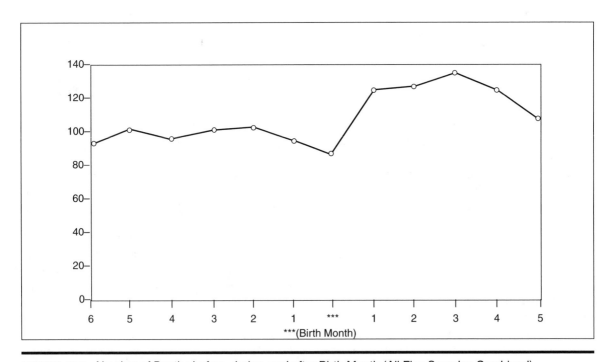

FIGURE 16.1 Number of Deaths before, during, and after Birth Month (All Five Samples Combined)

ery and facilitate compliance with prescribed medical regimens.

In a number of the studies that have been cited, it is possible to suggest alternatives to the social support explanation for findings. For example, the birth weight findings of Morris et al. (1973) might be due to a reporting artifact, in that high school graduate mothers appreciate the significance of low birth weight and therefore tend to over-report their small babies as unwanted, while the less well-educated mothers do neither. Similarly, the excess of suicides among sons not currently married described by Burch (1972) could conceivably be related to unresolved maternal ties, rather than to a lack of social support. At the other extreme, such studies as those of Nuckolls et al. (1972), de Araujo et al. (1973), Egbert et al. (1964), or my own on job termination are considerably less amenable to alternative interpretations because the social support was measured in advance, the stress was defined, and the outcomes were sufficiently specific to avoid major confounding. The crux of the matter seems to be that, although one or two of the studies presented might turn out on further investigation to be truly irrelevant, the series is so long and so diverse that it demands attention.

I may well have missed important findings both positive and negative. I would welcome additions to my files from readers who can identify such omissions. However, it should be clear that I have focused on the interaction of social support with environmental stress and have intentionally omitted a modest volume of studies that demonstrate a simple direct effect of social support on health. These studies are mostly included in the reviews by Gore (1973), Kaplan et al. (1973), and Pinneau (1975). The effect on tuberculosis is noted by Chen and Cobb (1960). The full range of data on coronary heart disease has never been assembled in one place. This deserves attention, for the collective effect of the full set is impressive. These data are not presented here because they are mostly reported as main effects rather than as moderating the effects of social stress.

What remains is to consider possible mechanisms [intervening variables] for the observed protective effects. At the present time, the most attractive theory about the nature of this phenomenon involves pathways through facilitation of coping and adaptation. (Coping in my language means manipulation of the environment in the service of self and adaptation means change in the self in an attempt to improve person-environment fit.) It would not be unreasonable to suppose that esteem support would encourage a person to cope, i.e., to go out and attempt to master a problem. Likewise, emotional support and a sense of belonging might provide the climate in which self-identity changes can most readily take place.

As evidence that mastery of a new task takes place best under supportive conditions, I would draw attention to the classical experiment of Coch and French (1948) in the pajama factory. They found that "participation" markedly reduced the time needed to get back to full production after a change in the nature of the task. An invitation from management to participate in the planning and implementation of a change is certainly direct esteem support. Participation may incidentally increase other forms of support, but that is not central to the argument that esteem support facilitates coping.

Parsons' (1958) study clarified the sick role. Since successful role changes involve identity changes, it is logical to presume that movement in and out of the sick role is assisted by those things that facilitate the relevant identity changes. Clearly, social support facilitated remaining in treatment (Baekeland and Lundwall, 1975) and may speed recovery (Egbert, Battit, Welch, and Barrett, 1964). The hypothesis is strong but, as far as I know, untested that social support facilitates identity change, which, in turn, facilitates role change.

Further research on the proposed mechanism through which social support might operate is clearly indicated. In addition, there is an obvious need for further investigation of the moderating effects of social support on the consequences of the following transitions: entry into primary school, entry into college, first job, marriage, residential change, and bereavement. Surely, investigation will proceed on the effect of social support on the outcome of medical treatment because the results are likely to point to methods for reducing the costs of medical care. This review has focused on acute stress. There remains an important question as to whether social support can moderate the effects of chronic stress such as that experienced by air traffic controllers (Cobb and Rose, 1973).

There appears to be enough evidence on the importance of social support to warrant action, although, of course, all the details as to the circum-

stances under which it is effective are not yet worked out. Following the behest of Stephen Smith (1874) cited at the beginning of this review, we should start now to teach all our patients, both well and sick, how to give and receive social support. Only in rare instances of clear psychiatric disability should this instruction require a psychiatrist. It seems to me that this is the real function for which Richard Cabot designed the profession of medical social work.

REFERENCES

Angyal, A. 1965. *Neurosis and Treatment: A Holistic Theory* (edited by E. Hanfmann and R. M. Jones). New York, Wiley.

Antonovsky, A. 1974. Conceptual and methodological problems in the study of resistance resources and stressful life events, in *Stressful Life Events: Their Nature and Effects,* Chap. 15 (edited by B. S. Dohrenwend and B. P. Dohrenwend). New York, Wiley.

Baekeland, F. and Lundwall, L. 1975. Dropping out of treatment: a critical review. *Psychological Bulletin* 82:738–783.

Berle, B. B., Pinsky, R. H., Wolf, S., and Wolf, H. G. 1952. Berle index: a clinical guide to prognosis in stress disease. *Journal of the American Medical Association* 149:1624–1628.

Blau, Z. S. 1973. *Old Age in a Changing Society.* New York, New Viewpoints.

Braceland, F. J. 1947. Psychiatric lessons from World War II. *American Journal of Psychiatry* 103:587–593.

Brown, G. W., Bhrolchain, M. N., and Harris, T. 1975. Social class and psychiatric disturbance among women in an urban population. *Sociology* 9:225–254.

Burch, J. 1972. Recent bereavement in relation to suicide. *Journal of Psychosomatic Research* 16:361–366.

Caplan, G. 1974. *Support Systems and Community Mental Health.* New York, Behavioral Publications.

Chambers, W. N. and Reiser, M. F. 1953. Emotional stress in the precipitation of congestive heart failure. *Psychosomatic Medicine* 15:38–60.

Chen, E. and Cobb, S. 1960. Family structure in relation to health and disease. *Journal of Chronic Diseases* 12:544–567.

Cobb, S. 1974. Physiological changes in men whose jobs were abolished. *Journal of Psychosomatic Research* 18:245–258.

Cobb, S., Kasl, S. V., French, J. R. P., Jr. and Norstebo, G. 1969. The intrafamilial transmission of rheumatoid arthritis. VII: Why do wives with rheumatoid arthritis have husbands with peptic ulcer? *Journal of Chronic Diseases* 22:279–293.

Cobb, S. and Rose, R. M. 1973. Hypertension, peptic ulcer and diabetes in air traffic controllers. *Journal of the American Medical Association* 224:489–492.

Coch, L. and French, J. R. P., Jr. 1948. Overcoming resistance to change. *Human Relations* 11:512–532.

de Araujo, G., van Arsdel, P. P., Holmes, T. H., and Dudley, D. L. 1973. Life change, coping ability and chronic intrinsic asthma. *Journal of Psychosomatic Research* 17:359–363.

Dytrych, Z., Matejcek, Z., Schuller, V., David, H. P., and Friedman, H. L. 1975. Children born to women denied abortion. *Family Planning Perspective* 7:165–171.

Egbert, L .D., Battit, G. E., Welch, C. E., and Barrett, M. K. 1964. Reduction of post-operative pain by encouragement and instruction of patients. *New England Journal of Medicine* 270:825–827.

Engel, G. L. 1976. Psychologic factors in instantaneous cardiac death. *New England Journal of Medicine* 294:664–665.

Forssman, H. and Thuwe, I. 1966. One hundred and twenty children born after application for therapeutic abortion refused. *Acta Psychiatrica Scandinavica* 42:71–88.

French, J. R. P., Jr., Rodgers, W., and Cobb, S. 1974. Adjustment as person-environment fit, in Coelho, G.

V., Hamburg, D. A., and Adams, J. E., *Coping and Adaptation*. New York, Basic Books.

Fromm, E. 1955. *The Sane Society*. New York. Rinehart.

Gerber, I., Wiener, A., Battin, D., and Arkin, A. 1975. Brief therapy to the aged bereaved, in *Bereavement: Its Psychosocial Aspects* (edited by B. Schoenberg et al.). New York, Columbia University Press.

Gore, S. 1973. The influence of social support and related variables in ameliorating the consequences of job loss. Doctoral dissertation, University of Pennsylvania.

Gruenberg, E., Snow, H. B., and Bennett, C. L. 1969. Preventing the social breakdown syndrome, in *Social Psychiatry*, Vol. 47 (edited by F. C. Redlich). Baltimore, ARNMD.

Haynes, R. B. and Sackett, D. L. 1974. *A Workshop/Symposium: Compliance with Therapeutic Regimens-Annotated Bibliography*. Department of Clinical Epidemiology and Biostatistics, McMaster University Medical Centre, Hamilton, Ontario.

Holmes, T. H., Joffe, J. R., and Ketcham, J. W. et al. 1961. Experimental study of prognosis. *Journal of Psychosomatic Research* 5:235–252.

Hultin, M. and Ottosson, M. O. 1971. Perinatal conditions of unwanted children. *Acta Psychiatrica Scandinavica* (Suppl.) 221:59–76.

Jackson, J. K. 1954. The problem of alcoholic tuberculous patients, in Sparer, P. F., *Personality, Stress and Tuberculosis*. New York, International Universities Press.

Jessner, L., Blom, G. E., and Waldfogel, S. 1952. Emotional implications of tonsillectomy and adenoidectomy on children. *Psychoanalytic Study of Children* 7:126–169.

Kaplan, B. H., Cassel, J. C., and Gore, S. 1973. Social support and health. Paper presented at meetings of American Public Health Association, Nov. 9.

Kramer, M., Pollack, E. S., Redick, R. W., and Locke, B. Z. 1972. *Mental Disorders/Suicide*. Cambridge, Harvard University Press.

Lambert, K. 1973. Agape as a therapeutic factor in analysis. *Journal of Analytical Psychology* 18:25–46.

Leigh, H., Hofer, M. A., Cooper, J., and Reiser, M. F. 1972. A psychological comparison of patients in "open" and "closed" coronary care units. *Journal of Psychosomatic Research* 16:449–457.

Leighton, A. H. 1959. *My Name Is Legion*. New York, Basic Books.

Leighton, A. H. 1971. *Come Near*. New York, Norton.

Lowenthal, M. E. and Haven, C. 1968. Interaction and adaptation: intimacy as a critical variable. *American Sociology Review* 33:20–30.

MacLeod, G. K. and Pressin, J. A. 1973. The continuing evolution of health maintenance organizations. *New England Journal of Medicine* 228:439–443.

Mather, H. G. 1974. Intensive care. *British Medical Journal* 2:322.

Mather, H. G. et al. 1971. Acute myocardial infarction: home and hospital treatment. *British Medical Journal* 3:334–338.

Menninger, W. C. 1947. Psychiatric experience in the war 1941–1946. *American Journal of Psychiatry* 103:587–593.

Moos, R. M. and Insel, P. M. 1974. *Issues in Social Ecology*. Palo Alto, National Press Books.

Morris, N. M., Udry, J. R., and Chase, C. L. 1973. Reduction of low birth weight rates by prevention of unwanted pregnancies. *American Journal of Public Health* 63:935–938.

Murray, H. A. et al. 1938. *Explorations in Personality*. New York, Oxford.

Nuckolls, K. B., Cassel, J., and Kaplan, B. H. 1972. Psychosocial assets, life crisis and the prognosis of pregnancy. *American Journal of Epidemiology* 95:431–441.

Parkes, C. M. 1972. *Bereavement: Studies of Grief in Adult Life*. New York, International Universities Press.

Parsons, T. 1958. Definition of health and illness in the light of American values and social structure, in patients. *Physicians and Illness* (edited by E. G. Jaco). Glencoe, Free Press.

Peabody, F. W. 1927. The care of the patient. *Journal of the American Medical Association* 88:877–882.

Phillips, D. P. and Feldman, K. A. 1973. A dip in deaths before ceremonial occasions: some new relationships between social integration and mortality. *American Sociology Review* 38:678–696.

Pinneau, S. R. 1975. Effects of social support on psychological and physiological strains. Dissertation, University of Michigan.

Quinn, R. P. 1973. Personal communication.

Reid, D. D. 1947. Some measures of the effect of operational stress on bomber crews, in *Great Britain Air Ministry, Psychological Disorders in Flying Personnel of the R.A.F.* London, His Majesty's Stationery Office.

Rose, A. M. 1956. Factors in mental breakdown in combat, in *Mental Health and Mental Disorder—A*

Sociological Approach (edited by A. M. Rose). London, Routledge and Kegan Paul.

Smith, S. 1874. On the limitations and modifying conditions of human longevity, the basis of sanitary work, in *Public Health Reports and Papers* (presented at the meetings of the American Public Health Association in the year 1873). New York. Riverside.

Stein, Z. and Susser, M. 1967. Social factors in the development of sphincter control. *Developmental Medical Child Neurology* 9:692–706.

Swank, R. L. 1949. Combat exhaustion: a descriptive and statistical analysis of causes, symptoms and signs. *Journal of Nervous Mental Disorders* 109:475–508.

Weiss, R. S. 1969. The fund of sociability. *Transactions* 6:36–43.

PART 7

INTERACTION

The building blocks of society are groups. Groups, in turn, are structured around sets of **statuses**. Although in everyday English the word *status* can be equivalent to *prestige*, sociologists prefer to think of a status as meaning a *social position* within a group. For example, a family group may contain two or more of the following statuses: husband, wife, mother, father, son, daughter, brother, sister, grandfather, grandmother, aunt, uncle, and cousin (to name some, but not all, of the possibilities). Associated with each status is at least one social **role**. A role is the active manifestation of the status; it involves expectations as to how the person holding a particular status should behave, what sorts of activities he or she will engage in. For example, one of my key statuses, *professor*, involves the roles of lecturer, advisor, college committee member, and researcher.

If I know some of your statuses, I can tell you much about your day-to-day interactions with other people. For example, as a college student, you probably treat your professors with a fair amount of deference or respect: When the professor begins class, you usually quickly quiet down if you've been talking with a classmate; when you want to ask a question, you often raise your hand and wait to be called upon; when you address your professor, you likely use his or her last name, prefaced with a title (e.g., "Dr. Zicker," "Professor Anderson," "Mr. Flores," "Mrs. Trimble"). In short, belonging to particular groups, holding particular statuses within these groups, and playing particular roles associated with these statuses induces us to interact with other people in particular ways.

However, our interactions are far from fully determined by the particular statuses and roles involved. For example, some professors enact the role of lecturer with verve and excitement, while others put everyone in the room asleep (figuratively for most, literally for a few!). Occasionally, a particular interaction we've undergone many times *emerges* into something quite unexpected. For example, let's say you ask your biology instructor, Dr. Morookian, questions in class from time to time. You are used to raising your hand, having him smile and acknowledge you, and asking your question. You're also used to him making a quick reply, often incorporating it into his lecture. But then, one beastly-ghastly day, you have a question and raise your hand; just as the word "what" is about to roll off your tongue, you uncouthly—even if unintentionally—erupt with a loud belch, and "what" comes out as "wHAAAAt!" The other students laugh, and Dr. Morookian turns beet red in sort of a sympathetic response to your self-inflicted embarrassment. Egad! You forget what you were going to say!

Analytically, we can separate out scores of factors that can determine the nature and outcome of any particular social interaction. Many of these factors are elucidated in Part 7; I will discuss just six of them here.

Stanley Milgram (1933–1984) illustrates the first the situation: the *context of the interaction*, and the norms and behavioral expectations associated with it. For example, your instructor might not ask you a personal question in class; however, later while the two of you are walking together across campus, she may ask you something personal ("Joe, are your parents divorced?"). In Milgram's classic study of obedience, ordinary citizens become torturers because they find themselves in a situation in which they had never before found themselves. ("Torturer? How could that be?" Go read his selection.) The Carnegie Mellon University study of the Internet (Robert Kraut *et al.*) also shows the power of social context in determining the nature of interaction and its consequences. More specifically, it reveals that the context of sitting in front of a computer screen instead of in the actual presence of someone (or communicating via the telephone) constrains the quality of the interaction, thereby increasing the odds of feeling lonely and depressed. For example, Kraut *et al.* observe that "on-line friends are less likely than friends developed at school, work, church, or in the neighborhood to be available for help with tangible favors, such as offering small loans, rides, or baby-sitting. Because on-line friends are not embedded in the same day-to-day environment, they will be less like to understand the context for conversation, making discussion more difficult and rending support less applicable."

Pamela Fishman, formerly of the University of California at Santa Barbara, describes a second factor: the *power differences between or among the interactants.* In this case, she demonstrates that when men and women interact, the nitty-gritty "work" of keeping the interaction running smoothly falls largely on the latter. She shows how women go about this work, and she argues that the inequality in this area of life reflects women's overall inequality in society: Women not only tend to get the short end of the stick in the work world but in simple conversations, too.

A third determinative factor is illustrated in the selection by Harry T. Reiss (University of Rochester in New York), John B. Nezlek (College of William and Mary in Williamsburg, Virginia), and Ladd Wheeler (University of New South Wales in Sydney, Australia). Their data supports the notion that attractive men tend to receive more positive feedback in their encounters with women, and this, in turn, makes them more confident and better able to negotiate dates. In short, as individuals begin to interact regularly, a process of *bargaining, exchanging,* and *negotiating* images or identities of each other and of rights and duties in the relationship develops. For example, a woman raised with conventional morality may begin having sexual intercourse with her boyfriend (something he really wants) if he agrees to view her as a good and moral woman, one who is only allowing premarital sex to occur because she's in love. The bargaining, exchanging, and negotiating may take only the first half of an evening or it may take years (depending, of course, on many other factors, some of which are discussed below, e.g., the long-term goals of the interactants). In sustained interactions and in the development of a relationship, the norm of *reciprocity* (I do something for you, you repay the favor; you do something for me, I repay the favor) always comes into play.

A fourth determinant of the nature of a particular interaction is the *goals* of the interactants. For example, two young men enter a CD-tape store to buy the latest Madonna album. One is married and happy and faithful. The other is single and looking for love. They both notice that the attractive young saleswoman isn't wearing a wedding ring. Which of the two men do you think will have the simple goal of buying the album and going home as quickly as possible? Which do you think will linger at the cash register, make small talk, and perhaps try to "get something going" with the young woman?

The preceding scenario at the CD-tape store illustrates a fifth determinant of interaction, the *status cues* invoked by the interactants. Status cues are anything that alerts us to the particular statuses someone holds—clothing, jewelry, job title, style of speech, mannerisms, skin color (see the discussion of Joe R. Feagin's research in Part 1!), and so on. The free and single young man in our example would be much less likely to linger if the young saleswoman were wearing a wedding band. Erving Goffman's (1922–1982) classic studies have repeatedly demonstrated how status cues are part of the information we use when entering the presence of others to help us know how to act.[1]

Goffman's research also highlights a sixth determinant of interaction, the *credibility of the identity each interactant is trying to establish*. We manage information about ourselves to shape how we want others to view us and act toward us. To wit, one would rather show an attractive photo of oneself than an ugly photo; one would rather share the fact that one received an A on an exam than a D; one would rather play a song one knew well on the guitar at a party than a song one was just in the process of learning. Other people will tend to accept the identity a person is trying to establish if other information confirms it. If so, the interaction may proceed smoothly; if not, the interaction may get rough, perhaps terminating prematurely in embarrassment. For example, I may want others to treat me as a cool cookie, but if in the heat of a fast-moving conversation I begin to stammer and blush, the gap between the impression I would like to give and the one I am actually giving off may be so great that others begin not wanting to deal with me, indeed to avoid me.

---

[1]See, for example, his *The Presentation of Self in Everyday Life* (New York: Doubleday, 1959).

CHAPTER 17

OBEDIENCE TO AUTHORITY

STANLEY MILGRAM

Obedience is as basic an element in the structure of social life as one can point to. Some system of authority is a requirement of all communal living, and it is only the man dwelling in isolation who is not forced to respond, through defiance or submission, to the commands of others. Obedience, as a determinant of behavior, is of particular relevance to our time. It has been reliably established that from 1933–1945 millions of innocent persons were systematically slaughtered on command. Gas chambers were built, death camps were guarded, daily quotas of corpses were produced with the same efficiency as the manufacture of appliances. These inhumane policies may have originated in the mind of a single person, but they could only be carried out on a massive scale if a very large number obeyed orders.

Obedience is the psychological mechanism that links individual action to political purpose. It is the dispositional cement that binds men to systems of authority. Facts of recent history and observation in daily life suggest that for many persons obedience may be a deeply ingrained behavior tendency, indeed, a prepotent impulse overriding training in ethics, sympathy, and moral conduct. C. P. Snow (1961) points to its importance when he writes:

> When you think of the long and gloomy history of man,
> you will find more hideous crimes have been commit-

ted in the name of obedience than have ever been committed in the name of rebellion. If you doubt that, read William Shirer's Rise and Fall of the Third Reich. The German Officer Corps were brought up in the most rigorous code of obedience . . . in the name of obedience they were party to, and assisted in, the most wicked large scale actions in the history of the world [p. 24].

While the particular form of obedience dealt with in the present study has its antecedents in these episodes, it must not be thought all obedience entails acts of aggression against others. Obedience serves numerous productive functions. Indeed, the very life of society is predicted on its existence. Obedience may be ennobling and educative and refer to acts of charity and kindness, as well as to destruction.

GENERAL PROCEDURE

A procedure was devised which seems useful as a tool for studying obedience (Milgram, 1961). It consists of ordering a naive subject to administer electric shock to a victim. A stimulated shock generator is used, with 30 clearly marked voltage levels that range from 15 to 450 volts. The instrument bears [written] designations that range from Slight Shock to Danger: Severe Shock. The responses of the victim, who is a trained confederate of the experimenter, are standardized. The orders to administer shocks are given to the naive subject in the context of a "learning experiment" ostensibly set up to study the effects of punishment on memory. As the experiment proceeds the naive subject is commanded to administer increasingly more intense shocks to the victim, even to the

From "Behavioral Study of Obedience," *Journal of Abnormal and Social Psychology,* 1963, 67(4), pp. 371–378. Copyright © 1963 by the American Psychological Association. Copyright renewed 1991 by Alexandra Milgram. Reprinted by permission. Footnotes have been incorporated as endnotes or deleted.

point reaching the level marked Danger: Severe Shock. Internal resistances become stronger, and at a certain point the subject refuses to go on with the experiment. Behavior prior to this rupture is considered "obedience," in that the subject complies with the commands of the experimenter. The point of rupture is the act of disobedience. A quantitative value is assigned to the subject's performance based on the maximum intensity shock he is willing to administer before he refuses to participate further. Thus for any particular subject and for any particular experimental condition the degree of obedience may be specified with a numerical value. The crux of the study is to systematically vary the degree of obedience to the experimental commands.

The technique allows important variables to be manipulated at several points in the experiment. One may vary aspects of the source of command, content and form of command, instrumentalities for its execution, target object, general social setting, etc. The problem, therefore, is not one of designing increasingly more numerous experimental conditions, but selecting those that best illuminate the *process* of obedience from the sociopsychological standpoint.

RELATED STUDIES

The inquiry bears an important relation to philosophic analyses of obedience and authority (Arendt, 1958; Friedrich, 1958; Weber, 1947), an early experimental study of obedience by Frank (1944), studies in "authoritarianism" (Adorno, Frenkel-Brunswick, Levinson, & Sanford, 1950; Rokeach, 1961), and a recent series of analytic and empirical studies in social power (Cartwright, 1959). It owes much to the long concern with *suggestion* in social psychology, both in its normal forms (e.g., Binet, 1900) and in its clinical manifestations (Charcot, 1881). But it derives, in the first instance, from direct observation of a social fact; the individual who is commanded by a legitimate authority ordinarily obeys. Obedience comes easily and often. It is a ubiquitous and indispensable feature of social life.

METHOD

Subjects

The subjects were 40 males between the ages of 20 and 50, drawn from New Haven and the surrounding communities. Subjects were obtained by a newspaper advertisement and direct mail solicitation. Those who responded to the appeal believed they were to participate in a study of memory and learning at Yale University. A wide range of occupations is represented in the sample. Typical subjects were postal clerks, high school teachers, salesmen, engineers, and laborers. Subjects ranged in educational level from one who had not finished high school, to those who had doctorate and other professional degrees. They were paid $4.50 [equivalent to about $50 in 1993] for their participation in the experiment. However, subjects were told that payment was simply for coming to the laboratory, and that the money was theirs no matter what happened after they arrived. Table 17.1 shows the proportion of age and occupational types assigned to the experimental condition.

Personnel and Locale

The experiment was conducted on the grounds of Yale University in the elegant interaction laboratory. (This detail is relevant to the perceived legitimacy of the experiment. In further variations, the experiment was dissociated from the university, with consequences for performance.) The role of experimenter was played by a 31-year-old high school teacher of biology. His manner was impassive, and his appearance somewhat stern throughout the experiment. He was dressed in a gray technician's coat. The victim was played by a 47-year-old accountant, trained for the role; he was of Irish-American stock, whom most observers found mild-mannered and likable.

Procedure

One naive subject and one victim (an accomplice) performed in each experiment. A pretext had to be devised that would justify the administration of elec-

TABLE 17.1 Distribution of Age and Occupational Types in the Experiment

OCCUPATIONS	NUMBER 20–29 YEARS	NUMBER 30–39 YEARS	NUMBER 40–50 YEARS	PERCENTAGE OF TOTAL (OCCUPATIONS)
Workers, skilled and unskilled	4	5	6	37.5
Sales, business and white-collar	3	6	7	40.0
Professional	1	5	3	22.5
Percentage of total (age)	20	40	40	

Note: Total *N* = 40.

tric shock by the naive subject. This was effectively accomplished by the cover story. After a general introduction on the presumed relation between punishment and learning, subjects were told:

> But actually, we know very little *about the effect of punishment on learning, because almost no truly scientific studies have been made of it in human beings.*
>
> *For instance, we don't know how* much *punishment is best for learning—and we don't know how much difference it makes as to who is giving the punishment, whether an adult learns best from a younger or older person than himself—or many things of that sort.*
>
> *So in this study we are bringing together a number of adults of different occupations and ages. And we're asking them to be teachers and some of them to be learners.*
>
> *We want to find out just what effect different people have on each other as teachers and learners, and also what effect* punishment *will have on learning in this situation.*
>
> *Therefore, I'm going to ask one of you to be the teacher here tonight and the other to be the learner.*
>
> *Does either of you have a preference?*

Subjects then drew slips of paper from a hat to determine who would be the teacher and who would be the learner in the experiment. The drawing was rigged so that the naive subject was always the teacher and the accomplice always the learner. (Both slips contained the word "Teacher.") Immediately after the drawing, the teacher and the learner were taken to an adjacent room and the learner was strapped into an "electric chair" apparatus.

The experimenter explained that the straps were to prevent excessive movement while the learner was being shocked. The effect was to make it impossible for him to escape from the situation. An electrode was attached to the learner's wrist, and electrode paste was applied "to avoid blisters and burns." Subjects were told that the electrode was attached to the shock generator in the adjoining room.

In order to improve credibility the experimenter declared, in response to a question by the learner: "Although the shocks can be extremely painful, they cause no permanent tissue damage."

Learning Task. The lesson administered by the subject was a pair-associate learning task. The subject read series of word pairs to the learner, and then read the first word of the pair along with four terms. The learner was to indicate which of the four terms had originally been paired with the first word. He communicated his answer by pressing one of the four switches in front of him, which in turn lit up one of the four numbered quadrants in an answer box located atop the shock generator.

Shock Generator. The instrument panel consists of 30 lever switches set in a horizontal line. Each switch is clearly labeled with a voltage designation that ranges from 15 to 450 volts. There is a 15-volt increment from one switch to the next going from left to right: Slight Shock, Moderate Shock, Strong Shock, Very Strong Shock, Intense Shock, Extreme Intensity Shock, Danger: Severe Shock. (Two switches after this designation are simply marked XXX.)

Upon depressing a switch: a pilot light corresponding to each switch is illuminated in bright red; an electric buzzing is heard; an electric blue light, labeled "voltage energizer," flashes; the dial on the voltage meter swings to the right; various relay clicks are sounded.

The upper left-hand corner of the generator is labeled Shock Generator, Type ZLB, Dyson Instrument Company, Waltham, Mass. Output 15 Volts–450 Volts.

Details of the instrument were carefully handled to insure an appearance of authenticity. The panel was engraved by precision industrial engravers, and all components were of high quality. No subject in the experiment suspected that the instrument was merely a simulated shock generator.

Sample Shock. Each naive subject is given a sample shock on the shock generator, prior to beginning his run as teacher. This shock is always 45 volts, and is applied by pressing the third switch of the generator. The shock is applied to the wrist of the naive subject, and has its source in a 45-volt battery wired into the generator. This further convinces the subject of the authenticity of the generator.

Shock Instructions. The subject is told to administer a shock to the learner each time he gives a wrong response. Moreover, and this is the key command, the subject is instructed to "move one level higher on the shock generator each time the learner flashes a wrong answer." He is also instructed to announce the voltage level before administering a shock. This serves to continually remind subjects of the increasing intensity of shocks administered to the learner.

Preliminary and Regular Run. Pretests revealed that the procedure of reading words and administering shocks requires some practice before it can be handled smoothly. Therefore, immediately preceding the regular run, the teacher is given a preliminary series of 10 words to read to the learner. There are 3 neutral words in the practice series (i.e., words that the learner answers correctly), so that shocks are admin-

istered for 7 of the words, with the maximum shock at 105 volts (moderate shock). Almost all subjects master the procedure by the time the preliminary run is over.

Subjects are then presented with a second list, and are told that the procedure is the same as for the first list; the experimenter adds, however:

When you get to the bottom of the list, repeat it over again, and continue giving shocks, until the learner has learned all the pairs correctly.

The experimenter instructs the subject to,

start from 15 volts and increase the shock level one step each time the learner gives a wrong answer.

Feedback from the Victim. In all conditions the learner gives a predetermined set of responses to the word pair test, based on a schedule of approximately three wrong answers to one correct answer. In the present experimental condition no vocal response or other sign of protest is heard from the learner until Shock Level 300 is reached. When the 300-volt shock is administered, the learner pounds on the wall of the room in which he is bound to the electric chair. The pounding can be heard by the subject. From this point on, the learner's answers no longer appear on the four-way panel.

At this juncture, subjects ordinarily turn to the experimenter for guidance. The experimenter instructs the subject to treat the absence of a response as a wrong answer, and to shock the subject according to the usual schedule. He advises the subjects to allow 5–10 seconds before considering no response as a wrong answer, and to increase the shock level one step each time the learner fails to respond correctly. The learner's pounding is repeated after the 315-volt shock is administered; afterwards he is not heard from, nor do his answers reappear on the four-way signal box.

Experimenter Feedback. At various points in the experiment the subject may turn to the experimenter for advice on whether he should continue to administer shocks. Or he may indicate that he does not wish to go on. It was important to standardize the experimenter's responses to these inquiries and reactions.

If the subject indicated his unwillingness to go on, the experimenter responded with a sequence of "prods," using as many as necessary to bring the subject into line.

> Prod 1: *Please continue.* or *Please go on.*
> Prod 2: *The experiment requires that you continue.*
> Prod 3: *It is absolutely essential that you continue.*
> Prod 4: *You have no other choice, you must go on.*

The prods were always made in sequence: Only if Prod 1 had been unsuccessful, could Prod 2 be used. If the subject refused to obey the experimenter after Prod 4, the experiment was terminated. The experimenter's tone of voice was at all times firm, but not impolite. The sequence was begun anew on each occasion that the subject balked or showed reluctance to follow orders.

Special Prods.   If the subject asked if the learner was liable to suffer permanent physical injury, the experimenter said:

> *Although the shocks may be painful, there is no permanent tissue damage, so please go on. [Followed by Prods 2, 3, and 4 if necessary.]*

If the subject asked if the learner did not want to go on, the experimenter replied:

> *Whether the learner likes it or not, you must go on until he has learned all the word pairs correctly. So please go on. [Followed by Prods 2, 3, and 4 if necessary.]*

Dependent Measures

The primary dependent measure for any subject is the maximum shock he administers before he refuses to go any further. In principle this may vary from 0 (for a subject who refuses to administer even the first shock) to 30 (for a subject who administers the highest shock on the generator). A subject who breaks off the experiment at any point prior to administering the thirtieth shock level is termed a *defiant* subject. One who complies with experimental commands

fully, and proceeds to administer all shock levels commanded, is termed an *obedient* subject.

Further Records.   With few exceptions, experimental sessions were recorded on magnetic tape. Occasional photographs were taken through one-way mirrors. Notes were kept on any unusual behavior occurring during the course of the experiments. On occasion, additional observers were directed to write objective descriptions of the subjects' behavior. The latency and duration of shocks were measured by accurate timing devices.

Interview and Dehoax.   Following the experiment, subjects were interviewed; open-ended questions, projective measures, and attitude scales were employed. After the interview, procedures were undertaken to assure that the subject would leave the laboratory in a state of well being. A friendly reconciliation was arranged between the subject and the victim, and an effort was made to reduce any tensions that arose as a result of the experiment.

RESULTS

Preliminary Notions

Before giving an account of the experimental results, it is instructive to consider how persons predict others will perform when commanded to administer powerful shocks to another person. Fourteen Yale seniors, all psychology majors, were provided with a detailed description of the experimental situation. They were asked to reflect carefully on it, and to predict the behavior of 100 hypothetical subjects. More specifically, they were instructed to plot the distribution of obedience of "100 Americans of diverse occupations, and ranging in age from 20 to 50 years," who were placed in the experimental situation.

There was considerable agreement among the respondents on the expected behavior of hypothetical subjects. All respondents predicted that only an insignificant minority would go through to the end of the shock series. (The estimates ranged from 0 to 3%;

i.e., the most "pessimistic" member of the class predicted that of 100 persons, 3 would continue to the most potent shock available on the shock generator—450 volts.) The class mean was 1.2%. The question was also posed informally to colleagues of the author, and the most general feeling was that few if any subjects would go beyond the designation Very Strong Shock.[1]

Results of Experiment I

Subjects Accept Situation.   With few exceptions subjects were convinced of the reality of the experimental situation, that they were administering shocks to another person, and the most potent shocks were extremely painful. In the post-experimental interview subjects were asked: "How painful to the learner were the last few shocks that you administered to him?" Subjects were instructed to indicate their answers on a printed 14-point scale ranging from "Not at all painful" to "Extremely painful." The modal response was 14 (Extremely painful) with the mean at 13.42.

Signs of Extreme Tension.   Many subjects showed signs of nervousness in the experimental situation, and especially upon administering the more powerful shocks. In a large number of cases the degree of tension reached extremes that are rarely seen in sociopsychological laboratory studies. Subjects were observed to sweat, tremble, stutter, bite their lips, groan, and dig their fingernails into their flesh. These were characteristic rather than exceptional responses to the experiment.

One sign of tension was the regular occurrence of nervous laughing fits. Fourteen of the 40 subjects showed definite signs of nervous laughter and smiling. The laughter seemed entirely out of place, even bizarre. Full-blown, uncontrollable seizures were observed for 3 subjects. On one occasion we observed a seizure so violently convulsive that it was necessary to call a halt to the experiment. The subject, a 46-year-old encyclopedia salesman, was seriously embarrassed by his untoward and uncontrollable behavior. In the post-experimental interviews subjects took pains to point out that the laughter did not mean they enjoyed shocking the victim.

Distribution of Scores.   It had been conjectured that persons would not, in general, agree to administer shocks beyond the level designated as Very Strong Shock. The distribution of maximum shocks for this experiment is shown in Table 17.2. The obtained distribution of scores deviated radically from the prediction.

Upon command of the experimenter, each of the 40 subjects went beyond the expected breakoff point. No subject stopped prior to administering Shock Level 20. (At this level—300 volts—the victim kicks on the wall and no longer provides answers to the teacher's multiple-choice questions.)

Of the 40 subjects, 5 refused to obey the experimental commands beyond the 300-volt level. Four more subjects administered one further shock, and then refused to go on. Two broke off at the 330-volt level, and 1 each at 345, 360, and 375 volts. Thus a total of 14 subjects defied the experimenter. It is instructive to reprint their remarks at the point of defiance, as transcribed from the tape recordings:

> *[0124] I think he's trying to communicate, he's knocking . . . Well it's not fair to shock the guy . . . these are terrific volts. I don't think this is very humane. . . . Oh, I can't go on with this; no, this isn't right. It's a hell of an experiment. The guy is suffering in there. No, I don't want to go on. This is crazy. [Subject refused to administer more shocks.]*
>
> *[0123] He's banging in there. I'm gonna chicken out. I'd like to continue, but I can't do that to a man. . . . I'm sorry I can't do that to a man. I'll hurt his heart. You take your check . . . No really, I couldn't do it.*

These subjects were frequently in a highly agitated and even angered state. Sometimes, verbal protest was at a minimum, and the subject simply got up from his chair in front of the shock generator, and indicated that he wished to leave the laboratory.

Of the 40 subjects, 26 obeyed the orders of the experimenter to the end, proceeding to punish the victim until they reached the most potent shock available

TABLE 17.2 Distribution of Breakoff Points

VERBAL DESIGNATION AND VOLTAGE INDICATION	NUMBER OF SUBJECTS FOR WHOM THIS WAS MAXIMUM SHOCK
Slight shock	
15	0
30	0
45	0
60	0
Moderate shock	
75	0
90	0
105	0
120	0
Strong shock	
135	0
150	0
165	0
180	0
Very strong shock	
195	0
210	0
225	0
240	0
Intense shock	
255	0
270	0
285	0
300	5
Extreme intensity shock	
315	4
330	2
345	1
360	1
Danger: severe shock	
375	1
390	0
405	0
420	0
XXX	
435	0
450	26

on the shock generator. At that point, the experimenter called a halt to the session. (The maximum shock is labeled 450 volts, and is two steps beyond the designation: Danger: Severe Shock.) Although obedient subjects continued to administer shocks, they often did so under extreme stress. Some expressed reluctance to administer shocks beyond the 300-volt level, and displayed fears similar to those who defied the experimenter; yet they obeyed.

After the maximum shocks had been delivered, and the experimenter called a halt to the proceedings, many obedient subjects heaved sighs of relief, mopped their brows, rubbed their fingers over their eyes, or nervously fumbled cigarettes. Some shook their heads, apparently in regret. Some subjects had remained calm throughout the experiment, and displayed only minimal signs of tension from beginning to end.

DISCUSSION

The experiment yielded two findings that were surprising. The first finding concerns the sheer strength of obedient tendencies manifested in this situation. Subjects have learned from childhood that it is a fundamental breach of moral conduct to hurt another person against his will. Yet, 26 subjects abandon this tenet in following the instructions of an authority who has no special powers to enforce his commands. To disobey would bring no material loss to the subject; no punishment would ensue. It is clear from the remarks and outward behavior of many participants that in punishing the victim they are often acting against their own values. Subjects often expressed deep disapproval of shocking a man in the face of his objections, and others denounced it as stupid and senseless. Yet the majority complied with the experimental commands. This outcome was surprising from two perspectives: first, from the standpoint of predictions made in the questionnaire described earlier. (Here, however, it is possible that the remoteness of the respondents from the actual situation, and the difficulty of conveying to them the concrete details of the experiment, could account for the serious underestimation of obedience.)

But the results were also unexpected to persons who observed the experiment in progress, through one-way mirrors. Observers often uttered expressions of disbelief upon seeing a subject administer more powerful shocks to the victim. These persons had a full acquaintance with the details of the situation, and yet systematically underestimated the amount of obedience that subjects would display.

The second unanticipated effect was the extraordinary tension generated by the procedures. One might suppose that a subject would simply break off or continue as his conscience dictated. Yet, this is very far from what happened. There were striking reactions of tension and emotional strain. One observer related:

> *I observed a mature and initially poised businessman enter the laboratory smiling and confident. Within 20 minutes he was reduced to a twitching, stuttering wreck, who was rapidly approaching a point of nervous collapse. He constantly pulled on his earlobe, and twisted his hands. At one point he pushed his fist into his forehead and muttered: "Oh God, let's stop it." And yet he continued to respond to every word of the experimenter, and obeyed to the end.*

Any understanding of the phenomenon of obedience must rest on an analysis of the particular conditions in which it occurs. The following features of the experiment go some distance in explaining the high amount of obedience observed in the situation.

1. The experiment is sponsored by and takes place on the grounds of an institution of unimpeachable reputation, Yale University. It may be reasonably presumed that the personnel are competent and reputable. The importance of this background authority is now being studied by conducting a series of experiments outside for New Haven, and without any visible ties to the university.

2. The experiment is, on the face of it, designed to attain a worthy purpose—advancement of knowledge about learning and memory. Obedience occurs not as an end in itself, but as an instrumental element in a situation that the subject construes as significant, and meaningful. He may not be able to see its full significance, but

he may properly assume that the experimenter does.

3. The subject perceives that the victim has voluntarily submitted to the authority system for the experimenter. He is not (at first) an unwilling captive impressed for involuntary service. He has taken the trouble to come to the laboratory presumably to aid the experimental research. That he later becomes an involuntary subject does not alter the fact that, initially, he consented to participate without qualification. Thus he has in some degree incurred an obligation toward the experimenter.

4. The subject, too, has entered the experiment voluntarily, and perceives himself under obligation to aid the experimenter. He has made a commitment, and to disrupt the experiment is a repudiation of this initial promise of aid.

5. Certain features of the procedure strengthen the subject's sense of obligation to the experimenter. For one, he has been paid for coming to the laboratory. In part this is canceled out by the experimenter's statement that:

    Of course, as in all experiments, the money is yours simply for coming to the laboratory. From this point on, no matter what happens, the money is yours.[2]

6. From the subject's standpoint, the fact that he is the teacher and the other man the learner is purely a chance consequence (it is determined by drawing lots) and he, the subject, ran the same risk as the other man in being assigned the role of learner. Since the assignments of positions in the experiment was achieved by fair means, the learner is deprived of any basis of complaint on this count. (A similar situation obtains in Army units, in which—in the absence of volunteers—a particularly dangerous mission may be assigned by drawing lots, and the unlucky soldier is expected to bear his misfortune with sportsmanship.)

7. There is, at best, ambiguity with regard to the prerogatives of a psychologist and the corresponding rights of his subject. There is a vagueness of expectation concerning what a psychologist may require of his subject, and when he is overstepping acceptable limits. Moreover, the experiment occurs in a closed setting, and thus provides no opportunity for the subject to remove these ambiguities by discussion with others. There are few standards that seem directly applicable to the situation, which is a novel one for most subjects.

8. The subjects are assured that the shocks administered to the subject are "painful but not dangerous." Thus they assume that the discomfort caused the victim is momentary, while the scientific gains resulting from the experiment are enduring.

9. Through Shock Level 20 the victim continues to provide answers on the signal box. The subject may construe this as a sign that the victim is still willing to "play the game." It is only after Shock Level 20 that the victim repudiates the rules completely, refusing to answer further.

These features help to explain the high amount of obedience obtained in this experiment. Many of the arguments raised need not remain matters of speculation, but can be reduced to testable propositions to be confirmed or disproved by further experiments.[3] . . .

POSTSCRIPT[4]

[Eventually,] almost a thousand adults were individually studied in this obedience research, and there were many specific conclusions regarding the variables that control obedience and disobedience to authority. Some of these have been discussed briefly in the preceding sections, and more detailed reports will be released subsequently.

There are now some other generalizations I should like to make, which do not derive in any strictly logical fashion from the [experiment] as carried out, but which, I feel, ought to be made. They are formulations of an intuitive sort that have been forced on me by observation of many subjects responding to the pressures of authority. The assertions represent a painful alteration in my own thinking; and since they were acquired only under the repeated impact of direct observation, I have no illusion that they will be generally accepted by persons who have not had the same experience.

With numbing regularity good people were seen to knuckle under the demands of authority and perform actions that were callous and severe. Men who are in everyday life responsible and decent were seduced by the trappings of authority, by the control of their perceptions, and by the uncritical acceptance of the experimenter's definition of the situation, into performing harsh acts.

What is the limit of such obedience? At many points we attempted to establish a boundary. Cries from the victim were inserted; not good enough. The victim claimed heart trouble; subjects still shocked him on command. The victim pleaded that he be let free, and his answers no longer registered on the signal box; subjects continued to shock him. At the outset we had not conceived that such drastic procedures would be needed to generate disobedience, and each step was added only as the ineffectiveness of the earlier techniques became clear. . . .

The results, as seen and felt in the laboratory, are to this author disturbing. They raise the possibility that human nature, or—more specifically—the kind of character produced in American democratic society, cannot be counted on to insulate its citizens from brutality and inhumane treatment at the direction of malevolent authority. A substantial proportion of peo-

ple do what they are told to do, irrespective of the content of the act and without limitations of conscience, so long as they perceive that the command comes from a legitimate authority. If in this study an anonymous experimenter could successfully command adults to subdue a fifty-year-old man, and force on him painful electric shocks against his protests, one can only wonder what government, with its vastly greater authority and prestige, can command of its subjects. There is, of course, the extremely important question of whether malevolent political institutions could or would arise in American society. The present research contributes nothing to this issue. In an article titled "The Dangers of Obedience," Harold J. Laski [1929] wrote:

> . . . civilization means, above all, an unwillingness to inflict unnecessary pain. Within the [sphere] of that definition, those of us who heedlessly accept the commands of authority cannot yet claim to be civilized. . . .
>
> Our business, if we desire to live a life not utterly devoid of meaning and significance, is to accept nothing which contradicts our basic experience merely because it comes to us from tradition or convention or authority. It may well be that we shall be wrong; but our self-expression is thwarted at the root unless the certainties we are asked to accept coincide with the certainties we experience. That is why the condition of freedom in any state is always a widespread and consistent skepticism of the canons upon which power insists.

NOTES

1. Milgram later conducted a more systematic study, asking forty psychiatrists at a leading medical school to make the same prediction; like the fourteen Yale seniors, the psychiatrists also predicted that few, if any, of the subjects would give the maximum shock. See "Some Conditions of Obedience and Disobedience to Authority," *Human Relations,* 18(1) (February 1965).

2. Forty-three subjects, undergraduates at Yale University, were run in the experiment without payment. The results are very similar to those obtained with paid subjects.

3. See "Some Conditions of Obedience and Disobedience to Authority."

4. From "Some Conditions of Obedience and Disobedience to Authority." Reprinted by permission of Alexandra Milgram. This postscript may cast some light on the inter-ethnic group carnage in the former Yugoslavian state of Bosnia-Herzegovnia in the early 1990s.

REFERENCES

Adorno, T., Frenkel-Brunswick, E. L., Levinson, D. J., & Sanford, R. N. 1950. *The authoritarian personality.* New York: Harper.

Arendt, H. What was authority? 1958. In C. J. Friedrich (Ed.). *Authority.* Cambridge: Harvard University Press. Pp. 81–112.

Binet, A. 1900. *La suggestibilité.* Paris: Schleicher.

Cartwright, S. (Ed.). 1959. *Studies in social power.* Ann Arbor: University of Michigan Institute for Social Research.

Charcot, J. M. 1881. *Oeuvres completes.* Paris: Bureaux du Progres Medical.

Frank, J. D. 1944. Experimental studies of personal pressure and resistance. *Journal of General Psychology,* 30, 23–64.

Friedrich, C. J . (Ed.). 1958. *Authority.* Cambridge: Harvard University Press.

Laski, Harold J. 1929. The dangers of obedience. *Harper's Monthly Magazine* 159, June, 1–10.

Milgram, S. *Dynamics of obedience.* 1961. Washington: National Science Foundation, 25 January. (Mimeo)

Milgram, S. 1965. Some conditions of obedience and disobedience to authority. *Human Relations,* 18:1, February.

Rokeach, M. 1961. Authority, authoritarianism, and conformity. In I. A. Berg & B. M. Bass (Eds.), *Conformity and Deviation.* New York: Harper. Pp. 230–257.

Snow, C. P. 1961. Either-or. *Progressive* (Feb) 24.

Weber, M. 1947. *The Theory of Social and Economic Organization.* Oxford: Oxford University Press.

CHAPTER 18

INTERNET PARADOX
A SOCIAL TECHNOLOGY THAT REDUCES A SOCIAL INVOLVEMENT AND PSYCHOLOGICAL WELL-BEING?

ROBERT KRAUT, MICHAEL PATTERSON, VICKI LUNDMARK, SARA KIESLER, TRIDAS MUKOPADHYAY, AND WILLIAM SCHERLIS

Fifteen years ago, computers were mainly the province of science, engineering, and business. By 1998, approximately 40% of all U.S. households owned a personal computer; roughly one third of these homes had access to the Internet. Many scholars, technologists, and social critics believe that these changes and the Internet, in particular, are transforming economic and social life (e.g., Anderson, Bikson, Law, & Mitchell, 1995; Attewell & Rule, 1984; King & Kraemer, 1995). However, analysts disagree as to the nature of these changes and whether the changes are for the better or worse. Some scholars argue that the Internet is causing people to become socially isolated and cut off from genuine social relationships, as they hunker alone over their terminals or communicate with anonymous strangers through a socially impoverished medium (e.g., Stoll, 1995; Turkle, 1996). Others argue that the Internet leads to more and better social relationships by freeing people from the constraints of geography or isolation brought on by stigma, illness, or schedule. According to them, the Internet allows people to join groups on the basis of common interests rather than convenience (e.g., Katz & Aspden, 1997; Rheingold, 1993).

Arguments based on the attributes of the technology alone do not resolve this debate. People can

use home computers and the Internet in many different ways and for many purposes, including entertainment, education, information retrieval, and communication. If people use the Internet mainly for communication with others through email, distribution lists, multiuser dungeons (MUDs), chats, and other such applications, they might do so to augment traditional technologies for social contact, expanding their number of friends and reducing the difficulty of coordinating interaction with them. On the other hand, these applications disproportionately reduce the costs of communication with geographically distant acquaintances and strangers; as a result, a smaller proportion of people's total social contacts might be with family and close friends. Other applications on the Internet, particularly the World Wide Web, provide asocial entertainment that could compete with social contact as a way for people to spend their time.

Whether the Internet is increasing or decreasing social involvement could have enormous consequences for society and for people's personal well-being. In an influential article, Putnam (1995) documented a broad decline in civic engagement and social participation in the United States over the past 35 years. Citizens vote less, go to church less, discuss government with their neighbors less, are members of fewer voluntary organizations, have fewer dinner parties, and generally get together less for civic and social purposes. Putnam argued that this social disengagement is having major consequences for the

From *American Psychologist* 53 (September 1998), pp. 1017–1031. Copyright © American Psychological Association. Reprinted by permission.

social fabric and for individual lives. At the societal level, social disengagement is associated with more corrupt, less efficient government and more crime. When citizens are involved in civic life, their schools run better, their politicians are more responsive, and their streets are safer. At the individual level, social disengagement is associated with poor quality of life and diminished physical and psychological health. When people have more social contact, they are happier and healthier, both physically and mentally (e.g., S. Cohen & Wills, 1985; Gove & Geerken, 1977).

Although changes in the labor force participation of women and marital breakup may account for some of the declines in social participation and increases in depression since the 1960s, technological change may also play a role. Television, an earlier technology similar to the Internet in some respects, may have reduced social participation as it kept people home watching the set. By contrast, other household technologies, in particular, the telephone, are used to enhance social participation, not discourage it (Fischer, 1992). The home computer and the Internet are too new and, until recently, were too thinly diffused into American households to explain social trends that originated over 35 years, but, now, they could either exacerbate or ameliorate these trends, depending on how they are used.

The goal of this article is to examine these issues and to report early empirical results of a field trial of Internet use. We show that within a diverse sample during their first year or two on-line, participants' Internet use led to their having, on balance, less social engagement and poorer psychological well-being. We discuss research that will be needed to assess the generality of the effects we have observed and to track down the mechanisms that produce them. We also discuss design and policy implications of these results, should they prove stable.

CURRENT DEBATE

Since the introduction of computing into society, scholars and technologists have pondered its possible social impact (e.g., Bell, 1973; Jacobson & Roucek,

1959; Leavitt & Whisler, 1958; Short, Williams, & Christie, 1976). With its rapid evolution, large numbers of applications, wealth of information sources, and global reach to homes, the Internet has added even more uncertainty. People could use the Internet to further privatize entertainment (as they have purportedly done with television), to obtain previously inaccessible information, to increase their technical skills, and to conduct commercial transactions at home—each are somewhat asocial functions that would make it easier for people to be alone and to be independent. Alternatively, people could use the Internet for more social purposes, to communicate and socialize with colleagues, friends, and family through electronic mail and to join social groups through distribution lists, newsgroups, and MUDs (Sproull & Faraj, 1995).

Internet for Entertainment, Information, and Commerce

If people use the Internet primarily for entertainment and information, the Internet's social effects might resemble those of television. Most research on the social impact of television has focused on its content; this research has investigated the effects of TV violence, educational content, gender stereotypes, racial stereotypes, advertising, and portrayals of family life, among other topics (Huston et al., 1992). Some social critics have argued that television reinforces sociability and social bonds (Beniger, 1987, pp. 356–362; McLuhan, 1964, p. 304). One study comparing Australian towns before and after television led to increases in social activity (Murray & Kippax, 1978). However, most empirical work has indicated that television watching reduces social involvement (Brody, 1990; Jackson-Beeck & Robinson, 1981; Maccoby, 1951; Neuman, 1991). Recent epidemiological research has linked television watching with reduced physical activity and diminished physical and mental health (Andersen, Crespo, Bartlett, Cheskin, & Pratt, 1998; Sidney et al., 1998).

If watching television does indeed lead to a decline in social participation and psychological well-being, the most plausible explanation faults time displacement. That is, the time people spend watching TV is time they are not actively socially engaged. Basing their estimates on detailed time diaries. Robinson and Godbey (1997; see also Robinson, 1990) reported that a typical American adult spends three hours each day watching TV; children's TV watching is much higher (Condry, 1993). Although a large percentage of TV watching occurs in the presence of others, the quality of social interaction among TV viewers is low. People who report they are energetic and happy when they are engaged in active social interaction also report they are bored and unhappy when they are watching TV (Kubey & Csikszentmihalyi, 1990). Lonely people report watching TV more than others (Canary & Spitzberg, 1993), and people report using TV to alleviate loneliness (Rubinstein & Shaver, 1982; Rook & Peplau, 1982). Although we cannot disentangle the direction of causation in this cross-sectional research, a plausible hypothesis is that watching TV causes both social disengagement and worsening of mood.

Like watching television, using a home computer and the Internet generally imply physical inactivity and limited face-to-face social interaction. Some studies, including our own, have indicated that using a home computer and the Internet can lead to increased skills and confidence with computers (Lundmark, Kiesler, Kraut, Scherlis, & Mukopadhyay, 1998). However, when people use these technologies intensively for learning new software, playing computer games, or retrieving electronic information, they consume time and may spend more time alone (Vitalari, Venkatesh, & Gronhaug, 1985). Some cross-sectional research suggests that home computing may be displacing television watching itself (Danko & McLachlan, 1983; Kohut, 1994) as well as reducing leisure time with the family (Vitalari et al., 1985).

Internet for Interpersonal Communication

The Internet, like its network predecessors (Sproull & Kiesler, 1991), has turned out to be far more social than television, and in this respect, the impact of the Internet may be more like that of the telephone than of TV. Our research has shown that interpersonal

communication is the dominant use of the Internet at home (Kraut, Mukopadhyay, Szczypula, Kiesler, & Scherlis, 1998). That people use the Internet mainly for interpersonal communication, however, does not imply that their social interactions and relationships on the Internet are the same as their traditional social interactions and relationships (Sproull & Kiesler, 1991), or that their social uses of the Internet will have effects comparable to traditional social activity.

Whether social uses of the Internet have positive or negative effects may depend on how the Internet shapes the balance of strong and weak network ties that people maintain. Strong ties are relationships associated with frequent contact, deep feelings of affection and obligation, and application to a broad content domain, whereas weak ties are relationships with superficial and easily broken bonds, infrequent contact, and narrow focus. Strong and weak ties alike provide people with social support. Weak ties (Granovetter, 1973), including weak on-line ties (Constant, Sproull, & Kiesler, 1996), are especially useful for linking people to information and social resources unavailable in people's closest, local groups. Nonetheless, strong social ties are the relationships that generally buffer people from life's stresses and that lead to better social and psychological outcomes (S. Cohen & Wills, 1985; Krackhardt, 1994). People receive most of their social support from people with whom they are in most frequent contact, and bigger favors come from those with stronger ties (Wellman & Wortley, 1990).

Generally, strong personal ties are supported by physical proximity. The Internet potentially reduces the importance of physical proximity in creating and maintaining networks of strong social ties. Unlike face-to-face interaction or even the telephone, the Internet offers opportunities for social interaction that do not depend on the distance between parties. People often use the Internet to keep up with those whom they have preexisting relationships (Kraut et al., 1998). But they also develop new relationships on-line. Most of these new relationships are weak. MUDs, listservs, newsgroups, and chat rooms put people in contact with a pool of new groups, but these on-line "mixers" are typically organized around specific topics, activities, or demographics and rarely revolve around local community and close family and friends.

Whether a typical relationship developed on-line becomes as strong as a typical traditional relationship and whether having on-line relationships changes the number or quality of a person's total social involvements are open questions. Empirical evidence about the impact of the Internet on relationships and social involvement is sparse. Many authors have debated whether the Internet will promote community or undercut it (e.g., Rheingold, 1993; Stoll, 1995; Turkle, 1996) and whether personal relationships that are formed on-line are impersonal or as close and substantial as those sustained through face-to-face interaction (Berry, 1993; Heim, 1992; Walther, Anderson, & Park, 1994). Much of this discussion has been speculative and anecdotal, or is based on cross-sectional data with small samples.

CURRENT DATA

Katz and Aspden's national survey (1997) is one of the few empirical studies that has compared the social participation of Internet users with nonusers. Controlling statistically for education, race, and other demographic variables, these researchers found no differences between Internet users' and nonusers' memberships in religious, leisure, and community organizations or in the amount of time users and nonusers reported spending communicating with family and friends. From these data, Katz and Aspden concluded that "[f]ar from creating a nation of strangers, the Internet is creating a nation richer in friendships and social relationships" (p. 86).

Katz and Aspden's (1997) conclusions may be premature because they used potentially inaccurate, self-report measures of Internet usage and social participation that are probably too insensitive to detect gradual changes over time. Furthermore, their observation that people have friendships on-line does not necessarily lead to the inference that using the Internet increases people's social participation or psychological well-being; to draw such a conclusion, one needs to know more about the quality of their on-line

relationships and the impact on the off-line relationships. Many studies show unequivocally that people can and do form on-line social relationships (e.g., Parks & Floyd, 1995). However, these data do not speak to the frequency, depth, and impact of on-line relationships compared with traditional ones or whether the existence of on-line relationships changes traditional relationships or the balance of people's strong and weak ties.

Even if a cross-sectional survey were to convincingly demonstrate that Internet use is associated with greater social involvement, it would not establish the causal direction of this relationship. In many cases, it is as plausible to assume that social involvement causes Internet use as the reverse. For example, many people buy a home computer to keep in touch with children in college or with retired parents. People who use the Internet differ substantially from those who do not in their demographics, skills, values, and attitudes. Statistical tests often under-control for the influence of these factors, which in turn can be associated with social involvement (Anderson et al., 1995; Kohut, 1994; Kraut, Scherlis, Mukopadhyay, Manning, & Kiesler, 1996).

A LONGITUDINAL STUDY OF INTERNET USE

The research described here uses longitudinal data to examine the causal relationship between people's use of the Internet, their social involvement, and certain likely psychological consequences of social involvement. The data come from a field trial of Internet use, in which we tracked the behavior of 169 participants over their first one or two years of Internet use. It improves on earlier research by using accurate measures of Internet use and a panel research design. Pleasures of Internet use were recorded automatically, and measures of social involvement and psychological well-being were collected twice, using reliable self-report scales. Because we tracked people over time, we can observe change and control statistically for social involvement, psychological states, and demographic attributes of the trial participants that existed prior to their use of the Internet. With these statistical controls and measures of change, we can draw stronger causal conclusions than is possible in research in which the data are collected once.

METHOD

Sample

The HomeNet study consists of a sample of 93 families from eight diverse neighborhoods in Pittsburgh, Pennsylvania. People in these families began using a computer and the Internet at home either in March 1995 or March 1996. Within these 93 families, 256 members signed consent forms, were given email accounts on the Internet, and logged on at least once. Children younger than 10 and uninterested members of the households are not included in the sample.

Each year's subsample was drawn from four school or neighborhood groups so that the participants would have some preexisting communication and information interests in common. The first year's participants consisted of families with teenagers participating in journalism classes in four area high schools. The second year's participants consisted of families in which an adult was on the Board of Directors of one of four community development organizations.

Families received a computer and software, a free telephone line, and free access to the Internet in exchange for permitting the researchers to automatically track their Internet usage and services, for answering periodic questionnaires, and for agreeing to an in-home interview. The families used Carnegie Mellon University's proprietary software for electronic mail, MacMail II, Netscape Navigator 2 or 3 for web browsing, and ClarisWorks Office. At least two family members also received a morning's training in the use of the computer, electronic mail, and the World Wide Web.

None of the groups approached about the study declined the invitation, and over 90% of the families contacted within each group agreed to participate. Because the recruitment plan excluded households or individuals with active Internet connections, the data represent people's first experiences with Internet use, and for all but a few of the households, their first experience with a powerful home computer.

Some participants left the study to attend college, because they moved, or for other reasons. Of the 256 individuals who completed the pretest questionnaire, 169 (66%) from 73 households also completed the follow-up questionnaire. Table 18.1 provides descriptive statistics on the sample that completed both a pretest and posttest questionnaire. Compared with participants who completed only the pretest questionnaire, participants who completed both were wealthier ($53,300 vs. $43,600 annual household income, $r = .20$, $p < .01$), more likely to be adults (74% vs. 55%, $r = .16$, $p < .01$), and less lonely (1.98 vs. 2.20 on a 5-point scale, $r = -.13$, $p < .05$). They did not differ on other measures.

Because estimates of communication within the family were based on reports from multiple family members, we have data for 231 individuals for this measure.

Data Collection

We measured demographic characteristics, social involvement, and psychological well-being of participants in the HomeNet trial on a pretest questionnaire, before the participants were given access to the Internet. After 12 to 24 months, participants completed a follow-up questionnaire containing the measures of social involvement and psychological well-being. During this interval, we automatically recorded their Internet usage using custom-designed logging programs. The data reported here encompass the first 104 weeks of use after a HomeNet family's Internet account was first operational for the 1995 subsample and 52 weeks of use for the 1996 subsample.

Demographic and control variables. In previous analyses of this sample, we found that the demographic factors of age, gender, and race were associated empirically with Internet usage (Kraut et al., 1998). Others have reported that household income is associated with Internet usage (Anderson et al., 1995). We used those demographic factors as control variables in our equations. Also, as a control variable that might influence participants' family communication, social network, social support, and loneliness, we

TABLE 18.1   Description of the Sample

VARIABLE	N	M	SD
Household income (dollars in thousands)	164	54.46	22.79
Race (White = 1, minority = 0)	167	0.75	0.43
Age (teen = 1, adult = 0)	169	0.28	0.45
Gender (female = 1, male = 0)	169	0.56	0.50
Social extraversion (1–5 scale)	169	3.66	0.80
Household size (individuals in household at pretest)	231	4.08	1.02
Family communication T1 (mean hours per day)	231	4.29	2.67
Family communication T3 (mean hours per day)	231	4.51	2.65
Local social network T1 (number of people)	166	23.94	17.87
Local social network T3 (number of people)	166	22.90	16.58
Distant social network T1 (number of people)	166	25.43	27.30
Distant social network T3 (number of people)	166	31.73	31.04
Social support T1 (1–5 scale, 16 items)	164	3.97	0.51
Social support T3 (1–5 scale, 16 items)	166	3.97	0.56
Loneliness T1 (1–5-point scale, 3 items)	165	1.99	0.71
Loneliness T3 (1–5-point scale, 3 items)	163	1.89	0.73
Stress T1 (mean of hassles reported of 49 items)	169	0.23	0.15
Stress T3 (mean of hassles reported of 49 items)	169	0.23	0.17
Depression T1 (0–3 scale, 15 items)	167	0.73	0.49
Depression T3 (0–3 scale, 15 items)	164	0.62	0.46
Internet usage T2 (mean hours per week)	169	2.43	4.94

Note: The units of the means and standard deviations for Internet hours and family communication are weekly hours

included a measure of social extraversion in those analyses (e.g., "I like to mix socially with people"; Bendig, 1962). A few other controls used in single analyses are described below.

Internet usage.   Software recorded the total hours in a week in which a participant connected to the Internet. Electronic mail and the World Wide Web were the major applications that participants used on the Internet and account for most of their time on-line. Internet hours also included time that participants read distribution lists such as listservs or Usenet newsgroups and participated in real-time communication using Web chat lines, MUDs, and Internet Relay Chat. For the analyses we report here, we averaged weekly Internet hours over the period in which each participant had access to the Internet, from the pretest up to the time he or she completed the follow-up questionnaire. Our analyses use the log of the variable to normalize the distribution.

Personal electronic mail use.   We recorded the number of e-mail messages participants sent and received. To better distinguish the use of the Internet for interpersonal communication rather than for information and entertainment, we excluded e-mail messages in which the participant was not explicitly named as a recipient in our count of received mail. These messages typically had been broadcast to a distribution list to which the participant had subscribed. We believe these messages reflect a mix of interpersonal communication and information distribution.

World Wide Web use.   We recorded the number of unique World Wide Web domains or sites accessed per week (a domain or site is an Internet protocol address, such as www.disney.com). Our metric for total volume of World Wide Web use is the number of different domains accessed during the week. The average number of weekly domains visited and the average number of weekly hypertext mark-up language (html) pages retrieved were very highly correlated ($r = .96$).

Social involvement and psychological well-being. Before participants gained access to the Internet and again (depending on sample) approximately 12 to 24 months later, they completed questionnaires assessing their social involvement and psychological well-being. We used four measures of social involvement: family communication, size of local social network, size of distant social network, and social support. To measure family communication, we asked participants to list all the members of their household and to estimate the number of minutes they spent each day communicating with each member. Pairs reported similar estimates ($r = .73$), and their estimates were averaged. The total amount of family communication for each participant is the sum of the minutes communicating with other family members. Extreme values (greater than 400 minutes) were truncated to 400 minutes. Because the measure was skewed, we took its log in the analyses that follow, to make the distribution more normal. Family communication is partly determined by the number of family members and is interdependent within households, so we controlled statistically for these group effects by including family as a dummy variable in the analyses involving family communication.

To measure the size of participants' local social network, we asked them to estimate the "the number of people in the Pittsburgh area . . . whom you socialize with at least once a month,." The size of their distant social network was defined as "the number of people outside of the Pittsburgh area whom you seek out to talk with or to visit at least once a year." Because both measures had some outliers, they were truncated (at 60 for the local circle and 100 for the distant circle); because they were skewed, we took their log in the analyses that follow.

Social support is a self-report measure of social resources that theoretically derive from the social network. To measure participants' levels of social support, we asked them to complete 16 items from S. Cohen, Mermelstein, Kamarck, and Hoberman's (1984) Interpersonal Support Evaluation List (Cronbach's $\alpha = .80$), which asks people to report how easy it is to get tangible help, advice, emotional support, and companionship, and how much they get a sense of belonging from people around them (e.g., "There is someone I could turn to for advice about changing my job or finding a new one").

We used three measures of psychological well-being that have been associated with social involvement: loneliness, stress, and depression. Participants completed three items (Cronbach's $\alpha = .54$) from the UCLA Loneliness Scale (Version 2), which asks people about their feelings of connection to others around them (e.g., "I can't find companionship when I want it" (Russell, Peplau, & Cutrona, 1980). To measure stress we used Kanner, Coyne, Schaefer, and Lazarus' (1981) Hassles Scale. Participants reported whether they experienced one or more of 49 possible daily life stressors in the preceding month; the stressors ranged from having one's car break down, to not liking school, to illness in the family. Because stress is often a trigger for depression, this measure was also included as a control variable in analyses involving depression. Participants completed 15 items from the Center for Epidemiologic Studies Depression (CES-D; Radloff, 1977) Scale (Cronbach's $\alpha = .86$) measuring depression in the general population. The scale asks respondents to report feelings, thoughts, symptoms, and energy levels associated with mild depression (e.g., "I felt that everything I did was an effort," "I felt I could not shake off the blues, even with help from family and friends").

Analysis

Our data analysis examined how changes in people's use of the Internet over 12 to 24 months was associated with changes in their social involvement and psychological well-being. We statistically controlled their initial levels of social involvement and psychological well-being, as well as certain demographic and control variables. Figure 18.1 describes the logic of our analysis as a path model (Bentler, 1995).

We used path analysis to test the relationships among variables measured at three time periods: pretest questionnaire at Time 1 (T1), Internet usage during Time 2 (T2), and posttest questionnaire at Time 3 (T3). The statistical associations among demographic characteristics, social involvement, and psychological well-being measured at T1 and Internet use measured at T2 provide an estimate of how much preexisting personal characteristics led people to use the Internet. The link between social involvement and psychological well-being at T1 and T3 reflects stability in involvement and well-being. Evidence that using the Internet changes social involvement and psychological well-being comes from the link between Internet use at T2 and social involvement and psychological well-being at T3. Because this analysis controls for a participant's demographic characteristics and the initial level of the outcome variables, one can interpret the coefficients associated with the link between Internet use at T2 and outcomes at T3 as the effect of Internet use on changes in social involvement and psychological well-being (J. Cohen & Cohen, 1983). By using longitudinal data, measuring Internet use over an extended period, and measuring the outcome variables at two time periods, we can

evaluate the possibility that initial social involvement or psychological well-being led to Internet use. We explicitly tested this possibility in the link between involvement and well-being at T1 and Internet use at T2; this link is controlled when we test the link between Internet use at T2 and outcome link at T3.

RESULTS

Table 18.1 presents the means and standard deviations of the demographic variables, measures of Internet use, social involvement, and psychological well-being used in this study. Table 18.2 presents a correlation matrix showing the relationships among these variables.

[Multivariable] relationships [are presented] graphically in Figures 18.2 to 18.4.

Social Involvement

Family communication.   Figure 18.2 documents a path model in which the amount of time participants communicated with other members of their households is the dependent variable. . . .
For purposes of clarity, only links with coefficients significant at the .05 level or less are included in Figure 18.2. . . .

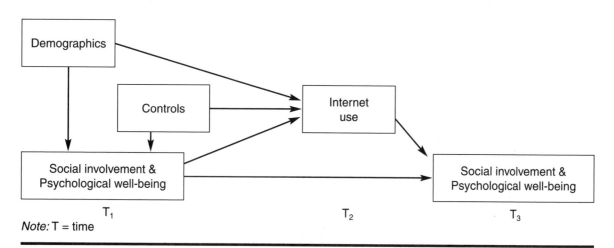

Note: T = time

FIGURE 18.1   Logic of Social Impact Analyses

TABLE 18.2 Correlations Among Variables

VARIABLE	1	2	3	4	5	6	7	8	9	10	11	12	13	14	15	16	17	18	19	20	21
1. Household income (dollars in thousands)	—																				
2. Race (White = 1, minority = 0)	.28	—																			
3. Age (teen = 1, adult = 0)	-.03	.08	—																		
4. Gender (female = 1, male = 0)	-.14	-.20	.03	—																	
5. Social extraversion (1–5 scale)	.11	.00	.12	.19	—																
6. Household size (people in household at pretest)	.27	.16	.16	-.07	.17	—															
7. Family communication T1 (mean hours per day)	-.14	-.01	-.07	.18	.09	.28	—														
8. Family communication T3 (mean hours per day)	-.03	-.10	-.28	.14	-.09	.01	.40	—													
9. Local social network T1 (number of people)	-.05	-.02	.27	.03	.07	.13	.09	.01	—												
10. Local social network T3 (number of people)	-.06	-.02	.24	.04	.12	.17	.20	.01	.56	—											
11. Distant social network T1 (number of people)	.14	.14	.02	.02	.06	.00	.09	.01	.30	.17	—										
12. Distant social network T3 (number of people)	.18	.27	.16	-.17	.06	.07	.06	.03	.16	.36	.38	—									
13. Social support T1 (1–5 scale, 16 items)	.12	.05	.05	.22	.34	.04	.25	.05	.16	.08	.06	.10	—								
14. Social support T3 (1–5 scale, 16 items)	.14	.13	.05	.18	.30	.14	.12	.04	.10	.14	.19	.13	.57	—							
15. Loneliness T1 (1–5 scale, 3 items)	-.09	-.07	-.18	-.08	-.37	-.12	-.25	-.10	-.21	-.19	-.08	-.18	-.61	-.48	—						
16. Loneliness T3 (1–5 scale, 3 items)	.07	-.08	-.05	-.21	-.36	-.07	-.15	-.05	-.30	-.23	-.15	-.12	-.49	-.67	.55	—					
17. Stress T1 (mean of hassles reported of 49 items)	-.01	-.01	-.15	.09	.04	.07	.06	.10	.03	.00	.07	-.09	-.08	-.01	.13	.09	—				
18. Stress T3 (mean of hassles reported of 49 items)	-.02	.13	.01	.05	.01	-.01	-.05	-.03	.07	.06	.00	.08	-.09	.10	.05	.01	.60	—			
19. Depression T1 (0–3 scale, 15 items)	.07	.05	.33	.10	-.14	.14	-.07	.03	.16	.12	.04	.08	-.26	-.12	.22	.24	.37	.30	—		
20. Depression T3 (0–3 scale, 15 items)	-.07	-.15	.14	.03	.00	-.06	-.08	-.20	-.07	-.06	-.13	-.11	-.12	-.36	.25	.36	.21	.31	.32	—	
21. Internet usage T2 (mean hours per week)	.06	.17	.23	-.07	-.10	-.07	-.09	-.08	-.07	-.11	-.08	-.05	-.01	-.04	-.09	.15	-.14	.04	.07	.15	—

Note: N for household size and family communication = 231. Other Ns vary between 163 and 169. Family communication, social networks, and Internet use have been logged before computing correlations.

When $r = .15$, $p = .05$; when $r = 17$, $p = .025$; when $r = .20$, $p = .01$.

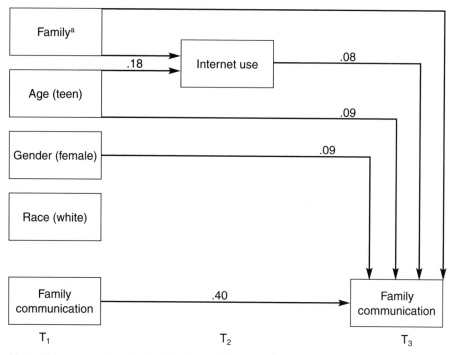

Note: Entries are standardized beta coefficients. All paths shown are significant at $p \leq .05$. T = time.

FIGURE 18.2   Influence of Internet Use on Family Communication

The analysis of family communication showed that teenagers used the Internet more hours (T2) than did adults, but Whites did not differ from minorities, and female participants did not differ from male participants in their average hours of use. Different families varied in their use of the Internet . . . but the amount of communication that an individual family member had with other members of the family did not predict subsequent Internet use. Family communication was stable over the period from T1 to T3. Whites increased their family communication more than minorities did. Adults increased their communication more than teens, and women/girls increased their communication in the family more than men/boys did. For our purposes, the most important finding is that greater use of the Internet was associated with subsequent declines in family communication.

Size of participants' social network. . . .   Greater social extroversion and having a larger local social circle predicted less use of the Internet during the next 12 or 24 months. Whites reported increasing their distant social circles more than minorities did, and teens reported increasing their distant circles more than adults did; these groups did not differ in changes to their local circles. Holding constant these control variables and the initial sizes of participants' social circles, greater use of the Internet was associated with subsequent declines in the size of both the local social circle ($p < .05$) and, marginally, the size of the distant social circle ($p < .07$).

Social support.   The social-circle measures ask respondents to estimate the number of people with whom they can exchange social resources. Howev-

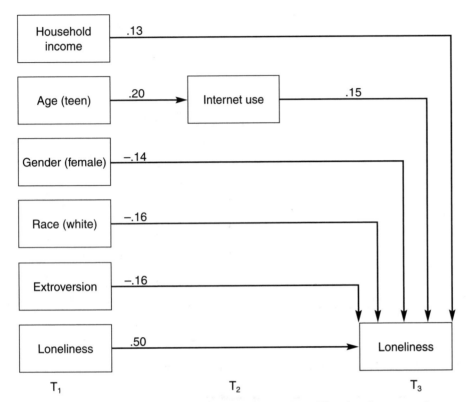

Note: Entries are standardized beta coefficients. T = time. All paths shown are significant at $p \leq .05$.

FIGURE 18.3   Influence of Internet Use on Loneliness

er, the definition provided to participants may have focused their attention primarily on people with whom they had face-to-face contact, thus leading to a biased view of social resources if the Internet allowed for the substitution of on-line contacts for face-to-face ones. The social support and loneliness measures are more direct measures of the consequences of having social contact and are not inherently biased by the medium of communication.

The social support measure and the loneliness measure have some items with comparable content (e.g., "I can find companionship when I want it" is on the loneliness scale and "When I feel lonely, these are several people I can talk to" is on the social support scale). Also, the two measures are correlated (r = .60). However, whereas the loneliness scale focuses on psychological feelings of belonging, the social

support scale includes components measuring the availability of tangible resources from others (e.g., a loan), intangible resources from others (e.g., advice), and reflected esteem (e.g., respect for abilities. . . . Although the association between Internet use and subsequent social support was negative, the effect did not approach statistical significance ($p > .40$).

Psychological Well-Being

Loneliness.   Figure 18.3 summarizes the results [involving loneliness]. Note that initial loneliness did not predict subsequent Internet use. Loneliness was stable over time. People from richer households increased loneliness more than did those from poorer households, men increased loneliness more than did women, and minorities increased loneliness more than did Whites. Controlling for these personal char-

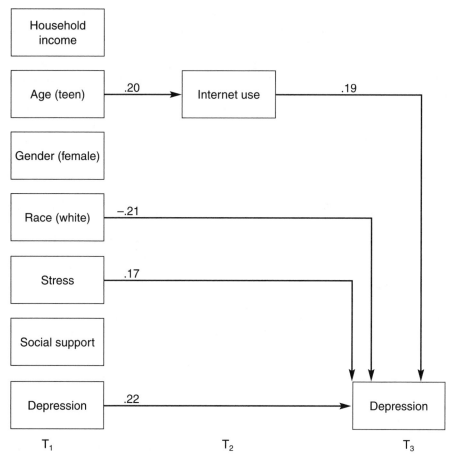

Note: Entries are standardized beta coefficients. T = time. All paths shown are significant at $p \leq .07$.

FIGURE 18.4   Influence of Internet Use on Depression

acteristics and initial loneliness, people who used the Internet more subsequently reported larger increases in loneliness. The association of Internet use with subsequent loneliness was comparable to the associations of income, gender, and race with subsequent loneliness.

Stress.   [T]he analysis involving self-reports of daily "hassles," an index of the extent of daily life stress [revealed that the] occurrence of these stressors was stable over the interval we studied. People who used the Internet more reported experiencing a greater number of daily life stressors in a subsequent period,

an increase that is marginally significant ($p = .08$). The Hassle Scale (S. Cohen et al., 1984) is a simple mean of a large number of stressors. We tried to gain more insight into the detailed changes that were occurring in participants' lives by conducting an exploratory, post hoc analysis to identify the particular stressors that increased with Internet use. We conducted separate analysis for each potential stressor. . . . Under this analysis, no single stressor changed reliably from its baseline. The implication is that even though use of the Internet may increase aggregate stress, it does not do so through a common route across the sample.

Depression. Figure 18.4 shows the significant variables [predicting depression], and social support is often a buffer protecting against depression, we included both the hassle and social support measures at T1 as covariates. The stability of depression in this sample was lower than the stability of other outcomes measured, but was comparable to its stability in other general populations (Radloff, 1977). Initial depression did not predict subsequent Internet use. Minorities reported more increases in depression than did Whites, and those with higher initial stress reported greater increases in depression. For the purposes of this analysis, the important finding is that greater use of the Internet was associated with increased depression at a subsequent period, even holding constant initial depression and demographic stress. This negative association between Internet use and depression is consistent with the interpretation that use of the Internet caused an increase in depression. Again, it is noteworthy that depression at T1 did not predict using the Internet subsequently.

DISCUSSION

Evaluating the Causal Claim

The findings of this research provide a surprisingly consistent picture of the consequences of using the Internet. Greater use of the Internet was associated with small, but statistically significant declines in social involvement as measured by communication within the family and the size of people's local social networks, and with increases in loneliness, a psychological state associated with social involvement. Greater use of the Internet was also associated with increases in depression. Other effects on the size of the distant social circle, social support, and stress did not reach standard significance levels but were consistently negative.

Our analyses are consistent with the hypothesis that using the Internet adversely affects social involvement and psychological well-being. The panel research design gives us substantial leverage in inferring causation, leading us to believe that in this case, correlation does indeed imply causation. Initial Internet use and initial social involvement and psychological well-being were included in all of the models assessing the effects of Internet use on subsequent social and psychological outcomes. Therefore, our analysis is equivalent to an analysis of change scores, controlling for regression toward the mean, unreliability, contemporaneous covariation between the outcome and the predictor variables, and other statistical artifacts (J. Cohen & Cohen, 1983). Because initial social involvement and psychological well-being were generally not associated with subsequent use of the Internet, these findings imply that the direction of causation is more likely to run from use of the Internet to declines in social involvement and psychological well-being, rather than the reverse. The only exception to this generalization was a marginal finding that people who initially had larger local social circles were lighter users of the Internet. . . .

Although the evidence is strong that using the Internet caused declines in social participation and psychological well-being within this sample, we do not know how generalizable the findings are across people, time, or outcomes. The sample examined here was selected to be diverse, but it was small and not statistically representative of any particular geographic region or population. In addition, the sample consisted of families with at least one member engaged in a preexisting face-to-face group (students working on a high school newspaper or adults on the board of a community development organization). If the sample had consisted of those who were already isolated (e.g., homeless or elderly people), social interaction on the Internet might have increased social participation and psychological well-being rather than decreased them.

Moreover, the sample examined people in their first one or two years on-line, starting in 1995 or 1996; whether results would have been the same at different points in their experience or at different points in the history of the Internet is unclear. Some of the teenagers, for example, reported that the Internet lost its appeal as they became immersed in the more serious work of college. The Internet itself changed during the course of this research. For example, group-oriented software, like America Online's

Instant Messenger or Mirabilis' ICQ, which allow people to monitor the availability of selected individuals and to immediately swap messages with them when they go on-line, was not available during the early days of this trial.

Finally, we can generalize our results only to outcomes related to social behavior. In particular, we are not reporting effects of the Internet on educational outcomes or on self-esteem related to computer skill learning. Participants gained computer skills with more Internet usage. Several parents of teenagers who had spent many hours on-line judged that their children's positive educational outcomes from using the Internet outweighed possible declines in their children's social interaction. Future research will be needed to evaluate whether such trade-offs exist.

Possible Causal Mechanisms

To this point, we have attempted to establish the existence of a phenomenon—that Internet use causes declines in social involvement and psychological well-being. We have not, however, identified the mechanisms though which this phenomenon occurs. There are at least two plausible and theoretically interesting mechanisms, but we have little evidence from our current research to establish which, if either, is correct.

Displacing social activity.   The time that people devote to using the Internet might substitute for time that they had previously spent engaged in social activities. According to this explanation, the Internet is similar to other passive, nonsocial entertainment activities, such as watching TV, reading, or listening to music. Use of the Internet, like watching TV, may represent a privatization of entertainment, which could lead to social withdrawal and to declines in psychological well-being. Putnam (1995) made a similar claim about television viewing.

The problem with this explanation is that a major use of the Internet is explicitly social. People use the Internet to keep up with family and friends through electronic mail and on-line chats and to make new acquaintances through MUDs, chats, Usenet news-groups, and listservs. Our previous analyses showed that interpersonal communication was the dominant use of the Internet among the sample studied in this research (Kraut et al., 1998). They used the Internet more frequently for exchanging electronic mail than for surfing the World Wide Web and, within a session, typically checked their mail before looking at the Web; their use of electronic mail was more stable over time than their use of the World Wide Web; and greater use of e-mail relative to the Web led them to use the Internet more intensively and over a longer period (Kraut et al., 1998). Other analyses, not reported here, show that even social uses of the Internet were associated with negative outcomes. For example, greater use of electronic mail was associated with increases in depression.

Displacing strong ties.   The paradox we observe, then, is that the Internet is a social technology used for communication with individuals and groups, but is associated with declines in social involvement and the psychological well-being that goes with social involvement. Perhaps, by using the Internet, people are substituting poorer quality social relationships for better relationships, that is, substituting weak ties for strong ones (e.g., Granovetter, 1973; Krackhardt, 1994). People can support strong ties electronically. Indeed, interviews with this sample revealed numerous instances in which participants kept up with physically distant parents or siblings, corresponded with children when they went off to college, rediscovered roommates from the past, consoled distant friends who had suffered tragedy, or exchanged messages with high school classmates after school.

However, many of the on-line relationships in our sample, and especially the new ones, represented weak ties rather than strong ones. Examples include a woman who exchanged mittens with a stranger she met on a knitting listserv, a man who exchanged jokes and Scottish trivia with a colleague he met through an on-line tourist website, and an adolescent who exchanged (fictional) stories about his underwater exploits to other members of a scuba diving chat service. A few participants met new people on-line and had friendships with them. For instance, one teenager met his prom date on-line, and another woman met a couple in Canada whom she subsequently visited during her summer vacation. However, interviews with participants in this trial suggest that making new friends on-line was rare. Even though it was welcomed when it occurred, it did not counteract overall declines in real-world communication with family and friends. Our conclusions resonate with Katz and Aspden's (1977) national survey data showing that only 22% of the respondents who had been using the Internet for two or more years had ever made a new friend on the Internet. Although neither we nor Katz and Aspden provide comparison data, we wonder whether, in the real world, only a fifth of the population make a friend over a two-year period.

On-line friendships are likely to be more limited than friendships supported by physical proximity. On-line friends are less likely than friends developed at school, work, church, or in the neighborhood to be available for help with tangible favors, such as offering small loans, rides, or babysitting. Because on-line friends are not embedded in the same day-to-day environment, they will be less likely to understand the context for conversation, making discussion more difficult (Clark, 1996) and rendering support less applicable. Even strong ties maintained at a distance through electronic communication are likely to be different in kind and perhaps diminished in strength compared with strong ties supported by physical proximity (Wellman & Wortley, 1990). Both frequency of contact and the nature of the medium may contribute to this difference. For example, one of our participants who said that she appreciated the e-mail correspondence she had with her college-aged daughter also noted that when her daughter was homesick or depressed, she reverted to telephone calls to provide support. Although a clergyman in the sample used e-mail to exchange sermon ideas with other clergy, he phoned them when he needed advice about negotiating his contract. Like that mother and clergyman, many participants in our sample loved the convenience of the Internet. However, this convenience may induce people to substitute less involving electronic interactions more involving real-world ones. The clergyman in the sample reported that his involvement with his listserv came at the expense of time with his wife.

Implications for Policy and Design

The negative effects of Internet use that we have documented here are not inevitable. Technologies are not immutable, especially not computing ones. Their effects will be shaped by how they are constructed by engineers, how they are deployed by service providers, and how they are used by consumers.

Designing technology and policy to avoid negative outcomes will depend on a more complete understanding of the mechanisms through which use of the Internet influences social involvement and psychological well-being. If we assume, for example, that the negative consequences of using the Internet occur at least partly because people spend more time and attention on weak ties and less time and attention on strong ties, then some design and policy solutions come easily to mind.

Most public policy discussion of the Internet has focused on its potential benefits as an information resource and as a medium for commercial exchange. Research funding also heavily favors the development of better resources for efficient information delivery and retrieval.

Both policy and technology interventions to better support the Internet's uses for interpersonal communication could right this imbalance. For example, recent legislation to limit taxes on the Internet favored the Internet for commercial transactions. There are not comparable policy initiatives to foster use of the Internet as an interpersonal communications medium (see Anderson et al., 1998). At the technological level, services for finding people are far less common, sophisticated, or accurate than services for finding information and products. On-line directories of e-mail addresses are far less comprehensive than on-line directories of telephone numbers. Search services on the Internet, such as Yahoo, Alta Vista, Infoseek, and Lycos, grew from sophisticated industrial and government-funded research programs in information retrieval. The initiative on digital libraries, funded by the National Science Foundation and the Defense

Advanced Research Projects Agency, has a goal of making pictures, graphs, and video images as easy to search and retrieve as text. Comparable search capabilities for finding people based on their attributes are far less well-supported. (See the research on collaborative filtering, e.g., Resnick & Varian, 1997, for an interesting exception).

The Interpersonal communication applications currently prevalent on the Internet are either neutral toward strong ties or tend to undercut rather than promote them. Because most websites, Usenet news groups, and listservs are topically organized, strangers are encouraged to read each others' messages and exchange communication on the basis of their common interests in soap operas, civil rights, stamp collecting, or other narrow topics. This communication is dominated by the designated topics and people are frequently discouraged by social pressures from straying from the topic. Although some of these groups are formed explicitly to provide support, and a few even encourage real-world friendships and tangible help, these are relatively few in comparison to the thousands of groups focused on professional advice, hobbies, and entertainment. Information and communication services that are geographically based and designed to support people who already know

and care about each other are even rarer. Some successful experiments at community-based on-line communication do exist (e.g., Carroll & Rosson, 1996) along with some successful commercial services that support preexisting social groups (e.g., "buddy lists" in America OnLine's Instant Messenger product). We believe these are valuable directions.

More intense development and deployment of services that support preexisting communities and strong relationships should be encouraged. Government efforts to wire the nation's schools, for example, should consider on-line homework sessions for students rather than just on-line reference works. The volunteers in churches, synagogues, and community groups building informational websites might discover that tools to support communication among their memberships are more valuable.

Both as a nation and as individual consumers, we must balance the value of the Internet for information, communication, and commerce with its cost. Use of the Internet can be both highly entertaining and useful, but if it causes too much disengagement from real life, it can also be harmful. Until the technology evolves to be more beneficial, people should moderate how much they use the Internet and monitor the uses to which they put it.

REFERENCES

Anderson, R. E., Crespo, C. J., Bartlett, S. J., Cheskin, L. J., & Pratt, M. (1998). Relationship of physical activity and television watching with body weight and level of fatness among children. *Journal of the American Medical Association, 279,* 938–942.

Anderson, R. H., Bikson, T. K., Law, S. A., & Mitchell, B. M. (Eds.) (1995). *Universal access to e-mail: Feasibility and societal implications.* Santa Monica, CA: Rand Corporation.

Attewell, P., & Rule, J. (1984). Computing and organizations: What we know and what we don't know. *Communication of the ACM, 27,* 1184–1192.

Bell, D. (1973). *The coming of post-industrial society: A venture in social forecasting.* New York: Basic Books.

Bendig, A. W. (1962). The Pittsburgh scales of social extraversion, introversion and emotionality. *The Journal of Psychology, 53,* 199–209.

Beniger, J. R. (1987). Personalization of mass media and the growth of pseudo-community. *Communication Research, 14,* 352–371.

Bentler, P. M. (1995). *EQS: Structural equations program manual.* Encino, CA: Multivariate Software, Inc.

Berry, W. (1993). *Sex, economy, freedom, and community.* New York: Pantheon.

Brody, G. H. (1990, April). Effects of television viewing on family interactions: An observational study. *Family Relations, 29,* 216–220.

Canary, D. J., & Spitzberg, B. H. (1993). Loneliness and media gratification, *Communication Research, 20,* 800–821.

Carroll, J., & Rosson, M. (1996). Developing the Blacksburg electronic village. *Communications of the ACM, 39*(12), 68–74.

Clark, H. H. (1996). *Using language*. New York: Cambridge University Press.

Cohen, J., & Cohen, P. (1983). *Applied multiple regression/correlation analysis for the behavioral sciences*. Hillsdale, NJ: Erlbaum.

Cohen, S., Mermelstein, R., Kamarck, T., & Hoberman, H. (1984). Measuring the functional components of social support. In I. G. Sarason & B. R. Sarason (Eds.). *Social support: Theory, research and applications* (pp. 73–94). The Hague, Holland: Martines Niijhotf.

Cohen S., & Wills, T. A. (1985). Stress, social support, and the buffering hypothesis. *Psychological Bulletin, 98,* 310–357.

Condry, J. (1993, Winter). Thief of time, unfaithful servant: Television and The American child. *Daedalus, 122,* 259–278.

Constant, D., Sproull, L., & Kiesler, S. (1996). The kindness of strangers: On the usefulness of weak ties for technical advice. *Organization Science, 7,* 119–135.

Danko, W. D., & MacLachlan, J. M. (1983). Research to accelerate the diffusion of a new invention. *Journal of Advertising Research, 23*(3), 39–43.

Fischer, C. S., (1992). *America calling*. Berkeley, CA: University of California Press.

Gove, W. R., & Geerken, M. R. (1977). The effect of children and employment on the mental health of married men and women. *Social Forces, 56,* 66–76.

Granovetter, M. (1973). The strength of weak ties. *American Journal of Sociology, 73,* 1361–1380.

Heim, M. (1992). The erotic ontology of cyberspace. In M. Benedikt (Ed.). *Cyberspace: First steps* (pp. 59–80). Cambridge, MA: MIT Press.

Huston, A. C., Donnersteinf, E., Fairchild, H., Feshbach, N., Katz, P., Murray, J., Rubinstein, E., Wilcox, B., & Zuckerman, D. (1992). *Big world, small screen: The role of television in American society*. Lincoln: University of Nebraska Press.

Jackson-Beeck, M., & Robinson, J. P. (1981). Television nonviewers: An endangered species? *Journal of Consumer Research, 7,* 356–359.

Jacobson, H. B., & Roucek, J. S., (1959). *Automation and society*. New York: Philosophical Library.

Kanner, A. D., Coyne, J. C., Schaefer, C., & Lazarus, R. S., (1981). Comparisons of two modes of stress measurement: Daily hassles and uplifts versus major life events. *Journal of Behavioral Medicine, 4,* 1–39.

Katz, J. E., & Aspden, P. (1997). A nation of strangers? *Communications of the ACM, 40*(12), 81–86.

King, J. L., & Kraemer, K. L., (1995). Information infrastructure, national policy, and global competitiveness. *Information Infrastructure and Policy, 4,* 5–28.

Kohut, A. (1994). *The role of technology in American Life*. Los Angeles Times Mirror Center for the People and the Press.

Krackhardt, D. (1994). The strength of strong ties: The importance of Philos in organizations. In N. Nohria & R. Eccles (Eds.). *Networks and organizations: Structure, form, and action*. Boston, MA: Harvard Business School Press.

Kraut, R., Mukopadhyay, T., Szczypula, J. Kiesler, S., & Scherlis, W. (1998). Communication and information: Alternative uses of the Internet in households. *In Proceedings of the CHI 98* (pp. 368–383) New York: ACM.

Kraut, R., Scherlis, W., Mukopadhyay, T., Manning, J., & Kiesler, S. (1996). The HomeNet field trial of residential Internet services. *Communication of the ACM, 39,* 55–63.

Kubey, R., & Csikszentmihalyi, M. (1990). *Television and the quality of life: How viewing shapes everyday experience*. Hillsdale, NJ: Erlbaum.

Leavitt, H. J., & Whisler, T. L. (1958, November–December). Management in the 1980s. *Harvard Business Review, 36,* 41–48.

Lundmark, V., Kiesler, S., Kraut, R., Scherlis, W., & Mukopadhyay, T. (1998). *How the strong survive: Patterns and significance of competence, commitment, and requests for external technical support in families on the Internet*. Unpublished manuscript.

Maccoby, E. E. (1951). Television: its impact on school children. *Public Opinion Quarterly, 15,* 421–444.

McLuhan, M. (1964). *Understanding media*. New York: McGraw-Hill.

Murray, J. P., & Kippax, S. (1978). Children's social behavior in three towns with differing television experience. *Journal of Communication, 28,* 18–29.

Neuman, S. B. (1991). *Literacy in the television age: The myth of the TV effect*. Norwood, NJ: Ablex.

Parks, M. R., & Floyd, K. (1995). Making friends in cyberspace. *Online Journal of Computer Mediated Communication, 1*(4). Available.

Putnam, R. (1995, January). Bowling alone: America's declining social capital. *Journal of Democracy, 6,* 65–78.

Radloff, L. (1977). The CES–D Scale: A self-report depression scale for research in the general population. *Applied Psychological Measurement, 1,* 385–401.

Resnick, P., & Varian, H. (1997). Recommender systems: Introduction to the special section. *Communications of the ACM, 40*(3), 56–58.

Rheingold, H. (1993). *The virtual community: Homesteading on the electronic frontier.* Reading, MA: Addison Wesley.

Robinson, J. P. (1990). Television's effects on families' use of time. In J. Bryant (Ed.), *Television and the American family* (pp. 195–209). Hillsdale, NJ: Erlbaum.

Robinson, J. P., & Godbey, G. (1997). *Time for life: The surprising ways Americans use their time.* University Park: The Pennsylvania State University Press.

Rook, K. S., & Peplau, L. A. (1982). Perspectives on helping the lonely. In L. A. Peplau & D. Perlman (Eds.). *Loneliness: A sourcebook of current theory, research and therapy* (pp. 351–378). New York: Wiley.

Rubinstein, C., & Shaver, P. (1982). *In search of intimacy.* New York: Delcorte.

Russell, D., Peplau, L., & Cutrona, C. (1980). The revised UCLA loneliness scale: Concurrent and discriminant validity evidence. *Journal of Personality and Social Psychology, 39,* 472–480.

Short, J., Williams, E., & Christie, B. (1976). *The social psychology of telecommunications.* London: Wiley.

Sidney, S., Sternfeld, B., Haskell, W. L., Jacobs, D. R., Chesney, M. A., & Hulley, S. B. (1998). Television viewing and cardiovascular risk factors in young adults. The CARDIA study. *Annals of Epidemiology, 6*(2), 154–159.

Sproull, L., & Faraj, S. (1995). Atheism, sex, and databases: The Net as a social technology. In B. Kahin & J. Keller (Eds.). *Public access to the Internet* (pp. 62–81). Cambridge, MA: MIT Press.

Sproull, L., & Kiesler, S. (1991). *Connections: New ways of working in the networked organization.* Cambridge, MA: MIT Press.

Stoll, C. (1995). *Silicon snake oil.* New York: Doubleday.

Turkel, S. (1996, Winter). Virtuality and its discontents: Searching for community in cyberspace. *The American Prospects, 24,* 50–57.

Vitalari, N. P., Venkatesh, A., & Gronhaug, K. (1985). Computing in the home: Shifts in the time allocation patterns of households. *Communications of the ACM, 28*(5), 512–522.

Walther, J. B., Anderson, J. F., & Park, D. W. (1994). Interpersonal anti-social communication. *Communication Research 21,* 460–487.

Wellman, B., & Wortley, S. (1990). Different strokes for different folks: Community ties and social support. *American Journal of Sociology, 96,* 558–588.

_____CHAPTER 19_____

INTERACTION: THE WORK WOMEN DO

PAMELA M. FISHMAN

The oppression of women in society is an issue of growing concern, both in academic fields and everyday life. Despite research on the historical and economic bases of women's position, we know little about how hierarchy is routinely established and maintained. This [essay] attempts to direct attention to the reality of power in daily experience. It is an analysis of conversations between men and women in their homes. The [chapter] focuses on how verbal interaction helps to construct and maintain the hierarchical relations between women and men.

Weber (1969:152 [pronounced "Vay-bur"]) provided the classic conception of power as the chances of one actor in a social relationship to impose his or her will on another. Recently, Berger and Luckmann (1967:109) have discussed power from a perspective which broadens the sense of "imposing one's will" on others. They define power as a question of potentially conflicting definitions of reality; that of the most powerful will be "made to stick." That particular people have the power to construct and enforce their definition of reality is due to socially prevalent economic and political definitions of reality.

Imposing one's will can be much more than forcing someone else to do something. Power is the ability to impose one's definition of what is possible, what is right, what is rational, what is real. Power is a product of human activities, just as the activities are themselves products of the power relations in the socioeconomic world.

Power usually is analyzed macrosociologically: it cannot be solely a result of what people do within the immediate situation in which it occurs. What people do in specific interactions expresses and reflects historical and social structural forces beyond the boundaries of their encounters. Power relations between men and women are the outcome of the social organization of their activities in the home and in the economy. Power can, however, be analyzed microsociologically, which is the purpose of this [essay]. Power and hierarchical relation are not abstract forces operating on people. Power must be a human accomplishment, situated in everyday interaction. Both structural forces and interactional activities are vital to the maintenance and construction of social reality.

Recent work on gender and the English language shows that the male-female hierarchy is inherent in the words we use to perceive and name our world: the use of the male generic "man" to refer to the human species (Miller and Swift, 1976); the addition of suffixes ("authoress," "actress," "stewardess") when referring to female practitioners (Miller and Swift, 1976); the asymmetrical use of first and last names (women are more often called by their first, men by their last, even when they are of equal rank) (Thorne and Henley, 1975); women's greater vocabulary for serving and cooking, men's for mechanics and sports (Conklin, 1974).[1] These studies of grammatical forms and vocabulary document the male-dominated reality expressed through our language.

Much less attention has been directed toward how male-female power relations are expressed in conversation.[2] By turning to conversation, we move to an analysis of the interactional production of a particular reality through people's talk.

This activity is significant for intimates. Berger and Kellner (1970: 64) have argued that at present, with the increasing separation of public and private spheres of life, intimate relationships are among the most important reality-maintaining settings. They apply this arrangement specifically to marriage. The process of daily interaction in the marital relationship is, ideally:

> . . . one in which reality is crystallized, narrowed, and stabilized. Ambivalences are converted into certainties. Typifications of self and other become settled. Most generally, possibilities become facticities.

In these relationships, in these trivial, mundane interactions, much of the essential work of sustaining the reality of the world goes on. Intimates often reconstruct their separate experiences, past and present, with one another. Specifically, the couple sustain and produce the reality of their own relationship, and, more generally, of the world.

Although Berger and Kellner have analyzed marriage as a reality-producing setting, they have not analyzed the interaction of marriage partners. I shall focus upon the interactional activities which constitute the everyday work done by intimates. It is through this work that people produce their relationship to one another, their relationship to the world, and those patterns normally referred to as social structure.

WORK IN INTERACTION[3]

Sometimes we think of interaction as work. At a party or meeting where silence lies heavy, we recognize the burden of interaction and respond to it as work. The many books written on "the art of conversation" call attention to the tasks involved in interaction. It is not simply an analogy to think of interaction as work. Rather, it is an intuitive recognition of what must be accomplished for interaction to occur.

Interaction requires at least two people. Conversation is produced not simply by their presence, but also by their display of their continuing agreement to pay attention to one another. That is, all interactions are potentially problematic and occur only through the continual, turn-by-turn, efforts of the participants.

The work of Sacks and his followers (Sacks et al., 1974; Schegloff and Sacks, 1974; Schegloff, 1972) attempts to specify how conversationalists work to accomplish such things as beginnings and endings. They have ignored, however, the interaction between intimates. Schegloff and Sacks (1974: 262) characterize intimates in home situations as "in continuing states of incipient talk." Thus, they contend that their analysis of the activities involved in opening and closing conversations, as well as those involved in keeping conversation going, do not apply to intimate conversations. But this perspective disregards the many conversations which do not begin with greetings nor end with good-byes. If one sees a movie with friends, conversation afterwards does not begin again with greetings. In social gatherings lulls occur and conversation must begin anew. In any setting in which conversation is possible, attempts at beginning, sustaining, and stopping talk still must be made. And these attempts must be recognized and oriented to by both parties for them to move between states of "incipient" and "actual" conversation.

In a sense, every remark or turn at speaking should be seen as an *attempt* to interact. It may be an attempt to open or close a conversation. It may be a bid to continue interaction: to respond to what went before and elicit a further remark from one's interlocutor. Some attempts succeed; others fail. For an attempt to succeed, the other party must be willing to do further interactional work. That other person has the power to turn an attempt into a conversation or to stop it dead.

METHOD

The data for this study consists of fifty-two hours of tape-recorded conversation between intimates in their homes. Three couples agreed to have a Uher 400 tape recorder in their apartments. They had the right to censor the taped material before I heard it. The apartments were small, so that the recorders picked up all conversation from the kitchen and living room as well as the louder portions of talk from the bedroom and bath. The tapes could run for a four-hour period without interruption. Though I had timers to switch the tapes on and off automatically, all three couples insisted on doing the switching manually. The segments of uninterrupted recording vary from one to four hours.

The three couples had been together for varying amounts of time—three months, six months, and two years. The two couples who had been together the longest were recently married. All were white and professionally oriented, between the ages of twenty-five and thirty-five. One woman was a social worker and the other five people were in graduate school. Two of the women were avowed feminists and all three men as well as the other women described themselves as sympathetic to the woman's movement.

The tape recorders were present in the apartments from four to fourteen days. I am satisfied that the material represents natural conversation and that there was no undue awareness of the recorder. The tapes sounded natural to me, like conversations between my husband and myself. Others who have read the transcripts have agreed. All six people also reported that they soon began to ignore the tape recorder. Further, they were apologetic about the material, calling it trivial and uninteresting, just the ordinary affairs of everyday life. Finally, one couple said they forgot the recorder sufficiently to begin making love in the living room while the recorder was on. That segment and two others were the only ones the participants deleted before handing the tapes over to me.

I listened to all of the tapes at least once, many two or more times. During this period, I observed general features and trends of the interactions as a whole. Three transcripts were chosen from five hours of transcribed conversations for closer, turn-by-turn analysis of the progress of concrete, interactional activities. I chose these three because they were good examples of conversation that appeared to be problematic for the man, for the woman, and for neither.

PRELIMINARY EVIDENCE

Some evidence of the power relations between couples appeared while I was still in the process of collecting the tapes. During casual conversations with the participants after the taping, I learned that in all three couples the men usually set up the tape recorders and turned them on and off. More significantly, some of the times that the men turned the recorders on, they did so without the women's knowledge. The reverse never occurred.

To control conversation is not merely to choose the topic. It is a matter of having control over the definition of the situation in general, which includes not only what will be talked about, but whether there will be a conversation at all and under what terms it will occur. In various scenes, control over aspects of the situation can be important. The addition of a tape recorder in the home is an example of a new aspect to the routine situation. The men clearly had and actively maintained unilateral control over this new feature in the situation.

In this research, there is also the issue of a typically private interaction becoming available to a third party, the researcher. Usually the men played the tapes to censor them, and made the only two attempts to exert control over the presentation of the data to me. One case involved the "clicks" that are normally recorded when the recorder is turned off. Since more than one time segment was often on the same side of a tape, I relied on the clicks, as well as my sense of the conversation, to know when a new time segment began. One man carefully erased nearly all the clicks on the tapes, making it difficult to separate out recordings at different time periods.

The second instance was a more explicit illustration of male censorship. Early on, I made the error of asking a couple to help transcribe a segment of their tape. The error was doubly instructive. First, I saw that the participants could rarely hear or understand the problem areas any better than I even though they had been "on the spot," and were hearing their own voices. Second, the man kept wanting to know why I was interested in the segment, repeatedly guessing what I was looking for. At the time, I only knew that it was an example of decision-making and did not know specifically what I wanted. He never accepted this explanation. He became irritated at my continued attempt at literal transcription and kept insisting that he could give me the sense of what occurred and that the exact words were unimportant. He continued the attempt to determine the meaning of the interaction retrospectively, with constant references to his motives for saying this or that. It took hours to withdraw from the situation, as he insisted on giving me the help that I had requested.

The preliminary data suggest that the men are more likely than the women to control conversation. The men ensured that they knew when the tape recorder was on and, thus, when their interaction was available to a third party. They were unconcerned, however, if the women also knew. Further, in at least two cases they attempted to control my interpretation of the tapes.

FINDINGS: INTERACTIONAL STRATEGIES

Textual analysis revealed how interactants do the work of conversation. There are a variety of strategies to insure, encourage, and subvert conversation.

Asking Questions

There is an overwhelming difference between male and female use of questions as a resource in interaction. At times I felt that all women did was ask questions. In seven hours of tapes the three men asked fifty-nine questions, the women one hundred and fifty, nearly three times as many.

Other research (Lakoff, 1975) notes that women ask more questions then men. Lakoff has interpreted this question-asking as an indication of women's insecurity, a linguistic signal of an internal psychological state resulting from the oppression of women. But a psychological explanation is unnecessary to reveal why women ask more questions than men. Since questions are produced in conversations, we should look first to how questions function there.

Questions are interactionally powerful utterances. They are among a class of utterances, like greetings, treated as standing in a paired relation; that is, they evoke further utterance. Questions are paired with answers (Sacks, 1972). People respond to questions as "deserving" answers. The absence of an answer is noticeable and may be complained about. A question does work in conversation by opening a two part sequence. It is a way to insure a minimal interaction—at least one utterance by each of two participants. It guarantees a response.

Once I noted the phenomenon of questions on the tapes, I attended to my own speech and discovered the same pattern. I tried, and still do try, to break myself of the "habit," and found it very difficult. Remarks kept coming out as questions before I could rephrase them. When I did succeed in making a remark as a statement, I usually did not get a response. It became clear that I asked questions not merely out of habit nor from insecurity but because it was likely that my attempt at interaction would fail if I did not.

Asking "D'ya Know"

In line with the assumption that children have restricted rights to speak in the presence of adults, Harvey Sacks (1972) describes a type of question used extensively by children as a conversational opening: "D'ya know what?" As with other questions, it provides for a next utterance. The archetype is, "D'ya know what?" "What?" "Blahblah (answer)." Sometimes, of course, the adult answers with an expectant look or a statement like, "Tell me what." Whatever the exact form of that first response, the idea is that the first question sets off a three-part sequence, Q-Q-A, rather than a simple Q-A sequence.

Sacks points out that the children's use of this device is a clever solution to their problem of insuring rights to speak (at the same time, their use of this strategy acknowledges those restricted rights). In response to the "What?" the children may say what they wanted to say in the first place. Finding such three-part "D'ya know" sequences in interaction informs us both about the work of guaranteeing interaction and the differential rights of the participants. In the five hours of transcribed material, the women used this device twice as often as the men.

Attention Beginnings

The phrase, "This is interesting," or a variation thereof, occurs throughout the tapes. When conversation is not problematic, the work of establishing that a remark is interesting ideally is done by both interactants, not one. The first person makes a remark, the second person orients to and responds to the remark, thus establishing its status as something worthy of joint interest or importance. All this occurs without the question of its interest ever becoming explicit.[4] The use of "This is really interesting" as an introduction shows that the user cannot assume that the remark itself will be seen as worthy of attention. At the same time, the user tries single-handedly to establish the interest of their remarks. The user is saying, "Pay attention to what I have to say, I can't assume that you will." In the five hours of transcribed material, the women used this device ten times, the men seven.[5]

There are also many instances of "y'know" interspersed throughout the transcripts. While this phrase does not compel the attention of one's partner as forcefully as "This is interesting" does, it is an attempt to command the other person's attention. The phrase was used thirty-four times by the women and three times by the men in the transcribed conversations.

Minimal Response

Another interaction strategy is the use of the minimal response, when the speaker takes a turn by saying "yeah," "umm," "huh," and only that. Men and women both do this, but they tend to use the minimal response in quite different ways. The male usages of the minimal response displayed lack of interest. The monosyllabic response merely filled a turn at a point when it needed to be filled. For example, a woman would make a lengthy remark, after which the man responded with "yeah," doing nothing to encourage

her, nor to elaborate. Such minimal responses are attempts to discourage interaction.

The women also made this type of minimal response at times, but their most frequent use of the minimal response was as "support work." Throughout the tapes, when the men are talking, the women are particularly skilled at inserting "mm's," "yeah's," "oh's," and other such comments throughout streams of talk rather than at the end. These are signs from the inserter that she is constantly attending to what is said, that she is demonstrating her participation, her interest in the interaction and the speaker. How well the women do this is also striking—seldom do they mistime their insertions and cause even slight overlaps. These minimal responses occur between the breaths of a speaker, and there is nothing in tone or structure to suggest they are attempting to take over the talk.

Making Statements

Finally, I would like to consider statements, which do nothing to insure their own success, or the success of the interaction. Of course, a statement does some interactional work: it fills a space and may also provide for a response. However, such statements display an assumption on the part of the speaker that the attempt will be successful as is: it will be understood, the statement is of interest, there will be a response. It is as if speakers can assume that everything is working well; success is naturally theirs.

In the transcribed material, the men produced over twice as many statements as the women, and they almost always got a response, which was not true for the women. For example: many times one or both people were reading, then read a passage aloud or commented on it. The man's comments often engendered a lengthy exchange, the woman's comments seldom did. In a discussion of their respective vitas, the man literally ignored both long and short comments from the woman on her vita, returning the conversation after each remark of hers back to his own. Each time, she respectfully turned her attention back to his vita, "as directed." Listening to these conversations, one cannot conclude from the substance of the remarks that the men talk about more interesting things than the women. They take on that character by virtue of generating interaction.

INTERACTIONAL PROGRESS

The simple narration of the use of strategies obscures one important quality of interaction, its progression. The finding and frequency of strategies are of interest, but setting the use of strategies in the developing character of interaction reveals more about the differential work done by the sexes.

In the transcript [Figure 19.1], a short segment of conversation is reproduced.[6] It is from the transcript originally chosen for analysis because the conversation appeared problematic for the woman. We can see why from the transcript: she documents her problems by the use of strategies that insure some type of response.

This segment is the beginning of an interaction during which the woman is reading a book in her academic specialty and the man is making a salad. The woman's opening remarks set up two "d'ya know" sequences, demonstrating her lack of certainty, before anything has been said, that the man will pay attention. A safe assumption, since the conversation never gets off the ground. The "d'ya know" only solves the minimal problem of getting a response. She cannot get a continuing conversation going.

Her second attempt at a conversation, in set 5, is a two-fold one, using both the "d'ya know" strategy and an attention beginning of "That's very interesting." This double attempt to gain his participation manages to evoke one statement of continuation out of him in set 8, but her follow-up calls forth only silence.

Her third attempt, in set 10, uses the attention beginning which had some small success the last time. She adds a few "y'know's" throughout her utterance, asking for attention. She finally achieves a minimal response, when she repeats something. Though she makes further attempts in the remainder of the interaction (not reproduced here), a conversa-

tion on the topic never does develop. After three or four more minutes, she finally gives up.

One might argue that because the man was making a salad he could not pay attention to the conversation. However, while still at work on the salad, the man introduces his own topic for conversation, remarking that then-President Nixon was a former lawyer for Pepsi-Cola. This topic introduction engenders a conversation when the woman responds to his remark. They go through a series of exchanges which end when he decides not to continue. This conversational exchange demonstrates that the man was willing to engage in discussion, but only on his own terms.

The transcript demonstrates how some strategies are used in actual conversation. It also documents the woman working at interaction and the man exercising his power by refusing to become a full-fledged participant. As the interaction develops and she becomes more sure of her difficulties, she brings more pressure to bear by an increased use of strategies. Even so, she is only able to insure immediate, localized responses, not a full conversational exchange.

CONCLUSIONS

There is an unequal distribution of work in conversation. We can see from the differential use of strategies that the women are more actively engage din insuring interaction than the men. They ask more questions and use attention beginnings. Women do support work while the men are talking and generally do active maintenance and continuation work in conversations. The men, on the other hand, do much less active work when they begin or participate in interactions. They rely on statements, which they assume will get responses, when they want interaction. Men much more often discourage interactions initiated by women than vice versa.

Several general patterns of male-female interactional work suggest themselves. The women seemed to try more often, and succeeded less often than the men. The men tried less often and seldom failed in their attempts. Both men and women regarded topics

F: I didn't know that. (=)   Um you know that ((garbage disposal on)) that organizational
1
M: Hmmm? (=)

F: stuff about Frederick Taylor and Bishopsgate and all that stuff? (=)   ⌐In the early
2
M: UmHm ((yes))⌐

F: 1900s people were trying to fight favoritism to the schools (4)
3
M: That's what we needed. (18) I

F:
4
M: never did get my smoked oysters. I'm going to look for ((inaudible)) (14) Should we try the

F   OK. That's a change. (72) Hmm. That's very interesting. Did
5
M: Riviera French Dressing? (=)

F: you know that teachers used to be men until about the 1840s when it became a female occupa-
6
M:

F: tion? (2)   Because they needed more teachers because of the increased enroll-
7
M: Nhhmm ((no)) (=)

F: ment. (5)   Yeah, relatively and the status (7)
8
M: And then the salaries started going down probably. (=)

F: ⌐There's two bottles I think⌐
9
M: Um, it's weird. We're out of oil again.   ⌊Now we have to buy that.⌋ ((whistling)) (8) Dressing

F: It does, yeah. (76) That's really interesting. They didn't start
10
M: looks good. See? (2) See, babe? (1)

F: using the test to measure and find the you know categorize and track people in American
11
M:

F: schools until like the early 1990s after the army y'know introduced their array alpha things
12
M:

F: to the draftees (?) And then it caught on with the schools and there was a lot of opposition right
13
M:

F: at the beginning to that, which was as sophisticated as today's arguments. The same argu-
14
M:

F: ments, y'know (=)   But it didn't work and they came (4)   ⌐heh
15
M: Yeah (=)   Leslie White is probably right.⌐

FIGURE 19.1   Transcript of an Interaction

introduced by women as tentative; many of these were quickly dropped. In contrast, topics introduced by the men were treated as topics to be pursued; they were seldom rejected. The women worked harder than the men in interaction because they had less certainty of success. They did much of the necessary work of interaction, starting conversations and then working to maintain them.

The failure of the women's attempts at interaction is not due to anything inherent in their talk, but to the failure of the men to respond, to do interactional work. The success of the men's remarks is due to the women doing interactional work in response to attempts by the men. Thus, the definition of what is appropriate or inappropriate conversation becomes the man's choice. What part of the world the interactants orient to, construct and maintain the reality of, is his choice, not hers. Yet the women labor hardest in making interactions go.

It seems that, as with work in its usual sense, there is a division of labor in conversation. The people who do the routine maintenance work, the women, are not the same people who either control or benefit from the process. Women are the "shitworkers" of routine interaction, and the "goods" being made are not only interactions, but, through them, realities.

Through this analysis of the detailed activity in everyday conversation, other dimensions of power and work in interaction are suggested. Two interrelated aspects concern women's availability and the maintenance of gender. Besides the problems women have generating interactions, they are almost always available to do the conversational work required by men and necessary for interactions. Appearance may differ by case: sometimes women are required to sit and "be a good listener" because they are not otherwise needed. At other times, women are required to fill silences and keep conversation moving, to talk a lot. Sometimes they are expected to develop others' topics and at other times they are required to present and develop topics of their own.

Women are required to do their work in a very strong sense. Sometimes they are required in ways that can be seen in interaction, as when men use interactional strategies such as attention beginnings and questions, to which the women fully respond. There are also times when there is no direct, situational evidence of "requirement" from the man, and the woman does so "naturally." "Naturally" means that it is a morally required and highly sanctionable matter not to do so. If one does not act "naturally," then one can be seen as crazy and deprived of adult status. We can speculate on the quality of doing it "naturally" by considering what happens to women who are unwilling to be available for the various jobs that the situation requires. Women who successfully control interactions are derided and doubt is cast on their status of female. They are often considered "abnormal"—terms like "castrating bitch," "domineering," "aggressive," and "witch" may be used to identify them. When they attempt to control situations temporarily, women often "start" arguments. Etiquette books are filled with instructions to women on how to be available. Women who do not behave are punished by deprivation of full female status. One's identity as either male or female is the most crucial identity one has. It is the most "natural" differentiating characteristic there is.

Whereas sociologists generally treat sex as an "ascribed" rather than as an "achieved" characteristic, Garfinkel's (1967, ch. 5) study of a transsexual describes one's gender as a continual, routine accomplishment. He discusses what the transsexual Agnes has shown him, that one must continually give off the appearance of being male or female in order for your gender to be unproblematic in a given interaction. Agnes had to learn these appearances and her awareness of them was explicit. For "normally sexed" people, it is routine.

The active maintenance of a female gender requires women to be available to do what needs to be done in interaction, to do the shitwork and not complain. Since interactional work is related to what constitutes being a woman, with what a woman *is*, the idea that it *is* work is obscured. The work is not seen as what women do, but as part of what they are. Because this work is obscured, because it is too often seen as an aspect of gender identity rather than of gender activity, the maintenance and expression of male-female power relations in our everyday conversations are hidden as well. When we orient instead to the activities involved in maintaining gender, we are able to discern the reality of hierarchy in our daily lives.

The purpose of this study has been to begin an exploration of the details of concrete conversational activity of couples in their homes from the perspective of the socially structured power relationship between males and females. From such detailed analysis we see that women do the work necessary for interaction to occur smoothly. But men control what will be produced as reality by the interaction. They already have, and they continually establish and enforce, their rights to define what the interaction, and reality, will be about.

NOTES

1. An excellent summary and analysis of this literature can be found in Thorne and Henley's introduction to their book, *Language and Sex: Difference and Dominance* (Thorne and Henley, 1975). Miller and Swift's (1976) encyclopedic work, *Words and Women*, catalogues the innumerable ways our language upholds the inferior position of women.

2. A notable exception is the work on interruptions in conversation by West (1977), West and Zimmerman (1977), and Zimmerman and West (1975). Hirschman (1973, 1974) has also examined the interactive production of language in male-female settings.

3. Throughout this [essay], I use the terms interaction and conversation interchangeably, although it is not meant to suggest that conversation covers all the essential components of interaction.

4. The notion that joint expression of interest is a necessary feature of conversation is discussed by Garfinkel (1967:39–42).

5. Unlike the use of questions and "D'ya know," which were randomly scattered throughout the transcripts, six of the seven male usages occurred during one lengthy interaction. The conversation had been chosen because it was one of the very few cases when the man was having trouble maintaining interaction. In contrast, four of the female usages were from one transcript and the other six were scattered. My impression from listening to all the tapes was that a complete count would show a much larger proportion of female to male usage than the ten to seven figure indicates.

6. The numbers in parentheses indicate number of seconds of a pause; "(=)" means the pause was less than one second. My own comments on the tape are in double parentheses. M and F stand for male and female speaker, respectively. The conversation is presented in paired exchanges, sections 1–15. The sections ideally would be joined up in ticker tape fashion and would read like a musical score. Brackets between lines indicate overlapping talk.

REFERENCES

Berger, Peter and Hansfried Kellner. 1970. "Marriage and the construction of reality." Pp. 50–72 in Hans Peter Dreitzel, ed., *Recent Sociology* No. 2. London: Macmillan.

Berger, Peter and Thomas Luckmann. 1967. *The Social Construction of Reality.* New York: Anchor Books.

Conklin, N. F. 1974. "Toward a feminist analysis of linguistic behavior." *The University of Michigan Papers in Women's Studies* 1(1): 51–73.

Garfinkel, Harold. 1967. *Studies in Ethnomethodology.* Englewood Cliffs, New Jersey: Prentice-Hall.

Hirschman, Lynette. 1974. "Analysis of supportive and assertive behavior in conversations." Paper presented at Linguistic Society of America.

———. 1973. "Female-male differences in conversational interaction." Paper presented at Linguistic Society of America.

Lakoff, Robin. 1975. *Language and Woman's Place.* New York: Harper Colophon Books.

Miller, Casey and Kate Swift. 1976. *Words and Women.* New York: Anchor Press.

Sacks, Harvey. 1972. "On the analyzability of stories by children." Pp. 325–345 in John Gumperz and Dell Hymes, eds., *Directions in Sociolinguistics: The Ethnography of Communication.* New York: Holt, Rinehart and Winston.

Sacks, Harvey, Emmanuel Schegloff and Gail Jefferson. 1974. "A simplest systematics for the organization of turn-taking for conversation." *Language* 50: 696–735.

Schegloff, Emmanuel. 1972. "Sequencing in conversational openings." Pp. 346–380 in John Gumperz and Dell Hymes, eds., *Directions in Sociolinguistics: The Ethnography of Communication*. New York: Holt, Rinehart, and Winston.

Schegloff, Emmanuel and Harvey Sacks. 1974. "Opening up closings." Pp. 197–215 in Roy Turner, ed., *Ethnomethodology*. Middlesex, England: Penguin Education.

Thorne, Barrie and Nancy Henley. 1975. *Language and Sex: Difference and Dominance*. Rowley, Massachusetts: Newbury House.

Weber, Max. 1969. *The Theory of Social and Economic Organization*. New York: Free Press.

West, Candace. 1977. "Against our will: Negotiating interruption in male-female conversation." Paper presented at New York Academy of Science meeting of Anthropology, Psychology and Linguistics, Sections, October 22, New York, New York.

West, Candace and Don Zimmerman. 1977. "Women's place in everyday talk: Reflections on parent-child interaction." *Social Problems* 24:521–529.

Zimmerman, Don and Candace West. 1975. "Sex roles, interruptions and silences in conversation." Pp. 105–129 in Barrie Thorne and Nancy Henley, eds., *Language and Sex: Difference and Dominance*. Rowley, Massachusetts: Newbury House.

CHAPTER 20

PHYSICAL ATTRACTIVENESS IN SOCIAL INTERACTION

HARRY T. REIS
JOHN NEZLEK
LADD WHEELER

This article reports research on the relationship between physical attractiveness and the everyday social interaction of first-year college students over an 8-month period. The data collection technique used was the developed by Wheeler and Nezlek (1977), which requires subjects to complete a short fixed-format record for every interaction of 10 minutes or longer that occurs during a specified interval. The major questions were: (a) Do normal levels of physical attractiveness affect quantitative and qualitative aspects of social participation? (b) Are the effects the same for females and males? (c) Do the effects change over time?

Adams (1977), outlining a "developmental social psychology of beauty," suggested four assumptions about the relationship between inner behavioral processes and outer appearance. The first is that people have different expectations about attractive and unattractive others and that these expectations are consistent across numerous social situations. This is the well-known physical attractiveness stereotype that "what is beautiful is good" (Dion, Berscheid, & Walster, 1972). The second assumption is that physically attractive people receive more favorable social exchanges. The third assumption is that these more favorable social exchanges create differential social images, self-expectations, and interpersonal styles.

The final assumption (Adams, 1977) is that "attractive people will be more likely to manifest confident interpersonal behavior patterns than [will] less attractive individuals" (p. 218).

Although evidence is provided for each of these assumptions, an implication derived from all of them, namely that attractive individuals should be more socially successful across a wide variety of social situations, has not been tested. Our first prediction, then, was that physically attractive people should have more social encounters with the opposite sex and perhaps with the same sex and should find these encounters more rewarding.

We based this prediction on two assumptions. The first was that our culture teaches us that physical beauty if both important and desirable, particularly in opposite-sex interaction. If attractive people are in greater demand as dating partners (e.g., Brislin & Lewis, 1968, Tesser & Brodie, 1971; Walster, Aronson, Abrahams, & Rottmann, 1966), then they ought to participate in more, and more pleasing, social events. The second assumption was that the more attractive are more socially skilled and confident or that such behavior is elicited from them by others. These is some evidence for both of these possibilities. Goldman and Lewis (1977) used a blind, anonymous telephone call to ascertain that more attractive individuals of both sexes were in fact rated as more socially skillful and likable by their conversants, who could not have known their appearance. Snyder, Tanke, and Berscheid (1977) reversed the procedure and told male telephone callers that a female target person was

From *Journal of Personality and Social Psychology* 38, #4 (1980), pp. 604–617. Reprinted by permission. Footnotes have been deleted.

either unattractive or attractive, when in fact all the targets were of equal attractiveness. Independent judges' ratings of just the target's half of the conversation revealed her to be more friendly, likable, and sociable when she was believed to be unattractive. These studies suggest that stereotypes about physical beauty may have important consequences for people's social behavior and skills, necessitating further research on the relationship between attractiveness and actual everyday social interaction (as distinguished from studies assessing attractiveness stereotypes or first encounters in the lab).

Our second question was whether physical attractiveness is more important to the social behavior of males or females. Despite the pervasive cultural belief that it is more important for a female to be attractive than for a male, the evidence is mixed. Walster et al. (1966) found that a self-report popularity index correlated with attractiveness more highly for females (.46) than for males (.31), and Berscheid, Dion, Walster, and Walster (1971) found that attractiveness and estimated number of dates in the last year correlated more highly for females (.61) than for males (.25). On the other hand, Byrne, Ervin, and Lamberth (1970) found that a date's physical attractiveness correlated more highly with the attraction responses of female subjects than with those of male subjects, although the males *claimed* that a date's attractiveness was more important for them. Given these conflicting results, our second prediction was that physical attractiveness would affect the social participation of females and males equally. One qualification to this hypothesis is in order. Given Deaux's (1977) assertion that sex-stereotypic self-presentations are more likely in more "social" situations, we would expect attractive males to have more self-initiated interactions, whereas attractive females would participate in more other-initiated encounters.

Our third question concerned the lasting effects of physical attractiveness. Most of the physical attractiveness research has dealt with one-time interactions or with responses to photographs. In both cases the information is very limited, and we would expect attractiveness to have strong effects in the absence of other salient inputs. Many theorists, Berscheid and Walster (1974), for example, have speculated that as we receive more information about a person, the effect of attractiveness may diminish. The only evidence that we have been able to find is an experiment by Mathes (1975) in which attractiveness remained important over five separate encounters, even with competing additional information. Moreover, the theoretical position of Adams (1977) suggests that the attractiveness stereotype may be largely true, in which case attractiveness should remain socially important over time. This "kernel of truth" may of course be due to self-fulfilling prophecies (cf. Snyder et al., 1977). Our final prediction, then, was that the effects of physical attractiveness on social participation would persist over the academic year of the study.

The purpose of the present study is to investigate the nature and breadth of physical attractiveness effects in people's ongoing social lives. Despite the apparent relevance of appearance to social interaction, as discussed by Adams (1977) and Berscheid and Walster (1974), there has been little research relating attractiveness to aspects of social interaction, and we are aware of none that examines and distinguishes the various parameters of socializing as they relate to attractiveness.

The technique developed by Wheeler and Nezlek (1977) for studying social participation makes investigation of this aspect of attractiveness possible. Their procedure requires subjects to complete a short fixed-format record for every interaction of 10 minutes or longer that occurs during a specified interval. From their entries, indices of duration, satisfaction, intimacy, initiation, activity, location, and sex composition are assessed, both overall and after they have been broken down into various categories (same-, opposite-, and mixed-sex interactions, for example). These variables were selected in their research because they represented many of the essential features characterizing people's social encounters. For this reason, as well as for their success in Wheeler and Nezlek's study, they will be utilized here also. Using this approach, we assessed the interaction pattern of a group of first-year college students and then examined the relationship of these numerous indices with physical attractiveness in order to explore the three general predictions stated above.

METHOD

Subjects and General Overview

Subjects were 35 males and 36 females enrolled in a moderately sized, academically oriented northeastern university. All were in their first year of college and lived in dormitory rooms shared with one roommate. They completed the interaction records for four 10-day periods chosen to minimize overlap with exam periods and holidays: September 27 to October 6, December 1 to 10, January 24 to February 2, and April 5 to 14. Some subjects did not complete the records during all four intervals for various reasons (e.g., illness, trips home, etc.), yielding the following subsamples: Time 1—36 males, 35 females; Time 2—33 males, 34 females; Time 3—35 males, 35 females; Time 4—34 males, 34 females. Pictures were taken at the conclusion of the fourth time period and were rated at a nearby university.

Procedure

Subjects were recruited during summer orientation sessions for a "research project on social interaction." During a brief meeting, the importance of understanding interaction patterns was explained and the students' role as collaborators in this naturalistic research was stressed. Although subjects were told that if grant support was obtained they would receive $10 for each record-keeping period, they were asked to volunteer only if the opportunity to participate in some interesting research was sufficiently rewarding. To emphasize this goal, it was noted that the probability of funding was small. Our subjects' intrinsic motivation is evident in the fact that not one complained about the lack of payment when informed that funding had not been secured. No other academic or extrinsic incentives were involved.

Shortly after their arrival on campus in September, another meeting was held with subjects who had expressed an interest in participating. At that time, the interaction record was explained more fully. The record, a sample of which is shown in Figure 20.1, was to be completed for every interaction that lasted 10 minutes or longer. An interaction was defined as any encounter with another person(s) in which the participants attended to one another and adjusted their behavior in response to one another. Examples were provided (e.g., sitting next to someone in a lecture for 10 minutes was), and the various categories were discussed until everyone felt comfortable with the forms. A more detailed description may be found in Wheeler and Nezlek (1977). It was suggested to subjects that they fill out the records at a uniform time, such as before going to sleep. To encourage daily recording, subjects were asked to return their completed forms and pick up blank ones every few days. Throughout the study, a collaborative, nondeceptive atmosphere was maintained, which we believe aided the gathering of valid data. Confidentiality of the records was emphasized and closely guarded throughout. At the conclusion of each 10-day record period, a brief interview with one of our research assistants was held. During that session, the interviewer probed for difficulties, ambiguities, and potential sources of inaccurate data. In particular, subjects were urged to inform us of anything that might have impeded their accuracy.

Date _____ Time _____ a.m. _____
                            p.m. _____ Length _____
Initials _____ _____ _____ Male Group Female Group
                                  Mixed Group

Sex: _____ _____ _____ No _____
Initiator: Self   Other   Mutual   Unclear
Intimacy of Interaction   Intimate 7 6 5 4 3 2 1 Not Intimate
Satisfaction   Unpleasant 7 6 5 4 3 2 1 Pleasant
Location Mine Theirs Ours Driving On Campus
Off Campus
Nature Task Past-time Conversation Share Date Party
Date/Party Other

FIGURE 20.1 The interaction record form.

At the conclusion of the final interview, subjects were informed that we wished to photograph them in order to investigate the effects of physical attractiveness. They were told the slides would be evaluated at another university and would never be shown on this campus nor used for any other purposes. Further, they were allowed to reclaim their slides at any point. One subject declined to be photographed.

Uniform mid-thigh to over-the-head photographs were taken, with a beige background curtain. All subjects were asked to smile, and the most favorable of a minimum of 2 slides (as judged by the investigators) was used. Subjects had not been forewarned that they would be photographed; we sought photographs that would reflect their "everyday appearance." The 71 final slides were then grouped by sex and were randomly arranged within sex. They were judged by an introductory psychology class of 47 males and 49 females at another university 75 miles away. This university is essentially similar in its orientation and in the type of students it attracts. Although a group rating session was used, the need for independent ratings was highlighted, and the students remained silent throughout. They were instructed to use their own, personal standards of physical attractiveness. Each slide was judged on the same 1–15 scale, with the high end indicating greater attractiveness. To provide a general orientation, the entire set of slides was shown once. They were then rated on a second viewing, 25 sec per slide. All of the female slides were shown first, followed by the males.

Construction and Nomenclature of Interaction Variables

From the raw interaction records, composite indices were created in the following manner: *satisfaction*— mean reported satisfaction over all interactions; *intimacy*—mean reported intimacy over all interactions; *length*—mean reported length of all interactions; *per day*—mean reported number of interactions per day; *time per day*—mean reported length summed across all interactions per day; *list*—number of different individuals interacted with during the entire record-keeping period; *percentage*—percentage of all interactions falling into that category; *initiation*— proportion of all interactions that were self-, other, mutually or unclearly initiated (must sum to 1.00 for each subject); *nature*—proportion of all interactions that were tasks, passing time, conversations, sharing thoughts and feelings, dates/parties, or other activities (must sum to 1.00 for each subject).

Each of these categories was then subdivided in accordance with the sex composition of the encounter: *same sex*—interactions including up to three members of the same sex; *opposite sex*—interactions including up to three members of the opposite sex; *mixed sex*— interactions including three others, at least one of each sex; and *group*—interactions including more than three other people. *Overall* measures incorporate all interactions. The same- and opposite-sex categories were then further divided to distinguish the processes inherent in close and less close relationships. Interaction partners were first rank-ordered within each time period by the frequency of occurrence. Where duplicate sets of initials appeared, subjects were asked to provide distinguishing middle initials. Each of the interaction measures was then computed for subjects' three best friends (i.e., satisfaction, intimacy, etc., for those interactions in which the three most frequently reported partners participated) and other friends (i.e., those interactions including friends ranked fourth through last). The appropriateness of frequency to define closeness has been discussed earlier (Wheeler & Nezlek, 1977). In their sample, 93% of respondents named one of the three most frequent interactants as their best friend. It should be noted that some of the categories listed above contained no observations for some subjects. These entries were treated as missing data in the analyses.

RESULTS

Accuracy of the Interaction Records

All subject were interviewed individually after each data collection period. The record was examined for any peculiarities, subjective impressions were elicited, and a standardized interview was given. . . .

Although these self-reports cannot be construed as objective measures of accuracy, taken together they indicate that subjects felt the diaries were representative of their social lives. The linear time trend suggests that the record-keeping became easier over time, although the lack of effect on the percentage of interactions not recorded indicates that this was not due to differential reporting of interactions. Furthermore, mean differences were small when compared to the scale endpoints. When combined with the lack of sex differences, these data imply that our results are not likely to have been due to differential recording. It is useful to note further that these values are nearly identical to those reported by Wheeler and Nezlek (1977). Although the present study did not include sufficient pairs of interactants acquainted with each other to compute reliabilities, theirs did. Intraclass correlations for their subjects, sorted by sex and time, ranged from .67 to .84. As the present measures and procedures are highly similar, their data may be taken as evidence of adequate reliability.

Ratings of Physical Attractiveness

Before discussing the relationship of attractiveness and interaction, it will be useful to examine the nature of the ratings themselves. Male and female raters tended to agree on relative attractiveness ratings. Their mean ratings correlated .96 for male stimuli and .95 for female stimuli. This is consistent with reports of other studies (cf. Berscheid & Walster, 1974). However, mean differences appeared such that pictures of females were seen as more attractive than pictures of males . . . The respective means are shown in Table 20.1 and are similar to those found in previous research (e.g., Morse, Reis, Gruzen, & Wolff, 1974). The extremely high correlations indicate that the sexes agreed in their relative rankings.

For all analyses, mean physical attractiveness scores were obtained by averaging across all raters. Systematic sex-of-rater differences did not affect any of our results.[1]

TABLE 20.1   Mean Rating and Mean Variability of Stimulus Persons' Attractiveness

STIMULUS PERSONS	MALE RATERS	FEMALE RATERS
Mean attractiveness		
Males		
M	5.51	5.15
SD	1.24	1.52
Females		
M	6.31	6.64
SD	1.78	1.88
Mean standard deviations of attractiveness across raters		
Males	5.05	6.46
Females	5.83	6.81

There are 36 female and 35 male stimulus persons and 49 female and 47 male raters.

Attractiveness and Social Interaction

The present research concerned the relationship of physical attractiveness to interaction. A correlational approach is therefore more appropriate. Since the major hypothesis posited a simple linear relation, the first step was to compute Pearson product-moment correlations between mean physical attractiveness on the one hand and the interaction indices on the other, separately for all four time periods. The various social interaction parameters were broken down for overall, same, opposite, mixed, and group composition; their correlations with attractiveness are presented in Tables 20.2 through 20.4 and 20.6 through 20.8. Correlations for the three best and other friends breakdown are discussed only for those instances in which they deviated from the combined results and therefore shed additional light on the phenomena. Results for the primary dependent variables, interaction quantity and quality, will be presented first, followed by the secondary measures of initiation and nature of the interaction.

A brief note on the quantity of computations is in order. Of course, computation of such a massive set of correlations necessarily produces a substantial number of chance-generated significant correlations (using the .05 criterion, 1/20). The only possible control for spurious conclusion drawing will be internal consistency across time periods and variables. Consistent, repeated, and strong data patterns will be treated as meaningful results; isolated significant correlations will be noted but considered cautiously.

Interaction Quantity

Table 20.2 presents the correlations between interaction quantity and attractiveness for males. These results are strong and stroking. Physically attractive males socialized with more females, more frequently, longer per interaction and per day, and as a greater proportion of their total social participation. They also engaged in mixed-sex encounters more often and with a greater duration. By contrast, attractive males reported interacting with fewer other males, less often, and as a smaller proportion of their daily socializing, although the length of these encounters was unaffected. Interestingly, these decrements in same-sex involvement grew stronger over time, perhaps suggesting that as their first year of college progressed and academic/extracurricular pressure increased, social interaction necessarily became more selective. Early in the year, interaction with females was essentially irrelevant to time spent with other males; later it precluded it. Group interactions showed no significant relationships with appearance for males.

The corresponding correlations for females are shown in Table 20.3. Immediately apparent is the lack of significant relationships between interaction quantity and physical appearance. Only one correlation, that with the proportion of group interactions during the fourth time period, was significant at the $p < .05$ level. Since this general paucity of significant correlations was surprising, the data were further scrutinized for nonlinear relationships. No significant quadratic (i.e., either inverted or upright U-shaped bivariate frequency distributions) relationships were found. Thus, the results for interaction quantity may be summarized succinctly: For males, beauty related

positively to interaction with women and negatively with men; for females, there were no discernible correlates.

Interaction Quality

Table 20.4 presents the Pearson correlations between attractiveness and self-reported intimacy and satisfaction for both sexes. Looking at females and males simultaneously, perceived intimacy did not relate to

TABLE 20.2 Correlations of Interaction Quantity and Physical Attractiveness for Males

COMPOSITION/ VARIABLE	TIME 1	TIME 2	TIME 3	TIME 4
Same list	−.03	−.18	−.33	−.39
Opposite list	.59	.32	.52	.57
Same percent	−.62	−.49	−.68	−.69
Opposite percent	.57	.40	.63	.65
Mixed percent	.32	.29	.54	.49
Group percent	.16	.08	−.07	−.01
Overall per day	.23	.14	.22	.13
Same	−.25	−.20	−.46	−.60
Opposite	.60	.35	.65	.56
Mixed	.44	.29	.59	.49
Group	.22	.12	−.03	−.00
Overall length	.21	.35	.44	.31
Same	−.03	.07	−.09	.21
Opposite	.17	.26	.64	.70
Mixed	−.04	.47	.33	.00
Group	.14	.20	.35	.13
Overall time	.38	.35	.44	.30
Same	−.15	−.14	−.40	−.41
Opposite	.61	.40	.67	.60
Mixed	.49	.51	.65	.51
Group	.22	.26	.18	.12

*Note. n*s vary from 33 to 36. Two-tailed critical values of *r* for 31 *df* are as follows: $r = .29$ ($p < .10$); $r = .34$ ($p < .05$); $r = .44$ ($p < .01$). Length *n*s vary from 24 to 35 because some subjects had no interactions in either the group or opposite-sex categories.

TABLE 20.3 Correlations of Interaction Quantity and Physical Attractiveness for Females

COMPOSITION/ VARIABLE	TIME 1	TIME 2	TIME 3	TIME 4
Same list	.12	−.05	−.02	−.26
Opposite list	−.10	.26	.13	.00
Same percent	−.01	−.01	.05	−.16
Opposite percent	−.15	−.03	−.02	.10
Mixed percent	.24	.05	−.05	.09
Group percent	.22	.10	.09	.39
Overall per day	.11	.13	−.04	−.20
Same	.11	.09	.01	−.23
Opposite	−.16	.04	−.01	−.03
Mixed	.24	.14	−.07	−.08
Group	.22	.16	.06	.18
Overall length	−.02	−.12	−.11	.21
Same	−.04	−.05	−.04	−.21
Opposite	−.05	−.10	−.18	.32
Mixed	.21	−.15	−.21	.27
Group	.11	−.17	−.06	−.11
Overall time	.17	.00	−.14	−.04
Same	.04	.07	−.06	−.28
Opposite	−.09	−.05	−.00	.11
Mixed	.35	−.03	−.15	.11
Group	.19	.02	−.01	.25

Note. *n*s vary from 34 to 35. Two-tailed critical values of *r* for 32 *df* are as follows: *r* = .29 (*p* < .10); *r* = .34 (*p* < .05); *r* = .43 (*p* < .01). Length *n*s vary from 31 to 35 because some subjects had no interactions in the group category.

TABLE 20.4 Correlations of Interaction Quality and Physical Attractiveness

COMPOSITION/ VARIABLE	TIME 1	TIME 2	TIME 3	TIME 4
	Males			
Overall intimacy	.20	.17	.16	.23
Same	.19	.16	.08	.21
Opposite	.03	.16	.32	.25
Mixed	.27	.21	.10	.09
Group	.12	.16	−.02	.12
Overall satisfaction	.06	.10	.17	.28
Same	−.03	−.04	.03	.17
Opposite	−.17	.04	.36	.41
Mixed	−.00	.06	.14	.15
Group	.04	.08	.01	.19
	Females			
Overall intimacy	.21	−.05	.25	.15
Same	.24	.00	.27	.27
Opposite	.23	−.20	.37	.31
Mixed	.04	−.01	.24	.09
Group	.07	−.05	.34	.22
Overall satisfaction	.03	.01	.21	.25
Same	.04	.07	.29	.22
Opposite	.24	.08	.21	.41
Mixed	−.04	.01	.21	.26
Group	−.11	−.10	.16	.30

Note. *n*s vary from 33 to 36. Two-tailed critical values of *r* for 31 *df* are as follows: *r* = .29 (*p* < .10); *r* = .34 (*p* < .05); *r* = .44 (*p* < .01). Group *n*s and male opposite sex *n*s vary from 24 to 35 because some subjects had no interactions in those categories.

appearance. Satisfaction revealed the more intriguing pattern of an increasingly positive correlation with attractiveness over time, most apparently so in interactions including members of the opposite sex. All 10 satisfaction correlations increased in positivity from the first time period to the third and fourth, and although only 2 of the Time 4 correlations were significant at *p* < .05 (opposite-sex satisfaction for females and males), the remainder were in the appropriate direction approaching significance (for 7,

p < .15). Examination of the satisfaction-attractiveness correlations for best and other friends separately revealed that this increment occurred primarily for other friend relationships. For females, attractiveness maintained a steady correlation with three best opposite-sex friends satisfaction (.23, .07, .19, .12), whereas it increased steadily for other opposite-sex friends (−.15, .18, .23, .39). For males, attractiveness showed similarly small changes with the three best opposite-sex friends (−.08, .18, .30, .17) and large gains with other opposite sex friends (−.28, .07, .25, .58). Comparable results were found for females' same-sex relationships (three best: .07, .08, .20, .19; others: .01, .12, .41, .33), although not for males. Thus, the increasingly positive relationship between attractiveness and satisfaction over time seems to derive primarily from changes in more peripheral opposite-sex interactions.

Initiation of Interactions

Although Hypothesis 2 predicted equivalent relationships between attractiveness and interaction for both sexes, correlations for attractiveness and initiation were expected to differ by gender (See Table 20.5).

Results did not support this prediction; however, they were consistent with the data pattern that has emerged so far. That is, for males, initiation did relate to attractiveness, chiefly in opposite-sex encounters. For females, no meaningful tendencies

appeared. Table 20.6 lists the correlation between male- and female-rated attractiveness and the proportions of opposite-sex interactions falling into each of the initiation categories. As can be seen, beautiful males had a greater preponderance of interactions that they perceived as mutually initiated, and a lesser proportion of self- and other-initiated encounters.[2] Although the overall, same, mixed, and group initiation data did not reveal any set of results beyond chance expectation, it should be noted that a number of individual correlations were consistent with this trend, and none contradicted it. The following significant correlations with attractiveness were found for males: Time 1, overall other initiation; $r(33) = -.36$; Time 4, overall unclear initiation: $r(32) = .33$.

Nature of Interactions

The final set of interaction variables sorted all social events into six distinct categories: tasks, pastimes, conversations, sharing feelings, dates/parties, and others. This was done to examine qualitative

TABLE 20.5 Correlations of Attractiveness Variance With Satisfaction

COMPOSITION/ VARIABLE	TIME 1	TIME 2	TIME 3	TIME 4
		Males		
Overall satisfaction	−.02	−.04	.07	.16
Same	−.10	−.16	−.04	.08
Opposite	−.22	.10	.38	.35
Mixed	−.05	−.09	.02	.13
Group	.04	−.04	−.03	.13
		Females		
Overall satisfaction	.17	.33	.42	.35
Same	.23	.37	.47	.29
Opposite	.16	.27	.43	.40
Mixed	.01	.34	.37	.37
Group	.05	.48	.41	.39

Note. *n*s vary from 33 to 36. Two-tailed critical values of *r* for 31 *df* are as follows: *r* = .29 (*p* < .10); *r* = .34 (*p* < .05); *r* = .44 (*p* < .01). Group *n*s, and male opposite sex *n*s vary from 24 to 35 because some subjects had no interactions in those categories.

TABLE 20.6 Attractiveness as Correlated With Initiation of Opposite-Sex Interactions

VARIABLE	TIME 1	TIME 2	TIME 3	TIME 4
		Males		
Self-initiation	−.19	.08	−.11	−.49
Other initiation	−.34	−.23	.16	.05
Mutual initiation	.50	.25	.26	.29
Unclear initiation	.07	−.14	−.29	.30
		Females		
Self-initiation	−.12	−.25	.05	−.05
Other initiation	.04	−.01	−.22	−.10
Mutual initiation	.31	.11	.06	.09
Unclear initiation	−.35	.24	.26	.11

Note. *n*s vary from 33 to 36. Two-tailed critical values of *r* for 31 *df* are as follows: *r* = .29 (*p* < .10); *r* = .34 (*p* < .05); *r* = .44 (*p* < .01). Group *n*s, and male opposite sex *n*s vary from 24 to 35 because some subjects had no interactions in those categories.

differences in the manner in which attractive and less attractive individuals spend their social time. To control for quantity differences, each score represented the proportion of all interactions of that sex composition spent in that domain. Among other things, these variables will allow us to test in our data the one finding most often reported in the literature: that attractive individuals date more frequently.

Table 20.7 presents these correlations for males. More attractive men appear to be spending a larger proportion of their interactions in conversations and a smaller proportion in pastimes and, to a lesser extent, in tasks, the two activity-centered dimensions. This pattern was spread across all of the sex composition categories and time periods, although the results were most consistent for overall and same-sex interactions, as well as for the latter two time periods. There was also a less consistent tendency for attractive males to date/party relatively more frequently in mixed-sex settings. Comparison of the three best friend and other friend correlations did not reveal any distinguishing trends.

The corresponding correlations for females are listed in Table 20.8. As with their male counterparts, attractive females tended to occupy a lesser proportion of their interactions with tasks. They also reported proportionally fewer "other" activities and sharing feelings. In contrast, they experienced more prevalent date/party interactions, notably including more than one other person, as most party interactions might. In the literature, attractiveness typically reveals a positive correlation with the *number* of dates, and it does in our data as well. The number of mixed-sex–date/party interactions correlated .30, .10, .32, and .36 with attractiveness over the four time periods (all but the second figure are significant at $p < .08$). These dates/parties tended to involve peripheral rather than their three best male friends: the attractiveness–opposite-sex others–date/party correlations approached significance at $p < .11$ for Time 3 and Time 4, both $rs(33) = .26$. Thus, support for the hypothesis that attractive women date more often is contained in our data.

TABLE 20.7   Males' Attractiveness as Correlated With the Nature of Their Interactions

COMPOSITION/VARIABLE	TIME 1	TIME 2	TIME 3	TIME 4
Tasks:				
Overall	.10	.02	−.11	−.17
Same	−.01	−.05	.03	.03
Opposite	.21	.24	−.46	−.07
Mixed	.17	−.09	−.28	−.00
Group	.12	−.11	.22	.13
Pastime:				
Overall	−.27	−.38	−.49	−.43
Same	−.15	−.44	−.30	−.44
Opposite	.19	.09	−.08	−.39
Mixed	−.46	−.20	−.15	.16
Group	−.36	−.23	−.07	−.30
Converse:				
Overall	−.03	−.00	.30	.39
Same	−.02	.22	.22	.39
Opposite	.03	−.19	.41	.25
Mixed	.23	−.13	.14	.16
Group	.15	.00	−.16	.06
Share:				
Overall	.12	.19	.18	.20
Same	.11	.10	.15	.08
Opposite	−.15	.02	.22	.34
Mixed	−.03	.42	−.13	.11
Group	−.09	.08	−.11	−.04
Party/Date:				
Overall	.16	.27	.23	−.06
Same	.11	.05	−.15	−.19
Opposite	−.17	−.05	.07	.05
Mixed	.25	.39	.29	−.23
Group	.18	.21	.31	.06
Other:				
Overall	.03	.08	.12	.03
Same	.02	.06	.29	.10
Opposite	.03	.05	−.01	−.17
Mixed	.01	−.28	−.04	−.25
Group	−.21	−.24	−.00	.14

*Note. n*s and significance criteria are the same as in Table 20.1.

TABLE 20.8 Females' Attractiveness as Correlated With the Nature of Their Interactions

COMPOSITION/ VARIABLE	TIME 1	TIME 2	TIME 3	TIME 4
Tasks:				
Overall	−.12	−.11	−.17	−.12
Same	−.19	−.16	−.10	−.09
Opposite	−.28	−.10	−.25	.06
Mixed	−.08	−.04	−.43	−.21
Group	.13	−.11	−.08	−.33
Pastime:				
Overall	.04	.05	.16	.16
Same	.14	.01	.24	.08
Opposite	.02	.16	−.00	−.06
Mixed	.10	.01	.09	.09
Group	−.05	−.08	−.03	.13
Converse:				
Overall	−.13	.13	−.16	−.21
Same	−.19	.23	−.15	−.11
Opposite	.18	.25	.12	−.02
Mixed	−.10	−.00	.04	−.17
Group	−.09	.15	−.03	.04
Share:				
Overall	.05	−.33	.10	.11
Same	.15	−.35	.05	.19
Opposite	−.01	−.34	.01	−.02
Mixed	.11	−.13	.27	.17
Group	−.15	−.13	.25	.21
Party/Date:				
Overall	.29	.13	.29	.46
Same	.16	.26	.16	.10
Opposite	.05	−.09	.14	.12
Mixed	.06	.22	.28	.48
Group	.23	.20	.14	.30
Other:				
Overall	.17	.13	−.05	−.15
Same	.06	.18	−.25	−.38
Opposite	.22	.10	.20	.10
Mixed	.01	.06	−.19	−.20
Group	−.08	−.15	−.30	−.48

*Note. n*s and significance criteria are the same as in Table 20.3.

DISCUSSION

We will begin discussing and interpreting our results by summarizing the predominant trends that bear on our three initial hypotheses. (a) Physical attractiveness was strongly related to the quantity of social interaction for males, positively with the opposite sex and negatively with the same sex; no significant pattern emerged for females. (b) For both sexes, satisfaction, particularly with opposite-sex interactions, showed an increasing tendency over time to be positively correlated with attractiveness. (c) Females with more variable attractiveness ratings were more likely to be satisfied with their socializing. (d) Physically attractive males tended to have more mutually initiated and fewer self or other initiated interactions with the opposite sex. (e) Attractive males spent more of their interactions conversing and less in activities; attractive females also reported a lesser proportion of task interactions and more prevalent date/parties.

Thus, Hypothesis I was clearly supported, but only for males. Of course, this means that Hypothesis 2 was not supported, but the findings are interesting in that they challenge folk wisdom: Attractiveness was a more important concomitant of social interaction for males than for females. Finally, Hypothesis 3 was supported in that most correlations with attractiveness endured over time. Correlations that changed, such as those for satisfaction, grew stronger as the academic year progressed.

That male attractiveness was broadly and quite strongly related to the quantity of interaction is consistent with other results reported by Berscheid et al. (1971), Krebs and Adinolfi (1975), and Walster et al. (1966). Prettier males had more and longer interactions for more time per day with more different females, both alone and in mixed-sex company. In contrast, they had fewer interactions with fewer other males. In addition, interactions involving females occupied a greater proportion of their social lives. Apparently, these males expanded their opposite-sex contacts at the expense of, rather than as a supplement to, other same-sex socializing. Perhaps their beauty makes them more acceptable to female partners and therefore less likely or less able to seek companionship elsewhere. Attractive males may also have experienced more positive feedback in opposite-sex encounters in the past, producing greater confidence, enjoyment, and attraction to relationships with women. This explanation is favored by the finding that these interactions were more likely to be conversations than tasks or pastimes and that they tended to be mutually initiated. A conversation focuses attention on the people involved. Anxiety or general unease would lead one to seek "something to do" in order to avoid awkward unfilled moments or self-focusing (objective self-awareness). Similarly, greater reliance on mutual initiation implies less of a seeking or being-sought orientation and more of a natural progression of chance contacts into interactions lasting at least as long as our criterion of 10 minutes. Along with Goldman and Lewis's (1977) finding that attractive males were more socially skillful in anonymous telephone conversations, it appears that beautiful males' greater heterosexual contact reflects greater self-assurance and skill. Doubtless, social anxiety stems from prior experiences. However, critical self-assessments may lead unattractive males to withdraw from heterosexual contact, thereby "proving" their own hypothesis in the manner of a self-fulfilling prophecy. Skills and confidence require practice, and one simply comes to prefer interactions with other males. By avoiding contact with women, rejection, particularly without externalizing justifications that maintain self-esteem, is not possible (Jones & Berglas, 1978).

It is perplexing that our data revealed no similar relationships for females. Prior research and popular wisdom suggest more prevalent effects for females, with the exception of Byrne et al. (1970), who found that attraction correlated more strongly with their dates' physical beauty for female subjects than males. Supporting a "no relationship" conclusion over experimental artifact is our replication of the basic datum reported in prior research: Attractive females reported more date/party interactions. However, this did not extend to other quantitative indices of their social lives.

One potential explanation centers on male–female differences in orientation to social interaction, differences that Deaux (1977) has characterized in terms of self-presentational style. Males, according to Deaux, are likely to choose a *status-asserting* manner, seeking to establish a more dominant position for themselves. In contrast, females prefer an affiliative, or *status-neutralizing*, style that minimizes status differentials and instead builds egalitarian bonds. If one thinks of beauty as a social asset, then more attractive males would perceive their chances of acceptance as higher (Huston, 1973) and would consequently seek interaction with females to enhance their social status. Less attractive males would assess their lot less favorably and shun interaction with females, since there was little stature to be gained. (Interestingly, Morse et al., 1974, found that males who rated females' attractiveness more highly dated less.) A related alternative states that many males fear rejection by attractive women. For females, self-perceptions of beauty would be less important, since the choice of an interaction partner would not be based on developing status differentials, but instead on eliminating them. The interaction and relationship itself is the focus, rather than any gains in social standing. The absence of a particular type of interaction or partner then leads simply to choosing a substitute, since there is greater latitude in the scope of acceptable activities and partners. Attractiveness may therefore not be so relevant to whether, and in what manner, a female socializes . . .

From these data, nothing should be more apparent than the fact that physical attractiveness plays an important role in social participation, the nature of this effect being decidedly more complex than was initially suspected. The "what is beautiful is good" stereotype may well be the origin of meaningful variations in one's style, extent, and feelings about socializing. These would include social skills, social confidence, the manner of activities and relationships one chooses, and cognitons about those relationships and oneself. What first figures as a superficial, minimally consequential trait is thereby imbued with substantial importance. Considerably more research is therefore appropriate, paying attention not only to what people's implicit theories about physical attractiveness are but to the real-life ramifications of these beliefs as well. Such research entails the naturalistic study of people in a broad context as they go about their lives.

NOTES

1. To control for the possibility that the sex-of-rater differences might have affected these measures, mean attractiveness was also computed from standard scores, thereby equalizing the sex-of-rater means and standard deviations. None of the correlations differed from those presented by more than .01. Further, correlations calculated separately for subjects' ratings by male judges and by female judges revealed results virtually identical to those presented. Thus the sex-of-rater differences that emerged seem not to be related to social interaction. Copies of these analyses are available from the senior author on request.

2. Because of skew in the distributions, Spearman rank-order correlations were computed to ensure that these findings were not attributable to a few anomalous cases. All significant correlations remained significant in this analysis.

REFERENCES

Adams, G. R. Physical attractiveness research: Toward a developmental social psychology of beauty. *Human Development,* 1977, *20,* 217–239.

Berscheid, E., Dion, K. K., Walster, E., & Walster, G. W. Physical attractiveness and dating choice: A test of the matching hypothesis. *Journal of Experimental Social Psychology,* 1971, *7,* 173–189.

Berscheid, E., & Walster, E. Physical attractiveness. In L. Berkowitz (Ed.), *Advances in experimental social psychology* (Vol. 7). New York: Academic Press, 1974.

Brislin, R. W., & Lewis, S. A. Dating and physical attractiveness: Replication. *Psychological Reports,* 1968, *22,* 976.

Byrne, D., Ervin, C. R., & Lamberth, J. Continuity between the experimental study of attraction and real-life computer dating. *Journal of Personality and Social Psychology,* 1970, *16,* 157–165.

Deaux, K. Sex differences in social behavior. In T. Blass (Ed.), *Personality variables in social behavior.* Hillsdale, N.J.: Erlbaum, 1977.

Dion, K. K., Berscheid, E., & Walster, E. What is beautiful is good. *Journal of Personality and Social Psychology,* 1972, *24,* 285–290.

Goldman, W., & Lewis, P. Beautiful is good: Evidence that the physically attractive are more socially skillful. *Journal of Experimental Social Psychology,* 1977, *13,* 125–130.

Huston, T. L. Ambiguity of acceptance, social desirability, and dating choice. *Journal of Experimental Social Psychology,* 1973, *9,* 32–42.

Jones, E. E., & Berglas, S. Control of attributions about the self through self-handicapping strategies: The appeal of alcohol and the role of underachievement. *Personality and Social Psychology Bulletin,* 1978, *4,* 200–206.

Krebs, D., & Adinolfi, A. A. Physical attractiveness, social relations, and personality style. *Journal of Personality and Social Psychology,* 1975, *31,* 245–253.

Mathes, E. W. The effects of physical attractiveness and anxiety on heterosexual attraction over a series of five encounters. *Journal of Marriage and the Family,* 1975, *37,* 769–774.

Morse, S. J., Reis, H. T., Gruzen, J., & Wolff, E. The "eye of the beholder": Determinants of physical attractiveness judgments in the U.S. and South Africa. *Journal of Personality,* 1974, *42,* 528–542.

Snyder, M., Tanke, E. D., & Berscheid, E. Social perception and interpersonal behavior: On the self-fulfilling nature of social stereotypes. *Journal of Personality and Social Psychology,* 1977, *35,* 656–666.

Tesser, A., & Brodie, M. A note on the evaluation of a "computer date." *Psychonomic Science,* 1971, *23,* 300.

Walster, E., Aronson, V., Abrahams, D., & Rottmann, L. Importance of physical attractiveness in dating behavior. *Journal of Personality and Social Psychology,* 1966, *4,* 508–516.

Wheeler, L., & Nezlek, J. Sex differences in social participation. *Journal of Personality and Social Psychology,* 1977, *35,* 742–754.

PART 8

CRIME, DEVIANCE, AND SOCIAL CONTROL

Sociologists define *deviance* as a violation of social norms—the rules and expectations for behavior. Violations of *folkways*—minor rules of behavior—invoke small forms of disapproval. For example, if I do not bathe or shower for a week or so, I may have to endure the scrunched up faces of those I get close to (as they get a whiff of my body odor). Violations of more important norms—called *mores* (more-ays)—can lead to serious reproof. If I shoplift a can of deodorant and get caught, I may find myself being led from the store in handcuffs and confronting possible jail time and community-wide humiliation as the news spreads among my family and acquaintances that I've been arrested. Stealing is a violation of an important norm and can elicit major retribution.

In small and homogeneous societies in which everyone has the same skin color, the same language, the same religion, and so on, deciding what constitutes deviance is easy. In larger and more heterogeneous societies, however, what does and does not constitute a violation of norms is more problematic. As the saying goes "One man's meat is another man's poison." For example, many southeast Asian immigrants from rural backgrounds have been accustomed in their homelands to supplementing their diets with whatever they can forage from the environment. This practice, however, can lead to serious problems in the United States. For instance, when they fish they keep everything they catch. This often results in violations of the fish and game laws, which restrict the type, size, and number of fish any one angler can take. When arrested and taken to court, these immigrants often simply cannot understand what they've done wrong; in their minds, all that they've done is to support their families and put food on the table.

When the norms of two or more groups come into conflict, which will prevail? Not surprisingly, the answer is the norms of the more prosperous and powerful groups.

Social control signifies the means by which individuals and groups induce one another to follow prevailing norms of behavior. Social control may be *informal* and occur during the course of everyday interactions, or it may be *formal* and have the weight of authority behind it. Teachers, bishops, police officers, and judges are representative of formal social control. The many specific manifestations of social control are called *sanctions*. Sanctions may be positive or negative, either formal or informal. The following table displays examples of the various types of sanctions:

TYPE OF SOCIAL CONTROL

	INFORMAL	FORMAL
POSITIVE	• Smiles • Pats on the back • Acceptance into the group • Compliments and praise	• Awards and citations • Grades and diplomas • Pay raises and promotions • Religious confirmations
NEGATIVE	• Frowns • Scowls • Ostracism • Embarrassment	• Firings, pay cuts, demotions • Demerits, suspensions • Arrests, fines, jail terms • Excommunications

TYPE OF SANCTION

University of Arizona sociologist Travis Hirschi's classic study of delinquency is based on the theoretic idea of social control. More specifically, he demonstrates the importance of an individual's attachment to the group in keeping the individual in check, that is, in line with normative expectations for behavior. He emphasizes that the key question in the study of deviance is *not* "Why do individuals commit deviant acts?" but rather, "Why don't individuals commit deviant acts?" His answer is founded on a fundamental principle of human reality: People like being liked and like being accepted; to achieve these aims they conform to expectations of those whom they want to like and accept them. Thus, Hirschi found that adolescents who had strong ties to their families and to their schools were less likely to commit delinquent acts—because such acts are frowned upon by these two groups.

Hirschi's approach to deviance has become known as **control theory** in the language of modern-day social science. This theory consistently receives in empirical support, and one of the most important examples of this is presented in the essay by John H. Laub (of Northeastern University in Boston), Daniel S. Nagin (of Carnegie Mellon University in Pittsburgh), and Robert J. Sampson (of the University of Chicago). More particularly, they demonstrate that delinquent boys who end up getting married during their twenties are much less likely to commit criminal acts in adulthood compared to their counterparts who did not marry, especially when the marriages are of high quality—which is to say tight-knit and emotionally satisfying to both husbands and wives.

D. L. Rosenhan, of Stanford University, highlights the problem of normative definitions of proper conduct in a heterogeneous society like that of the United States—a society with a great deal of economic inequality and of ethnic and racial diversity. His essay is also reflective of an important perspective in the sociological study of deviance: **labeling theory**. One of the guiding postulates of labeling theory is that the less powerful members of a society have little control in defining societal norms. Thus, for example, the small and weak religious sect of Rastafarianism enjoins its members to smoke marijuana as a religious ritual; they would undoubtedly like to redefine marijuana as a relatively harmless drug and to eliminate all legal sanctions for its possession, use, or sale, but as they are so weak and so few in number, they cannot.

A second postulate of labeling theory is that the weaker members of a society are more likely to be singled out and punished for their "deviant" acts and, consequently, more likely to receive a deviant *label* (e.g., as "thief," "slut," "druggie," or whatever). The chain of effects after receiving a deviant label can be devastating: First, "straight" people may begin to avoid the "deviant." One of their fears, of course, is that they too will acquire a similar label if they are seen with him or her. Second, being denied acceptance by "straight" society, the "deviant" individual begins to hang around other outcasts in the search of friendship and emotional support. If these others often engage in deviant acts, the new "deviant" may begin to participate to win approval and acceptance. In time, the "deviant" individual may well come to accept the deviant label as a self-image: "I *am* a thief"; "I *am* a slut"; "I *am* a drug addict" and so on. Adding A (straight society shuns the "deviant") plus B (the "deviant" begins hanging out with other "deviants") plus C (the "deviant" accepts the label as descriptive of his or her true inner self), what would you expect to get? The answer, of course, is D, more deviance. Labeling theorists call deviance that arises from being labeled a "deviant" *secondary deviance*; they call the original deviant acts *primary deviance*. Do you see the conundrum, in this case a vicious circle, that the labeling perspective presents us with? We cannot tolerate serious deviance; say, burglary. So we catch and punish the burglar. But by doing so—by arresting him, publishing his name in the newspaper, putting him in prison and giving him a record that is publicly available—what have we done? Ensured that he continues to be a thief!

In most people's minds, the concept of deviance is negative. It invokes images of delinquency and crime and uncouth behavior. However, deviance may be "innovative." Émile Durkheim (1858–1917) was the first sociologist to clearly recognize that crime and deviance were a part of every society and that, indeed, they could serve positive functions. Among these functions two are paramount: First, the singling out and punishing of deviants encourages group solidarity—it brings members closer to one another ("we're not like that person"). Second, deviance may encourage social change, which can be very good for a society, as two examples from the last half of the twentieth century potently remind us. In the Civil Rights movement, many blacks (and whites) defied segregationist laws and got themselves arrested, beaten, and even murdered in the cause of promoting a more equitable, just, and productive society. Similarly, the post–World War II women's liberation movement involved many women (and men) violating conventional expectations of proper attire, behavior, and social and economic roles. Robert K. Merton emphasizes that a society's cultural goals may not be accompanied by realistic means for attaining them—at least not for everyone.[1] Those who want the accepted goals but do not have ready access to the accepted means to attain them may "innovate" and come up with their own means. Thus, for example, the inner-city adolescent whose family has few resources to send him to private school, help him get a job, or start a career and who attends a school where the majority of students will drop out may well find himself out on the streets as a young man, with few prospects. From the popular culture—television, movies, magazines—and from his friends and family he has absorbed the cultural goal of material success. Unable to achieve it by conventional means—that is, by getting an education and using his networks to get a good first job—he "innovates" and tries to reach it through criminal means (he steals, sells drugs, or whatever).

But the women who burned their bras in the 1960s were also innovators. They shared the cultural expectation of individual fulfillment and happiness and the cultural goal of doing socially productive work. However, the means that societal norms had open to them in 1960—getting married and being productive by having children and taking care of them and the husband and the house—were very constricting. And, indeed, even if every woman had wanted to follow this narrow path, American society was structured so that this was impossible. That is, the sex ratio (the number of males per every 100 women) was unbalanced, especially for those of marriageable age. For every

---

[1]See Robert K. Merton, "Social Structure and Anomie," in his *Social Theory and Social Structure*. Enlarged Edition (New York: The Free Press, 1968), especially pp. 185–203.

100 women in their twenties who wanted to get married in 1968, there were only 70 or 80 eligible males. What were the 5 million or so forced-to-be single women supposed to do? Crawl into a hole? Instead, large numbers of them engaged in and encouraged "deviance," that is, they tried to redefine the sex roles in American life such that "career woman" was no longer a mild epithet. Many women in college and in professional careers today think nothing of being there, least of all of being there as a mild form of deviance. They owe their thanks to the "deviant" innovators of the preceding generation.

_____CHAPTER 21_____

CONTROL THEORY AND JUVENILE DELINQUENCY

TRAVIS HIRSCHI

The more weakened the groups to which the [individual] belongs, the less he depends on them, the more he consequently depends only on himself and recognizes no other rules of conduct than what are founded on his private interests.[1]

Control theories assume that delinquent acts result when an individual's bond to society is weak or broken. Since these theories embrace two highly complex concepts, the *bond* of the individual to *society*, it is not surprising that they have at one time or another formed the basis of explanations of most forms of aberrant or unusual behavior. It is also not surprising that control theories have described the elements of the bond to society in many ways, and that they have focused on a variety of units as the point of control.

I begin with a classification and description of the elements of the bond to conventional society. I try to show how each of these elements is related to delinquent behavior and how they are related to each other. . . .

ELEMENTS OF THE BOND

Attachment

In explaining conforming behavior, sociologists justly emphasize sensitivity to the opinion of others[2]. . . . The process of becoming alienated from others often involves or is based on active interpersonal conflict. Such conflict could easily supply a reservoir of *socially derived* hostility sufficient to account for the aggressiveness of those whose attachments to others have been weakened.

Durkheim said it many years ago: "We are moral beings to the extent that we are social beings."[3] This may be interpreted to mean that we are moral beings to the extent that we have "internalized the norms" of society. But what does it mean to say that a person has internalized the norms of society? The norms of society are by definition shared by the members of society. To violate a norm is, therefore, to act contrary to the wishes and expectations of other people. If a person does not care about the wishes and expectations of other people—that is, if he is insensitive to the opinion of others—then he is to that extent not bound by the norms. He is free to deviate.

The essence of internalization of norms, conscience, or super-ego thus lies in the attachment of the individual to others. . . .

Commitment

"Of all passions, that which inclineth men least to break the laws, is fear. Nay, excepting some generous natures, it is the only thing, when there is the appearance of profit or pleasure by breaking the laws, that makes men keep them."[4] Few would deny that men on occasion obey the rules simply from fear of the consequences. This rational component in conformity we label commitment. What does it mean to say that a person is committed to conformity? In Howard S. Becker's formulation it means the following:

First, the individual is in a position in which his decision with regard to some particular line of action has consequences for other interests and activities not necessarily [directly] related to it. Second, he has placed himself in that position by his own prior actions. A third element is present though so obvious as not to be apparent: the committed person must be aware [of these other interests] and must recognize that his decision in this case will have ramifications beyond it.[5]

The idea, then, is that the person invests time, energy, himself, in a certain line of activity—say, getting an education, building up a business, acquiring a reputation for virtue. When or whenever he considers deviant behavior, he must consider the costs of this deviant behavior, the risk he runs of losing the investment he has made in conventional behavior . . . To the person committed to conventional lines of action, risking one to ten years in prison for a ten-dollar holdup is stupidity, because to the committed person the costs and risks obviously exceed ten dollars in value. . . .

The concept of commitment assumes that the organization of society is such that the interests of most persons would be endangered if they were to engage in criminal acts. Most people, simply by the process of living in an organized society, acquire goods, reputations, prospects that they do not want to risk losing. These accumulations are society's insurance that they will abide by the rules. Many hypotheses about the antecedents of delinquent behavior are based on this premise. For example, Arthur L. Stinchcombe's hypothesis that "high school rebellion . . . occurs when future status is not clearly related to present performance" suggests that one is committed to conformity not only by what one has but also by what one hopes to obtain.[6] Thus "ambition" and/or "aspiration" play an important role in producing conformity. The person becomes committed to a conventional line of action, and he is therefore committed to conformity.

Most lines of action in a society are of course conventional. The clearest examples are educational and occupational careers. Actions thought to jeopardize one's chances in these areas are presumably avoided. Interestingly enough, even nonconventional commitments may operate to produce conventional conformity. We are told, at least, that boys aspiring to careers in the rackets or professional thievery are judged by their "honesty" and "reliability"—traits traditionally in demand among seekers of office boys.[7]

Involvement

Many persons undoubtedly owe a life of virtue to a lack of opportunity to do otherwise. Time and energy are inherently limited: "Not that I would not, if I could, be both handsome and fat and well dressed, and a great athlete, and make a million a year, be a wit, a bon vivant, and a lady killer, as well as a philosopher, a philanthropist, a statesman, warrior, and African explorer, as well as a 'tone-poet' and saint. But the thing is simply impossible."[8] The things that William James here says he would like to be or do are all, I suppose, within the realm of conventionality, but if he were to include illicit actions he would still have to eliminate some of them as simply impossible.

Involvement or engrossment in conventional activities is thus often part of a control theory. The assumption, widely shared, is that a person may be simply too busy doing conventional things to find time to engage in deviant behavior. The person involved in conventional activities is tied to appointments, deadlines, working hours, plans, and the like, so the opportunity to commit deviant acts rarely arises. To the extent that he is engrossed in conventional activities, he cannot even think about deviant acts, let alone act out his inclinations.

This line of reasoning is responsible for the stress placed on recreational facilities in many programs to reduce delinquency, for much of the concern with the high school dropout, and for the idea that boys should be drafted into the Army to keep them out of trouble. So obvious and persuasive is the idea that involvement in conventional activities is a major deterrent to delinquency that it was accepted even by Sutherland: "In the general area of juvenile delinquency it is probable that the most significant difference between juveniles who engage in delinquency and those who do not is that the latter are provided abundant opportunities of a conventional type for satisfying their recreational interests, while the former lack those opportunities or facilities."[9] [In short,] "idle hands are the devil's workshop." . . .

Belief

Unlike the cultural deviance theory, the control theory assumes the existence of a common value system within the society or group whose norms are being violated. If the deviant is committed to a value system different from that of conventional society, there is, within the context of the theory, nothing to explain. The question is, "Why does a man violate the rules in which he believes?" It is not, "Why do men differ in their beliefs about what constitutes good and desirable conduct?" The person is assumed to have been socialized (perhaps imperfectly) into the group whose rules he is violating; deviance is not a question of one group imposing its rules on the members of another group. In other words, we not only assume the deviant *has* believed the rules, we assume he believes the rules even as he violates them.

How can a person believe it is wrong to steal at the same time he is stealing? . . . If both the deviant and the nondeviant believe the deviant act is wrong, how do we account for the fact that one commits it and the other does not?

Control theories . . . [answer this question] by hypothesis. Many persons do not have an attitude of respect toward the rules of society; many persons feel no moral obligation to conform regardless of personal advantage. We assume . . . that there is variation in the extent to which people believe they should obey the rules of society, and, furthermore, that the less a person believes he should obey the rules, the more likely he is to violate them . . . The keystone of this argument is of course the assumption that there is variation in belief in the moral validity of social rules. This assumption is amenable to direct empirical test and can thus survive at least until its first confrontation with data. For the present, we must return to the idea of a common value system with which this section was begun.

The idea of a common (or, perhaps better, a single) value system is consistent with the fact, or presumption, of variation in the strength of moral beliefs. We have not suggested that delinquency is based on beliefs counter to conventional morality; we have not suggested that delinquents do not believe delinquent acts are wrong. They may well believe these acts are wrong, but the meaning and efficacy of such beliefs are contingent upon other beliefs and, indeed, on the strength of other ties to the conventional order.

THE SAMPLE AND THE DATA

Western Contra Costa County is part of the San Francisco–Oakland metropolitan area, bounded on the south by Berkeley and on the west and north by San Francisco and San Paulo bays. In the hills to the east live professionals and executives who commute to Berkeley, Oakland, San Francisco, and the major city in the western part of the county, Richmond. The flatland between the hills and the bay is populated predominantly by manual workers and, since the beginning of World War II, by a Negro population that has grown from less than 1 to more than 12 percent.

The Sample

The sample on which the present study is based was drawn as part of the Richmond Youth Project from the 17,500 students entering the eleven public junior and senior high schools of this area in the fall of 1964.[10] This population was stratified by race, sex, school, and grade, producing 130 subgroups, such as seventh grade non-Negro boys at Granada Junior High School and tenth grade Negro girls at Richmond High School. In most cases, 85 percent of the Negro boys, 60 percent of the Negro girls, 30 percent of the non-Negro (largely Caucasian but with some Oriental and Mexican-American) boys, and 12 percent of the non-Negro girls were selected randomly for inclusion in the sample.[11] In a few schools, where these sampling fractions would not produce 25 Negro boys or 25 Negro girls, all Negro boys and girls in the school were included in the sample. This procedure produced a stratified probability sample of 5,545 students: 1,479 Negro boys, 2,126 non-Negro boys, 1,076 Negro girls, and 864 non-Negro girls. Of the 5,545 students in the original sample, complete data were eventually obtained on 4,077, or 73.5 percent. . . .

Of the several reasons for nonresponse to the questionnaire . . . failure to obtain permission from parents [was the most important]. The school administration required that permission be obtained from a parent or guardian of each child in the sample prior to administration of the questionnaire. After names and addresses were obtained from school records, a letter requesting such permission was sent to all parents. If no response was received within ten days, a follow-up letter was sent explaining the project in greater detail and again requesting permission to include the child in the sample. Finally, field workers called on most non-respondents to seek their permission. In the end, 359 students (6.5 percent of the original sample) were excluded from the survey because their parents refused permission, and an additional 303 students (5.5 percent) were excluded because their parents could not be contacted or failed to respond to the permission request. Before administration of the questionnaire began, then, 12 percent

of the original sample had been lost due to failure to obtain permission from a parent. (Actually, many permissions were undoubtedly denied at the request of the student. Several parents reported directly to us that although they were willing for their child to take part in the survey, the child himself refused to participate.)

By the spring of 1965, when the questionnaire was administered, 345 of the students selected in the fall of 1964 were no longer in the Richmond schools. These dropouts and those who transferred to other school systems are not properly part of the population sampled, since the population at issue is the in-school population during the spring of the school year. While the time gap between the selection of the sampling frame and the administration of the questionnaire makes the response rate look worse than it actually was, it should be noted that the sampling frame did not include students transferring into the school system during the same period.

Three hundred ninety-six students were absent during all administrations of the questionnaire, or did not complete enough of the questionnaire to allow data on them to be retained. (Unless the student completed at least two of the three sections of the questionnaire, he was classified as an absentee, and none of the answer sheets he completed was used in the analysis.)

Finally, screening of the answer sheets on which responses were recorded by the students resulted in the elimination of 65 additional cases as probably invalid. . . .

The Data

The data used in the present study come from three sources: school records, the questionnaire completed by the students, and police records.

School Records. The school records which served as a sampling frame contain, in addition to the race, sex, grade, and school information used in sampling, numerous academic achievement test scores and grade-point averages in selected subjects. All students in the district are given a battery of achievement tests in the eighth grade. Scores on these tests for students who were in the seventh grade at the time of administration of the questionnaire were added in the following year.

The Questionnaire.   The questionnaire was divided into three sections. For each section, an IBM answer sheet containing the student's name, grade, school, and identification number was prepared. Both faces of the answer sheet were numbered, and these numbers were referred to repeatedly in the questionnaire itself. . . . Inasmuch as the schools had assumed responsibility for the first administration of the questionnaire, the answer sheets, arranged in alphabetical order by grade, were sent to the schools. Sets of instructions for administration were provided each school. The more difficult questions, such as father's occupation, had been placed at the beginning of each section in order that the teacher could use them as examples in giving instructions to the students. Most of the schools administered the questionnaire one section at a time on three consecutive days, although at least one school administered all three sections during consecutive class periods.

Responsibility for follow-up administrations of the questionnaire was assumed by the research staff of the Richmond Youth Project, the schools having returned all of the questionnaires after one attempt at administration. On the first administration, more than 2,100 students failed to complete the questionnaire satisfactorily. These included students absent on the day the questionnaire was administered, students who did not have sufficient time to complete the questionnaire, and students whose answer sheets suggested misunderstanding of instructions or failure to take the questionnaire seriously.

Answer sheets returned by the schools were checked for completeness and for impossible or illegitimate marks. Lists of students to be included in the follow-up were then prepared by processing unsatisfactory answer sheets through an IBM 1230 mark-sensing machine. If the student had been absent during any portion of the first administration, his answer sheet pertaining to that portion was returned to him on the follow-up; if he had simply failed to complete sections of the questionnaire, his original answer sheet and a questionnaire booklet marked at the point he was to begin were provided; those students whose original answer sheets indicated misunderstanding or facetiousness were given clean answer sheets and special attention in follow-up trips to the school.

In most cases, the schools required that all students failing to complete the questionnaire on the first administration attend follow-up sessions during regular class periods. In some cases, however, attendance was voluntary, and the follow-up was administered before or after regular class sessions.

After the follow-up administrations of the questionnaire had been completed (a process requiring about six weeks), the answer sheets were again screened for reversals (the student marking the wrong side of the answer sheet, an error readily detectable from the pattern of responses), other types of errors, and apparent failure to take the questionnaire seriously. Given the varying range of permissible responses to items, the student merely checking the answer sheet without regard to the questionnaire items soon gave himself away, regardless of whether he was providing random or geometrical patterns of response. As mentioned earlier, 65 cases were eventually eliminated as a result of such checking. (Individual answer sheets were also discarded as a result of such checking, although the bulk of the data on such a student was retained.)

Police Data.   An alphabetical list of all 3,605 boys in the original sample was prepared, and records at the Richmond and San Paulo police departments and at the Contra Costa County Sheriff's Office were searched for evidence of contact with the police. Information was obtained on the total number of offenses a boy had committed; his age at first offense; the date of his most recent offense; the type of offenses committed. These data [provided] information on the bias in the sample with respect to delinquency, as well as an alternative measure of the dependent variable. . . .

Measures of Delinquency

A theory purporting to explain a variety of delinquent acts does not necessarily assume they are strongly related to each other. Thus petty theft may or may not be related to vandalism: given the opportunity to commit an act of vandalism, the theory suggests, the person currently committing petty thefts is more likely to succumb, as common sense holds. But no relation like that suggested by Reiss is required or supposed: "An adolescent boy or girl who is arrested for stealing almost always has also violated sexual conduct norms, and the reverse is usually the case as well."[12]

Among the many items on the questionnaire dealing with delinquent or deviant behavior were those listed below. These were included to serve as an index of delinquency.

1. Have you ever taken little things (worth less than $2) that did not belong to you?
2. Have you ever taken things of some value (between $2 and $50) that did not belong to you?
3. Have you ever taken things of large value (worth over $50) that did not belong to you?
4. Have you ever taken a car for a ride without the owner's permission?
5. Have you ever banged up something that did not belong to you on purpose?
6. Not counting fights you may have had with a brother or sister, have you ever beaten up on anyone or hurt anyone on purpose?

. . . In addition to their relations with each other, each item is related in the same manner and in the expected direction to such things as self-reported *truancy* (.24–.33),[13] self-reported school *suspensions* (.18–.28), self-reported *contacts with the police* (.28–.39), and official delinquency as measured by police records (.13–.29). An example of a relation between one of these items and delinquency as measured by official records is given in Table 21.1.

Only 15 percent of the boys who report they have never stolen anything of medium value have police records, whereas 46 percent of the boys who report stealing something of medium value during the previous year and prior to that have been picked up by the police. The six items intended for use as measures of "delinquency" thus have pragmatic validity—they differentiate between boys known to differ on some independently measured aspect of delinquency. . . .

THE SOCIAL DISTRIBUTION DELINQUENCY

Social Class

While the prisons bulge with the socioeconomic dregs of society, careful quantitative research shows again and again that relation between socioeconomic status and the commission of delinquent acts is small, or nonexistent. More than common sense is offended by a finding of no difference, as some of the first investigators to find it suggest in classic understatement: ". . . the findings have implications for those

TABLE 21.1   Official Offenses by Theft of Item of Medium Value—White Boys Only

"HAVE YOU EVER TAKEN SOMETHING OF MEDIUM VALUE ($2–$50) THAT DID NOT BELONG TO YOU?" (%)				
NUMBER OF OFFENSES IN PREVIOUS TWO YEARS	**NEVER**	**MORE THAN YEAR AGO**	**DURING LAST YEAR**	**DURING AND MORE**
None	85	73	61	55
One	9	14	19	21
Two or more	6	13	20	25
Totals	100	100	100	101
	(1,054)	(123)	(70)	(53)

etiological studies which rely upon the assumed class differential in delinquent behavior as a basis for a delinquency theory. . . ."[14]

If socioeconomic status is unrelated to delinquency, then consistency requires that "socioeconomic status" be removed from the dictionary of delinquency theory and research. A sociological language with this term removed is not easily used, as some of those reporting a zero relation between class and delinquency have found. Concern for the discrepancy between self-report and official measures of delinquency thus reflects justifiable concern for broader questions of sociological and criminological theory. Accepting the self-report findings at face value calls into question assumptions basic to such areas as stratification and the family;[15] accepting these findings would also appear simply and directly to falsify delinquency theories based on an assumed relation between social class and delinquency. . . .

Are the "criminal classes" really no more criminal than other social classes? Have the theorists, the police, the layman simply been wrong? The list of studies reporting no significant difference is impressive.[16] Furthermore, there are reasons for expecting a discrepancy between the correlates of self-reported and official measures of delinquency. Defenders of what might be called an official reaction hypothesis have long argued that the police and the courts create the statistical relations which generate and then confirm most sociological and common-sense theories of crime. And it *is* true that the lower-class boy is more likely to be picked up by the police, more likely to be sent to juvenile court, more likely to be convicted, and more likely to be institutionalized if convicted, when he has committed the same crime as a middle-class boy.[17]

The findings in the present sample are consistent with previous research: we are dealing with what is, at most, a very *small* relation that could easily be upset by random disturbances of sampling or definition. Father's occupation, for example, offers little in the way of confirmation of conventional theory. The sons of professionals and executives are least likely to have committed many delinquent acts (Table 21.2),

TABLE 21.2   Self-Reported Delinquency by Father's Occupation—White Boys Only (in percentage)

| | FATHER'S OCCUPATION[a] | | | | |
| | LOW | | | | HIGH |
SELF-REPORTED ACTS	1	2	3	4	5
None	62	53	56	49	61
One	16	26	25	28	25
Two or more	23	21	19	23	14
Total	101	100	100	100	100
	(151)	(156)	(390)	(142)	(282)[b]

[a]1 = unskilled labor; 2 = semiskilled labor; 3 = skilled labor, foreman, merchant; 4 = white collar; 5 = professional and executive.

[b]The total number of students will vary from table to table for several reasons. (1) The response rate was different for almost every item in the questionnaire, and students for whom data were not available on all items in a table are excluded from that table. (2) The table programs employed differed in their definition of "complete data." In one program, tables were based only on those cases for whom data were available on all items in the "run," regardless of the number of items in a particular table. (3) In tables in which self-reported and official delinquency were to be compared, I excluded boys 18 or older because in many cases their records had been removed from police files.

but the sons of white-collar workers are most likely to have committed one or more, and the sons of unskilled laborers are among the least delinquent groups in the sample.

There is much evidence for the validity of the measure of father's occupation as an indicator of socioeconomic status. It is related in the expected direction to such other measures of socioeconomic status as father's education, welfare status, and home ownership. Furthermore, the comparative distributions of father's occupation among Negroes and whites, and among the eleven schools in the study, reflect "known" differences.[18]

Father's education does no better, suggesting at best a trend in the direction of a negative relation between socioeconomic status and the commission of delinquent acts (Table 21.3). Along the same lines, an index of cultural objects in the home (maps, newspapers, news magazines, books, musical instruments) was found to be unrelated to the commission of delinquent acts.

For that matter, there appears to be little or no relation between the socioeconomic status of an area and its rate of self-reported delinquency. The percentages reporting one or more delinquent acts by school range from 36 percent in Portola, the junior high school highest in socioeconomic status, to 49 percent in El Cerrito, the senior high school highest in socioeconomic status. . . .

ATTACHMENT TO PARENTS

Control theory assumes that the bond of affection for conventional persons is a major deterrent to crime. The stronger this bond, the more likely the person is to take it into account when and if he contemplates a criminal act. The ability to take something into account, however, suggests the corollary ability to do something about it, and crimes are of course committed in the face of strong attachments to conventional others. Yet the attached person, by his greater efforts to avoid detection and by his unwillingness to take the risks the unattached freely takes, proves the potency of his attachment even as he commits the crime. In fact, when detection is certain, the attached person may hit upon unusual means for preventing those whose opinion he values from gaining knowledge of his act: "I intend to kill my wife after I pick her up from work. I don't want her to have to face the embarrassment that my actions will surely cause her."[19]

A persistent image in delinquency theory is that of a child *already* without a family—at least without a family whose unhappiness is of concern to him. Like most such images, this one contains much that is true. Since most delinquent acts are committed outside the home, since few delinquencies are committed at parental urging, and since most detected acts cause parents embarrassment and/or inconvenience, it is not surprising that an image of the delinquent as

TABLE 21.3   Self-Reported Delinquency by Father's Education—White Boys Only

SELF-REPORTED ACTS	FATHER'S EDUCATION				
	LESS THAN HIGH SCHOOL	HIGH SCHOOL GRADUATE	TRADE OR BUSINESS	SOME COLLEGE	COLLEGE GRADUATE
None	55	57	54	61	58
One	26	26	29	18	25
Two or more	19	17	17	21	17
Total	100	100	100	100	100
	(286)	(398)	(70)	(170)	(271)

not only physically but emotionally free of his parents has developed.

But a social vacuum is abhorrent to theories based on the assumption that the delinquent act is "positively" motivated.[20] If behavior is normatively oriented, if man requires social support for his actions, then there must be others who are willing to praise and reward that which parents condemn. As a consequence, in most sociological theories of delinquency the gang rushes in to fill the void created by estrangement from parents. The incontestable fact that most delinquent acts are committed with companions is taken as evidence supporting this view. Walter C. Reckless goes so far as to say: "There is almost every reason to admit that companionship is one of the most important, universal causes of crime and delinquency among males."[21] But the link between "companionship" and delinquency is still a matter of dispute, and the Gluecks, unimpressed by a mountain of sociological theory and research, and by their own data which shows a strong relation between delinquency and the delinquency of companions, could still argue that boys become delinquents *before* they choose their companions.[22]

And, indeed, studies of neglected children, of the psychopathic personality, appear to support the Gluecks' view. They suggest that the capacity to form attachments to others may be generally impaired so that the child who feels nothing for his parents is less likely to feel anything for anyone else. They suggest that the freedom that severance of the bonds to family creates is *not* immediately lost by being swallowed up in a new group, that there are those outside the "web of group affiliations" who have in some sense lost the capacity to belong. Delinquents may be with other boys when they commit their delinquent deeds, but this does not necessarily mean that these acts are a response to pressures emanating from a moral community.

For that matter, no good evidence has been produced to show that attachment to peers is actually conducive to delinquency. Unless delinquent behavior is valued among adolescents, there is no reason to believe that attachments to other adolescents

should produce results different from those obtaining from attachments to conventional *adults*. Predictions about the effects of peer attachments thus hinge on the assumed conventionality or non-conventionality of peers. If the peer "culture" requires delinquent behavior, then presumably attachment would foster conformity—that is, delinquency. However, if the peer culture is identical to conventional culture, then attachment to persons within this culture should foster conformity to conventional standards.

No such ambiguity adheres in predictions about the effect of attachments to teachers and the school. Teachers, by inclination and law, espouse conventional standards. Here, again, however, the question of the extent of carry-over from attitudes toward parents to attitudes toward teachers is of interest, as is the question of the relative importance of attachments to persons variously located in conventional society.

In this [chapter], I examine attachments to parents, teachers, and peers. Although I shall devote much of the analysis to factors affecting attachment (and some to the effects of attachment on other elements of the bond to conventional society), the burden of the argument rests on the relations between the various attachments and delinquency. I shall begin by assuming that all "others" are conventional and only later investigate the effects of attachment to persons not conforming to the conventional model.

Attachment to Conventional Parents

Although denied in some theories and ignored in others, the fact that delinquents are less likely than nondelinquents to be closely tied to their parents is one of the best documented findings of delinquency research.[23] As is true with most well-established relations in the field of delinquency, there are many ways of accounting for this relation.

In the light of the cultural deviance perspective, the child unattached to his parents is simply more likely to be exposed to "criminogenic influences." He is, in other words, more likely to be free to take up with a gang. His lack of attachment to his parents is, in itself, of no moral significance.[24]

Strain theory appears to have particular difficulty with the relation between attachment to parents and delinquency, and it is therefore largely ignored by strain theorists.[25] (If, for example, there are systematic differences in the adequacy of socialization between social classes, then no differences in pressures to deviate are required to explain the differential rates of deviation.)

It is in control theory, then, that attachment to parent becomes a central variable, and many of the variations in explanations of this relation may be found within the control theory tradition. Perhaps the major focus of attention has been on the link between attachment and the adequacy of socialization, the internalization of norms. As is well known, the emotional bond between the parent and the child presumably provides the bridge across which pass parental ideals and expectations.[26] If the child is alienated from the parent, he will not learn or will have no feeling for moral rules, he will not develop an adequate conscience or superego. Among those with a more psychoanalytic orientation, actual separation from the parent, especially the mother, is held to be more serious than lack of attachment to a physically present mother.[27] In fact, the maternal deprivation hypothesis has received endorsement reminiscent of that granted feeble-mindedness hypotheses in the early years of the twentieth century: ". . . on the basis of this varied evidence it appears that there is a very strong case indeed for believing that prolonged separation of a child from his mother (or mother-substitute) during the first five years of life stands foremost among the causes of delinquent character development and persistent misbehaviour."[28]

Like the feeble-mindedness hypothesis, this form of the maternal deprivation hypothesis can take little comfort from quantitative research based on reasonably large samples of noninstitutional populations. McCord and McCord and Nye both report no difference in delinquent behavior between those whose homes were broken later. And in the present data those living with both parents prior to age five are just as likely to have committed delinquent acts as children separated from one or both parents during this period.

Explanation of the effects of attachment to the parents on delinquent behavior by reference to the internalization of norms (or, as is common in social control theories, by reference to "internal" or "personal" control)" creates difficulties in explaining variations in delinquent activity over time. If the conscience is a relative constant built into the child at an early age, how do we explain the increase in delinquent activity in early adolescence and the decline in late adolescence? . . .

[This difficulty is] avoided if we ignore internalization and assume that the moral element in attachment to parents resides directly in the attachment itself. If the bond to the parent is weakened, the probability of delinquent behavior increases; if this bond is strengthened, the probability of delinquent behavior declines. Attachment may easily be seen as *variable* over persons and over time for the same person.

There are many elements of the bond to the parent, all of which may not be equally important in the control of delinquent behavior. Let us therefore look more closely at the process through which attachment to the parent presumably works against the commission of delinquent acts.

The child attached to his parents may be less likely to get into situations in which delinquent acts are possible, simply because he spends more of his time in their presence. However, since most delinquent acts require little time, and since most adolescents are frequently exposed to situations potentially definable as opportunities for delinquency, the amount of time spent with parents would probably be only a minor factor in delinquency prevention. So-called "direct control" is not, except as a limiting case, of much substantive or theoretical importance.[29] The important consideration is whether the parent is psychologically present when temptation to commit a crime appears. If, in the situation of temptation, no thought is given to parental reaction, the child is to his extent free to commit the act.

Which children are most likely to ask themselves, "What will my parents think?" Those who think their parents know where they are and what they are doing. Two items on the questionnaire bear directly on such virtual supervision: "Does your mother (father) know where you are when you are away from home?" And, "Does your mother (father) know whom you are with when you are away from home?" The response categories were: "Usually," "Sometimes," and "Never." The two mother items, which correlated .59, were combined, equally weighted, so that the mothers of boys obtaining a score of 4 "usually" know where they are and whom they are with. The relation between this index of supervision and self-reported delinquency is shown in Table 21.4.

The skewness of the distribution evident in the bottom row of Table 21.4, together with hindsight, suggests that the boys should have been allowed to report that their mothers "almost always" know where they are and whom they are with, since the majority of boys in the sample are, according to this measure, well and equally supervised. Even so, the range of virtual supervision present in the table is sufficient to produce marked variation in delinquent activity: children who perceive their parents as unaware of their whereabouts are highly likely to have committed delinquent acts. Although only 11 boys say their mothers never know where they are and whom they are with, all 11 have committed delinquent acts in the year prior to administration of the questionnaire. The majority of the sample who in this sense usually have their mothers with them are much less likely to have committed delinquent acts than those who, at least sometimes, feel they have moved beyond the range of parental knowledge or interest.

We assume that the supervision illustrated in Table 21.4 is indirect, that the child is less likely to commit delinquent acts not because his parents actually restrict his activities, but because he shares his activities with them; not because his parents actually know where he is, but because he perceives them as aware of his location. Following this line of reasoning, we can say that the more the child is accustomed to sharing his mental life with his parents, the more he is accustomed to seeking or getting their opinion about his activities, the more likely he is to perceive them as part of his social and psychological field, and the less likely he would be to neglect their opinion when considering an act contrary to law—which is, after all, a potential source of embarrassment and/or inconvenience to them.

Several items on the questionnaire are appropriate as measures of the intimacy of communication between parent and child. The boys were asked: "Do you share your thoughts and feelings with your mother (father)?" And, "How often have you talked over your future plans with your mother (father)?" Independent analysis reveals that these items are sufficiently correlated to justify combining them on empirical as well as conceptual grounds. They were combined, equally weighted, such that boys with highest scores often share their thoughts and talk over their plans with their parents, while the boys with the lowest scores never have such communication with their parents. This index, which I shall call an index of intimacy of communication (A), is correlated .25

TABLE 21.4 Self-Reported Delinquency by Mother's Virtual Supervision (in percentage)

	MOTHER'S SUPERVISION				
	LOW				HIGH
SELF-REPORTED ACTS	0	1	2	3	4
None	0	28	45	59	63
One	45	31	26	21	26
Two or more	55	41	29	20	12
Total	100	100	100	100	101
	(11)	(29)	(236)	(252)	(698)

with mother's virtual supervision, and .26 with father's virtual supervision.[30]

A second index of intimacy of communication (B), distinguished from the first by the fact that the flow of communication is from the parent to the child rather than from the child to the parent, was constructed from the following items: "When you don't know why your mother (father) makes a rule, will she explain the reason?" "When you come across things you don't understand, does your mother (father) help you with them?" And, "Does your mother (father) ever explain why she feels the way she does?"

As would be expected, the two indexes of intimacy of communication are strongly correlated (for mothers, the correlation is .42; for fathers, .52). The second index is even more strongly correlated with virtual supervision than the first (for mothers, $r = .35$; for fathers, $r = .40$). . . .

As Table 21.5 illustrates, the intimacy of communication between child and parent is strongly related to the commission of delinquent acts. Only 5 percent of the boys who often discuss their future plans and often share their thoughts and feelings with their fathers have committed two or more delinquent acts in the year prior to administration of the questionnaire, while 43 percent of those never communicating with their fathers about these matters have committed as many delinquent acts. As reported ear-

lier, however, those who spend much time talking with their parents are only slightly less likely than those who spend little time talking with their parents to have committed delinquent acts. All of which suggests that it is not simply the fact of communication with the parents but the focus of this communication that is crucial in affecting the likelihood that the child will recall his parents when and if a situation of potential delinquency arises.

If we assume that the child considers the reaction of his parents, he must then ask himself a further question: "Do I care what my parents will think?" Most studies of the effects of parent-child relations concentrate on this second question. Thus affectional identification, love, or respect is taken as the crucial element of the bond to the parent. Even if the child does in effect consider the opinion of his parents, he may conclude that parental reaction is not sufficiently important to deter him from the act (given, of course, a certain risk of detection). This conclusion is presumably more likely the less the child cares for his parents.

Since most items measuring aspects of parent-child relations reflect to some extent the favorability of the child's attitudes toward his parents, this dimension is both easy and difficult to measure. (The ubiquity of the favorability-unfavorability dimension may well be the reason that many analyses seem to suggest that everything the parent does "matters"

TABLE 21.5 Self-Reported Delinquency by Intimacy of Communication (A) with Father (in percentage)

SELF-REPORTED ACTS	LITTLE INTIMATE COMMUNICATION 0	1	2	3	MUCH INTIMATE COMMUNICATION 4
None	39	55	55	63	73
One	18	25	28	23	22
Two or more	43	20	17	15	5
Total	100	100	100	101	100
	(97)	(182)	(436)	(287)	(121)

Note: The comparable index of intimacy of communication with the mother is more badly skewed (boys are more likely to report intimate communication with the mother) and is slightly less strongly related to delinquency.

with respect to delinquency.) Perhaps the best single item in the present data is: "Would you like to be the kind of person your mother (father) is?"

As affectional identification with the parents increases, the likelihood of delinquency declines (Table 21.6). On the basis of measures available,[31] it appears reasonable to suggest that extent and nature of communication between the parent and the child are as important as feelings of affection for the parent. . . .

Consistent with much previous research, then, the present data indicate that the closer the child's relations with his parents, the more he is attached to and identifies with them, the lower his chances of delinquency. It is argued here that the moral significance of this attachment resides directly in the attachment itself. The more strongly a child is attached to his parents, the more strongly he is bound to their expectations, and therefore the more strongly he is bound to conformity with the legal norms of the larger system. . . .

Attachment and Exposure to Criminal Influences

A second approach to the cultural deviance perspective of the effects of attachment involves a choice between intervening variables. In control theory, lack of attachment to the parents is directly conducive to delinquency because the unattached child does not have to consider the consequences of his actions for his relations with his parents. In cultural deviance theory, in contrast, lack of attachment to the parents merely increases the probability that the child will be exposed to criminal influences, that he will learn the attitudes, values, and skills conducive to delinquency; a learning process must intervene: "If the family is in a community in which there is no pattern of theft, the children do not steal, no matter how much neglected or how unhappy they may be at home."[32]

It would perhaps be difficult to find a community in which there was no pattern of theft, and therefore difficult directly to falsify this proposition. However, this proposition assumes that certain experiences must intervene if attachment to the family is to influence delinquent conduct. If we can measure some of these experiences, we can determine whether they affect the influence of attachment to parents on the likelihood the child will *steal*.[33]

. . . [In short, both] cultural deviance theory and . . . control theory predict . . . [that] the delinquency of one's friends is strongly related to one's own record of delinquent conduct.

Table 21.7 indicates that three-fourths of those boys with four or more close friends who have been

TABLE 21.6   Self-Reported Delinquency by Affectional Identification with the Father (in percentage)

	"WOULD YOU LIKE TO BE THE KIND OF PERSON YOUR FATHER IS?"				
SELF-REPORTED ACTS	IN EVERY WAY	IN MOST WAYS	IN SOME WAYS	IN JUST A FEW WAYS	NOT AT ALL
None	64	65	58	48	41
One	21	24	25	30	22
Two or more	16	11	17	22	38
Total	101	100	100	100	101
	(121)	(404)	(387)	(172)	(138)

Note: The relation between identification with the mother and delinquency is somewhat stronger than the relation shown in the table. I do not combine the items for the two parents because such a combination has little, if any, additional effect. As discussed [later], part of the reason for the lack of additive effect is that the boys in the sample tend very strongly to have similar attitudes toward both parents.

TABLE 21.7   Self-Reported Delinquency by Friends' Contacts with the Police (in percentage)

	"HAVE ANY OF YOUR CLOSE FRIENDS EVER BEEN PICKED UP BY THE POLICE?"					
SELF-REPORTED ACTS	**NO**	**ONE**	**TWO**	**THREE**	**FOUR OR MORE**	**DON'T KNOW**
None	73	51	41	32	25	61
One	20	27	37	24	30	24
Two or more	7	21	21	44	45	15
Total	100	99	99	100	100	100
	(520)	(164)	(99)	(62)	(208)	(227)

picked up by the police have themselves committed delinquent acts in the previous year, while only slightly more than one-fourth of those with no delinquent friends have committed delinquent acts during the same period. Percentaged in the other direction, the table would show that of those boys committing two or more delinquent offenses 82 percent have had at least one close friend picked up by the police, while only 34 percent of those committing no delinquent acts have delinquent friends.[34]

The magnitude of this relation adds plausibility to the thesis that exposure to criminal influences must intervene if lack of attachment to the parent is to result in delinquency. However, a direct test of this hypothesis requires that we examine the effects of attachment to parents and "criminal influences" simultaneously, as in Table 21.8.

With respect to the issue at hand, Table 21.8 supports control theory. Regardless of the delinquency of his friends, the child attached to his father is less likely to commit delinquent acts. Among those with no delinquent friends and among those with several delinquent friends, the weaker the attachment to the father, the greater the likelihood of delinquency.

We should not allow selective emphasis to take us too far from the data, however, since in all other respects Table 21.8 offers impressive evidence in favor of a cultural deviance interpretation. Children unattached to their parents are much more likely to have delinquent friends (this fact is of course expectable also from social control perspective), and delinquency of companions is strongly related to delinquency regardless of the level of attachment to the father.

TABLE 21.8   Percentage Committing Two or More Delinquent Acts by Intimacy of Communication with Father and Delinquency of Friends

	NUMBER OF FRIENDS PICKED UP BY POLICE		
INTIMACY OF COMMUNICATION	**NONE**	**ONE–TWO**	**THREE OR MORE**
High	4 (190)	16 (85)	30 (63)
Medium	9 (184)	22 (88)	39 (77)
Low	11 (87)	23 (53)	53 (83)

NOTES

1. Émile Durkheim, *Suicide* (New York: Free Press, 1951), p. 209.

2. Books have been written on the increasing importance of interpersonal sensitivity in modern life. According to this view, controls from within have become less important than controls from without in producing conformity. Whether or not this observation is true as a description of historical trends, it is true that interpersonal sensitivity has become more important in *explaining* conformity. Although logically it should also have become more important in explaining nonconformity, the opposite has been the case, once again showing that Cohen's observation that an explanation of conformity should be an explanation of deviance cannot be translated as "an explanation of conformity has to be an explanation of deviance." For the view that interpersonal sensitivity currently plays a greater role than formerly in producing conformity, see William Goode, "Norm Commitment and Conformity to Role-Status Obligations," *American Journal of Sociology,* LXVI (1960), 246-258. And, of course, also see David Riesman, Nathan Glazer, and Reuel Denney, *The Lonely Crowd* (Garden City, New York: Doubleday, 1950), especially Part I.

3. See his *Moral Education* (New York: Free Press, 1961), p. 64.

4. See Thomas Hobbes, *Leviathan* (Oxford: Basil Blackwell, 1957), p. 195.

5. Howard S. Becker, "Notes on the Concept of Commitment," *American Journal of Sociology,* LXVI (1960), pp. 35–36.

6. Arthur L. Stinchcombe, *Rebellion in a High School* (Chicago: Quadrangle; 1964), p. 5.

7. Richard A. Cloward and Lloyd E. Ohlin, *Delinquency and Opportunity* (New York: Free Press, 1960), p. 147, quoting Edwin H. Sutherland, ed., *The Professional Thief* (Chicago: University of Chicago Press, 1937), pp. 211–213.

8. See William James, *Psychology* (Cleveland: World Publishing Co., 1948), p. 186.

9. See *The Sutherland Papers,* ed. Albert K. Cohen et al. (Bloomington: Indiana University Press, 1956), p. 37.

10. Sampling procedures are described in greater detail in Alan B. Wilson, Travis Hirschi, and Glen Elder, "Technical Report No.1: Secondary School Survey," mimeographed, Survey Research Center, Berkeley, 1965, pp. 3–21. The account presented here depends heavily on this source.

11. [In this section,] I refer to "non-Negro" students and to girls. [However,] in the analysis which follows, "non-Negro becomes "white," and the girls disappear. Subsequent reference to "white" boys is accurate, because the few Oriental and Mexican-American boys were removed from the non-Negro category. Since girls have been neglected for too long by students of delinquency, the exclusion of them is difficult to justify. I hope to return to them soon.

12. See Albert J. Reiss, "Sex Offenses of Adolescents," *Readings in Juvenile Delinquency,* ed. Ruth S. Cavan (Philadelphia: Lippincott, 1964), p. 229.

13. These figures define the range of correlation coefficients for the six items. The smallest correlation with truancy was .24; the largest was .33.

14. See F. Ivan Nye, James F. Short, Jr., and Virgil J. Olson, "Socioeconomic Status and Delinquent Behavior," *American Journal of Sociology,* LXIII (1958), 388.

15. See, for example, the ideal-type description of the lower class in Joseph A. Kahl, *The American Class Structure* (New York: Holt, Rinehart and Winston, 1964), pp. 210–215. For a brief description of how high-status parents are better able to socialize their children, see D. G. McKinley, *Social Class and Family Life* (New York: The Free Press, 1964), p. 57. These are of course, but two of the countless references that could be used to show how deeply the assumption of greater criminality among the lower classes is imbedded in American sociology.

16. Nye, Short, and Olson, "Socioeconomic Status"; Arthur L. Stinchcombe, *Rebellion in a High School* (Chicago: Quadrangle Books, 1964), pp. 81–87; Ronald L. Akers, "Socio-Economic Status and Delinquent Behavior: A Retest," *Journal of Research in Crime and Delinquency,* I (1964), pp. 38–46; Robert A. Dentler and Lawrence J. Monroe, "Social Correlates of Early Adolescent Theft," *American Sociological Review,* XXVI (1961), pp. 733–743. See also, Robert H. Hardt and George E. Bodine, *Development of Self-Report Instruments in Delinquency Research* (Syracuse University, Youth Development Center, 1965), p. 13.

17. Evidence in favor of the official reaction hypothesis was widely reported prior to the finding that there is little difference between social classes in self-reported delinquency rates (for a reasonably complete list of such studies, see Hardt and Bodine, *Development of Self-Report Instruments,* p. vi).

Actually, at any given stage of the adjudication process, the differences may not be large. In analyzing police dispositions of over 17,000 juveniles picked up in Oakland, California, during the 1950s, I could find only small differences in disposition between African Americans and whites, between children from broken and unbroken homes, and between children from high-rate (generally low socioeconomic status) and low-rate areas, when offense was held constant. For example, among those picked up on a first offense for *burglary,* the . . . percentages [cited in Table 21.9] were *arrested* (the most serious disposition).

In 21 of 29 comparisons, including those in this table, the Negro arrest rate is higher than the white rate, with the other variables having less effect on the severity of disposition. The magnitude of these differences does not seem to fit with anecdotal accounts of police bias, however. The fact is that the bias of the policeman is probably less important in generating differences than is the bias in police procedures, such as surveillance and interrogation. Irving Piliavin and Scott Briar suggest that, after the nature of the offense and prior record, the *demeanor* of the offender is the most important determinant of severity of disposition (see their "Police Encounters with Juveniles," *American Journal of Sociology,* LXX [1964], pp. 206–214). This variable too would presumably have much of its effect before the question of disposition in the formal sense arises. That is, boys whose demeanor is "inappropriate" are simply more likely to appear on police records. (The data upon which the table is based were made available to me by Piliavin and Briar.)

18. For example, of white boys analyzed, 47 percent of those in Portola Junior High in El Cerrito (a high SES school) report that their fathers are professionals or executives, while only 9 percent of those in Downer Junior High in Richmond (a low SES school) classify their fathers in this category.

19. See Charles Joseph Whitman, quoted by *Newsweek,* August 15, 1966.

20. See Muzafer Sherif and Carolyn W. Sherif, *Reference Groups: Explorations into Conformity and Deviation of Adolescents* (New York: Harper and Row, 1964), especially pp. 271–273.

21. See Walter C. Reckless, *The Crime Problem,* 3rd ed. (New York: Appleton-Century-Crofts, 1961), p. 311.

22. See Sheldon and Eleanor Glueck, *Unraveling Juvenile Delinquency* (Cambridge, Mass.: Harvard University Press, 1950), p. 164.

23. See F. Ivan Nye, *Family Relationships and Delinquent Behavior* (New York: Wiley, 1958), Chapter 8.

24. See Edwin H. Sutherland and Donald R. Cressey, *Principles of Criminology,* 7th ed. (Philadelphia: Lippincott, 1966), especially pp. 225–228.

25. Robert K. Merton suggests that persons in the social class with the highest rate of crime tend to be inadequately socialized. However, Cloward and Ohlin are more consistent in this regard and explicitly deny variations in the adequacy of socialization as a cause of delinquency. For Merton's position, see *Social Theory and Social Structure* (New York: The Free Press, 1957), p. 141 [also, see Merton's essay in Part 8—Ed.]. One of the clearest statements in the literature with respect to the varying assumptions of the strain, cultural deviance, and control theories on this point may be found in Richard A. Cloward and Lloyd E. Ohlin, *Delinquency and Opportunity* (New York: The Free Press, 1960), p. 106.

26. David G. McKinley, *Social Class and Family Life* (New York: The Free Press, 1964), p. 57. McKinley argues that the higher the status of the parent, the stronger the emotional bond between the parent and the child.

27. See Kate Friedlander, *The Psycho-Analytical Approach to Juvenile Delinquency* (New York: International Universities Press, 1947), p. 70.

28. John Bowlby, *Forty-Four Juvenile Thieves* (London: Bailliero, Tindall and Cox, 1946), p. 41, quoted by Barbara Wootton in *Social Science and Social Pathology* (New York: Macmillan, 1959), p. 137. Wootton's treatment of the mater-

TABLE 21.9   Percentage Arrested for Burglary as a First Offense

PARENTS TOGETHER				PARENTS NOT TOGETHER			
LOW RATE		HIGH RATE		LOW RATE		HIGH RATE	
WHITE	AFRICAN AMERICAN	WHITE	AFRICAN AMERICAN	WHITE	AFRICAN AMERICAN	WHITE	AFRICAN AMERICAN
31	29	32	40	42	45	31	45
(329)	(96)	(130)	(191)	(185)	(65)	(86)	(228)

nal separation studies is clearly "devastating"—but it is difficult to imagine any kind of social research that would satisfy the criteria of evaluation she uses. If the results are consistent and reasonably conclusive, Wootton does not hesitate to conclude that "homely truths" are lurking behind a "pretentious scientific facade."

29. Items measuring the amount of time spent talking with parents, working around the house, and the like, are related to the commission of delinquent acts in the expected direction, but these relations are uniformly weak.

30. Each index is constructed separately for each parent. The correlations are thus between, for example, intimacy of communication with *mother* and *mother's* virtual supervision.

31. Indexes of emotional attachment to the father and the mother produce relations only slightly stronger than that shown in Table 21.6. The items available for measuring attachment to the parents on the original questionnaire are a source of some uneasiness, since they are uniformly indirect. For example, the most direct items on the questionnaire are: "Does your father seem to understand you?" "Have you ever felt unwanted by your father?" And, "Would your father stick by you if you got into really bad trouble?" . . . Nevertheless, in a separate study of a subsample of the students used here, Irving Piliavin asked a series of direct questions about the child's emotional attachment to his parents (for example, "Are you interested in what your father thinks of you?"). The relations between Piliavin's items and delinquency appear to be no stronger than those reported here.

32. See Sutherland and Cressey, *Principles of Criminology*, p. 227.

33. Four of the six items in the self-report index involve theft.

34. In calculating these percentages, I have excluded the boys who had no knowledge of their friends' contacts with the police.

CHAPTER 22

TRAJECTORIES OF CHANGE IN CRIMINAL OFFENDING: GOOD MARRIAGES AND THE DESISTANCE PROCESS

JOHN H. LAUB
DANIEL S. NAGIN
ROBERT J. SAMPSON

When and how do criminal offenders desist? Although the relationship between age and criminal behavior has animated much recent research in criminology, the questions of change in criminal offending and the attendant issue of measuring such change have received little attention. We emphasize the central role of social bonds in the movement away from criminal and antisocial behavior patterns. The emergence of social bonds can be likened to an investment process in that social bonds do not arise intact and full-grown but develop over time like a pension plan funded by regular installments. As the investment in social bonds grows, the incentive for avoiding crime increases because more is at stake. Thus, while seminal events can dramatically alter longstanding patterns of behavior, we expect that desistance from crime will be gradual and will accompany the accumulation of social bonds (Horney, Osgood, and Marshall 1995: 671).

Sampson and Laub (1993) pose an age-graded theory of informal social control in which social bonding in the form of strong ties to work and family plans an important role in the movement away from crime for previously criminal youths. They find that

individuals who desist from crime are significantly more likely to have entered into stable marriages and steady employment. Thus, Sampson and Laub contend, marriage and work act as "turning points" in the life course and are crucial in understanding the processes of change. . . .

DATA AND METHODS

We analyze the criminal histories of 500 delinquent boys who were followed into adulthood by Glueck and Glueck (1950, 1968). The Gluecks' prospective study of the formation and development of criminal careers was initiated in 1940 and also included a control group of 500 nondelinquent boys. As our interest is in desistance from crime, we exclude the Gluecks' nondelinquent sample from our study.

The data collection process took place over 25 years, from 1940 through 1965. After an initial interview at age 14 (on average), subjects were followed up at ages 25 and 32. The data were collected using a multimethod strategy that included interviews with the subjects and their families and with key informants such as social workers, school teachers, neighbors, employers, and criminal justice officials (Glueck and Glueck 1950: 41–53). Interview data were supplemented by field investigations that gathered information from the records of public and private agencies. These data verified and amplified the case materials collected during the interviews (Glueck and Glueck 1950, 1968; Sampson and Laub 1993).

Key Measures

The following measures covering childhood, adolescence, and adulthood were selected (Sampson and Laub 1993:47–63; Sampson and Laub 1994:530–31).

Individual differences.   Measures of individual differences include verbal intelligence, personality traits, and childhood behaviors. *Verbal intelligence* was assessed using the Wechsler-Bellevue IQ test; scores were coded into eight categories ranging from 1 (120 and above) to 8 (59 and below). The mean verbal IQ score for the delinquent sample was 88.6 (Glueck and Glueck 1950:356).

From psychiatric assessments we used four dichotomous variables that tap *personality traits*; extroverted ("uninhibited in regard to motor responses to stimuli"); adventurous ("desirous of change, excitement, or risk"); egocentric ("self-centered"); and aggressive ("inclined to impose one's will on others").

To capture *childhood behaviors* we used a dichotomous indicator based on teachers' and parents' reports that the subject engaged in violent and habitual temper tantrums while growing up. Another measure of childhood behavior (difficult child) indicated whether the subject was overly restless and irritable.

Family differences.   Included here are *family poverty* (indicated by a combination of low income and reliance on public assistance), *family size* (number of children), and *parental criminality and alcohol abuse* (determined from official records and interview data). In addition, we used three measures of family process—*parental style of discipline, mother's supervision*, and *parent-child attachment*. Parenting style was measured by summing three variables describing the discipline and punishment practices of mothers and fathers to create a measure that combined mother's and father's discipline—*erratic/harsh discipline*.

Adolescent behavior.   *Antisocial conduct in adolescence* was measured in two ways. One indicator is the *average annual frequency of arrests* up to age 17 while not incarcerated. A second measure is a composite "unofficial" scale (ranging from 1 to 26) of self-, parent-, and teacher-reports of delinquent behavior (e.g., stealing, vandalism) and other misconduct (e.g., truancy, running away) not necessarily known to the police. In addition, we use self-reported *age of onset of misbehavior* to create a dichotomous variable (coded 1 if age of onset is earlier than age 8). Finally, *attachment to school* is a composite measure that combines the boy's attitude toward school and his academic ambition.

Adult criminal behavior.   Information on *criminal activity through age 32* was drawn from official criminal histories at the state and national levels.

Adult social bonds.   All of the social bond measures were taken from the age-32 interview. *Job stability* is measured by a standardized composite scale of employment status, stability of most recent employment, and work habits. *Attachment to spouse* is a standardized composite scale derived from interview data describing the general conjugal relationship during the following-up period plus a measure of the cohesiveness of the family unit. (For details, see Sampson and Laub 1993:143–45.)

In addition to *marital status at age 32*, we included a variable from the age 25 interview indicating whether a child was born within seven months of the date of marriage and the birth was not recorded as premature or if pregnancy at marriage is acknowledged by the couple. We label this variable *"shotgun" marriage.*

Measuring Adult Desistance

We anticipate that individuals who enter early into a marriage that subsequently evolves into a strong attachment, hereafter referred to as an "ex-post good marriage," will desist the soonest. Testing this dynamic prediction requires that we operationalize the concept of desistance. Our perspective empha-sizes gradual change, that is, we do not expect crim-inal activity to drop abruptly to zero. Rather we expect a gradual decline toward zero or a very low rate of offending.

Consider two hypothetical offending trajectories. In both trajectories, the individual's rate of offending rises throughout adolescence, reaches a peak at about age 18, and declines thereafter. However, for one individual, the rate of decline is rapid, so that by age 25 his rate of offending is negligible. In contrast, the rate of decline for the second individual is more gradual, so that by age 32 his rate is substantially less than at age 18 but is still far from zero. By any reasonable conception of desistance, the former indi-vidual has desisted, but not the latter. . . .

RESULTS

First-Stage Analysis

Exploratory analysis suggested that a four-group model best fit the data. Figure 22.1 shows the four offending trajectories identified by the model. Although individuals in this sample were selected on the basis of their being active delinquents in their youth, by age 32 the distribution of their offending mirrors that of the general population—it is skewed right. Group 1 is a small but prominent group of high-rate chronic offenders. Based on the maximum probability rules described above, only 11 individu-als were assigned to this group. Another 95 individu-als were assigned to Group 2, which includes chronic offenders who offend at a more modest rate. Finally,

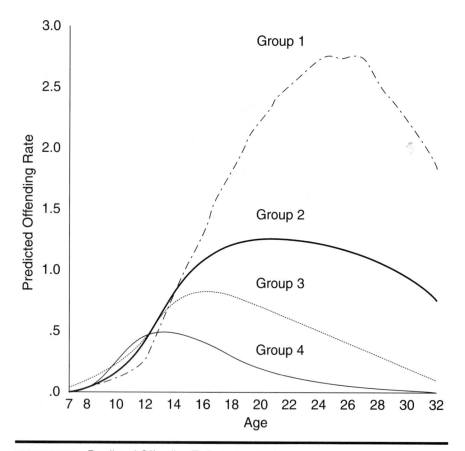

FIGURE 22.1   Predicted Offending Trajectories, by Age

Groups 3 and 4 constitute the largest share of the sample, 220 and 154 individuals, respectively. These individuals have either effectively desisted or are near desistance by age 32.

Figure 22.2 compares the actual and predicted offending trajectories for each group. The correspondence between actual and predicted is generally close for all four groups.

Group 1 includes individuals who remain high-rate offenders throughout the adult observation period. Their peak average offending rate of nearly 3 arrests per year occurs at age 25 and declines only to about 2 arrests per year by age 32. This group constitutes only a small percentage of the sample—2.8 percent based on the model's parameters. Group 2 also is comprised of individuals who can be characterized as chronic offenders. This group, which accounts for an estimated 25.7 percent of the sample, differs from Group 1 only in degree: Through the adult years the estimated average offending rate of Group 2 is about 60 percent of that of Group 1. Otherwise Group 2's offending trajectory mirrors that of Group 1, reaching

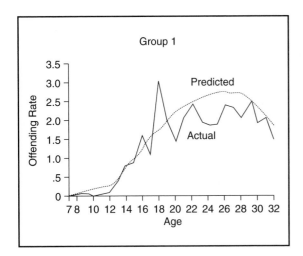
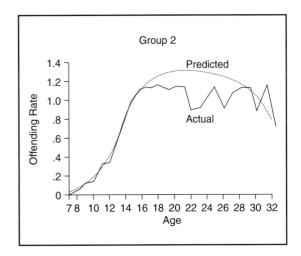
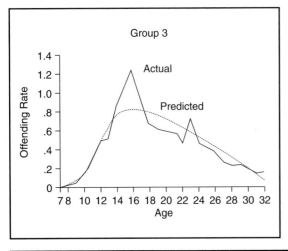
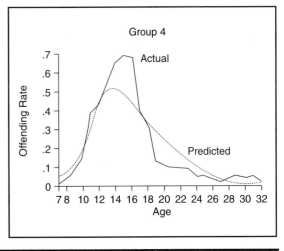

FIGURE 22.2 Actual and Predicted Offending Rates by Age, for Groups

a peak at about age 25 and slowly declining thereafter. But even at age 32, those in Group 2 average about .8 arrests per year.

Groups 3 and 4 are the largest groups making up an estimated 42.5 percent and 28.9 percent of the sample, respectively. While both groups have modestly high rates of offending through their teenage years, by age 32 the average arrest rates are small: For Group 4 it approaches 0 (.02 arrests per year). Figure 22.1 indicates that effectively this group has

desisted from offending for nearly a decade. At age 32 the estimated offending rate of Group 3 is only .1 arrests per year, which implies an average time between arrests of about 10 years. The effective desistance of Group 3 members by age 32 appears to have occurred more gradually than that for Group 4 members, as throughout their twenties those in Group 3 have modestly high arrest rates.

Table 22.1 presents group means on a variety of individual characteristics, behaviors, and life-course

TABLE 22.1   Comparison of Group Means for Selected Characteristics, by Group Membership

CHARACTERISTIC	GROUPS 1 AND 2	GROUP 3	GROUP 4
Individual Differences in Childhood			
Verbal IQ	5.63	5.49	5.44
Percent extroverted	67.0	53.1	55.8
Percent adventurous*	66.0	52.7	50.6
Percent egocentric	12.3	15.9	9.7
Percent aggressive	14.2	15.9	15.6
Percent tantrums	44.3	41.4	34.4
Percent difficult	55.8	60.9	57.9
Family Differences in Childhood			
Poverty	.10	.08	.00
Family size*	6.00	5.34	5.23
Parental crime/alcohol abuse	2.06	1.94	2.04
Erratic discipline	.13	−.15	−.08
Supervision	1.39	1.47	1.42
Attachment to family	3.07	3.13	3.10
Adolescent Behavior			
Arrest frequency*	.45	.45	.37
Unofficial delinquency*	15.6	14.0	13.6
Percent attached to school*	21.6	35.9	39.7
Percent early onset	15.4	14.1	9.6
Adult Social Bonds			
Percent divorce/separation by age 32*	38.5	18.9	10.3
Percent "shotgun" marriage*	40.8	34.4	18.4
Percent married by age 32*	30.8	50.7	80.3
Quality of marriage at age 32*	−2.01	−.47	.69
Job stability at age 32*	−3.16	−1.37	.50
Number of Cases	106	220	154

*Differences are jointly significant at *p* < .05 level.

outcomes. We combine Groups 1 and 2 because of the small numbers in Group 1. Consider first the "unofficial" delinquency measure under "Adolescent Behavior." Although Groups 1 and 2 had more adolescent delinquent activity than did members of Groups 3 and 4, the difference is modest—15.6 for Groups 1 and 2 versus 14.0 for Group 3 and 13.6 for Group 4. Thus, *conditional upon having a juvenile record*, the intensity of adolescent delinquency seems to be only moderately predictive of eventual desistance. This important point is often overlooked in discussions of desistance from crime in adulthood.

The variables measuring individual and family differences in childhood were selected because research on the Gluecks' data (Sampson and Laub 1993) as well as on other data (Loeber and Stouthamer-Loeber 1986; Nagin and Farrington 1992; Nagin, Farrington, and Moffitt 1995) has shown that these childhood factors predict juvenile delinquency, and in some instances, predict adult criminality. Our concern, however, is with desistance.

Only family size distinguishes the groups—on average the desisters come from somewhat smaller families, 5.5 and 5.2 for Groups 3 and 4, respectively, versus 6.0 for Groups 1 and 2. None of the other variables measuring family factors—poverty, parental criminality, and childrearing practices—distinguish the groups; only one of the individual characteristics—whether the boy was judged "adventurous"—differentiates the groups. The percentages of subjects who in childhood were extroverted, egocentric, aggressive, difficult, or prone to temper tantrums all fail to differentiate the Group 1 and 2 nondesisters from the two desister groups. We suspect that the limited capacity of these childhood factors to differentiate group membership stems from the relatively small differences across groups in the intensity of their adolescent delinquency. Put differently, while prior research has shown that childhood and family differences are "sturdy" predictors of antisocial behavior (Robins 1978), the capacity of these differences to predict future desistance from such behavior seems to be limited. Nagin et al. (1995) also found that these variables had a limited capacity to predict desistance among active offenders in a

more contemporary sample of 411 British males born in 1951–1954.

The variables measuring adult social bonds show that desister groups (Groups 3 and 4) are significantly and substantially less likely to be divorced or separated or to have been involved in "shotgun" marriages. They also have significantly higher scores on two indices of social bonds—the quality of the marriage bond at age 32 for those who are married and job stability for the period from age 25 to 32.

The pronounced association between membership in Group 3 and 4 and the strength of adult social bonds is consistent with our view of change over time; but it is also consistent with a selection process view. . . .

Second-Stage Analysis

In the second stage of our analysis, we test two key predictions on gradual change: (1) Individuals who early on become involved in marriages that evolve into good marriages will desist from crime the soonest, and (2) as a result of the growing investment in ex-post good marriages, the magnitude of the preventive effect of the marital bond will grow over time. [Multivariable analyses confirm both of these predictions.] . . .

CONCLUSION AND IMPLICATIONS

Several conclusions flow from our analyses. First, there are distinct trajectories of individual offending that diverge markedly from the aggregate age-crime curve. Four offender groups characterize the delinquent sample from Glueck and Glueck (1950). Although two of these groups follow the conventional age-crime curve with sharp declines in offending in adulthood (Farrington 1986; Hirschi and Gottfredson 1983), two groups do not. In fact, at least one group and probably a (small) second group of men continue to offend at a fairly high and relatively flat rate even as they age into their thirties. These findings emerge from a group of highrate juvenile offenders. The delinquents in the Gluecks' study were serious, persistent offenders, and consequently, they were remanded to juvenile institutions. yet as they age, the heterogeneity in offending patterns becomes sharper, so that by age 32 the skewness of offending that we observe in general population samples is evident in this group too (albeit at a higher level of overall offending).

The second finding, implied but not compelled by the first, is that childhood and juvenile characteristics are insufficient for predicting the patterns of future offending in a high-rate group of juvenile offenders. The divergent pathways that unfold over time can be predicted by concurrent events in the transition to young adulthood. Recall that many of the staple variables of delinquency theory (e.g., being a difficult child, low IQ, living in poverty, poor parental supervision) were unable to differentiate offending trajectories into mid-adulthood. These findings suggest that many of the classic predictors of the onset and frequency of delinquency may not explain desistance.

The third major finding concerns the timing and quality of marriage: Early marriages characterized by social cohesiveness led to a growing preventive effect.

Consistent with the informal social control theory of Sampson and Laub (1993) and Nagin and Paternoster (1994), the data support the investment-quality character of good marriages. The effect of a good marriage takes time to appear, and its grows slowly over time until it inhibits crime. Our findings accord well with studies using contemporary data.

For example, Horney et al. (1995) showed that large *within-individual* variations in criminal offending for a sample of high-rate convicted felons were systematically associated with local life circumstances (e.g., employment and marriage). As they noted, *some* of the time, *some* high-rate offenders enter into circumstances like marriage that provide the potential for informal social control. When they do, and in our case when marital unions are cohesive, the investment has a significant preventive effect on offending (Farrington and West 1995). "Good" things sometimes happen to "bad" actors, and when they do desistance has a chance. Of course, our perspective suggests that outcomes are always in doubt, but that is even more reason not to give up hope based on negative returns from the early years alone.

REFERENCES

Farrington, David P. 1986. "Age and Crime." Pp. 189–250 in *Crime and Justice*, vol. 7, edited by M. Tonry and N. Morris. Chicago, IL: University of Chicago Press.

Farrington, David P. and Donald J. West. 1995. "The Effects of Marriage, Separation, and Children on Offending by Adult Males." Pp. 249–81 in *Current Perspectives on Aging and Life Cycle*, vol. 4, *Delinquency and Disrepute in the Life Course*, edited by Z. Smith Blau and J. Hagan. Greenwich, CT: JAI Press.

Glueck, Sheldon and Eleanor Glueck. 1950. *Unraveling Juvenile Delinquency*. New York: Commonwealth Fund.

———. 1968. *Delinquents and Nondelinquents in Perspective*. Cambridge, MA: Harvard University Press.

Hirschi, Travis and Michael Gottfredson. 1983. "Age and the Explanation of Crime." *American Journal of Sociology* 89:552–84.

Horney, Julie, D. Wayne Osgood, and Ineke Haen Marshall. 1995. "Criminal Careers in the Short-Term: Intra-individual Variability in Crime and Its Relation to Local Life Circumstances." *American Sociological Review* 60: 655–73.

Laub, John H. and Robert J. Sampson. 1993. "Turning Points in the Life Course: Why Change Matters to the Study of Crime." *Criminology* 31:301–25.

Loeber, Rolf and Magda Stouthamer-Loeber. 1986. "Family Factors as Correlates and Predictors of Juvenile Conduct Problems and Delinquency." Pp. 29–149 in *Crime and Justice*, vol. 7, edited by M. Tonry and N. Morris. Chicago, IL: University of Chicago Press.

Nagin, Daniel S. and David P. Farrington. 1992. "The Stability of Criminal Potential from Childhood to Adulthood." *Criminology* 30:235–60.

Nagin, Daniel S. and Ray Paternoster. 1994. "Personal Capital and Social Control: The Deterrence Implications of Individual Differences in Criminal Offending." *Criminology* 32:581–606.

Nagin, Daniel S., David P. Farrington, and Terrie E. Moffitt. 1995. "Life Course Trajectories of Different Types of Offenders." *Criminology* 33:111–39.

Robins, Lee N. 1978. "Sturdy Childhood Predictors of Adult Behavior: Replications from Longitudinal Studies." *Psychological Medicine* 8:611–22.

Sampson, Robert J. and John H. Laub. 1993. *Crime in the Making: Pathways and Turning Points through Life.* Cambridge, MA: Harvard University Press.

———. 1994. "Urban Poverty and the Family Context of Delinquency: A New Look at Structure and Process in a Classic Study." *Child Development* 65:523–40.

CHAPTER 23

ON BEING SANE IN INSANE PLACES

D. L. ROSENHAN

If sanity and insanity exist, how shall we know them?

The question is neither capricious nor itself insane. However much we may be personally convinced that we can tell the normal from the abnormal, the evidence is simply not compelling. It is commonplace, for example, to read about murder trials wherein eminent psychiatrists for the defense are contradicted by equally eminent psychiatrists for the prosecution on the matter of the defendant's sanity. More generally, there are a great deal of conflicting data on the reliability, utility, and meaning of such terms as "sanity," "insanity," "mental illness," and "schizophrenia." Finally, as early as 1934, Benedict suggested that normality and abnormality are not universal.[1] What is viewed as normal in one culture may be seen as quite aberrant in another. Thus, notions of normality and abnormality may not be quite as accurate as people believe they are.

To raise questions regarding normality and abnormality is in no way to question the fact that some behaviors are deviant or odd. Murder is deviant. So, too, are hallucinations. Nor does raising such questions deny the existence of the personal anguish

that is often associated with "mental illness." Anxiety and depression exist. Psychological suffering exists. But normality and abnormality, sanity and insanity, and the diagnoses that flow from them may be less substantive than many believe them to be.

At its heart, the question of whether the sane can be distinguished from the insane (and whether degrees of insanity can be distinguished from each other) is a simple matter: do the salient characteristics that lead to diagnoses reside in the patients themselves or in the environments and contexts in which observers find them? From Bleuler, through Kretchmer, through the formulators of the recently revised *Diagnostic and Statistical Manual of the American Psychiatric Association,* the belief has been strong that patients present symptoms, that those symptoms can be categorized, and, implicitly, that the sane are distinguishable from the insane. More recently, however, this belief has been questioned. Based in part on theoretical and anthropological considerations, but also on philosophical, legal, and therapeutic ones, the view has grown that psychological categorization of mental illness is useless at best and downright harmful, misleading, and pejorative at worst. Psychiatric diagnoses, in this view, are in the minds of the observers and are not valid summaries of characteristics displayed by the observed.[2]

Gains can be made in deciding which of these is more nearly accurate by getting normal people (that

From *Science* 179 (January 1973), pp. 250–258. Copyright © 1973 by the American Association for the Advancement of Science. Reprinted by permission. Some footnotes have been incorporated as additional endnotes or deleted. The reader should contrast the findings on mental hospitals in this essay with the findings reported by Weinstein in Part 2.

is, people who do not have, and have never suffered, symptoms of serious psychiatric disorders) admitted to psychiatric hospitals and then determining whether they were discovered to be sane and, if so, how. If the sanity of such pseudopatients were always detected, there would be prima facie evidence that a sane individual can be distinguished from the insane context in which he is found. Normality (and presumably abnormality) is distinct enough that it can be recognized wherever it occurs, for it is carried within the person. If, on the other hand, the sanity of the pseudopatients were never discovered, serious difficulties would arise for those who support traditional modes of psychiatric diagnosis. Given that the hospital staff was not incompetent, that the pseudopatient had been behaving as sanely as he had been outside of the hospital, and that it had never been previously suggested that he belonged in a psychiatric hospital, such an unlikely outcome would support the view that psychiatric diagnosis betrays little about the patient but much about the environment in which an observer finds him.

This article describes such an experiment. Eight sane people gained secret admission to 12 different hospitals. Their diagnostic experiences constitute the data of the first part of this article; the remainder is devoted to a description of their experiences in psychiatric institutions. Too few psychiatrists and psychologists, even those who have worked in such hospitals, know what the experience is like. They rarely talk about it with former patients, perhaps because they distrust information coming from the previously insane. Those who have worked in psychiatric hospitals are likely to have adapted so thoroughly to the settings that they are insensitive to the impact of that experience. And while there have been occasional reports of researchers who submitted themselves to psychiatric hospitalization,[3] these researchers have commonly remained in the hospitals for short periods of time, often with the knowledge of the hospital staff. It is difficult to know the extent to which they were treated like patients or like research colleagues. Nevertheless, their reports about the inside of the psychiatric hospital have been valuable. This article extends those efforts.

PSEUDOPATIENTS AND THEIR SETTINGS

The eight pseudopatients were a varied group. One was a psychology graduate student in his 20's. The remaining seven were older and "established." Among them were three psychologists, a pediatrician, a psychiatrist, a painter, and a housewife. Three pseudopatients were women, five were men. All of them employed pseudonyms, lest their alleged diagnoses embarrass them later. Those who were in mental health professions alleged another occupation in order to avoid the special attentions that might be accorded by staff, as a matter of courtesy or caution, to ailing colleagues.[4] With the exception of myself (I was the first pseudopatient and my presence was known to the hospital administrator and chief psychologist and, so far as I can tell, to them alone), the presence of pseudopatients and the nature of the research program was not known to the hospital staffs.[5]

The settings were similarly varied. In order to generalize the findings, admission into a variety of hospitals was sought. The 12 hospitals in the sample were located in five different states on the East and West coasts. Some were old and shabby, some were quite new. Some were research-oriented, others not. Some had good staff-patient ratios, others were quite understaffed. Only one was a strictly private hospital. All of the others were supported by state or federal funds or, in one instance, by university funds.

After calling the hospital for an appointment, the pseudopatient arrived at the admissions office complaining that he had been hearing voices. Asked what the voices said, he replied that they were often unclear, but as far as he could tell they said "empty," "hollow," and "thud." The voices were unfamiliar and were of the same sex as the pseudopatient. The choice of these symptoms was occasioned by their apparent similarity to existential symptoms. Such symptoms are alleged to arise from painful concerns about the perceived meaninglessness of one's life. It is as if the hallucinating person were saying, "My life is empty and hollow." The choice of these symptoms was also determined by the *absence* of a single report of existential psychoses in the literature.

Beyond alleging the symptoms and falsifying name, vocation, and employment, no further alterations of person, history, or circumstances were made. The significant events of the pseudopatient's life history were presented as they had actually occurred. Relationships with parents and siblings, with spouse and children, with people at work and in school, consistent with the aforementioned exceptions, were described as they were or had been. Frustrations and upsets were described along with joys and satisfactions. These facts are important to remember. If anything, they strongly biased the subsequent results in favor of detecting sanity, since none of their histories or current behaviors were seriously pathological in any way.

Immediately upon admission to the psychiatric ward, the pseudopatient ceased simulating *any* symptoms of abnormality. In some cases, there was a brief period of mild nervousness and anxiety, since none of the pseudopatients really believed that they would be admitted so easily. Indeed, their shared fear was that they would be immediately exposed as frauds and greatly embarrassed. Moreover, many of them had never visited a psychiatric ward, even those who had, nevertheless had some genuine fears about what might happen to them. Their nervousness, then, was quite appropriate to the novelty of the hospital setting, and it abated rapidly.

Apart from that short-lived nervousness, the pseudopatient behaved on the ward as he "normally" behaved. The pseudopatient spoke to patients and staff as he might ordinarily. Because there is uncommonly little to do on a psychiatric ward, he attempted to engage others in conversation. When asked by staff how he was feeling, he indicated that he was fine, that he no longer experienced symptoms. He responded to instructions from attendants, to calls for medication (which was not swallowed), and to dining-hall instructions. Beyond such activities as were available to him on the admissions ward, he spent his time writing down his observations about the ward, its patients, and the staff. Initially these notes were written "secretly," but as it soon became clear that no one much cared, they were subsequently written on standard tablets of paper in such public

places as the dayroom. No secret was made of these activities.

The pseudopatient, very much as a true psychiatric patient, entered a hospital with no foreknowledge of when he would be discharged. Each was told that he would have to get out by his own devices, essentially by convincing the staff that he was sane. The psychological stresses associated with hospitalization were considerable, and all but one of the pseudopatients desired to be discharged almost immediately after being admitted. They were, therefore, motivated not only to behave sanely, but to be paragons of cooperation. That their behavior was in no way disruptive is confirmed by nursing reports, which have been obtained on most of the patients. These reports uniformly indicate that the patients were "friendly," "cooperative," and "exhibited no abnormal indications."

THE NORMAL ARE NOT DETECTABLY SANE

Despite their public "show" of sanity, the pseudopatients were never detected. Admitted, except in one case, with a diagnosis of schizophrenia, each was discharged with a diagnosis of schizophrenia "in remission" [the one different diagnosis was "manic-depressive psychosis"]. The label "in remission" should in no way be dismissed as a formality, for at no time during any hospitalization had any question been raised about any pseudopatient's simulation. Nor are there any indications in the hospital records that the pseudopatient's status was suspect. Rather, the evidence is strong that, once labeled schizophrenic, the pseudopatient was stuck with that label. If the pseudopatient was to be discharged, he must naturally be "in remission"; but he was not sane, nor, in the institutions view, had he ever been sane.

The uniform failure to recognize sanity cannot be attributed to the quality of the hospitals, for, although there were considerable variations among them, several are considered excellent. Nor can it be alleged that there was simply not enough time to observe the pseudopatients. Length of hospitalization ranged from 7 to 52 days, with an average of 19 days. The pseudopatients were not, in fact, carefully observed, but this failure clearly speaks more to traditions within psychiatric hospitals than to lack of opportunity.

Finally, it cannot be said that the failure to recognize the pseudopatients' sanity was due to the fact that they were not behaving sanely. While there was clearly some tension present in all of them, their daily visitors could detect no serious behavioral consequences—nor, indeed, could other patients. It was quite common for the patients to "detect" the pseudopatients' sanity. During the first three hospitalizations, when accurate counts were kept, 35 of a total of 118 patients on the admissions ward voiced their suspicions, some vigorously. "You're not crazy. You're a journalist, or a professor [referring to the continual note taking]. You're checking up on the hospital." While most of the patients were reassured by the pseudopatient's insistence that he had been sick before he came in but was fine now, some continued to believe that the pseudopatient was sane throughout his hospitalization.[6] The fact that the patients often recognized normality when staff did not raises important questions.

Failure to detect sanity during the course of hospitalization may be due to the fact that physicians operate with a strong bias toward what statisticians call the type 2 error. This is to say that physicians are more inclined to call a healthy person sick (a false positive, type 2) than a sick person healthy (a false negative, type 1). The reasons for this are not hard to find: it is clearly more dangerous to misdiagnose illness than health. Better to err on the side of caution, to suspect illness even among the healthy.

But what holds for medicine does not hold equally well for psychiatry. Medical illnesses, while unfortunate, are not commonly pejorative. Psychiatric diagnoses, on the contrary, carry with them personal, legal, and social stigmas. It was therefore important to see whether the tendency toward diagnosing the sane insane could be reversed. The following experiment was arranged at a research and teaching hospital whose staff had heard these findings but doubted that such an error could occur in their hospital. The staff was informed that at some time during the following 3 months, one or more pseudopatients would attempt to be admitted into the psychiatric hospital. Each staff member was asked to rate each patient who presented himself at admissions or on the ward according to the likelihood that the patient was a pseudopatient. A 10-point scale was used, with a 1 and 2 reflecting high confidence that the patient was a pseudopatient.

Judgments were obtained on 193 patients who were admitted for psychiatric treatment. All staff who had had sustained contact with or primary responsibility for the patient—attendants, nurses, psychiatrists, physicians, and psychologists—were asked to make judgments. Forty-one patients were alleged, with high confidence, to be pseudopatients by at least one member of the staff. Twenty-three were considered suspect by at least one psychiatrist. Nineteen were suspected by one psychiatrist *and* one other staff member. Actually, no genuine pseudopatient (at least from my group) presented himself during this period.

The experiment is instructive. It indicates that the tendency to designate sane people as insane can be reversed when the stakes (in this case, prestige and diagnostic acumen) are high. But what can be said of the 19 people who were suspected of being "sane" by one psychiatrist and another staff member? Were these people truly "sane," or was it rather the case that in the course of avoiding the type 2 error the staff tended to make more errors of the first sort—calling the crazy "sane"? There is no way of knowing. But one thing is certain: any diagnostic process that lends itself so readily to massive errors of this sort cannot be a very reliable one.

THE STICKINESS OF PSYCHODIAGNOSTIC LABELS

Beyond the tendency to call the healthy sick—a tendency that accounts better for diagnostic behavior on admission than it does for such behavior after a lengthy period of exposure—the data speak to the massive role of labeling in psychiatric assessment. Having once been labeled schizophrenic, there is nothing the pseudopatient can do to overcome the tag. The tag profoundly colors others' perceptions of him and his behavior.

From one viewpoint, these data are hardly surprising, for it has long been known that elements are given meaning by the context in which they occur. Gestalt psychology made this point vigorously, and Asch demonstrated that there are "central" personality traits (such as "warm" versus "cold") which are so powerful that they markedly color the meaning of other information in forming an impression of a given personality.[7] "Insane," "schizophrenic," "manic-depressive," and "crazy" are probably among the most powerful of such central traits. Once a person is designated abnormal, all of his other behaviors and characteristics are colored by that label. Indeed, that label is so powerful that many of pseudopatients' normal behaviors were overlooked entirely or profoundly misinterpreted. Some examples may clarify this issue.

Earlier I indicated that there were no changes in the pseudopatient's personal history and current status beyond those of name, employment, and, where necessary, vocation. Otherwise, a veridical description of personal history and circumstances was offered. Those circumstances were not psychotic. How were they made consonant with the diagnosis of psychosis? Or were those diagnoses modified in such a way as to bring them into accord with the circumstances of the pseudopatient's life, as described by him?

As far as I can determine, diagnoses were in no way affected by the relative health of the circumstances of a pseudopatient's life. Rather, the reverse occurred: the perception of his circumstances was shaped entirely by the diagnosis. A clear example of such translation is found in the case of a pseudopatient who had had a close relationship with his mother but was rather remote from his father during early childhood. During adolescence and beyond, however, his father became a close friend, while his relationship with his mother cooled. His present relationship with his wife was characteristically close and warm. Apart from occasionally angry exchanges, friction was minimal. The children had rarely been spanked. Surely there is nothing especially pathological about such a history. Indeed, many readers may see a similar pattern in their own experiences, with the markedly distinguished consequences. Observe, however, how such a history was translated in the psychopathological context, this from the case summary prepared after the patient was discharged.

> *This white 39-year-old male . . . manifests a long history of considerable ambivalence in close relationships, which begins in early childhood. A warm relationship with his mother cools during his adolescence. A distant relationship to his father is described as becoming very intense. Affective stability is absent. His attempts to control emotionality with his wife and children are punctuated by angry outbursts and, in the case of the children, spankings. And while he says that he has several good friends, one senses considerable ambivalence embedded in those relationships also. . . .*

The facts of the case were unintentionally distorted by the staff to achieve consistency with a popular theory of the dynamics of a schizophrenic reaction. Nothing of an ambivalent nature had been described in relations with parents, spouse, or friends. To the extent that ambivalence could be inferred, it was probably not greater than is found in all human relationships. It is true the pseudopatient's relationships with his parents changed over time, but in the ordinary context that would hardly be remarkable—indeed, it might very well be expected. Clearly, the meaning ascribed to his verbalizations (that is, ambivalence, affective instability) was determined by the diagnosis: schizophrenia. An entirely different meaning would have been ascribed if it were known that the man was "normal."

All pseudopatients took extensive notes publicly. Under ordinary circumstances, such behavior would have raised questions in the minds of observers, as, in fact, it did among patients. Indeed, it seemed so certain that the notes would elicit suspicion that elaborate precautions were taken to remove them from the ward each day. But the precautions proved needless. The closest any staff member came to questioning these notes occurred when one pseudopatient asked his physician what kind of medication he was receiving and began to write down the response. "You needn't write it," he was told gently. "If you have trouble remembering, just ask me again."

If no questions were asked of the pseudopatients, how was their writing interpreted? Nursing records for three patients indicate that the writing was seen as an aspect of their pathological behavior. "Patient engages in writing behavior," was the daily nursing comment. Given that the patient is in the hospital, he must be psychologically disturbed. And given that he is disturbed, continuous writing must be a behavioral manifestation of that disturbance, perhaps a subset of the compulsive behaviors that are sometimes correlated with schizophrenia.

One tacit characteristic of psychiatric diagnosis is that it locates the sources of aberration within the individual and only rarely within the complex of stimuli that surrounds him. Consequently, behaviors that are stimulated by the environment are commonly misattributed to the patient's disorder. For example, one kindly nurse found a pseudopatient pacing the long hospital corridors. "Nervous, Mr. X?" she asked. "No, bored," he said.

The notes kept by pseudopatients are full of patient behaviors that were misinterpreted by well-intentioned staff. Often enough, a patient would go "berserk" because he had, wittingly or unwittingly, been mistreated by, say, an attendant. A nurse coming upon the scene would rarely inquire even cursorily into the environmental stimuli of the patient's behavior. Rather, she assumed that his upset derived from his pathology, not from his present interactions with other staff members. Occasionally, the staff might assume that the patient's family (especially when they had recently visited) or other patients had stimulated the outburst. But never were the staff found to assume that one of themselves or the structure of the hospital had anything to do with a patient's behavior. One psychiatrist pointed to a group of patients who were sitting outside the cafeteria entrance half an hour before lunchtime. To a group of young residents he indicated that such behavior was characteristic of the oral-acquisitive nature of the syndrome. It seemed not to occur to him that there were very few things to anticipate in a psychiatric hospital besides eating.

A psychiatric label has a life and an influence of its own. Once the impression has been formed that the patient is schizophrenic, the expectation is that he will continue to be schizophrenic. When a sufficient amount of time has passed, during which the patient has done nothing bizarre, he is considered to be in remission and available for discharge. But the label endures beyond discharge, with the unconfirmed expectation that he will behave as a schizophrenic again. Such labels, conferred by mental health professionals, are as influential on the patient as they are on his relatives and friends, and it should be no surprise to anyone that the diagnosis is on all of them as a self-fulfilling prophecy. Eventually, the patient himself accepts the diagnosis, with all of its surplus meanings and expectations, and behaves accordingly.

The inferences to be made from these matters are quite simple. Much as Zigler and Phillips have demonstrated that there is enormous overlap in the symptoms presented by patients who have been variously diagnosed, so there is enormous overlap in the behaviors of the sane and the insane.[8] The sane are not "sane" all of the time. We lose our tempers "for no good reason." We are occasionally depressed or anxious, again for no good reason. And we may find it difficult to get along with one or another person—again for no reason that we can specify. Similarly, the insane are not always insane. Indeed, it was the impression of the pseudopatients while living with them that they were sane for long periods of time—that the bizarre behaviors upon which their diagnoses were allegedly predicated constituted only a small fraction of their total behavior. If it makes no sense to label ourselves permanently depressed on the basis of an occasional depression, then it takes better evidence than is presently available to label all patients insane or schizophrenic on the basis of bizarre behaviors or cognitions. It seems more useful, as Mischel has pointed out, to limit our discussions to *behaviors,* the stimuli that provoke them, and their correlates.[9]

It is not known why powerful impressions of personality traits, such as "crazy" or "insane," arise. Conceivably, when the origins of and stimuli that give rise to a behavior are remote or unknown, or when the behavior strikes us as immutable, trait labels regarding the behavior arise. When, on the other hand, the origins and stimuli are known and available, discourse is limited to the behavior itself. Thus, I may hallucinate because I am sleeping, or I may hallucinate because I have ingested a peculiar drug. These are termed sleep-induced hallucinations, or dreams, and drug-induced hallucinations, respectively. But when the stimuli to my hallucinations are unknown, that is called craziness, or schizophrenia—as if that inference were somehow as illuminating as the others.

THE EXPERIENCE OF PSYCHIATRIC HOSPITALIZATION

The term "mental illness" is of recent origin. It was coined by people who were humane in their inclinations and who wanted very much to raise the station of (and the public's sympathies toward) the psychologically disturbed from that of witches and "crazies" to one that was akin to the physically ill. And they were at least partially successful, for the treatment of the mentally ill *has* improved considerably over the years. But while treatment has improved, it is doubtful that people really regard the mentally ill in the same way that they view the physically ill. A broken leg is something one recovers from, but mental illness allegedly endures forever.[10] A broken leg does not threaten the observer, but a crazy schizophrenic? There is by now a host of evidence that attitudes toward the mentally ill are characterized by fear, hostility, aloofness, suspicion, and dread.[11] The mentally ill are society's lepers.

That such attitudes infect the general population is perhaps not surprising, only upsetting. But that they affect the professionals—attendants, nurses, physicians, psychologists, and social workers—who treat and deal with the mentally ill is more disconcerting, both because such attitudes are self-evidently pernicious and because they are unwitting. Most mental health professionals would insist that they are sympathetic toward the mentally ill, that they are neither avoidant nor hostile. But it is more likely that an exquisite ambivalence characterizes their relations with psychiatric patients, such that their avowed impulses are only part of their entire attitude. Negative attitudes are there too and can easily be detected. Such attitudes should not surprise us. They are the natural offspring of the labels patients wear and the places in which they are found.

Consider the structure of the typical psychiatric hospital. Staff and patients are strictly segregated. Staff have their own living space, including their dining facilities, bathrooms, and assembly places. The glassed quarters that contain the professional staff, which the pseudopatients came to call "the cage," sit out on every dayroom. The staff emerge primarily for caretaking purposes—to give medication, to conduct a therapy or group meeting, to instruct or reprimand a patient. Otherwise, staff keep to themselves, almost as if the disorder that affects their charges is somehow catching.

So much is patient-staff segregation the rule that for four public hospitals in which an attempt was made to measure the degree to which staff and patients mingle, it was necessary to use "time out of the staff cage" as the operational measure. While it was not the case that all time spent out of the cage was spent mingling with patients (attendants, for example, would occasionally emerge to watch television in the dayroom), it was the only way which one could gather reliable data on time for measuring.

The average amount of time by attendants outside of the cage was 11.3 percent (range, 3 to 52 percent). This figure does not represent only time spent mingling with patients, but also includes time spent on such chores as folding laundry, supervising patients while they shave, directing ward clean-up, and sending patients to off-ward activities. It was the relatively rare attendant who spent time talking with patients or playing games with them. It proved impossible to obtain a "percent mingling time" for nurses, since the amount of time they spent out of cage was too brief. Rather, we counted instances of emergence from the cage. On the average, daytime nurses emerged from the cage 11.5 times per shift including instances when they left the ward entirely (range, 4 to 39 times). Late afternoon and night nurses were even less available, emerging on the average 9.4 times per shift (range, 4 to 41 times). Data on early morning nurses, who arrived usually after midnight and departed at 8 a.m., are not available because patients were asleep during most of this period.

Physicians, especially psychiatrists, were even less available. They were rarely seen on the wards. Quite commonly, they would be seen only when they arrived and departed, with the remaining time being spent in their offices or in the cage. On the average, physicians emerged on the ward 6.7 times per day (range, 1 to 17 times). It proved difficult to make an accurate estimate in this regard, since physicians often maintained hours that allowed them to come and go at different times.

The hierarchical organization of psychiatric hospitals has been commented on before,[12] but the latent meaning of that kind of organization is worth noting again. Those with the most power have least to do with patients, and those with the least power are most involved with them. Recall, however, that the acquisition of role-appropriate behaviors occurs mainly through the observation of others, with the most powerful having the most influence. Consequently, it is understandable that attendants not only spend more time with patients than do any other members of the staff—that is required by their station in the hierarchy—but also, insofar as they learn from their superiors' behavior, spend as little time with patients as they can. Attendants are seen mainly in the cage, which is where the models, the action, and the power are.

I turn now to a different set of studies, those dealing with staff response to patient-initiated contact. It has long been known that the amount of time a person spends with you can be an index of your significance to him. If he initiates and maintains eye contact, there is reason to believe that he is considering your requests and needs. If he pauses to chat or actually stops and talks, there is added reason to infer he is individuating you. In four hospitals, the pseudopatient approached the staff member with a request which took the following form: "Pardon me, Mr. [or Dr. or Mrs.] X, could you tell me when I will be eligible for grounds privileges?" (or ". . . . when I will be presented at the staff meeting?" or ". . . . when I am likely to be discharged?"). While the content of

the question varied according to the appropriateness of the target and the pseudopatient's (apparent) current needs, the form was always a courteous and relevant request for information. Care was taken never to approach a particular member of the staff more than once a day, lest the staff member become suspicious or irritated. In examining these data, remember that the behavior of the pseudopatients was neither bizarre nor disruptive. One could indeed engage in good conversation with them.

The data for these experiments are shown in Table 23.1, separately for physicians (column 1) and for nurses and attendants (column 2). Minor differences between these four institutions were overwhelmed by the degree to which staff avoided continuing contacts that patients had initiated. By far, their most common response consisted of either a brief response to the question, offered while they were "on the move" and with head averted, or no response at all.

The encounter frequently took the following bizarre form: (pseudopatient) "Pardon me, Dr. X. Could you tell me when I am eligible for grounds privileges?" (physician) "Good morning, Dave. How are you today?" (Moves off without waiting for a response.)

It is instructive to compare these data with data recently obtained at Stanford University. It has been alleged that large and eminent universities are characterized by faculty who are so busy that they have no time for students. For this comparison, a young lady approached individual faculty members who seemed to be walking purposefully to some meeting or teaching engagement and asked them the following six questions.

1. "Pardon me, could you direct me to Encina Hall?" (at the medical school: ". . . . to the Clinical Research Center?").
2. "Do you know where Fish Annex is?" (there is a Fish Annex at Stanford).
3. "Do you teach here?"
4. "How does one apply for admission to the college?" (at the medical school: ". . . . to the medical school?").

TABLE 23.1 Self-Initiated Contact by Pseudopatients with Psychiatrists and Nurses and Attendants, Compared to Contact with Other Groups

CONTACT	PSYCHIATRIC HOSPITALS		UNIVERSITY CAMPUS (NONMEDICAL)	UNIVERSITY MEDICAL CENTER PHYSICIANS		
	PSYCHIATRISTS	NURSES AND ATTENDANTS	FACULTY	"LOOKING FOR A PSYCHIATRIST"	"LOOKING FOR AN INTERNIST"	NO ADDITIONAL COMMENT
Responses						
Moves on, head averted (%)	71	88	0	0	0	0
Makes eye contact (%)	23	10	0	11	0	0
Pauses and chats (%)	2	2	0	11	0	10
Stops and talks (%)	4	0.5	100	78	100	90
Mean number of questions answered (out of 6)	*	*	6	3.8	4.8	4.5
Number of respondents	13	47	14	18	15	10
Number of attempts	185	1,283	14	18	15	10

*Not applicable.

5. "Is it difficult to get in?"
6. "Is there financial aid?"

Without exception, as can be seen in Table 23.1 (column 3), all of the questions were answered. No matter how rushed they were, all respondents not only maintained eye contact, but stopped to talk. Indeed, many of the respondents went out of their way to direct or take the questioner to the office she was seeking, to try to locate "Fish Annex," or to discuss with her the possibilities of being admitted to the university.

Similar data, also shown in Table 23.1 (columns 4, 5, and 6), were obtained in the hospital. Here too, the young lady came prepared with six questions. After the first question, however, she remarked to 18 of her respondents (column 4), "I'm looking for a psychiatrist," and to 15 others (column 5), "I'm looking for an internist." Ten other respondents received no inserted comment (column 6). The general degree of cooperative responses is considerably higher for these university groups than it was for pseudopatients in psychiatric hospitals. Even so, differences are apparent within the medical school setting. Once having indicated that she was looking for a psychiatrist, the degree of cooperation elicited was less than when she sought an internist.

POWERLESSNESS AND DEPERSONALIZATION

Eye contact and verbal contact reflect concern and individuation; their absence, avoidance and depersonalization. The data I have presented do not do justice to the rich daily encounters that grew up around matters of depersonalization and avoidance. I have records of patients who were beaten by staff for the sin of having initiated verbal contact. During my own experience, for example, one patient was beaten in the presence of other patients for having approached an attendant and told him, "I like you." Occasionally, punishment meted out to patients for misdemeanors seemed so excessive that it could not be justified by the most radical interpretations of psychiatric canon. Nevertheless, they appeared to go unquestioned. Tempers were often short. A patient who had not heard a call for medication would be roundly excoriated, and the morning attendants would often wake patients with, "Come on, you m——— f———s, out of bed!"

Neither anecdotal nor "hard" data can convey the overwhelming sense of powerlessness which invades the individual as he is continually exposed to the depersonalization of the psychiatric hospital. It hardly matters *which* psychiatric hospital—the excellent public ones and the very plush private hospital were better than the rural and shabby ones in this regard, but, again, the features that psychiatric hospitals had in common overwhelmed by far their apparent differences.

Powerlessness was evident everywhere. The patient is deprived of many of his legal rights by dint of his psychiatric commitment.[13] He is shorn of credibility by virtue of his psychiatric label. His freedom of movement is restricted. He cannot initiate contact with the staff, but may only respond to such overtures as they make. Personal privacy is minimal. Patient quarters and possessions can be entered and examined by any staff member, for whatever reason. His personal history and anguish is available to any staff member (often including the "grey lady" and "candy striper" volunteer) who chooses to read his folder, regardless of their therapeutic relationship to him. His personal hygiene and waste evacuation are often monitored. The water closets may have no doors.

At times, depersonalization reached such proportions that pseudopatients had the sense that they were invisible, or at least unworthy of account. Upon being admitted, I and other pseudopatients took the initial physical examinations in a semipublic room, where staff members went about their own business as if we were not there.

On the ward, attendants delivered verbal and occasionally serious physical abuse to patients in the presence of other observing patients, some of whom (the pseudopatients) were writing it all down. Abusive behavior, on the other hand, terminated quite abruptly when other staff members were known to be coming. Staff are credible witnesses. Patients are not.

A nurse unbuttoned her uniform to adjust her brassiere in the presence of an entire ward of viewing men. One did not have the sense that she was being seductive. Rather, she didn't notice us. A group of staff persons might point to a patient in the dayroom and discuss him animatedly, as if he were not there.

One illuminating instance of depersonalization and invisibility occurred with regard to medications. All told, the pseudopatients were administered nearly 2100 pills, including Elavil, Stelazine, Compazine, and Thorazine, to name but a few. (That such a variety of medications should have been administered to patients presenting identical symptoms is itself worthy of note.) Only two were swallowed. The rest were either pocketed or deposited in the toilet. The pseudopatients were not alone in this. Although I have no precise records on how many patients rejected their medications, the pseudopatients frequently found the medications of other patients in the toilet before they deposited their own. As long as they were cooperative, their behavior and the pseudopatients' own in this matter, as in other important matters, went unnoticed throughout.

Reactions to such depersonalization among pseudopatients were intense. Although they had come to the hospital as participant observers and were fully aware that they did not "belong," they nevertheless found themselves caught up in and fighting the process of depersonalization. Some examples: a graduate student in psychology asked his wife to bring his textbooks to the hospital so he could "catch up on his homework"—this despite the elaborate precautions taken to conceal his professional association. The same student, who had trained for quite some time to get into the hospital, and who had looked forward to the experience, "remembered" some drag races that he had wanted to see on the weekend and insisted that he be discharged by that time. Another pseudopatient attempted a romance with a nurse. Subsequently, he informed the staff that he was applying for admission to graduate school in psychology and was very likely to be admitted, since a graduate professor was one of his regular hospital visitors. The same person began to engage in psychotherapy with other patients—all of this as a way of becoming a person in an impersonal environment.

THE SOURCES OF DEPERSONALIZATION

What are the origins of depersonalization? I have already mentioned two. First are attitudes held by all of us toward the mentally ill—including those who treat them—attitudes characterized by fear, distrust, and horrible expectations on the one hand, and benevolent intentions on the other. Our ambivalence leads, in this instance as in others, to avoidance.

Second, and not entirely separate, the hierarchical structure of the psychiatric hospital facilitates depersonalization. Those who are at the top have least to do with patients, and their behavior inspires the rest of the staff. Average daily contact with psychiatrists, psychologist[s], residents, and physicians combined ranged from 3.9 to 25.1 minutes, with an overall mean of 6.8 (six pseudopatients over a total of 129 days of hospitalization). Included in this average are time spent in the admission interview, ward meetings in the presence of a senior staff member, group and individual psychotherapy contacts, case presentation conferences, and discharge meetings. Clearly, patients do not spend much time in interpersonal contact with doctoral staff. And doctoral staff serve as models for nurses and attendants.

There are probably other sources. Psychiatric installations are presently in serious financial straits. Staff shortages are pervasive, staff time at a premium. Something has to give, and that something is patient contact. Yet, while financial stresses are realities, too much can be made of them. I have the impression that the psychological forces that result in depersonalization are much stronger than the fiscal ones and that the addition of more staff would not correspondingly improve patient care in this regard. The incidence of staff meetings and the enormous amount of record-keeping on patients for example, have not been as substantially reduced as has patient contact. Priorities exist, even during hard times. Patient contact is not a significant priority in the traditional psychiatric hospital, and fiscal pressures do not account for this. Avoidance and depersonalization may.

Heavy reliance upon psychotropic medication tacitly contributes to depersonalization by convincing staff that treatment is indeed being conducted that further patient contact may not be necessary. Even here, however, caution needs to be exercised in understanding the role of psychotropic drugs. If patients were powerful rather than powerless, if they were viewed as interesting individuals rather than diagnostic entities, if they were socially significant rather than social lepers, if their anguish truly and wholly compelled our sympathies and concerns, would we not *seek* contact with them, despite the availability of medications? Perhaps for the pleasure of it all?

CONSEQUENCES OF LABELING AND DEPERSONALIZATION

Whenever the ratio of what is known to what needs to be known approaches zero, we tend to invent "knowledge" and assume that we understand more than we actually do. We seem unable to acknowledge that we simply don't know. The needs for diagnosis and medication of behavioral and emotional problems are enormous. But rather than acknowledge that we are just embarking on understanding, we continue to label patients "schizophrenic," "manic-depressive," and "insane," as if in those words we had captured the essence of understanding. The facts of the matter are that we have known for a long time that diagnoses are often not useful or reliable, but we have nevertheless continued to use them. We now know that we cannot distinguish insanity from sanity. It is depressing to consider how that information will be used.

Not merely depressing, but frightening. How many people, one wonders, are sane but not recognized as such in our psychiatric institutions? How many have been needlessly stripped of their privileges of citizenship, from the right to vote and drive to that of handling their own accounts? How many have pleaded insanity in order to avoid the criminal consequences of their behavior, and, conversely, how many would rather stand trial than live interminably at a psychiatric hospital—but are strongly thought to be mentally ill? How many have been stigmatized by well-intentioned, but nevertheless erroneous, diagnoses? On the last point, recall again that a "type 2 error" in psychiatric diagnosis does not have the same consequences it does in medical diagnosis. A diagnosis of cancer that has been found to be in error is cause for celebration. But psychiatric diagnoses are rarely found to be in error. The label sticks, a mark of inadequacy forever.

Finally, how many patients might be "sane" outside the psychiatric hospital but seem insane in it—not because craziness resides in them, as it were, but because they are responding to a bizarre setting, one that may be unique to institutions which harbor nether people? Goffman [see note 2] calls the process of socialization to such institutions "mortification"—an apt metaphor that includes the processes of depersonalization that have been described here. And while it is impossible to know whether the pseudopatients' responses to these processes are characteristic of all inmates—they were, after all, not real patients—it is difficult to believe that these processes of socialization to a psychiatric hospital provide useful attitudes or habits of response for living in the "real world."

SUMMARY AND CONCLUSIONS

It is clear that we cannot distinguish the sane from the insane in psychiatric hospitals. The hospital itself imposes a special environment in which the meanings of behavior can easily be misunderstood. The consequences to patients hospitalized in such an environment—the powerlessness, depersonalization, segregation, mortification, and self-labeling—seem undoubtedly counter-therapeutic.

I do not, even now, understand this problem well enough to perceive solutions. But two matters seem to have some promise. The first concerns the proliferation of community mental health facilities, of crisis intervention centers, of the human potential movement, and of behavior therapies that, for all of their own problems, tend to avoid psychiatric labels, to focus on specific problems and behaviors, and to retain the individual in a relatively non-pejorative environment. Clearly, to the extent that we refrain from sending the distressed to insane places, our impressions of them are less likely to be distorted. (The risk of distorted perceptions, it seems to me, is always present, since we are much more sensitive to an individual's behaviors and verbalizations than we are to the subtle contextual stimuli that often promote them. At issue here is a matter of magnitude. And, as I have shown, the magnitude of distortion is exceedingly high in the extreme context that is a psychiatric hospital.)

The second matter that might prove promising speaks to the need to increase the sensitivity of mental health workers and researchers to the *Catch 22* position of psychiatric patients. Simply reading materials in this area will be of help to some such workers and researchers. For others, directly experiencing the impact of psychiatric hospitalization will be of enormous use. Clearly, further research into the social psychology of such total institutions will both facilitate treatment and deepen understanding.

I and the other pseudopatients in the psychiatric setting had distinctly negative reactions. We do not pretend to describe the subjective experiences of true patients. Theirs may be different from ours, particularly with the passage of time and the necessary process of adaptation to one's environment. But we can and do speak to the relatively more objective indices of treatment within the hospital. It could be a mistake, and a very unfortunate one, to consider that what happened to us derived from malice or stupidity on the part of the staff. Quite the contrary, our overwhelming impression of them was of people who really cared, who were committed and who were uncommonly intelligent. Where they failed, as they sometimes did painfully, it would be more accurate to attribute those failures to the environment in which they, too, found themselves than to personal callousness. Their perceptions and behavior were controlled by the situation, rather than being motivated by a malicious disposition. In a more benign environment, one that was less attached to global diagnosis, their behaviors and judgments might have been more benign and effective.

NOTES

1. See R. Benedict, *Journal of General Psychology* 10, 59 (1934).

2. See, for example, E. Goffman, *Asylums* (Doubleday, Garden City, N.Y., 1961) and T. J. Scheff, *Being Mentally Ill: A Sociological Theory* (Aldine, Chicago, 1966).

3. See, for example, A. Barry, *Bellevue Is a State of Mind* (Harcourt Brace Jovanovich, New York, 1971).

4. Beyond the personal difficulties that the pseudopatient is likely to experience in the hospital, there are legal and social ones that, combined, require considerable attention before entry. For example, once admitted to a psychiatric institution, it is difficult, if not impossible, to be discharged on short notice, state law to the contrary notwithstanding. I was not sensitive to these difficulties at the outset of the project, nor to the personal and situational emergencies that can arise, but later a writ of habeas corpus was prepared for each of the entering pseudopatients and an attorney was kept "on call" during every hospitalization. I am grateful to John Kaplan and Robert Bartels for legal advice and assistance in these matters.

5. However distasteful such concealment is it was a necessary first step to examining these questions. Without concealment, there would have been no way to know how valid these experiences were; nor was there any way of knowing whether whatever detections occurred were a tribute to the diagnostic acumen of the staff or to the hospital's rumor network. Obviously, since my concerns are general ones that cut across individual hospitals and staffs, I have respected their anonymity and have eliminated clues that might lead to their identifications.

6. It is possible, of course, that patients have quite broad latitudes in diagnosis and therefore are inclined to call many people sane, even those whose behavior is patently aberrant. However, although we have no hard data on this matter, it was our distinct impression that this was not the case. In many instances, patients not only singled us out for attention, but came to imitate our behaviors and styles.

7. See S. E. Asch, *Journal of Abnormal Social Psychology* 41, 258 (1946); *Social Psychology* (Prentice-Hall, New York, 1952).

8. See E. Zigler and L. Phillips, *Journal of Abnormal Social Psychology* 63, 69 (1961).

9. See W. Mischel, *Personality and Assessment* (Wiley, New York, 1968).

10. The most recent and unfortunate instance of this tenet is that of Senator Thomas Eagleton. [After it came to public light that he had spent time in a mental hospital, Senator Eagleton was forced to withdraw himself as a U.S. vice-presidential candidate on the Democratic ticket in the 1972 election campaign.—Ed.]

11. See T. R. Sarbin and J. C. Mancuso, *Journal of Clinical Consulting Psychology* 35, 159 (1970); J. C. Nunnally, Jr., *Popular Conceptions of Mental Health* (Holt, Rinehart & Winston, New York, 1961).

12. See A. H. Stanton and M. S. Schwartz, The Mental Hospital: A Study of Institutional Participation in Psychiatric Illness and Treatment (Basic, New York, 1954).

13. See D. B. Wexler and S. E. Scoville, *Arizona Law Review* 13, 1 (1971).

PART 9

INEQUALITY

Of the many variables that concern sociologists, none is more important than social class. One's social class is associated with a multitude of lifestyle variables: from healthiness to longevity, from job stability to leisure-time pursuits, from tastes in food to tastes in sex, from what one reads to whom one befriends.

The major indicators of social class, income and wealth, are on our minds constantly; indeed, most of us envision many of our immediate and long-term problems being solved by money. The same is true for society: Many of our most pressing contemporary social problems—from health care to education quality to the elderly—are rooted in the unequal distributions of income and wealth.

Among the more important issues in the study of social class are the following. First, why are all societies—capitalist and socialist, democratic and totalitarian, small and large, historical and contemporary—*stratified*, that is, containing gross inequalities in income, wealth, power, and prestige? Second, given any particular system of social stratification, who is most likely to succeed? Who is most likely to fail? Finally, what are the consequences of being located in one or another position in the social class system—that is, what does it mean to be poor? Working class? Middle class? Upper-middle class? Rich? With varying emphases, each of the selections in Part 9 is concerned with each of these issues. Here, however, I will concentrate only on the first.

In the last half of the nineteenth century, Karl Marx (1818-1863) developed the basic ideas behind what today is known as the *conflict perspective* on social stratification. Its explanation as to why all societies are stratified begins with the fundamental and true assumption that as individuals, and as groups of individuals, we have differing interests. Consider the following examples:

- Employees and employers have the common goal of creating the best product or service possible, so that the company can compete and survive in the marketplace, which ensures that they, in turn, can earn money and thrive. However, they also have differing interests: Employers want to reinvest profits in the company after paying dividends to investors, and to keep as large a share as possible for themselves. On the other side, employees want good wages, paid vacations, and benefits in the areas of health care, disability, and retirement. If each group pursues its interests keenly, the result will be competition over company profits, which sometimes results in strikes and other forms of intense conflict, even violence if strikers are replaced by "scabs."

- Professors and college students have the common goal of getting students educated and graduated. Nevertheless, they have at least two points of contention if both pursue their respective interests vigorously. First and foremost, students want to pay the minimum for their educations; all things equal, they'd rather pay $8,000 for tuition than $18,000. However, in most institutions of higher learning the biggest budget item is staff salaries. What do you think: Would professors rather be paid $3,000 per course or $30,000? Second, most students want As. It would be a very happy lot indeed if 30 out of 30 students in a class received an A as the final course grade. But that could put the professor under a cloud of suspicion about his or her grading standards. Very likely the dean of the faculty would call the professor in and note the following: Students are unequal in ability. Students are unequal in their interest levels in any particular course. Students are unequal in their study habits. "Why, then," the dean would ask, "do they have *equal* grades?" A couple more classes with 100 percent As and the professor might well be looking for another job—indeed, another profession.

• Physicians and patients have in common the good health of the patients. But they also have several areas of dispute. Perhaps foremost is the fee schedule. All things equal, patients would rather pay $10 than $60 for an office visit, and $1,000 for an operation rather than $4,000. However, the physician would obviously prefer the latter fees.

The conflict perspective assumes that individuals and groups that pursue their interests vigorously will eventually end up in states of competition and conflict. Pick up any daily newspaper and the truth of this assumption is obvious. Accounts of conflict—labor strikes, coups d'etat, wars, business competition, and sporting events—abound.

What will determine the outcome of any particular conflict? The answer seems obvious, and it is: Those individuals and those groups with the greatest number of resources will tend to win out, whether the competition is between two men for a woman or two companies for a contract or two nations at war. Resources comprise anything that can be of assistance in a fray; money, knowledge, technology, size, experience, and allies are just a few examples.

Eventually, with each side applying the resources at its disposal, conflicts are resolved, but then the parties will have new conflicting interests: Losers will want to try to get back what they've lost, winners will want to solidify their gains. In a closed system, the cycle, repeated over many generations, will result in a social-class structure, that is, in stratification: The rich will tend to get richer and the poor poorer. This cycle is sketched here:

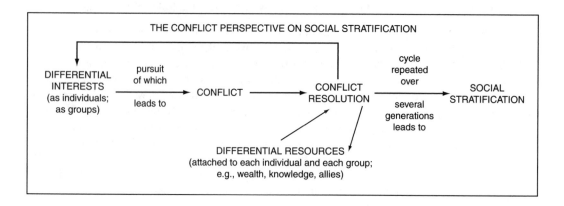

Marx's essay in Part 1, we may recall, offers the following example of this cyclical process: The landowners of England and Scotland were the heart of the upper class from the fifteenth through the eighteenth centuries. As the textile industry developed and they saw more profit in using their land for sheep grazing rather than for tilling, they used their power and influence to expropriate the peasants from their historic holdings and convert these holdings into sheep pastures. The weaker class, the peasants, were forced into states of privation and compelled to migrate to cities, where they toiled for low wages in the textile mills converting wool and cotton into cloth. In short, the rich stayed rich or got richer, and the poor got more miserably poor.

The same processes are evident in contemporary society. For example, Marvin E. Olsen's research reveals that the poorer half of American society suffered during the decade of the 1980s.[1] Much of this suffering was due to the influence of the rich and powerful on federal fiscal and economic policies. Studies conducted by the Federal Reserve Board and by the U.S. Bureau of the Census confirm Olsen's findings.[2]

Caroline Hodges Persell and Peter Cookson, Jr. write in the tradition of the conflict perspective. Their essay in Part 9 reveals that the nation's most elite schools, whose student bodies are comprised largely from the upper and upper-middle classes, operate to ensure that their students gain admission to the nation's most elite colleges and universities—thereby ensuring that the most prosperous families will remain that way.

Leonard Beeghley of the University of Florida also writes in this tradition. His article demonstrates how election laws and practices in the United States benefit the more affluent classes. It is all the more persuasive in that he demonstrates how changes in these laws and practices over the past 100 years have enhanced the affluent classes' domination of the political system.

The *functionalist perspective* on social stratification also addresses the issue of why all societies are stratified. In a classic article that appeared in the first two editions of *Empirical Approaches to Sociology*, Kingsley Davis and Wilbert E. Moore developed the basic ideas behind this perspective.[3] The functionalist explanation begins with the fundamental and true assumption that society's most important positions—those critical to the survival and well-being of its members—cannot be filled by just anyone. Thus, for example, many people can mow grass, but few can perform heart surgery. Moreover, society's most important positions are very demanding; they require major investments of time, study, hard work, talent, and skill. The question then becomes: How do we get individuals to "pay the price" it takes to pursue careers in society's most important jobs? The answer seems obvious: We motivate them by rewarding them unequally; that is, we accord each of these important positions great amounts of income, power, and prestige. In time, a society finds certain positions more or less permanently established near the top of its reward system and others near the bottom. Those individuals who fill the former become members of the more affluent classes, while those that fill the

[1]Marvin E. Olsen, "The Affluent Prosper While Everyone Else Struggles," *Sociological Focus* 23 (May 1990): 73–87.

[2]See "Reagan Era a Boon for the Nation's Rich," *Providence Journal*, 7 January 1992, p.1 (originally appearing in the *Los Angeles Times*); and "Poverty Rolls Grew by 2.1 Million in Past Year," *Providence Journal*, 4 September 1992, p. 1 (originally appearing in the *New York Times*).

[3]See their "Some Principles of Stratification," *American Sociological Review* 10(2) (April 1945): 242–249.

latter are relegated to the less affluent classes. We may sketch the causal logic of the functionalist perspective as follows:

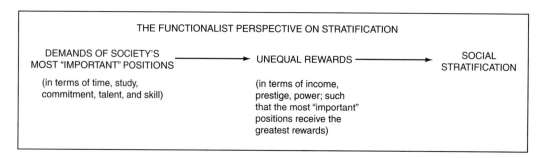

> THE FUNCTIONALIST PERSPECTIVE ON STRATIFICATION
>
> DEMANDS OF SOCIETY'S ⟶ UNEQUAL REWARDS ⟶ SOCIAL
> MOST "IMPORTANT" POSITIONS   STRATIFICATION
>
> (in terms of time, study,   (in terms of income,
> commitment, talent, and skill)   prestige, power; such
>   that the most "important"
>   positions receive the
>   greatest rewards)

There is truth in the functionalist perspective. Consider yourself. Why are you in college? Most likely because you believe the time and energy spent studying will pay off, and you intend to place yourself in a position that will garner significant income, prestige, and power.

However, to fully understand social stratification, one needs to combine both the conflict and functionalist perspectives. Physicians and corporate executives do not get high salaries just because their positions are so important and demanding and capable of being filled by so few. Once a position becomes invested with a degree of income, prestige, and power, individuals filling it will use its resources to help maintain its resources (i.e., the income, prestige, and power). Thus, for example, at the beginning of the twentieth century, medical doctors used their resources to influence state legislatures to outlaw and/or highly restrict other healing practitioners such as chiropractors and homeopathic doctors. And, true to the conflict perspective, it was only when the latter increased their resources and made effective use of them that laws and social conventions were changed allowing for the freer practicing of the healing arts. Thus, for example, in the 1970s chiropractors courted public opinion, lobbied legislatures, and used the courts to promote and eventually win their right to receive medical insurance benefits such as Blue Cross.

In his classic essay reprinted here in Part 9, James Davis presents findings on social mobility that reflect the explanatory power of both theoretical perspectives on inequality. On the one hand, Davis finds a father's occupational prestige greatly predicts that of the son's; thus, for example, the odds are about 2 to 1 that the son of a white-collar worker will end up doing white-collar work and, similarly, the odds are about 2 to 1 that the son of a blue-collar worker will end up holding down a blue-collar job. However, Davis also observes that there is still a great deal of mobility across generations *both* up and down occupational prestige scales—implying that coming from a prosperous background does not ensure success, just as coming from a less affluent background does not ensure that an individual remains toward the bottom of the stratification system. The 2 to 1 odds of remaining in the same place in the social class system as one's parents would be accounted for by those factors emphasized by the conflict perspective; while the explanation of the upward and downward movement of children compared to their parents would include factors contained in the functionalist perspective, for example, the willingness of individuals to "pay the price" (or, as it were, to *not* pay the price) required for economic success (e.g., staying in school; working hard; and having effective work habits, strong leadership ability, and high ambition).

Davis's work is extended and refined in the more contemporary research of Stephen W. Raudenbush, of Michigan State University, and Rafa M. Kasim of the University of Alabama at Birmingham. Their findings are best interpreted using both perspectives on inequality: On the one hand they find that reading ability correlates significantly with labor-force outcomes, with individuals with higher ability tending to earn more than individuals with lower ability, as would be predicted by the functionalist perspective. However, when reading ability is held constant, there still remains a large gap between the labor-force success of African American men and white (European-heritage) men, and between men and women in general—even when controls are added for education, credentials, and seniority. In other words, an African American man with the same reading ability, same amount of schooling, same educational degree, and work experience as his white counterpart is very likely to earn less income. Similarly, a woman with the same reading ability, same amount of schooling, same educational degree, and work experience as her male counterpart is very likely to earn less income. Such findings indicate the persistence of racial and gender discrimination, as would be predicted by the conflict perspective.

_____CHAPTER 24_____

UP AND DOWN
OPPORTUNITY'S LADDER

JAMES DAVIS

"Mobility" is one of the few social science terms that means exactly what it says—movement of some kind. Geographic mobility is the clearest example. If you are born in Mobile, Alabama and move away you are "mobile," but if you are born in Mobile and stay there until you die you are "immobile." Social mobility is a bit less obvious since it entails so many dimensions. Generally, sociologists define it as how far one has moved or down life's ladder, and you don't have to be a sociologist to be aware of people who are "rising in the world," "on the skids," "going places," "drop outs," and so forth.

Defining that initial rung on the social mobility ladder is a bit tricky, because at birth we all are unemployed, illiterate, and broke. Such deprivation is universal, but if the baby's parents are "up there" we don't feel quite so sad, while if the baby's parents are clinging to a bottom rung, things don't look as promising. Thus, the convention has developed of assigning *parental* scores as starting values. If your dad was a bootblack and you are now a physician, sociology says you have experienced "upward intergenerational occupational mobility"—73 points worth, as we shall see.

Of the ladders available for objective research, occupation has received most scrutiny. When sociologists talk about "social mobility" they usually mean intergenerational occupational mobility. And they are, ahem, usually talking about males. We don't have good beginning rungs for women because so few

James Davis, "Up and Down Opportunity's Ladder." *Public Opinion*, June/July 1982: 11–15, 48–51. Copyright © 1982 American Enterprise Institute. Reprinted by permission.

mothers had jobs. In the National Opinion Research Center (NORC) General Social Surveys, a series of national samplings during the 1970s, just half (50.4 percent) of the respondents said "yes" to "Did your mother ever work for pay for as long as a year, after she was married?" Needless to say, current scholars are redressing this imbalance. The early results suggest the main themes of mobility research are androgynous, but in the first half of this report I will stick to the classic data and thus talk mostly about males.

Mobility research is not new. Pitirim Sorokin's 1927 volume, *Social Mobility*, is still worth reading, but the quantity and quality of mobility data changed enormously after World War II, when nationwide studies began. The landmark here is Peter Blau and Otis D. Duncan's 1967 book, *The American Occupational Structure*, a sophisticated and encyclopedic analysis of CPS (the Census Bureau's Current Population Survey) data from a probability sample of some twenty thousand U.S. men. The Blau-Duncan study is known as OCG-I for "Occupational Change in a Generation." A decade later in 1973, David Featherman and Robert Hauser gave us OCG-II, a thirty thousand case replication. Whether, like *Rocky* or *Superman*, we have further OCG treats in store is unknown, but a third data base was emerged on its own. Beginning in 1972, NORC began a series of samplings of American adults known as the General Social Survey (GSS). Most of the GSS questions are reported word for word, year after year—not for lack of imagination but to catch social trends. One can pool GSSs to obtain a large sample—some 12,000 cases if one pools the eight surveys from 1972 through 1980. GSS 1982 is just completed, but we haven't seen any results yet.

After this brief introduction, let me turn to the daunting assignment of summarizing the findings of dozens of books and articles and analyzing the data. Necessarily painting with rather broad brush strokes, I say it looks like this:

1. Americans are frequent border-crossers
2. There is a lot more downward mobility than one might expect
3. But more of us move into the top levels than move out
4. Points 1, 2, and 3 shouldn't lead one to ignore the high amount of class continuity
5. Which is both promoted and mitigated by the "educational two-step."

AMERICANS ARE FREQUENT BORDER-CROSSERS

Comparing current situations with earlier ones, the General Social Survey and the Michigan election studies tell us:

No more than 10 to 15 percent of those surveyed shift out of their original religion

A bit less than 15 percent shift regions

About 30 percent shift political party

About a third have shifted from one state to another

About a third cross the white collar v. blue collar/ farm line, going one way or the other.

Occupational mobility is not rare. It is about as common as inter-state or inter-party mobility, and a lot more common than movement across the subcultural fault lines of religion and region.

DOWNWARD MOBILITY

Table 24.1 gives several examples of the classic way to examine mobility data, a nine-celled percentage table with fathers and sons each sorted into white collar, farm, and blue collar. For example, the fifth line of data says that in OCG-II, of 5,855 sons of farm fathers, 25.7 percent now have white collar jobs, 15 percent are still farming, and 59.3 percent have blue collar jobs.

Sticking with nonfarm jobs for the moment and squinting just a bit, I say each study is consistent with this proposition: "About a third of the white collar sons move down to blue, and about a third of blue collar sons move up to white collar." The ascent of the blues is, of course, "The American Dream," but the descent of the white collars is seldom lauded in Labor Day speeches on our open society. Yet the probabilities are similar in either direction. Not all descents are sickening plummets, I grant you. Indeed, as we will see, the top of the blue collar group (Craftsmen) have occupational prestige scores on a par with the bottom of the white collar (Clerical and Sales). True enough, but most white collar fathers are among the more prestigious "Professional and Managerial" group and most blue fathers are within the less prestigious "Operatives, Service Workers, Laborers" group rather than Craftsmen. Taking the *top* of the whites and the *bottom* of the blues and combining OCG-I and OCG-II, 16 percent of the Professional and Managerial sons ended up in Operative-Service-Labor, while 22 percent of the Operative-Service-Labor sons ended up in Professional and Managerial. For nonfarm workers, the chances of downward mobility are about the same as the chances for upward mobility.

MOVING INTO THE TOP LEVELS

If the white collars have about the same chance of moving down as the blue collars have of moving up, why do we hear only about upward mobility? Perhaps part of our sense of progress comes from the astounding increase in real incomes in this century. Contemporary blue collar workers live a lot better than pre-World War II white collar workers. But another part comes from a profound mathematical principle: if you apply the same percentage to a larger number you will get more cases than if you apply it to a smaller number. Look again at Table 24.1. About half of us come from blue collar homes and only about a quarter from white collar homes. Most of this difference can be accounted for by occupational structure, but some of it is due to fertility. Blue collar families generate more sons for the tables than

TABLE 24.1   The Standard Brand, Contemporary U.S., Father-Son Mobility Table

	SON'S JOB					
FATHER'S JOB	**WHITE COLLAR**	**FARM**	**BLUE COLLAR**	**TOTAL**	**N**	**ORIGINS**
(A) OCG-I (1962)						
White Collar	69.8%	1.4%	28.8%	100%	4,290	24.4%
Farm	22.9	22.3	54.9	100	5,141	29.2
Blue Collar	36.5	1.7	61.9	100	8,180	46.4
					17,611	100.0
(B) OCG-II (1973)						
White Collar	66.1	.1	32.9	99	7,232	27.6
Farm	25.7	15.0	59.3	100	5,855	22.3
Blue Collar	38.1	1.1	60.9	100	13,148	50.1
					26,235	100.0
(C) GSS (1972–1976)*						
White Collar	66.5	.5	32.9	100	762	25.6
Farm	24.4	19.9	55.7	100	734	24.6
Blue Collar	35.4	.8	63.8	100	1,483	49.8
					2,974	100.0
(D) GSS (adjusted for education)						
White Collar	54.0	1.2	44.7	100	762	25.6
Farm	34.2	17.6	48.3	100	734	24.6
Blue Collar	37.7	.8	61.5	100	1,483	49.8
					2,979	100.0

*Calculated from tables in John W. Meyer, Nancy Brandon Tuma, and Krzystof Zagorski, "Educational and Occupational Mobility: A Comparison of Polish and American Men," *American Journal of Sociology* (1979), 84:978–986.

the same number of white collar families. Consequently, there are roughly twice as many sons who moved from blue to white as moved from white to blue.

And then there are the farm sons. If asked to nominate one single social trend to characterize America in the last century, I would opt for "Land Rush"—a rush of farmers and farm sons to get off the land. GSS data, for example, suggest that among Americans born around 1890, half had farmer fathers while among those in the birth cohort of 1955 (in their early twenties during the GSS years 1972–1980)

the figure is down to 6 percent. Rural southern blacks, Yankee adolescents on stony hillsides, and Scandinavian lads from the endless prairies: all had this in common—as adults the vast majority were working in cities, most (about 55 percent in Table 24.1) as blue collar workers, but a sizable minority (about 25 percent) as white collar. Farm sons were more likely to end up as white collar workers than as farmers! Since nobody (one percent or less) from nonfarm origins ends up working in agriculture, the land rush added considerably to the number of people crossing into white collar jobs. Averaging over the three studies and fudging a weensy bit to make things tidy:

> 50 percent stayed in their father's group (immobile)
>
> 25 percent moved from farm or blue collar into white (up)
>
> 10 percent moved from white collar to blue (down)
>
> 15 percent moved from farm to blue (down)

These four numbers can be combined and rearranged into several pretty patterns:

> (25% + 10% = 35%) i.e., the one-third crossing the white collar line one way or the other
>
> (25% + 10% + 15% = 50%) Half the sons are mobile if you use a three-way split
>
> 25% ÷ 10% = 2.5%) More than twice as many move into white collar as move out
>
> (15% − 10% = 5%) Most entrants into blue collar stratum came from farm
>
> (15% + 10% = 25%) If you consider movement from farm to blue collar as downward mobility (more on this later), upward mobility (25% moving from farm or blue collar into white) and downward mobility are about equally common.

Assuming the rates stay the same, the *rate by origin* principle allows us to speculate about the future of mobility. Three predictions: (1) As white collar jobs increase vis-à-vis blue collar, downward mobility will increase and upward mobility decrease in absolute terms; (2) the evaporation of farm origins will reduce downward mobility more than it reduces upward; and (3) these two trends either will or won't cancel each other out and the rates may or may not stay the same.

While "just" half the sons remain in their paternal stratum, they are considerably more likely to end up there than sons from other strata. At the top, two-thirds of the white collar sons stay put, but that is a lot more than the one-third or less of blue collar or farm sons who scale those heights. And, of course, the opposite occurs for blue collar jobs, where blue collar sons end up with more than their fair share. In less

technical language, "them as has, gets." The consequence is a perpetuation of family privilege and of family underprivilege.

Statistically, we are talking about a positive correlation between the prestige of father's and son's occupations. These correlations may well be the most studied statistic in sociology. I have seen dozens of them. The numbers vary with the sample and the particular statistics used, but they are always positive: in any community, region, ethnic group, or whatever in the United States, it is safe to bet that the higher the prestige of the father, the higher the prestige of the son or daughter.

Whether this goes on more than two generations has not been well studied. My guess (drawing on unpublished research by Christopher Jencks and NORC) is that there is very little correlation between prestige of grandfathers and grandsons, and what there is is explained by father's occupation. As the old American aphorism goes, "shirt sleeves to shirt sleeves in three generations." The American pattern seems to be one of moderate continuity but not of dynasties or a permanent underclass.

THE "EDUCATIONAL TWO-STEP"

How do fathers pass on the occupational baton (or short end of the stick)? We know it isn't direct inheritance of jobs. If you remove the minority of cases where fathers and sons have exactly the same job titles, the patterns in Table 24.1 change little. Instead, the key variable turns out to be schooling—the number of years of formal education.

When a third variable strongly influences a correlation, statistical rules say it must have an important association with both. Thus, the contribution of schooling to father-son occupational inheritance consists of two separate steps, a relation between father's occupation and education and a second relation between son's occupation and education.

Step one can be called the liberals' step, since it makes the United States look bad and would cost a lot of money to change. Table 24.2a uses GSS data to illustrate the strong differences in schooling still present in America:

More than 60 percent of white collar sons have a year or more of college, in contrast to 32 percent of blue collar and 18 percent of farm sons.

Almost 60 percent of farm sons failed to finish high school in contrast to 36 percent of blue collar and 15 percent of white collar.

Most white collar sons have a year or more of college, most farm sons never finished high school, and blue collar sons are evenly split between college, high school, and less than high school.

Americans don't feel comfortable about discussing it, but we still have sharp class differences in schooling. As best we can tell, these differences are not going away. (Race differences in schooling are going away, but that's another matter.) Younger birth cohorts do have strikingly higher levels of education.

For the birth cohorts of 1900, 1910, 1920, 1930, and 1940 the portions with 12 or more years of schooling are estimated as 23 percent, 36 percent, 50 percent, 58 percent, and 72 percent.

Step two of the educational two-step runs from education to occupation, and it should please the conservatives since it suggests the system is working fairly and wonderfully and it would be a shame to monkey with it. More exactly, Table 24.2b shows that when one looks at the occupational effects of education and father's stratum simultaneously, education is very important and class origins not very important.

In each origin stratum, the proportion of white collar sons rises dramatically with education.

In each educational level, the effects of father's stratum are moderate at best.

TABLE 24.2 Educational Attainment and Occupational Mobility (GSS)

(a) Father's Occupation and Son's Education

| | SON'S EDUCATION | | | | | | | | |
FATHER'S OCCUPATION	0–8	9–11	12	13–15	16+	TOTAL	0–11	13+	N
White Collar	5.0%	9.7%	22.6%	28.3%	34.4%	100%	14.7%	62.7%	762
Blue Collar	15.7	20.3	32.0	18.3	13.8	100	36.0	32.1	1,483
Farm	41.0	17.8	23.0	8.6	9.5	100	58.8	18.1	734
									2,979

(b) Father's Occupation, Son's Education, and Son's Occupation
(Proportion of Sons in the White Collar Jobs)

| | SON'S EDUCATION | | | | |
FATHER'S OCCUPATION	0–8	9–11	12	13–15	16+
White Collar	28.9%	33.8%	51.2%	67.1%	90.8%
	(38)*	(74)	(172)	(216)	(262)
Blue Collar	12.1	18.3	25.9	53.7	84.8
	(232)	(301)	(474)	(272)	(204)
Farm	11.6	12.2	25.4	46.0	80.0
	(301)	(131)	(169)	(63)	(70)

*Numbers in parentheses represent the total cases for the proportions above.

A blue collar or farm son with a college degree
has a better chance at a white collar job than a
white collar son without a degree.

Liberals (rightly) decry the gross class differences in schooling, and conservatives (rightly) point
with pride to the palpable meritocratic effects of
schooling in every origin stratum, but the sociologist
is interested in how these two steps combine to influence father-son inheritance. Table 24.1d shows what
happens to the data in Table 24.1c after a little experiment. Let us give the sons in each paternal stratum
of Table 24.1c the same educational attainments—
through a statistical procedure called "direct stan-
dardization," not, I hasten to say, through federal
handouts. Then let's see what this does to inheritance. Comparing Tables 24.1c and 24.1d we see the
adjustment eliminates about half the inheritance. For
example, in Table 24.1c white collar sons have a
31.1% advantage in white collar jobs compared with
sons of blue collar workers ($66.5 - 35.4 = 31.1$) but
when class differences in education are eliminated
statistically their advantage drops to 16.3% ($54.0 -
37.7 = 16.3$). Other statistics, other data sets, and other
occupational measures give slightly different numbers, but one can routinely explain half or more of the
father-son occupational prestige correlation by son's
schooling.

The American system of education acts powerfully and simultaneously to:

—preserve class differences across generations
because the well-born go much farther in
school and schooling is crucial for good jobs;
—cancel out class differences across generations
because not all well-born go far in school (a
third of white collar sons have no college), a
number of lower status sons get a lot of schooling (a third of blue collar sons have some college) and schooling is more important than
class origins in getting good jobs.

These then are the main themes in mobility
research: an impressive amount of intergenerational
mobility in all directions, rates of downward mobility almost as large as rates of upward mobility, more

movement into the very top than out of it because of
origin distributions and the secular decline in farming, a persistent positive correlation between father's
and son's occupational prestige, and the powerful
effect of schooling both in transmitting status across
generations and in promoting mobility. . . .

While Americans seem inhibited about discussing social class, quite the opposite seems true for
ethnicity. I suspect we all hold the following beliefs
about our own group: (1) We started at the very bottom; (2) We are especially hard working and self-
sacrificing; (3) We have come a long way but not as
far as we deserve; and (4) Among us, unlike other
groups, Mamma really runs the family. Similarly in
the intellectual world much more is published than
known about ethnicity and we do not have the classic data bases comparable to those in Table 24.1.
However, Andrew Greeley of NORC pioneered in
studying ethnicity by pooling national surveys and
unpublished results from the GSS, allowing us to
follow his lead with more recent samples. Table 24.3
lays out the key facts.

Since the results here are in terms of "occupational prestige scales" rather than white-blue-farm, we
must detour briefly to consider measurement. Tables
like Table 24.1 treat large occupational categories
(collars) but one may also study mobility in terms of
specific occupations (e.g. physicians or bootblacks).
To do so, the jobs must be placed on a single scale of
prestige or "social standing." This turns out to be
much easier than one might think. One of the remarkable conclusions of modern sociological research is
the high agreement on the prestige of occupations.
When one asks the man or woman in the street to
judge the social standing of specific jobs, one finds
striking consensus across time (1925 to today), occupational strata, educational levels, regions, sexes, even
nations of the world. Consequently, sociologists have
developed prestige scales for occupations. The GSS
uses the Hodge-Segal-Rossi scale, which runs from a
low of 9 points (bootblacks) to a high of 82 (physicians).

The left-hand column of Table 24.3 gives the
average (mean) prestige score for fathers of the
twenty-nine groups, that is, how they lined up at the

TABLE 24.3 Occupational and Education Scores of Ethnic Groups

GROUP	OCCUPATIONAL PRESTIGE		CHANGE IN RANK	SCHOOLING
	FATHER'S	OWN		
(1) Jewish	45.3	46.6	0	48.8
(2) ScotPN	45.1	46.1	0	35.0
(3) FrncPN	45.1	43.1	−4	32.2
(4) EnglPS	42.9	43.3	−2	21.0
(5) EnglPN	42.0	42.3	−5	23.3
(6) SwedeP	41.8	40.2	−6	8.6
(7) DanesP	41.8	42.7	−1	18.9
(8) FrncPS	41.3	45.1	+4	11.4
(9) IrishC	41.2	41.9	−2	22.8
(10) ScotPS	41.0	44.6	+5	19.2
(11) EngliC	40.8	46.0	+8	33.7
(12) NorwyP	40.3	42.6	+3	15.0
(13) GermnC	40.1	39.6	−2	0.9
(14) GermnP	40.1	39.8	+1	− 1.6
(15) FrnchC	40.0	39.6	−1	17.3
(16) IrshPN	39.8	39.1	−1	0.4
(17) IrshPS	39.4	39.1	−1	−21.1
(18) FrcanC	37.9	36.0	−5	−15.1
(19) DutchP	37.9	37.3	−2	−28.8
(20) CzechC	36.7	39.7	+6	− 2.1
(21) ItalyC	36.3	38.2	+2	− 7.1
(22) Amerin	35.8	34.2	−3	−23.3
(23) BlckSN	34.9	29.9	−5	−35.2
(24) PolesC	34.3	38.0	+4	−10.5
(25) PrrcoC	34.0	30.7	−2	−57.9
(26) BlckNN	32.9	35.4	+2	1.2
(27) FinnsP	32.6	36.2	+5	−19.5
(28) BlckSS	32.1	28.6	−1	−46.3
(29) MexcoC	30.5	32.1	+3	−31.9

Note: N = North, S = South, C = Catholic, P = Protestant.

starting gate. Since the mean age of the respondents is about forty-five and fathers average thirty years older than their children, the typical father in these data was born around the turn of the century and the typical respondent (we are dealing with both men and women in this section) was born just at the beginning of the Great Depression. The figures can thus be seen as a rough estimate of how the twenty-nine groups stood in occupational prestige in the first third of the 20th century. Top position went to the Jews with a mean of 45.3. The Poles' position, 34.3, is distinctly lower, and the anchor spot went to Mexican Catholics with a score of 30.5. The rankings, by and large, confirm our social stereotypes:

Of the bottom eight positions all but two went to nonwhites (the three black groups and Indians) or Latins (Mexicans and Puerto Ricans).

While the Catholic group spans a larger range than the stereotype (from nine to thirty) none of the Catholic groups was in the top quarter. Of the top eight positions, five went to the older Protestant groups (Scotch, French, English), both northern and southern.

There are some surprises:

Even a generation ago Jews had the highest prestige of any ethnic group.

The Scandinavians showed a wide range in prestige origins from rank six (Swedes) to rank twenty-seven (Finns).

The Protestant Irish, both northern and southern, were distinctly farther down the ladder (ranks sixteen and eighteen) than the other old Protestant groups, these being the famous "Scotch-Irish" or less affectionately, "Hill Billies." They started—and remained—below the rank of the later arriving Irish Catholics.

While Table 24.3 shows that Jews and Mexican Catholics started out 14.8 points apart, it is hard to say whether 14.8 is big or small. I think it is small—or at least smaller than most of us would expect.

One yardstick is the distribution of individuals. In the cumulative GSS, 25 percent of the individuals report father scores above 45 and 22 percent report father scores below 30.5. Thus, while Jews were the highest prestige group in the parental generation, their average score was at the "bottom of the top quarter" for all Americans. Comfortable, maybe, but hardly aristocratic. Similarly, almost a quarter of all Americans had parental prestige scores lower than those of Mexican Catholics, whose position was uncomfortable, maybe, but hardly down and out. While the twenty-nine ethnic groups were spread out in their original scores, they were all spread through the middle of the U.S. distribution. None of them could be termed patricians and none pariahs.

If the first striking feature of the group data is the small range of the original status differences, the second is the large size of the inheritance or stability.

If one calculates a scale known in the sociology business as a "Pearson product moment correlation (r)" for father's and own jobs, one obtains an r of + .870, which is in two words, a whopper. Since a high correlation between origins and destinations means low mobility, the theme here is one of relative immobility. For example, if we simply subtract father's score from own job using the data in Table 24.3 (e.g., for Jews 46.6 − 45.3 = +1.3), the median change is ±1.6. Thus, the typical movement of an ethnic group is up or down less than two points on another scale, the Hodge-Segal-Rossi scale. Only two groups shifted five or more points: English Catholics moved up from 40.8 to 46.0, while blacks who moved from South to North dropped from 34.9 to 29.9.

When talking about individuals, the theme was "a lot of continuity and a lot of mobility" but when talking about ethnic groups the theme seems to be "a lot of continuity and some mobility."

Even a correlation of .870 is not perfect and the groups did not cross the finish line in perfect follow-the-leader form. The third column in Table 24.3 shows the change in *rank* for each group. For example, Mexican Catholics started at rank twenty-nine, ended up in rank twenty-six, and got a rank change score of +3. Four groups increased their rank by five or more points (Finnish Protestants, Southern Scotch Protestants, Czech Catholics, and English Catholics), and four groups fell back five or more ranks (black migrants from South to North, French Canadian Catholics, English Northern Protestants, and Swedish Protestants).

How do you zoom past your competitors? Hard work? Tough mammas? Maybe, but again schooling has a definite impact. So we tune up another two-step, this time at the group level.

Step one says the higher the paternal status of a group, the higher the education of its sons and daughters. The index I used is simply the percentage with a year or more of college minus the percentage with zero to eleven years of schooling. Thus, Jews have 62.3 percent with some college and 13.5 percent with zero to eleven giving an index of +48.8. Puerto Ricans, at the other extreme, have 8.8 percent with some college and 66.7 percent with zero to eleven years giving an index of −57.9. The other twenty-seven groups lie between these scores. The product moment correlation between "Fathers" and "Schooling" in Table 24.3 equals +.837, which is substantial. You can reach the same conclusion without any calculations by inspecting the right hand column in Table 24.3. With one exception, all the minus signs are lower than the positive scores—that is, except for German Protestants, children from the top sixteen groups were more likely to have some college than to be high school dropouts, while for the bottom thirteen groups "high school dropouts" outnumber those with a year or more of college.

The second half of the educational two-step (à la Table 24.2b) requires us to demonstrate that the educational level of an ethnic group affects its occupational prestige, *controlling* for father's prestige.

The left-hand column in Table 24.4 rearranges the twenty-nine ethnic groups and the educational score predicted by using father's job in a regression equation. High scores mean the group went a lot farther in school than one would predict from their fathers' jobs; negative scores mean the group did not obtain as much schooling as one would predict. The highest "over-achievers" are northern-born, northern-living blacks. Their educational score is not smashing (a value of 1.2 and rank fourteen), but they got an awful lot of schooling considering their parental starting point at rank twenty-six. Other overachievers by ten or more points are English Catholics, Finnish Protestants, Polish Catholics, Jews, Mexican Catholics, and French Catholics. At the opposite end, southern-born blacks (migrant or not), French Canadian Catholics, Dutch Protestants, Southern Irish Protestants, and Puerto Rican Catholics all fell ten or more points short of their predicted scores.

Is there a pattern here? I find it interesting that seven of ten Catholic groups are overachievers, as are seven of fourteen Protestant groups and the one out of four nonwhite groups who didn't attend southern schools.

Intriguing, but the question is whether schooling-net-of-father's-occupation affects prestige. Look at the right hand column in Table 24.4 where the change in rank data are repeated. Again, the plus signs are up toward the top and the minus signs toward the bottom. More exactly:

Of the ten groups which moved up two or more ranks, nine are overachievers.

Of the nine groups which moved zero, one, or two ranks, five are overachievers.

Of the ten groups which moved down two or more ranks, two are overachievers.

As with individuals, schooling is simultaneously the key mobility mechanism (as shown by the strong association between "overachievement" and change

TABLE 24.4 Education and Mobility

ETHNIC GROUP	SCHOOLING NET OF FATHER'S JOB	CHANGE IN RANK
(26) BlckNN	32.73	+2
(11) EngliC	22.35	+8
(27) FinnsP	13.66	+5
(24) PolesC	13.43	+4
(1) Jewish	13.02	0
(29) MexcoC	12.66	+3
(15) FrnchC	10.29	−1
(9) IrishC	9.28	−2
(20) CzechC	8.81	+6
(10) ScotPS	6.77	+5
(12) NorwyP	6.37	+3
(21) ItalyC	5.98	+2
(5) EnglPN	5.44	−5
(7) DanesP	2.12	−1
(3) FrncPN	1.31	−1
(2) ScotPN	0.31	0
(4) EnglPS	− 1.75	−2
(8) FrncPS	− 2.66	+4
(16) IrshPN	− 5.52	−1
(13) GermnC	− 6.65	−2
(22) Amerin	− 7.51	−3
(6) SwedeP	− 8.18	−6
(14) GermnP	− 9.15	+1
(28) BlckSS	−10.42	−1
(18) FrcanC	−10.71	−5
(23) BlckSN	−14.52	−5
(19) DutchP	−24.41	−2
(17) IrshPS	−24.85	−1
(25) PrrcoC	−32.34	−2

Note: N = North, S = South, C = Catholic, P = Protestant.

in rank) and the key mechanism in maintaining the ethnic "peck order" (as shown by the reduction of the father-own correlation from +.870 to +.324 when education is controlled).

EDUCATION BEGETS PRESTIGE

Some groups moved up, some groups moved down, some groups stayed put. How, overall, did the pattern change? If we think of the ranks in terms of a top quarter, a bottom quarter, and a large middle, I draw four conclusions:

At the bottom, the four nonwhite and two Latin Catholic groups ended up about where they started while the Poles and Finns moved up.

At the top, Jews remained in the number one spot and the old Protestant groups, if anything, improved their standing as the southern Scotch and French moved into the top quarter while only the northern English moved down.

Among the non-Latin Catholics, the English zoomed up into the top quarter, but the other groups mostly remained in the middle half.

Among the Scandinavians and German Protestants, the trend was toward the middle half as the Swedes dropped from the top quarter and the Finns moved up toward the middle.

As in the case of individual mobility, the ethnic mobility results have something for every ideological taste. The highest prestige group is so far from the top and the lowest group so far from the bottom that ethnic differences in occupational prestige must be characterized as moderate. Schooling is the key to ethnic mobility: groups who get more schooling move up in the pack, groups who get less fall back—whatever their odd cooking habits and weird religions. Statistically, educational attainment is a much better predictor of a group's current prestige than is its original (father's) prestige.

All this is true and cheery, and yet, the amount of schooling a group gets is still powerfully influenced by the paternal occupational level. A generation of "rapid social change" still shows "old Protestants" (ScotPN, FrncPS, ScotPS, EnglPS, and FrncPN) in five of the seven top ranks and blacks, Latins, and American Indians in the bottom six positions. The issues and problems of "border crossing" for the contemporary United States are not limited to the Immigration Service.

CHAPTER 25

COGNITIVE SKILL AND ECONOMIC INEQUALITY: FINDINGS FROM THE NATIONAL ADULT LITERACY SURVEY

STEPHEN W. RAUDENBUSH
RAFA M. KASIM

In all modern societies, differences in social origins (e.g., social class, gender, and ethnic, cultural, or linguistic background) predict inequalities in adult employment and earnings. The sources of such inequality have received enormous attention in economics and sociology (see reviews by Carnoy, 1995; Ferber, 1995; Ganzeboom, Treiman, & Ultee, 1991; Kerckhoff, 1995). Research in many countries shows that social origins are related to schooling experience, which, in turn, is related to employment and earnings. Thus, unequal educational attainment is a crucial link between inequality of social origin and inequality of adult economic status. A question of fundamental and enduring interest, therefore, is whether and to what extent investments in schooling can equalize economic opportunity.

U.S. policymakers, journalists, and educators, in particular, have long claimed that improvement of educational opportunity holds the key to reducing inequality of economic opportunity (see reviews by Bowles & Gintis, 1976; Levin & Kelly, 1994), and decades of research provide some support for that argument. While it is well known that the socioeconomic status (SES), of the family at birth is statistically related to adult SES, this relationship has, in

many studies, been largely "explained" by unequal access to schooling (Blau & Duncan, 1967; Duncan, Featherman, & Duncan, 1972; Sewell & Hauser, 1975). Thus, the statistical evidence suggests that two individuals of different SES at birth could nonetheless expect nearly equal access to jobs and earnings as adults if they had obtained the same level of schooling and credentials. Levin and Kelley (1994) wisely warn us not to extrapolate the longitudinal consequences of public investments in education from such research;[1] nevertheless, this finding provides encouragement to the claim that understanding social inequality in access to schooling is crucial to understanding social inequality in adult economic status.

Despite this link between educational opportunity and adult economic status, gender and ethnicity inequities continue to be a puzzle. Gender and ethnic gaps in economic outcomes remain large even after controlling for inequality in access to schooling (Card & Krueger, 1993; Carnoy, 1995; Rivera-Batiz, 1992). Levels of educational attainment are now similar for men and women, yet the gender gap in earnings remains large. Furthermore, although on average African Americans and Hispanic Americans attain fewer years of schooling and fewer degrees than do European Americans, large ethnic gaps in access to employment and earnings remain even after taking into account such differences in educational attainment. For example, African Americans and Hispanic Americans can expect lower pay than can European Americans who have the same gender and education-

From *Harvard Educational Review* 68(1) (1998) pp. 33–42, 44–47, 56, 64–69. Copyright © 1998 by the President and Fellows of Harvard College. Reprinted by permission. Some footnotes have been incorporated as additional endnotes or deleted.

al background. In fact, gender and ethnic inequality are inextricably linked, with the magnitude of these "ethnic gaps" varying by gender, and the ethnic gaps remaining considerably larger for men than for women (Carnoy, 1995).

In this article, we consider alternative explanations for this puzzle. The first contends that quantitative measures of education, such as years of schooling and degrees obtained, inadequately capture the cognitive knowledge and skills that have become decisive in the modern labor market. An extreme version of this view, popularized especially by Herrnstein and Murray (1994), claims that inherited differences in cognitive ability have created an aristocracy of intelligence, and that such differences explain ethnic differences in economic success. A more mainstream view accepts the centrality of cognitive skill in the modern labor market, but takes a more environmental viewpoint. In this view, educational policy should equalize the quality of schooling and not just the quantity. Such educational equalization would presumably eliminate gender and ethnic inequality in access to good jobs and high pay.[2]

If one accepts the proposition that cognitive skill is important to labor market success and the key to understanding current group inequality, then the role for affirmative action in the labor market is diminished or nonexistent. Few would hold employers responsible for rectifying inequality in cognitive skills. Thus, the main target for affirmative action policy would be the educational system, which is primarily responsible for producing cognitive skill.

A second explanation for gender and ethnic inequality in economic success emphasizes preferences rather than skills as the active ingredient. According to this view, people vary in their preferences for different kinds of work, and therefore select occupations that have varied job security and earnings. In particular, women are widely held to select occupations that pay less than do occupations preferred by men. These gender differences in preference are believed to constitute an important part of the gender gap in earnings (Ferber, 1995). If true, the "preference explanation" is likely to be more impor-

tant for understanding gender inequality than for understanding ethnic inequality.

The emphasis on gender differences in occupational preference implies a small or nonexistent need for affirmative action in the workplace, as it is plausible to expect parents and teachers to broaden the occupational aspirations of girls. Asking employers to reshape the occupational aspirations of their female workers appears a less promising strategy for reform.

We see, then, that an emphasis on either cognitive skills or preferences as keys to understanding ethnic and gender inequality tends to erode the basis for affirmative action in the workplace. Both explanations, however, are based on assumptions that can, to some degree, be tested empirically. In this article, we examine these assumptions. To the extent that the evidence contradicts these assumptions, alternative explanations for persistent inequality must be considered, including those based on social competition, labor market discrimination, residential segregation, and noncognitive skill. These alternative explanations have quite different implications for educational and economic policy.

ASSUMPTIONS UNDERLYING THE EMPHASIS ON COGNITIVE SKILL

Several key assumptions underlie the premise that differences in cognitive skill underlie group differences in employment and pay. First, there must be a single meritocratic labor market, one that distributes jobs and pay strictly on the basis of worker qualifications. If the labor market is not meritocratic—for example, if it distributes rewards partly on the basis of ascriptive characteristics such as gender or ethnicity—the benefit to currently disadvantaged groups of equalizing cognitive skills would be limited. Moreover, this explanation assumes that cognitive skills are of preeminent importance in the modern labor market. Finally, it assumes that disadvantaged groups, in particular ethnic minorities, suffer for deficits in such cognitive skills. In sum, according to this reasoning, the importance of cognitive skills in a meritocratic labor market, combined with inequalities in access to cognitive skills, accounts for the lion's share of inequality in economic outcomes. Critics of this view would reject one or more of these assumptions.

Is There a Single, Meritocratic Labor Market?

According to human capital theory (Becker, 1964), wage offers in a competitive market equal a worker's marginal productivity, which is determined by job-related knowledge and skill (Velloso, 1995). A prominent criticism of the human capital view denies that there is a single labor market in which all workers freely compete to sell their human capital. Rather, critics have argued, the labor market is subdivided as a function of occupations and industries into sectors or "segments" with varying pay and benefits (Doeringer & Piore, 1971); a worker's productivity and pay are determined more by the job and its technology than by the human capital of the worker (Velloso, 1995); and social groups compete to control access to scarce and favored jobs (Tomaskovic-Devey, 1993). Moreover, these critics contend that residential segregation based on race may spatially separate minority groups from the primary labor market, creating a secondary labor market consisting primarily of low-paying and insecure jobs (Kain, 1968; Massay & Denton, 1993; Wilson, 1996). In sum, it can be argued that economic inequalities, as a function of social origin, arise because disadvantaged groups are systematically denied access to the better jobs via occupational, industrial, and residential segregation. In addition, it may be argued that disadvantaged groups are denied equal access to promotions and pay raises within a given occupation (Carnoy, 1995).

Are Cognitive Skills of Preeminent Importance in the Labor Market?

Many studies have indicated that cognitive skills, as measured by scores on IQ or achievement tests, are only modestly helpful in predicting labor-force outcomes once years of education are controlled (see reviews by Bowles & Gintis, 1996; Levin & Kelley, 1994). Moreover, cognitive skills have accounted for

only part of the contribution of education and credentials to employment and earnings in prior research. In their review of thirteen studies of the relationship between cognitive skills and earnings, Bowles and Gintis (1996) found that cognitive skills accounted, on average, for only about 25 percent of the contribution of education to earnings. The implication is that skills not measured by cognitive tests, such as noncognitive skills, attitudes, and habits, may be highly significant in determining the productivity of the worker, and therefore may be strongly rewarded in a labor market operating on the human capital model.[3] If so, one would not expect social inequality in cognitive skill to account for social inequality in economic outcomes, even in a meritocratic labor market.

Do Economically Disadvantaged Social Groups Lag Far Behind More Advantaged Groups in Job-Related Cognitive Skills?

Although many studies have found ethnic differences in cognitive test scores (Coleman, Hoffer, & Kilgore, 1982; Lee & Bryk, 1989), it is not clear that such differences are sufficiently large to account for large observed ethnic differences in employment and earnings, even under the assumption that such skills are of great importance to productivity. Moreover, gender differences in cognitive skill are typically found to be very small (often favoring women); thus, cognitive skill gaps cannot account for gender gaps in economic outcomes. If social inequality in cognitive skill is not sufficiently large to account for social inequality in employment and earnings, some other explanation is required.

ASSUMPTIONS UNDERLYING THE EMPHASIS ON PREFERENCES

If cognitive skill differences cannot plausibly explain gender differences in earnings, gender differences in occupational preference may provide a more promising explanation (Ferber, 1995). Ethnic differences in occupational preference may exist as well, and these differences may help explain ethnic inequality, though that idea is not prominent in the research literature.

It is difficult to distinguish occupational segregation that arises from preference from occupational segregation that arises because of discriminatory hiring practices. In 1940, 60 percent of all Black women in the U.S. labor force worked as domestic servants, and 40 percent of the Black men worked as agricultural laborers (Allen & Farley, 1986). These facts are incomprehensible without understanding the pervasive racial and gender discrimination characterizing the economy at that time. It is far more difficult in the 1990s to disentangle preference and discrimination. It is quite clear, however, that occupational preference cannot explain gender and ethnic inequalities that lie within occupations. We can, therefore, test the limits of the occupational-preference argument by examining within-occupation inequality in employment and pay by gender and ethnicity. Indeed, if gender and ethnic inequalities are found within occupations, and if these inequalities cannot be explained by differences in cognitive skill, then neither the cognitive skill explanation nor the occupational preference explanation will be adequate for understanding inequality. Other explanations, involving either discrimination in promotions and pay within occupations or group differences in noncognitive skills, would be required.

THE NATIONAL ADULT LITERACY SURVEY

The National Adult Literacy Survey (NALS), conducted by the U.S. National Center for Educational Statistics to describe job-related cognitive skills of the adult population, provides a unique opportunity to evaluate key assumptions underlying beliefs that job-related cognitive skills or occupational preferences are key to understanding persistent social inequalities in economic outcomes. The survey uses a sophisticated, individually administered, multifaceted assessment of adult literacy operationalized to tap key aspects of job-related cognitive knowledge and skill. In addition, it provides detailed information on the social background, education experience, and occupations of a large, nationally representative sample of U.S. adults in 1992.

Using this data source, we addressed the following empirical questions:

1. How Important Is Cognitive Skill, as Indicated by the Literacy Assessment in the NALS, in Reducing the Risk of Unemployment and Predicting Earnings?

Even if gender or ethnic inequality in cognitive skills are large, such inequalities will translate into social inequality in economic outcomes only if these skills are important in the labor market.

Answering this question is vital not only for understanding economic inequality, but also for evaluating arguments about the centrality of cognitive skills in improving worker productivity more generally. It is widely asserted that improving the cognitive skills of the labor force by increasing the quantity and quality of education is the key to any nation's economic future (Johnston & Packer, 1987; National Commission on Educational Excellence, 1983; Statistics Canada, 1996). Yet research reviewed by Levin and Kelley (1994) and Bowles and Gintis (1996) suggests that the link between cognitive skills and earnings is modest and accounts for only a fraction of the association between education and earnings. The NALS data create the opportunity to assess the association between cognitive skills and earnings for a large, nationally representative sample of the entire adult work force in the United States.

2. How Large Are the Differences in Cognitive Skills Between Groups?

No matter how important cognitive skills are in the labor market, inequality in these skills as a function of ethnicity and gender must be quite large if it is to account for the large gaps in economic outcomes among these groups.

3. How Important Is Group Inequality in Cognitive Skills for Understanding Social Inequality in Labor-Force Outcomes?

The answer to this question depends on the answers to the first two questions. If cognitive skills are sufficiently important in the labor market and if group inequality in these skills is sufficiently large, then inequality in cognitive skills will statistically "explain" economic inequality between groups.

Rivera-Batiz (1992) found that ethnic inequalities in the quantitative skills of young adults were sufficiently large to account for a large portion of the gap among ethnic groups in the risk of unemployment. The residual gap in the risk of unemployment between African Americans and European Americans remained ambiguous: thought the estimated gap was fairly large, it was nonsignificant, and the results remained inconclusive because the sample size was small. The current study enlarges this inquiry in three ways: a) we include the entire adult labor force; b) the NALS data include a much larger sample, enabling us to estimate gaps unexplained by cognitive skills with more precision; and c) we are able to include earnings and unemployment as outcomes.

4. To the Extent that Cognitive Skill Differences Do Not Account for Ethnic and Gender Differences in Economic Outcomes, Does the Remaining Inequality Lie Between Occupations, within Occupations, or Both?

Recall that a prominent explanation of gender inequality in pay was based on gender differences in occupational preference. Gender differences in occupational preference would indeed lead to some degree of occupational segregation by gender, with disproportionate numbers of women located in occupations with low pay. Statistically, the gender gap in pay would be a between-occupation phenomenon. Such preferences would presumably have no impact on gender differences within occupations. Hence, if large gender differences in pay exist within occupations, the data will contradict the assertion that occupational preference accounts for gender inequality. Similarly, the existence of large ethnic gaps in outcomes within occupations would undermine the importance of occupational preference as an explanation of ethnic inequality.[4]

The partitioning of inequality between and within occupations can also partially test the theory that social groups struggle to control access to favored occupations. Under that theory, group membership, not job-related skill, would, to some degree, determine occupational access. If this is true, cognitive skill differences between social groups would not be adequate to account for group differences in access to favored occupations. Social segregation in the labor market would be pronounced, and the gender and/or ethnic composition of occupations would be related to outcomes even after controlling for worker cognitive skills. If we find, however, that group differences in cognitive skills do explain group differences in access to such occupations, then it becomes harder to argue that the job market is unfair in this way.[5]

DATA AND METHODS

Sample and Measures

The target population of this study in all U.S. adults between the ages of twenty-five and fifty-nine who were in the labor force in 1992; that is, people working full time or who wished to work full time at the time of the interview. Our analytic sample included 12,492 people and is described in Table 25.1.

Key variables for the analysis were of four types: social origin, human capital, occupation, and labor force outcomes.

Social origins include age, parent education, gender, and ethnicity. Indicator variables were computed for each ethnic group;[6] thus, the means in Table 25.1 are proportions. We see, then, that 70.1 percent of the sample were European American, 16.9 percent African American, 10.4 percent Hispanic American, and 1.6 percent Asian American. Between occupations, the proportion female, proportion African American, and proportion Hispanic as compiled for each occupation by the U.S. Bureau of Labor Statistics reflect occupational segregation by gender and ethnicity.

Human capital includes educational attainment (years of schooling), credentials obtained (a "GED" or general education diploma equivalent to a high school degree, a regular high school degree, an associates degree [or some college experience], a bachelors

TABLE 25.1 Description of the Sample

		N	MEAN	STANDARD DEVIATION
Social Origin	Age	12492	38.970	9.152
	Parent Education (Yrs.)	12492	10.932	3.532
	Female	12492	0.482	0.500
	African American	12492	0.169	0.375
	Asian American	12492	0.016	0.126
	European American	12492	0.701	0.458
	Hispanic American	12492	0.104	0.306
	Other	12492	0.010	0.099
Human Capital	Educational Attainment (Yrs.)	12492	13.275	0.777
	GED	12492	0.874	0.332
	High School Diploma	12492	0.836	0.370
	Associates Degree	12492	0.398	0.490
	Bachelors Degree	12492	0.268	0.443
	Masters Degree	12492	0.093	0.290
	Log Labor-Force Experience	12492	2.907	0.519
	Average Literacy	12492	286.108	60.958
Occupational Segregation	Proportion Female	460	0.35	0.29
	Proportion Black	460	0.09	0.06
	Proportion Hispanic	460	0.08	0.06
Labor-Force Outcomes	Log Wages	11912	6.037	0.710
	Unemployment	12492	0.084	0.28

degree, or a masters or higher); labor-force experience (age minus 5 minus years of schooling);[7] and a composite measure of adult literacy. Literacy in NALS is conceptualized as the ability to comprehend prose, extract and use information from documents, and draw inferences from quantitative information (Kirsch, Jungleblut, Jenkins, & Kolstad, 1993; Sum, 1994). Literacy was assessed individually in the homes of the sample adults.

Literacy. NALS has adopted the view that literacy is neither a dichotomy (literate/nonliterate) nor a minimum competency, but, rather, that literacy "encompasses a broad range of skills that adults use in accomplishing the many different types of literacy tasks associated with work, home, and community contexts" (Kirsch et al., 1993, p. 3). The assessment involves three subscales: prose literacy (knowledge and skill involved in understanding editorials, news stories, prose, and fiction); document literacy (knowledge and skills needed for job applications, payroll forms, transportation schedules, maps, tables, and graphs); and quantitative literacy (arithmetic operations used alone or sequentially, using numbers embedded in print materials, etc.). Tasks within each subscale vary widely in difficulty to allow classification at five levels. For example, a level-5 task in the prose subscale requires high-level inferences from complex information; tasks in the document subscale require a search of complex displays to make text-based inferences; and level-5 tasks in the quantitative subscale require the respondent to disembed features of a problem from text and to determine operations needed to solve it. To achieve these assessment goals, 165 literacy tasks were constructed. Most tasks require a brief written or oral response or require respondents to explain how they would set up and solve a problem. Of course, all 165 tasks could not be administered to every respondent because the time required per assessment would be excessive. . . .

Despite the sophistication of the literacy assessments in NALS, it could not have captured all aspects of job-related cognitive skills. We consider the resulting uncertainty in the Discussion section. Henceforth we refer to our measure of cognitive skills as "literacy," as measured by NALS.

Occupation.   Sample respondents were classified into occupations defined by the Dictionary of Occupational titles (three-digit codes). Sample members were found to be in one of 460 distinct occupations. The three-digit codes produced a relatively fine-grained definition of occupations; our aim was to produce occupational classes that were as internally homogeneous as possible so that outcome variation could be partitioned between and within occupations. Nevertheless, some occupational heterogeneity remained within these 460 classes, and our interpretations regarding "within-occupation" variation must be qualified by recognizing this heterogeneity. We return to this issue in the Discussion section.

Labor-force outcomes include the natural logarithm of wages per week and employment status (1 = unemployed; 0 = employed). The relatively high rate of unemployment (8.4%) in Table 25.1 reflects the recessionary nature of the period during which the data were collected (early 1992) and the exclusion from the sample of individuals working part time who did not wish to work full time. The mean of log wages of 6.037 corresponds to a wage of $419 per week.

Bivariate Relationships

An inspection of the relationships between pairs of variables make a seemingly strong prima facie case that a) literacy is important for labor force outcomes; b) social background and ethnicity are related to inequality in literacy; and c) social and ethnic economic inequalities mirror these ethnic differences in literacy. Inequality in literacy thus becomes a plausible explanation for social and ethnic economic inequality. Let us consider the evidence for each assertion.

Relationship Between Literacy and Labor-force Outcomes.   We see from Table 25.2A that literacy is moderately correlated with log wages (r = .39): individuals with higher literacy scores earn more than do individuals with lower scores. Moreover, a large "literacy gap" exists between the employed and the unemployed (Table 25.2B). Clearly, literacy is related to labor-force outcomes.

Social and Ethnic Inequality in Literacy.   We see that SES of family of origin, as indicated by years of parent education, is quite strongly positively correlated with literacy (r = .51; Table 25.2A). Also, a literacy gap exists between European Americans, m = 305.7, and African Americans, m = 247.3 (Table 25.3). The mean difference between these two groups of 58.4 is almost one standard deviation ("sd") (note, sd = 61.0 for literacy in Table 25.1). An even larger gap between European Americans and Hispanic Americans of 83.5 points is about 1.4 standard deviation units. Note, however, the similarity in literacy means of men and women. Thus, we see clear evidence of literacy inequality as a function of family SES and ethnicity (but not gender).

Social and Ethnic Inequality in Labor-Force Outcomes.   Inspection of Table 25.3 reveals that social and ethnic inequality in labor-force outcomes roughly parallel social and ethnic inequality in literacy. We see that parent education is positively associated with log wages (r = .22, Table 25.2A), and negatively associated with the probability of unemployment (note that positive mean difference in parent education between the employed and unemployed in Table 25.2B). Table 25.3 shows large log wage differentials among ethnic groups. The mean difference between European Americans and African Americans (6.13–5.83 = .30) is more than .40 standard deviation units,[8]

TABLE 25.2A Bivariate Correlations

	LOG WAGES	PARENT EDUCATION	EDUCATIONAL ATTAINMENT
Literacy	.39	.51	.66
Log Wages		.22	.41
Parent Education		.51	

TABLE 25.2B Literacy, Parent Education, and Educational Attainment by Employment Status

	UNEMPLOYED			EMPLOYED		
TOTAL N = 12492	**N**	**M**	**SD**	**N**	**M**	**SD**
Literacy	1055	259.39	62.11	11437	288.57	60.26
Parent Education	1055	10.30	3.66	11437	10.99	3.51
Educational Attainment	1055	12.23	2.82	11437	13.37	2.75

while the mean difference between European Americans and Hispanic Americans is somewhat larger. Ethnic differences in the probability of unemployment are more dramatic: note from Table 25.3 that the unemployment rate of African Americans is nearly double that of European Americans.

It is tempting to put these three pieces of evidence together into an interpretation of social and ethnic inequality in labor-force outcomes. According to this interpretation, literacy is critical for obtaining jobs and good pay, and large social and ethnic inequalities in access to good pay and job security are linked to similar inequalities in literacy. Although it is tempting to adopt this explanation based on the bivariate evidence, we must resist this temptation and consider why a deeper analysis is required. The required analysis is both multivariate and multilevel.

[Such analyses] . . . indicate that adult literacy is an important "explainer" of SES and ethnic inequality in earnings. That is, estimated inequalities associated with SES of family origin and ethnicity, inequalities not explained by labor-force experience, education, and credentials, are either partially or fully explained by adding literacy to the model. Nevertheless, a disturbing gap between African American males and European American males remains

unexplained by literacy. To be sure, literacy has helped account for a good part of this gap, but the remaining gap is non-trivial.

In contrast to ethnic and SES gaps, important gender gaps, predictably, are not explained by literacy differences, simply because gender gaps in literacy are either small (in the case of African Americans) or virtually nonexistent (in the case of European Americans and Hispanic Americans).

Correlates of Unemployment

When we examined inequality in the risk of unemployment, the results showed parallels to the findings for earnings, yet some important differences also emerge.

In sum, we found inequality in adult literacy to provide an important part of the explanation of inequalities in earnings and unemployment as a function of social background and ethnicity. Gaps not explainable by differences in education were in every case partly or completely explained by literacy. The most important exception involved inequalities in earnings and unemployment between African Americans and European Americans. Especially among males, large inequalities remained even after con-

TABLE 25.3 Literacy, Log Wages, Unemployment, and Educational Attainment by Ethnicity and Gender

		LITERACY[A]		LOG WAGES[B]		PROPORTION UNEMPLOYED[A]		EDUCATIONAL ATTAINMENT[A]		PARENT EDUCATION[A]	
	N	M	SD	M	SD	M	SD	M	SD	M	SD
Ethnicity											
European American	8751[a] 8443[b]	305.7	46.7	6.13	.70	.069	.253	13.73	2.38	11.68	2.92
African American	2113[a] 1931[b]	247.3	52.0	5.83	.68	.137	.344	12.73	2.38	10.14	3.32
Hispanic American	1302[a] 1229[b]	222.2	79.4	5.74	.66	.094	.293	10.91	4.09	7.34	4.67
Asian American	203[a] 194[b]	267.7	66.1	6.21	.75	.094	.292	14.81	2.84	10.53	4.73
Others	123[a] 115[b]	263.5	65.7	5.78	.71	.179	.385	12.70	3.02	9.90	3.92
Gender											
Female	6027[a] 5708[b]	286.7	57.0	5.85	.68	.088	.284	13.29	2.59	10.93	3.45
Male	6465[a] 6204[b]	285.5	64.4	6.21	.79	.081	.272	13.26	2.94	10.93	3.61

[a]Statistics for literacy, proportion unemployed, educational attainment, and parent education are based on the entire sample, n = 12,492.

[b]Statistics for log wages are based on those who had worked at least one week during the prior year, n = 11,912.

trolling for adult literacy. Nor was inequality in literacy a plausible explanation for gender differences in earnings. Other explanations, then, are required to understand inequality associated with African American ethnicity and female gender.

Differences in Occupational Preference as an Explanation of Economic Inequality

Gender and ethnic differences in occupational preference offer a possible explanation for corresponding gaps in economic outcomes. Persons having similar levels of adult literacy will choose occupations that vary in job security and earnings. If such differences in preference are associated with gender and ethnicity, they will produce differences in outcomes. Out data suggest, however, that such differences in preferences are not powerful explainers of gender and ethnic differences in outcomes. This conclusion is based on three findings:

- about two-thirds of the gender gap in earnings lies within rather than between occupations;
- similarly, about two-thirds of the earnings gap between African American and European American males lies within occupations; and

• essentially all of the gap between African Americans and European Americans in unemployment lies within occupations.

Occupational preference cannot account for inequality within occupations. Because most inequality in outcomes lie within occupations (controlling for education, literacy, and the other predictors), occupational preferences can at most explain only a fraction of the inequalities in outcomes found in these data.

Alternative Explanations

To the extent explanations of inequality based on cognitive skill and occupational preference fail to account for manifest inequalities in earnings and unemployment, other explanations are required.

• *Social competition and occupational segregation* Past research and theory reviewed earlier suggest that social groups may compete for control of access to favored occupations, leading to occupational segregation on the basis of ethnicity and gender and then to inequality in pay and job security. Our data cannot distinguish between the validity of this explanation and the validity of the explanation based on group differences in occupational preference. Both would lead to sizable gender and ethnic gaps associated with occupational segregation. While our data provide some evidence of such gender and ethnic segregation effects after controlling for literacy, most of the gender and ethnic inequality in earnings and all of the inequality in unemployment were found to lie within occupations. Thus, our data put a limit on the importance of theories that emphasize occupational discrimination.

• *Labor-market discrimination within occupations* We have seen that substantial gaps between African American and European American men and between men and women remain unexplained by education, credentials, labor-force experience, and literacy, and that

these gaps lie largely within occupations. Thus, our data are consistent with the hypothesis that gender and ethnic discrimination within occupations remain salient in the U.S. economy. Our data cannot readily distinguish, however, between such an explanation and alternatives, including those based on non-cognitive skills and residential segregation on the basis of ethnicity. Stronger evidence of discrimination comes from controlled experiments (Dickens, Kane, & Schultz, 1995), in which job candidates with identical resumes are dispatched to interviews.

IMPLICATIONS FOR EDUCATIONAL POLICY AND AFFIRMATIVE ACTION

The findings of this study support the contention that understanding ethnic inequality in cognitive skills as indicated by the adult literacy assessment in NALS is vital to understanding corresponding inequality in employment and earnings. Equalizing access to years of schooling and even to educational credentials is not sufficient. There are clearly important differences in cognitive skills among persons sharing the same education backgrounds, and these differences are linked to prospects for employment and earnings. This finding lends urgency to the task of improving the quality of schooling and of non-school educative environments, especially for Hispanic American and African American youth.

At the same time, we view these findings as lending support to continued vigorous affirmative action in the workplace. Inequality in literacy is far from sufficient for understanding ethnic and gender inequality in the labor market. Nor can theories of gender or ethnic differences in occupational preference provide powerful explanations of economic inequality. Even if parents and schools were successful in eliminating gender and ethnic differences in cognitive skills and occupational preferences, the evidence suggests that substantial inequality in employment and earnings would persist. Neither these data nor other available data can pinpoint the source of the unexplained inequality. We therefore face the familiar problem of decision-making under uncertainty. One might presume that labor-market discrimination is no longer prevalent, that unexplained differences between men and women and between African Americans and European Americans reflect unmeasured job-relevant differences, including noncognitive skills. Given that labor-market discrimination based on gender and ethnicity has been pervasive throughout our history, however, it is much more defensible to assume that group differences not explained by literacy reflect, at least in part, the continuing effects of inequality of opportunity for females and for ethnic minorities. . . .

More research is certainly warranted. Nevertheless, policy ought to attend to the best available evidence, and that evidence suggests that disturbingly large ethnic and gender inequalities in access to jobs and pay persist even after taking into account education, credentials, and cognitive skills. In light of historical inequalities, such evidence of current inequality supports a renewed and aggressive effort to secure opportunities for minorities and women in the workplace, as well as in school.

NOTES

1. Studies such as those cited above, as well as the present study, can tell us little about how changes in educational policy would affect the future distribution of occupational and economic success. It is hard to predict, for example, how the labor market would respond to large changes in the schooling and credentials of the work force. These studies do a better job at estimating the expected consequences of a person's decision to obtain education, holding constant current labor-market conditions.

2. See review by Levin and Kelly (1994).

3. Following Parsons (1959) and Dreeben (1967), Bowles and Gintis (1996) theorize that educational persistence produces noncognitive skills and orientations valuable to employers. Employers may view highly educated workers as well-socialized for work, or, in the words of P. Meyer, as "persistent, dependable, consistent, punctual, and tactful" (Bowles, Gintis, & Meyer, 1975). If education helps workers compete in the labor market primarily by inculcating such attitudes and values, it becomes less plausible to believe that increasing the quantity and quality of education for disadvantaged groups will have a major impact on inequality, or that such an effect could be explained by cognitive skills.

4. The occupational-preference argument predicts important differences in pay between occupations that vary in gender composition. However, a finding of such between-occupation differences does not validate the preferences argument because such differences could also reflect gender discrimination in access to better paying occupations.

5. Thus, a finding that literacy "explains" ethnic and gender differences between occupations would undermine the argument that occupational discrimination is key to understanding group differences. However, to the extent literacy cannot account for such differences between occupations, the results would be considered ambiguous (see prior note).

6. For example, the variable "female" = 1 if the respondent is female and 0 if male. The mean of this variable is therefore the proportion female in the sample, which, according to Table 25.1, is .482 or 48.2%.

7. In studies of wage differences among earners, labor-force experience is conventionally inducted by time elapsed since the completion of full-time schooling, unless more detailed information is available.

8. This mean difference in log wages is equivalent to a weekly wage differential of $119 per week, and indicates that African Americans, on average, earn about 74 percent of what European Americans earn. This difference is highly statistically significant.

REFERENCES

Allen, W., & Farley, R. (1986). The shifting social and economic tides of Black America, 1950–1980. *Annual Review of Sociology, 12,* 277–306.

Becker, G. (1964). *Human capital.* New York: Columbia University Press.

Blau, P., & Duncan, O. (1967). *The American occupational structure.* New York: John Wiley.

Bowles, S., & Gintis, H. (1976). *Schooling in capitalist America.* New York: Basic Books.

———. (1996). *Productive skills, labor discipline, and the returns to schooling.* Unpublished manuscript.

Bowles, S. Gintis, H., & Meyer, P. (1975). The long shadow of work: Explaining the economic return to education. *Insurgent Sociologist* (Summer).

Card, D., & Krueger, A. (1993). Trends in relative Black-White earnings revisited. *American Economical Review, 83*(2), 85–91.

Carnoy, M. (1995). Race earnings differentials. In M. Carnoy (Ed.), *International encyclopedia of economics of education* (2nd ed., pp. 235–242). New York: Elsevier Science.

Coleman, J., Hoffer, T., & Kilgore, S. (1992). *High school achievement: Public, Catholic and other schools compared.* New York: Basic Books.

Dickens, W., Kane, T., & Schultz, G. (1995). Does 'The Bell Curve' ring true? *Brookings Review, 12*(3), 18–23.

Doeringer, P., & Piore, M. (1971). *Internal labor markets and manpower analysis.* Lexington, MA: D. C. Heath.

Dreeben, R. (1967). *On what is learned in school.* Reading, MA: Addison-Wesley.

Duncan, O., Featherman, D., & Duncan, B. (1972). *Socioeconomic background and achievement.* New York: Seminar Press.

Ferber, M. (1995). Gender differences in earnings. In M. Carnoy (Ed.), *International encyclopedia of economics of education* (2nd ed., pp. 242–247). New York: Elsevier Science.

Ganzeboom, H., Treiman, D., & Ultee, W. (1991). Comparative intergenerational stratification research: Compensation, reinforcement, or neutrality? *Annual Review of Sociology, 17,* 277–302.

Herrnstein, R. J., & Murray, C. (1994). *The bell curve: Intelligence and class structure in American life.* New York: Free Press.

Johnston, W. B., & Packer, A. (1987). *Workforce 2000: Work and workers for the 21st century.* Indianapolis, IN: Hudson Institute.

Kain, J. F. (1968). Housing segregation, Negro employment, and metropolitan decentralization. *Quarterly Journal of Economics, 82,* 175–197.

Kerckhoff, A. (1995). Institutional arrangements and stratification processes in industrial societies. *Annual Review of Sociology, 21,* 175–197.

Kirsch, I., Jungleblut, A., Jenkins, L., & Kolstad, S. (1993). *Adult literacy in America: A first look at the results of the National Adult Literacy Survey.* Washington, DC: U.S. Department of Education, National Center for Education Statistics.

Lee, V. E., & Bryk, A. S. (1989). A multilevel model of the social distribution of educational achievement. *Sociology of Education, 62,* 172–192.

Levin, H. M., & Kelly, C. (1994). Can education do it alone? *Economics of Education Review, 13*(2), 97–108.

Massey, D., & Denton, N. (1993). *American apartheid: Segregation and the making of the underclass.* Cambridge, MA: Harvard University Press.

National Commission on Educational Excellence. (1983). *A nation at risk.* Washington, DC: U.S. Government Printing Office.

Parsons, T. (1959). The school class as a social system. *Harvard Educational Review, 29,* 297–318.

Rivera-Batiz, F. L. (1992). Quantitative literacy and the likelihood of employment among young adults in the United States. *Journal of Human Resources, 27,* 313–328.

Sewell, W. H., & Hauser, R. M. (1975). *Education, occupations, and earnings: Achievement in the early career.* New York: Academic Press.

Sum, A. (1994). *Literacy in the labor force: A report on the results of the National Adult Literacy Survey.* Washington, DC: U.S. Department of Education, National Center for Education Statistics.

Statistics Canada. (1996). *Reading the future: A portrait of literacy in Canada.* Ottawa: Human Resources Department Canada.

Tomaskovic-Devey, I. (1993). The gender and race composition of jobs and the male/female, White/Black pay gaps. *Social Forces, 72*(1), 45–76.

Velloso, J. (1995). Income distribution and education. In M. Carnoy (Ed.), *International encyclopedia of economics of education* (2nd ed., pp. 230–234). New York: Elsevier Science.

Wilson, W. J. (1996). *When work disappears: The world of the new urban poor.* New York: Knopf.

_____CHAPTER 26_____

SOCIAL CLASS AND LIFE CHANCES
CHARTERING AND BARTERING:
ELITE EDUCATION AND SOCIAL
REPRODUCTION

CAROLINE HODGES PERSELL AND PETER W. COOKSON, JR.

The continuation of power and privilege has been the subject of intense sociological debate. One recurring question is whether the system of mobility is open or whether relationships of power and privilege are reproduced from one generation to the next. If reproduction occurs, is it the reproduction of certain powerful and privileged families or groups (cf. Robinson, 1984)? Or, does it involve the reproduction of a structure of power and privilege which allows for replacement of some members with new recruits while preserving the structure?

The role of education in these processes has been the subject of much dispute. Researchers in the status attainment tradition stress the importance for mobility of the knowledge and skills acquired through education, thereby emphasizing the meritocratic and open basis for mobility (e.g., Alexander and Eckland, 1975; Alexander et al., 1975; Blau and Duncan, 1967; Haller and Portes, 1973; Kerckhoff, 1984; Otto and Haller, 1979; Sewell et al., 1969, 1970; Wilson and Portes, 1975). On the other hand, theorists such as Bowles and Gintis (1976) suggest education inculcates certain non-cognitive personality traits which serve to reproduce the social relations within a class structure; thus they put more emphasis on non-meritocratic features in the educational process.

Collins (1979) also deals with non-meritocratic aspects when he suggests that educational institutions develop and fortify status groups, and that differently valued educational credentials protect desired market positions such as those of the professions. In a related vein, Meyer (1977) notes that certain organizational "charters" serve as "selection criteria" in an educational or occupational marketplace. Meyer defines "charter" as "the social definition of the products of [an] organization" (Meyer, 1970: 577). Charters do not need to be recognized formally or legally to operate in social life. If they exist, they would create structural limitations within a presumably open market by making some people eligible for certain sets of rights that are denied to other people.

Social observers have long noted that one particular set of schools is central to the reproduction and solidarity of a national upper class, specifically elite secondary boarding schools (Baltzell, 1958, 1964; Domhoff, 1967, 1970, 1983; Mills, 1956). As well as preparing their students for socially desirable colleges and universities, traditionally such schools have been thought to build social networks among upper class scions from various regions, leading to adult business deals and marriages. Although less than one percent of the American population attends such schools, that one percent represents a strategic segment of American life that is seldom directly studied. Recently, Useem (1984) reported that graduates of 14 elite boarding schools were much more likely than non-graduates to become part of the "inner circle" of

Reprinted from *Social Problems* 33, no. 2 (December 1986): 114–29, by permission. © 1986 by the Society for the Study of Social Problems.

Fortune 500 business leaders. This evidence suggests that elite schools may play a role in class reproduction.

Few researchers have gained direct access to these schools to study social processes bearing on social reproduction. The research reported here represents the first systematic study of elite secondary boarding schools and their social relations with another important institution, namely colleges and universities.

The results of this research illustrate Collins' view that stratification involves networks of "persons making bargains and threats . . . [and that] the key resource of powerful individuals is their ability to impress and manipulate a network of social contacts" (1979:26). If such were the case, we would expect to find that upper class institutions actively develop social networks for the purpose of advancing the interests of their constituencies.

By focusing on the processes of social reproduction rather than individual attributes or the results of intergenerational mobility, our research differs from the approaches taken in both the status attainment and status allocation literature. Status attainment models focus on individual attributes and achievement, and allocation models examine structural supports or barriers to social mobility; yet neither approach explores the underlying processes. Status attainment models assume the existence of a relatively open contest system, while reproduction and allocation models stress that selection criteria and structural barriers create inequalities, limiting opportunities for one group while favoring another (Kerckhoff, 1976, 1984). Neither attainment nor allocation models show how class reproduction, selection criteria, or structural opportunities and impediments operate in practice.

Considerable evidence supports the view that structural limitations operate in the labor market (e.g., Beck et al., 1978; Bibb and Form, 1977; Stolzenberg, 1975) but, with the exception of tracking, little evidence has been found that similar structural limitations exist in education. Tracking systems create structural impediments in an open model of educational attainment (Oakes, 1985; Persell, 1977; Rosenbaum, 1976, 1980), although not all research supports this conclusion (e.g., Alexander et al., 1978; Heyns, 1974).

In this paper we suggest that there is an additional structural limitation in the key transition from high school to college. We explore the possibility that special organizational "charters" exist for certain secondary schools and that a process of "bartering" occurs between representatives of selected secondary schools and some college admissions officers. These processes have not been clearly identified by prior research on education and stratification, although there has been some previous research which leads in this direction.

EMPIRICAL LITERATURE

Researchers of various orientations concur that differences between schools seem to have little bearing on student attainment (Averch et al., 1972; Jencks et al., 1972; Meyer, 1970, 1977). Indeed, Meyer (1977) suggests the most puzzling paradox in the sociology of American education is that while schools differ in structure and resources, they vary little in their effects because all secondary schools are assumed to have similar "charters." Meyer believes that no American high school is specially chartered by selective colleges in the way, for instance, that certain British Public Schools have been chartered by Oxford and Cambridge Universities. Instead, he suggests that "all American high schools have similar status rights (and therefore) variations in their effects should be small" (Meyer, 1977:60).

Kamens (1977:217–18), on the other hand, argues that "schools symbolically redefine people and make them eligible for membership in societal categories to which specific sets of rights are assigned." The work of Alexander and Eckland (1977) is consistent with this view. These researchers found that students who attended high schools where the social status of the student body was high also attended selective colleges at a greater rate than did students at other high schools, even when individual student academic ability and family background were held constant (Alexander and Eckland, 1975). Their research and other work finding a relationship between curricular track placement and college attendance (Alexander et al., 1978; Alexander and McDill, 1976; Jaffe and Adams, 1970; Rosenbaum, 1976, 1980) suggest that differences between schools may affect stratification outcomes.

Research has shown that graduation from a private school is related to attending a four-year (rather than a two-year) college (Falsey and Heyns, 1984), attending a highly selective college (Hammack and Cookson, 1980), and earning higher income in adult life (Lewis and Wanner, 1979). Moreover, Cookson (1981) found that graduates of private boarding schools attended more selective colleges than did their public school counterparts, even when family background and Scholastic Aptitude Test (SAT) scores were held constant. Furthermore, some private colleges acknowledge the distinctive nature of certain secondary schools. Klitgaard (1985: Table 2.2) reports that students from private secondary schools generally had an advantage for admission to Harvard over public school graduates, even when their academic ratings were comparable. Karen (1985) notes that applications to Harvard from certain private boarding schools were placed in special colored dockets, or folders, to set them apart from other applications. Thus, they were considered as a distinct group. Not only did Harvard acknowledge the special status of certain schools by color-coding their applicants' folders, attendance at one of those schools provided an advantage for acceptance, even when parental background, grades, SATs, and other characteristics were controlled (Karen, 1985).

NETWORKS AND THE TRANSMISSION OF PRIVILEGE

For these reasons we believe it is worth investigating whether certain secondary schools have special organizational charters, at least in relation to certain colleges. If they do, the question arises, how do organizational charters operate? Network analysts suggest that "the pattern of ties in a network provides significant opportunities and constraints because it affects the relative access of people and institutions to such resources as information, wealth and power" (Wellman, 1981:3). Furthermore, "because of their structural location, members of a social system differ greatly in their access to these resources" (Wellman, 1981:30). Moreover, network analysts have suggested that class-structured networks work to preserve upper class ideology, consciousness, and life-style (see, for example, Laumann, 1966: 132–36).

We expect that colleges and secondary schools have much closer ties than has previously been documented. Close networks of personal relationships between officials at certain private schools and some elite colleges transform what is for many students a relatively standardized, bureaucratic procedure into a process of negotiation. As a result, they are able to communicate more vital information about their respective needs, giving selected secondary school students an inside track to gaining acceptance to desired colleges. We call this process "bartering."

SAMPLE AND DATA

Baltzell (1958, 1964) noted the importance of elite secondary boarding schools for upper class solidarity. However, he was careful to distinguish between those boarding schools that were truly socially elite and those that had historically served somewhat less affluent and less powerful families. He indicates that there is a core group of eastern Protestant schools that "set the pace and bore the brunt of criticism received by private schools for their so-called 'snobbish,' 'undemocratic' and even 'un-American' values" (Baltzell, 1958:307–08). These 16 schools are: Phillips (Andover) Academy (MA), Phillips Exeter Academy (NH), St. Paul's School (NH), St. Mark's School (MA), Groton School (MA), St. George's School (RI), Kent School (CT), The Taft School (CT), The Hotchkiss School (CT), Choate Rosemary Hall (CT), Middlesex School (MA), Deerfield Academy (MA), The Lawrenceville School (NJ), The Hill School (PA), The Episcopal High School (VA), and Woodberry Forest School (VA). We refer to the schools on Baltzell's list as the "select 16."[1]

In 1982 and 1983, we visited a representative sample of 12 of the select 16 schools. These 12 schools reflect the geographic distribution of the select 16 schools. In this time period we also visited 30 other "leading" secondary boarding schools drawn from the 1981 *Handbook of Private Schools'* list of 289 "leading" secondary boarding schools. This sample is representative of leading secondary boarding schools nationally in location, religious affiliation, size, and the sex composition of the student body. These schools are organizationally similar to the select 16 schools in offering only a college preparatory curriculum, in being incorporated as non-profit organizations, in their faculty/student ratios, and in the percent of boarders who receive financial aid. They differ somewhat with respect to sex composition, average size, the sex of their heads, and number of advanced placement courses (see Table 26.1). However, the key difference between the select 16 schools and the other "leading" schools is that the former are more socially elite than the latter. For instance, in one of the select 16 boarding schools in 1982, 40 percent of the current students' parents were listed in *Social Register.*[2]

All 42 schools were visited by one or both of the authors. Visits lasted between one and five days and included interviews with administrators, teachers, and students. Most relevant to this study were the lengthy interviews with the schools' college advisors. These interviews explored all aspects of the college counseling process, including the nature and content of the advisors' relationships with admissions officers at various colleges. At a representative sample of six of the select 16 schools and a representative sample of 13 of the other "leading" schools a questionnaire was administered to seniors during our visits.[3] The questionnaire contained more than 50 items and included questions on parental education, occupation, income, number of books in the home, family travel, educational legacies as well as many questions on boarding school life and how students felt about their experiences in school. Overall, student survey and school record data were collected on 687 seniors from the six select 16 schools and 658 seniors from other leading schools. Although not every piece of data was available for every student, we did obtain 578 complete cases from six select 16 schools and 457 cases from ten leading schools.[4] School record data included student grade point averages, Scholastic Aptitude Test (SAT) scores, class rank, names of colleges to which students applied, names of colleges to which students were accepted, and names of colleges students will attend. This material was supplied by the schools after the seniors graduated, in the summer or fall of 1982 and 1983. With this population

TABLE 26.1   Comparison of Population and Two Samples of Boarding Schools*

	TOTAL POPULATION (N = 289)	OTHER BOARDING SCHOOL SAMPLE (N = 30)	SELECT 16 SAMPLE (N = 12)
Percent with College Preparatory Curriculum	100	100	100
Percent with No Religious Affiliation	65	70	67
Percent Incorporated, Not-for-profit	83	90	83
Average Faculty/Student Ratio	0.17	0.15	0.15
Average Percent of Boarders Aided	15	16	18
Percent of Schools which are All-Boys	28	17	33
Percent of Schools which are All-Girls	17	28	0
Percent Coeducational Schools	55	55	67
Percent with Male Heads	92	73	100
Average Number of Advanced Courses	3.5	4.8	6.7
Average Size	311	322	612

*Computed from data published in the *Handbook of Private Schools* (1981).

actual enrollment matches school reports with high reliability. The record data have been linked with questionnaire data from the seniors and with various characteristics of the college. The college students planned to attend were coded as to academic selectivity, Ivy League, and other characteristics not analyzed here.[5]

CHARTERING

Historical evidence shows that the select 16 schools have had special charters in relation to Ivy League colleges in general, and Harvard, Yale, and Princeton in particular. In the 1930s and 1940s, two-thirds of all graduates of 12 of the select 16 boarding schools attended Harvard, Yale, or Princeton (Karabel, 1984). But, by 1973, this share had slipped noticeably to an average of 21 percent, although the rate of acceptance between schools ranges from 51 percent to 8 percent (Cookson and Persell, 1978; Table 4). In the last half century, then, the proportion of select 16 school graduates who attended Harvard, Yale, or Princeton dropped substantially.

This decrease was paralleled by an increase in the competition for admission to Ivy League colleges. According to several college advisors at select 16 boarding schools, 90 percent of all applicants to Harvard in the 1940s were accepted as were about half of those in the early 1950s. In 1982, the national acceptance rate for the eight Ivy League schools was 26 percent, although it was 20 percent or less at Harvard, Yale, and Princeton (National College Data Bank, 1984).

The pattern of Ivy League college admissions has changed during this time. Ivy League colleges have begun to admit more public school graduates. Before World War II at Princeton, for example, about 80 percent of the entering freshmen came from private secondary schools (Blumberg and Paul, 1975:70). In 1982, 34 percent of the freshman class at Harvard, 40 percent of Yale freshmen, and 40 percent of Princeton freshmen were from non-public high schools (National College Data Bank, 1984).

This shift in college admissions policy, combined with increased financial aid and an inflationary trend

in higher education that puts increased emphasis on which college one attends, contributes to the larger number [of] applications to certain colleges nationally. Thus, while in the past decade the number of college-age students has declined, the number of students applying to Ivy League colleges has increased (Mackay-Smith, 1985; Maeroff, 1984; Winerip, 1984).

In view of these historical changes, is there any evidence that the select 16 schools still retain special charters in relation to college admissions? When four pools of applications to the Ivy League colleges are compared, the acceptance rate is highest at select 16 schools, followed by a highly selective public high school, other leading boarding schools, and finally the entire national pool of applications (Table 26.2).[6]

While we do not have comparable background data on all the applicants from these various pools, we do know that the students in the highly selective public high school have among the highest academic qualifications in the country.[7] Their combined SAT scores, for example, average at least 150 points higher than those of students at the leading boarding schools. On that basis they might be expected to do considerably better than applicants from boarding schools: which they do at some colleges but not at Harvard, Yale, or Princeton.

The most revealing insights into the operation of special charters, however, are provided by a comparison between select 16 boarding schools and other leading boarding schools—the most similar schools and the ones on which we have the most detailed data.

Students from select 16 schools apply to somewhat different colleges than do students from other leading boarding schools. Select 16 school students were much more likely to apply to one or more of the eight Ivy League and at least one of the other highly selective colleges than were students from other leading boarding schools (Table 26.3). Among those who applied, select 16 students were more likely to be accepted than were students from other boarding schools, and, if accepted, they were slightly more likely to attend.

Before we can conclude that these differences are due to a school charter, we need to control for

TABLE 26.2   Percent of Applications That Were Accepted at Ivy League Colleges from Four Pools of Applications

COLLEGE NAME	SELECT 16 BOARDING SCHOOLS[a] (1982–83)	SELECTIVE OTHER LEADING BOARDING SCHOOLS[b] (1982–83)	PUBLIC HIGH SCHOOLS[c] (1984)	NATIONAL GROUP OF APPLICANTS[d] (1982)
Brown University				
Percent Accepted	35	20	28	22
Number of Applications	95	45	114	11,854
Columbia University				
Percent Accepted	66	29	32	41
Number of Applications	35	7	170	3,650
Cornell University				
Percent Accepted	57	36	55	31
Number of Applications	65	25	112	17,927
Dartmouth				
Percent Accepted	41	21	41	22
Number of Applications	79	33	37	8,313
Harvard University				
Percent Accepted	38	28	20	17
Number of Applications	104	29	127	13,341
Princeton University				
Percent Accepted	40	28	18	18
Number of Applications	103	40	109	11,804
University of Pennsylvania				
Percent Accepted	45	32	33	36
Number of Applications	40	19	167	11,000
Yale University				
Percent Accepted	40	32	15	20
Number of Applications	92	25	124	11,023
Overall Percent Accepted	42	27	30	26
Total Number of Applications	613	223	960	88,912

[a]Based on school record data on the applications of 578 seniors.
[b]Based on school record data on the applications of 457 seniors.
[c]Based on data published in the school newspaper.
[d]Based on data published in the *National College Data Bank* (1984).

parental SES[8] and student SAT scores.[9] This analysis is shown in Table 26.4. One striking finding here is the high rate of success enjoyed by boarding school students in general. At least one-third and as many as 92 percent of the students in each cell of Table 26.4 are accepted. Given that the average freshman combined SAT score is more than 1175 at these colleges and universities, it is particularly notable that such a large proportion of those with combined SAT scores of 1050 or less are accepted.

TABLE 26.3   Boarding School Students' College Application, Chances of Acceptance, and Plans to Attend

A. PERCENT OF BOARDING SCHOOL SAMPLES WHO APPLIED		IVY LEAGUE COLLEGES	HIGHLY SELECTIVE COLLEGES
Select 16 Boarding Schools	%=	61	87
	N=	(353)	(502)
Other Leading Boarding Schools	%=	28	61
	N=	(129)	(279)

B. PERCENT OF APPLICANTS WHO WERE ACCEPTED		IVY LEAGUE COLLEGES	HIGHLY SELECTIVE COLLEGES
Select 16 Boarding Schools	%=	54	84
	N=	(191)	(420)
Other Leading Boarding Schools	%=	36	64
	N=	(47)	(178)

C. PERCENT OF ACCEPTEES WHO PLAN TO ATTEND		IVY LEAGUE COLLEGES	HIGHLY SELECTIVE COLLEGES
Select 16 Boarding Schools	%=	79	81
	N=	(151)	(340)
Other Leading Boarding Schools	%=	53	77
	N=	(25)	(137)

TABLE 26.4   Percent of Students Who Applied to the Most Highly Selective Colleges Who Were Accepted, with SAT Scores, SES, and School Type Held Constant*

STUDENT SOCIO-ECONOMIC STATUS		STUDENT COMBINED SAT SCORES					
		HIGH (1580–1220)		MEDIUM (1216–1060)		LOW (1050–540)	
		SELECT 16 SCHOOLS	OTHER LEADING BOARDING SCHOOLS	SELECT 16 SCHOOLS	OTHER LEADING BOARDING SCHOOLS	SELECT 16 SCHOOLS	OTHER LEADING BOARDING SCHOOLS
High	%=	87	70	80	64	65	53
	N=	(93)	(33)	(73)	(36)	(34)	(30)
Medium	%=	89	71	85	76	44	35
	N=	(100)	(28)	(66)	(46)	(18)	(51)
Low	%=	92	72	78	69	55	33
	N=	(72)	(25)	(51)	(32)	(33)	(49)

*Based on student questionnaires and school record data on 1035 seniors for whom data were available.

In general, high SAT scores increase chances of acceptance, but the relationship is somewhat attenuated under certain conditions. Students with low SAT scores are more likely to be accepted at highly selective colleges if they have higher SES backgrounds, especially if they attend a select 16 school. These students seem to have relatively high "floors" placed under them, since two-thirds of those from select 16 schools and more than half of those from other schools were accepted by one of the most selective colleges.[10]

The most successful ones of all are relatively low SES students with the highest SATs attending select 16 schools—92 percent of whom were accepted. Students from relatively modest backgrounds appear to receive a "knighting effect" by attending a select 16 school. Thus, select 16 schools provide mobility for some individuals from relatively less privileged backgrounds. To a considerable degree all students with high SATs, regardless of their SES, appear to be "turbo-charged" by attending a select 16 school compared to their counterparts at other leading schools.

At every level of SATs and SES, students' chances of acceptance increase if they attend a select 16 school. Such a finding is consistent with the argument that a chartering effect continues to operate among elite educational institutions. The historical shifts toward admitting more public school students on the part of Ivy League colleges and the increased competition for entry, described above, have meant that more effort has been required on the part of select 16 schools to retain an advantage for their students. We believe that certain private boarding schools have buttressed their charters by an increasingly active bartering operation.

BARTERING

Normally, we do not think of the college admissions process as an arena for bartering. It is assumed that colleges simply choose students according to their own criteria and needs. Few students and no high schools are thought to have any special "leverage" in admissions decisions. Our research revealed, however, that select 16 boarding schools—perhaps because of their perennial supply of academically able and affluent students—can negotiate admissions cases with colleges. The colleges are aware that select 16 schools attract excellent college prospects and devote considerable attention to maintaining close relationships with these schools, especially through the college admissions officers. Secondary school college advisors actively "market" their students within a context of tremendous parental pressure and increasing competition for admission to elite colleges.

SELECT 16 COLLEGE ADVISORS AND IVY LEAGUE ADMISSIONS DIRECTORS: THE OLD SCHOOL TIE

Of the 11 select 16 school college advisors on whom data were available, 10 were graduates of Harvard, Yale, or Princeton. Of the 23 other leading boarding school college advisors on whom data were available, only three were Ivy League graduates, and none of them was from Harvard, Yale, or Princeton. College advisors are overwhelmingly white men. At the select 16 schools only one (an acting director) was a woman, and at other schools five were women. Some college advisors have previously worked as college admissions officers. Their educational and social similarity to college admissions officers may facilitate the creation of social ties and the sharing of useful information. Research shows that the exchange of ideas most frequently occurs between people who share certain social attributes (Rogers and Kincaid, 1981).

College advisors at select 16 schools tend to have long tenures—15 or more years is not unusual. On the other hand, college advisors at other schools are more likely to have assumed the job recently. A college advisor at one select 16 school stressed the "importance of continuity on both sides of the relationship." Thus, it is not surprising that select 16 schools hold on to their college advisors.

Select 16 college advisors have close social relationships with each other and with elite college admissions officers that are cemented through numerous face-to-face meetings each year. All of the select

16 schools are on the East Coast, whereas only 70 percent of the other leading boarding schools are in that region. However, even those leading boarding schools on the East Coast lack the close relationships with colleges that characterize the select 16 schools. Thus, geography alone does not explain these relationships.

The college advisors at most of the boarding schools we studied have personally visited a number of colleges around the country. Boarding schools often provide college advisors with summer support for systematic visits, and a number of geographically removed colleges offer attractive incentives, or fully paid trips to their region (e.g., Southern California). These trips often take place during bitter New England winters, and include elegant food and lodging as well as a chance to see colleges and meet admissions officers.

However, the college advisors at select 16 schools are likely to have visited far more schools (several mentioned that they had personally visited 60 or 70 schools) than college advisors at other schools (some of whom had not visited any). They are also much more likely to visit regularly the most selective and prestigious colleges.[11]

Numerous college admissions officers also travel to these boarding schools to interview students and meet the college advisors. The select 16 schools have more college admissions officers visit than do other schools; more than 100 in any given academic year is not unusual. College advisors have drinks and dinner with selected admissions officers, who often stay overnight on campus. As one college advisor noted, "We get to establish a personal relationship with each other." Moreover, Ivy League colleges bring students from select 16 schools to their campus to visit for weekends.

By knowing each other personally, college advisors and admissions officers "develop a relationship of trust," so that they can evaluate the sources as well as the content of phone calls and letters. We observed phone calls between college advisors and admissions officers when we were in their offices. Several college advisors mentioned, "It helps to know personally the individual you are speaking or writing to," and one college advisor at a select 16 school said, "I have built up a track record with the private colleges over the years."

Virtually all of the select 16 school college advisors indicated that in the spring—before colleges have finished making their admissions decisions—they take their application files and drive to elite colleges to discuss "their list." They often sit in on the admissions deliberations while they are there. In contrast, the other schools' college advisorys generally did not make such trips. Such actions suggest the existence of strong social networks between select 16 school college advisors and elite college admissions officers.

HOW THE SYSTEM WORKS: "FINE TUNING" THE ADMISSIONS PROCESS

Bartering implies a reciprocal relationship, and select 16 schools and elite colleges have a well-developed system of information exchange. Both sides have learned to cooperate to their mutual benefit. College advisors try to provide admissions officers with as much information about their students as possible to help justify the acceptance of a particular applicant. Select 16 schools have institutionalized this process more than other schools. The most professional operation we found was in a select 16 school where about half the graduating class goes to Harvard, Yale, or Princeton. There, the college advisor interviews the entire faculty on each member of the senior class. He tape-records all their comments and has them transcribed. This produces a "huge confidential dossier which gives a very good sense of where each student is." In addition, housemasters and coaches write reports. Then the college advisor interviews each senior, dictating notes after each interview. After assimilating all of these comments on each student, the college advisor writes his letter of recommendation, which he is able to pack with corroborative details illustrating a candidate's strengths. The thoroughness, thought, and care that go into this process insures that anything and everything positive that could be said about a student is included, thereby maximizing his or her chances for a favorable reception at a college.[12]

Information also flows from colleges to the secondary schools. By sitting in on the admissions process at colleges like Harvard, Princeton, and Yale, select 16 school college advisors say they "see the wealth and breadth of the applicant pool." They get a firsthand view of the competition their students face. They also obtain a sense of how a college "puts its class together," which helps them to learn strategies for putting forward their own applicants.

By observing and participating in the admissions process, select 16 school college advisors gain an insider's view of a college's selection process. This insider's knowledge is reflected in the specific figures select 16 advisors mentioned in our conversations with them. One select 16 college advisor said that a student has "two and one half times as good a chance for admission to Harvard if his father went there than if he did not." Another said, "While 22 percent in general are admitted to Ivy League colleges, 45 percent of legacies are admitted to Ivy League colleges." In both cases, they mentioned a specific, quantified statement about how being a legacy affected their students' admissions probabilities.[13] Similarly, several select 16 school college advisors mentioned the percentages of the freshman class at Harvard and Yale that were from public and private schools, and one even mentioned how those percentages have changed since 1957. College advisors at other schools do not lace their conversations with as many specific figures nor do they belong to the special organization that some of the select 16 schools have formed to share information and strategies.

The special interest group these schools have formed is able to negotiate with the colleges to their students' advantage. For instance, the college advisors explained that select 16 school students have greater competition than the average high school student and carry a more rigorous course load.[14] Therefore, this group persuaded the colleges that their students should not receive an absolute class rank, but simply an indication of where the students stand by decile or quintile. Colleges may then put such stu-

dents in a "not ranked" category or report the decile or quintile rank. No entering student from such a secondary school is clearly labeled as the bottom person in the class. To our knowledge, only select 16 schools have made this arrangement.

Armed with an insider's knowledge of a college's desires, select 16 school college advisors seek to present colleges with the most appropriate candidates. As one select 16 school college advisor said, "I try to shape up different applicant pools for different colleges," a process that has several components. First, college advisors try to screen out hopeless prospects, or as one tactfully phrased it, "I try to discourage unproductive leads." This is not always easy because, as one said, "Certain dreams die hard." College advisors in other schools were more likely to say that they never told students where they should or should not apply.

One select 16 school requires students to write a "trial college essay" that helps the college advisor ascertain "what kind of a student this is." From the essay he can tell how well students write, determine whether they follow through and do what they need to do on time, and learn something about their personal and family background. With faculty and student comments in hand, college advisors can begin to assemble their applicant pools. One thing they always want to learn is which college is a student's first choice, and why. This is useful information when bartering with colleges.

Some college advisors are quite frank when bartering; for example, the select 16 college advisor who stressed, "I am candid about a student to the colleges, something that is not true at a lot of schools where they take an advocacy position in relation to their students. . . . We don't sell damaged goods to the colleges." College advisors at other schools did not define their role as one of weeding out candidates prior to presenting them to colleges, although they may do this as well. It would seem then that part of the gate-keeping process of admission to college is occurring in select 16 secondary schools. College advisors, particularly those with long tenures at select 16 schools, seem quite aware of the importance of maintaining long-term credibility with colleges, since credibility influences how effectively they can work for their school in the future.

While the children of certain big donors (so-called "development cases") may be counseled with special care, in general the college advisors have organizational concerns that are more important than the fate of a particular student. Several select 16 school college advisors spoke with scorn about parents who see a rejection as the "first step in the negotiation." Such parents threaten to disrupt a delicate network of social relationships that link elite institutions over a considerable time span.

At the same time, college advisors try to do everything they can to help their students jump the admissions hurdle. One select 16 school college advisor said,

> I don't see our students as having an advantage (in college admissions). We have to make the situation unequal. We do this by writing full summary reports on the students, by reviewing the applicants with the colleges several times during the year, and by traveling to the top six colleges in the spring. . . . [Those visits] are an advocacy proceeding on the side of the students. The colleges make their decisions on our students and those from [another select 16 school] because they have the most information on these students.

Another select 16 college advisor said, "We want to be sure they are reading the applications of our students fairly, and we lobby for our students." A third select 16 college advisor made a similar statement, "When I drive to the [Ivy League] colleges, I give them a reading on our applicants. I let them know if I think they are making a mistake. There is a lobbying component here."

Select 16 college advisors do not stop with simply asking elite college admissions officers to reconsider a decision, however. They try to barter, and the colleges show they are open to this possibility when the college admissions officer says, "Let's talk about your group." One select 16 college advisor said he stresses to colleges that if his school recommends someone and he or she is accepted, that student will come. While not all colleges heed this warranty, some do.

One select 16 college advisor said, "It is getting harder than it used to be to say to an admissions officer, 'take a chance on this one,' especially at Harvard which now has so many more applications." But it is significant that he did not say that it was impossible. If all else fails in a negotiation, a select 16 college advisor said, "We lobby for the college to make him their absolute first choice on the waiting list." Such a compromise represents a chance for both parties to save face.

Most public high school counselors are at a distinct disadvantage in the bartering process because they are not part of the interpersonal network, do not have strategic information, and are thus unable to lobby effectively for their students. One select 16 advisor told us about a counselor from the Midwest who came to an Ivy League college to sit in on the admissions committee decision for his truly outstanding candidate—SATs in the 700s, top in his class, class president, and star athlete. The select 16 college advisor was also there, lobbying on behalf of his candidate—a nice undistinguished fellow (in the words of his advisor, "A good kid,") with SATs in the 500s, middle of his class, average athlete, and no strong signs of leadership. After hearing both the counselors, the Ivy League college chose the candidate from the select 16 school. The outraged public school counselor walked out in disgust. Afterwards, the Ivy League college admissions officer said to the select 16 college advisor, "We may not be able to have these open meetings anymore." Even in the unusual case where a public school counselor did everything that a select 16 boarding school college advisor did, it was not enough to secure the applicant's admission. Despite the competitive environment that currently surrounds admission to elite colleges, the admission officers apparently listen more closely to advisors from select 16 boarding schools than to public school counselors.

CONCLUSIONS AND IMPLICATIONS

The graduates of certain private schools are at a distinct advantage when it comes to admission to highly selective colleges because of the special charters and highly developed social networks these schools possess. Of course, other factors are operating as well. Parental wealth (which is not fully tapped by a measure of SES based on education, occupation, and income), preference for the children of alumni, Advanced Placement (AP) coursework, sports ability especially in such scarce areas as ice hockey, crew, or squash, and many other factors also influence the process of college admission. Elite boarding schools are part of a larger process whereby more privileged members of society transmit their advantages to their children. Attendance at a select 16 boarding school signals admissions committees that an applicant may have certain valuable educational and social characteristics.

Significantly, neither the families nor the secondary schools leave the college admissions process to chance or to formal bureaucratic procedures. Instead, they use personal connections to smooth the process, and there is reason to believe that those efforts affect the outcomes. The "knighting effect" of select 16 schools helps a few low SES, high SAT students gain admission to highly selective colleges, evidence of sponsored mobility for a few worthy youngsters of relatively humble origins. Our findings are consistent with Kamens' (1974) suggestion that certain schools make their students eligible for special social rights. Furthermore, the interaction between social background, SATs, and select 16 school attendance suggests that both individual ability and socially structured advantages operate in the school–college transition.

These results illustrate Collins' (1979) view that stratified systems are maintained through the manipulation of social contacts. They show one way that networks and stratification processes are interconnected. College access is only one aspect of the larger phenomenon of elite maintenance and reproduction. Elite boarding schools no doubt contribute as well to the social contacts and marriage markets of their graduates. What this instance shows is that reproduction is not a simple process. It involves family and group reproduction as well as some structural replacement with carefully screened new members. There is active personal intervention in what is publicly presented as a meritocratic and open competition. The internal processes and external networks described here operate to construct class privileges as well as to transmit class advantages, thereby helping to reproduce structured stratification within society.

If this example is generalizable, we would expect that economically and culturally advantaged groups might regularly find or create specially chartered organizations and brokers with well-developed networks to help them successfully traverse critical junctures in their social histories. Such key switching points include the transition from secondary school to college, admission to an elite graduate or professional school, obtaining the right job, finding a mentor, gaining a medical residency at a choice hospital (Hall, 1946, 1948, 1949), getting a book manuscript published (Coser et al., 1982), having one's paintings exhibited at an art gallery or museum, obtaining a theatrical agent, having one's business considered for venture capital or bank support (Rogers and Larsen, 1984), being offered membership in an exclusive social club, or being asked to serve on a corporate or other board of directors (Useem, 1984).

In all of these instances, many qualified individuals seek desired, but scarce, social and/or economic opportunities. Truly open competition for highly desired outcomes leaves privileged groups vulnerable. Because the socially desired positions are finite at any given moment, processes that give an advantage to the members of certain groups work to limit the opportunities of individuals from other groups.[15] In these ways, dominant groups enhance their chances, at the same time that a few worthy newcomers are advanced, a process which serves to reproduce and legitimate a structure of social inequality.

NOTES

1. Others besides Baltzell have developed lists of elite private schools, including Baird (1977), Domhoff (1967, 1970, 1983), and McLaughlin (1970).

2. We were not able to compute the percent of students in *Social Register* for every school because most schools do not publish the names of their students. Hence, we were

not able to look their families up in *Social Register*. We do know that less than .000265 percent of American families are listed in *Social Register*. See Levine (1980) for an historical discussion of the social backgrounds of students at several of the select 16 schools.

3. We asked to give the student questionnaires at nine of the 12 select 16 schools and six of those nine schools agreed. At the other leading schools, we asked to give the questionnaires at 15 and 13 schools agreed.

4. Three leading schools did not supply the college data.

5. Following Astin et al. (1981:7), we measured selectivity with the average SAT scores of the entering freshmen.

6. The entire national applicant pool includes the relatively more successful subgroups within it. If they were excluded, the national acceptance rate would be even lower.

7. Students admitted to this selective public high school must be recommended by their junior high school to take a competitive entrance exam, where they must score very well. The school was among the top five in the nation with respect to the number of National Merit Scholarships won by its students, and each year a number of students in the school win Westinghouse science prizes. This school was selected for purposes of comparison here because academically it is considered to be among the very top public schools in the nation. However, it does not have the social prestige of the select 16 boarding schools.

8. SES was measured by combining father's education, father's occupation, and family income into a composite SES score. These SES scores were then standardized for this population, and each student received a single standardized SES score.

9. The combined verbal and mathematics scores were used.

10. We performed separate analyses for boys and girls to see if sex was related to admission to a highly selective college when type of boarding school, SATs, and SES were held constant, and generally it was not. Girls who attend either select 16 or other leading boarding schools do as well or better in their admission to college as do their male counterparts, with the single exception of girls at

select 16 schools in the top third on their SATs and SES. In that particular group, 92 percent of the boys but only 77 percent of the girls were accepted at the most highly selective colleges. Since that is the only exception, boys and girls are discussed together in the text of the paper.

11. Our field visits and interviews with college advisors at two highly selective public high schools and three open admission public high schools show that college advisors at even the most selective public high schools generally do not personally know the admissions officers at colleges, particularly at the most selective and Ivy League colleges, nor do they talk with them over the phone or in person prior to their admissions decisions.

12. Such a procedure requires considerable financial and personal resources. Select 16 schools have more capital-intensive and professional office services supporting their college admissions endeavor than other schools. Most of them have word processors, considerable professional staff, and ample secretarial and clerical help.

13. We did not ask students what colleges their parents attended so we could not control for college legacy in our analysis. Future research on the admissions process should do so.

14. One way select 16 schools establish their reputations as rigorous schools is through the numbers of their students who succeed on the Advanced Placement (AP) Exams given by the College Entrance Examination Board. Compared to other secondary schools, select 16 schools offer larger numbers of advanced courses, encourage more students to take them, coach students very effectively on how to take the test, and maintain contacts with the people who design and read AP exams so that they know what is expected and can guide students accordingly. (See Cookson and Persell, 1985, for more discussion of these processes.) Other schools are much less likely than select 16 ones to have teachers who have graded AP exams or to know people who have helped to write the tests.

15. See Parkin (1979) for a discussion of social closure as exclusion and usurpation.

REFERENCES

Alexander, Karl L., Martha Cook, and Edward L. McDill. 1978. "Curriculum Tracking and Educational Stratification: Some Further Evidence." *American Sociological Review* 43: 47–66.

Alexander, Karl L., and Bruce K. Eckland. 1975. "Contextual Effects in the High School Attainment Process." *American Sociological Review* 40: 402–16.

———. 1977. "High School Context and College Selectivity: Institutional Constraints in Educational Stratification." *Social Forces* 56: 166–88.

Alexander, Karl L., Bruce K. Eckland, and Larry J. Griffin. 1975. "The Wisconsin Model of Socioeconomic Achievement: A Replication." *American Journal of Sociology* 81: 324–42.

Alexander, Karl L., and Edward L. McDill. 1976. "Selection and Allocation within Schools: Some Causes and Consequences of Curriculum Placement." *American Sociological Review* 41: 963–80.

Astin, Alexander W., Margo R. King, and Gerald T. Richardson. 1981. *The American Freshman: National Norms for Fall 1981.* Los Angeles: Laboratory for Research in Higher Education, University of California.

Averch, Harvey A., Steven J. Carroll, Theodore S. Donaldson, Herbert J. Kiesling, and John Pincus. 1972. *How Effective Is Schooling? A Critical Review and Synthesis of Research Findings.* Santa Monica, Calif.: The Rand Corporation.

Baird, Leonard L. 1977. *The Elite Schools.* Lexington, Mass.: Lexington Books.

Baltzell, E. Digby. 1958. *Philadelphia Gentlemen.* New York: Free Press.

———. 1964. *The Protestant Establishment.* New York: Random House.

Beck, E. M., Patrick M. Horan, and Charles M. Tolbert II. 1978. "Stratification in a Dual Economy." *American Sociological Review* 43: 704–20.

Bibb, Robert C., and William Form. 1977. "The Effects of Industrial, Occupational and Sex Stratification on Wages in Blue-Collar Markets." *Social Forces* 55: 974–96.

Blau, Peter, and Otis D. Duncan. 1967. *The American Occupational Structure.* New York: Wiley.

Blumberg, Paul M., and P. W. Paul. 1975. "Continuities and Discontinuities in Upper-Class Marriages." *Journal of Marriage and the Family* 37: 63–77.

Bowles, Samuel, and Herbert Gintis. 1976. *Schooling in Capitalist America.* New York: Basic Books.

Collins, Randall. 1979. *The Credential Society.* New York: Academic Press.

Cookson, Peter Willis, Jr. 1981. "Private Secondary Boarding School and Public Suburban High School Graduation: An Analysis of College Attendance Plans." Unpublished Ph.D. dissertation. New York University.

Cookson, Peter W., Jr., and Caroline Hodges Persell. 1978. "Social Structure and Educational Programs: A Comparison of Elite Boarding Schools and Public Education in the United States." Paper presented at the annual meeting of the American Sociological Association, San Francisco.

———. 1985. *Preparing for Power: America's Elite Boarding Schools.* New York: Basic Books.

Coser, Lewis A., Charles Kadushin, and Walter W. Powell. 1982. *Books: The Culture & Commerce of Publishing.* New York: Basic Books.

Domhoff, G. William. 1967. *Who Rules America?* Englewood Cliffs: Prentice-Hall.

———. 1970. *The Higher Circles.* New York: Vintage.

———. 1983. *Who Rules America Now?* Englewood Cliffs: Prentice-Hall.

Falsey, Barbara, and Barbara Heyns. 1984. "The College Channel: Private and Public Schools Reconsidered." *Sociology of Education* 57: 111–22.

Hall, Oswald. 1946. "The Informal Organization of the Medical Profession." *Canadian Journal of Economics and Political Science* 12: 30–41.

———. 1948. "The Stages of a Medical Career." *American Journal of Sociology* 53: 327–36.

———. 1949. "Types of Medical Careers." *American Journal of Sociology* 55:243–53.

Haller, Archibald O., and Alejandro Portes. 1973. "Status Attainment Processes." *Sociology of Education* 46: 51–91.

Hammack, Floyd M., and Peter W. Cookson, Jr. 1980. "Colleges Attended by Graduates of Elite Secondary Schools." *The Educational Forum* 44: 483–90.

Handbook of Private Schools. 1981. Boston: Porter Sargent Publishers, Inc.

Heyns, Barbara. 1974. "Social Selection and Stratification Within Schools." *American Journal of Sociology* 79: 1434–51.

Jaffe, Abraham, and Walter Adams. 1970. "Academic and Socio-Economic Factors Related to Entrance and Retention at Two- and Four-Year Colleges in the Late 1960s." New York: Bureau of Applied Social Research, Columbia University.

Jencks, Christopher, Marshall Smith, Henry Acland, Mary Jo Bane, David Cohen, Herbert Gintis, Barbara Heyns, and Stephan Michelson. 1972. *Inequality.* New York: Basic Books.

Kamens, David. 1974. "Colleges and Elite Formation: The Case of Prestigious American Colleges." *Sociology of Education* 47: 354–78.

———. 1977. "Legitimating Myths and Educational Organizations: The Relationship Between Organizational Ideology and Formal Structure." *American Sociological Review* 42: 208–19.

Karabel, Jerome. 1984. "Status-Group Struggle, Organizational Interests, and the Limits of Institutional Autonomy: The Transformation of Harvard, Yale, and Princeton 1918–1940." *Theory and Society* 13: 1–40.

Karen, David. 1985. "Who Gets into Harvard? Selection and Exclusion." Unpublished Ph.D. dissertation. Department of Sociology, Harvard University.

Kerckhoff, Alan c. 1976. "The Status Attainment Process: Socialization or Allocation?" *Social Forces* 55: 368–81.

———. 1984. "The Current State of Social Mobility Research." *Sociological Quarterly* 25: 139–53.

Klitgaard, Robert. 1985. *Choosing Elites.* New York: Basic Books.

Laumann, Edward O. 1966. *Prestige and Association in an Urban Community: An Analysis of an Urban Stratification System.* Indianapolis: Bobbs-Merrill.

Levine, Steven B. 1980. "The Rise of American Boarding Schools and the Development of a National Upper Class." *Social Problems* 28: 63–94.

Lewis, Lionel S., and Richard A. Wanner. 1979. "Private Schooling and the Status Attainment Process." *Sociology of Education* 52: 99–112.

Mackay-Smith, Anne. 1985. "Admissions Crunch: Top Colleges Remain Awash in Applicants Despite a Smaller Pool." *The Wall Street Journal* (April 2): 1, 14.

Maeroff, Gene I. 1984. "Top Eastern Colleges Report Unusual Rise in Applications." *The New York Times* (February 21): A1, C10.

McLaughlin, James. 1970. *American Boarding Schools: A Historical Study.* New York: Charles Scribner's Sons.

Meyer, John. 1970. "The Charter: Conditions of Diffuse Socialization in School." Pp. 564–78 in *Social Processes and Social Structure,* edited by W. Richard Scott. New York: Holt, Rinehart.

———. 1977. "Education as an Institution." *American Journal of Sociology* 83: 55–77.

Mills, C. Wright. 1956. *The Power Elite.* London: Oxford University Press.

National College Data Bank. 1984. Princeton: Peterson's Guides, Inc.

Oakes, Jeannie. 1985. *Keeping Track: How Schools Structure Inequality.* New Haven: Yale University Press.

Otto, Luther B., and Archibald O. Haller. 1979. "Evidence for a Social Psychological View of the Status Attainment Process: Four Studies Compared." *Social Forces* 57: 887–914.

Parkin, Frank. 1979. *Marxism and Class Theory: A Bourgeois Critique.* New York: Columbia University Press.

Persell, Caroline Hodges. 1977. *Education and Inequality.* New York: Free Press.

Robinson, Robert V. 1984. "Reproducing Class Relations in Industrial Capitalism." *American Sociological Review* 49: 182–96.

Rogers, Everett M., and D. Lawrence Kincaid. 1981. *Communications Networks: Toward a New Paradigm for Research.* New York: Free Press.

Rogers, Everett M., and Judith K. Larsen. 1984. *Silicon Valley Fever: The Growth of High-Tech Culture.* New York: Basic Books.

Rosenbaum, James E. 1976. *Making Inequality: The Hidden Curriculum of High School Tracking.* New York: Wiley.

———. 1980. "Track Misperceptions and Frustrated College Plans: An Analysis of the Effects of Tracks and Track Perceptions in the National Longitudinal Survey." *Sociology of Education* 53: 74–88.

Sewell, William H., Archibald O. Haller, and Alejandro Portes. 1969. "The Educational and Early Occupational Attainment Process." *American Sociological Review* 34: 82–91.

Sewell, William H., Archibald O. Haller, and George W. Ohlendorf. 1970. "The Educational and Early Occupational Status Achievement Process: Replication and Revision." *American Sociological Review* 35: 1014–27.

Social Register. 1984. New York: Social Register Association.

Stolzenberg, Ross M. 1975. "Occupations, Labor Markets and the Process of Wage Attainment." *American Sociological Review* 40: 645–65.

Useem, Michael. 1984. *The Inner Circle: Large Corporations and the Rise of Business Political Activity in the U.S. and U.K.* New York: Oxford University Press.

Wellman, Barry. 1981. "Network Analysis from Method and Metaphor to Theory and Substance." Working Paper Series 1B, Structural Analysis Programme, University of Toronto.

Wilson, Kenneth L., and Alejandro Portes. 1975. "The Educational Attainment Process: Results from a National Sample." *American Journal of Sociology* 81: 343–63.

Winerip, Michael. 1984. "Hot Colleges and How They Get That Way." *New York Times Magazine* (November 18): 68ff.

_____CHAPTER 27_____

SOCIAL CLASS AND
POLITICAL PARTICIPATION

LEONARD BEEGHLEY

Among traditional conceptions of democracy is the idea that the political process should be pluralist. First, people should act within the rules to influence public policy. These rules stipulate that unruliness (any form of disruption or violence) is not appropriate because procedures exist for changing policies. When such procedures are followed, so the ideology holds, decisions about societal goals, priorities, and resource distribution are accepted, even by those whose interests are harmed. Second, access to the political arena should be open: anyone can compete for power, and today's losers may be tomorrow's winners. As a result of this competitive process, it is said, officials are held accountable for decisions and conflicts are resolved without unruliness.

Adherence to these fundamental values, we are told, makes the U.S. different from other nations (Dahl, 1967). Yet voting, the primal democratic act, has very low rates of participation in the U.S., both historically and in comparison to other Western democracies. This fact, which reflects class differences, suggests that fundamental American values are unrealized and that a potential source of instability exists if those who are left out of the political process come to believe they have little recourse but unruliness.

Why do class differences in the rate of political participation exist? In exploring this question, I take

seriously Durkheim's (1982:128) dictum that it is "in the nature of the society itself that we must seek the explanation of social life." Thus, my theoretical orientation is that the organization of society affects the range of options people have and that such choices are external and coercive over individuals. From this theoretical vantage point, I will try to explain why social facts produce different rates of participation in various classes and what such variations imply.

This approach is different from most research on participation which focuses on how correlates explain some portion of the variance individual action. For example, Verba and Nie (1972) describe a "standard socioeconomic model" that shows that the best predictors of a person's political participation are socioeconomic status and a set of psychological correlates, called "civic orientations." While this information is very important to understanding the political process, it is not dealt with here. Rather, I will show that the rate of political participation is a societal characteristic and its explanation requires assessment of factors located in the social structure. . . .

A structural analysis of participation contributes to understanding in two ways. First, it juxtaposes and makes sense of data that are extant but often unconnected and seemingly "elusive." Second, it goes beyond common sense interpretations of the "standard socioeconomic model" by looking at the findings in a broader context. . . . I want to explain how social structure influences the range of choices people have, thereby producing varying rates of behavior among those in different locations in the society. This is . . . a common sociological concern. . . .

From *Sociological Forum* 1(3) (Summer 1986), pp. 496–513. Reprinted by permission of the author and Plenum Publishing Corporation. Some footnotes have been deleted.

SOCIAL CLASS AND POLITICAL PARTICIPATION

While voting has great significance, political participation is a multidimensional process. In looking at class variations in participation, I use Olsen's (1982) typology . . . : the first three categories (cognitive, expressive, and organizational) serve as preconditions for participation in the next three categories (electoral, partisan, and governmental). In addition, organizational participation provides a basis for what I will call interest representation, having one's interests protected as a function of group membership. I shall focus on the extreme cases: the poor, who display the lowest rate of all forms of participation, and the rich, who display the highest.

Cognitive Participation

Citizens obtain information about issues by watching television news, listening to radio, talking with friends and coworkers, reading newspapers and magazines, and responding to contacts from the political parties or groups to which they belong. Thus, people participate by developing knowledge of public issues. All observers report that cognitive participation, as indicated by exposure to the media or any measure of political awareness, is class related (Olsen, 1982:77; Miller, Miller, and Schneider, 1980:306–311). Thus, the lower the socioeconomic status, the lower the rate of cognitive participation. This fact means a smaller proportion of the poor and a higher proportion of the rich have the information necessary to be active. Further, since the poor are more reliant on less intellectually demanding media (such as television) and belong to groups at much lower rates, the quality of their information is lower (Graber, 1976).

Expressive Participation

In addition to obtaining information, citizens also express opinions to others. Such exchanges are political acts in that people mutually inform and persuade each other. Again, all observers report that expressive participation, as indicated by political conversations or any measure of "communal activity" is class related (Olsen, 1982:77; Verba and Nie, 1972:132). Further, ethnographic data suggest that the poor display a higher level of social isolation than do the nonpoor (Howell, 1973; Stack, 1974). Thus, the lower the socioeconomic status, the lower the rate of expressive participation. Since conversation is an energizing act, this fact means that fewer of the poor and more of the rich are stimulated to be active in other ways. In addition, the poor are more likely to have friends who are less informed and belong to groups with fewer resources. Therefore, the quality of their information is lower than that of other classes.

Organizational Participation

Americans are joiners; more than 60 percent of all adults belong to some voluntary organization. Group participation is related to political participation, even when the object of the group is manifestly nonpolitical (Verba and Nie, 1972:174–209). This is because organizations provide a forum within which people discuss issues and stimulate each other to participate. Further, groups often become politically mobilized when their interests or those of their members are affected. As before, all observers report that organizational participation is class related, no matter what measure is used (Olsen, 1982:77; Verba and Nie, 1972:204). Thus, the lower the socioeconomic status, the lower the rate of group participation. As a result, fewer of the poor and more of the rich have the information and motivation to be active politically in other ways.

More significantly, group membership provides people with a means for interest representation. For example, members of such occupations as auto workers, physicians, bankers, farmers, and even sociologists, belong to organizations that disseminate information, thereby making it easier to vote, to appear on party mailing lists, and to lobby legislative and bureaucratic office-holders. Similarly, people with special interests, such as gun owners, municipal bond owners, owners of timber, coal, and other resources, also belong to groups which represent their particular needs. Thus, many persons need only join and, of course, pay dues, in order to have their interests protected by the group and its representatives. This fact illustrates the reality underlying Alford and Friedland's [1975] notion of "power without participation," . . . middle-class and rich persons often participate by having their interests represented for them.

In sum, these three modes of participation—gaining information, talking with others, and joining groups—provide a basis for subsequent types of action, either directly by individuals or through their representatives.

Electoral Participation

In the presidential elections of 1972, 1976, and 1980, an average of 54 percent of the eligible adult population voted (U.S. Bureau of the Census, 1984:492). Thus, the necessary majority to choose the president and other public officers elected at the same time is about a quarter of the electorate. Turnout during off-year elections is even lower. For example, only 35 percent of those eligible actually cast ballots in U.S. House of Representatives races. The figure was only 16 percent in Georgia, the lowest in the nation (U.S. Bureau of the Census, 1984:492). Part of the reason for such low turnouts is the large number of "safe"—relatively uncontested—House seats. However, since most gubernatorial elections occur in off-years, these figures mean that the governors of most states and many other public agents are chosen by only 15 to 20 percent of all eligible citizens. . . . I shall argue that (within limits) such officials represent the interests of those who vote.

Table 27.1 shows the relationship between socioeconomic status and two indicators of electoral participation. First, the percent of all adults reporting registration and voting in 1980 decreased as their income decreased. Second, the gap between the percent registered and percent voting widened as income declined. Thus, the lower the socioeconomic status, the lower the rate of electoral participation. This fact suggests that the poor have little influence on public policy because elected officials are not dependent on their votes.

Although the figures are not shown in Table 27.1, most nonvoters come from lower income groups. Thus, one-third of those who did not participate in the 1980 election had family incomes of less than $10,000 in that year and another one-third had family incomes between $10,000 and $20,000 (U.S. Bureau of the Census, 1982:66). Those not participating in the electoral process are the poor and the near poor.

TABLE 27.1 Participation in 1980 Presidential Elections by Family Income

1 FAMILY INCOME LEVEL	2 ADULTS REPORTED REGISTERED (%)	3 ADULTS REPORTED VOTED (%)	4 DIFFERENCE BETWEEN COLUMNS 2 AND 3
< $5,000	51	40	11
$5,000–9,999	58	49	9
$10,000–14,999	64	55	9
$15,000–19,999	67	60	7
$20,000–24,999	74	67	7
> $25,000	79	74	5

Source: U.S. Bureau of the Census (1982:66).

Partisan Participation

Political partisans identify with and work for a candidate. The range of participation varies from casual to intense, from wearing a button, to doing volunteer work, contributing money, advising candidates on strategy, writing position papers, organizing demonstrations, and other activities designed to influence the selection of decision makers. All observers report that partisan participation is class related, regardless of the measure used (Olsen, 1982:77; Verba and Nie, 1972:80, 100). Consider campaign contributions, one of the most important forms of partisan activity: only 13 percent of the population donated any amount of money to 1980 Congressional campaigns, and this was an all-time high. These individuals accounted for 67 percent of House and 78 percent of Senate candidates' funds (Alexander, 1984). The majority of these contributors are rich, white, and male (Berg, Eastland, and Jaffe, 1981). Thus, the lower the socioeconomic status, the lower the rate of partisanship. This fact means that lower class people have little influence because elected officials and government administrators are not dependent on their monetary contributions.

Government Participation

The range of efforts to influence government (lobbying) can vary from making a phone call to a school board member to visiting a Congressperson in Washington. But few citizens lobby very often and those who do are primarily middle and upper class (Olsen, 1982; Miller, Miller, and Schneider, 1980:305). Thus, the lower the socioeconomic status, the lower the rate of government participation. This fact means that lower class people have little influence because elected officials and government administrators do not hear from them.

The six political roles sketched above are interrelated. They are presented so as to show increasing levels of political activity by individuals and, at the same time, to suggest the importance of interest representation. Only about 11 percent of the population are complete activists (Verba and Nie, 1972:119),

engaging in all roles. They are overwhelmingly from middle and upper class backgrounds and, given the significance of group membership, elected officials are very dependent on them for support. As a result, their interests are well represented while those of the poor are ignored.

SOME HISTORICAL AND COMPARATIVE DATA

Yet this need not be the case. I focus here on voting, partly because of its intrinsic importance but also because the necessary data are available. Voting rates in the U.S. are very low today compared to the past and to those existing in other democracies.

Among those who were eligible, voting levels were very high in the U.S. during the last quarter of the nineteenth century. For example, Burnham (1980) shows that during the period 1874–1892 an average of 79 percent of all eligible citizens voted in presidential elections, while 65 percent voted in off-year congressional elections. In the non-Southern and most densely populated states, however, average turnout rates for presidential elections were even higher: for example, 93 percent in Indiana, 92 percent in New Jersey and Ohio, 89 percent in New York, 83 percent in Pennsylvania. In off-year congressional elections, these same states had average turnouts of 84 percent in Indiana, 77 percent in New Jersey and Ohio, 68 percent in New York, and 71 percent in Pennsylvania. Such figures indicate that nearly all eligible citizens were mobilized to vote in those states where most of the population lived. Thus, class variation in electoral participation was far less than today, at least in the north. But it does not follow that the poor were better represented in the nineteenth century because many groups denied voting rights at that time were impoverished (e.g., blacks and immigrants).

In comparison to the U.S., the voting profile by social class is much different in other Western democracies. For example, in most Western European nations the lower classes have voting levels as high or higher than the middle and upper classes. For example, Table 27.2 depicts voter turnout in Sweden

TABLE 27.2   Voter Turnout in Sweden, 1979, by Income

1979 INCOME (SWEDISH CROWNS)	1979 VOTER TURNOUT (%)
Less than 10,000	89
10,000–29,999	86
30,000–49,999	91
50,000 or more	90

Source: National Central Bureau of Statistics (1981:418).

in 1979 by income and shows that electoral participation does not vary appreciably along class lines. Turnout levels have been between 80 and 90 percent in all Swedish elections since World War II (Burnham, 1980), a pattern common throughout Western Europe (Powell, 1980).

These examples show clearly that class variation in voting is not inevitable. My argument is that the only way to understand why contemporary American society displays such differences in electoral and other forms of participation is to look at structural factors.

HOW STRUCTURAL FACTORS PRODUCE CLASS VARIATIONS IN PARTICIPATION

The poor display the lowest rate of all forms of participation for three reasons, all structural: they have fewer political resources, fewer psychological resources, and the organization of the electoral process inhibits their participation. While the notions of political and psychological resources may seem to refer to individual characteristics, the distribution of these factors varies according to location in the social structure.

Level of Political Resources

The most important political resource in the U.S. is clearly money. Beeghley (1983:23) shows that a family of four living at the poverty line in 1981 had $2.12 per person for food each day and $516 per month to pay for rent, utilities, and all other needs. Such families have little money for newspapers and other print media. However, 98 percent of all Americans do have television sets (U.S. Bureau of the Census, 1984:592), so the poor rely heavily on television, the least informative medium, for information. In addition, their budgets do not allow much for transportation to meetings, so expressive, organizational, electoral, partisan and governmental participation is difficult.

Most importantly, the budget for a poor family does not include money for campaign contributions. While this is also true for families living well above the poverty line, the poor are least able to donate. As a result, they are least likely to appear on candidate or party mailing lists, and least likely to be contacted and mobilized to participate (Zipp, Landerman, and Luebke, 1982). Since contact increases both cognitive and expressive participation, and, hence, motivation to vote, display partisanship, and lobby, the poor are excluded from one of the main avenues of involvement in a pluralist system.

The importance of campaign contributions cannot be overstated, for elected public officials attend to those who contribute to campaigns and to voters, in that order (Green and Waldman, 1982). Nonvoters are ignored, mainly because there is a high correlation between level of campaign spending and winning elections. As a result, there is also a high correlation between social class and access to public officials. And access means influence. At every stage of the legislative, rule making, and rule enforcing process, the rich have more influence than any other class (Green and Waldman, 1982). This is why public policy generally favors their interests.

Another important factor affecting participation is membership in organizations. Belonging has two consequences: (1) Attending meetings provides people with information and motivation to participate in other ways, and (2) depending on the organization, simply joining insures interest representation. But group membership requires social and economic resources the poor often lack: decent clothing, energy, transportation, literacy, child care, time, freedom from fear, money for dues, etc. For those with little money these problems often become insurmountable obstacles to membership.

Attending meetings is difficult for those who lack education, fear for their personal safety, and work at physically tiring jobs. Individuals who do not read well or speak correctly feel out of place and so withdraw from situations, such as voluntary organizations, in which these deficiencies are obvious. In addition, crime also affects meeting attendance, since in many poor neighborhoods people are afraid to go out at night. Middle class white people often avoid poor areas, especially at night and especially if the areas are black neighborhoods. Yet the residents of these areas, who are far more likely to be victimized by crime, often avoid going out at night also. Finally, the nature of the work people do affects their ability to attend meetings, simply in terms of the amount and kind of energy people have. Thus, at the end of a long day, white-collar people are often so psychologically tired that they want to work off excess physical energy, which means going to a meeting at night may be inconvenient but it is not physically difficult. In contrast, blue-collar employees are often so physically exhausted at the end of the day that they have less ability to attend a meeting. Thus, differences in education, fear of crime, and type of work (among other variables) help explain why the poor join associations and attend meetings at lower rates—and, hence, display lower levels of political participation.

Another result of group membership is interest representation. By joining, paying dues, and maintaining contributions to a group's political action committee, people participate by employing others to protect their interests. Although few citizens ever lobby government officials directly, this category of participation is misleading because thousands of lobbyists are paid to do this task. Thus, while very few farmers, physicians, bankers, or sociologists go to

Washington, their associations systematically try— often successfully—to influence public policy.

In sum, because of their location in society, poor people have fewer political resources (money, time, energy, education, freedom from fear) that are necessary for participation in a pluralist system. Thus, regardless of their formal right to obtain information, express their opinions, join groups, vote, contribute to campaigns, and lobby officials, the poor have less input to public policy than any other class. As a result, their interests are ignored.

Level of Psychological Resources

Political participation is also affected by a variety of psychological resources which fewer poor persons possess: feelings of competence, beliefs that political decisions can be made in one's own interests, and a generalized sense that political issues are important. These are the civic orientations referred to in Verba and Nie's "standard socioeconomic model." Instead of looking at individuals, however, I am interested in how the distribution of these characteristics across social class relates to different rates of behavior.

The psychological resources described above are distributed differently by class. Measures of political efficacy commonly show that the poor think they have less say in political decisions and less influence over decision makers than members of any other class (Miller, Miller, and Schneider, 1980:125–238). And they are right, of course, for impoverished persons typically do not control their own destiny. For example, they do not have job protection if they are fired unjustly or legal aid if they are denied unemployment compensation. They do not have legal or monetary resources if they are evicted from their homes illegally or if landlords do not maintain their dwellings properly. If they are female, they have less access to contraception or abortion and, hence, cannot control what happens to their own bodies (Beeghley, 1983). As a result, their sense of competence in solving problems, even the most personal ones, is low. In this context, the structure of the electoral process exacerbates the precarious position of the poor, creating barriers to participation.

The Structure of the Electoral Process

Electoral procedures are so designed that the poor are least able to participate. Where possible, I will illustrate this fact by comparing the U.S. and Western European societies.

Election Day.   In most Western European nations, election day either occurs on Sunday or is a national holiday, which means that there is leisure time available to vote. This fact helps to explain why electoral participation rates are very high, usually between 80 and 90 percent, and class differences are minimal.

In the U.S., election day is Tuesday and, partly as a result, participation rates are much lower and class differences are great. Voting during the week is a structural barrier to participation. Those who overcome this obstacle in the greatest numbers have longer lunch hours, leave-time built into their jobs, more physical energy at the end of the day, child care available, and belief in their own competence. These traits, however, are class related, which is why participation is also class related.

Voting   Procedures.   Voting   procedures   have become more complex. In the nineteenth century, citizens simply dropped a printed ticket into the ballot box, a practice making it almost impossible to vote a split ticket. The "Australian ballot," which identifies all the candidates for each office on one piece of paper and requires citizens to mark their choices, was introduced in all states around the turn of the century. This procedure significantly changed the electoral process, making it easier to vote a split ticket. Because citizens can exercise more choice, this change seems inherently democratic. But it also requires greater knowledge and reading skill, which is one reason why electoral participation rates began to decline around 1900 (Burnham, 1980).[1] The paradox, of course, is that a reform designed to increase democracy produced less of it, if by democracy one means the ability of all citizens to participate in making decisions facing the society. In general, the more complex the ballot, the more difficult it is to vote.

More   recently,   the   introduction   of   voting machines and computer punch cards to speed tabulating results has complicated electoral procedures still more. While few data are available, these changes probably inhibit electoral participation rates among those who are less sophisticated, especially the poor.

Registration Requirements.   In Western European nations, the state automatically registers all citizens to vote, a fact that partly accounts for high electoral participation rates. In the U.S., citizens are responsible for their own registration. Requiring the first act as a condition for the second is a structural barrier to electoral participation.

Registration is often more difficult than voting, for it usually involves a trip to city hall or the county seat during inconvenient hours and well in advance of election day, before the candidates and the issues are salient to many citizens (Rosenstone and Wolfinger, 1978). All these factors are structural barriers to electoral participation, and they affect the poor most of all. The registration requirement was introduced at the turn of the century and, according to some observers, it is a major reason for the decline in electoral participation rates since that time (Burnham, 1980).

There are several plausible estimates of the effect of the registration requirement. Rosenstone and Wolfinger (1978) estimate that if laws had allowed registration up to election day, required extended hours beyond normal work time during the week, required offices to remain open on weekends, and allowed deputy regulation or registration within each precinct, then an additional twelve million people or 9 percent of the electorate would have voted in 1972. Yankelovich (1973) argues that registration kept twenty-six million people, or 19 percent of the electorate, from the polls in 1972. Some additional evidence is available from Ohio, for not all counties in that state have registration requirements. Burnham (1980) shows that turnout in counties without such requirements is 10 to 15 percent higher than in counties where registration is a prerequisite for voting.

The usual rationale for registration requirements is that it prevents corruption. Although there are some famous nineteenth-century examples of election fraud, mainly in a few large cities, it now appears that most elections at that time were relatively honest (Jensen, 1971). In addition, there is no evidence of election fraud in Ohio or in North Dakota, which also does not require registration. Nor does it appear to be a problem in Sweden, Germany, Great Britain, and other Western European nations.

Separation of Local, State, and Federal Elections. Americans go to the polls for different purposes in different elections. Partly as a result, participation rates are very low and class differences are great. State and federal elections are generally separated: only fourteen states ever schedule gubernatorial contests in presidential election years (Jewell and Olson, 1978:50). Similarly, local elections are usually separated from other contests: only 17 percent of all cities larger than twenty-five thousand people hold elections concurrently with either state or federal campaigns (Karnig and Walter, 1977). Finally, many areas hold bond and special district elections at different times. With so much diverse election activity, many people find it difficult to obtain information about candidates and issues and to maintain an interest in voting. Those who are most capable and, in fact, cast ballots at the greatest rate, have access to more demanding media, have friends and colleagues who are interested in these various contests, belong to groups with a stake in the outcomes, and have the time, energy, and money to vote and engage in partisan activities. Such persons are overwhelmingly middle class and rich.

The Frequency of Elections. The separation of electoral contests means that Americans go to the polls often. In one study of six states, citizens voted twice a year between 1972 and 1976 (Boyd, 1981). Frequent trips to the polls are difficult for the poor, especially in view of all the obstacles cited earlier. Furthermore, nineteen states purge their polls of nonvoters every two years (Wolfinger and Rosenstone, 1980), which means that citizens who focus on the "more important" federal elections will often have to

re-register and, prior to so doing, will not have their interests represented at the local level. Such persons are most likely to be poor.

As a last note, Alford and Friedland (1975) emphasize how frequently office holders (both elected and administrative) violate the wishes of citizens—using poll data as their evidence. They conclude that elections mean little. But poll data are misleading because a random sample of the population does not vote. Actually, office holders respond very well to those citizens who either elect them (voters and contributors) or systematically lobby them. They often neglect the interests of nonparticipants.

In sum, while individuals can choose to vote or not, the process is so organized that low rates of participation by the poor are inevitable. Given their location in society, members of this stratum are least capable of voting on Tuesdays, coping with voting procedures, getting registered, overcoming the problem posed by separate elections, and getting to the polls frequently. Low rates of participation would be expected even if the poor did not lack political and psychological resources, and when these traits are coupled with the structure of the electoral process, the effect is cumulative. Thus, for those who live poorly in the U.S., the pluralist system may be open in principle but it is closed in fact.

WHY STRUCTURAL FACTORS PRODUCE CLASS VARIATIONS IN PARTICIPATION

Although participation in the U.S. is positively related to class, this situation is not inevitable. Both historical and comparative findings indicate that such variation need not exist. These observations lead to a structural analysis: different rates of participation result from social facts external and coercive over individuals. Now I wish to suggest why: the issue is power and the benefits that flow from it. My hypothesis is that the higher the rate of participation displayed by a class, then the more benefits its members receive. This assertion does not imply a conspiracy. Rather, it merely recognizes that public policies are not accidents; they reflect decisions made by people who have opportunities to pursue and interests to protect. Thus, as in every society, politics have a class basis in the U.S. (Weber, 1968).

When the current structure of the electoral process was decided upon at the turn of the century, choices were made that produced declining electoral participation, especially among the poor. This result benefitted both middle class reformers and the rich, who began to dominate the political process and continue to do so today. Similarly, the reorganization of campaign finance laws in recent years insures that political resources continue to depend on location in the social structure. The result also benefits the middle class and rich at the expense of other classes. Evidence of their domination can be seen in two ways: Attempts to change the electoral process and thereby reduce class differences in rates of participation are defeated and public policies that benefit the nonpoor are adopted.

Proposals aimed at changing the electoral process so that voting would be easier are regularly introduced and defeated in Congress (Rosenstone and Wolfinger, 1978). For example, bills allowing voters to register by postcard rather than in person were defeated in 1971, 1973, 1975, and 1976. A bill to establish election day registration was defeated in 1977. These decisions do not occur in a political vacuum. A reasonable interpretation of this pattern is that many elected public officials and their constituents have a stake in low turnouts and the exclusion of the poor from the democratic political process.

The nature of the resulting benefits can be suggested by looking at public policies. There are nearly two hundred income transfer programs funded by the federal government and it has been estimated that 80 percent of all expenditures for these programs go to the nonpoor; that is, they are added to the incomes of working class, middle class, and rich people (Lawrence and Leeds, 1978).[2] Agricultural price supports are one example. Such programs provide income support for farmers by making up the difference between the actual market price of commodities and specified target prices. Growers of goods such as wheat, corn, grain, sorghum, barley, cotton, soybeans, tobacco, rice, wool and mohair, sugar, milkcows, and

even bees are eligible for income transfers under certain conditions. In most cases, however, payments to one firm or farm corporation are limited to $50,000 from all programs combined. What is important to remember is that these benefits are added on top of all other income. In comparison, the average family receiving Aid for Families with Dependent Children had $5,400 in disposable income, including food stamps, in 1981 (Beeghley, 1983: 55). Agricultural price supports are not considered public assistance, but in reality they can be seen as a form of guaranteed annual income.

The total cost of supporting the income of farmers was $4.0 billion in 1981, rose to $13.3 billion in 1982, and ballooned to $20.6 billion in 1983 (Executive Office of the President 1984:5–57). This figure does not count billions more in low interest and guaranteed loans made to farmers. During this same period, outlays for public assistance were being cut back drastically. Nearly all the money for agricultural price supports goes to large farmers and farm corporations; small farmers (who need it most) see very little of it. This pattern of increasing farm price supports at a time when government transfers to the nonvoting segment of the population were declining demonstrates the political power of farmers, farm corporations, and farm interest groups. For these income transfers protect agricultural interests from low prices, natural disasters, and even their own mistakes. Here is an example.

The proposed Dairy Production Stabilization Act of 1983 would have reduced price supports in the dairy industry by about 12 percent. It would also have reduced both government costs incurred for storing dairy products and consumer prices. This bill was defeated by a vote of 250–174. Of those representatives who received more than $1,000 in campaign contributions from dairy political action committees (PACs), 95 percent voted against the bill. This is true even for those representatives whose districts have no milk production whatsoever: 97 percent of those receiving more than $1,000 voted against the bill (Public Voice, 1985).

Now there is nothing inherently wrong with agricultural price supports. A case can be made that farm prosperity is in the national interest. My point is merely that these policies reflect the class interest of those who are most capable of making such arguments because a high proportion of them participate in the political roles outlined earlier. And people who participate benefit. Note, however, the way in which they participated in this case: through having their interests represented by such PACs as Associated Milk Producers, Inc., Mid-America Dairymen, Inc., and Dairymen, Inc. (Public Voice, 1985). Simply by belonging, farmers had representatives who lobbied and funneled campaign contributions to members of Congress. In addition, of course, members in such organizations provided farmers with information and motivation necessary for their individual lobbying efforts.

The significance of this example (many more are possible) is that those who benefit from public policy have little interest in changing the social structure so that all are equally able to participate. As noted before, the issue here is not the common good, but power: the maintenance of the political power of the middle class and the rich. Although the organization of the political process insures that the ideal expressed by the term pluralism cannot be met, those who dominate the political process do not define the situation as requiring change.

This fact leads to two paradoxes (Coser, 1967: 53–110). The first paradox is that, on the one hand,

poor persons are told, and for the most part come to believe, that the only legitimate means of influencing public policy is by learning about the issues, joining organizations, voting, contributing money and working for candidates, and lobbying public officials; yet, on the other hand, these modes of participation are effectively closed to them. It is sometimes the case that their only realistic alternative is some form of unruliness (Gamson, 1975; Williams, 1977). Nonetheless, pluralism (as ideology, not fact) means that any unruliness will nearly always be condemned as illegal and immoral by the majority of the population. The second paradox is that, on the one hand, pluralist norms are a means for making societal decisions and resolving conflict without violence; on the other hand, however, they constitute a system of political control that operates to keep members of the lower class in their place.

In sum, my argument is that these paradoxes are built into the American political process. The distribution of political and psychological resources and the organization of the electoral process constitute a normative environment that, as Durkheim would say, is external and coercive to individuals; it is the social context in which data showing class variations in participation must be evaluated. Without such information, the nature of the American political system cannot be fully understood.

NOTES

1. One can argue persuasively that the public good is served by the Australian ballot, even if its complexity results in lower participation by the poor. But this assertion should be made in full knowledge of whose interests are being served.

2. Economists use the term income transfer to refer to government spending that does not add to the Gross National Product because neither goods nor services are obtained in exchange (Samuelson, 1977).

REFERENCES

Alexander, Herbert E. 1984. *Financing Politics: Money, Elections, and Political Reform.* Washington, DC: Congressional Quarterly Press.

Alford, Robert R. and Roger Friedland. 1975. "Political participation and public policy." In A. Inkeles, J. C. Coleman, and N. Smelser (eds.), *Annual Review of Sociology:* 429–479. Palo Alto, CA: Annual Reviews, Inc.

Beeghley, Leonard. 1983. *Living Poorly in America.* New York: Praeger.

Berg, Larry, Larry Eastland and Sherry Jaffe. 1981. "Characteristics of large campaign contributors." *Social Science Quarterly* 62 (September): 409–423.

Boyd, Richard W. 1981. "Decline of U.S. voter turnout: Structural explanations." *American Politics Quarterly* 9 (April): 133–159.

Burnham, Walter Dean. 1980. "The appearance and disappearance of the American voter." In Richard Rose (ed.), *Electoral Participation:* 35–73. Beverly Hills, CA: Sage.

Coser, Lewis A. 1967. *Continuities in the Study of Social Conflict.* New York: Free Press.

Dahl, Robert A. 1967. *Pluralist Democracy in the United States: Conflict and Consent.* Chicago: Rand McNally.

Durkheim, Emile. 1982. *The Rules of Sociological Method.* New York: Free Press.

Executive Office of the President. 1984. *Budget of the United States Government, Fiscal 1985.* Washington, DC: U.S. Government Printing Office.

Gamson, W. A. 1975. *The Strategy of Social Protest.* Homewood, IL: Dorsey Press.

Graber, Doris. 1976. "Press and TV as opinion sources in presidential campaigns." *Public Opinion Quarterly* 40 (Fall): 285–303.

Green, Mark and Michael Waldman. 1982. *Who Runs Congress?* 4th ed. New York: Dell.

Howell, Joseph. 1973. *Hard Living on Clay Street.* Garden City, NY: Doubleday.

Jensen, Richard. 1971. *The Winning of the Midwest.* Chicago: University of Chicago Press.

Jewell, Michael E. and David M. Olson. 1978. *American State Political Parties and Elections.* Homewood, IL: Dorsey Press.

Karnig, A. D. and B. O. Walter. 1977. "Municipal elections: Registration, incumbent success, and voter participation." In *Municipal Year Book:* 41–85. Washington, DC: International City Management Association.

Lawrence, William J. and Stephen Leeds. 1978. *An Inventory of Federal Income Transfer Programs.* White Plains, NY: Institute for Socioeconomic Studies.

Miller, Warren E., Arthur H. Miller and J. Schneider. 1980. *American National Election Studies Data Sourcebook, 1952–78.* Cambridge MA: Harvard University Press.

National Central Bureau of Statistics. 1981. *Statistical Abstract of Sweden.* Stockholm: National Central Bureau of Statistics.

Olsen, Marvin E. 1982. *Participatory Pluralism.* Chicago: Nelson-Hall.

Powell, G. Bingham. 1980. "Voter turnout in thirty democracies." In Richard Rose (ed.), *Electors Participation:* 5–34. Beverly Hills, CA: Sage.

Public Voice for Food and Health Policy. 1985. *Who's Milking Whom? Dairy Money, Dairy Votes, Dairy Production.* Washington, DC: Public Voice.

Rosenstone, Steven J. and Raymond E. Wolfinger. 1978. "The effect of registration laws on voter turnout." *American Political Science Review* 72 (March):22–45.

Samuelson, Paul A. 1977. *Economics.* 10th ed. New York: McGraw-Hill.

Stack, Carol. 1974. *All Our Kin.* New York: Harper.

U.S. Bureau of the Census. 1982. "Voting and registration in the election of November, 1980." *Current Population Reports,* Series P-20, No. 320. Washington, DC: U.S. Government Printing Office.

_____. 1984. *Statistical Abstract of the United States, 1982–83.* Washington, DC: U.S. Government Printing Office.

Verba, Sidney and Norman H. Nie. 1972. *Participation in America: Political Democracy and Social Equality.* New York: Harper and Row.

Weber, Max. 1968. *Economy and Society.* New York: Bedminster Press.

Williams, Robin M., Jr. 1977. *Mutual Accommodation: Ethnic Conflict and Cooperation.* Minneapolis: University of Minnesota Press.

Wolfinger, Raymond E. and Steven J. Rosenstone. 1980. *Who Votes?* New Haven, CT: Yale University Press.

Yankelovich, Daniel. 1973. *A Study of the Registration Process in the United States.* New York: Yankelovich, Inc.

Zipp, John F., Richard Landerman, and Paul Luebke. 1982. "Political parties and political participation: A reexamination of the standard socioeconomic model." *Social Forces* 60 (June): 1140–1153.

PART 10

RACE AND ETHNICITY

The concept of *race* includes social and biological elements. Generally speaking, sociologists are most interested in the social component and in its consequences.

The first "black" Miss America, Vanessa Williams, provides an example of the importance of the social element in the definition of race. I remember vividly when her picture appeared in the newspaper the day after she won the pageant in 1984. After scrutinizing her photograph, a close friend asked me, "What's *black* about her?" Her skin was nearly white (perhaps as dark as a European from the Mediterranean—say a Greek or a southern Italian); her hair and face looked like a Barbie doll's. I told my friend, good sociologist that I am, that what made her "black" was that her parents were "black" (obviously very light brown) and everyone in the community had considered them so.

American soldiers in the Vietnam War provide a second example of the social nature of racial definitions. The Vietnamese made no serious distinction between white and black soldiers. Neither looked Asian; both spoke English. Socially, they were treated alike. Thus, for example, if a Vietnamese woman was predisposed to date an American, black or white made no difference.

The pre-1960s southern United States provides a third illustration. Many states below the Mason-Dixon line had laws against "miscegenation" (intermarriage between the races). What constituted a "Negro" varied from state to state, but in some states it was as little as 1/32 black. Such definitions were as impractical as they were sinister. A person with one "black" grandparent and three "white" grandparents, who is therefore black, can pass for white, pure and simple. And because the personal costs of being the victim of prejudice and discrimination were so high, this biologic fact prompted many light-skinned blacks to deny the black part of their ancestry and pass themselves off as whites. Of course, this would require leaving the community of their birth, where many people would know their true ancestry.

Similar to race, *ethnicity* is a concept combining social and biologic elements. And, as in the case of race, the social element is what interests sociologists most. It is partly revealed in the ability of "ethnic" Americans to pass themselves off as nonethnic. For example, many southern and eastern European immigrants—and perhaps even more of their descendants—"anglicized" their surnames to deflect prejudice and discrimination. Gino Oliveri, whose parents were from Calabria, could become Eugene Oliver.

Racial and ethnic differences would be of little interest to most sociologists if it were not for the pervasive prejudice, discrimination, and conflict that are entwined with such differences. *Prejudice* is a mindset that involves invidious distinctions about groups of people: *Those* people are not like *us*—they are lazy; *they* are not like *us*—they cheat one another; and so on. Prejudice provides a foundation for, but is not the same thing as, *discrimination*. While prejudice is a mindset, discrimination is *behavior* that favors one group over another for no objective reason.

Prejudice and discrimination encourage conflict among groups. The conflict may be minor and subside if *assimilation* (the melding of two or more groups into one) occurs. It may be larger and result in a system of *accommodation* ("We'll live side by side, but will follow certain rules to make sure our groups don't mix too much; e.g., we'll live in separate neighborhoods"). The rules in such a case will, of course, be set by the more powerful of the groups. In its worst form, accommodation amounts to slavery; in its best form, it amounts to *cultural pluralism*—the acceptance of diversity by most members of a society, with few or no strings attached. Finally, the conflict may be enormous and result in the *banishment* or even the *annihilation* (i.e., *genocide*) of a weaker group.

The pervasive and brutal ethnic conflicts of the 1990s, as typified in Rwanda and Burundi in Africa and in the former states of Yugoslavia (Bosnia/Serbia/Croatia/Kosovo), reveal fundamental principles of social life: Ethnic pride fuels intra- and intersocietal conflict. Ethnic group membership partly determines how others treat you, as well as your chances for economic success. Ethnic group identification is strengthened when the group has a distinct language or dialect; when it has a different religion; when it experiences few intergroup marriages; when it is physically segregated (on a large scale, in its own province or territory; on a smaller scale, in its own neighborhoods); and when its members are forced to rely on one another for material support due to discrimination against them on the part of society's dominant group. Such principles are pertinent in understanding how ethnicity affects social and political affairs not only in developing countries in eastern Europe, Africa, and Asia, but also in the United States and other developed countries.

Each of the selections in Part 10 deals with race and ethnicity as they involve prejudice, discrimination, and conflict. In his classic study of the economic roots of discrimination, Norval D. Glenn—of the University of Texas–documents in his essay reprinted here that whites in the United States have benefited from African Americans being kept low in the occupational structure. Given a constant occupational structure, keeping African Americans down has necessarily kept whites up. The extent of these gains has depended upon the percentage of the employed labor that is African American. For instance, whites benefited little if only one or two percent of the workers are African American. But even moderate discrimination aided whites appreciably where half of the workers have been African American.

Glenn's study is related to another economic-based cause of prejudice and discrimination, *downward social mobility*. In an article published in an earlier edition of *Empirical Approaches to Sociology*, Bettelheim and Janowitz argued—and documented with survey data on U.S. servicemen—that as particular members of the dominant racial or ethnic group in a society experience (or fear) the loss of income, power, or prestige, they are more tempted to blame others; in short, minority groups can become convenient scapegoats.[1] When most of the members of the dominant group in a society experience downward mobility, the prejudice can be overwhelming and lead to atrocities such as Germany's annihilation of the Jews during World War II.

---

[1]Bruno Bettelheim and Morris Janowitz, "Ethnic Tolerance: A Function of Social and Personal Control," pp. 381–392 in Gregg Lee Carter (ed.), *Empirical Approaches to Sociology: Classic and Contemporary Readings*, 2nd edition (Boston: Allyn & Bacon, 1998).

Farley's analyses of the Detroit Areas Surveys have revealed the enduring nature of racial prejudice and discrimination in the United States.[2] Drive through any major American city, and you will find African Americans tending to live in one set of neighborhoods, Latinos in another set, and whites in a third. Everyone knew that this reality was not merely a matter of choice; it was not, that is, that each of these groups simply chose to live apart from the others. Everyone knew that systematic housing discrimination was at work and was partly responsible for the segregated layout of urban neighborhoods. But what everyone knew was very hard to prove scientifically until the Detroit Area Surveys of 1976 and 1992, which showed that it has been whites' unwillingness to live in neighborhoods populated by more than a small percentage of African Americans that has kept our cities racially segregated.[3]

Kasarda demonstrates how the plight of many blacks in the United States worsened in the 1980s, despite tremendous reductions in discrimination during the 1960s and 1970s.[4] His research helps us understand the underlying causes of the cataclysmic rioting in Los Angeles in the spring of 1992, as well as other inner-city riots that have occurred sporadically in the United States throughout the 1990s. Although Kasarda recognizes that there are many causes for the continued impoverishment and forlornness of inner-city residents,[5] his main focus has been on the mismatch between the low education of many inner-city blacks and the high educational demands of recent urban jobs, which are concentrated in white-collar service sectors. Loss of employment opportunities, in turn, had devastating effects on African American families—generating desertions, separations, out-of-wedlock births, single-parent homes, welfare dependency, and crime.

---

[2]See, for example, Reynolds Farley, Charlotte Steeh, Maria Krysan, Tara Jackson, and Keith Reeves, "Stereotypes and Segregation: Neighborhoods in the Detroit Area," *American Journal of Sociology* 100 (1994), pp. 750–780.

[3]Two other critical studies were the "Housing Market Practices Surveys" conducted by the United States Department of Housing and Urban Development. These studies demonstrated that realtors systematically discriminated against African Americans and Latinos, directing them toward minority neighborhoods and away from white ones. See Ronald E. Wienk, Clifford E. Reid, John C. Simonson, and Frederick J. Eggers, *Measuring Racial Discrimination in American Housing Markets: The Housing Market Practices Survey* (Washington, DC: U.S. Department of Housing and Urban Development), April 1979; and Margery Austin Turner, Raymond J. Struyk, and John Yinger, *Housing Discrimination Study: Synthesis* (Washington, DC: The Urban Institute), August 1991.

[4]See, for example, his "Urban Industrial Transition and the Underclass," *Annals of the American Academy of Political and Social Science* 501 (January 1989): 26–47.

[5]For example, Kasarda addresses the issue of why Asians and some Latino groups have fared fairly well in recent years, while the situations of many blacks have worsened. His data reveal that many Asian and some Latino groups have carved out specialized economic enclaves (e.g., restauranting, laundering, green groceries). Importantly, the success of these enclaves is linked to ethnic social customs emphasizing mutual support. For example, many Asian small businesses do not have to rely on white banks to gain financing. Asian businessmen (and in a few instances businesswomen) pool their resources and lend to one another. Furthermore, ethnic-enclave establishments hire almost exclusively their own members, many of whom would likely face employment discrimination by firms outside their enclave. Kasarda proposes that such a system of mutual support would be an important means by which blacks could improve their collective lot.

Kasarda's research meshes well with that of Wilson,[6] who emphasizes two causes of inner-city black impoverishment that are discrimination-related. First, even though they enjoy the protection of antidiscrimination laws, many African Americans are suffering from the discrimination that their parents and grandparents endured. That is, their parents and grandparents were prevented from developing wealth and social connections that they could pass on to their children; such advantages can be crucial in obtaining a higher education, starting a family business, or landing a first job. Second, the lessening of housing discrimination has allowed an exodus of middle-class blacks from the ghetto. This exodus has two deleterious effects on poor black employment: First, many individuals hear about jobs and find work from those already in the labor market. With the employed minority middle classes leaving the ghetto, poor minorities are bereft of these job-landing networks. Second, the minority middle classes have traditionally provided mainstream role models that help to keep alive the perception that education is meaningful, that steady employment is a viable alternative to welfare, and that family stability is the norm, not the exception. What results is a vicious circle of poverty formation: As the black middle and working classes leave the ghetto, those left behind lose their job-finding networks and role models for working. As this happens, they fall into a lifestyle of unemployment, which, in turn, generates poverty, crime, poor schools, and other social problems. These problems encourage the middle classes all the more to flee the ghetto, and the vicious circle continues.

My own research using over-time census data on the inner-city neighborhood of "South Providence" in Providence, Rhode Island,[7] largely confirms the thinking of Kasarda and Wilson. During the 1970s and 1980s, the American economy, in general, and the South Providence economy, in particular, were restructured drastically. Most significant for African Americans was the deindustrialization of the urban economies in the Midwest and Northeast (including South Providence) and the massive loss of production jobs. Moreover, the restructuring occurred at the same time that upsurges of immigrants from Latin America, Asia, and Africa were entering the workforce and competing with native African Americans for low-skill and entry-level jobs in the urban economy.

One might find an optimistic twist in the implied argument that middle-class African Americans are escaping the "ghetto" and that the race problem in the United States is becoming more and more restricted to poor, inner-city African American neighborhoods. However, Norman Fainstein, of Vassar College, demonstrates in his Part 10 essay that racial segregation has changed little in the United States over the past three decades. Further, he convincingly argues that residential segregation is the root of the "race problem" and that middle-class African Americans suffer under its yoke nearly as much as their poor counterparts.

Fainstein's findings would imply that African Americans of all social classes are more likely than their white counterparts to suffer from mistrust and unhappiness. Indeed, this is confirmed by the research of Michael Hughes (Virginia Polytechnic Institute and State University) and Melvin E. Thomas (North Carolina State University) that is reprinted here. Hughs's and Thomas's analyses of

---

[6]See, for example, Wilson's *The Truly Disadvantaged* (Chicago: University of Chicago Press, 1987), as well as his *When Work Disappears: The World of the New Urban Poor* (New York: Alfred A. Knopf, 1996).
[7]Gregg Lee Carter, "Social Disintegration in Inner-City Black Neighborhoods of the Frostbelt: The Example of South Providence," *Research in Urban Economics 9* (1993): 115–140.

General Social Survey[8] data reveal that even though the lives of many African Americans have improved immensely over the past three decades, their quality of life and overall happiness still lag substantially behind those of whites, generally speaking.

There may be further basis for optimism, however, in observing that education can bring many African Americans into the middle-class, thereby improving not only their own lot but also the nature of race relations, in that black-white problems become less complex—that is, more a matter of simply skin-color differences and less a matter of economic differences (and those cultural differences that are rooted in such differences). Indeed, this optimism is partially validated in the findings presented in Part 10 by Abigail Thernstrom (a senior fellow at the Manhattan Institute) and Stephan Thernstrom (a professor of history at Harvard University). They document that over the last several decades African Americans have steadily become more white collar, more middle-class, and more suburban. Coming hand-in-hand with such progress have been improvements in race relations—to wit, in 1964 fewer than one in five whites reported having a black friend, but by 1989 more than two out of three did. The Therstroms document many other such advances.

Dutch social scientists Matthijs Kalmijn (Ultrecht University) and Gerbert Kraaykamp (Nymegen University) offer further evidence in Part 10 that we can be at least cautiously optimistic about U.S. race relations. More specifically, they show that African Americans are making significant gains in their "cultural capital"—that is, in their participation in high-brow cultural activities such as art, classical music, museum and theater attendance, and reading literature. This, in turn, has increased their likelihood of academic success, and has ultimately reduced black-white differences in educational attainment. In the context of legal and institutional changes that increase opportunities for African Americans, increased educational attainment has and will continue to improve their well-being and reduce some of the key differences between white and black in U.S. society.

---

[8]Except for the years 1979, 1981, and 1992, the General Social Survey (GSS) was conducted annually between 1972 and 1994 by the National Opinion Research Center at the University of Chicago. For each of the survey years, approximately 1,600 adult Americans were asked about their family backgrounds, personal histories, behaviors, and attitudes toward a variety of issues. Beginning in 1996, the survey became biennial and expanded to a sample size of approximately 3,000. Because the National Opinion Research Center uses rigorous scientific sampling strategies and has a high response rate, it is safe to assume that the data are of a very high quality. For more information on the GSS, see its web site at http://www.icpsr.umich.edu/gss/.

_____CHAPTER 28_____

OCCUPATIONAL BENEFITS TO WHITES FROM THE SUBORDINATION OF AFRICAN AMERICANS

NORVAL D. GLENN

That whites in the United States benefit to some extent from African Americans being kept low in the occupational structure may seem obvious. Given a constant occupational structure, keeping African Americans down will necessarily keep whites up. However, . . . the belief that whites gain occupationally at all from the subordination of African Americans is a hypothesis only, and one which is investigated in this paper.

If the hypothesized occupational gains do accrue to whites, the extent of these gains depends upon . . . the percentage of the employed labor which is African American. For instance, whites will benefit little if only 1 or 2 percent of the workers are African American. But even moderate discrimination will aid whites appreciably where half of the workers are African American. . . .

The localities used for testing this hypothesis were the 151 Standard Metropolitan Areas which had 100,000 or more people in 1950, and the workers included were only those in nonagricultural occupations. Limiting the study to the metropolitan nonagricultural labor force very roughly controlled for several factors which influence white occupational status. For instance, the occupational status of whites

in metropolitan areas is generally higher than the status of whites in smaller cities and is markedly higher than the status of rural whites. Therefore, if states or counties were used as units of analysis, differences in the distribution of whites among communities of different sizes would account for much if not most of the variation in whites' status.

Two techniques of analysis were used. First the SMAs were divided into 14 classes according to the relative size of their African American populations in 1950, and the distributions of employed white male and female workers in each class among the nine non-agricultural occupational groups were compiled. [Note that the] relative size of the total African American population was used because the data were originally tabulated for another study, for which the former variable was the more relevant. A partial replication of the present study with data on the relative size of the employed African American labor force produced very nearly the same results reported here and revealed that a complete replication was not necessary.

To save space and make the pattern of variation more apparent, the 14 original classes were collapsed into four and the nine occupational groups were collapsed into five broad categories for presentation of the data here (see Table 28.1). Since the male and female patterns of variation were almost identical, only the male data are shown. An index of occupational status (abbreviated IOS) was computed separately for each sex for employed whites and employed African Americans, and the index values for males

From *American Sociological Review*, 1963. Vol. 28 (June): 443–448. Copyright © 1963 American Sociological Association. Reprinted by permission. Throughout this chapter, the terms "Negro" and "Negroes" have been replaced with the more contemporary "African American" and "African Americans." Footnotes have been either deleted or incorporated into the body of the text.

are shown in Table 28.1. The index is computed by assigning a value to each occupational group according to the median education of its workers as of 1950 and the median income in 1949. The value is above 100 if both the education and income of experienced workers in the occupational group were above parity (defined as the median education and income of all experienced workers); and the value is below 100 if both education and income were below parity. Each worker is assigned value of his occupational group, and the IOS for a number of workers is the average of their individual values. More specifically, the, formula for the index is:

IOS for an occupational group = $\dfrac{a/A+b/B*100}{2}$

[where]

a = median income of experienced workers in the occupational group in 1949.

A = median income of all experienced workers in 1949.

b = median years of school completed by experienced workers in the occupational group as of 1950.

B = median years of school completed by all experienced workers as of 1950.

The male index values are computed from male income and education data, and the female values are computed from female data.

Correlation analysis was the second technique used. IOS values were computed for white employed male workers in each of the 151 SMAs, and Pearsonian coefficients of correlation were computed between the IOS and the percentage of the population African American separately for the Southern, the Border, and the Northern and Western SMAs. These are given in Table 28.2. So many factors aside from the percentage of the population African American are likely to influence white occupational status that any attempt to control for all of these would be futile. In fact, most of these are not measurable in any precise

TABLE 28.1 Occupational Distribution of Employed White Males in Standard Metropolitan Areas with 100,000 or More People, by Percentage of the Population African American, 1950

	PERCENTAGE AFRICAN AMERICAN			
Occupation	**0–2.9**	**3–9.9**	**10–24.9**	**25 and up**
Professional, technical, and kindred workers; and managers, officials, and proprietors, except farm	21.6	24.8	23.8	26.9
Clerical, sales and kindred workers	16.4	17.8	18.5	21.5
Craftsmen, foremen, and kindred workers	23.2	22.4	24.2	25.4
Operatives and kindred workers; and service workers except private household	31.0	28.1	27.8	22.7
Private household workers, and laborers (except farm and mine)	7.8	6.9	5.7	3.5
Total	100.0	100.0	100.0	100.0
White IOS	112	114	114	117
African American IOS	94	96	94	94
Ratio of white to African American IOS	1.19	1.19	1.21	1.24
Number of SMAs				
Southern	0	0	9	21
Border	2	8	14	0
Northern and Western	52	34	10	0
Total	54	43	33	21

TABLE 28.2   Pearsonian Correlations, by Region

	ZERO-ORDER	WITH SIZE OF TOTAL POPULATION HELD CONSTANT
Between percentage of the population African American and the white IOS		
South (N=30)	+.441	+.464
Border (N=24)	+.499	+.417
North and West (N=97)	+.276	+.203
Between percentage of the population African American and the median income of white persons		
South (N=30)	+.315	+.367
Border (N=24)	+.541	+.429
North and West (N=97)	+.484	+.424

manner. However, one variable was controlled for, the total size of the populations of the SMAs. This variable is known to be positively associated with white occupational status, and there was reason to suspect that outside of the South, population size might be commonly and highly enough associated with the two variables being investigated to produce a spurious correlation between them. The partial correlations with population size held constant are also given in Table 28.2. . . .

FINDINGS

The white IOS both for males and females increased appreciably from the lower to the upper end of the scale of percentage of the population African American. . . . [Moreover,] the percentage of white workers in seven of the nine occupational groups varied in an approximately linear fashion with the percentage of the population African American. The percentage of whites who were craftsmen, foremen, and kindred workers remained almost constant, and professional and technical workers increased very slightly but not consistently up the scale. The percentages of whites in the other three more desirable

occupational groups varied directly with the relative size of the African American population, and the percentages in the four least desirable ones varied inversely. The failure of white professional workers to increase consistently up the scale can be attributed to African Americans' providing considerable professional service (such as teaching) for themselves and a generally lower proportion of professional and technical workers in the Southern SMAs.

The percentage of the population African American and the white IOS were positively correlated in each region, but the correlations were only moderate among the Southern and Border SMAs and small among the Northern and Western ones. Since the relative size of the African American population is only one of many factors which influence white occupational status, it is not surprising that the correlations were not higher. In the North and West, African Americans were numerous enough to affect white status appreciably only in a few SMAs, so a very large proportion of the variation in white status is accounted for by factors other than the relative size of the African American population. Holding constant the size of the total populations of the SMAs affected the correlations little, but it did reduce somewhat the values for the Border and the Northern and Western SMAs. . . .

In [sum,] . . . gains to whites from discrimination against African Americans [in] the occupational [arena] . . . are important. The rewards of higher occupational status are not merely monetary but include greater prestige, more pleasant working conditions, greater authority and independence, and other advantages. Furthermore, a given amount of money income was probably greater "real income" in those SMAs with the larger African American populations. Data are not available which allow an accurate comparison of costs of living in the different SMAs in or around 1950. However, domestic help undoubtedly cost less in the Southern SMAs, as probably did almost all services and goods produced by local labor. Whites in the Southern SMAs almost certainly enjoyed a more favorable style of life than did whites in the SMAs in which a smaller percent-age of the people were African Americans.

CONCLUSIONS

The data presented here leave little doubt that in 1950 whites in American metropolitan areas which had large African American populations were benefiting occupationally from the presence and low status of African Americans. These data suggest that American whites in general were and still are benefiting from anti–African American discrimination.

The findings of this study lend credence to the view that discrimination and its supporting prejudice persist mainly because majority people gain from them. One should not go so far as to attribute the perpetuation of discrimination entirely to its functions to the majority, nor should the many known and possible dysfunctions of discrimination to the majority be overlooked. However, one should also avoid viewing discrimination as merely a self-perpetuating carry-over from a past era which will certainly and rapidly disappear. . . . [Indeed,] the tradition of discrimination against African Americans apparently receives continuous reinforcement from the present self-interests of the majority.

CHAPTER 29

THE CONTINUING SIGNIFICANCE OF RACE REVISITED:

A STUDY OF RACE, CLASS, AND QUALITY OF LIFE IN AMERICA, 1972 TO 1996

MICHAEL HUGHES
MELVIN E. THOMAS

More than a decade ago, we (Thomas and Hughes 1986) demonstrated that the subjective well-being of African Americans in the United States was significantly and consistently lower than it was for whites over the 14-year period from 1972 to 1985. In the intervening years, evidence has accumulated that African American mental health and self-esteem is as good as or better than that of whites (Kessler et al. 1994; Porter and Washington 1989, 1993; Williams, Takeuchi, and Adair 1992). Yet racial inequality remains a persistent feature of American life (Bennett 1995; Thomas, Herring, and Horton 1994). Whether and how African Americans' well-being may have changed since 1985 is unclear. We update our 1986 study using data from all General Social Surveys conducted over the 25-year period from 1972 through 1996.

BACKGROUND

The Original Study

In 1986 we found that African Americans' sentiments about society and their place in it, what Schuessler (1982) termed "social life feelings," were consider-

From *American Sociological Review* 63 (December 1998), pp. 785–795. Copyright © American Sociological Association. Reprinted by permission. Some footnotes have been incorporated as additional endnotes or deleted.

ably less positive than were those of whites (Thomas and Hughes 1986). We found that African Americans were less satisfied, less happy, more mistrustful, more anomic, had less happy marriages, and rated their physical health worse than whites. Controls for socioeconomic status, marital status, and age did not eliminate these differences. In addition, racial differences on these variables did not narrow significantly between 1972 and 1985, and trends were the same for African Americans of different class levels. Comparisons with research done in the years 1957 through 1972 (Bracy 1976) indicated that there had been no improvement in African Americans' happiness and satisfaction over nearly a 30-year period.

These findings were particularly noteworthy because the years 1972 through 1985 overlapped with a period of significant improvement in civil rights and social status for African Americans. The racial disparity in quality of life over these years strongly suggested that lingering social and economic disadvantages exerted a powerful negative effect on the subjective well-being of African Americans (Farley and Allen 1987; Feagin 1991; Feagin and Sikes 1994; Willie 1979).

Other Research on Well-Being

Recent research has challenged the idea that African Americans' subjective well-being is worse than that of whites. For example, analyses of data from the

Epidemiologic Catchment Area (ECA) study (Robins and Regier 1991; Somervell et al. 1989; Williams et al. 1992), the National Comorbidity Survey (NCS) (Kessler et al. 1994), and the 1994 National Household Survey on Drug Abuse (U.S. Department of Health and Human Services 1996) show that, in general, African Americans are not more likely than whites to have psychiatric disorders. Studies show that African Americans have lower rates than do whites on indicators of depression (Robins and Regier 1991; Somervell et al. 1989; U.S. Department of Health and Human Services 1996), affective disorders, substance-use disorders, comorbidity (three or more disorders) (Kessler et al. 1994), and drug use and drug dependency (Warner et al. 1995). In addition, an analysis of the ECA data found that race did not magnify the negative effect of social class on mental disorder (Williams et al. 1992).

African Americans and whites do not differ in self-esteem (for reviews see Cross 1991; Porter and Washington 1989). Furthermore, African Americans' racial self-esteem is very positive, and their tendency to reject negative racial stereotypes and embrace positive ones is associated with higher self-esteem (Hughes and Demo 1989).

These findings stand in sharp contrast not only to our previous study (Thomas and Hughes 1986) but also to a large body of literature arguing that racism has produced identity problems, psychopathology, anger, and rage among African Americans (e.g., Cose 1993; Grier and Cobbs 1968; Kardiner and Ovesey 1951; Proshansky and Newton 1968). The findings also contradict the idea that racial inequality, which can lead to a reduced sense of personal control (Hughes and Demo 1989), is therefore associated with psychological distress (Mirowsky and Ross 1989).

How can we interpret this apparent contradiction? One possibility is that well-being among African Americans has improved, and that examining recent data on quality of life would show smaller racial differences in well-being, paralleling differences shown for mental disorder and self-esteem. Nonsignificant trends showing convergence between blacks and whites on five of six indicators of well-being in our 1986 study support this interpretation.

Another possibility, however, is that self-reports of quality of life measure dimensions of social life feelings that are distinct from psychiatric diagnoses and self-esteem. Schuessler and Freshnock (1978; also see Schuessler 1982) showed that psychiatric dimensions such as depression and anxiety are different from life satisfaction, pessimism (e.g., anomia), cynicism (e.g., mistrust), and personal morale (e.g., happiness). Such quality-of-life measures are based on respondents' evaluations of the quality of their life experiences not on psychiatric or social standards (Campbell 1981; Campbell, Converse, and Rodgers 1976).[1] Rather than contrasting a serious debilitating or painful condition with its absence, quality-of-life measures indicate both how positive and how negative one's life experience is (Campbell et al. 1976).

Self-esteem, the belief that one is a worthwhile person, is conceptually distinct from both quality of life and mental disorder (Rosenberg 1979; 1981). It is influenced primarily by interactions with significant others (Rosenberg 1979, 1981) that are somewhat insulated from macro-social inequality (Hughes and Demo 1989). Clearly, people can think highly of themselves, be in good psychiatric health, but also be dissatisfied with their quality of life.

Of course, distinct and different do not mean unrelated. Because psychiatric, self-esteem, and quality-of-life indicators tap life feelings that can be relatively positive or negative, they should be correlated. But if they are indeed separate dimensions, they may have different correlations with predictor variables, including race, as is the case cross different dimensions of social life feelings (Schuessler 1982). Different patterns for various outcome variables could indicate that different processes affect various dimensions of life experience.

Observers have long noted considerable resilience in the African American community (e.g., Coles 1964; Cross 1991). The low rates of psychopathology and high levels of self-esteem that coexist with dissatisfaction, anomia, mistrust, and unhappiness may reflect this resilience (also see McCarthy and Yancey 1971; Rosenberg 1979; Yancey, Rigsby, and McCarthy 1972).

DATA AND METHODS

Samples

The data for this study come from African American and white respondents interviewed for the General Social Surveys (GSS) collected over the years 1972 through 1996. The GSS has been conducted for every year during this time period, except during 1979, 1981, 1992, and 1995. Each sample was designed to be representative to noninstitutionalized adults 18 years of age or over in the United States. For most years the sample size is approximately 1,500, with roughly 170 of these respondents being African Americans. African Americans were oversampled in 1982 and 1987 (in our analyses a weighting procedure is used to adjust for this). Recent variations in sampling procedures and questionnaire construction have resulted in some variation in the effective sample size from that indicated here (for details about sampling, weights, and sample ballots, see Davis and Smith 1996).

Variables

Except for two differences in how the data were coded, our six dependent variables are identical to those used in 1986 (Thomas and Hughes 1986); a *life satisfaction index*, a *general happiness item*, a *marital happiness item*, a *mistrust index*, an *anomia index*, and a *self-rated physical health item* (see Appendix A for descriptions of variables). The differences are: (1) The variables in the *trust* index in the original study have been coded so that this index is a *mistrust* index in the present study, and (2) all dependent variables have been standardized to a mean of 100 and a standard deviation of 10.

Data for all six dependent variables are not available for all years of the GSS. In each of our analyses we use all available data and the findings show the years for which data are available.

Control variables in the present study also are the same as those used in 1986 (Thomas and Hughes 1986); *education, family income* (standardized within survey year),[2] *work status* (employed versus unemployed), *marital status* (married versus not currently married), and *age*. Income, education, and employment variables were selected as controls to test the hypothesis that racial differences in socioeconomic status could account for any association between race and quality of life. Marital status and age were included to adjust for the racial differences in these variables, both of which are associated with quality of life. Gender is not included as a control variable because including it with these other control variables does not influence the findings. . . .

FINDINGS

Racial Differences in Quality of Life

[Multivariable analyses] revealed that there are substantial and significant racial differences in all six quality-of-life variables: African American respondents indicate lower life satisfaction, happiness, and marital happiness, and greater anomia and mistrust (where differences are greatest), and worse health. . . .

Figure 29.1 shows the dependent variables for blacks and whites by year, adjusted for controls. The absence of a data marker on a graph indicates that data were not available for that year.

Except for curvilinear effects of year on all variables but marital happiness, these patterns are very similar to those from our previous study (Thomas and Hughes 1986) and indicate no significant alteration in the black disadvantage in quality of life from 1972 to 1996. There are consistent racial differences over time in happiness, marital happiness, anomia, and mistrust, and nearly consistent differences in life satisfaction and health. On anomia and mistrust, where trends for blacks and whites differ significantly, blacks remain substantially disadvantaged, although measures for whites have come a little closer to those for blacks in recent years.

It appears that blacks' life satisfaction exceeded that of whites in 1994. However, the 1994 GSS included only 48 blacks and 389 whites with complete data on life satisfaction.[3] In that year, with a larger effective sample size for the happiness analysis (313 blacks and 2,201 whites), the black disadvantage in happiness was substantial. On the health

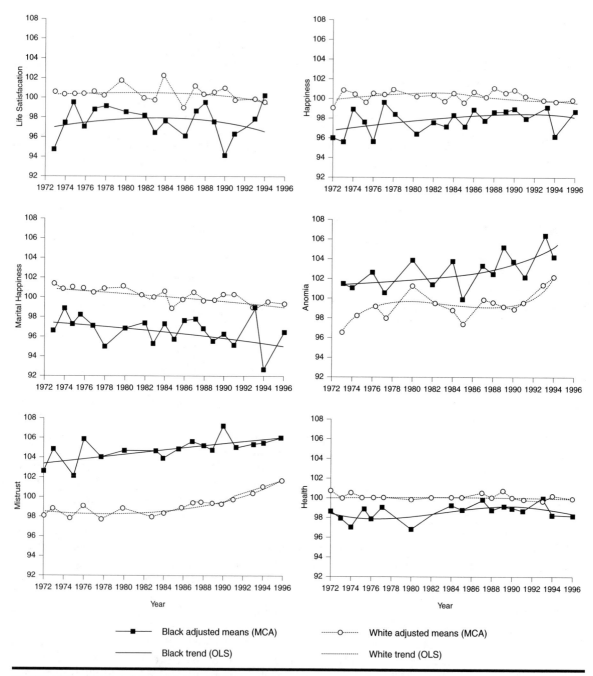

FIGURE 29.1 Quality-of-Life Variables by Year and Race, Controlling for Income, Education, Work Status, Marital Status, and Age: General Social Surveys, 1972-1996

variable, where racial differences are smaller than for other life-quality variables, the adjusted mean health ratings for blacks exceeded those of whites by a small amount in one year (1993).

The curvilinear associations in our analyses could be due to the effects of events, measurement error (e.g., the effect of question context), or sampling error. If these fluctuations represent real changes in quality of life, they suggest that slight improvements in the early to mid-1980s, particularly for whites, have eroded in the late 1980s and early 1990s. The design of our analysis does not allow us to determine what, if any, events or processes are responsible for these changes.

Are Racial Differences Declining for the Black Middle Class?

If, as suggested by Wilson's (1978) thesis about the declining significance of race, life chances have been improving more for middle- and upper-class blacks than for those in the lowest classes, life quality among upper status blacks may have become more like that of whites. . . .

We investigated this possibility but found that the results of these analyses show that trends over time in quality of life by race do not vary by education or income. This indicates that life quality has not improved more for African Americans in the upper and middle classes than for those in the lower classes.

DISCUSSION AND CONCLUSION

In 1986 we (Thomas and Hughes 1986) found that race significantly influenced quality of life in the United States from 1972 to 1985. Here we have demonstrated that blacks' disadvantage in quality of life continues into the 1990s. Analyses of the interactions between race and survey year variables show that trends for blacks and whites in life satisfaction, happiness, marital happiness, and health are parallel. Trends for blacks and whites differ on anomia and mistrust, but a large black disadvantage persists in spite of the fact that whites have recently become a little more like blacks on these dimensions. In short,

evidence indicates that African Americans have experienced consistently lower quality of life than have whites between 1972 and 1996, and there is no indication in the GSS data that African American quality of life is improving to the level experienced by whites. In addition, trends for middle- and upper-status African Americans did not differ from those of other African Americans. . . .

In sum [it] is clear is that being black in U.S. society results in a lower quality of life than does being white. Also clear is the substantial degree of racial inequality in U.S. society (Bennett 1995) and the continuing experience of racism in the lives of African Americans (Feagin 1991; Feagin and Sikes 1994). The coexistence of these facts suggests that racial differences in quality of life are produced by racial inequality and the experiences it produces, but exact processes linking these factors have yet to be uncovered.

In 1986 we (Thomas and Hughes 1986) concluded our paper by echoing Willie's (1979) comment that racial discrimination in wages constitutes a racial "tax" on blacks for not being white. We suggested that evidence on well-being variables indicated that the tax was psychological as well. Our present findings suggest that this tax, whose existence can be documented as early as the 1950s, has persisted undiminished into the 1990s.

APPENDIX A. DESCRIPTIONS OF VARIABLES USED IN THE ANALYSIS

The six variables below were standardized to a mean of 100 and a standard deviation of 10:

The *life satisfaction* index is an additive index consisting of five items asking respondents how much satisfaction they get from their (1) family life, (2) friendships, (3) nonworking activities (hobbies, etc.), (4) city or place where they live, and (5) health and physical condition (Cronbach's alpha = .68). Each of the five items was coded from 1 (low satisfaction) to 7 (high satisfaction). Scores were then summed and standardized.

The general *happiness* item is a single item: "Taken all together, how would you say things are these days—would you say you are very happy, pretty happy, or not too happy?"

Marital happiness is a single item: "Taking all things together, how would you describe your marriage? Would you say that your marriage is very happy, pretty happy, or not too happy?" Prior to standardizing, both the general happiness and the marital happiness items were coded as follows: 1 = not too happy, 2 = pretty happy, and 3 = very happy.

The *mistrust* index is an additive index constructed from three items asking respondents (1) if they would say that most of the time people try to be helpful, or that they are mostly looking out for themselves; (2) if they thought most people would try to take advantage of them if they got the chance, or would try to be fair; and (3) if they would generally say that most people could be trusted or that you could not be too careful in dealing with people (Cronbach's alpha = .66). Prior to standardizing the index, the component items were coded as follows: a trusting response = 1, an ambivalent response = 2, and a mistrusting response = 3.

The *anomia* index is an additive index of three items asking respondents: (1) In spite of what some people say, the lot (situation/condition) of the average man is getting worse, not better; (2) It is hardly fair to bring a child into the world with the way things look for the future; and (3) Most public officials (people in public office) are not really interested in the problems of the average man (Cronbach's alpha = .54). Before standardizing, anomic responses were coded 1; other responses were coded 0.

The self-rating of *physical health* is a single item: "Would you say your own health, in general, is excellent, good, fair or poor?" Prior to standardizing, responses were coded 1 = poor, 2 = fair, 3 = good, 4 = excellent.

NOTES

1. Recent studies showing that blacks have similar or lower rates of mental disorder than whites (Kessler et al. 1994; Robins and Regier 1991; Sommervell et al. 1989; U.S. Department of Health and Human Services 1996; Williams et al. 1992) use dichotomous measures of mental disorder—the Diagnostic Interview Schedule [DIS] (Robins et al. 1981) and the Comprehensive International Diagnostic Interview [CIDI] (Robins et al. 1988)—that attempt to mimic a psychiatric interview and generate diagnoses consistent with the third edition of the American Psychiatric Association's *Diagnostic and Statistical Manual of Mental Disorders* (Murphy 1995). These measures use self-reports, but the judgments of whether a person is likely to be ill are those of the clinicians and researchers who developed the criteria and measuring instruments, not those of the person being interviewed. Not qualifying for a disorder says nothing about the quality of one's life, except that serious mental disorder is absent.

2. The family income variable represents relative differences in income within each year. For the purposes of the present study, this variable controls for changes in the income dimension of social class over time, but it does not adjust for absolute gains in income.

3. Because of budget constraints, the GSS questionnaire is designed to ask some questions of only a subset of respondents. In 1994, only 511 respondents were asked the life-satisfaction questions.

REFERENCES

Bennett, Claudette E. 1995. "The Black Population in the United States: March 1994 and 1993." Pp. 20–480 in *U.S. Bureau of the Census, Current Population Reports*. Washington, DC: U.S. Government Printing Office.

Bracy, James H. 1976. "The Quality of Life Experience of Black People." Pp. 443–69 in *The Quality of American Life: Perceptions, Evaluations, and Satisfactions*, edited by A. Campbell, P. E. Converse, and W. L. Rodgers. New York: Russell Sage.

Campbell, Angus. 1981. *The Sense of Well Being in America*. New York: McGraw-Hill.

Campbell, Angus, Phillip E. Converse, and Willard L. Rodgers. 1976. *The Quality of Life in America*. New York: Russell Sage Foundation.

Coles, Robert. 1964. *Children of Crisis: A Study of Courage and Fear*. New York: Dell.

Cose, Ellis. 1993. *The Rage of a Privileged Class*. New York: Harper Collins.

Cross, William E. 1991. *Shades of Black: Diversity in African-American Identity*. Philadelphia, PA: Temple University Press.

Davis, James A. and Tom W. Smith. 1996. *General Social Survey Cumulative Codebook*. Chicago, IL: National Opinion Research Center.

Farley, Reynolds and Walter R. Allen. 1987. *The Color Line and Quality of Life in America*. New York: Russell Sage Foundation.

Feagin, Joe R. 1991. "The Continuing Significance of Race: Antiblack Discrimination in Public Places." *American Sociological Review* 56:101–16.

Feagin, Joe R. and Melvin P. Sikes. 1994. *Living with Racism: The Black Middle-Class Experience*. Boston, MA: Beacon.

Grier, William H. and Price M. Cobbs. 1968. *Black Rage*. New York: Bantam.

Hughes, Michael and David H. Demo. 1989. "Self-Perceptions of Black Americans: Self-Esteem and Personal Efficacy." *American Journal of Sociology* 95:132–59.

Kardiner, Abram and Lionel Ovesey. 1951. *The Mark of Oppression*. New York: Norton.

Kessler, Ronald C., Katherine A. McGonagle, Shanyang Zhao, Christopher B. Nelson, Michael Hughes, Suzann Eshleman, Hans-Ulrich Wittchen, and Kenneth S. Kendler. 1994. "Lifetime and 12-Month Prevalence of *DSM-III-R* Psychiatric Disorders in the United States." *Archives of General Psychiatry* 51:8–19.

McCarthy, John D. and William L. Yancey. 1971. "Uncle Tom and Mr. Charlie: Metaphysical Pathos in the Study of Racism and Personal Disorganization." *American Journal of Sociology* 76:648–72.

Mirowsky, John and Catherine E. Ross. 1989. *Social Causes of Psychological Distress*. New York: Aldine de Gruyter.

Murphy, Jane M. 1995. "Diagnostic Schedules and Rating Scales in Adult Psychiatry." Pp. 253–71 in *Textbook in Psychiatric Epidemiology*, edited by M. T. Tsuang, M. Tohen, and G. E. P. Zahner. New York: John Wiley and Sons.

Porter, Judith R. and Robert E. Washington. 1979. "Black Identity and Self-Esteem: A Review of Studies of Black Self-Concept." *Annual Review of Sociology* 5:53–74.

———. 1989. "Developments in Research on Black Identity and Self-Esteem." *Revue Internationale de Psychologie Sociale* 2:339–53.

———. 1993. "Minority Identity and Self-Esteem." *Annual Review of Sociology*. 19:139–61. Proshansky, Harold and Peggy Newton. 1968. "The Nature and Meaning of Negro Self-Identity," Pp. 178–218 in *Social Class, Race, and Psychosocial Development*, edited by M. Deutsch, I. Katz, and A. R. Jensen. New York: Holt, Rinehart, and Winston.

Prohansky, Harold and Peggy Newton. 1968. "The Nature and Meaning of Negro Self-Identity." Pp. 178–218 in *Social Class, Race, and Psychosocial Development*, edited by M. Deutsch, I. Katz, and A. R. Jensen. New York: Holt, Rinehart, and Winston.

Robins, Lee N. and Darrel A. Regier, eds. 1991. *Psychiatric Disorders in America: The Epidemiologic Catchment Area Study*. New York: Free Press.

Robins, Lee N., John E. Helzer, Jack Croughan, and Kathryn S. Ratcliff. 1981. "The NIMH Diagnostic Interview Schedule: Its History, Characteristics and Validity. *Archives of General Psychiatry*. 38:381–89.

Robins, Lee N., John Wing, Hans-Ulrich Wittchen, John E. Helzer, Thomas F. Babor, Jay Burke, Anne Farmer, Assen Jablenski, Roy Pickens, Darrel A. Regier, Norman Sartorius, and Leland H. Towle. 1988. "The Composite International Diagnostic Interview: An Epidemiologic Instrument Suitable for Use in Conjunction with Different Diagnostic Systems and in Different Cultures." *Archives of General Psychiatry* 45:1069–77.

Rosenberg, Morris. 1979. *Conceiving the Self*. New York: Basic Books.

———. 1981. "The Self-Concept: Social Product and Social Force." Pp. 593–624 in *Social Psychology: Sociological Perspectives*, edited by M. Rosenberg and R. H. Turner. New York: Basic Books.

Schuessler, Karl F. 1982. *Measuring Social Life Feelings*. San Francisco, CA: Jossey-Bass.

Schuessler, Karl F. and Larry Freshnock. 1978. "Measuring Attitudes toward the Self and Others in Society." *Social Forces*. 56:1228–44.

Somervell, P. D., Philip Leaf, Myrna Weissman, Dan Glazer, and Martha Livingston Bruce. 1989. "The Prevalence of Major Depression In Black and White Adults in Five United States Communities." *American Journal of Epidemiology* 130:725–35.

Thomas, Melvin E., Cedric Herring, and Hayward Derrick Horton. 1994. "Discrimination over the Life Course:

A Synthetic Cohort Analysis of Earnings Differences between Black and White Males." *Social Problems* 41:608–28.

Thomas, Melvin E. and Michael Hughes. 1986. "The Continuing Significance of Race: A Study of Race, Class, and Quality of Life in America, 1972–1985." *American Sociological Review* 51:830–41.

U.S. Department of Health and Human Services. 1996. *Mental Health Estimates from the 1994 National Household Survey on Drug Abuse*. Advance Report 15, July. Rockville, MD: National Clearing House for Alcohol and Drug Information.

Warner, Lynn A., Ronald C. Kessler, Michael Hughes, James C. Anthony, and Christopher B. Nelson. 1995. "Prevalence and Correlates of Drug Use and Dependence in the United States." *Archives of General Psychiatry* 52:219–29.

Williams, David R., David T. Takeuchi, and Russell K. Adair. 1992. "Socioeconomic Status and Psychiatric Disorder among Blacks and Whites." *Social Forces* 71:179–94.

Willie, Charles V. 1979. *The Caste and Class Controversy*. Bayside, NY: General Hall.

Wilson, William Julius. 1978. *The Declining Significance of Race*. Chicago, IL: University of Chicago Press.

Yancey, William L., Leo Rigsby, and John D. McCarthy. 1972. "Social Position and Self-Evaluation: The Relative Importance of Race." *American Journal of Sociology*. 78:338–59.

CHAPTER 30

RACE, CULTURAL CAPITAL, AND SCHOOLING:

AN ANALYSIS OF TRENDS IN THE UNITED STATES

MATTHIJS KALMIJN
GERBERT KRAAYKAMP

Differences in schooling are a key factor in the debate on racial inequality in American society. As is well known, the Black-White gap in schooling has narrowed over the course of this century, but even in recent cohorts, Blacks remain at a disadvantage. Although American research has examined several causes underlying this trend (Farley and Allen 1989), the European tradition of research on cultural capital may provide another answer. using individual survey data on cultural socialization, we examine the link between racial inequality in schooling, on the one hand, and exclusion in the cultural domain, on the other hand. More specifically, we assess whether race-specific trends in educational attainment in the 20th century are related to changes in exposure to Euro-American high-status culture in Black and White families.

CULTURAL CAPITAL AND RACIAL INEQUALITY

Racial Differences in Schooling

The American history of racial inequality in schooling can be roughly divided into three periods (Smith 1984). Shortly after Emancipation in 1863, there were signs that schooling was expanding more rapidly

From *Sociology of Education* 69, (January 1996): 22–34.

among Blacks than among Whites. During Reconstruction, the difference in average years of schooling completed by Black and White men declined form 4.39 for men born before 1865, to 3.18 for men born in the 1880s. This period of convergence was followed by a 20-year period of divergence. After 1896, educational opportunities for Blacks were blocked by the so-called separate-but-equal doctrine. As a consequence of this doctrine, all public schools became segregated by race, and Black schools received considerably less governmental support than did White schools. The salaries of teachers in White schools, for example, were about twice as high as those of teachers in Black schools, and pupil-to-pupil ratios in Black schools were 1.7 times as high as in White schools (Card and Krueger 1992). The gap in years of schooling for Black men in the second period increased from 3.02 for men born in the 1880s to 3.46 for men born at the beginning of the 20th century. In the third and longest period, Black-White differences in schooling declined again, even though school segregation persisted until 1954, when it was finally declared unconstitutional in *Brown v. Board of Education*. The schooling gap in the third period decreased from 3.46 for men born at the beginning at this century to .83 for men born in the 1950s. Similar patterns are observed for women (Smith 1984).

Despite the long-term decline of educational inequality in the third period, a racial gap in educational attainment remains. In 1988, the gap between

Blacks and Whites aged 25–34 in years of completed schooling was still .66 years (Farley and Allen 1989). This difference seems modest, but a small difference in average years of schooling is caused by large underlying differences in high school and college completion. For example, in 1988, 83 percent of Black men aged 25–34 were high school graduates, compared to 91 percent of White men. For college graduates, the proportions were 15 percent for Blacks and 28 percent for Whites.

Several factors help explain why a gap in schooling exists. First, the quality and financial support of precollege education in predominantly Black schools has generally been lower than that of predominantly White schools (Card and Krueger 1992). As a result Black students are often not as well prepared to enter and complete college as are White students. A second explanation focuses on racial differences in family background. On average, Black parents have lower levels of schooling and lower family incomes than do White parents. Blacks are also more likely than are Whites to grow up in broken homes and to have more siblings on average. Since all these factors affect children's schooling, part of the gap in schooling can be explained by the less favorable family resources of Black students (Duncan 1968; Grusky and DiPrete 1990; Haveman and Wolfe 1994). Third, with regard to the more recent turnaround in racial inequality, racial differences in schooling can be linked to problems of the inner-city population. The most prominent hypothesis in this respect was suggested by Wilson (1987), who argued that the exodus of Black middle-class families from the inner city has left lower-class blacks with few role models of achievement. In this line of reasoning, the prevalence of unemployment, low-quality jobs, and illegal sources of income in the inner city has lowered the motivation of Black youths to invest in schooling.

Cultural Capital and Educational Inequality

A second and different line of research on educational inequality has focused on the effects of cultural capital on educational attainment. Cultural capital usually refers to socialization into high-brow cultural activities, and this concept includes a variety of tastes and behaviors, such as interest in art and classical music, attendance at theaters and museums, and reading literature. The leading proponent of this tradition is the French sociologist Bourdieu. One of Bourdieu's (1973) contributions to stratification research was the development of a new answer to the old question of how socioeconomic advantages are transmitted across generations. In general, Bourdieu argued that in a time of the rapid expansion of higher education, cultural capital arose as a new ascriptive force in the status-attainment process. More specifically, he contended that children from high socioeconomic backgrounds are more often exposed to highbrow cultural activities at home and that those who acquire cultural capital at home are more likely to do well in school and subsequently to have better chances of achieving high levels of schooling than others. Together, these arguments imply that differences in cultural capital explain part of the association between the socioeconomic positions of parents and their children.

Cultural capital is believed to be an asset in the schooling process for several reasons: Children who are exposed to cultural capital may be better prepared to master academic material, may develop a greater taste for learning abstract and intellectual concepts, and may be favored directly by teachers over children who have less cultural capital. A lack of cultural capital may discourage students to stay in school (self-selection) may hamper their accomplishments while in school (indirect exclusion), or may lead to a lack of recognition from teachers (teacher selection). Although there is a debate about which of these mechanisms is most likely to operate, empirical studies have generally underscored the role of cultural capital in the schooling process.

In one of the first systematic American empirical studies on cultural capital, DiMaggio (1982) showed that a student's involvement in art, music, and literature is positively correlated with his or her grades in high school, even after the influence of prior ability and father's education is taken into account. In a later study, DiMaggio and Mohr (1985) also found significant effects of the respondents' cultural capital on years of schooling completed (after controlling for father's education and occupational prestige) and noted that differences in cultural capital explained about 14 percent of the effect of father's education on a respondent's schooling. A drawback of these two studies is that they focused entirely on the cultural interests and activities of students. Thus, it remains somewhat uncertain whether the measures of cultural capital are causally prior to outcomes in schooling. Another way to measure cultural capital is to use indicators of parents' cultural participation (Teachman 1987). This is a somewhat stronger measure because parents' cultural activities are unlikely to be affected by their children's schooling. Using a large longitudinal data set on high school seniors, Teachman found positive effects of parental cultural resources on children's educational attainment.

In European countries, researchers generally have found similar results. For the Netherlands, De Graaf (1986) showed that parental cultural capital has significant effects on educational attainment, after controlling for father's and mother's schooling and father's occupational prestige; cultural capital explained 9 percent (oldest cohort) to 14 percent (youngest cohort) of the effect of parental socioeconomic status (SES) on educational attainment. De Graaf (1988) found positive results for West Germany as well, although the effect of cultural capital was limited to success at the highest level of secondary schooling (the gymnasium). In a comparative study, Mateju (1990) stated that cultural capital explained part of the effect of parental SES on schooling in Czechoslovakia (13 percent), Hungary (20 percent), and the Netherlands (21 percent). Similar results for Hungary were found by Ganzeboom, De Graaf, and Robert (1990).

In sum, both American and European studies have underscored the role of cultural capital in the schooling process. Socialization into high-status culture appears to have a strong effect on educational attainment. At the same time, however, the degree to which cultural capital explains the association between socioeconomic origins and destinations is relatively modest: in the range of 15 percent.

Synthesis and Research Questions

So far, few studies have applied notions of cultural capital to ethnic or racial differences in schooling. Most studies have focused either on European countries, where ethnic minorities are small, or on the United States, but have limited the analyses to Whites. An exception is Farkas, Grobe, Sheehan, and Shuan (1990), who examined the interaction between teachers and students of different ethnic groups from a cultural capital perspective. A more relevant exception for our aims is DiMaggio and Ostrower's (1990) comparison of Black-White differences in cultural participation. Although that study did not address inequality in socioeconomic outcomes per se, it presented several findings that served as a starting point for our analysis. Using the 1982 Survey of Public Participation in the Arts, DiMaggio and Ostrower showed that there are important racial differences in arts consumption. On the one hand, Whites are more likely to attend classical music, opera, and ballet performances and to visit art museums and historical monuments. On the other hand, Blacks are more likely to engage in traditional African American art forms, such as listening to jazz and blues, attending jazz and blues concerts, and watching these art forms on television. Although a large part of these differences can be attributed to Black-White differences in schooling, the effects of race remain significant after the influence of father's and mother's educational attainment is taken into account.

A more important finding, at least from our perspective, is that similar differences exist when one focuses on childhood experiences: Socialization into highbrow cultural activities is more common in White families than in Black families, even after differences in parental education are taken into account. DiMaggio and Ostrower (1990) further claimed that over time, there has been no convergence between Blacks and Whites with respect to participation in highbrow cultural activities. They interpreted this finding as being an indication of "cultural resistance." That is, in the face of increased socioeconomic opportunities, Blacks have remained attached to traditional Black art forms to maintain their cultural identity. Hence, despite the long-term convergence of Blacks and Whites in several other respects, such as income, education, and intermarriage, DiMaggio and Ostrower argued that Blacks have maintained their distance from traditional White culture. This model of resistance is in contrast to the cultural behavior of Whites. DiMaggio and Ostrower pointed out that over time, Whites have become integrated into traditional Black culture, such as jazz, blues, and soul music.

In this article we answer the following three questions:

1. How have cultural resources changed across birth cohorts of Blacks and Whites?
2. To what extent can these changes be explained by changes in family background?
3. Have changes in family background and cultural resources contributed to the Black–White convergence in schooling?

If cultural capital is relevant for the influence of class background on educational attainment, as previous work has shown, it should be relevant for other ascriptive factors, such as race, as well. Following DiMaggio and Ostrower (1990), we argue that cultural capital (as measured in studies of educational attainment) is part of the Euro-American cultural tradition and that selection or self-selection on the basis of cultural capital in the schooling career can be understood as a mechanism through which racial inequality in American society is strengthened. In contrast to DiMaggio and Ostrower's hypothesis of cultural resistance, however, we expected that as intergroup contact has increased and overt racial discrimination has decreased, racial segmentation with respect to tastes and lifestyles has also declined. If such a convergence in cultural resources has occurred, we expected it to have contributed to the convergence in schooling. In a more general sense, we tried to examine whether segmentation with respect to cultural tastes and lifestyles in American society has implications for trends in racial inequality. Hence, our analysis focuses not so much on why Whites have an advantage over Blacks in schooling, but more on the question of why Blacks have been catching up over time.

THE DATA

The data we analyzed came from the 1982 and 1985 waves of the Survey of Public Participation in the Arts (SPPA) that contains a set of questions on arts consumption, parental background, and cultural socialization. The survey was done in conjunction with the National Crime Survey and was a random probability sample of the American population. The 1982 and 1985 questions we used were formulated in an identical fashion, and questions on parents' participation in the arts were directed to a subset of the sample. We limited our comparisons to Black and non-Hispanic White men and women aged 25 and over, since some younger persons would still be enrolled in school. The total number of respondents was 6,248, 5,660 of whom were non-Hispanic White and 588 were Black.

The SPPA is unique in providing data on cultural socialization, but it also has limitations. As is the case in most surveys containing questions on family background, no retrospective information is available on parental income. Although parental income has important effects on educational attainment, studies in the Netherlands (Ganzeboom 1982) have shown that income has little effect on the consumption of high-status culture once the influence of education has been taken into account. As a result, our model is incomplete, but our estimates of the effect of cultural socialization on schooling are hardly biased. Similar arguments can be made about other determinants of schooling, such as the number of siblings and family structure. The only concern that remains is the omission of father's occupation, which has a small effect on both cultural socialization and children's schooling (Ganzeboom 1982).

DESCRIPTIVE ANALYSES

We start out by describing how cultural socialization and schooling have changed across birth cohorts and how these trends differ for Blacks and Whites. The top panel of Figure 30.1 presents mean levels of schooling by race and birth cohort. Our cohorts ranged from persons born in 1900 to persons born in 1960. Respondent's schooling was measured in sin-

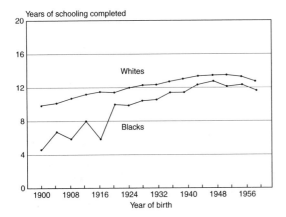

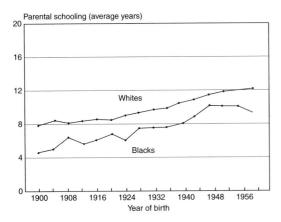

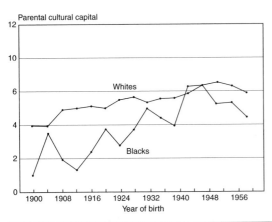

FIGURE 30.1   Years of Schooling Completed, Parental Schooling, and Parental Cultural Capital, by Race and Year of Birth: Survey of Public Participation in the Arts, 1982–1985

gle years of completed schooling, ranging from 0 for no schooling to 20 years for Ph.D.s ($M = 12.2$; $SD = 3.2$). Our results are generally consistent with findings from other studies: a rapid increase in educational attainment and a steady narrowing of the racial gap since the beginning of this century. It should be kept in mind that selective mortality from older cohorts may have led to a modest understatement of the true trend.

The middle panel of Figure 30.1 depicts trends in parental education. Father's and mother's schooling were measured in six categories. We recoded categories to the weighted midpoints in years of schooling (using data on the respondent's education broken down by sex). In 14 percent of the cases, educational data on both parents were missing. Missing values were imputed, using data on years of schooling by race, birth cohort, and sex as published in Smith (1984). From Figure 30.1, it is clear that the average level of parental education has increased during the 20th century for both Whites and Blacks. Hence, family resources have become more favorable for both races, though there appears to have been little convergence.

Our results are consistent with what several other researchers have found on the basis of larger data sets (Farley and Allen 1989; Smith 1984). What makes the SPPA survey unique is that it allowed us to examine trends in parental cultural capital. Following Lamont and Lareau (1988:156), cultural capital can be defined as "institutionalized, i.e., widely shared high status cultural signals (attitudes, preferences, formal knowledge, behaviors, goods, and credentials) used for social and cultural exclusion." Although limited in scope, our data contain several key indicators of high-status cultural behavior. More specifically, we considered four parental activities: whether parents attended performances of classical music, plays, and art museums and encouraged the respondent to read books (not for school). All items are respondents' reports of what parents did when the respondents were aged 15. Possible answers were "never," "occasionally," and "often." For the lack of other information, we assumed equal distances between categories. Subsequently, we used the unweighted average of scores on the four variables as an index of parental cultural capital. The index ranges from 0 (for no exposure at all) to 2 (for "often" on all four items) and has a reliability of $\alpha = .73$, which is reasonable for a scale of four items. For purposes of presentation, we multiplied the index by 10 ($M = 5.5$; $SD = 5.0$).

The bottom panel of Figure 30.1 presents mean levels of cultural capital broken down by birth cohort and race. Since our scale pertains to the same age (age 15) for all respondents, differences among birth cohorts provide a view of trends that is not confounded by age effects. In this respect, our analyses improve on DiMaggio and Ostrower's (1990) comparison of *respondent's* current cultural participation across birth cohorts. Figure 30.1 shows that across cohorts, there has been a clear increase in parental cultural capital. In most cohorts, however, the mean for Blacks is well below the mean for Whites, indicating that Blacks are disadvantaged with respect to cultural capital. The cohort averages fluctuate because of the relatively small number of Blacks in most cohorts, but at first glance, the racial gap in acquired cultural capital appears to have narrowed.

In sum, there has been an increase in schooling and family resources for both Blacks and Whites. For Blacks, however, the increase in schooling and parental cultural capital has occurred at a faster rate, leading to a convergence in both domains. Thus changes in racial inequality in the cultural domain contributed to changes in the inequality of schooling. . . . [Multivariable analyses that strongly support conclusion have been deleted.—Ed.]

Trends in Cultural Capital

Our first research question was, How have cultural resources changed across birth cohorts for Blacks and Whites? To answer this question, we [use multivariable analyses] . . . show[ing] that in 1900, Blacks had 2.67 points less cultural capital than did Whites. Since the mean of the scale is 5.5, this finding indicates that Blacks were at a notable disadvantage at the beginning of the 20th century. When considering trends, we observed that among Whites, there has been a significant increase in cultural capital of .40

points per decade; over the entire period (until the 1960 cohort), this finding implies an increase of 2.37 points. Among Blacks, the increase is greater (.77). Hence, cultural resources have increased at a faster rate for Black children than for White children. More specifically, the racial difference in cultural capital has declined by $.77 - .40 = .37$ per decade. This convergence is statistically significant (*t*-value is 2.9). This finding implies that for cohorts born in 1960, almost no difference between Blacks and Whites remains ($2.674 - 6 \times .37 = .42$). This result is consistent with the convergence observed in the bottom panel of Figure 30.1. . . .

Trends in Educational Attainment

Although the net gain in cultural capital among Blacks may be important in its own right, its relevance ultimately depends on how it has affected racial inequality in other domains of the stratification system. Therefore, we examined what part of the educational difference between Blacks and Whites can be explained by differences in cultural capita: [Multivariable] models for individual differences in educational attainment . . . [reveal] that in the 1900 cohort, Blacks had 4.3 fewer years of schooling than did Whites. Among Blacks, there has been a strong increase in schooling of 1.27 years per decade. Among Whites, there has been an increase as well, but not as strong (.63 years per decade). When comparing these two trends, we observed that the convergence in schooling is $1.27 - .63 = .65$ per decade. This convergence is statistically significant (*t*-value is 8.5). That Blacks have made gains in schooling relative to Whites is consistent with cohort comparisons using larger data sets (Smith 1984) . . .

DISCUSSION

When using parental characteristics to examine trends in cultural capital, we found a significant increase in participation in traditionally Euro-American culture. That this increase has been faster among Blacks than among Whites and persists after Black-White differences in parental education are taken into account shows that there has been a certain degree of racial integration in the cultural domain. This finding is consistent with changes in other dimensions of racial integration, such as intermarriage (Kalmijn 1993); occupational segmentation; and, to some extent, income differences (Farley and Allen 1989). In addition, we found that in all cohorts and for both races, more exposure to cultural capital is associated with higher levels of schooling after other background characteristics are taken into account. This finding confirms Bourdieu's (1973) thesis of cultural reproduction and extends it to an important ethnic minority in American society. Furthermore, we observed that the integration of Blacks in traditionally Euro-American culture has made a positive though modest contribution to the Black-White convergence in schooling.

Our findings give rise to two more general conclusions. With respect to growing racial equality in American society, we conclude that the integration of Blacks in Euro-American high culture has made a positive contribution to the relative gains of Blacks in the educational system. However, we also believe that the role of cultural capital is modest in comparison to the well-known influence of legal and institutional changes in American society, such as school desegregation, busing, scholarships for Blacks, and affirmative action. How the effect of cultural integration on schooling compares to the role of the improved economic position of Blacks is difficult to assess at this point. To answer this questions, we would need specific information on both the cultural and financial resources in the parental home.

With respect to Bourdieu's thesis, we believe that our findings point to another way in which cultural capital may operate. Previous studies showed that cultural socialization generally explains a significant part of the influence of class background on socioeconomic achievement. This finding has generally been interpreted in terms of reproduction or the persistence of inequality. According to this reasoning, ascriptive variables like father's occupation and education maintain their force in modern societies through the process of cultural socialization. In this article, we focused on a different and more persistent ascriptive force in modern society—race—and reached a somewhat different conclusion. By showing that cultural capital explains part of the Black–White convergence in schooling, we illustrated that cultural capital may also serve as a route to upward mobility for less privileged groups in society.

REFERENCES

Bourdieu, Pierre. 1973. "Cultural Reproduction and Social Reproduction." Pp. 71–112 in *Knowledge, Education, and Cultural Change*, edited by R. Brown. London: Tavistock.

Card, David and Alan W. Krueger. 1992. "School Quality and Black–White Relative Earnings: A Direct Assessment." *Quarterly Journal of Economics* 107: 151–200.

De Graaf, Paul M. 1986. "The Impact of Financial and Cultural Resources on Educational Attainment in the Netherlands." *Sociology of Education* 59:237–46.

———. 1988. "Parents' Financial and Cultural Resources and Transition to Secondary School in the Federal Republic of Germany." *European Sociological Review* 4:209–21.

DiMaggio, Paul. 1982. "Cultural Capital and School Success: The Impact of Status Culture Participation on the Grades of U.S. High School Students." *American Sociological Review* 47:189–201.

DiMaggio, Paul and John Mohr. 1985. "Cultural Capital, Educational Attainment, and Marital Selection." *American Journal of Sociology* 90:1231–61.

DiMaggio, Paul and Francie Ostrower. 1990. "Participation in the Arts by Black and White Americans." *Social Forces* 68:753–78.

Duncan, Otis Dudley. 1968. "Inheritance of Poverty or Inheritance of Race?" Pp. 85–110 in *Perspectives on Poverty: On Understanding Poverty*, edited by Daniel P. Moynihan. New York, Basic Books.

Farkas, George, Robert P. Grobe, Daniel Sheehan, and Yuan Shuan. 1990. "Cultural Resources and School Success: Gender, Ethnicity, and Poverty Groups within an Urban School District." *American Sociological Review* 55:127–42.

Farley, Reynolds and Walter R. Allen. 1989. *The Color Line and the Quality of Life in America*. New York: Oxford University Press.

Ganzeboom, Harry B. G. 1982. "Explaining Differential Participation in High-Cultural Activities: A Confrontation of Information-Processing and Status-Seeking Theories." Pp. 186–205 in *Theoretical Models and Empirical Analyses*, edited by Werner Raub. Utrecht: E.S.-Publications.

Ganzeboom, Harry B. G., Paul M. De Graaf, and Peter Robert. 1990. "Cultural Reproduction Theory on Socialist Ground." *Research in Social Stratification and Mobility* 9:79–104.

Grusky, David G. and Thomas A. DiPrete. 1990. "Recent Trends in the Process of Stratification." *Demography* 27:617–37.

Haveman, Robert and Barbara Wolfe. 1994. *Succeeding Generations: On the Effects of Investments in Children*. New York: Russell Sage Foundation.

Kalmijn, Matthijs. 1993. "Trends in Black/White Intermarriage." *Social Forces* 72:119–46.

Lamont, Michèle and Annette Lareau. 1988. "Cultural Capital: Allusions, Gaps and Glissandos in Recent Theoretical Developments." *Sociological Theory* 6:152–68.

Mateju, Peter. 1990. "Family Effect on Educational Attainment in Czechoslovakia, the Netherlands and Hungary." Pp. 187–210 in *Social Reproduction in Eastern and Western Europe*, edited by J. L. Peschar. Groningen, the Netherlands: Oomo.

Smith, James P. 1984. "Race and Human Capital." *American Economic Review* 74: 685–98.

Teachman, Jay D. 1987. "Family Background, Educational Resources, and Educational Attainment." *American Sociological Review* 52:548–57.

Wilson, William Julius. 1987. *The Truly Disadvantaged: The Inner City, the Underclass, and Public Policy*. Chicago: University of Chicago Press.

CHAPTER 31

BLACK GHETTOIZATION AND
SOCIAL MOBILITY

NORMAN FAINSTEIN

Some images about race confront us every day when we turn on our television sets: teenage mothers on welfare, crack addicts, drive-by shootings, rundown neighborhoods, children dying in tenement-house fires, the MTV rap world of fast girls and violent boys. Such images reflect and reinforce popular identification of African Americans with the worst-off and the most socially "deviant" segments of the black poor—the members of the so-called underclass—and with the places where they live—the black ghetto.

The prominent black sociologist, William Julius Wilson, minces no words as he describes the "underclass" in his influential book, *The Truly Disadvantaged*:

Today's ghetto neighborhoods are populated almost exclusively by the most disadvantaged segments of the black urban community, that heterogeneous grouping of families and individuals who are out of the mainstream of the American occupational system. Included in this group are individuals who lack training and skills and either experience long-term unemployment or are not members of the labor force, individuals who are engaged in street crime and other forms of aberrant behavior, and families that experience long-term spells of poverty and/or welfare dependency. These are the populations to which I refer when I speak of the underclass. *I use this term to depict a reality not captured in the more standard designation* lower class.[1]

Thanks to Wilson—and a host of other scholars, journalists, foundations, and government agencies—the study of the underclass has provided a raison d'être for refocusing attention on race and poverty.[2] But it has also reproduced in academic jargon, buttressed by powerful statistical tools, the very image that it has sought to clarify and explain, if not dispel. While the literature on the subject is too vast to review here in any detail, it is worth outlining the basic feature of the underclass interpretation of how race and economics intersect.[3]

The "underclass" comprises people who used to be called down and out, individuals who for various reasons do not work and apparently behave "antisocially" in other respects, as well. By focusing on the rather small core of people perennially disattached from the official labor market, researchers inevitably ignore the majority of low-income people who do work, although at wages that keep them in economic deprivation.[4] Rather than offering a theory of the labor market, of how and why it seems to be generating more and more low-wage and underground jobs, rather than examining the continual movement in and out of work at the bottom of our economy, underclass theory tries to explain the personal and environmental attributes of the permanently unemployed. Correlated with the joblessness of such people are a host of the other characteristics of the urban poor that are readily visible in the television picture of "the ghetto."

Depending on the politics of the analyst, the blame for the underclass is lodged either with government programs that have bred dependency and corrupted the morals of the poor or with an economy that has literally left the poor behind: some combination of suburbanization of new jobs and deindustrialization has created a spatial mismatch and brought skill levels up beyond the educational attainment of inner-city residents (thereby effecting a skills mismatch).[5]

All sides downplay race as a factor, even though the underclass seems to be mainly African American, and most attention is focused on central-city, lower-class black neighborhoods. These neighborhoods are increasingly "isolated" from mainstream society and economy, with their inhabitants ever more "concentrated" in a pathological environment. To students of social history, the imagery of the underclass inhabiting its packed ghettos is quite familiar: it resonates almost perfectly with previous models of the undeserving poor and their disease-laden districts, of the slum (which needed to be cleared), and of the pathological immigrant ghetto.[6]

There is, however, an important twist to the idea of the underclass as it is played out these days by social scientists, one that did not exist in past theories of slum life. The argument is now made that the very pathology of the "ghetto" and its impoverished, isolated residents has been produced, in good part, by the success of upwardly and outwardly mobile black households. Thus, many scholars have detailed the growth of a black middle class as well as the exodus of such families from the worst—"ghetto"—neighborhoods. Increasing class inequality among blacks has, in this view, combined with residential mobility to leave "behind" the large residuum that is the "ghetto poor," deprived of the "better elements" who used to provide role models and institutional ballast.[7]

By an unstated logic, therefore, the underclass not only results from the increasing bifurcation of black society, but reaffirms by its existence the reality of black success. It would not be too much to say, in fact, that the sociology of the underclass tells whites that working and middle-class blacks, including, of course, black professionals, are *not* the underclass, that the appropriate lens with which to examine the economic situation of African Americans is class, not race.

But that lens distorts: Race has not gone away. It remains a biting reality for African Americans, perhaps especially for those who have achieved some economic success. To see this, we need to free our minds from the television and social science equation of racial and economic stratification with the impoverished ghetto and the underclass. Instead of imagining dilapidated black neighborhoods and their downtrodden and sometimes "dangerous" inhabitants, we might think of another picture, this one drawn by the 1990 census of a city known for its large black working and middle class: Washington, DC. A century ago W. E. B. Du Bois spoke of the "color line" that divided the races, in the North as well as the South, regardless of income and occupation. Washington's neighborhoods today remain divided by that same color line. While few cities are so perfectly bisected by a single racial fault line, most are just as segregated as the nation's capital. Moreover, residential segregation is no mere remnant of a racist past. It is a glaring sign of the continued racial segmentation of our society today. As I will show, segregation plays a critical role in redefining class for African Americans and in reducing their prospects for upward economic mobility.

THE REALITIES OF CONTINUED ECONOMIC DEPRIVATION AND RESIDENTIAL SEGREGATION

The economic success of any social group, in this case African Americans, over an extended period of time can best be understood, on the one hand, in terms of a changing structure of economic opportunity and, on the other hand, in terms of the resources possessed by group members as they compete with others for economic advantage. Both within their lifetimes and between generations, some members of a group will experience upward mobility in a changing opportunity structure, and others downward mobility. Group success is a reflection, on balance, of net upward mobility. The same applies to a particular stratum, like the black poor. Poverty will decrease if the resources possessed by lower-income blacks provide them with sufficient advantages to be upwardly mobile on average in relation to other low-income groups. By thinking of poverty, or any other status, as an instantaneous picture of dynamic processes centrally rooted in the economy, we will not just better understand the reasons for continued black poverty, but also better explain the competitive situation of all African Americans.

The American economy has traversed two distinct periods since the Depression. The first, which extended from 1940 to 1973, witnessed steady improvement in the economic condition of the typical American, with a general reduction in overall inequality along the way. The second, through which we have now suffered for two decades, has been associated with real overall growth as measured by GNP and related indicators (although at a much slower rate than earlier), yet with no improvement for the typical American because economic inequality increased sharply and the wealthiest households reaped all the benefits of such growth as there has been.[8]

In this kind of situation, African Americans, who were disadvantaged at the start, could not be expected to make much economic progress along the way. So it is unremarkable that black median household income increased by less than $100 between 1973 and 1991, with the typical black household remaining at only 59–60 percent of the income of a typical white household (see Table 31.1). The black middle class, those with incomes of $25,000–50,000, *contracted* slightly during the period, as did the white. And while upper-middle-class and elite black households grew in these eighteen years, they still composed but 12 percent of all black households, compared with more than 27 percent of white households. By contrast, the percentage of blacks in poverty has *not* increased since 1973, but it remains very high, at more than two-fifths of all black households. These data explain why it is so important to examine the economic situation of all African Americans, not just to concentrate obsessively on the nonworking poor. The reality is that the entire black income structure has remained relatively unchanged in shape and unimproved relative to that of whites.

TABLE 31.1 Race and Income Structure, 1967–91: Annual Household Income in Constant (1991) Dollars

	POVERTY ≤14,999	MARGINAL 15–24,999	MIDDLE 25–49,999	UPPER MIDDLE 50–99,999	ELITE ≥100,000	MEDIAN
Black Distribution						
1967	46.7	24.9	23.3	4.7	0.5	16,228
1973	42.0	21.7	28.1	7.7	0.6	18,713
1979	42.4	20.4	26.6	10.0	0.5	18,650
1985	44.0	20.3	25.5	9.5	0.8	18,758
1991	42.4	19.1	26.6	10.8	1.1	18,807
White Distribution						
1967	24.4	19.8	40.5	13.5	1.8	27,949
1973	22.2	16.6	38.1	20.2	2.9	31,791
1979	21.9	17.4	36.1	21.3	3.3	31,766
1985	22.3	17.3	34.4	21.9	4.1	31,529
1991	21.9	17.3	33.3	22.7	4.8	31,569

Source: U.S. Bureau of the Census, *Current Population Reports*, Series P-60, no. 180 (1992), Table B-2.

Note: The median income of all U.S. households was $26,801 in 1967, $30,333 in 1973, $30,297 in 1979, $29,896 in 1985, and $30,126 in 1991.

It should be noted, however, that even during the period of most rapid economic growth, the gap between blacks and whites was closed mainly because of the transformation of the southern economy from semifeudal to industrial. A good indicator is provided by the ratio of black to white median family income between 1950 and 1990. Over these forty years there was no gain for the median black family; the improvement in the 1960s was lost by 1974. What is more, outside of the South the *relative* position of black families actually deteriorated between the early fifties and the early nineties. Of course, real median family income was much higher in 1990 than in 1950, so the typical family, whether black or white, saw its standard of living improve. Only in these "absolute" terms were blacks *on average* socially mobile.

Popular images—and the more sophisticated discussion of the underclass—have managed to avoid confrontation with evidence about income distribution and economic reorganization, even in the face of an abundance of empirical and theoretical work in these areas. The same may be said about the most omnipresent and long-standing reality about African Americans—their residential segregation. The color line that bisects Washington may be seen everywhere in America by those who care to look. In fact, throughout most of the twentieth century blacks have stood alone in the extent of their physical separation, regardless of time, place, or class attributes.[9]

The 1990 census shows that blacks remain highly segregated, particularly in the large metropolitan areas where most are concentrated (see Table 31.2). Even the small declines in some places are probably an artifact of the expansion of black neighborhoods into adjacent areas, which appear to be racially integrated at the moment of the census count.[10] Particularly disquieting for people who believe that the black middle class has become integrated are the figures in the lower panel of Table 31.2. These show that blacks in New York City with household incomes of at least $100,000 a year are as highly segregated as blacks in poverty. While findings from the 1990 census are just now appearing, extensive analyses of the 1980 and 1970 censuses show that blacks throughout America were residentially segregated whatever their social class.

In Table 31.3 we look at evidence of black-white segregation using both income and education as indicators of social class. The first column shows the degree of segregation of blacks at specified income or education levels from whites of any incomes or education. For example, the index number is .79 for blacks with incomes of $50,000 or more in 1980. This means that 79 percent of these black persons would have had to move from their census tracts in order to match the distribution of whites as a whole within their metropolitan area. It is apparent from the data that blacks at every class are equally isolated from white society. In the second column, we look at segregation with class controlled for both blacks and whites, in other words, at the level of interracial segregation of blacks and whites with the same incomes or educations. Again, race overwhelms class. Middle-class blacks, working-class blacks, and poor blacks are equally segregated from their white class counterparts. Clearly, higher class standing does little to buy African Americans a racially integrated environment. When better-off African Americans move out of the most impoverished black neighborhoods, nearly all move into other segregated areas.

Blacks are ghettoized through political and economic processes that establish residential segregation as a sign of, and basis for, group subordination. The black ghetto—like the Jewish ghetto of the Middle Ages—encompasses the entire population bearing an ascriptive attribute, in this case skin color, which signifies a deeply rooted set of historical and contemporary relations. The black ghetto is continually and mainly intentionally reproduced by white Americans and the institutions that they dominate. Earlier in the century, the black ghettos were established through a combination of violent white communal resistance to integration and a host of well-known governmental processes, including legal restrictions on interracial sales, explicit policies by the Federal Housing and the Veterans Administrations, and the activities of municipal governments in zoning, urban redevelopment, and public housing construction. Banks, realtors, and rental agents all played their parts.[11]

TABLE 31.2   Racial Segregation in 1980 and 1990: Index of Segregation (D) of Blacks from All Other Groups

	1990	1980	DIFFERENCE
Ten largest metropolitan areas in 1990			
New York	.82	.82	.00
Los Angeles–Long Beach	.73	.76	.03
Chicago	.86	.89	.03
Philadelphia	.77	.77	.00
Detroit	.88	.90	.02
Washington, D.C.	.66	.66	.00
Houston	.67	.74	.07
Nassau-Suffolk County	.76	.76	.00
Boston	.68	.71	.03
Atlanta	.68	.75	.07
Metropolitan Statistical Areas (MSAs) by size			
All	.69	.74	.05
Large MSAs	.74	.78	.04
Medium MSAs	.64	.69	.05
Small MSAs	.58	.61	.03
New York City			
All black households	.84	.84	.00
Incomes below $15,000	.86	.87	.01
Incomes above $100,000	.88	.88	.00

Source: Roderick J. Harrison and Daniel H. Weinberg, "Racial and Ethnic Residential Segregation in 1990," Table 1; and "Changes in Racial and Ethnic Segregation, 1980–1990," Tables 1, 2, and 12; U.S. Bureau of the Census, 1992. Andrew A. Beveridge and Hyun Sook Kim, "Patterns of Residential Segregation in New York City, 1980 to 1990: Preliminary Analysis," New York Metropolitan Area Demographics Laboratory, Queens College, 1992.

Note: Figures for metropolitan areas are values of the index of dissimilarity (D), a measure of residential segregation. The index shows the proportion of black households that would have to change census tracts within a metropolitan area in order to be distributed in the same manner as the comparative nonblack population. D ranges between zero and 1.00. In the distribution of D, 0–.30 is considered low, .30–.60 moderate, and .60–1.00 high. Thus, all values of D in this table are, in fact, in the high range.

For New York City, D is again the measure of segregation, but in this case with block groups rather than census tracts as the unit of area. Since block groups are smaller and therefore more homogeneous than census tracts, D is likely to be slightly higher. The subcategories for New York City measure, respectively, the segregation of blacks in poverty and those with elite incomes from all other groups. Incomes are expressed in constant (1990) dollars. The categories used for comparison between 1990 and 1980 are not perfectly identical, however, so changes in D for specific income groups are approximations, while comparisons between categories in either 1980 or 1990 are exact.

TABLE 31.3 Segregation of African Americans from Whites: Index of Racial Residential Segregation (D) in Standard Metropolitan Areas (SMAs) with Largest Black Populations, 1980

	INDEX OF SEGREGATION FROM WHITE PERSONS	
	REGARDLESS OF INCOME OR EDUCATION OF WHITE PERSONS	WHITE PERSONS WITH SAME INCOME OR EDUCATION
Black persons		
Family income		
Under $10,000	.79	.76
$15,000–19,999	.76	.75
$25,000–34,999	.77	.76
$50,000 or more	.79	.79
Education		
9–11 years	.83	.77
High-school graduate	.78	.76
Some college	.75	.74
College graduate	.72	.71

Source: (First column) Nancy A. Denton and Douglas S. Massey, "Residential Segregation of Blacks, Hispanics, and Asians by Socioeconomic Status and Generation," *Social Science Quarterly* 69 (1988): Table 1; (second column) Reynolds Farley and Walter R. Allen, *The Color Line and the Quality of Life in America* (New York: Russel Sage Foundation, 1987), Table 5.10.

Note: Both columns exhibit values of the index of dissimilarity (D), a measure of residential segregation. It measures the number of black households that would have to change census tracts within a metropolitan area in order to be distributed in the same manner as the comparative white population. D ranges between zero and 1.000. (In this table, D is rounded off to 100ths and ranges between zero and 1.00.) For the distribution of D, 0–.300 is considered low, .300–.600 moderate, and .600–1.000 high. Thus, all values of D in this table are, in fact, in the high range.

The columns are drawn from two somewhat different but overlapping samples. The first comprises the 10 metropolitan areas with the largest black populations in 1980. Here D shows how many black persons with a particular characteristic of family income or personal education would have to be redistributed to match the distribution of *all* whites among census tracts in each SMA. The final number is a weighted average of D for all ten SMAs. The second column uses the same methodology for the 16 SMAs with the largest black populations. But here D measures the redistribution of black persons requires to match the distribution of white persons with the *same* characteristic. For example, the number .71 in the lower right-hand corner of the table means that 71 percent of college-educated black persons would need to change census tracts in order to match the distribution of college-educated white persons.

They continue to do so today, even when official government policy supports integration. While a majority of whites claim to oppose discrimination, most also would not want to live in an integrated neighborhood.[12] White behavior—buttressed by an institutional system of governmental fragmentation and decentralization of political power[13]—seems hardly to have changed at all:

Two decades after the passage of the Fair Housing Act, levels of black segregation remain exceedingly high in large urban areas. . . . This high level of seg-

regation cannot be explained by blacks' objective socioeconomic characteristics, their housing preferences, or their limited knowledge of white housing markets. Rather, it is linked empirically to the persistence of discrimination in housing markets and to continuing antiblack prejudice.[14]

Segregation, as we have seen, is hardly limited to just the most impoverished neighborhoods that some now call the "ghetto," thereby usurping the term, implicitly and quite innocently suggesting that other black neighborhoods are not ghettoized.[15]

William Julius Wilson was right when he emphasized the intersection of race and poverty in his 1990 presidential address to the American Sociological Association, arguing that we should stop speaking about the underclass and instead use the term *ghetto poor*.[16] His explanation of black poverty would have been much improved, however, if he had also considered the significance of the ghettoized working class, the ghettoized middle class, and yes, the ghettoized rich.

RACIAL SEGREGATION AND SOCIAL MOBILITY

Whatever advantages blacks have gleaned from ghettoization—mainly in political representation—constitute a silver lining in an otherwise dark cloud that has negatively affected communal life, economic success, and, most generally, the political situation of blacks and whites alike. For ghettoization is not compatible with racial equality; separation, as it has been established in the American system, reflects and supports subordination.

At least since the Depression, numerous studies have recognized the inherent evil of ghettoization in isolating blacks of *every* social class, in breeding black resentment and feelings of inferiority, in contributing to social pathology and to white prejudice. A pathbreaking postwar national study committed to integration by Robert Weaver, who would go on to become the first African American cabinet officer as secretary of the nascent Department of Housing and Urban Development, concluded:

The modern American ghetto is a Black Belt from which the occupants can escape only if they move into another well-defined Negro community. . . . This ghetto has all incomes and social classes. Its inhabitants are better prepared and more anxious than ever before to enter the mainstream of American life. Residential segregation, more than any other single institution, is an impediment to their realization of the American dream.[17]

Two decades later St. Claire Drake could stress that "the spatial isolation" of Negroes from whites "increased consciousness of their separate subordinate position, for no whites were available to them as neighbors, schoolmates, or friends"; rather, blacks encountered whites in the superordinate positions of landlords and street-level bureaucrats such as police officers and school officials.[18] Indeed, it was this situation of continuing subordination across the class structure that helped precipitate the movement for "community control" of black neighborhoods in the sixties and seventies.[19]

Over the years there has been much social science research that has attempted to identify the immediate effects of segregation and its long-term consequences for black well-being. With regard to the former, there is clear and relatively unambiguous evidence. Blacks face a highly segmented housing market that poorly fits the standard economic model. In that market, they are the victims of continual racial discrimination by sellers, realtors, landlords, and lending institutions. Two results follow: compared with whites at similar income levels, they get less housing for the money in whatever jurisdictions they find themselves, and they are excluded from jurisdictions with higher levels of public services and better-quality schools.[20]

Another immediate consequence of segregation that has been much examined in the case of the black poor is that blacks are concentrated in central cities at a level far beyond what one might expect from their incomes relative to that of whites. Given the decentralization of jobs over the last several decades, analysts at least since the days of the 1968 Kerner Commission Report have identified a spatial mismatch between residence and employment opportunities. The validity of this argument is supported more by repetition than by evidence, however. That there is a mismatch is without doubt, but in a time when everyone drives to work, the consequences of disproportionate concentration of black residences within the *centers* of decentralized metropolitan labor markets is unclear, whether with regard to unemployment or wages.[21]

Racial segregation has also been indicted—correctly I think—as the main cause of an increase of concentrated, inner-city black poverty.[22] But the further claim that such poverty can be explained by increasing spatial separation of social classes within the ghetto (understood simply as the black part of metropolitan areas) needs to be scrutinized. For it suggests that there has been a heightening of *class* segregation among blacks, and that the effect has been mainly to isolate the black poor. What does the evidence show about class separation among blacks and about trends in those figures?

The answer depends upon how we think about class separation. If we employ the same kind of indicator as we commonly do in measuring overall *racial* separation, the index of dissimilarity that reflects the *unevenness* of a spatial distribution, then we discover that blacks and whites have quite similar scores; in each case, indexes typically are at the low or moderate levels. Researchers in the fifties and sixties were surprised at this finding because they had expected much less spatial separation among blacks.[23] But the fact remains that by measures of unevenness, blacks and whites have had similar patterns at least since 1940, and nothing much has changed recently.[24]

Measures of unevenness in the distribution of classes within racial groups tell us only part of what we want to know about spatial contact or isolation of classes. The problem with these measures is that they are *not* sensitive to the relative sizes of different groups. Actual spatial contact (or isolation) depends not just upon the unevenness of a distribution but also upon the relative size of groups. Let me give a concrete example. Suppose that poor and nonpoor blacks were distributed in the 1940s within northern cities in more or less the same way as they are now; the

index of dissimilarity between these classes would not have changed. But fifty years ago roughly 60 percent of that black population was poor, while today's figure is closer to 30 percent. Accordingly, the chances of a poor black having contact with nonpoor blacks would have *increased* substantially over the period, simply as a result of the changing proportions of the poor and nonpoor. Of course, if *both* the evenness of the distribution and the proportions of each group changed over the years, one would have no way of knowing a priori how much change there had been in contact. For this reason, we need a measure of contact that is sensitive to how a population is distributed spatially as well as to its relative size. Such a measure is P*, which reflects the percentage of individuals of one group—say poor blacks—living in the same census tract as the average individual of another group—say nonpoor blacks.

Unfortunately, there have been very few studies over the years that have utilized a measure of probable contact like P*, in part because until recently nobody much cared about class contact and isolation within races. The only large-scale study that looked at several measures of class and examined class contact among blacks and among whites was carried out for the Chicago metropolitan area in 1970.[25] It showed, as we would expect, that while black and white occupational and income groups were spatially distributed in a similar way, patterns of class contact were quite different within each race. Compared with blacks, whites were more likely to be in higher occupational categories. For that reason, the average white at the upper end of the class scale was likely to have much less contact with lower-class whites than would blacks of similar class standing with lower-class blacks. The converse was also true. Poor blacks—being relatively much more numerous than poor whites—were less likely to have contact with better-off blacks than were poor whites with better-off whites. For example, the average black unskilled manual worker lived in a census tract in which 8 percent of the black population was employed in professional or managerial occupations; the average white unskilled manual worker lived in tracts where 23 percent of his white neighbors were professionals or managers. The same kinds of results were found when class was measured by income or education.

While we would like more comparative and longitudinal data, these findings are likely to be quite generally true in other places and after 1970, as well.[26] For they are almost inevitable. So long as levels of racial segregation remain little changed, and so long as the black economic structure remains depressed compared with the white—and we have seen hardly any change in either dimension since 1970—then this pattern of class contact among blacks will remain. As we saw, upper-income blacks were no more likely to live near whites than were low-income blacks. But the proportion of blacks who are lower income is much greater than the proportion of whites at those levels. Therefore, the typical better-off black household, unable to move into an integrated or white neighborhood at its own class level, is forced to live in a black neighborhood in which many lower-class blacks also live. Put another way, the spatial payoffs of upward mobility are lower for blacks than for whites because of racial segregation.

These are exactly the findings of a second study that analyzes class contact among blacks and whites.[27] Douglas Massey and his colleagues present evidence from Philadelphia, a city with black neighborhoods at every class level. Using several different indicators of social class, they show that middle-class whites are much less likely than middle-class blacks to encounter people with so-called underclass attributes in their neighborhoods. For example, a middle-income black family is about three times as likely as a similar white family to have neighbors who are on welfare. Equally important, the study examines in great detail other measures of the quality of life in neighborhoods occupied by working-class and middle-class blacks versus those occupied by whites of similar class. It finds that class simply does not buy blacks the environment that it buys whites in a society where class stratification is expressed spatially:

High status blacks, like whites, seek to convert past socioeconomic attainments into improved residential

circumstances. However, very few blacks are successful in achieving these locational outcomes. The vast majority live in segregated neighborhoods where blacks have long been, or are rapidly becoming, the majority, areas characterized by high crime, poor schools, economic dependency, unstable families, dilapidated housing, and poor health. All evidence indicates that blacks are no different than whites in trying to escape such an environment, when they are able. They are just less able.[28]

The authors suggest that the relative social heterogeneity of middle-income black neighborhoods reduces the ability of the black middle class to reproduce itself through cultural capital transmission:

Because of residential segregation, middle class blacks must send their children to public schools with children far below their own class standing, children with more limited cognitive, linguistic, and social skills. Given the strong effect of peer influences and environment on aspirations, motivation, and achievement, it is hardly surprising that so many young black people, even those from middle class families, fail to achieve high test scores or educational distinction.[29]

But do the reduced spatial payoffs of black social mobility actually reduce black mobility itself? In a vicious cycle, does racial segregation contribute to the high proportion of blacks in poverty and thereby to the costs for better-off black households of not being able to move into more class-homogeneous neighborhoods? This question points in almost the opposite direction from the problematic posed in many studies of the underclass, where the supposed absence of better-off households is advanced as an explanation of poverty.

The contemporary social science argument according to which "solid" working- and middle-class families will uplift the poor recapitulates the rationale of the settlement house. But popular opinion tends toward a very different metaphor, that of the bad apples that spoil the barrel. In this image too many lower-class households intrude upon the lives of those African Americans who might otherwise be socially mobile. Particularly in the critical years of adolescence, when undesirable school and street environments can pull children down, better-off black households cannot sufficiently distance themselves at any point in time from impoverished ones. Among the poor as well, those making the first moves toward mobility are forced by the segregation of all blacks to live in a spatially and culturally compressed environment, one that cannot possibly facilitate mobility. In this way, racial residential segregation rests as a critical—but of course, not the sole—cause of inadequate black social mobility, and thereby of continued poverty among a large lower class.

Nearly every black and white family in America assumes that inferior neighbors will drag them down and tries to distance itself from those beneath it. Social scientists, however, have failed to demonstrate that bad apples do spoil the barrel. Thus, Christopher Jencks and Susan Mayer have conducted an exhaustive review of all of the sociological evidence compiled in the seventies and eighties.[30] In trying to determine the social consequences of growing up in a poor neighborhood they conclude—not surprisingly—that neighborhoods matter, although how they matter is highly dependent on particular institutional settings. The most unambiguous evidence, which extends back a quarter century to the Coleman Report,[31] is that a child does better if he or she attends a school where classmates are predominantly of a higher social class. Beyond that, however, the sociological picture of schooling becomes quite fuzzy, even though nearly everyone concerned about the education of their *own* children tries to keep them away from kids with poor performance or behavior—both correlated with a lower social class. As to other "social consequences," Jencks and Mayer come to conclusions that are laden with qualifiers.

One body of evidence that has so far pointed clearly toward the effect of a "good" environment derives from the so-called Gautreaux decision, which required that federally subsidized housing be made available to low-income people in the suburbs of Chicago.[32] It appears that, other things being equal, poor black and Latino families who moved from inner-city neighborhoods have done better in school and in the labor market than those like them who

stayed behind.[33] But it is a long step from this and similar studies to a convincing demonstration of just how ghettoization affects social mobility.

THE SOCIAL CONSTRUCTION OF BLACK "OTHERNESS"

Beyond the technical reasons I have enumerated for the weakness of social science evidence, I would argue that ghettoization has produced a political atmosphere and a mentality in both races that affect a host of other factors, from motivation on the part of black children to discrimination by white employers to the whole character of American social policy. This atmosphere gums up nearly all empirical social science research, even while it cannot itself be demonstrated "scientifically."

For African Americans, ghettoization makes a daily symbolic statement of group subordination. Blacks are contained, separated, isolated—and their "otherness" is derived from the immutable physical attribute of skin color. The ghetto is at once the reflection, the reminder, and the component of the larger construction in American history, that of race itself as a "natural" social category. The inescapability of race and of the likelihood of racial subordination results, for many, in alienation from American institutions and thereby contributes to individual self-fulfilling prophesies of academic and economic failure. Collectively, Afrocentrism, even to the point of some advocates demanding all-black schools, has both widened the racial divide and played into the hands of white segregationists.

For whites, the physical ghettoization of nearly all blacks, along with the media focus on the "worst" black neighborhoods and the most socially deviant elements in them, has reinforced a stereotyped image of black people. By blurring or eliminating class differences among blacks, and by equating blacks with criminals and welfare mothers, whites are freed from guilt or even sympathy. In the white mentality, the social problems of race and economic inequality become reduced to a single, colored, televisioned image of the black "ghetto," at once a dangerous place and an undeserving population.

AMERICAN LOGIC

THIS MAN is not responsible for THIS MAN
even if they do belong in the same race.

THIS MAN is responsible for all that THIS MAN
does because they belong to the same race.

FIGURE 31.1   American Logic (*Source: The Crisis,* June 1913)

The encapsulation of the black lower classes in our central cities functions very effectively not only to obscure more general processes of spatial and social stratification—to reify them into categories like "inner city" and "the poor"—but to reduce a much larger issue of the place of African Americans in America to a single question: What are we to do about the black poor—that is, about welfare, crime, and idleness? I do not know if there is a way out of this impasse. Yet I remain convinced that residential segregation is simultaneously cause and effect of the segmentation of our society. In Gramsci's terms, the ghetto is the basis for a social trench, a physical arrangement transformed into a sociopolitical boundary and barrier. Blacks under attack from superior white power are defined, homogenized, and ultimately demoralized by their containment behind that trench, one that whites built and some blacks now maintain. The 1913 illustration of the color line found in *The Crisis* (Figure 31.1) reminds us of the frightening continuity of the American racial pattern.

NOTES

1. William Julius Wilson, *The Truly Disadvantaged* (Chicago: University of Chicago Press, 1987), 7–8.
2. See Carole Marks, "The Urban Underclass," *Annual Review of Sociology* 17 (1991): 445–66.

3. See Norman Fainstein, "Race, Class, and Segregation: Discourses about African Americans," *International Journal of Urban and Regional Research* 17, no. 3 (1993).

4. By the time the various qualifiers are attached to individuals that make them members of the underclass, as opposed to just suffering from low income, the "real" underclass shrinks to less than 2 percent of the "poor" (Erol Rickets, "The Nature and Dimensions of the Underclass," in *The Metropolis in Black and White*, ed. George Galster and Edward Hill [New Brunswick, N.J.: Rutgers University Center for Urban Policy Research, 1992], 51).

5. For an exposition of mismatch theory, see John Kasarda, "Urban Industrial Transformation and the Underclass," in "The Ghetto Underclass: Social Science Perspectives," *Annals* 501, ed. William Julius Wilson (January 1989): 33–57. I offer a detailed critique in Norman Fainstein, "The Underclass/Mismatch Hypothesis as Explanation for Black Economic Deprivation," *Politics and Society* 15, no. 4 (1986): 403–51.

6. See David Ward, *Poverty, Ethnicity, and the American City* (New York: Cambridge University Press, 1989), and Michael Katz, ed., *The Underclass Debate—Views from History* (Princeton, N.J.: Princeton University Press, 1993).

7. See Elijah Anderson, *Streetwise* (Chicago: University of Chicago Press, 1989), 58–59.

8. U.S. House of Representatives, Committee on Ways and Means, *Overviews of Entitlement Programs* (Washington, D.C., 1991), appendix J, table 23; Bennett Harrison and Lucy Gorham, "What Happened to African American Wages in the 1980s?" in *Metropolis in Black and White*, ed. Galster and Hill, 56–71.

9. Reynolds Farley and Walter Allen, *The Color Line and the Quality of Life in America* (New York: Sage, 1987); Douglas S. Massey and Nancy A. Denton, *American Apartheid* (Cambridge, Mass.: Harvard University Press, 1993).

10. Roderick J. Harrison and Daniel H. Weinberg, "Changes in Racial and Ethnic Segregation, 1980–1990," U.S. Bureau of the Census (Washington, D.C., 1992), 17.

11. See Massey and Denton, *American Apartheid*, chap. 4, and G. Thomas Kingsley and Margery Austin Turner, eds., *Housing Markets and Residential Mobility* (Washington, D.C.: Urban Institute Press, 1993).

12. Reynolds Farley, "Neighborhood Preferences and Aspirations among Blacks and Whites," in *Housing Markets and Residential Mobility*, ed. Kingsley and Turner, 161–92.

13. Gregory Weiher, *The Fractured Metropolis: Political Fragmentation and Metropolitan Segregation* (Albany, SUNY Press, 1991).

14. Douglas Massey, "American Apartheid: Segregation and the Making of the Underclass," *American Journal of Sociology* 96, no. 2 (1990): 354. Massey supports his conclusion with numerous references that I cannot detail here.

15. Until the terms of discourse were turned by the underclass school, the word *ghetto* was used to characterize segregated black neighborhoods encompassing a variety of class strata, and residential segregation was viewed as distorting the whole range of black-white relations. It was in this sense that Kenneth Clark called Harlem in the fifties and sixties a "dark ghetto," which he identified with "institutionalized pathology" as he excoriated Harlem's institutions and leaders, not least of all its black politicians and community elites (Kenneth Clark, *Dark Ghetto* [New York: Harper and Row, 1965], 81).

16. William Julius Wilson, "Studying Inner-City Social Dislocations," *American Sociological Review* 56 (February 1991): 1–14.

17. Robert Weaver, *The Negro Ghetto* (New York: Harcourt, Brace, 1948), 7.

18. St. Claire Drake, "The Social and Economic Status of the Negro in the United States," in *The Negro American*, ed. Talcott Parsons and Kenneth B. Clark (Boston: Houghton Mifflin, 1966), 7–8.

19. Norman Fainstein and Susan Fainstein, *Urban Political Movements* (Englewood Cliffs, N.J.: Prentice-Hall, 1974).

20. Besides the work cited earlier, see Gary Orfield and Carole Ashkinaze, who show just how segregation in the Atlanta region works to reduce the quality of schooling, housing, and public services for African Americans, including those of the middle class (Gary Orfield and Carole Ashkinaze, *The Closing Door* [Chicago: University of Chicago Press, 1991]). An excellent analysis of data from the seventies is provided by Mark Schneider and John Logan, "Suburban Racial Segregation and Black Access to Public Resources," *Social Science Quarterly* 63 (1982): 762–70.

21. An extensive review of evidence on spatial mismatch is provided by Harry J. Holzer, "The Spatial Mismatch Hypothesis: What Has the Evidence Shown?" *Urban Studies* 28, no. 1 (1991): 105–22. Also see the discussion in Susan Fainstein and Norman Fainstein, "The Racial Dimension in Urban Political Economy," *Urban Affairs Quarterly* 25 (December 1989): 187–99.

22. Douglas S. Massey and Mitchell L. Eggers, "The Ecology of Inequality: Minorities and the Concentration of Poverty, 1970–1980," *American Journal of Sociology* 95, no. 5 (1990): 1153–88.

23. Karl E. Taeuber and Alma F. Taeuber, *Negroes in Cities* (Chicago: Aldine, 1965); Nathan Kantrowitz, *Ethnic*

and Racial Segregation in the New York Metropolis (New York: Praeger, 1973).

24. Reynolds Farley, "Residential Segregation of Social and Economic Groups among Blacks, 1970–1980," in *The Urban Underclass*, ed. Christopher Jencks and Paul E. Peterson (Washington, D.C.: Brookings Institution, 1991), 274–98. Preliminary analyses by Andrew Beveridge of the 1990 data for the New York metropolis show little change from the 1980 patterns (Sam Roberts, "Shifts in Eighties Failed to Ease Segregation," *New York Times*, July 15, 1992, B1).

25. Bridgette Mach Erbe, "Race and Socioeconomic Segregation," *American Sociological Review* 40 (December 1975): 801–12.

26. Using individual data from the neighborhood files of the 1970 census, Wayne Villemez found that at a given income level, blacks are less able to achieve class segregation than whites (Wayne Villemez, "Race, Class, and Neighborhood: Differences in the Residential Return on Individual Resources," *Social Forces* 59, no. 2 [1980]: 414–30).

27. Douglas S. Massey, Gretchen A. Condron, and Nancy A. Denton, "The Effects of Residential Segregation on Black Social and Economic Well-Being," *Social Forces* 66 (September 1987): 29–56.

28. Ibid., 52.

29. Ibid., 54.

30. Christopher Jencks and Susan Mayer, "The Social Consequences of Growing Up in a Poor Neighborhood," in National Resource Council, *Inner-City Poverty in the United States* (Washington, D.C.: National Academy Press, 1990), 111–86.

31. James S. Coleman et al., *Equality of Educational Opportunity* (Washington, D.C.: GPO, 1966).

32. Mary Davis, "The Gautreaux Assisted Housing Program," in *Housing Markets and Residential Mobility*, ed. Kingsley and Turner, 243–54.

33. James E. Rosenbaum, "Black Pioneers—Do Their Moves to the Suburbs Increase Economic Opportunity for Mothers and Children?" *Housing Policy Debate* 2, no. 4 (1991): 1179–1213; James E. Rosenbaum and Susan J. Popkin, "Employment and Earnings of Low-Income Blacks Who Move to Middle-Class Suburbs," in *The Urban Underclass*, ed. Jencks and Peterson, 342–56.

CHAPTER 32

RACIAL PROGRESS

ABIGAIL AND STEPHAN THERNSTROM

In the Perrywood community of Upper Marlboro, MD, near Washington, DC, homes cost between $160,000 and $400,000. The lawns are green and the amenities appealing—including a basketball court.

Low-income teen-agers from Washington started coming there. The teens were black, and they were not welcomed. The homeowners' association hired off-duty police as security, and they would ask the ballplayers whether they "belonged" in the area. The association's newsletter noted the "eyesore" at the basketball court.

But the story has a surprising twist: many of the homeowners were black too. "We started having problems with the young men, and unfortunately they are our people," one resident told a reporter from the Washington *Post*. "But what can you do?"

The homeowners didn't care about the race of the basketball players. They were outsiders—intruders. As another resident remarked, "People who don't live here might not care about things the way we do. Seeing all the new houses going up, someone might be tempted."

It's a telling story. Lots of Americans think that almost all blacks live in inner cities. Not true. Today many blacks own homes in suburban neighborhoods—not just around Washington, but outside Atlanta, Denver, and other cities as well.

That's not the only common misconception Americans have about race. For some of the misinformation, the media are to blame. A reporter in *The Wall Street Journal*, for instance, writes that the eco-nomic gap between whites and blacks has widened. He offers no evidence. The picture drawn of racial relations is even bleaker. In one poll, for instance, 85 percent of blacks, but only 34 percent of whites, agreed with the verdict in the O. J. Simpson murder trial. That racially divided response made headline news. Blacks and whites, media accounts would have us believe, are still separate and hostile. Division is a constant theme, racism another.

To be sure, racism has not disappeared, and race relations could—and probably will—improve. But the serious inequality that remains is less a function of racism than of the racial gap in levels of educational attainment, single parenthood and crime. The bad news, has been exaggerated, and the good news neglected. Consider these three trends.

A BLACK MIDDLE CLASS HAS ARRIVED

Andrew Young recalls the day he was mistaken for a valet at the Waldorf-Astoria Hotel in New York City. It was an infuriating case of mistaken identity for a man who was then U.S. ambassador to the United Nations.

But it wasn't long ago that most blacks *were* servants—or their equivalent. On the eve of World War II, a trivial five percent of black men were engaged in white-collar work of any kind, and six out of ten African American women were employed as domestics.

In 1940 there were only 1000 practicing African American lawyers; by 1995 there were over 32,000, about four percent of all attorneys (for overall changes in white-collar employment see Figure 32.1).

From *Reader's Digest*, Large edition, (March 1998), pp. 57–62. Reprinted by permission.

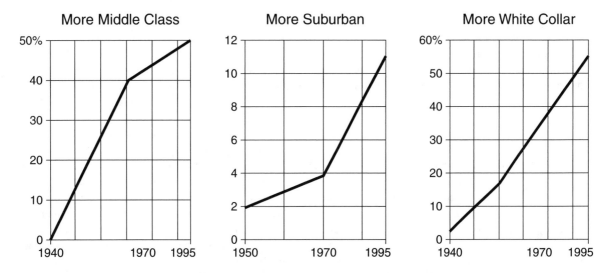

Source: U.S. Bureau of Census. Chart 1: Percent of black families with incomes at least double the poverty line; some calculations by Reynolds Farley and William H. Frey. Chart 2: African American suburban dwellers, in millions. Chart 3: Percent of employed African Americans with white-collar jobs.

FIGURE 32.1   A Steady Climb for Black Americans

Today almost three-quarters of African American families have incomes above the government poverty line. Many are in the middle class, according to one useful index—earning double the government's poverty level; in 1995 this was $30,910 for a two-parent family with two children and $40,728 for a two-parent family with four children. Only one black family in 100 enjoyed a middle-class income by 1940; by 1995 it was 49 in 100 (see Figure 32.1). And more than 40 percent of black households also own their homes. That's a huge change.

The typical white family still earns a lot more than the black family because it is more likely to collect two paychecks. But if we look only at married couples—much of the middle class—the white-black income gap shrinks to 13 percent. Much of that gap can be explained by the smaller percentage of blacks with college degrees, which boost wages, and the greater concentration of blacks in the South, where wages tend to be lower.

BLACKS ARE MOVING TO THE SUBURBS

Following the urban riots of the mid-1960s, the Presidential Kerner Commission concluded that the nation's future was menaced by "accelerating segregation"—black central cities and whites outside the core. That segregation might well blow the country apart, it said.

It's true that whites have continued to leave inner cities for the suburbs, but so, too, have blacks. The number of black suburban dwellers in the last generation has almost tripled to 10.6 million. In 1970 metropolitan Atlanta, for example, 27 percent of blacks lived in the suburbs with 85 percent of whites. By 1990, 64 percent of blacks and 94 percent of whites resided there (see Figure 32.1).

This is not phony integration, with blacks moving from one all-black neighborhood into another. Most of the movement has brought African Americans into neighborhoods much less black than those left behind, thus increasing integration. By 1994 six in ten whites reported that they lived in neighborhoods with blacks.

Residential patterns do remain closely connected to race. However, neighborhoods have become more racially mixed, and residential segregation has been decreasing.

BIGOTRY HAS DECLINED

Before World War II, Gunnar Myrdal roamed the South researching *An American Dilemma*, the now-classic book that documented the chasm between the nation's ideals and its racial practices. In one small Southern city, he kept asking whites how he could find "Mr. Jim Smith," an African American who was principal of a black high school. No one seemed to know who he was. After he finally found Smith, Myrdal was told that he should have just asked for "Jim." That's how great was white aversion to dignifying African Americans with "Mr." or "Mrs."

Bigotry was not just a Southern problem. A national survey in the 1940s asked whether "Negroes should have as good a chance as white people to get any kind of job." A majority of whites said that "white people should have the first chance at any kind of job."

Such a question would not even be asked today. Except for a lunatic fringe, no whites would sign on to such a notion.

In 1964 less than one in five whites reported having a black friend. By 1989 more than two of three did. And more than eight of ten African Americans had a white friend.

What about the last taboo? In 1963 ten percent of whites approved of black-white dating; by 1994 it

was 65 percent. Interracial marriages? Four percent of whites said it was okay in 1958; by 1994 the figure had climbed more than elevenfold, to 45 percent. These surveys measure opinion, but behavior has also changed. In 1963 less than one percent of marriages by African Americans were racially mixed. By 1993, 12 percent were.

Today black Americans can climb the ladder to the top. Ann M. Fudge is already there; she's in charge of manufacturing, promotion, and sales at the $2.7-billion Maxwell House Coffee and Post Cereals divisions of Kraft Foods. So are Kenneth Chenault, president and chief operating officer at American Express, and Richard D. Parsons, president of Time Warner, Inc. After the 1988 Democratic Convention, the Rev. Jesse Jackson talked about his chances of making it to the White House. "I may not get there," he said. "But it is possible for our children to get there now."

Even that seems too pessimistic. Consider how things have improved since Colin and Alma Powell packed their belongings into a Volkswagen and left for Fort Devens, Mass., for Fort Bragg, N.C. "I remember passing Woodbridge, Va.," General Powell wrote in his autobiography, "and not finding even a gas-station bathroom that we were allowed to use." That was in 1962. In 1996 reliable polls suggest he could have been elected President.

Progress over the last half-century has been dramatic. As Coretta Scott King wrote not long ago, the ideals for which her husband, Martin Luther King, Jr., died have become "deeply embedded in the very fabric of America."

PART 11

GENDER

Gender issues have appeared throughout *Empirical Approaches to Sociology*: in Durkheim's study of male-female differences in suicide rates; in Carter and Hesse-Biber's discussion of eating disorders of college-age women, in Mirowsky and Ross's examination of gender differences in psychological distress; and in Fishman's investigation of the power differences between women and men in everyday conversations. The selections in Part 11 buttress these readings, while bringing into sharper focus the social roots of gender identification and of male-female inequality.

Margaret Mead (1901–1978) had a profound influence on the intellectual development of sociology. Her research on gender socialization and gender roles revolutionized our thinking on what it means to be a "man" versus a "woman." Although no one doubted that socialization played a part, most Americans and Europeans believed that sex roles had been largely genetically (or even divinely) determined. That is, men were thought to be by nature aggressive, tough, and oriented toward matters away from the home (from hunting to politics). On the other hand, women were conceived as the weaker sex—physically, mentally, and, in some areas of life, morally; they were by nature passive, nurturing, and oriented toward matters of the home (especially the love and care of children). Mead reasoned that if what makes men act like "men" and what makes women like "women" is genetically determined, then in all societies we should find men acting more or less the same (aggressive, etc.) and women also acting more or less the same (nurturing, etc.). She chose isolated islands in the South Pacific to study because she wanted to find societies that were uncontaminated with the culture and traditions of the West, whose societies have become similar in many aspects because of trade, migrations, and conquests.[1]

What Mead uncovered forced us to rethink the origins of gender roles. She found one tribe in which both men and women acted "feminine" (according to western standards): Both sexes took care of the children and neither sex was aggressive. In a second tribe, she found both sexes acting "masculine" (again, according to western standards): Neither sex enjoyed taking care of children; both sexes were tough and aggressive (coitus often amounted to rape). And, in a third tribe, she found males acting "feminine" and females acting "masculine": Men took care of the children and adorned their bodies with jewelry, while women went to the sea to fish and support the family. In sum, gender roles are socially produced.

---

[1] See Margaret Mead, *Sex and Temperament in Three Primitive Societies* (New York: William Morrow, 1935), and her *Male and Female: A Study in the Sexes in a Changing World* (New York: William Morrow, 1949).

In the early 1980s, Mead's research came under heavy attack from the respected anthropologist, Derek Freeman,[2] who questioned her methods and findings. For example, he accused Mead of having relied too much on a single informant and having spent too much time close to her comfortable house and not enough time "in the field" rubbing shoulders with the natives. Anthropologists and sociologists debated and assessed Freeman's accusations for several years. The outcome was a realization that Mead had made some errors but that many of her findings and conclusions, including those presented above, were solid. For example, anthropologist Nancy McDowell studied the Mundugumor (the tribe in which Mead found both sexes acting "masculine") during three extended field trips between 1972 and 1981, and she found the people just as "harsh and aggressive" as Mead had said they were.[3]

Mead's findings have also received confirmation from an entirely different direction. John Money and his colleagues at Johns Hopkins University (including his co-author in the "classic" essay presented here, Anke A. Ehrhardt) examined gender identification and gender roles from a genetic perspective. In particular, they studied hermaphrodites (individuals born with both male and female genitalia) and related aberrations involving sex organs. The upshot of their research reveals that socialization, rather than biology/genetics, is the key to understanding gender identification. For example, XY (genetically male) hermaphrodites raised as females come to identify themselves as "women" and have no desire to become "men"; similarly, XX (genetically female) hermaphrodites raised as males grow up to act like "men" and have no desire to realize their genetic code to be "female."[4]

---

[2]Derek Freeman, *Margaret Mead and Samoa: The Making and Unmaking of Anthropological Myth* (Cambridge, MA: Harvard University Press), 1983.

[3]Nancy McDowell, *The Mundugumor,* as cited in Jane Howard, *Margaret Mead, A Life* (New York: Ballentine Books), 1984, pp. 138-139.

[4]John Money's writings on David Reimer, an infant who accidentally lost his penis during circumcision at 8 months old and who was subsequently raised as a "girl" under Money's guidance, received extreme criticism in the media during the early part of 2000. During the 1970s, Money reported that Reimer was being successfully raised as a girl, when in fact he was not; indeed, he eventually opted to become a "boy" during adolescence. This failed experiment was used to raise the petard of "biology/genes" as the key determinant of gender identity. However, Money's research on hermaphrodites, reported in part here, negates this stance. Moreover, according to many scholars, the Reimer case should not be overemphasized—mainly because it represents a sample of one. Moreover, "the causes of the trauma and Reimer's boyish" personality "are not at all necessarily a result of David's 'true male psyche' as implied. Many girls are not comfortable with the feminine gender role either. Furthermore, David Reimer wasn't raised like most girls are raised. He went through a traumatic relationship with a researcher that broke many dominant cultural norms. . . . People attempted to raise David as a girl, but it seems to me that he was treated uniquely from day one and there was so much emphasis put on how his genitals differed from both males and females that it is no surprise that he chose to identify with the more impowered gender role of boy/man. I think his unusual treatment as a patient, the power relations involved vis-à-vis both gender and the doctor/researcher vs. patient/subject, and the focus put on his physiology are all too confounded with being raised as a girl to claim that we know anything about which was influential in making David 'boyish.' Certainly physiology and the cultural meanings we attach have important interactive effects. But to say so is quite different from saying there is a natural male psyche" (Lisa Jones, "David Reimer, Gender, and Biology," teachsoc@vance.irss.unc.edu, February 17, 2000). For Reimer's tragic-yet-inspiring biography, see John Colapinto, *As Nature Made Him* (New York: HarperCollins, 2000).

Simon Davis, of the University of British Columbia, demonstrates how powerful traditional conceptions of gender and of gender roles still are. Despite the transformation of women's work roles in the past three decades (from homemakers to wage earners), many people still desire traditional traits in their potential spouses. More particularly, Davis's study of personal advertisements revealed that men tend to want soft, beautiful, sexy women and that women tend to want materially successful men.

Katherine M. Haskins and H. Edward Ransford (both of the University of Southern California) also demonstrate how powerful traditional gender roles still are. They show that societal expectations for women to be thin and attractive carry over into the work world; in particular, women in high-status white-collar jobs are more likely to be successful if they are trim. Their fundamental conclusion is that even though women in general face discrimination, overweight women experience a "uniquely high degree of discrimination."

Part 11 ends with an empirically argued essay that draws the connection between gender inequality in the work world, on the one hand, and gender socialization in the contexts of the family, school, peer groups, and the media on the other hand. More specifically, Sharlene Hesse-Biber (Boston College) and I show how gender socialization still encourages many traditional stereotypes of desirable behavior for men and women. Such stereotypes reinforce traditional gender arrangements—ones that result in men being more likely than women to be economically successful. For example, most children see both mother and father in the workforce, but they also see household chores still predominantly done by their mothers. Despite greater gender egalitarianism in education philosophy and programs, girls are still "shortchanged" in the modern school; to wit, in coeducational classrooms, teachers give boys more attention and encouragement to be assertive. Regarding peers, youth culture encourages boys to be athletic and not overly expressive, while girls are encouraged to be beauty-oriented and demure; such a culture reinforces the idea that males achieve status through accomplishment, while females achieve status by appearance and beauty. Finally, the media often reinforces traditional gender stereotypes; for example, women in television are much more likely than men to be portrayed as submissive and unsuccessful.

The upshot of all these gender socialization influences is that in high school, noncollege-oriented boys are much more likely to take vocational courses that will lead them into high-paying blue-collar trades (plumbing, carpentry, electrician work), while girls are much more likely to take vocational courses that prepare them for low-paying office work (file clerk, bookkeeper, bank teller). The situation is similar at the college level, with men more likely than women to major in fields (e.g., engineering, computer science) that lead to high-paying jobs.

_____CHAPTER 33_____

SOCIALIZATION, GENETICS, AND GENDER ROLES

JOHN MONEY AND ANKE A. EHRHARDT

In human beings, no one yet knows the influence on pregnancy of drugs or foods, or even the mother's own, perhaps anomalous placental hormones, or anomalous hormones or hormone deficiency from another maternal source, on the central nervous system of the fetus and the subsequent gender-dimorphic behavior of the child, boy or girl.[1] [T]herefore . . . it is premature to attribute all aspects of gender-identity to the postnatal period of gender-identity differentiation.

Nonetheless, the evidence of human hermaphroditism makes it abundantly clear that nature has ordained a major part of human gender-identity differentiation to be accomplished in the postnatal period.[2] It then takes place, as does the development of native language, when a prenatally programmed disposition comes in contact with postnatal, socially programmed signals. The test cases are matched pairs of hermaphrodites, chromosomally, gonadally, and otherwise diagnostically the same, but antithetical in sex assignment, biographical history, and gender identity. The contrast between two such young adult individuals in gender role and gender identity is so complete that the ordinary person meeting them socially or vocationally has no clues as to the remarkable contents of their medical histories.

A similar extraordinary contrast has been observed even when a child born as a normal male

was surgically reassigned as a female, following an accidental burn in circumcision by cautery. The burn totally ablated [obliterated] the penis. The child is not yet postpubertal and erotically mature, so that the final word remains to be written. Meanwhile, in gender behavior, she is quite gender-different from her identical twin brother (see [later] for further details). . . .

GENETIC DIMORPHISM

X and Y Chromosomes

The dimorphism which will eventually appear in the differentiation of gender identity and behavior is represented at the very beginning of life in the dimorphism of the sex-determining chromosomes, X and Y. The presence of two X chromosomes (XX) in the egg fertilized by the sperm heralds the differentiation of a female, if all goes well, and if the developmental program proceeds according to Nature's preferred plan. Alternatively, an X chromosome plus a Y (XY) herald that a male will be differentiated, if all goes well.

It is not invariable that all does go well in Nature. There are deviations from the preferred plan—of diverse types and for various and sundry reasons. Extra X or Y chromosomes may be added, or one taken away. A chromosome may be broken or otherwise distorted. Even without such a mishap, the conditions in which the earliest stages of cellular and embryonic differentiation take place may be altered and atypical, so that the normal masculine or feminine course of differentiation is interfered with, ending up with an individual whose sexual differentiation is paradoxical or discordant with the XX or XY chromosomal pattern in the cells.

All the occasions when Nature's preferred chromosomal plan for sexual differentiation is deviated from are extremely important for the theory of gender identity, for they give one a chance to investigate the relationship between genetics and the sexual dimorphism of behavior—that is to say, they provide a glimpse into the genetics of masculinity and femininity of behavior.

In the case of human development, the glimpse cannot be created at will, as in planned breeding experiments, because of the ethical limitations that we human beings place on our unwarranted interference with one another's lives. One must rely instead on Nature's own experiments—the quirks and errors of chromosome sorting that occur spontaneously. . . .

GENDER DIMORPHISM IN ASSIGNMENT AND REARING

Dimorphism of Behavior, Parental and Cultural

It is easy to get trapped in circular argument as to whether boys and girls develop different patterns of preferred behavior because they are treated differently, or whether they are treated differently because they demonstrate different behavioral patterns right from the beginning. The [scientific] evidence ,. . . shows rather conclusively that there are in human beings some gender-dimorphic behavior differences based on antenatal hormonal history, but that these differences do not automatically dictate or totally preordain the course of postnatal dimorphism of behavioral differentiation. [Later we] produce further evidence of the weighty importance of postnatal events in determining how the prenatal determinants or dispositions will be incorporated into the final gender-dimorphic behavioral product.

The purpose of the present chapter is to assemble some evidence that demonstrates the proposition that cultural tradition does indeed prescribe what no one seriously doubts, namely, that parents behave differently toward and have different expectations of their infant sons and daughters. . . .

The evidence is drawn from . . . the testimony of . . . parents who actually went through the experience of treating a baby as a son for the first seventeen months of life, and, thereafter, following an obligatory sex reassignment, as a daughter.

Rearing of a Genitally Malformed, Sex-Reassigned Infant as a Girl

The diagnosis established for this baby born with ambiguous genitalia was that of genetic male (46,XY) with a . . . microphallus [minuscule penis]. The phallus was 1 cm long [about ⅓ inch], so small as to resemble a slightly enlarged clitoris, and like a clitoris, it did not carry a urinary canal. The urinary opening was at the base of this organ in approximately the female position. The scrotum was incompletely fused in the midline, but each half of it contained a palpable testis.

Though a female sex assignment was suggested to the parents at the time of birth, the suggestion was revoked after a few days. A specialist consultant, on the basis of the presence of testes, had decided that the child should live as a boy, despite the absence of a penis. Thenceforth, the parents lived through several months of indecision, while medical opinions differed as to the wisdom of assigning the baby as a boy. By the time the child was seventeen months old, following the necessary consultations, a decision was finalized to reassign the child as a girl. The first stage of surgical feminization of the genitalia was successfully completed. The second, vaginoplasty, would follow in teenage years, after pubertal growth and feminization of the body shape by means of estrogen replacement therapy.

Both parents were in their late twenties when they had their second child, at which time the older brother was twenty-two months of age. The older boy had been born with a defect of the penis, a second degree hypospadias [abnormal urethral opening], which had been successfully repaired.

At the time of sex reassignment, the parents were given the same type of advice and counseling as indicated in the preceding case example, with particular attention to what to tell the older brother (Money,

Potter, and Stoll, 1969). He needed to know that by no caprice of fate would a reassignment of sex be required of him.

The follow-up since sex reassignment has been nearly three years. Meantime the parents have been informative regarding their experience of making the change from rearing a son to rearing a daughter.

The first change was related to different clothes. The baby received a completely new set of female clothing and her hair was allowed to grow long. Another recent immediate change was a completely new set of girl's toys.

Shortly after the sex reassignment, the parents noted a marked change in the brother who was about 3½ years of age at that time. The parents had explained to the boy that his baby brother really was a baby sister and that the doctors had made a mistake. Subsequently, they showed him the surgically feminized genitalia and he had no difficulty in accepting the sex reassignment. The father reported: "My wife tells me, she has noticed a marked difference in his behavior towards his new sister . . . she sees a very evident degree of protectionism, now, on his part towards his sister, and a marked tendency to treat her much more gently. Whereas, before, he was just as likely to stick his foot out and trip her as he went by, he now wants to hold her hand to make sure she doesn't fall." The parents were not aware of making a special point that their son should treat his sister differently from the time she had been a boy. The only reason they could think of for the change in his behavior was that he copied other boys' behavior towards their sisters.

Two months after the sex reassignment, the mother reported that she and her husband thought the girl had really changed in her ways and had become much more feminine. They allowed that it may have something to do with their own perception, but that they thought it was a clear-cut, objective observation. The father described at that time his own feelings: "It's a great feeling of fun for me to have a little girl. I have completely different feelings towards this child as a girl than as a boy." He had noticed a change in his behavior towards his daughter compared to his son: "I treat my son quite differently—

wrestling around, playing ball." He said that he had done the same with the second child before sex reassignment. Now he avoided such things with the girl. He attempted to distinguish between "things you associate with fun for boys, and things for girls."

During a follow-up visit when the child was two years and three months old, the mother reported that her daughter imitated many things from her such as doing dishes, cooking, kitchen work on her own kitchen sink and, in general, activities that are related to the woman's household role. At the same time, the child participated in boys' play activities and games together with boys, as do many tomboyish girls. Her mother was concerned whether she should discourage any tomboyish activity to a larger degree than she was doing. She was advised rather to let the child follow her own impulses in order not to evoke a rebellious counter-reaction. Similar advice was offered to the mother three months later, when she became concerned that her daughter would say occasionally that she was a boy and not a girl. The mother was told that it would be better not to contradict the child, but to put the child's comment into a girl's perspective by saying that lots of girls wanted to become boys, sometimes.

At age three, the girl's behavior still seemed quite tomboyish to her mother who noticed that she tended to be louder and more aggressive than other little girls they came in contact with. She also still seemed to have more physical energy expenditure. The parents were quite aware that they were perhaps somewhat oversensitive about their daughter's behavior, that they kept comparing her too much with other little girls of her age. At age three, the girl also had clearly feminine wishes. For Christmas, she wanted glass slippers, so that she could go to the ball like Cinderella, and a doll. The parents were delighted. The girl continued to receive typically girlish toys from her parents. She continued more and more to show feminine interests, as in helping her mother.

The father gave an example, when the girl was three years old, of how girls and boys are differently treated with respect to rehearsal of their adult roles as a female or male romantic partner. The family had established the habit of dancing together to the record-player, after the father arrived home from work. The father usually picked his daughter up, or danced with her, holding her close to him, while the boy was doing rock and roll dancing of a more solo type, maybe including his mother as a partner. At first, the girl wanted to copy her brother, but then she began to enjoy the favoritism of dancing with her father.

Regarding toilet habits, the girl tried standing up to urinate (though because of the genital deformity, the standing position had always been impossible) and had been told that little girls usually sit down on the toilet. At age three, this habit had faded, and the girl preferred to sit down on the toilet.

[This case] of sex reassignment illustrate that parents do indeed have different criteria of what to reinforce in the behavior and responses of boys and girls. These criteria apply to clothing, adornment and general appearance; to body movements and positions; to play and the rehearsal of future roles as romantic partner, and wife and mother, or husband and father; to genital play and sex education, and to academic and vocational choice. Some gender-conforming behavior is openly and explicitly reinforced by adults and other children, whereas in other instances the reinforcements are more subtle and covert.

GENDER IDENTITY DIFFERENTIATION

Terminology

Gender identity . . . is the private experience of gender role; and gender role is the public manifestation of gender identity. There is no single term to signify gender identity/role, which is a semantic handicap. Nevertheless, "gender identity" can be read to mean "gender identity/role," unless the context signifies otherwise. . . . Gender identity . . . differentiates generally so as to be rather remarkably fixed in adulthood. Typically, it differentiates as primarily or exclusively masculine in boys, and feminine in girls. Possibly, however, differentiation may be unfinished as either completely masculine or completely feminine, but ambiguous instead. . . .

Matched Pairs of Hermaphrodites

Informative as they are, even large numbers of case biographies of genetic male hermaphrodites reared as girls do not give the final and conclusive answer as to the postnatal effect of the sex of rearing on gender-identity differentiation. By themselves alone, these biographies might lead one to the hypothesis that the very ambiguity of the hermaphroditic condition predisposes the child to differentiate a feminine identity. For this reason, matched pairs of hermaphrodites, concordant for diagnosis but discordant for sex of rearing, are particularly instructive.

Matched pairs of hermaphrodites demonstrate conclusively how heavily weighted is the contribution of the postnatal phase of gender-identity differentiation. To use the Pygmalion allegory, one may begin with the same clay and fashion a god or a goddess. Certain conditions must be met:

1. It is absolutely prerequisite that the parents have no doubt or ambiguity as to whether they are raising a son or a daughter. Uncertainty, if it exists at the time of birth, must be resolved in such a way that the parents follow the same train of reasoning as the experts who guide them. They then reach the same decision, instead of having to accept an instruction on faith, with no guarantee whether it is correct or in error.

2. The sooner that the first stages of corrective genital surgery are initiated, the better. Parents need the reassurance of the baby's sexual appearance. They cannot raise a baby as a girl, despite ovaries and a uterus internally, if it has a penis externally—which can happen. Conversely, they cannot raise as a boy a baby that has a urogenital opening in the female position and a phallic organ no bigger than a large clitoris. Relatives and baby-sitters are equally nonplussed and, moreover, gossipy. When the limitations of surgical technique require delays between the progressive stages of surgical reconstruction, the prognosis needs to be given to the parents and, eventually, to the child himself or herself.

3. At the usual age of puberty, and in concordance with statural growth, the gender-appropriate sex hormones should be administered, estrogen for the girl, and androgen for the boy. Girls with breasts too small can have them enlarged with a silicone implant; and boys without testes can have silicone prosthetic testes implanted.

4. In age-graded steps, a hermaphroditic child should be kept diagnostically and prognostically informed with suitably simplified concepts and explanations. Ideally, this information will be interconnected with the ordinary sex education of childhood. For example, knowledge of motherhood by pregnancy versus motherhood by adoption will be familiar in advance of prognostications of fertility. Never make prophecies, only probability statements: even the most distant ray of hope should never be extinguished! Moreover, all lay people know examples of unfulfilled medical prophecies, and today's prophecies may be tomorrow's fallacies. For example, the sterility of castration today may be the fertility of an implanted ovum tomorrow. Children respond with trust when they are entrusted. Prepared with the truth, they rehearse in their fantasies a future that will not bring the anguish of surprise and disillusionment— even a difficult future like the one that will require an artificial penis for vaginal penetration. Uninformed of his medical situation, a child makes guesswork inferences on the basis of what is done to him or her and of what is so easily overheard in clinics and examining rooms. Adults claim that they withhold information to protect the child, whereas actually they only spare themselves from their communicational ineptitude and anxiety.

When the foregoing conditions have been met, then it is to all intents and purposes predictable that each member of a matched pair of hermaphrodites, discordant for sex of assignment and rearing, will be discordant also for gender identity. Even if the prediction is not universally valid, then it is frequently so and, in each instance, with remarkable completeness. . . .

[Two] Matched Pairs of Biographies

The [two] pairs of cases herewith presented are chosen because all [four] are concordant for diagnosis but different in biography. In each case the diagnosis is genetic female [i.e., all had the XX chromosomal pattern] with the adrenogenital syndrome. At birth the genitalia were ambiguous. In each pair, despite the sameness of genetic, gonadal, and fetal hormonal sex, one has a masculine, the other a feminine gender identity.

First Matched Pair. In the first pair, the diagnosis was established early enough to permit the suppression, by hormonal regulation with cortisone, of accelerated statural growth and premature, masculinizing puberty during the years of childhood.

The child raised as a girl was actually announced as a boy at the time of birth, because of the appearance of the genitals. The correct diagnosis was established by the age of two months and a sex reannouncement was decided upon. The parents were counseled on how to negotiate a sex reannouncement within the family and the community (Money, Potter, and Stoll, 1969), which they accomplished successfully. Today it is known that the first stage of surgical feminization could have been safely carried out without delay, but at the time it was delayed as a precaution against a surgically induced crisis of adrenal insufficiency, until the age of two years. Thereafter, the child had an unremarkable childhood, medically, except for taking a daily maintenance dosage of cortisone pills. At the age of thirteen breast development began. The menses failed to appear on time, as is occasionally the case in the adrenogenital syndrome, and did not begin until age twenty.

During childhood, the child developed behaviorally as a girl with tomboyish activity interests, in the fashion now considered typical for children with the adrenogenital syndrome, though not so as to become conspicuously different from other girls of her age. In teenage [years], academic and career interests had priority over dating, romance, and going steady. There was no romantic inclination toward either boys or girls, but rather a projection into the future of the boyfriend and married stage of life. Otherwise, everything about this girl was very attractively feminine to all who interviewed and knew her.

The second member of the first matched pair was given an improvised diagnosis at birth and pronounced a male with a hypospadiac phallus and undescended testes. Three stages of surgical masculinization ended in failure, as urine backed up into the internally opening vagina with ensuing infection. At age three and a half, the correct diagnosis was established and the case was referred to Johns Hopkins. At this time the child was terror stricken at being once again in a hospital. He said that a nurse would cut off his wee wee, and that his baby sister had had hers cut off. But his big brother in the Air Force would bring him a new wee wee. His terror abated when, with plastic clay and water, he was shown how an imperfect penis could be repaired.

It was decided to allow the boy to continue living as a boy. The appropriate surgery was done, and during childhood cortisone therapy corrected the abnormal activity of the adrenal cortices and permitted statural growth to be normal. At the age of puberty, masculinization was induced by means of androgen therapy. Artificial testes were implanted in the empty scrotum.

The boy's family life, as he approached teen age, was tortured. His parents fought. The father was incapacitated by multiple sclerosis. The wife won points by reminding him that he was not the father of this particular child, and the boy himself heard what she said.

In teenage, the boy was an academic underachiever, and he tended to seek the company of quasi-delinquents where he could achieve status of sorts as a rebel. He was accepted by the other boys as one of them. He was not overly aggressive. Psychosexually, the significant finding was that all of his romantic feelings and approaches were toward girls, despite his trepidation at the prospect of attempting intercourse with too small a penis and prosthetic testes that could be recognized on palpation as not soft enough.

Second Matched Pair.   The criterion that separates the second from the first matched pair of children with the adrenogenital syndrome, their gender identities respectively concordant with assigned sex and rearing [everyone treated the boy as a "boy," and he thought of himself as a "boy"; likewise for the girl—everyone treated her as a "girl," and she thought of herself as a "girl"], is that hormonal sex in both children of the second pair was, at age twelve, discordant with gender identity. The girl was masculinized, and the boy feminized. The boy's female chromosomal and gonadal sex were also discordant with his gender identity [he was XX and had enlarged breasts and an empty scrotum].

The boy was aged thirteen at the time depicted, and had to his disgust manifested breast growth since the age of eleven. Diagnostically, he was still believed at age eleven to be a genetic male with the adrenogenital syndrome, though a rather atypical case since the testes were not present in the scrotum, and the urinary opening was slightly misplaced away from the tip of the rather small phallus. He had been on treatment with cortisone since age 3 1/2 years. The gonads being in fact ovaries, the therapy with cortisone permitted them at age eleven to secrete estrogen in the fashion typical for a female at puberty, and hence to induce breast growth. Menstrual bleeding had not yet begun when the boy was seen at age thirteen. The correct chromosomal status (46,XX) had been ascertained at age twelve, and soon thereafter the boy was referred for a decision as to whether to attempt or avoid a sex reassignment.

The decision was against a reassignment, and for the same reason as it would be for the vast majority of thirteen-year-old American boys. His mother said: "He has a sister, and they are completely different. He does not think like a girl, and he does not have the same interests. Right now, the one thing that made me very sure, is that he has a girlfriend. And that to me was a relief, because that was just the clincher that he wasn't a girl." The mother had some months earlier been told the diagnosis. For the father, the boy was very much a son, and they shared many evenings, weekends, and vacations with rifle and rod. The boy's other recreational interest, shared with a boyfriend, was motor-bike racing in the dry river bed. He gave an authentic biographical account of the early phase of teen-aged romantic attraction, and had a particular girlfriend. He experienced erotic arousal, which included the slow secretion of genital moistness, from being with her, and also from girl watching. This finding was all the more significant in view of the fact that adrenocortical androgen production was low, on account of suppression with cortisone. Subsequent replacement therapy with testosterone as well as cortisone, following gonadectomy and hysterectomy, would eventually lower the threshold of erotic arousal and increase its frequency and genital carry-through, in masturbation, for instance. Meantime, masturbation was reported as nonexistent, though not morally disapproved. Phlegmatic by temperament, the boy had at first assumed that he would have to get used to having a chest with breasts on it. "I was very overjoyed," he said, when first hearing of the possibility of mastectomy; "I really couldn't wait until I could get here." He is due to return soon for his first follow-up examination in person since the termination of a feminizing hormonal puberty and its replacement with androgenization.

With respect to discordant hormonal sex, it is equally remarkable in this pair of cases that hormonal feminization did not feminize the boy's masculine gender identity, and that the great excess of premature hormonal masculinization in the girl did not masculinize her feminine gender identity. She was twelve years old at the time depicted. Like other girls in her untreated predicament, she reacted to the masculinization of her body as a deformity and wanted to be rid of it. Hormonal therapy with cortisone was begun at age twelve. It suppressed adrenocortical androgen secretion and released the ovaries to secrete estrogen. Feminine body development then ensued. She became an attractively good-looking young woman. Narrow hips and mildly short stature remained unchanged, as the epiphyses of the bones had already fused under the influence of precocious masculinization. These two signs alone remained as reminders of the past, except for a small amount of coarse facial hair, requiring removal by electrolysis. The voice was husky, but so used as to be not mistaken as masculine on the telephone.

Surgical feminization at age twelve entailed exteriorization of the vaginal opening and removal of the enlarged clitoris. The capacity for orgasm was not lost. The proof came fifteen years later, upon the establishment of a sexual relationship and marriage. It is not unusual for romance to blossom late in the treated adrenogenital syndrome in girls. In this particular case, there seemed to be an additional impediment, characteristic of girls who mature masculinized and with an uncorrected genital deformity. Even after good surgical and hormonal feminization of appearance has been achieved, such a girl is diffident and fearful of rejection—as though the old body image will not fade and be replaced by the new one. Inchoately, the girl acts as if her first lover will magically decipher her old body image and know that she used to be some sort of freak. Surmounting the barrier is a protracted business, and is achieved when intercourse in a love affair is finally ventured, with success.

Chromosomes, Hormones, and Gender Identity

The foregoing . . . matched pairs of hermaphrodites, and many others like them, concordant for diagnosis and discordant for gender identity, wreck the assumption that gender identity as male or female is preordained by the sex (XX or XY) chromosomes. Clearly it is not.

The . . . pairs also prohibit the assumption that gender identity is automatically preordained by prenatal hormonal history. . . .

Like hormonal status prenatally, hormonal status after birth does not have a preordained influence on the masculinity or femininity of gender identity. The evidence from hermaphroditism is confirmed by that from adolescents or adults who undergo spontaneous changes in sex-hormone balance, as from a hormone-producing tumor. Thus a boy who grows breasts wants them removed. He does not want to change his status and live as a girl, though he may worry as to whether fate may be turning his body, though not his mind, into that of a girl. Likewise, in reverse, for the girl who grows a beard and gets a deep voice and body hair. . . .

The ultimate test of the thesis that gender identity differentiation is not preordained *in toto* by either the sex chromosomes, the prenatal hormonal pattern, or the postnatal hormonal levels would be undertaken if one had the same ethical freedom of working in experiments with normal babies as with animals. Since planned experiments are ethically unthinkable, one can only take advantage of unplanned opportunities, such as [those offered by the study of surgically altered hermaphrodites].

NOTES

1. *Dimorphism* is from the Greek word *dimorphos,* meaning "two forms"; in this case, it means that the human species has two distinct forms: male and female.—Ed.

2. A *hermaphrodite* is one having the sex organs of both male and female.—Ed.

REFERENCES

Money, John, Reynolds Potter, and Clarice S. Stoll. 1969. "Sex Reannouncement in Hereditary Sex Deformity: Psychology and Sociology." *Social Science and Medicine* 3:207–216.

CHAPTER 34

MEN AS SUCCESS OBJECTS
AND WOMEN AS SEX OBJECTS:
A STUDY OF PERSONAL ADVERTISEMENTS

SIMON DAVIS

Previous research has indicated that, to a large extent, selection of opposite-sex partners is dictated by traditional sex stereotypes (Urberg, 1979). More specifically, it has been found that men tend to emphasize sexuality and physical attractiveness in a mate to a greater extent than women (e.g., Deaux & Hanna, 1984; Harrison & Saeed, 1977; Nevid, 1984); this distinction has been found across cultures, as in the study by Stiles and colleagues (1987) of American and Icelandic adolescents.

The relatively greater preoccupation with casual sexual encounters demonstrated by men (Hite, 1987, p. 184) may be accounted for by the greater emotional investment that women place in sex; Basow (1986, p. 80) suggests that the "gender differences in this area (different meaning attached to sex) may turn out to be the strongest of all gender differences."

Women, conversely, may tend to emphasize psychological and personality characteristics (Curry & Hock, 1981; Deaux & Hanna, 1984), and to seek longevity and commitment in a relationship to a greater extent (Basow, 1986, p. 213).

Women may also seek financial security more so than men (Harrison & Saeed, 1977). Regarding this last point, Farrell (1986, p. 25) suggests that the tendency to treat men as success objects is reflected in the media, particularly in advertisements in women's magazines. On the other hand, men themselves may reinforce this stereotype in that a number of men still

apparently prefer the traditional marriage with working husband and unemployed wife (Basow, 1986, p. 210).

Men have traditionally been more dominant in intellectual matters, and this may be reinforced in the courting process: Braito (1981) found in his study that female coeds feigned intellectual inferiority with their dates on a number of occasions. In the same vein, Hite, in her 1981 survey, found that men were less likely to seek intellectual prowess in their mates (p. 108).

The mate selection process has been characterized in at least two ways. Harrison and Saeed (1977) found evidence for a matching process, where individuals seeking particular characteristics in a partner were more likely to offer those characteristics in themselves. This is consistent with the observation that "like attracts like" and that husbands and wives tend to resemble one another in various ways (Thiessen & Gregg, 1980). Additionally, an exchange process may be in operation, wherein a trade-off is made with women offering "domestic work and sex for financial support" (Basow, 1986, p. 213).

With respect to sex stereotypes and mate selection, the trend has been for "both sexes to believe that the other sex expects them to live up to the gender stereotype" (Basow, 1986, p. 209).

Theoretical explanations of sex stereotypes in mate selection range from the sociobiological (Symons, 1987) to radical political views (Smith, 1973). Of interest in recent years has been demographic influences, that is, the lesser availability of

From *Sex Roles* 23 (1/2) (July 1990), pp. 43–50. Reprinted with permission of Plenum Publishing Corporation.

men because of population shifts and marital patterns (Shaevitz, 1987, p. 40). Age may differentially affect women, particularly when children are desired; this, combined with women's generally lower economic status [particularly when unmarried (Halas, 1981, p. 124)], may mean that the need to "settle down" into a secure, committed relationship becomes relatively more crucial for women.

The present study looks at differential mate selection by men and women as reflected in newspaper companion ads. Using such a forum for the exploration of sex stereotypes is not new; for instance, in the study by Harrison and Saeed (1977) cited earlier, the authors found that in such ads women were more likely to seek financial security and men to seek attractiveness; a later study by Deaux and Hanna (1984) had similar results, along with the finding that women were more likely to seek psychological characteristics, specific personality traits, and to emphasize the quality and longevity of the relationship. The present study may be seen as a follow-up of this earlier research, although on this occasion using a Canadian setting. Of particular interest was the following: Were traditional stereotypes still in operation, that is, women being viewed as sex objects and men as success objects (the latter defined as financial and intellectual accomplishments)?

METHOD

Personal advertisements were taken from the *Vancouver Sun,* which is the major daily newspaper serving Vancouver, British Columbia. The *Sun* is generally perceived as a conservative, respectable journal—hence it was assumed that people advertising in it represented the "mainstream." It should be noted that people placing the ads must do so in person. For the sake of this study, gay ads were not included. A typical ad would run about 50 words, and included a brief description of the person placing it and a list of the attributes desired in the other party. Only the parts pertaining to the attributes desired in the partner were included for analysis. Attributes that pertained to hob-

bies or recreations were not included for the purpose of this study.

The ads were sampled as follows: Only Saturday ads were used, since in the *Sun* the convention was for Saturday to be the main day for personal ads, with 40–60 ads per edition—compared to only 2–4 ads per edition on weekdays. Within any one edition *all* the ads were included for analysis. Six editions were randomly sampled, covering the period of September 30, 1988, to September 30, 1989. The attempt to sample through the calendar year was made in an effort to avoid any unspecified seasonal effect. The size of the sample (six editions) was large enough to meet goodness-of-fit requirements for statistical tests.

The attributes listed in the ads were coded as follows:

1. *Attractive:* specified that a partner should be, for example, "pretty" or "handsome."
2. *Physique:* similar to 1; however, this focused not on the face but rather on whether the partner was "fit and trim," "muscular," or had "a good figure." If it was not clear if body or face was being emphasized, this fell into variable (1) by default.
3. *Sex:* specified that the partner should have, for instance, "high sex drive," or should be "sensuous" or "erotic," or if there was a clear message that this was an arrangement, for sexual purposes ("lunchtime liaisons—discretion required").
4. *Picture:* specified that the partner should include a photo in his/her reply.
5. *Profession:* specified that the partner should be a professional.
6. *Employed:* specified that the partner should be employed, e.g., "must hold steady job" or "must have steady income."
7. *Financial:* specified that the partner should be, for instance, "financially secure" or "financially independent."
8. *Education:* specified that the partner should be, for instance, "well educated" or "well read," or should be a "college grad."
9. *Intelligence:* specified that the partner should be "intelligent," "intellectual," or "bright."

10. *Honest:* specified, for instance, that the partner should be "honest" or have "integrity."
11. *Humor:* specified "sense of humor" or "cheerfulness."
12. *Commitment:* specified that the relationship was to be "long term" or "lead to marriage," or some other indication of stability and longevity.
13. *Emotion:* specified that the partner should be "warm," "romantic," "emotionally supportive," "emotionally expressive," "sensitive," "loving," "responsive," or similar terms indicating an opposition to being cold and aloof.

In addition to the 13 attribute variables, two other pieces of information were collected: The length of the ad (in lines) and the age of the person placing the ad. Only if age was exactly specified was it included; if age was vague (e.g., "late 40s") this was not counted.

Variables were measured in the following way: Any ad requesting one of the 13 attributes was scored once for that attribute. If not explicitly mentioned, it was not scored. The scoring was thus "all or nothing," e.g., no matter how many times a person in a particular ad stressed that looks were important it was only counted as a single score in the "attractive" column; thus, each single score represented one person. Conceivably, an individual ad could mention all, some, or none of the variables. Comparisons were then made between the sexes on the basis of the variables, using percentages and chi-squares. Chi-square values were derived by cross-tabulating gender (male/female) with attribute (asked for/not asked for). Degrees of freedom in all cases equaled one. Finally, several of the individual variables were collapsed to get an overall sense of the relative importance of (a) physical factors, (b) employment factors, and (c) intellectual factors.

RESULTS

A total of 329 personal ads were contained in the six newspaper editions studied. One ad was discarded in that it specified a gay relationship, leaving a total sample of 328. Of this number, 215 of the ads were placed by men (65.5%) and 113 by women (34.5%).

The mean age of people placing ads was 40.4. One hundred and twenty-seven cases (38.7%) counted as missing data in that the age was not specified or was vague. The mean age for the two sexes was similar: 39.4 for women (with 50.4% of cases missing) and 40.7 for men (with 32.6% of cases missing).

Sex differences in desired companion attributes are summarized in Table 34.1. It will be seen that for 10 of the 13 variables a statistically significant difference was detected. The three largest differences were found for attractiveness, professional and financial status. To summarize the table: in the case of attractiveness, physique, sex, and picture (physical attributes) the men were more likely than the women to seek these. In the case of professional status, employment status, financial status, intelligence, commitment, and emotion (nonphysical attributes) the women were more likely to seek these. The women were also more likely to specify education, honesty, and humor, however not at a statistically significant level.

The data were explored further by collapsing several of the categories: the first 4 variables were collapsed into a "physical" category, Variables 5–7 were collapsed into an "employment" category, and Variables 8 and 9 were collapsed into an "intellectual" category. The assumption was that the collapsed categories were sufficiently similar (within the three new categories) to make the new larger categories conceptually meaningful; conversely, it was felt the remaining variables (10–13) could not be meaningfully collapsed any further.

Sex differences for the three collapsed categories are summarized in Table 34.2. Note that the Table 34.2 figures were not derived simply by adding the numbers in the Table 34.1 categories: recall that for Variables 1–4 a subject could specify all, one, or none; hence simply adding the Table 34.1 figures would be biased by those individuals who were more effusive in specifying various physical traits. Instead, the Table 34.2 categories are (like Table 34.1) all or nothing: whether a subject specified one or all four of the physical attributes it would only count once.

TABLE 34.1   Gender Comparison for Attributes Desired in Partner

	GENDER		
VARIABLE	DESIRED BY MEN (*N* = 215)	DESIRED BY WOMEN (*N* = 113)	CHI SQUARE
1. Attractive	76 (35.3%)	20 (17.7%)	11.13[a]
2. Physique	81 (37.7%)	27 (23.9%)	6.37[a]
3. Sex	25 (11.6%)	4 (3.5%)	6.03[a]
4. Picture	74 (34.4%)	24 (21.2%)	6.18[a]
5. Profession	6 (2.8%)	19 (16.8%)	20.74[a]
6. Employed	8 (3.7%)	12 (10.6%)	6.12[a]
7. Financial	7 (3.2%)	22 (19.5%)	24.26[a]
8. Education	8 (3.7%)	8 (7.1%)	1.79[b]
9. Intelligence	22 (10.2%)	24 (21.2%)	7.46[a]
10. Honest	20 (9.3%)	17 (15.0%)	2.44[b]
11. Humor	36 (16.7%)	26 (23.0%)	1.89[b]
12. Commitment	38 (17.6%)	31 (27.4%)	4.25[a]
13. Emotion	44 (20.5%)	35 (31.0%)	4.36[a]

[a]Significant at the .05 level.
[b]Not significant.

Thus, each score represented one person. In brief, Table 34.2 gives similar, although more exaggerated results to Table 34.1. (The exaggeration is the result of only one item of several being needed to score within a collapsed category.) The men were more likely than the women to specify some physical attribute. The women were considerably more likely to specify that the companion be employed, or have a profession, or be in good financial shape. And the women were more likely to emphasize the intellectual abilities of their mate.

One can, incidentally, also note from this table an overall indication of attribute importance by collapsing across sexes, i.e., it is apparent that physical

TABLE 34.2   Gender Comparison for Physical, Employment, and Intellectual Attributes

	GENDER		
VARIABLE	DESIRED BY MEN (*N* = 215)	DESIRED BY WOMEN (*N* = 113)	CHI SQUARE
Physical (collapsing variables 1–4)	143 (66.5%)	50 (44.2%)	15.13[a]
Employment (collapsing variables 5–7)	17 (7.9%)	47 (41.6%)	51.36[a]
Intellectual (collapsing 8 and 9)	29 (13.5%)	31 (27.4%)	9.65[a]

[a]Significant at the .05 level.

characteristics are the most desired regardless of sex.

DISCUSSION

Sex Differences

This study found that the attitudes of the subjects, in terms of desired companion attributes, were consistent with traditional sex role stereotypes. The men were more likely to emphasize stereotypically desirable feminine traits (appearance) and deemphasize the nonfeminine traits (financial, employment, and intellectual status). One inconsistency was that emotional expressiveness is a feminine trait but was emphasized relatively less by the men.

Women, on the other hand, were more likely to emphasize masculine traits such as financial, employment, and intellectual status, and valued commitment in a relationship more highly. One inconsistency detected for the women concerned the fact that although emotional expressiveness is not a masculine trait, the women in this sample asked for it, relatively more than the men, anyway. Regarding this last point, it may be relevant to refer to Basow's (1986, p. 210) conclusion that "women prefer relatively androgynous men, but men, especially traditional ones, prefer relatively sex-typed women."

These findings are similar to results from earlier studies, e.g., Deaux and Hanna (1984), and indicate that at this point in time and in this setting sex role stereotyping is still in operation.

One secondary finding that was of some interest to the author was that considerably more men than women placed personal ads—almost a 2:1 ratio. One can only speculate as to why this was so; however, there are probably at least two (related) contributing factors. One is that social convention dictates that women should be less outgoing in the initiation of relationships: Green and Sandos (1983) found that women who initiated dates were viewed less positively than their male counterparts. Another factor is that whoever places the ad is in a "power position" in that they can check out the other person's letter and photo, and then make a choice, all in anonymity; one could speculate that this need to be in control might be more an issue for the men.

Methodological Issues

Content analysis of newspaper ads has its strengths and weaknesses. By virtue of being an unobtrusive study of variables with face validity, it was felt some reliable measure of gender-related attitudes was being achieved. That the mean age of the men and women placing the ads was similar was taken as support for the assumption that the two sexes in this sample were demographically similar. Further, sex differences in desired companion attributes could not be attributed to differential verbal ability in that it was found that length of ad was similar for both sexes.

On the other hand, there were some limitations. It could be argued that people placing personal ads are not representative of the public in general. For instance, with respect to this study, it was found that the subjects were a somewhat older group—mean age of 40—than might be found in other courting situations. This raises the possibility of age being a confounding variable. Older singles may emphasize certain aspects of a relationship, regardless of sex. On the other hand, there is the possibility that age differentially affects women in the mate selection process, particularly when children are desired. The strategy of controlling for age in the analysis was felt problematic in that the numbers for analysis were fairly small, especially given the missing data, and further, that one cannot assume the missing cases were not systematically different (i.e., older) from those present.

REFERENCES

Basow, S. 1986. *Gender stereotypes, Traditions and alternatives.* Brooks/Cole Publishing Co.

Braito, R. 1981. The inferiority game: Perceptions and behavior. *Sex Roles,* 7, 65–72.

Curry, T., & Hock, R. 1981. Sex differences in sex role ideals in early adolescence. *Adolescence,* 16, 779–789.

Deaux, K., & Hanna, R. 1984. Courtship in the personals column: The influence of gender and sexual orientation. *Sex Roles,* 11, 363–375.

Farrell, W. 1986. *Why men are the way they are.* New York: Berkley Books.

Green, S., & Sandos, P. 1983. Perceptions of male and female initiators of relationship. *Sex Roles,* 9, 849–852.

Halas, C. 1981. *Why can't a woman be more like a man?* New York: Macmillan Publishing Co.

Harrison, A., & Saeed, L. 1977. Let's make a deal: An analysis of revelations and stipulations in lonely hearts advertisements. *Journal of Personality and Social Psychology,* 3,5, 257–264.

Hite, S. 1981. *The Hite report on male sexuality.* New York: Alfred A. Knopf.

Hite, S. 1987. *Women and love: A cultural revolution in progress.* New York: Alfred A. Knopf.

Nevid, J. 1984. Sex differences in factors of romantic attraction. *Sex Roles,* 11, 401–411.

Shaevitz, M. 1987. *Sexual static.* Boston: Little, Brown & Co.

Smith, D. 1973. Women, the family and corporate capitalism. In M. Stephenson (Ed.), *Women in Canada.* Toronto: New Press.

Stiles, D., Gibbon, J., Hardardottir, S., & Schnellmann, J. 1987. The ideal man or women as described by young adolescents in Iceland and the United States. *Sex Roles,* 17, 313–320.

Symons, D. 1987. An evolutionary approach. In J. Geer & W. O'Donohue (Eds.), *Theories of human sexuality.* New York: Plenum Press.

Thiessen, D., & Gregg, B. 1980. Human assortive mating and genetic equilibrium: An evolutionary perspective. *Ethology and Sociobiology,* 1, 111–140.

Urberg, K. 1979. Sex role conceptualization in adolescents and adults. *Developmental Psychology,* 15, 90–92.

CHAPTER 35

THE RELATIONSHIP BETWEEN WEIGHT AND CAREER PAYOFFS AMONG WOMEN

KATHERINE M. HASKINS AND H. EDWARD RANSFORD

INTRODUCTION

A number of authors have noted that a stigma is attached to being overweight in our society and that this limits an individual's opportunities (Cahnman, 1968; Mayer, 1968; Allon, 1975; Larkin and Pines, 1979; Benson *et al.,* 1980; DeJong, 1980; Seid, 1989; Register and Williams, 1990; Gortmaker *et al.*, 1993). In this respect, weight, like race, class, and gender, is a stratification variable of the general society. In this study we explore the question of whether or not overweight women in organizations face greater barriers to desirable jobs and higher incomes than "ideal weight" women when qualifications and experience are controlled. That is, does social inequality by weight in the general society carry over to organizations?

Women overall face discrimination. Overweight women may experience a uniquely high degree of discrimination. Our society places great emphasis on thinness and attractiveness for women. Historically, American women have put a great deal of money and effort into "the pursuit of personal beauty" (Banner, 1983). Bell (1975) argues that for women, it is primarily their bodies that determine sexual value. However, personality, occupational success, and intelligence define sexual attractiveness for men. In terms of job discrimination, being overweight and female may limit opportunities more than being overweight and male.

Although studies exist that suggest overweight persons would likely suffer disadvantages in hiring and promotions (Frieze *et al.*, 1990; Benson *et al.*, 1980; Larkin and Pines, 1979), only a few studies, to our knowledge, examine the extent to which being overweight does affect job and income payoffs for women. In a recent study of over 10,000 young men and women between the ages of 16 and 24, researchers found obese women earn $6710 less in annual income than thinner women. Obese women also are 20% less likely to be married, finish about half a year less in education and have household poverty rates 10% higher than their slimmer counterparts. By contrast, overweight men were 11% less likely to be married but did not suffer economically from their weight (Gortmaker *et al.*, 1993). Similarly, in a study of males and females ages 18–25 taken from the youth sample of the National Longitudinal Surveys, obesity was found to have a significant negative effect on wages for women but not for men. The study controlled for human capital variables (Register *et al.*, 1990). Both of these studies involved very youthful samples. We need to know if women of a wider age spectrum suffer economic penalties for weight. Further, no studies, of which we are aware, examine the effect of overweight on career payoffs among women in male-dominated managerial and professional occupations, or in occupations in which women have contact with many clients outside the organization.

From *Sociological Forum*, 14(2) (1999): 295–318. Reprinted by permission of Plenum Publishing Corporation. Some footnotes have been incorporated as additional endnotes or deleted.

We will address these omissions by examining the extent to which weight limits career payoffs among a sample of women in one major manufacturing organization. Specifically, we expect that overweight women will be in lower occupational and income levels that ideal weight women, especially so in male-dominated occupations and occupations involving contact outside the organization. Three somewhat overlapping theoretical traditions provide a conceptual background for these predictions: stigma, stratification, and organizational theory.

THEORETICAL CONTEXT

Stigma and Stratification

Not until recently in history has thinness been so highly associated with physical attractiveness (banner, 1983; Powdermaker, 1975; Seid, 1989). In the second half of the 1800s, thin women were subject to ridicule and stigma. Similar to the products available today to make one thinner, products then promised to add pounds and produce more rounded, more feminine bodies. Historically, women's shapes have always been important. However, the ideal standards and their definitions have changed drastically.

Our study draws on Goffman's concept of stigma. Stigma "refer(s) to an attribute that is deeply discrediting . . ." (Goffman, 1963:3). he described three distinct types of stigma: "abominations of the body," "blemishes of the individual character," and "tribal stigma of race, nation, and religion." Although Goffman did not discuss the issue of weight, DeJong (1980) notes that being significantly overweight is an "abomination of the body" and is stigmatized. Overweight persons are ridiculed and negatively evaluated by others (Allon, 1975; Cahnman, 1968; Mayer, 1968; Seid, 1989).

Goffman (1963) connects stigma to stratification when he notes that because of a sigma, life chances are reduced for the possessor. To rationalize this differential treatment, society constructs a supporting ideology. There is a rationale that justifies the stigma and differential treatment accorded to overweight persons. They are believed to be lazy, with no willpower,

self-control, or self-discipline (Allon, 1975; Harmetz, 1975; Kalisch, 1975; Maddox *et al., 1968*; Seid, 1989). In other words, weight can be seen as a stratification variable in the sense that obesity affects the unequal distribution of power, privilege, and prestige, and in the sense that an ideology exists to justify the unequal distribution of these resources (Jeffries and Ransford, 1980). Evidence suggests that persons of ideal weight are preferred to overweight persons in employment hiring practices and employment opportunities (Benson *et al.*, 1980; Larkin and Pines, 1979).

Stratification in Organizations

The setting of this research is a large aerospace organization. In the Weberian tradition, organizations are ideally based on rationality with decisions dependent on considerations of productivity and efficiency (Weber, 1978). From this "ideal type" perspective, an individual's access to career payoffs within an organization is based solely on the individual's performance, expertise, and contribution. Stratification variables of the general society, some which are "irrationally" based on physical characteristics such as race, age, gender, and weight, should not carry over to the internal workings of organizations. Instead, organizations should have a neutralizing effect on the discriminatory practices of external society.

Sociological studies on stratification and organizations have not supported this view. Miller (1986) argued that organizations can take stratification variable of the general society and emphasize or shape them into limited opportunities and rewards within the organization. Miller found that gender and race were important stratification variables in the organizations he studied. Similarly, Roos (1992) notes that if universalism were to characterize any institutional sector, it should be the professions; yet gender discrimination, based on ideology, prejudice, and traditionalism, remains present in the professions. A study examining the careers of men and women engineers showed that gender roles operate within organizations and limit the opportunities of female engineers (McIlwee and Robinson, 1992). England *et al.* (1988), demonstrated that, net of human capital, skill demands, and working conditions, women experience pay discrimination by virtue of being in predominantly female occupations. Similarly, Kanter's classic work on organizations (1977) indicates that opportunities for women to move into male-dominated occupations are limited, and the few who do reach such positions are often typecasted into narrow stereotyped roles. We argue that weight discrimination and gender discrimination present in the general society extend to the organization. In other words, gatekeepers within the organization may limit overweight women's access to certain occupations and higher income.

HYPOTHESES

1. It is hypothesized that women who are at or below their desirable weight will have higher incomes and occupational positions than women who are overweight with human capital variables controlled. The control variables are educational attainment, entry occupation, length of service, age, and father's occupation. We expect some of these control variables will have a stronger effect on income and occupational status than weight. But, it is predicted that weight will have a net effect after the more traditional determinants are controlled. This prediction is based on the premise that overweight women are likely to encounter direct discrimination by top officers and administrators. Note that these hypotheses have to do with weight discrimination at higher socioeconomic status levels. We suspect that weight will have much less influence (or no influence) on entrance into clerical or blue-collar jobs.

Gatekeepers could be "discriminating" or making selections on the basis of weight because, echoing societal preferences, they prefer female employees at or near ideal weight. Another possible explanation is that the employer may perceive the person's weight as a proxy for some nonobservable productivity-related characteristics such as discipline, intelligence, competence, or self-control. Then it would be perceived potential for productivity that influences the employer's decision.

A third possibility is that women at or near their ideal weight will represent the organization well.

Some research suggests that those who are more attractive elicit more favorable responses from others (Kaslow and Schwartz, 1978). In a study of professional women who were both successful and highly attractive in physical appearance and personality characteristics, the women believed their attractiveness was a valuable asset for initiating interaction. These women also believed they were selected for positions of high visibility because of their attractiveness (Kaslow and Schwartz, 1978).

Throughout this paper we are assuming that a socioeconomic status (SES) gap by weight (human capital variables controlled) is due to discrimination. In addition to discrimination, social psychological explanations can be stated. For instance, a self-fulfilling prophecy may be operating. High-level administrators may expect more of women who are thin and attractive and, as a result, come to behave differently toward them. Then, these women may actually come to behave differently. Conversely, it could be argued that a negative self-fulfilling prophecy may be operating for overweight women—they are seen as incapable of moving up, and thus they do not. Further, in addition to direct discrimination within the organization, it may be that physically attractive women (and, thus, possibly also thin women) are more socially skilled and self-confident (Kaslow and Schwartz, 1978). Perhaps attractive, thin women are more likely to put themselves in situations where they are noticed.

2. We hypothesize that the effect of weight on career payoffs will be especially strong when the woman is in a frontstage position that involves contact outside the organization. It is in these jobs that weight may be particularly important for career payoffs. Women at or near their desirable weight may present a more favorable image of the company to outsiders and elicit more favorable responses from others.

3. We hypothesize that the effect of weight on career payoffs will be especially strong when women are in traditionally male-dominated occupations. Our argument is that there may be heightened ambiguities and challenges for women in such roles. A special effect may be required. Like ethnic newcomers to managerial positions (Silbert, 1985; Willie, 1982), a woman may have to do twice as well and be twice as good as her male counterparts to prove herself capable. In such a situation, everything must be in tip-top shape (weight, human capital variables, motivation, etc.) to make the best possible impression.

Also, the job may require some ideal blend of masculine and feminine virtues. Some articles suggest that women in managerial positions are expected to be outgoing, assertive, and competitive. Yet, if too assertive, they are harshly judged as nonfeminine (Kanter, 1977; Lawrence, 1985). In today's culture, thinness is an embodiment of femininity, yet it also demonstrates control over the body and self-discipline, traditionally male virtues. The ideal weight may help to mediate some of these conflicts. Thinness may send out messages that the woman has mastered both masculine and feminine virtues. Thinner women may be perceived as both feminine and having power and control over their bodies (Bordo, 1989).

It is also quite possible that overweight women are less likely to reach male-dominated, higher status occupations because they are more likely to be isolated from informal occupational experiences and contacts that are part of the screening process so important for career mobility. The literature on gender and organizations indicates that women are more isolated and less likely to be placed on the fast track required for promotion (Lawrence, 1985; Miller *et al.*, 1975). It is highly plausible that weight adds an additional increment of disadvantage such that overweight women are even more isolated than women as a whole. In this sense, discrimination by weight may be systemic, involving cumulative disadvantages over time. Overweight women are less likely to be groomed for upward mobility, especially in male-dominated occupations.

SAMPLE AND MEASUREMENT OF VARIABLES

Sample

The setting of this research is Bilby Corporation. Bilby (a pseudonym) is a large industrial organization in the aerospace industry contracting predominantly with the United States Department of Defense. All of its companies combined employee approxi-

mately 85,000 people. Bilby was chosen because of its size and because it has women in a variety of occupational categories. This organization is composed of about 25% women and 75% men.

The population (3910 women from one of Bilby's local companies) was stratified by length of employment and occupation. A cross-tabular table was constructed with length of employment by occupation for the entire population. This table was the basis for systematic disproportional probability sampling. Because such a large proportion of the population was clerical (47%), a strictly random sample, though representative of the organization, would result in mostly clerical respondents. Since we were interested especially in women in higher levels of the organization, women in occupations that represent a smaller proportion of women in the population, such as managers (7%), were oversampled. A certain amount of representativeness is sacrificed in order to ensure an adequate number of cases in all occupational categories.

A mailed questionnaire was administered to a sample of 918 women employees in 1988. Two waves of the questionnaire were sent in an effort to maximize participation. The response rate was 33%, yielding 306 respondents. Although this response rate is typical for mailed questionnaires (Selltiz *et al.*, 1976: 297), we were concerned that the two thirds who did not respond might be atypical in some way. (There was no further follow-up contact with those who did not respond.) We looked at the response rates separately by occupation and length of service. The lowest response rates were among blue-collar workers; while only about 15% of blue-collar workers responded, 39% of professionals, 44% of managers, and 49% of clerical workers responded. Since much of our analysis focuses on weight discrimination in white-collar ranks, and on several occasions the white-collar and blue-collar respondents are analyzed separately, we argue that the response rate is better for the arena of discrimination we are examining most closely—a 44% response rate for professional, managerial, and clerical workers combined.

The response rates for length of service categories indicate that those who worked at Bilby the longest were least likely to complete the question-naire. For those who worked there less than 5 years, the response rate was 57% compared to 45% for 5–9 years, 23% for 10–19 years, and 21% for 20 years or more. Perhaps long-time employees are the most loyal. They may choose not to respond to prevent revealing any company secrets or faults.

It is possible that some chose not to respond because weight is a sensitive issue. The cover letter on the questionnaire indicated the topic of this paper in general terms. One could argue that overweight persons would be less likely to respond. Still, our sample shows a fairly large number of overweight women who did respond (27% by the objective mea-sure of weight and 31% by the subjective measure of weight). Moreover, we would argue that overweight women would be just as likely to respond as others in order to voice their protest to the weight–career issue, that is, to state that overweight people are treat-

ed unfairly. Additionally, it could be argued that only those who believe weight has an effect on occupation and income participated. Yet, open-ended responses of subjects suggested an even split of those saying weight was important, and weight makes no differ-ence. In short, our sample did not appear to overrep-resent or underrepresent women of different weights or with a particular view on weight.

A demographic profile of the respondents is pre-sented in Table 35.1 Note that the disproportional sampling method resulted in 52% of the sample being in professional or managerial positions. This is in contrast to only 30% of women in the Bilby popula-tion being in such positions.

Measurement of the Independent Variable

Weight.   The measurement of weight is based on self-reported weight, height (without shoes), and

TABLE 35.1   Demographic Profile of the Sample

Personal income		Current occupation	
$10,000–14,999	1%	Professional and technical	25%
$15,000–19,999	6%	Managers, officials, and administrators	27%
$20,000–24,999	11%	Clerical	32%
$25,000–29,999	22%	Blue collar	15%
$30,000–39,999	38%		
$40,000–59,999	19%		
$60,000 and up	2%		
Age		Race	
20 or below	18%	White	80%
3039	30%	Black	8%
40–49	28%	Hispanic	5%
50–59	15%	Others	7%
60 or above	9%		
Objective weight		Subjective Weight	
Overweight[a]	27%	Overweight	31%
Slightly overweight[b]	24%	Slightly overweight	40%
Ideal weight and underweight[c]	49%	Ideal weight and underweight	29%

[a]Respondent's weight is 10% of more over upper limit of ideal range (Metropolitan Table, 1983).

[b]Respondent's weight is between 1% and 9.9% over upper limit of ideal range (Metropolitan Table, 1983).

[c]Respondent's weight is within or below ideal range (Metropolitan Table, 1983).

frame size. Self-reported weight and height are recoded to reflect the respondent's percent above or below the desirable weight standard according to the 1983 Metropolitan Life Insurance Company tables (Metropolitan Life Foundation, 1983). We are assuming that most self-report answers are truthful. However, self-reports may not be totally accurate when a truthful response would be embarrassing. Hence, some of our respondents (such as those who are very overweight), could have understated their weight. Unlike some studies that have calculated overweight as the percentage above the midpoint of the ideal weight range (U.S. Department of Health and Human Services, 1985), we defined overweight as percentage above the upper limit of that range. To define overweight as being above one precise weight does not allow, for individual variations in body type. We reasoned that a social perception of overweight is much more likely to occur when the person is above the upper limit. All those within the ideal weight range for a given height and frame were coded 0, while those above or below ideal limits were coded as a percent above or below. For example, the Metropolitan Table lists a range of 117–132 pounds for a medium-frame woman of 5 feet 4 inches in height. If a respondent weighed 144 pounds, she would be 12 pounds over the upper limit (or .091% above) and would receive a score of .091. This measure is the primary measure of weight and is seen as a more objective measure. In regression analysis, the variable is continuous. For cross-tabular analysis, 105 or more over the upper limit of the ideal range was operationally defined as "overweight." This cutting point is more generous than the cutoff for obesity used in other studies—weight exceeding 20% of the standard weight or midpoint of the interval (Register and Williams, 1990).[1]

Subjective Weight. We were interested in seeing how our measure corresponds with a subjective measure of weight. Respondents were asked to classify their weight as somewhat overweight, slightly overweight, just right, or underweight. Table 35.1 compares the objective and subjective definitions. Some fairly large discrepancies appear with lower percentages of women subjectively judging their weight to be "just right" or "underweight" (29%) than the objective measure (49%). Either our objective measure is "generous" (only significantly overweight women are so classified), or women, drawing on a cultural ideal of thinness, are harshly judging themselves overweight whey they are still at or below their desirable weight. Perhaps both of these dynamics are operating. Given the multitude of cultural messages surrounding thinness in our society, we felt safer in employing the objective measure of weight as our leading measure. However, we also summarize findings with the subjective measure.

Entry Weight. Entry weight is included in the analysis in order to determine causal time order (i.e., that weight came before occupational placement and income). Entry weight is measured the same as current weight except that respondents are asked to report their weight at the time they entered Bilby. A caution is in order: retrospective questions can be faulty for measuring the past. This may be especially true for a culturally loaded topic such as weight. For example, some women may state more continuity in weight over time than in fact exists.

Measurement of the Dependent Variables

Personal Income. Respondents reported their personal income by choosing one of seven categories on the questionnaire. The income categories are shown in Table 35.1.

Occupation. Respondent's current occupation was coded as upper-level professional/managerial (4), entry-level professional/managerial (3), clerical (2), and blue collar (1). Our theory notes that weight should matter especially in the professional and managerial categories. Desiring more precision at this end of the scale, we separated upper-level and entry-level professional and managerial jobs. "Senior Engineer" and "Director of Accounting" are examples of upper-level professional and managerial occupations; "Junior Engineer" and "Program Manager" are examples of entry-level professional and managerial occupations.

Measurement of Specification Variables

Contact Outside the Firm.   Outside contact, or frontstage occupation, was measured by the following item: "Does your job require you to have a great deal of contact with people who do not work for Bilby?" Response choices were "a great deal," "sometimes," "rarely," and "never."

Traditionally Male-Dominated Occupations.   Using their current occupation titles, the respondents were coded to either traditionally male dominated or not traditionally male dominated. A source from Bilby Corporation was consulted on the questionable job titles. Most of the blue-collar occupations were labeled "male dominated," though some were classified "nonmale dominated." Examples of blue-collar, male-dominated job titles are Molded Plastic Tool Builder and Flightline Mechanic; Electrical Bench Assembler and Inspector illustrate the nonmale-dominated, blue-collar jobs. The clerical positions were identified as "nonmale dominated." This means that it is primarily in the professional, technical, and managerial occupations that there is variance on the male-dominated dimension. Examples of high-status, male-dominated positions are Research Scientist, Senior Engineer, Physicist, and Director International Marketing; job titles such as Senior Buyer and Manager Human Resources illustrate nonmale-dominated, high-status positions.

Although this variable was not created as another measure of top status jobs, there is a connection. With the exception of the blue-collar jobs, a disproportionate number of the male-dominated positions are in fact the higher status jobs. This is a function of the work world in general where women have been excluded from the upper echelons of the hierarchy.

Human Capital Control Variables

The human capital variables were measured as follows: *educational attainment* was measured by the item, "What was the last grade or year of school you completed?" (nine levels were listed from none to advanced degree (e.g., M.S., Ph.D.); *entry occupation* was measured by the question, "What was your occupational title at your first job at Bilby _____?"; *length of service* was tapped by the question "How long have you been working at Bilby _____ years _____ months?"; *age* was measured by the question "What is your birthdate month _____ day _____ year _____?"; father's occupation was measured by the question, "What is/was your father's occupation title (Please be exact _____)?" Finally, to measure entry weight, the question was asked "Estimate your weight five years ago _____ pounds 10 years ago _____ pounds, when you began working at Bilby _____ pounds."

FINDINGS

We have predicted that career payoffs, in the forms of income and occupational status, will be affected by weight. Some of our respondents ($N = 81$ or 26%) made interesting comments on this hypothesis in the open-ended section of the questionnaire. One group felt weight has no effect on income and occupation:

> *Weight problems do not affect work, only social life! I have never had a tiny little rear end or thin thighs and men still judge those things. These inferences regarding my career and professional capabilities exhibit a shallow 1950s moral attitude. I would hate to think that my advancement opportunities were based on cheesecake (or too much cheesecake).*
>
> *I have been fortunate to work for people who judge their subordinates based on contribution to the organization and not looks or physical attributes.*

Many others, however, comments that they believe weight does indeed affect career payoffs. Some examples of these responses follow:

> *Since my health and weight have never been a problem. I do not see them as affecting my career. However, I have seen other women who are overweight being affected by virtue of not being looked upon as management material. Being fat is not only social suicide but career suicide as well. Management's perception is a lack of control and self-esteem.*
>
> *Appearance, especially weight, has a lot to do with advancing. I have been normal size and have advanced. But since I have been heavy no one wants*

me. I have a high IQ and my productivity is extremely high. But, no one cares. There are more men here and they look down on heavy women. They would rather promote and have cute, thin airheads.

The differences expressed in these two points of view (weight has no effect vs. weight matters) made us eager to examine the quantitative data with [multivariable] techniques, that is, to examine the hypothesis that weight affects occupation and income with human capital factors controlled. . . . [Such] analyses showed no support for this hypothesis. . . . [In short, when] length of service, age, and entry occupation are controlled, weight has not effect on income.

We reasoned that weight might have an effect on income among women in professional/managerial positions only. It is in these upper, more highly competitive occupations that screening would be more intense and gatekeepers would be more apt to look for ideal combinations of education, attractiveness (weight), and experience.

[But] findings showed that weight does indeed have a significant effect on income among women in entry-level professional and managerial occupations but not in upper-level professional and managerial occupations. This suggests that within the category "entry-level professional and managerial," some jobs

are paying more than others and ideal-weight women are more likely to be in these better paying positions. Weight has no effect on income for blue-collar and clerical workers.

Weight and Occupational Status

The data in Table 35.2 support the hypothesis that a woman's weight affects her occupation. Although [a multivariable analysis revealed that] weight is not nearly as strong a predictor . . . of occupation as education or entry occupation; weight is an important and significant predictor of occupation for this sample. . . .

That weight is still a significant predictor of occupation, with powerful human capital variables in the equation, suggests that the stratification effects of weight in the general society are being carried through to the organization.

Our theory suggests that weight should be most strongly related to occupational position at the higher professional and managerial levels where screening by appearance would be more intense. Table 35.2 [reveals that,] as expected, those at or below desirable weight are more likely to be in the professional and managerial levels. When the entry-level and upper-level categories are combined, the difference

TABLE 35.2   Crosstabular Analysis: Occupation Status by Weight

OCCUPATION	WEIGHT			TOTAL %	N
	OVERWEIGHT[a]	SLIGHTLY OVER[b]	IDEAL OF BELOW[c]		
Blue collar	25%	20%	7%	15%	(45)
Clerical	37%	37%	28%	32%	(97)
Entry level Professional/managerial	25%	30%	41%	34%	(101)
Upper level Professional/managerial	14%	14%	24%	19%	(56)
Total %	27%	24%	49%		
N	(81)	(71)	(147)		
Tau B = .22 $p < .01$					

[a]Respondent's weight is 10% or more over upper limit of ideal range (Metropolitan Table, 1983).

[b]Respondent's weight is between 1% and 9.9% over upper limit of ideal range (Metropolitan Table, 1983).

[c]Respondent's weight is within or below ideal range (Metropolitan Table, 1983).

is striking. Sixty-five percent of the thinner women are in professional and managerial positions compared to only 39% of the overweight women. For blue-collar workers, the reverse trend is apparent; only 7% of thinner women work in blue-collar positions while 25% of overweight women do. There is no relationship for clerical workers; that is, about the same percentage of ideal weight, slightly overweight, and overweight women hold clerical jobs. . . .

DISCUSSION

Does the stratification based on weight that is present in the general society extend to the inner workings of workplace organizations? Specifically, do overweight women face greater barriers to desirable jobs and higher incomes that "ideal weight" women? These questions have been the central concern of this paper.

We predicted that, for women, stratification based on weight would be carried over into the organization. Indeed, it was found that career payoffs for women are in part dependent on body weight. Even with very strong determinants of income and occupation held constant, weight is a stratification variable for women in this organization. It affects their lives and limits their opportunities within the organization as it does in the external society.

The finding that weight does have an effect on career payoffs in this organization needs to be qualified. The effect on occupation was significant for the entire sample. But for income, it was significant only for women in entry-level professional/managerial positions. Among women in upper-level professional/ managerial, clerical and blue-collar jobs, there was no relationship. These findings seem consistent with the notion that weight would matter most for women pushing into the upper echelons and top positions. Women in these positions need to "have everything together" because gatekeepers are more likely to screen them more carefully.

We were curious as to why weight did not affect income at upper-level professional and managerial jobs. Perhaps at the top level, length of service

(seniority) is the most important factor in determining income and overrides weight. . . .

It was predicted that the relationship between weight and occupational status would be stronger among women in traditionally male-dominated occupations. The data [not shown here] clearly supported this prediction. Of particular importance is that the effects of the more "rational" employment criteria such as education, entry occupation and age, also increased in the male-dominated occupations. Length of service was the only variable that did not increase in strength. It is also the least related to qualifications. It seems that not only weight but also most of the qualifications variables, which are the "rational" determinants of occupation, matter more for women in traditionally male-dominated occupations. [One interpretation] . . . is that women have to have everything together (weight and human capital) to secure jobs in these categories. . . .

Current feminist thought has something to say about the complexity of these male-dominated job environments. To men, the embodied femininity of thin women means they are controllable (Bordo, 1989; Haug, 1987; Henley, 1977). Seen this way, thin women may fit in better in a male-dominated work environment because men are not threatened by them. Yet, thin women with excellent credentials may also send out signals of self-empowerment and that may seem more threatening. Bordo (1989:18) addresses this contradiction describing it as a "double-bind." Women are expected to be traditionally feminine in the sense of being nurturing and other-oriented. Yet today, women in the workplace are also expected to be skilled at self-control, determination, emotional discipline, and self-mastery, that is, the traditionally male virtues. They must meet these dual and conflicting demand. While thinness is the embodiment of femininity, it also displays control over the body and self-discipline that are "masculine" traits. According to Bordo (1989:19), thinness "offer(s) the illusion of meeting, through the body, the contradictory demands of the contemporary ideology of femininity." Again, thinness may send out a message that the woman has mastered both masculine and feminine virtues. . . .

The Context of Bilby Corporation

An important question is the degree to which this study can be generalized to other organizations. The aerospace industry is sometimes stereotyped as more gender conservative than others, that is, aerospace is viewed by some as a man's world dominated by an "old-boy network." Indeed several of our respondents noted this on the open-ended section of the questionnaire. If the aerospace industry is more conservative than other industries, one would expect the association between weight and career payoffs among women to be stronger than would be found in other organizations. However, this gender conservatism could be offset by the fact of government contract work and Equal Opportunity constraints (and monitoring) to hire the most qualified. In short, aerospace may be a contextually specific environment. This research needs replication in other organizations.

CONCLUDING REMARKS

The limits of this study point to other areas for future research. For instance, would the results be different for males? The literature suggests that at least part of the gatekeeper's assessment will be affected differentially by gender. Women receive harsher judgments on the weight criterion (Mahoney and Finch, 1976; Seid, 1989; Register *et al.*, 1990; Gortmaker *et al.*, 1993). A sample of both males and females would allow the direct comparisons that this study does not provide. Or, would the findings be stronger or weaker in an industry other than aerospace? Designing a study that compared organizations in terms of external constraints of Equal Opportunity Employment requirements and in terms of the internal conser-

vatism of the organization would specify better the weight-SES relationship.

Finally, we feel it is important to design a study that would illuminate the processes by which weight affects career payoffs. Perhaps there are different levels of screening going on for the top, most competitive positions. First, qualifications such as education and experience may be considered. At a second level of sorting, more personal attractiveness characteristics such as weight may be come important for women. Perhaps male-dominated occupations are the point at which weight becomes particularly important for women. As a whole, these jobs are more demanding and competitive.

What does it mean that organizations discriminate against women on the basis of weight? Some argue that organizations exist to perpetuate the power of the dominant group, that corporations are a tool used by the elite to preserve their power (Morgan, 1986; Moore, 1987). It is well documented that, despite their advances, women remain relatively powerless within the workplace (Ghiloni, 1987; Moore, 1987; Kanter, 1977). Moore (1987: 62) describes the corporate elite as a "uniformly white male world . . . with a large pool of other white males with similar backgrounds and values to draw from." Gender stratification within the organization is far from gone. We suggest that discrimination on the basis of a women's weight is part of a broader scope of gender relations. The data in this research are consistent with the interpretation that there is a "glass ceiling" effect for women aspiring to entry-level and top professional and managerial male-dominated positions. Our findings indicate that women within ideal weight ranges may more easily penetrate this glass ceiling.

NOTES

1. It is difficult to state exactly at what point discrimination would begin. By our definition of 10% or more above the upper limit, a women 5 feet 4 inches tall and weighing 146 pounds would be classified as overweight. It could be argued that such a woman would not necessarily suffer discrimination with such a small amount over the ideal weight.

REFERENCES

Allon, Natalie. 1975. "The stigma of overweight in everyday life." In George A. Bay (ed.). *Obesity in Perspective: A Conference* (Pp. 83–102). Washington, DC: U.S. Government Printing Office.

Banner, Lois. 1983. *American Beauty.* Chicago: University of Chicago Press.

Bell, Inge Powell. 1975. "The double standard: Age." In Jo Freeman (ed.), *Women: A Feminist Perspective* (Pp. 233–244). Palo Alto, CA: Mayfield Publishing.

Benson, Peter L., Drew Severs, John Tatgenhorst, and Nancy Loddengaard. 1980. "The social costs of obesity: A nonreactive field study." *Social Behavior and Personality* 8:91–96.

Bordo, Susan R. 1989. "The body and the reproduction of femininity: A feminist appropriation of Foucault." In Alison M. Jaggar and Susan R. Bordo (eds.), *Gender/Body/Knowledge: Feminist Reconstructions of Being and Knowing* (Pp. 13–33). New Brunswick, NJ: Rutgers University Press.

Cahnman, Werner J. 1968. "The stigma of obesity." *Sociological Quarterly* 9:283–299.

DeJong, William. 1980. "The stigma of obesity: The consequences of naive assumptions concerning the causes of physical deviance." *Journal of Health and Social Behavior* 21:75–87.

England, Paula, George Farkas, Barbara S. Kilbourne, and Thomas Dou. 1988. "Explaining occupational sex segregation and wages: Findings from a model with fixed effects." *American Sociological Review* 53:544–558.

Frieze, Irene H., Josephine E. Olsen, and Deborah C. Good. 1990. "Perceived and actual discrimination in the salaries of male and female managers." *Journal of Applied Social Psychology* 20: 46–67.

Ghiloni, Beth W. 1987. "The Velvet Ghetto: Women, power and the corporation." In G. William Domhoff and Thomas R. Dye (eds.), *Power Elites and Organizations* (Pp. 21–36). Newbury Park, CA: Sage Publications.

Goffman, Erving. 1963. *Stigma: Notes on the Management of Spoiled Identity.* Englewood Cliffs, NJ: Prentice-Hall.

Gortmaker, Steven L., Aviva Must, James M. Perrin, Arthur M. Sobel, and William H. Dietz. 1993. "Social and economic consequences of overweight in adolescence and young adulthood." *New England Journal of Medicine* 329:1008–1012.

Harmetz, Alijean. 1975. "Oh, how we're punished for the crime of being fat." In Brent Q. Haten (ed.), *Over-weight and Obesity: Causes, Fallacies, Treatment* (Pp. 73–76). Provo, UT: Brigham Young University Press.

Haug, Frigga. 1987. *Female Sexualization: A Collective Work of Memory.* Thetford, Norfolk: Thetford Press.

Henley, Nancy M. 1977. *Body Politics: Politics, Sex and Nonverbal Communication.* New York: Simon and Schuster.

Jeffries, Vincent and H. Edward Ransford. 1980. *Stratification: A Multiple Hierarchy Approach.* New York: Allyn and Bacon.

Kalisch, Beatrice J. 1975. "The stigma of obesity." In Brent Q. Hafen (ed.), *Overweight and Obesity: Causes, Fallacies, Treatment* (Pp. 77–80). Provo, UT: Brigham Young University Press.

Kanter, Rosabeth M. 1977. *Men and Women of the Corporation.* New York: Basic Books.

Kaslow, Florence W. and Lita L. Schwartz. 1978. "Self perceptions of the attractive, successful female professional." *Intellect* 106:313–315.

Larkin, Judith C. and Harvey A. Pines. 1979. "No fat persons need apply: Experimental studies of the overweight and hiring preferences." *Sociology of Work and Occupations* 6:312–327.

Lawrence, John. 1985. "Subtle sexism still pervades the workforce." *Los Angeles Times,* Sept. 22. 1985.

Maddox, George L., Kurt Back, and Veronica R. Liederman. 1968. "Overweight as social deviance and disability." *Journal of Health and Social Behavior* 9:287–298.

Mahoney, E. R. and M. D. Finch. 1976. "The dimensionality of body-cathexis." *Journal of Psychology* 92:277–279.

Mayer, Jean. 1968. *Overweight: Causes, Cost and Control.* Englewood Cliffs, NJ: Prentice Hall.

McIlwee, Judith S. and J. Gregg Robinson. 1992. *Women in Engineering: Gender, Power and Workplace Culture.* Albany: State University of New York Press.

Metropolitan Life Foundation. 1983. "1983 Metropolitan Height and Weight Tables." *Statistical Bulletin* 64:3–8.

Miller, Jon. 1986. *Pathways in the Workplace: The Effects of Gender and Race on Access to Organizational Resources.* Cambridge: Cambridge University Press.

Miller, Jon, Sanford Labovitz, and Lincoln Fry. 1975. "Inequities in the organizational experiences of women and men." *Social Forces* 54:365–381.

Moore, Gwen. 1987. "Women in the old-boy network: The case of New York State Government." In G. William

Domhoff and Thomas R. Dye (eds.), *Power Elites and Organizations* (Pp. 63–84). Newbury Park, CA: Sage Publications.

Moore, Mary E., Albert J. Stunkard, and Leo Srole. 1962. "Obesity, social class and mental illness." *Journal of the American Medical Association* 181:962–966.

Morgan, Gareth. 1986. *Images of Organization.* London: Sage Publications.

Powdermaker, Hortense. 1975. "An anthropological approach to the problem of obesity." In Brent Q. Haten (ed.), *Overweight and Obesity: Causes, Fallacies, Treatment* (Pp. 143–151). Provo, UT: Brigham Young University Press.

Register, Charles A. and Donald R. Williams. 1990. "Wage effects of obesity among young workers." *Social Science Quarterly* 71:130–141.

Roos, Patricia A. 1992. "Breaking down barriers: Women's entry into the professions." *Contemporary Sociology* 21:573–576.

Seid, Robert P. 1989. *Never Too Thin: Why Women Are at War with their Bodies.* New York: Prentice-Hall.

Selltiz, Claire, Lawrence S. Wrightsman, and Stuart W. Cook. 1976. *Research Methods in Social Relations.* New York: Holt, Rinehart and Winston.

Silbert, Susan. 1985. "Making it to the top: A study of black partners in major law firms." Ph.D. dissertation, Department of Sociology, University of Southern California, Los Angeles, CA.

U.S. Department of Health and Human Services. 1985. *Health Promotion and Disease Prevention, United States, 1985.* Hyattsville, MD: Center for Health Statistics, Series 10, No. 163:74.

Weber, Max. 1978. *Economy and Society.* Berkeley: University of California Press.

Willie, Charles V. 1982. "The inclining significance of race." In Norman R. Yetman and C. Hoy Steele (eds.), *Majority and Minority: The Dynamics of Race and Ethnicity in American Life* (Pp. 393–398). Boston: Allyn and Bacon.

_____CHAPTER 36_____

GENDER INEQUALITY AND SOCIALIZATION: THE INFLUENCES OF FAMILY, SCHOOL, PEERS, AND THE MEDIA

GREGG LEE CARTER
SHARLENE HESSE-BIBER

Sex is biologically determined at conception by the type of sperm that fertilizes the egg. A "Y" sperm produces a male, an "X" sperm yields a female. In contrast, **gender** is determined socially; it is the societal meaning assigned to male and female. Each society emphasizes particular roles that each sex should play, although there is wide latitude in acceptable behaviors for each gender. These gender roles are powerful and coercive. Consider, for example, the necessity most young men feel either to work or go to school: this is a product of their having been socialized into believing that these are really the only two life choices open to them. That most young men do not wear make-up, put on lipstick, or shave their armpits is also a product of gender socialization (these aren't things "real men" do). On the other hand, although many young women feel the motivation to enter the work world or attend school, many of them also feel that marriage and devotion to children and home are acceptable; moreover, many women see little problem with adorning themselves with make-up and lipstick, as well as shaving their axillas. These attitudes are also a product of gender socialization. In this chapter, we will explore the ways in which socialization for gender roles ultimately generates inequalities between the sexes in income, prestige, power,

and life chances in general. Our focus is on U.S. society, but the basic arguments are applicable to most societies (see Soroka and Bryjak, 1994, chap. 8, for international examples).

GENDER ROLES—PRODUCTS OF BIOLOGY OR SOCIALIZATION

In the long view of history, there were powerful biology-related reasons why women were restrained to household duties or other work taking place within or near the home. Until the last few hundred years in economically developed societies, as still today in many developing nations, infant mortality rates were extremely high. For a society to survive, birth rates had to be very high, and cultural norms arose that encouraged women to marry young and to "be fruitful and multiply." And this is exactly what occurred: women married soon after puberty and were much of the time either pregnant or nursing, until menopause or death, whichever came first. However, with the advent of public sanitation—especially preventing sewage from contaminating drinking water—and other public health measures such as childhood immunization and fortifying food staples with micronutrients (e.g., adding vitamins A and D to milk products), infant and childhood mortality rates have dropped dramatically, and so too birth rates. Now the typical American woman can expect to have only one or two children during her lifetime.

Low birth rates have freed women from having to concentrate so heavily on the roles of mother and keeper of the house. However, some students of society, coming from the perspectives of evolutionary psychology and sociobiology, contend that tens of thousands (if not hundreds of thousands) of years of enacting such roles have left their genetic, hormonal, and related biologic impacts on women. In short, they contend that women are inherently better suited than men to raise children and are inherently less fit for the worlds of politics and work (see, for example, Allen and Gorski, 1992; Goldberg, 1974; Gorman, 1992; LeVay, 1993; Parsons et al., 1955, and Rossi, 1977). Evolution thus not only partly explains the way social arrangements (including gender inequality) are, in this view, but also the way they should be.

Scientific studies on the relationship between female-versus-male genes, hormones, and other biologic traits, on the one hand, and of behavioral differences between men and women, on the other hand, show these two sets of variables correlate only weakly, at best (for reviews see, for example, Deaux, 1992; Fausto-Sterling, 1992; Jacklin, 1989; Kelly, 1991, ch. 4; McCoy, 1985; Shapiro, 1990; Tavris and Wade, 1984; and Tavris, 1992). Females tend to score better on tests of verbal ability, while males tend to test better in mathematical and visual-spatial ability; furthermore, females are much less likely to act out their feelings of aggression. But such differences are often small, and, in many studies, statistically insignificant. "Collectively, research findings presently do not support the conclusion that women and men are significantly different in temperament or in intellectual abilities" (Soroka and Bryjak, 1994, p. 228).

Among the most convincing studies showing that biological differences in the sexes do not provide a blueprint for gender roles—and consequently for gender inequality—are those having to do with the behaviors of individuals whose gender socialization does not match their genetic sex (XX females raised as "boys"; XY males raised as "girls"). For example, children with ambiguous genitalia at birth (some aspects indicative of being a male, other aspects of being a female) who were later discovered through genetic testing to have been assigned the "incorrect"

gender (e.g., an XX female having been raised a "boy") acted in accordance with their socially encouraged gender roles and not according to their genetics. Thus, for example, when a 13-year-old boy was discovered to have an XX chromosomal pattern (he had been referred to a sex specialist after it was discovered he was experiencing menstrual bleeding), the proposition that he should undergo sex reassignment was completely nixed by both the teenager and his family:

> *The decision was against a reassignment [for] the same reason as it would be for the vast majority of thirteen-year-old American boys. His mother said: "He has a sister, and they are completely different. He does not think like a girl, and he does not have the same interests. Right now, the one thing that made me very sure, is that he has a girlfriend. And that to me was a relief, because that was just the clincher that he wasn't a girl."* . . . *For the father, the boy was very much a son, and they shared many evenings, weekends, and vacations with rifle and rod. The boy's other recreational interest, shared with a boyfriend, was motorbike racing in the dry riverbed. He gave an authentic biographical account of the early phase of teen-aged romantic attraction, and had a particular girlfriend. He experienced erotic arousal . . . from being with her, and also from girl watching (Money and Ehrhardt, 1994, p. 483).*

(This particular boy eventually had all of the female sex organs surgically removed and was given testosterone therapy to masculinize his appearance.)

Studies of isolated cultures, such as those in the islands of the South Pacific, also provide convincing evidence that biologic differences in the sexes do not provide a blueprint for gender roles. Indeed, such studies reveal that many of the "masculine" behaviors associated with the male sex in Western society (e.g., aggressiveness, emotional coolness, and being oriented more toward the worlds of politics and work outside the home than toward childcare and work within the home) do not characterize these other men. Similarly, many traits that are "feminine" by Western standards (e.g., nonaggressiveness, emotionality, the desire to nurture, and being child- and home-oriented) do not characterize these women. For example, Margaret Mead found in New Guinea that

Mundugumor women actively dislike childbearing, and they dislike children. Children are carried in harsh opaque baskets that scratch their skins, later on their mother's shoulders, well away from the breast. Mothers nurse their children standing up, pushing them away as soon as they are the least bit satisfied. . . . Women are masculinized to a point where every feminine feature is a drawback (1994, pp. 468–469).[1]

Her study of such isolated tribes led to her the fundamental conclusion that "male and female personality are socially produced" (1994, p. 471).

Taken together, biologic and cross-cultural anthropological research demonstrate that gender roles are malleable and that there are no inherent or universal reasons why current social and economic arrangements should involve so much gender inequality. Indeed, such research makes it clear that the fountainhead of gender role expectations is *socialization*. This is the process of learning how to think about and act in particular situations and particular social roles. By way of gender socialization, individual learn what men are supposed to do and what women are supposed to do. Such socialization is entwined with almost every aspect of society, but four domains in which it occurs are especially important: the family, the educational system, peer groups, and the media.

The Family

An individual's first gender socialization experiences happen at home. Parents transmit gender information both directly (e.g., "big boys don't cry") and indirectly by way of the toys they buy (e.g., dolls for girls, road racers for boys) and the activities they encourage their children to pursue (e.g., many more girls take ballet than play youth football). Such transmission may sometimes be unintentional (e.g., encouraging nurturance in girls to a far greater degree than in boys, as was observed by Frisch, 1977, and Smith and Lloyd, 1978, who found this to be the case even for mothers who espoused egalitarianism between the sexes and other liberal ideals).

Parents typically begin gender socialization as soon as the child's sex is known. A study of the home environments of infants between 5 and 25 months found that the number and variety of toys were similar between the sexes, but that boys were provided with more sports equipment, tools, and large and small vehicles, while girls had more dolls, fictional characters, and child furniture (Pomerleau et al., 1990). These differences appear critical to later child development and ultimately to gender inequality. Infants who are encouraged to play with dolls and child furniture, or sports equipment and tools, will be more likely to choose these objects as they grow older:

They are familiar with these objects, and they know what can be done with them. They have also learned that these objects are appropriate for them, and for children of their own gender. Also, repetitive play with some types of objects is likely to promote the development of specific skills, abilities, and behaviors in male and female children, and in parent–child interaction. Tools, cars, and sports equipment elicit more active play than dolls, doll houses, and domestic objects . . . The times are changing. However, the changes do not seem to occur quickly enough to provide equal opportunities for girls and boys during their early development (Pomerleau et al., p. 366).

Hundreds of studies conducted over the past three decades have repeatedly demonstrated that children have developed gender stereotypes and gender-role expectations well before the age of five, and further, that many of these stereotypes have changed only marginally during the "gender aware" 1970s, 80s, and 90s (see Pomerleau et al., 1990 and Albert and Porter, 1988, for reviews of some of this literature). By age three, almost all children have developed a gender identity ("I'm a boy" or "I'm a girl"), and many—if not most—prefer playing in sex-segregated groups. By age five, girls prefer dolls, doll accessories, soft toys, drawing, painting, cutting, and pasting—while boys prefer blocks, small vehicles, tools, and roughhouse play. When pictures of children of their age group whom they do not know are presented to them, four-to-ten year-olds predict that girls will prefer "feminine" toys (dolls, etc.) and boys "masculine" toys (toy race cars, etc.) (Martin, 1989). During middle childhood and early teens, parents are much more likely to sign their daughters up for dance classes, and even though female participation in team sports has grown enormously since the Educational Amendments Acts of 1972 (its Title IX provisions mandate equal opportunity for boys and girls to participate in sports), boys are still more likely to be encouraged to play sports, especially team sports (Malec, 1997), and to have their gender identities more powerfully shaped by sports (Messner, 1992).

Sociologists have long recognized that much social learning occurs via role models. And despite the huge increase in women's labor-force participation, the role models in many families support traditional gender stereotypes. In particular, regardless of the work status of their mothers (not employed outside of house, employed part-time, employed full-time), many children see household chores still predominantly done by their mothers. Indeed, even though many men have come to support (at least in theory) the concept of sharing housework responsibilities equally, they often view their contribution as "helping out" their wives; women are held responsible if essential tasks are not done (Abbott and Wallace, 1997, p. 153; Oakley, 1982). Moreover, regardless of the willingness of many modern men to share in housework, women still most often end up doing more. Children are also likely to witness power imbalances in the interactions between their fathers and mothers. For example, Fishman's (1983) intensive analysis of conversational patterns between husbands and wives revealed that women try harder to communicate but succeed less. Both men and women regard topics introduced by women as tentative, and more often than not they are dropped. In contrast, topics introduced by men are almost always produced as reality by the interaction. They already have, and they continually establish and enforce, their rights to define what the interaction, and reality, will be about" (p. 405).

The effects of gender socialization in the family are cumulative. Gender-role expectations and stereotypes increase with age, and within the home many— if not most—children learn that boys and girls, men

and women, differ in the levels of independence, aggression, activity, strength, fearlessness, dominance, obedience, expressiveness, concern with physical appearance, nurturance, intellectual ability, and mechanical competence. Moreover, even though race, ethnicity, and social class can influence gender socialization (as we will discuss later), such influence is often relatively minor. In other words, children from a wide variety of social and economic backgrounds develop many of the same gender stereotypes.

The family is also the locus for decisions as to where and how children will be educated, and schooling has enormous consequences for gender socialization.

The Educational System

School has traditionally been one of the strongest arenas in which gender socialization has occurred. Prior to the mid-1970s, virtually all aspects of the curriculum and of extracurricular activities reinforced traditional gender roles. Textbooks and readers showed males in many occupations and females mainly as housewives and mothers. Sentences referring to both sexes used the male pronoun almost exclusively. Both fiction and nonfiction tended to focus on male characters and their exploits, females were usually depicted in supportive and ancillary roles. Boys were encouraged (or required) to take metal- and woodworking shop; technical-vocational education prepared them to work as carpenters, plumbers, mechanics, auto-body repairmen, and in other skilled trades. Girls were encouraged (or required) to take courses in home economics; those not headed for college were trained to take dictation, to write in shorthand, and to do filing and typing. Guidance counselors encouraged girls to pursue traditional female occupations (secretary, nurse, elementary school teacher) and boys to pursue traditional male occupations (mechanic, engineer, lawyer, white-collar office worker). Girls' sports were treated as much less important than boys'. Only as cheerleaders were girls in the spotlight at sports events.

In response to the feminist movement of the 1960s and its manifold repercussions (from legislation attempting to ensure sexual equality in pay, to women entering the workforce, to changing cultural norms that transformed "career woman" from an epithet to a compliment, to scientific studies showing the pervasiveness of gender stereotypes in the educational process and the negative consequences thereof), schools began changing in the 1970s. The changes were directed at promoting equal opportunities for the sexes in all areas of the curriculum and in extracurricular activities. And to a large degree, this has occurred. For example, public schools that once required either home economics (for girls) or shop (for boys) now require that both sexes take both courses (Giele, 1988, p. 303). Differences in the scores of male and female high school students have narrowed for some tests of mathematical ability (e.g., on the National Assessment of Education Progress examinations; see National Center for Education Statistics, 1996a, p. 121). Children's books now portray more women in nontraditional roles. Girls' participation in school sports programs has increased dramatically—in 1972, there were fewer than 300,000 girls participating in high-school sports programs, compared to more than 3.6 million boys, a ratio of about 1:12; however, by 1995, there were 2.2 million girls involved in high-school sports, compared to 3.5 million boys, a ratio of about 2:3 (Malec, 1997). Girls now have accessible to them more team sports than in years past: not only basketball, field hockey, softball, and volleyball, but even the most "macho" sports—including soccer, ice hockey, lacrosse, and rugby. Individual sports such as gymnastics, swimming, tennis, and track are now more widely available.

The change in girls' sports participation is more important than the average person might think. Social scientists have long contended that team sports provide boys with valuable learning environments that have an impact on future economic success. Team sports cultivate social skills: learning to deal with diversity in memberships in which each person is doing a special task; learning to coordinate actions and maintain cohesiveness among group members; learning to cope with impersonal rules; learning to work for collective as well as personal goals; developing one's strategic thinking; gaining experience in leadership positions; learning to deal with interpersonal competition in a forthright manner; experiencing face-to-face confrontations—often involving a close friend—and learning how to depersonalize the attack; learning self-control and keeping one's "cool" under fire (Lever, 1978, pp. 480–481).

Nevertheless, the changes in schooling aimed at equalizing opportunity and life chances between the sexes are far from complete. As just noted, girls are still only about two-thirds as likely as boys to participate in school sports programs. Although improved, many texts and readers still most commonly depict women in domestic roles and as more helpless, more emotional, and less adventuresome than men (Ferree and Hall, 1990; Peterson and Kroner, 1992; Peterson and Lach, 1990; Purcell and Stewart, 1990)—thereby perpetuating "the cultural stereotype that men tend to be stronger, more active, and working in the world to solve problems, whereas women are more likely to be weaker, more passive, and focusing their interests around home and family" (Sullivan, 1997, p. 252). In a series of recent reports, the American Association of University Women (1990, 1991, 1992) has documented that schools are still a place where many girls are "shortchanged." In particular, these reports reveal that boys are much more likely than girls to say they are "pretty good at a lot of things" and to list their talents as the thing they like most about themselves, while girls, on the other hand, list aspects of their physical appearance. Moreover, boys are much less likely to say they are "not good enough" or "not smart enough" to achieve their career goals. The reports also make it clear that the sources of these disparities in feelings of competence are rooted in classroom experiences. Teachers give boys more attention and more encouragement to be assertive. Furthermore, as girls advance through school, their interest in mathematics and the hard sciences decreases, and those girls who take such courses are only half as likely as boys to feel competent in them. These latter findings are highly significant, for other studies have shown "that a loss of confidence in math usually *precedes* a drop in achievement, rather than vice versa," and indeed a difference in level of confidence, rather than ability, "may help explain why the number of female physical and computer scientists actually went down during the 1980s" (Orenstein, 1997, p. 44). A final factor related to the historical short-changing of girls in the sciences and mathematics—but one that has almost been ameliorated—has been the lack of same-sex role models. Until the early 1980s, only 25 percent of the teachers in these fields were female (National Science Foundation, 1982); however, in recent years, the number of female teachers in these areas has grown dramatically, to about 42 percent of high-school science teachers and 51 percent of high-school math teachers (National Center for Education Statistics, 1996b, Table 2.10). However, comparing the average mathematical scores of males and females on the Scholastic Assessment Test over the past two decades reveals little consistent change in the gap between boys and girls (see Figure 36.1); for example, the difference between the sexes was 41 points in 1971 (M = 507, F = 466), and 40 points in 1995 (M = 503, F = 463).

The Special Case of Single-Sex Schools.   Research on mixed- versus single-sex high schools reveals that girls prosper in the latter (Riordan, 1990, 1997; Lockheed and Klein, 1985). Female cognitive development is greater; female occupational aspirations and their ultimate attainment are increased; female self-confidence and self-esteem are magnified. Moreover, in such schools, females receive better treatment in the classroom; they are more likely to be encouraged to explore—and to have access to—wider curriculum opportunities; and teachers have greater respect for their work. Finally, females attending single-sex schools have "more egalitarian attitudes toward the role of women in society than do their counterparts in mixed-sex schools" (Riordan, 1997, p. 178). Single-sex schools accrue these benefits for girls for a variety of reasons, including the following: (1) a diminished emphasis on "youth culture," which centers on athletics, social life, physical attractiveness, heterosexual popularity, and negative attitudes toward academics; (2) the provision of more successful same-sex role models (the top students in all subjects and all extracurricular activities will be girls); (3) a reduction in sex bias in teacher–student interaction (there are not boys around that can be "favored"); and (4) elimination of sex stereotypes in peer interaction (generally, cross-sex peer interaction in school involves male dominance, male leadership, and, often, sexual harassment).

Peer Groups

Child and adolescent peer groups are powerful agents of socialization. Even though there are many cross-gender activities and many cross-gender groups, peers

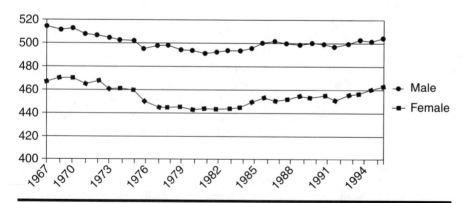

FIGURE 36.1   Scholastic Assessment Test Math Score Averages for College-Bound High School Seniors, by Sex, 1967–1995. *Source:* National Center for Education Statistics, 1996a, p. 127)

from the earliest ages (2 or 3) on through high school tend to congregate in same-sex groups and to engage in gender-appropriate behavior. "Both boys and girls who select gender-appropriate toys are more likely to have other children play with them" (Renzetti and Curran, 1995, p. 99).

As just noted, studies of single-sex schools have revealed that one of the reasons for their success is their de-emphasizing youth cultures and the kinds of peer pressures involved therein. Such cultures are imbued with traditional gender stereotypes—boys are to be athletic, tough, and not overly expressive; girls are to be beauty-oriented and demure. Good grades are O.K., but they should not be flaunted, as this is what nerds, dweebs, and geeks get. For both sexes, to be "cool" is to be physically attractive and heterosexually popular. Youth cultures generally yield more favorable results for males in the long run. With the greater emphasis on sports for males and "looks" for females, the message being sent is that a woman's status is determined by her appearance, a man's by his accomplishment.

Dating patterns during adolescence reinforce this depiction of reality. Girls often date older boys, who because of their age have acquired more knowledge and experience. One impact is that both sexes begin thinking that males are more sophisticated and worldly and are on firmer ground when they act aggressive. The idea that males should be more aggressive is bolstered by the fact that boys are supposed to "ask out" girls—that is, to be the initiators in the dating game. Further, boys are most often expected to supply the transportation, picking up the girl at her home and then driving to the movie theater or restaurant or party.

Studies of peer interactions reveal that females learn to act in ways that suggest they are less powerful and more vulnerable than males. Females learn that to get along with males they must be willing to accept interruptions and to defer to male decisions on the choice and character of conversations (see Fishman, 1983; and Thorne, Kramarae, and Henley, 1983). They also learn that to be successful in heterosexual interactions their body language must send out signals that they are demure: they should not sit with their legs wide apart; they should not recline

with their hands behind their head and elbows thrusting outward; during conversation, they should smile often, tilt their heads, be attentive looking, avert their gazes, and nod their heads often. In the words of body language expert Janet Lee Mills (1985, p. 8–9), to be successful in social interaction, a woman must learn "to be passive, accommodating, affiliative, subordinate, submissive, and vulnerable." Such traits win her "popularity, dates, and admiration in her social life." Mills notes that these traits are exactly opposite to those encouraged in males, those that produce success in the business world—that is, being active, dominant, aggressive, confident, competent, and tough. Figure 36.2 displays five photographs starkly illustrating Mills's observations on the differences in body language that we have learned to expect from males versus females.

Finally, although the "double standard" regarding sex has diminished considerably, Lees (1986) has shown that adolescent males control adolescent females by threatening to label them as promiscuous. It is still all right for young men to "sow their oats," but young women who try to become sexually powerful are labeled "sluts" and "easy lays." This remnant of the double standard serves to maintain traditional gender stereotypes (Abbott and Wallace, 1997, p. 125).

The Media

Images of gender in the mass media—newspapers, magazines, television, and the motion pictures—partly reflect the relationships and behavior of males and females in the dominant society. However, the media also act as an agent of gender socialization that can shape our expectations and perceptions. Very often the media reinforce traditional gender stereotypes (e.g., men as aggressive, active, problem-solvers vs. women as passive and more interested in relationships than in work, politics, and power) or overemphasize certain aspects of them to the point of distortion (e.g., promoting the notion that many men use their fists and guns on a daily basis to solve problems, which makes women love these men a lot more than they otherwise would).

FIGURE 36.2 Illustrations of "Proper" Male versus "Proper" Female Body Language. In which photograph does the man's posture seem appropriate? In which does the woman's? Note: Male nonverbal behavior typically includes very few affiliative displays, such as smiles and head cants, and many power cues, such as expanded limb positions and serious facial expressions. Female nonverbal behavior, however, is ordinarily just the opposite, containing many affiliative displays and few power cues. The overall impression males create is one of power, dominance, high status, and activity, particularly in contrast to the overall impression females create, which is one of submissiveness, subordination, low status, and passivity. *Source:* Mills, 1985, pp. 11–12; used by permission.

Newspapers and news magazines are largely the province of men. Men are twice as likely as women to read these publications (*Media Report to Women*, 1993a), and stories about men and written by men predominate. Eighty-five percent of front-page news stories focus on men; men author two-thirds of front-page stories and three-quarters of opinion pieces; women predominate in the "non-news" (sometimes called "soft") sections of the daily paper (*Media Report to Women*, 1993b, 1993c). When women do appear in "hard" news stories, aspects of their gender that would be considered trivial for men are often highlighted. Stories involving women very often include descriptions of their physical appearance and family status. For example, the *Washington Post's* characterizations of the candidates in a Pennsylvania senatorial race

> described the Democratic candidate Lynn Yeakel, as a *"feisty and feminine 50-year-old with the unmistakable Dorothy Hamill wedge of gray hair and the dazzling silk suit of lime, tangerine, and blue."* In addition, it was noted that she was a congressman's daughter, currently married to a stockbroker, and formerly a full-time mother. In contrast, her opponent, Republication Senator Arlen Specter, was described as a *"crime-busting district attorney and mayoral hopeful."* The profile of Specter did not mention his hair or wardrobe (Renzetti and Curran, 1995, p. 156; also see Media Report to Women, *1992*).

Nonnews magazines are purchased and read by women much more than by men—in ratios that are estimated to be from 2:1 to 3:1 (Audits and Surveys, 1991). Analyses of the advertisements, editorials, and stories in the most popular women's magazines reveal that themes of getting and keeping a man and making oneself beautiful have been dominant since the 1940s (Cantor, 1987; Ferguson, 1983; Galzer, 1980; McCracken, 1993; Phillips, 1978; Synnott, 1991—as cited in Simon and Henderson, 1997); moreover, even though many articles about career and job concerns began appearing in the 1980s, achievement in the work world is "often presented as being dependent on physical attractiveness, e.g., 'dressing for success,' applying the right make-up, or fixing one's hair a particular way" (Renzetti and Curran, 1995, pp. 160–161).

Analyses of gender on television reveal that women play only about one in every three roles and that this figure has not changed since the early 1950s (Gerbner, 1993). Moreover, despite women being shown in recent years as working outside of the home and doing nontraditional jobs (e.g., police officer), they are depicted much more often than men as submissive and unsuccessful (Metzger, 1992). When they are successful (such as Murphy Brown), they become so at the risk of being failures with men and in their domestic lives (Japp, 1991). Further, compared to males, females are much more likely to be young, blond, thin, and scantily clad; and when depicted as older women they are much more likely to be shown as societal outcasts and social misfits (Fejes, 1992; Metzger, 1992; Silverstein et al., 1986).

Television advertising perpetuates gender stereotyping to a greater degree than the programs being sponsored (Fejes, 1992; Lazier-Smith, 1989; McCracken, 1993; Strate, 1992). Men are shown in a wide variety of roles, and as in control (or if not in control, with the distinct possibility of being so if they would only buy the product at hand). Women are depicted as "sweet young things" (whether shown in the work world or not) or as housewives and mothers. Women demonstrate household products, while the voice-overs are overwhelmingly male (because the male voice is the voice of authority; see Renzetti and Curran, 1995, pp. 173–174).

Although it is difficult to tease out the direction of the causal arrow (which factor is causing which factor), the amount of time spent in front of the television set correlates with espousing gender stereotypes (Comstock and Paik, 1991). Social psychology experiments tend to support the television → stereotyping model as opposed to its reverse (that those with strong gender stereotypes tend to watch more television). For example, Geis et al. (1984) found that when female students were shown commercials in which gender stereotypes were prevalent, they were later much more likely to project images of themselves in traditional statuses (e.g., wife, mother) than

other female students shown commercials that depicted women having nontraditional statuses and playing
nontraditional roles (compare similar findings in Morgan, 1972).

CONSEQUENCES OF GENDER SOCIALIZATION
FOR CAREER CHOICES

Gender socialization in each of these domains—the
educational system, the family, the peer group, and
the media—undoubtedly strongly influences choice
of career. Here we focus on the effects of such socialization in the schools

As we have already noted, one reason why
schools have historically been so important in creation and maintenance of gender roles is sex-based
curriculum tracking. Boys not oriented toward college either were placed in or encouraged to take
courses that would prepare them for blue-collar
trades; girls either were placed in or encouraged to
take courses that would prepare them to be secretaries, receptionists, file clerks, cashiers, or sales
workers. Blue-collar occupations, which are end
always have been predominantly male, traditionally
and presently pay considerably better wages that
low-level office and retail work. For example, among
the blue-collar trades, we find the following median
annual salaries for 1996: automotive mechanic—
$30,905, carpenter—$30,480, electrician—$35,446,
plumber—$35,585, and tool & die maker—$35,416;
while in fields noncollege-oriented females typically
enter, we find bank tellers averaging $16,110 per year,
bookkeepers $23,427, cashiers $14,164, data entry
operators $19,495, file clerks $15,966, secretaries
$24,622, and word processors $21,554 (Economic
Research Institute, 1995, p. 300). Moreover, despite
the manifold changes in U.S. schools over the past
two decades that were intended to equalize opportunities for the sexes, we still find males seven times
more likely than females to be taking "trade and
industrial" vocational-education courses (National
Center for Education Statistics, 1996a, Table 134).

About 12 percent of high school seniors, both
males (11.9%) and females (11.6%), are in vocational-
education programs, and another 43 percent are tak-

ing college preparatory curricula. Females (44.2%)
are more likely than males (41.8%) to be in college
preparatory program (National Center for Education
Statistics, 1996a, Table 132). Moreover, females
(80.1%) are more likely than males (73.0%) to report
that they plan to go to college after high school
(National Center for Education Statistics, 1996a,
Table 138); and, indeed, they actually do—of the
approximately 1.6 million students entering college
full-time each year, 53.2 percent are females, and of
the nearly 7.2 million full-time undergraduate students currently enrolled in U.S. colleges and universities, 53.4 percent are female (National Center for
Education Statistics, 1996a, Table 174). Finally, as
of the mid-1990s, women receive 54.5 percent of the
1.2 million bachelor's degrees that are granted each
year (National Center for Education Statistics, 1996a,
Table 239). Such statistics are of great interest to students of gender inequality because, at the individual
level of analysis, the strongest predictor of annual
income is years of education. Now if females are
more likely to be enrolled in college preparatory programs in high school, are more likely to go on to college, and are more likely to graduate from college,
why then is there such a wide discrepancy between
the incomes of men and women? Put differently, why
do women appear to b getting less monetary return
on their investments in education?

Part of the answer rests in the types of education
men and women pursue, both at the undergraduate
and postgraduate levels. At the undergraduate level
(see Table 36.1), women are significantly more likely than men to major in traditional "female" fields of
study (elementary education, English, home economics, paralegal training, library science, and the performing arts)—all of which lead to careers that pay
substantially less than careers arising from those
majors men are significantly more likely to choose
(business, computer science, engineering, the physical
sciences, medicine, dentistry, and law). The median
annual salary for public elementary school teachers
is $33,946 (considerably less for private schools), for
example, and for public secondary school teachers,
$35,405 (again, much less at private schools); for
librarians, $34,738; registered nurses, $35,256; and

TABLE 36.1   Bachelor's Degrees by Sex of Student and Field of Study, 1993–1994.

	TOTAL	MEN	WOMEN	PERCENT WOMEN
All Fields	1,169,275	532,422	636,853	54.5
Agriculture and natural resources	18,070	11,748	6,322	35.0
Agricultural sciences	6,432	3,750	2,682	41.7
Conservation and renewable natural resources	6,679	4,387	2,292	34.4
Architecture and related programs	8,975	5,764	3,211	35.8
Area, ethnic, and cultural studies	5,573	1,958	3,615	64.9
Biological sciences/life sciences	51,383	25,050	26,333	51.3
Business management, administrative services and marketing operations/marketing and distribution	246,654	129,161	117,493	47.7
Communications and communications technologies	51,827	21,359	30,468	58.8
Computer and information sciences	24,200	17,317	6,883	28.5
Education, total	107,600	24,450	83,150	77.3
General teacher education, total	61,017	6,699	54,318	89.1
Adult and continuing education	89	20	69	77.6
Elementary education	48,733	4,642	44,091	90.5
Junior high/intermediate/middle school education	1,378	298	1,080	78.4
Pre-elementary/early childhood/kindergarten education	6,474	164	6,310	97.5
Secondary education	3,746	1,537	2,209	59.0
Teacher education, general program, other	597	38	559	93.7
Engineering and engineering-related technologies	78,225	66,597	11,628	14.9
English language and literature/letters	53,924	18,425	35,499	65.9
Foreign languages and literatures	14,378	4,304	10,074	70.1
Health professions and related sciences, total	74,421	13,062	61,359	82.5
Pre-dentistry studies	70	46	24	34.3
Pre-medicine studies	756	438	318	42.1
Medical basic sciences	245	94	151	61.7
Nursing	39,076	3,735	35,341	90.5
Home economics and vocational home economics	15,522	1,933	13,589	87.6
Law and legal studies, total	2,171	648	1,523	70.2
Pre-law studies	239	120	119	49.8
Paralegal/legal assistant	1,028	154	874	85.1
Liberal arts and sciences, general studies and humanities	33,397	13,117	20,280	60.8
Library science	62	5	57	92.0
Mathematics	14,396	7,735	6,661	46.3
Multi/interdisciplinary studies	25,167	9,058	16,109	64.1
Parks, recreation, leisure, and fitness studies	11,470	5,823	5,647	49.3
Philosophy and religion	7,546	4,844	2,702	35.9
Physical sciences and science technologies	18,400	12,223	6,177	33.6
Precision production trades, total	420	308	112	26.7

(continued)

TABLE 36.1   continued.

	TOTAL	MEN	WOMEN	PERCENT WOMEN
Protective services	23,009	14,169	8,840	38.5
Psychology	69,259	18,642	50,617	73.1
Public administration and services	17,815	3,919	13,896	78.1
R.O.T.C. and military technologies	19	16	3	15.8
Social sciences and history	133,680	72,006	61,674	46.2
Theological studies/religious vocations	5,434	4,125	1,309	24.1
Transportational and material moving	3,923	3,500	423	10.8
Visual and performing arts	49,053	19,538	29,515	60.2

Source: National Center for Education Statistics, 1996a, pp. 258–273.

social workers, $30,000 (with an M.S.W., $20,000 for those with only a B.S.W.); while in predominantly male careers, we find chemical engineers making $56,682; civil engineers, $47,734; computer programmers, $36,350; electrical engineers, $53,876; dentists, $100,000; financial analysts, $46,950; lawyers, $67,900; marketing managers, $52,555; physicians, $156,000; and systems programmers, $64,824 (Economic Research Institute, 1995, p. 300; Bureau of Labor Statistics, 1996c, pp. 118, 134, 156).

At the graduate level, just as at the undergraduate level, we find more female than male students: of the slightly more than 2 million postgraduate students studying full- and part-time for masters degrees, Ph.D.s, and professional degrees (dentistry, laws, medicine), 53 percent are women (National Center for Education Statistics, 1996a, Table 174). However, just as at the undergraduate level, women are more likely to be enrolled in graduate programs that will put them in careers that pay less. A social worker with a masters degree averages $30,000 a year, as just noted, while the average private attorney makes $67,000 a year; nurse practitioners with graduate degrees average $50,000 and physicians $156,000. Figure 36.3 compares the distribution of men and women receiving doctorates in the high-paying fields of business, engineering, computer science, mathematics, and the physical sciences, as well as in the lower paying fields of education, English, and foreign languages and literature. These data clearly show that women predominate in the fields of study that lead to lower-

paying careers, while men predominate in the fields that lead to higher-paying careers. Moreover, women are more likely than men to be enrolled in masters programs (see Figure 36.4). Masters degrees yield smaller income returns than doctoral (e.g., Ph.D., D.B.A., Ed.D.) and professional degrees—the postgraduate programs in which men predominate. Of the dozens of professional careers detailed in the Bureau of Labor Statistics (1996c) *Occupational Outlook Handbook,* in every instance it is noted that individuals with doctorates make more than their colleagues with only masters degrees.

Why women are less likely to go into the professions, engineering, and the hard sciences undoubtedly is related to the socialization influences that occur in the contexts of high school, the family, peer groups, and the media. And when looking at postgraduate programs (the Ph.D. and professional degrees), we can include the additional factor of women being more likely to be married and more likely to be involved in the care of their young children—thereby deterring them from enrolling and completing degrees in these programs.

RACIAL, ETHNIC, AND CLASS VARIATIONS IN GENDER SOCIALIZATION

Although we might suspect that the gender socialization processes described above vary by race, ethnicity, and class, there has been little research in the area—and the studies that have been done have produced

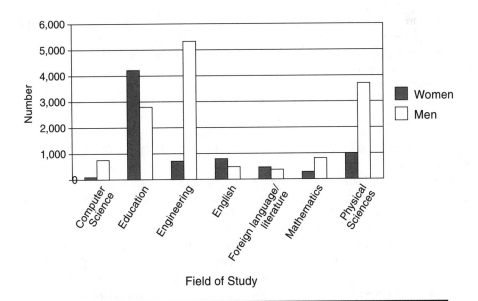

FIGURE 36.3   Doctorates Awarded in 1993–4 by Sex for Selected Fields of Study. Note: Percentage female: Computer Science—15.4; Education—60.8; Engineering—11.1; English—57.7; Foreign Language/Literature—59.9; Mathematics—21.9; Physical Science—21.7 *Source:* National Center for Education Statistics, 1996a, pp. 258–265.

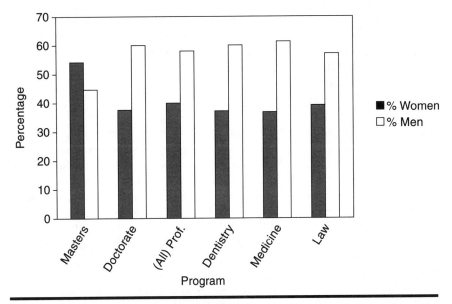

FIGURE 36.4   Postgraduate Degrees in 1994 by Type of Program and Sex. *Source:* National Center for Education Statistics, 1996a, pp. 258, 281.

contradictory findings." Much more research is needed to elucidate the rich diversity of gender socialization practices and their outcomes among various races
and classes" (Renzetti and Curran, 1995, pp. 99–100).
We present here some tentative findings.

Women of Color

In the words of one student of gender socialization,
"many of the characteristics associated with the feminine stereotype—dependence on men, weakness, and
learned helplessness, for example—simply are not
typical of women of color" (Anderson, 1993, p. 38).
One difference between white and African American
girls is the greater emphasis placed on female self-
sufficiency in African American homes and the expectation that a woman's role includes material support
of the family, whether she is a single parent or married. African American children in two-parent homes
are also more likely to witness more egalitarianism
in the division of household labor and in decision-
making. Research has shown that African American
children, regardless of sex, "are expected to be
assertive, independent, and emotionally expressive"
(Figueira-McDonough, 1985, p. 124; also see Hale-
Benson, 1986). One key exception occurs within
Black Muslim families, in which male dominance in
both public and private life is an essential part of their
credo. Another important variation: poor African
American men face discrimination that may prevent
them from fulfilling the traditional male role of
provider; as a result, some "develop roles of exaggerated masculinity—the 'tough guy' or the 'player
of women'" (Scarpitti, Andersen, and O'Toole, 1997,
p. 219; also see Oliver, 1984).

An expected empirical consequence of such differences in gender socialization would be the greater
likelihood that African American women work,
compared with white women. Indeed, this has always
been the case. However, the gender-role expectations
having changed for white girls and women over the
past two decades such that the desire to combine work
and family have become the norm, we would expect
this difference to narrow or disappear.

At least one study, Isaaks (1980), found the
same differences for Latino children as just detailed
for African American children: in short, that they are
exposed to—and consequently subscribe to—fewer
bipolar gender stereotypes (e.g., males as tough,
females as demure). However, other researchers have
found "at least as much, if not more, gender stereotyping among blacks and Hispanics as among whites"
(Renzetti and Curran, 1995, p. 101). Indeed, Hale-
Benson's (1986) study revealed that African
American boys are encouraged—especially by their
peers—to be athletic, sexually competent, street
smart, and tough, while African American girls are
socialized into "a very strong motherhood orientation" (as quoted in Renzetti and Curran, 1995, p. 100).
General Social Survey data consistently show that
African Americans are slightly more likely than
whites to agree with the statement that "women
should take care of running their homes and leave running the country up to men" (NORC, 1991–1994,
1994, 1996).

As for Asian American women, it has often been
noted that they are socialized "in the context of a culture with devalued and subordinate roles for women"
(Scarpitti, Andersen, and O'Toole, 1997, p. 219).
However, the present gender socialization picture is
surely much more complicated, considering the number of prominent female Asian American role models in various fields.

Social Class

Most studies of the impact of race and ethnicity on
gender socialization have used middle-class samples,
so firm conclusions on the effects of social class on
gender socialization are few. A number of studies
have shown a modest negative relationship between
education and gender stereotyping (Burns and Homel,
1989; Lackey, 1989; Brooks-Gunn, 1986), and, as
evidenced in Figure 36.5, recent national survey data
support this conclusion. However, one major study
(Bardwell et al., 1986) found white children to be
exposed to greater gender stereotyping as one
moves up the social class scale; similarly, Figueira-

Years of Education

	0–11	12	13–15	16+
Disagree	67%	81%	86.7%	93.5%
	(207)	(439)	(451)	(476)
Agree	33%	19%	13.3%	6.5%
	(102)	(103)	(69)	(33)
	100%	100%	100%	100%
	(309)	(542)	(520)	(509)

N = 1880

FIGURE 36.5 Relationship between Educational Attainment and Agreeing or Disagreeing with the Statement that "Women should take care of running their homes and leave running the country up to men." *Source:* NORC, 1996.

McDonough (1985) found that African American girls raised in middle-class homes were more likely to express traditional gender views (e.g., girls should not be aggressive) than their counterparts raised in poor homes.

To the degree that career choices are dictated by socialization and to the degree that there exists a strong pattern to this process that cuts across racial and ethnic origins, we would expect to find more similarities than differences among contemporary working women of different racial and ethnic origins—and indeed we do (for example, women of all racial/ethnic backgrounds are much more likely than their male counterparts to be secretaries and much less likely to be mechanics).

SUMMARY

It is not biologic determinism but the socialization of individuals, which occurs within the contexts of the family, the educational system, the peer group, and the popular media, that ultimately has dramatic influences on gender inequality and the fates of working women. Although in recent years each of these con-

texts has become much more egalitarian, the framework for interpreting reality that is created and encouraged is one still strongly favoring many traditional stereotypes of desirable behavior for men and women. Such stereotypes reinforce traditional gender arrangements—arrangements that result in men being much more likely than women to become economically successful.

Parents are still more likely to give their sons toys that elicit more active and aggressive play and to their daughters toys that reinforce the gender stereotype of females having primary concern with home and family matters. Parental role models reinforce these stereotypes too; although most children see both mother and father in the workforce, they also see household chores still predominantly done by their mothers. Children are also likely to witness power imbalances in the interactions between their mother and father.

Schools are major arenas in which gender socialization occurs. Before 1970, virtually all aspects of the curriculum and extracurricular activities reinforced traditional gender roles. Since Title IX of the 1972 Education Amendments Act, dramatic changes in schools have taken place, with females gaining, though not yet attaining, much greater equality in both curricular and extracurricular activities. The most significant indicators of this equality are the narrowing between boys and girls in mathematical ability and in sports participation. These indicators are particularly important because success in mathematics is correlated with taking technical career tracks in college and entering traditionally male fields such as engineering and medicine, which pay considerably more than traditional female fields such as teaching and nursing. And team sports cultivate skills that are especially important for success in the workplace. Social scientists have long held that, in years gone by, girls were hurt in ways that eventually showed up economically by not participating in team sports. Despite greater gender egalitarianism in education philosophy and programs, girls are still "shortchanged" in the modern school. In coeducational classrooms, teachers give boys more attention and more encouragement to be assertive. Girls' sports participation is only two-thirds that of boys. And girls' SAT mathematics scores still fall 40 points shy of boys'. The overall impact is that boys are much less likely to say they are "not good enough" or "not smart enough" to achieve their career goals. These problems are minimized for the small percentage of girls attending single-sex schools, where girls end up having greater cognitive development, higher occupation occupational aspirations, and magnified self-confidence and self-esteem.

Child and adolescent peer groups are powerful agents of socialization, and they tend to encourage same-sex groups and gender-appropriate behavior. Youth culture encourages boys to be athletic and not overly expressive, while girls are encouraged to be beauty-oriented and demure. For both sexes, to be "cool" is to be physically attractive and heterosexually popular. The youth culture reinforces the idea that males achieve status through accomplishment, while females achieve status by appearance and beauty.

Although the media act as a mirror to reflect the relationships and behavior of males and females in the dominant society, they also influence our expectations and perceptions of gender roles. More often than not, the media reinforce traditional gender stereotypes—men are aggressive, active, problem-solvers, while women are passive and more interested in relationships than in work, politics, and power. Most non-news magazines oriented toward women often present female achievement in the work world as being dependent on physical attractiveness. Women in television are much more likely than men to be portrayed as submissive and unsuccessful. And when they are successful economically, television more often than not depicts an accompanying risk of being a failure in family life or with men.

Even though females have higher graduation rates from both high school and college, the educational tracks they take prepare them for jobs that pay less than those males are prepared for. In high school, noncollege-oriented boys are much more likely to take vocational courses that will lead them into high-paying blue-collar trades (plumbing, carpentry, electrician work), while girls are much more likely to take vocational courses that prepare them for low-paying office work (file clerk, bookkeeper, bank teller). The situation is similar at the college level: women are more likely than men to major in subjects (e.g., elementary education, English, home economics, paralegal training, library science, the performing arts) that lead to lower-paying jobs than the majors in which men predominate (e.g., business, computer science, engineering, the physical sciences). The situation remains the same even at the level of graduate school, with women more likely to enroll in programs that will put them in careers that pay less (doctorates in education, English, foreign languages and literature earn substantially less than doctorates in business, engineering, computer science, mathematics, and the physical sciences).

NOTES

1. In the early 1980s, Mead's research came under heavy attack from the respected anthropologist Derek Freeman (1983), who questioned her methods and findings. Anthropologists and sociologists debated and assessed Freeman's accusations for several years. The outcome was a realization that Mead had made some errors, but that many of her findings and conclusions, including those presented here, were solid. Anthropologist Nancy McDowell (1984, pp. 138–139) studies the Mundugumor during three extended field trips between 1972 and 1981, and she found the women there just as "harsh and aggressive" as Mead had said they were.

REFERENCES

Abbott, Pamela, and Clair Wallace. 1997. *An Introduction to Sociology: Feminist Perspectives.* NY: Routledge.

Albert, Alexa A., and Judith R. Porter. 1988. "Children's Gender-Role Stereotypes: A Sociological Investigation of Psychological Models." *Sociological Forum* 3(2):184–210.

Allen, Laura S., and Roger A. Gorski. 1992. "Sexual Orientation and the Sizes of the Anterior Commissure in the Human Brain." *Proceedings of the National Academy of Sciences* 89:7199–7202.

Anderson, Elaine A., and Jane W. Spruill. 1993. "The Dual Career Commuter Family: A Lifestyle on the Move." *Marriage and Family Review* 19(1–2):131–147.

Audits and Surveys. 1991. *The Study of Magazine Buying Patterns.* Port Washington, NY: Publishers Clearinghouse.

Bardwell, J. R., Coebran, S. W., and S. Walker. 1986. "Relationship of Parental Education, Race, and Gender to Sex Role Stereotyping in Five-Year-Old Kindergartners." *Sex Roles* 15:275–281.

Brooks-Gunn, Jeanne. 1986. "The Relationships of Maternal Beliefs About Sex Typing to Maternal and Young Children's Behavior." *Sex Roles* 14:21–35.

Bureau of Labor Statistics. 1971. *Current Population Survey March 1971 Supplement.* Washington, D.C.: Bureau of the Census.

———. 1996c. *Occupational Outlook Handbook, 1996–97 Edition* (Bulletin 2470). Washington, D.C.: U.S. Government Printing Office.

Burns, Alisa, and Ross Homel. 1989. "Gender Division of Tasks by Parents and Their Children." *Psychology of Women Quarterly* 13:113–125.

Cantor, Muriel. G. 1987. "Popular Culture and the Portrayal of Women: Content and Control." Pp. 190–214 in Beth B. Hess and Myra Marx Ferree (eds.), *Analyzing Gender.* Newbury Park, CA: Sage.

Comstock, George, and Haejung Paik. 1991. *Television and the American Child.* San Diego: Academic Press.

Deaux, Kay. 1992. "Sex Differences." Pp. 1749–1753 in Edgar F. Borgatta and Marie L. Borgatta (eds.), *Encyclopedia of Sociology*, Vol. 3. NY: Macmillan.

Economic Research Institute. 1995. *The 1996 Geographic Reference Report.* Washington, D.C.: Economic Research Institute.

Fausto-Sterling, Anne. 1992. *Myths of Gender: Biological Theories About Women and Men.* NY: Basic Books.

Fejes, Fred J. 1992. "Masculinity as Fact." Pp. 9–22 in Steve Craig (ed.), *Men, Masculinity, and Media.* Newbury Park, CA: Sage.

Ferguson, Marjorie. 1983. *Forever Feminine: Women's Magazines and the Cult of Femininity.* London: Heinemann.

Ferree, Myra Marx, and Elaine J. Hall. 1990. "Visual Images of American Society: Gender and Race In Introductory Sociology Textbooks." *Gender and Society* 4:500–533.

Figueira-McDonough, Josefina. 1985. "Gender, Race, and Class: Differences in Levels of Feminist Orientation." *Journal of Applied Behavioral Science* 21(2):121–142.

Fishman, Pamela M. 1983. "Interaction: The Work Women Do." *Social Problems* 25(April):397–406.

Freeman, Derek. 1983. *Margaret Mead and Samoa: The Making and Unmaking of Anthropological Myth.* Cambridge, MA: Harvard University press.

Frisch, Hannah L. 1977. "Sex Stereotypes in Adult-Infant Play." *Child Development* 48:1671–1675.

Geis, Florence L., V. Brown, J. Jennings Walstedt, and N. Porter. 1984. "TV Commercials as Achievement Scripts for Women." *Sex Roles* 10:513–525.

Gerbner. G. 1993. *Women and Minorities on Television: A Study in Casting and Fate—A Report to the Screen Actors Guild and the American Federation of Radio and Television Artists.* Philadelphia: Annenberg School of Communications, University of Pennsylvania.

Giele, Janet Z. 1988. "Gender and Sex Roles." Pp. 291–323 in Neil J. Smelser (ed.), *Handbook of Sociology.* Newbury Park, CA: Sage.

Glazer, Nathan. 1980. "Overworking the Working Woman: The Double Day in a Mass Magazine." *Women's Studies International Quarterly* 3:79–95.

Goldberg, Steven. 1974. *The Inevitability of Patriarchy.* NY: William Morrow.

Gorman, C. 1992. "Sizing Up the Sexes." *Time* (January 20):42–51.

Hale-Benson, Janice E. 1986. *Black Children: Their Roots, Culture, and Learning Styles* (Revised Edition). Provo, UT: Brigham Young University Press.

Isaaks; L.1980. *Sex Role Stereotyping as It Relates 10 Ethnicity, Age, and Sex in Young Children.* Commerce, TX: unpublished dissertation, East Texas State University.

Jacklin, Carol Nagy. 1989. "Female and Male: Issues of Gender." *American Psychologist* 44(2):127–133.

Japp, Phyllis M. 1991. "Gender and Work in the 1980s: Television's Working Women as Displaced Persons." *Women's Studies in Communication* 14:49–74.

Kelly, Rita Mae. 1991. *The Gendered Economy: Work, Careers, and Success*. Newbury Park, CA: Sage.

Lackey, Pat N. 1989. "Adults' Attitudes About Assignments of Household Chores to Male and Female Children." *Sex Roles* 20:271–281.

Lazier-Smith, Linda. 1989. "A New Genderation of Images of Women." Pp. 247–260 in P. J. Creedon (ed.), *Women in Mass Communication*. Newbury Park, CA: Sage.

Lees, Sue. 1986. *Losing Out: Sexuality and Adolescent Girls*. London: Hutchinson.

LeVay, Simon. 1993. *The Sexual Brain*. Cambridge, MA: MIT Press.

Lever, Janet. 1978. "Sex Differences in the Complexity of Children's Play and Games." *American Sociological Review* 42(August):471–483.

Lockheed, M. E., and S. S. Klein. 1985. "Sex Equity in Classroom Organization and Climate." Pp. 189–217 in Susan S. Klein (ed.), *Handbook for Achieving Sex Equity Through Education*. Baltimore: Johns Hopkins University Press.

Malec, Michael A. 1997. "Gender Equity in Athletics." Pp. 209–218 in Gregg Lee Carter (ed.), *Perspectives on Current Social Problems*. Boston: Allyn and Bacon.

Martin, Carol Lynn. 1989. "Children's Use of Gender-Related Information in Making Social Judgments." *Developmental Psychology* 25:80–88.

McCoy, N. L. 1985. "Innate Factors in Sex Differences. Pp. 74–86 in Alice G. Sargent (ed.), *Beyond Sex Roles*. 2nd ed. St. Paul, MN: West.

McCracken, Ellen. 1993. *Decoding Women's Magazines*. NY: St. Martin's Press.

McDowell, Nancy. 1984. *The Mundugumor*, as cited in Jane Howard, *Margaret Mead, A Media Report to Women*. 1992. "Report Traces Media's Polarizing Influence in Society, Politics." (Fall):8–9.

———. 1993a. "Newspaper Gender Gap Widening, Says Newspaper Association of American." (Spring):5.

———. 1993b. "Scoring the News Media: Underrepresentation of Women Continues." (Spring):2–3.

———. 1993c. "Briefs—The Associated Press in December." (Winter):5.

Messner, Michael. 1992. *Power at Play: Sports and the Problem of Masculinity*. Boston: Beacon.

Metzger, Gretchen. 1992. "T.V. Is A Blonde, Blonde World." *American Demographics* 5(November):51.

Mills, Janet Lee. 1985. "Body Language Speaks Louder Than Words." *Horizons* (February):8–12.

Money, John, and Anke A. Ehrhardt. 1996. *Man and Woman, Boy and Girl*. Northvale, NJ: Jason Aronson Publishers.

Morgan, Elaine 1972. *The Descent of Women*. NY Stein and Day.

National Center for Education Statistics. 1996a. *Digest of Education Statistics 1996*, NCES 96–133. Washington, D.C.: U.S. Government Printing Office.

———. 1996b. *Schools and Staffing Survey, 1993–94* (Public School Teacher Questionnaire). Washington, D.C.: U.S. Department of Education.

National Science Foundation. 1982. *Science and Engineering Education: Data and Information*. Washington, D.C.: National Science Foundation.

NORC (National Opinion Research Center). 1991–1994. *Cumulated General Social Survey, 1991–1994*. Chicago: National Opinion Research Center, University of Chicago.

———. 1994. *General Social Survey, 1994*. Chicago: National Opinion Research Center, University of Chicago.

———. 1996. *General Social Survey, 1996*. Chicago: National Opinion Research Center, University of Chicago.

Oakley, Ann. 1982. *Subject Women*. London: Fontana.

Oliver, William. 1984. "Black Males and the Tough Guy Image: The Dual Dilemma of Black Men." *Journal of Social Issues* 34(Winter):10–20.

Orenstein, Peggy. 1997. "Shortchanging Girls: Gender Socialization in Schools." Pp. 43–52 in Dana Dunn (ed.), *Workplace/Women's Place: An Anthology*. Los Angeles: Roxbury.

Parsons, Talcott, Robert Bales, James Olds, Morris Zilditch, and Philip E. Slater. 1955. *Family, Socialization, and Interaction Process*. NY: Free Press.

Peterson, Sharyl Bender, and Traci Kroner. 1992. "Gender biases in Textbooks for Introductory Psychology and Human Development." *Psychology of Women Quarterly* 16:17–36.

Peterson, Sharyl Bender, and Mary Alyce Lach. 1990. "Gender Stereotypes in Children's Books; Their Prevalence and Influence on Cognitive and Affective Development." *Gender and Education* 2(2):185–197.

Phillips, F. B. 1978. "Magazine Heroines: Is Ms. Just Another Member of the Family Circle?" Pp. 115–24 in G. Tuchman, A. K. Daniels, and J. Benet (eds.), *Hearth and Home*. NY: Oxford University Press.

Pomerleau, Andrée, Daniel Boduc, Gérard Malcuit, and Louise Cossette. 1990. "Pink or Blue: Environmental Gender Stereotypes in the First Two Years of Life." *Sex Roles* 22(5/6):359–367.

Purcell, Piper, and Lara Stewart. 1990. "Dick and Jane in 1989." *Sex Roles* 22(3/4):177–185.

Renzetti, Claire M., and Daniel J. Curran. 1995. *Women, Men, and Society.* 3rd ed. Boston: Allyn and Bacon.

Riordan, Cornelius. 1990. *Girls and Boys in School: Together or Separate?* NY: Teachers College Press.

———. 1997. "Minority Success and Single-Gender Schools." Pp. 175–193 in Gregg Lee Carter (ed.), *Perspectives on Current Social Problems.* Boston: Allyn and Bacon.

Rossi, Alice. 1977. "A Biosocial Perspective on Parenting" *Daedalus* 106:1–31.

Scarpitti, Frank R., Margaret L. Andersen, and Laura L. O'Toole. 1997. *Social problems.* 3rd ed. NY: Longman.

Shapiro, Laura. 1990. "Guns and Dolls." *Newsweek* 28 (May):56–65.

Silverstein, Brett, L. Perdue, B. Peterson, and E. Kelly. 1986. "The Role of the Mass Media in Promoting a Thin Standard of Bodily Attractiveness for Women." *Sex Roles* 14:519–532.

Simon, David R., and Joel H. Henderson. 1997. *Private Troubles and Public Issues: Social Problems in the Postmodern Era.* NY: Harcourt Brace.

Smith, Caroline, and Barbara Lloyd. 1978. "Maternal Behavior and Perceived Sex of Infant: Revisited." *Child Development* 49(4):1263–1266.

Soroka, Michael P., and George J. Bryjak. 1994. *Social Problems: A World at Risk.* Boston: Allyn & Bacon.

Strate, L. 1992. "Beer Commercials." Pp. 78–92 in S. Craig (ed.), *Men, Masculinity and Media.* Newbury Park, CA: Sage.

Sullivan, Thomas J. 1997. *Introduction to Social Problems.* 4th ed. Boston: Allyn and Bacon.

Travris, Carol. 1992. *The Mismeasure of Woman.* NY: Simon and Schuster.

Tavris, Carol, and Carole Wade. 1984. *The Longest War: Sex Differences in Perspective.* 2nd ed. NY: Harcourt Brace Jovanovich.

Thorne, Barrie, Cheris Kramarae, and Nancy Henley (eds.). 1983. *Language, Gender, and Society.* Rowley, MA: Newbury House.

PART 12

SOCIAL CHANGE
AND SOCIAL CONFLICT

We began this volume by trying to answer the question of what keeps society together and orderly in the face of seemingly endless social change. We noted that major instigators of change include advances in technology, immigration, urbanization, industrialization, economic booms and busts, baby booms and busts, war, and civil unrest. In Part 12, we return to the concept of social change and to the conflict that can precede and follow it.

In his classic essay on the "success of the unruly," William A. Gamson, of Boston College, argues that the poor, the working class, minority groups, traditional "outsiders," and new groups seeking to change the *status quo* and to gain advantages in American society increase their likelihood of success when they become "unruly" (e.g., demonstrate, strike, riot). His analysis reveals that this unruliness is most often successful when the challenging groups are strong—for example, numerous, well-organized, having the weight of public opinion on their side.

Marc Howard Ross, of Bryn Mawr College in Pennsylvania, discusses other structural and interpersonal factors that either encourage or discourage unruliness and violence within and between societies. He shows that *intra*societal conflict decreases the greater the number of *cross-cutting social ties* (e.g., marriages between individuals of different social backgrounds). Such ties promote the settlement of disputes by creating shared interests among groups and individuals. At the same time, however, cross-cutting ties increase *inter*societal conflict by providing a social basis for political unity and thereby emphasizing the boundaries of a society. Ross also finds that intersocietal conflict increases with socioeconomic and political complexity. At the interpersonal and psychosocial levels of analysis, he finds that "harsh" child-rearing practices and distant father-child ties promote conflict, both within and between societies.

Émile Durkheim, Karl Marx, and most of the other nineteenth century founding fathers of sociology were primarily concerned with the great disruptions that industrialization wrought on European and U.S. society. They showed how social order based on common values and face-to-face interactions was replaced by social order based on interdependence (due to the division of labor), bureaucracy, coercion (e.g., the rise of the legal system, the police, the courts, prisons, and other forms of institutionalized authority), and eventually a new system of values and norms that regulated individuals and gave order to society. The reconstituted social order lasted until the mid-1960s, when—according to Francis Fukuyama, of George Mason University, in his essay reprinted here—it began to crumble in the face of the information age. The crumbling is indicated by soaring rates of crime, divorce, and out-of-wedlock births, and by declining levels of trust—of major institutions, like government, and of people, in general. The causes, Fukuyama contends, can be found in the rise of the information age, which—by way of a complex causal skein that he details—resulted in the unintentional spread of unbridled individualism and its consequent encouraging of rule-breaking regarding marriage, crime, drug use, and so on. Such behavior destroys a society's *social capital*, that is, its shared values—which are, in turn, the prerequisite of all forms of group enterprise ("from running a grocery store to lobbying Congress to raising children"). Group enterprises are the foundation for communities, which both reflect and give orderliness to a society. The rule-breakings that Fukuyama identifies as most destructive concern sex (promiscuity has become rampant) and the family (especially men deserting their families or their children born out of wedlock); both of these are rooted in the large-scale movement of women into the paid labor force that began in the 1960s. Women, reasoned many men, no longer needed the traditional male "provider," as they could earn enough to take of both themselves and their children. Fukuyama's essay is the most polemical in this volume. After reading it, you should try to decide on your own whether his interpretations outpace his data.

William Graves III, of Bryant College, focuses on changes accompanying the introduction of computers into the workplace. His research confirms the notion that social order is not a given, but rather is negotiated and arises during social interaction. As has so often been the case throughout human history, new technologies change human relationships in fundamental ways, and such change is commonly accompanied by recalcitrance and protest. More specifically, Graves demonstrates how the introduction of computers in the workplace can upset organizational culture and hurt the productivity of individual workers unless great care is given to understanding the patterns of work that already exist and the values and norms that underpin them.

_____CHAPTER 37_____

THE SUCCESS OF THE UNRULY

WILLIAM A. GAMSON

This [chapter] examines the experiences of a representative collection of American voluntary groups that, between 1800 and 1945, have challenged some aspect of the status quo. It explores the strategies they used and the organizational characteristics that influenced the success of their challenges. The results raise some serious questions about the pluralist interpretation of the operation of power in American society. . . .

In May, 1937, shortly before Memorial Day, 78,000 steelworkers began a strike against the "Little Steel" companies of Bethlehem Steel. Republic Steel, Inland Steel, and Youngstown Sheet and Tube. The CIO-backed Steel Workers Organizing Committee (SWOC) was less than a year old at the time but had already signed collective bargaining agreements with the five largest U.S. Steel subsidiaries, and, by early May, SWOC had signed contracts with 110 firms.

The Little Steel companies, however, were prepared to resist. Under the leadership of Tom M. Girdler, president of Republic Steel, they refused to sign an agreement which they felt, in Girdler's words, "was a bad thing for our companies, for our employees; indeed for the United States of America" (Galenson, 1960, p. 96).

The decision to resist was made more ominous by the common practice of large employers of the time to stock arsenals of weapons and tear gas in anticipation of labor disputes. Much of our information comes from the report of the LaFollette Commit-

tee of the United States Senate,[1] which investigated the events surrounding the Little Steel strike. The committee report noted, for example, that during the years 1933 to 1937, over a million dollars' worth of tear gas and sickening gas was purchased by employers and law-enforcement agencies but that "all of the largest individual purchasers are corporations and that their totals far surpass those of large law-enforcement purchasers" (quoted in Sweeney, 1956, p. 20). The largest purchaser of gas equipment in the country was none other than the Republic Steel Corporation, which "bought four times as much as the largest law-enforcement purchaser." The Republic Steel arsenal included 552 revolvers, 61 rifles with 1325 rounds of ammunition, and 245 shotguns in addition to gas grenades (Sweeney, p. 33).

The Little Steel strike began on May 26, 1937, and for a few days prior to May 30, picketing and arrests occurred near Republic Steel's mill in south Chicago. On Memorial Day, after a mass meeting at strike headquarters, the strikers decided to march to the plant to establish a mass picket line. A crowd of about 1,000 persons, "headed by two bearers of American Flags, . . . started across the prairie toward the street which fronts on the mill. There was a holiday spirit over the crowd" (Sweeney, p. 33).

Chicago police were there in force and the paraders were commanded to disperse. Within a few minutes, seven strikers were dead, three lay fatally wounded, scores of others were seriously wounded, and 35 policemen were injured. The LaFollette Committee concluded on the basis of testimony from many eye-witnesses and photographs that "the first shots came from the police; that these were unprovoked, except perhaps by a tree branch thrown by the

From *The Strategy of Social Protest* (Homewood, IL: Dorsey, 1975), pp. ix, 1–6, 19–22, 72–88. Copyright © 1975 by William A. Gamson. Reprinted by permission. Some footnotes have been incorporated as endnotes or deleted.

strikers, and that the second volley of police shots was simultaneous with the missiles thrown by the strikers." The strikers fled after the first volley but were pursued by the police. Of the ten marchers who were fatally shot, ". . . seven received the fatal wound in the back, three in the side, none in front. . . . The medical testimony of the nature of the marchers' wounds indicates that they were shot in flight. . . . The police were free with their use of clubs as well as guns. . . . Suffice it to say that the evidence, photographic and oral, is replete with instances of the use of clubs upon marchers doing their utmost to retreat, as well as upon those who were on the ground and in a position to offer no show of resistance," the LaFollette Committee Report concluded (quoted in Galenson, 1960).

The "Memorial Day Massacre" at the Republic Steel Plant in Chicago was the most notorious but by no means the only violent clash in the Little Steel strike. The strike was effectively broken by these tactics. Within two weeks of the Memorial Day clash, the Republic Steel plant had resumed normal operation. Within another few weeks, other struck plants reopened as well and the strike was essentially over.

The victory of the companies was, as it turned out, only a temporary one. By the fall of 1941, all four Little Steel companies had agreed to recognize the SWOC, and in May, 1942, the Steel Workers Organizing Committee became the United Steelworkers of America. Today, the leaders of the union dine with Presidents and serve as labor spokesmen on a variety of governmental bodies. By any measure of membership of the polity, they are full-fledged and certified. In reading the bitter history of the Little Steel strike from the consciousness of today, it is difficult to credit the fact that these events occurred a mere generation ago, in the living memory of many readers or, at the very least, of their parents.

This particular challenger has, for better or worse, moved inside the salon. But the anterooms and corridors contain the battered hulks of less successful challengers. Their abortive careers also promise to tell us important things about the permeability of the American political system.

Take the Brotherhood of the Cooperative Commonwealth, for example. Born in the ferment of the 1890s, it was the brainchild of an obscure Maine reformer, Norman Wallace Lermond. "Its immediate and most important objective was to colonize *en masse* a sparsely inhabited Western state with persons desiring to live in socialist communities. Once established, the colonists would be in a position to capture control of the state's government and lay the foundation for a socialist commonwealth" (Quint, 1964).

Not much happened for the first year of its existence but Lermond was "a letter writing dynamo and he bombarded reformers throughout the country with appeals for assistance." He began to get some results. Imogene C. Fales, a New York reformer, "who was a charter member of innumerable humanitarian and socialist movements in the 1880s and 1890s, agreed to serve with Lermond as co-organizer" (Quint).

But the big catch for the fledgling challenging group was Eugene V. Debs. Debs had been recently released from his prison terms for defying the injunction against the American Railway Union which broke the Pullman strike. He was a genuine hero of the left, who was now, for the first time, espousing socialism. Debs was a thoroughly decent person who lacked the vituperative personal style so characteristic of many leftists. Furthermore, he was an extraordinarily effective platform speaker where, as Quint describes him, "the shining sincerity of his speeches and the flowing honesty of his personality more than compensated for the lack of knowledge of the more delicate points of Marxist theory. His soul was filled with a longing for social justice and he communicated this feeling to the audiences who gathered to hear him extol the new Social Democracy."

Debs became attracted to the colonization scheme. "Give me 10,000 men," Debs told a socialist convention, "aye, 10,000 in a western state with access to the sources of production, and we will change the economic conditions, and we will convince the people of that state, win their hearts and their intelligence. We will lay hold upon the reins of government and plant the flag of Socialism upon the State House" (quoted in Quint).

Many other socialists were appalled at what they considered a diversion of energy into a thoroughly impractical scheme. However, they were gentle with

Debs personally, hoping to woo him back to the true path. Even the normally vitriolic socialist leader, Daniel DeLeon, was unaccustomedly polite. "With warm esteem for the good intentions of Mr. Debs, but fully appreciative of the harm that more failures will do," he wrote, "we earnestly warn the proletariat of America once more not to embark on this chimera; not to yield out of love for the good intentions of Mr. Debs, greater respect for his judgment than it deserves" (Quint).

Gradually, Debs began relegating the colonization scheme to be one of several strategies rather than to *the* strategy of the socialist movement. The Brotherhood of the Cooperative Commonwealth did not particularly prosper. They did establish a colony, "Equality" in Edison, Washington, and later another at Burley, Washington, but these did not thrive. "By 1902, Equality contained 105 people, living on a very plain diet in two apartment houses, four log cabins, and fourteen frame houses, earning a bare subsistence by the sale of lumber and grain" (Quint). By 1914, there wasn't anything left of the colonization plans of the Brotherhood of the Cooperative Commonwealth.

How can we account for the different experiences of a representative collection of American challenging groups? What is the characteristic response to groups of different types and what determines this response? What strategies work under what circumstances? What organizational characteristics influence the success of the challenge?

The careers of challenging groups tell us about the permeability and openness of the American political system. To know who gets in and how is to understand the central issue in competing images of the American political experience.

THE PLURALIST IMAGE OF AMERICAN POLITICS

Until the turbulence of the 1960s caused many to rethink the issue, a particular interpretation of American politics dominated the thinking of most professional observers. It remains highly influential today if perhaps not as dominant as it once was in the face of a developing body of criticism. This interpretation presents an image of a highly open system with free access for would-be competitors. Furthermore, the image has behind it a well-developed and elegant body of theoretical ideas usually presented under the label "pluralist democracy" or simply "pluralism."

A democratic political system must be able to handle two great problems if it is to continue successfully: the danger of tyranny or domination by a minority, and responsiveness to unmet or changing needs among its citizens. Pluralist theory has the virtue of explaining how a political system can handle both of these problems simultaneously. To the extent that the American political system approximates the pluralist model, it is argued, it will produce regular and orderly change with the consent of the governed.

Those who support this interpretation are not unaware of urban riots and the considerable history of violent conflict in the United States. However, they tend to view such events as abnormalities or pathologies arising from the gap between an always imperfect reality and an ideal, abstract model. In other words, the occasional, admitted failures of American democracy to produce orderly change are caused by departures from the ideal conditions of pluralism. Furthermore, even a well-functioning thermostat sometimes produces temperatures that are momentarily too hot or too cold as it goes about giving us the proper temperature.

There is a vast literature on pluralism and the American political system, and the discussion here will not attempt to do it full justice. A particularly coherent and convincing statement of the case is made in Dahl's *Pluralist Democracy in the United States* (1967). Now Dahl is no mindless celebrator of the genius of American politics; he paints his subject with all its warts and blemishes. But the important point is that this darker side of American politics is viewed as blemish and not as the essence of his subject.

Dahl suggests (p. 24) that the "fundamental axiom in the theory and practice of American pluralism is . . . this: Instead of a single center of sovereign power there must be multiple centers of power, none of which is or can be wholly sovereign." Why is this so important? Because the "existence of multiple centers of power . . . will help to tame power, to secure the consent of all, and to settle conflicts peacefully."

The brilliance of pluralist thinking is illustrated by its ability to handle multiple problems simultaneously—the prevention of dominance by a single group or individual, responsiveness to the needs of its citizens, and the prevention of extreme or violent conflict. It deals with two very different threats to the political system. The first threat is that the delicate balance of competition will be destroyed by a temporarily ascendant group that will use its ascendancy to crush its competitors. The second threat is that in the stalemate of veto groups and countervailing power there will be ineffective government, leading to an accumulation of discontent that will destroy the legitimacy and threaten the stability of the existing system. . . .

"The flaw in the pluralist heaven," writes Schattschneider (1960, p. 35), "is that the heavenly chorus sings with a strong upper-class accent. Probably about 90 percent of the people cannot get into the pressure system." In one form or another, this theme is present in most writing that is critical of pluralist theory. . . . [To determine how "outsiders" have generated advantages in U.S. society and politics, I created a] . . . sample of challenging groups.

The universe of groups that this [chapter] addresses are all those challenging groups that surfaced in American society between 1800 and 1945. The members of this universe meet primary criteria: they are seeking the mobilization of an unmobilized constituency and their antagonist or target of influence lies outside of this constituency. We have restricted or clarified this universe further by adopting conventions dealing with the geographical breadth of the constituency, citizenship status, federations, splinter groups, and satellites.

There have been between five and six hundred challenging groups in American society that meet the criteria described here. We will focus on a sample of 53 of them. Shortly, I intend to defend the claim that these 53 groups are an equal probability sample of the defined universe of challenging groups in American society. But first, it will be use-

ful if the reader has at least a general descriptive sense of the variety and nature of the members of the sample.

The 53 challengers range from the narrowest of reform groups to the most sweeping of revolutionary groups. One group, the League of American Wheelmen, aimed only at the modest goal of eliminating a series of restrictions on the use of the bicycle and winning the right to ride on public highways. Later, flushed by success, their ambitions grew to include as well the improvement of public highways as they became participants in the "good roads movement." In contrast to these most finite of goals, the German-American Bund hoped to do no less than remodel the American political system along the lines of German National Socialism.

Some groups—for example, the American Association of University Professors—have such a respectable image today that they constitute an embarrassment to a book on social protest. Others—for example, the Tobacco Night Riders on the black patch area of Kentucky and Tennessee—look more disreputable by contemporary standards than they probably did at the time. But, then, even the most reputable of groups today was usually not considered such during its period of challenge.

Some of the 53 are famous and well-remembered—for example, Father Coughlin's National Union for Social Justice. Others—for example, the League of Deliverance, a group that aimed at excluding Chinese labor from the United States—are remembered only by a handful of professional students of American labor and nativist movements. . . .

We can divide them into four broad, descriptive categories. Twenty of the groups (38 percent) were occupationally based. The most obvious examples are unions of blue collar workers—for example, The Packinghouse Workers Organizing Committee and the American Labor Union, a forerunner of the International Workers of the World or "Wobblies." But the category also includes middle-class occupational groups (The American Federation of Teachers), craftsmen (The Union Trade Society of Journeymen Tailors and The National Brotherhood of Baseball

Players), and farm organizations (The Tobacco Night Riders and the Dairymen's League).

Seventeen of the groups (32 percent) were one form or another of a "reform group." Some of these groups—for example, the American Anti-Slavery Society, a leading abolitionist group—were considered very radical in their day. Some—for example, Theodore Roosevelt's Bull Moose Party and William Randolph Hearst's Independence League—were conventional political parties seeking electoral success. Some—for example, A. Philip Randolph's March on Washington Committee and the National Urban League—were civil rights groups. Some—for example, the Church Peace Union and the American Committee for the Outlawry of War—were peace groups. Some—for example, the Federal Suffrage Association and the American Proportional Representation League—sought specific institutional reforms in one area.

Ten of the groups (19 percent) were rooted in the socialist tradition. The sample includes the granddaddy of socialism in America, The International Workingmen's Association, or First International. Some of the socialist groups—for example, the National Student League—were campus-based. Some—for example, the Progressive Labor Party—were electorally oriented; while others—for example, the Revolutionary Workers League—strongly rejected the possibility of effecting change through the ballot box.

Finally, six of the groups (11 percent) were some variety of rightwing or nativist group. Electoral challengers—for example, the Native American or American Republican Party—are included here along with such classical right-wing challengers as the Christian Front against Communism and the German-American Bund. The distribution of the 53 groups is summarized in Figure 37.1.

The groups are also well distributed over time. A little over half (55 percent) began their careers in the 19th century, and every single decade except 1800–1810 and the 1870s is represented by at least one new challenger. Figure 37.2 shows the distribution of groups by decade and reveals the 1880s and

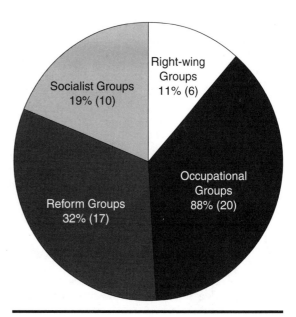

FIGURE 37.1   Distribution of Types of Groups in the Sample

the 1930s as the most productive of new challenges with the 1910s and 1890s not far behind. The 1830s are the major contributor in the pre-civil war period. The median length of a challenge period is about eight years, but there is great variability.

[Violence and Success]

It is a happy fact that we continue to be shocked by the appearance of violence in social protest. Apparently, frequency is no great cushion against shock for, at least in America, social protest has been liberally speckled with violent episodes. One can exaggerate the frequency—a majority of challenges run their course without any history of violence or arrests. But a very substantial minority—more than 25 percent—have violence in their history. The fact that violence is a common consort of social protest in the United States is not a matter of serious contention.

The consequences of violence are at issue. It is commonly believed to be self-defeating. Evaluating

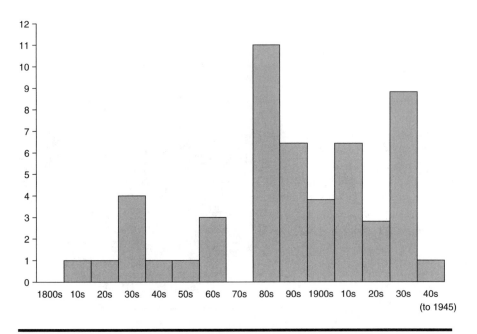

FIGURE 37.2   Distribution of Challenging Groups by Decade of Origin

the validity of this belief is made elusive by a tendency that we all have, social scientists and laymen alike, to allow our moral judgments to influence our strategic judgments and vice versa. Kaplowitz has suggested the following general hypothesis. If strategic rationality does not clearly specify a course of action as desirable but normative criteria do, people will tend to believe that the normatively desirable course of action is also strategically rational.

Violence is relatively unambiguous morally. At most, it is regarded as a necessary evil which may be justified in preventing or overcoming some even greater evil. And for many, the situations in which it is justified are scant to nonexistent. The issue depends on one's image of the society in which violence takes place. In a closed and oppressive political system that offers no nonviolent means for accomplishing change, the morality of violence is not as clear. But when it is believed that effective nonviolent alternatives exist, almost everybody would consider these morally preferable.

In the pluralist image of American society, the political system is relatively open, offering access at many points for effective nonviolent protest and efforts at change. With this premise, the use of violence by groups engaged in efforts at social change seems particularly reprehensible. The above reasoning should apply not only to violence as a means of influence but as a means of social control as well. The use of violence and other extralegal methods for dealing with protestors is also morally reprehensible.

While the moral issues may be clear, the strategic ones are ambiguous. There is not consensus on the set of conditions under which violence is a more or less effective strategy, and the issue has been seriously analyzed only in the international sphere. The Kaplowitz hypothesis, if correct, explains the strong tendency for people to believe that something so immoral as domestic violence is not a very effective strategy in domestic social protest. It also helps us to recognize that the fact that many people regard violence as self-defeating is no evidence that it is actually futile.

The pluralist view, then, acknowledges that collective violence has taken place in the United States with considerable frequency but argues that it is effective neither as a strategy of social influence when used by challenging groups nor as a strategy of repression when it is used by the enemies of such groups. We treat this view here as an hypothesis. It would be comforting to find that moral and strategic imperatives coincide, but the evidence discussed below suggests that they do not.

VIOLENCE USERS AND RECIPIENTS

I mean by the term "violence" deliberate physical injury to property or persons. This does not embrace such things as forceful constraint—for example, arrest—unless it is accompanied by beatings or other physical injury. It also excludes bribery, brainwashing, and other nasty techniques. To use the term violence as a catch-all for unpleasant means of influence or social control confuses the issue; other unpopular means need to stand forth on their own for evaluation, and we will explore some of these as well.

Among the 53 groups, there were 15 that engaged in violent interactions with antagonists, agents of social control, or hostile third parties. Eight of these groups were active participants; they themselves used violence. It is important to emphasize that these "violence users" were not necessarily initiators; in some cases they were attacked and fought back, and in still others the sequence of events is unclear. No assumption is made that the violence users were necessarily the aggressors in the violent interaction that transpired.

Whether they initiate violence or not, all of the violence users accept it, some with reluctance and some with apparent glee. Wallace Stegner (1949, pp. 255–56) describes some of the actions of Father Coughlin's Christian Front against Communism. "In Boston, a *Social Justice* truck went out to distribute the paper without benefit of the mails. When a *Boston Traveler* photographer tried for a picture, the truck driver kicked his camera apart while a friendly cop held the photographer's arms." In another incident in the Boston area, a printer named Levin was approached by Christian Fronters who handed him *Social Justice* and told him, "'Here, you're a Jew, Levin. You ought to read about what your pals have been doing lately. Take a look how your investments in Russia are coming.' . . . One morning, . . . Levin came down to his shop to find it broken open and its contents wrecked." In New York, as Stegner describes it (p. 252), Christian Fronters would start fights with passing Jews, would beat up one or two opponents, and then vanish. Another source, Charles Tull (1965, p. 207) writes, that "it was common for the Coughlinite pickets . . . to be involved in violence with their more vocal critics. . . . Street brawls involving Christian Fronters and Jews became frequent in New York City. . . ." Now these accounts are at best unsympathetic to the Christian Front. Some of the clashes may well have been initiated by opponents of the group. For example, Tull points out that the "most notable incident from the standpoint of sheer numbers occurred on April 8, 1939, when a crowd of several thousand people mobbed ten newsboys selling *Social Justice*." Although the Christian Fronters may have been passive recipients of violence in this particular case, on many other occasions they clearly played the role of active participant or more.

The active role is even clearer in the case of the Tobacco Night Riders. . . . "The Tobacco Night Riders were organized in 1906 as a secret, fraternal order, officially called 'The Silent Brigade' or 'The Inner Circle.' Their purpose was to force all growers to join the [Planters Protective] Association . . . and to force the [tobacco] trust companies to buy tobacco only from the association" (Nall, 1942).

The violence of the Night Riders was the most organized of any group studied. They "made their first show of armed forces at Princeton [Kentucky], on the morning of Saturday, December 1, 1906 when shortly after midnight approximately 250 armed and masked men took possession of the city and dynamited and burned two large tobacco factories. . . . Citizens in the business district opened windows and looked out on bodies of masked men hurrying along with guns on their shoulders. They saw other masked and armed men patrolling the sidewalks and street corners and they heard commands: 'Get back!' And if they did not obey, bullets splattered against the brick walls near by or crashed through the window panes above their heads. . . . Several squads of men had marched in along the Cadiz road and captured the police station, the waterworks plants, the courthouse, and the telephone and telegraph offices. They had disarmed the policemen and put them under guard, shut off the city water supply, and taken the places of the telephone and telegraph operators. . . . Within a few minutes the city was in control of the Riders and all communication with the outside was cut off." With their mission accomplished and the tobacco factories in flames, the men "mounted their horses and rode away singing 'The fire shines bright in my old Kentucky home'" (Nall, 1942, p. 69).

About a year later, the Night Riders struck again at the town of Hopkinsville, Kentucky. It is worth noting, since the argument here views violence as instrumental rather than expressive, that the Hopkinsville raid was twice postponed when it appeared that the town was prepared to resist. "The Night Riders were not cowards," Nall writes, "but their cause and methods of operation did not demand that they face a resistant line of shot and shell to accomplish their purposes." The Night Riders made heavy use of fifth columnists in the town to assure that their raid could be successful without bloodshed. As in the Princeton raid, they carried out the operation with precision, occupying all strategic points. During this raid, they "shot into the . . . residence of W. Lindsay Mitchell, a buyer for the Imperial Tobacco Company, shattering electric lights and windowpanes. A group entered the house and disarmed him just in time to keep him from shooting into their comrades. He was brought into the street and struck over the head several times with a gun barrel, sustaining painful wounds. The captain of the squad looked on until he considered that Mr. Mitchell had 'had enough' then rescued him and escorted him back to his door" (Nall, p. 78). After the raid, they reassembled out of town for a roll call and marched away singing. The sheriff and local military officer organized a small posse to pursue the raiders and attacked their rear, killing one man and

wounding another before the posse was forced to retreat back to Hopkinsville. One might have thought that the Night Riders would have retaliated for the attack made on them by the posse, and, indeed, Nall reports that "some of the Riders considered a second raid to retaliate . . . but such was not considered by the leaders. They had accomplished their purpose" (p. 82).

The Native American, or American Republican Party, a nativist group of the 1840s, was heavily implicated in less organized violence directed against Catholics. "Traversing the Irish section [of Philadelphia], the [nativist] mob was soon locked in armed conflict with equally riotous foreigners. The Hibernia Hose Company house was stormed and demolished; before midnight, more than thirty houses belonging to Irishmen had been burned to the ground. . . ." A few nights later, "roaming the streets, the rioters finally came to Saint Michael's Catholic Church. A rumor that arms were concealed within the building proved sufficient grounds for attack, and while the presiding priest fled in disguise, the torch was applied. . . ." The mob also burned St. Augustine's Church and "throughout the city, priests and nuns trembled for their lives" (Billington, 1963, pp. 225–26). Party leadership repudiated much of the mob action but especially deplored and emphasized the counterattacks: "the killing of natives by foreign mobs." The central involvement of American Republicans was, however, substantial and well-documented.

The other violence users were all labor unions involved in clashes with strikebreakers or police and militia called out to assist and defend the strikebreakers. Among the violence users, then, the challenging group is sometimes the initiator but not always; sometimes the leadership openly defends and advocates the practice but not always. To be classified as a violence user, it is only necessary that the group be an active participant in the violent interactions in which it is involved.

The recipients of violence were passive recipients—they were attacked and either did not or, because they had insufficient means, could not fight back. The International Workingmen's Association, the First International, is one example. In September,

1873, a major financial panic occurred in the United States, resulting in subsequent unemployment and economic dislocation. A mass demonstration was called for January 13, 1874, in the form of a march of the unemployed in New York City. To quote John Commons (1966, p. 220), "It was the original plan of the Committee that the parade should disband after a mass meeting in front of the city hall but this was prohibited by the authorities and Tompkins Square was chosen as the next best place for the purpose. The parade was formed at the appointed hour and by the time it reached Tompkins Square it had swelled to an immense procession. Here they were met by a force of policemen and, immediately after the order to disperse had been given, the police charged with drawn clubs. During the ensuing panic, hundreds of workmen were injured."

Abolitionists were frequent recipients of violence in the form of antiabolitionist riots. The object of the violence was primarily the property and meeting places of abolitionists rather than their persons, although there were frequent threats and some physical abuse as well. The National Female Anti-Slavery Society was victimized on various occasions, although the women themselves were never attacked. Once, when the hall in which they were scheduled to hold a meeting was set on fire by an antiabolitionist mob, the women sought refuge in the home of Lucretia Mott. "As the rioters swarmed through nearby streets, it seemed as if an attack on the Mott house were imminent but a friend of the Motts joined the mob, and crying, 'On to the Motts' led them in the wrong direction" (Lutz, 1968, p. 139). William Lloyd Garrison was attacked at one of the meetings and dragged through the streets. The American Anti-Slavery Society was similarly abused. Eggs and stones were thrown at the audience of several of their meetings. In Cincinnati, rioters attacked the shops and homes of abolitionists, particularly Englishmen. An abolitionist printer in Illinois, Elijah Lovejoy, was killed when he attempted to resist an antiabolitionist mob destroying his shop. Lovejoy's resistance was isolated and provoked a controversy in the fervently nonviolent Society. Lovejoy had had his printing presses destroyed three times, "his house was invad-

ed, and his wife was brought to the verge of hysterical collapse. When a fourth new press arrived, Lovejoy determined that he would protect it. . . . When his press was attacked he raised his pistol but was quickly gunned down by one of the mob." Even under such circumstances, "abolitionists in the American Anti-Slavery Society and elsewhere were divided on whether or not to censure Lovejoy's action" (Sorin, 1972, p. 91). They did not censure Lovejoy but reasserted their commitment to nonviolent means of achieving the end of slavery.

Members of the National Student League were attacked in the familiar manner of northern civil rights workers going south in the 1960s. In one instance, the cause was the bitter struggle of coal miners in Harlan County, Kentucky. "At Cumberland Gap, the mountain pass into Kentucky, the full impact of Kentucky law and order descended. The road was almost dark when the bus turned the corner over the boundary; out of the approaching night the scowling faces of a mob of more than 200 people greeted the visitors. Cars drove up and surrounded the bus; most of the throng were armed, wearing the badges of deputy sheriffs. . . . There were derisive cat-calls, then the ominous lynch-cry: 'String 'em up'" (Wechsler, 1935). Students were shoved and some knocked down, but none seriously injured on this occasion.

The recipients of violence, then, unlike the users, play essentially passive roles in the violent episodes in which they were involved. The success or failure of the violence users will enable us to say something about the effectiveness of violence as a means of influence; the success or failure of the violence recipients will help us to evaluate the effectiveness of violence as a means of social control.

THE RESULTS

What is the fate of these groups? Are the users of violence crushed by adverse public reaction and the coercive power of the state? Do the recipients of violence rouse the public sympathy with their martyrdom, rallying to their cause important bystanders who are appalled at their victimization and join them in their struggle?

Figure 37.3 gives the basic results. The violence users, it turns out, have a higher-than-average success rate. Six of the eight won new advantages, and five of these six established a minimal acceptance relationship as well. Of course, some paid their dues in blood in the process as we have seen in the descriptions above. The seven recipients of violence also paid such dues but with little or nothing to show for it in the end. One, The Dairymen's League, established a minimal acceptance relationship with its antagonist, but none of them were able to gain new advantages for their beneficiary. With respect to violence and success, it appears better to give than receive.

It is worth asking whether the different goals of these groups might account for the difference. The most relevant variable is whether the displacement of the antagonist is part of the goals. Two of the eight violence users have displacement goals, and two of the seven violence recipients do also. Figure 37.4 makes the same comparison as Figure 37.3 but only for those groups that are not attempting to replace their targets. It reveals that every violence user with more limited goals is successful, although the Night Riders were not accepted; every violence recipient was unsuccessful, although the Dairymen's League won minimal acceptance. The earlier result is, if anything, sharpened.

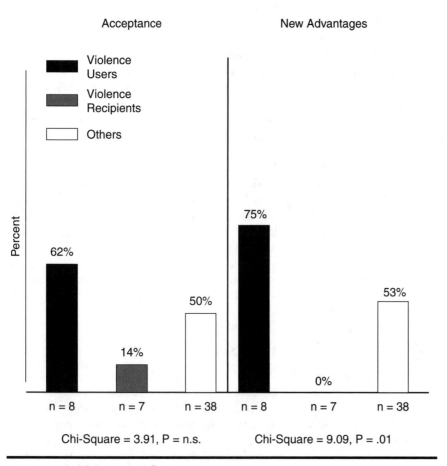

FIGURE 37.3 Violence and Outcome

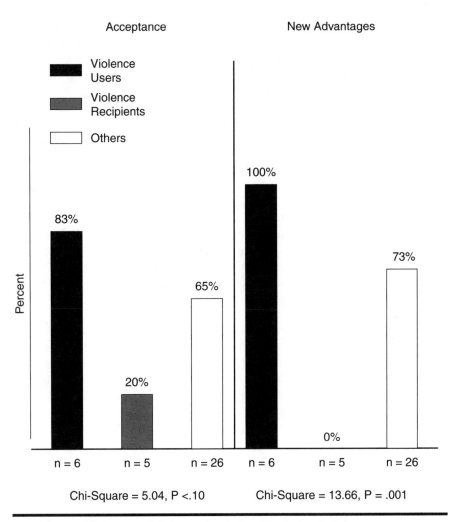

FIGURE 37.4   Violence and Outcome Excluding Displacing Groups

DOES VIOLENCE PAY?

Am I ready to conclude then that violence basically works? Not quite, or at least not in any simple fashion, and my caution is not due simply to the small number of cases involved and the real possibility of sampling error. It is easier to say what these data refute than what they prove.

Specifically, the data undermine the following line of thinking: violence is the product of frustration, desperation, and weakness. It is an act of last resort by those who see no other means of achieving their goals. In this view, the challenging group, frustrated by its inability to attract a significant following and gain some response from its targets of influence, turns to violence in desperation. However, this merely hastens and ensures its failure because its actions increase the hostility around it and invite the legitimate action of authorities against it.

When authorities use violence against challenging groups, there are similar dynamics in this argument. Frightened by the growing strength of the challenging group and unable to halt its rising power by legitimate means, tottering on their throne and unwilling to make concessions, the threatened authorities turn to repression. But this attempted repression simply adds fuel to the fire, bringing new allies to the cause of the challenging group and increasing its chances of ultimate success.

However compelling these images may be, they clearly do not fit the data presented here. The interpretation I would suggest is almost the opposite. As Eisinger (1973) puts it in discussing protest behavior in American cities, one hypothesis is that protest is as much a "signal of impatience as frustration." Violence should be viewed as an instrumental act, aimed at furthering the purposes of the group that uses it when they have some reason to think it will help their cause. This is especially likely to be true when the normal condemnation which attends to its use is muted or neutralized in the surrounding community, when it is tacitly condoned by large parts of the audience. In this sense, it grows from an impatience born of confidence and rising efficacy rather than the opposite. It occurs when hostility toward the victim renders it a relatively safe and costless strategy. The users of violence sense that they will be exonerated because they will be seen as more the midwives than the initiators of punishment. The victims are implicitly told, "See how your sins have provoked the wrath of the fanatics and have brought this punishment upon yourselves."

The size of the violence users and recipients supports this interpretation. The violence users tend to be large groups, the recipients small ones. Only one of the eight violence users is under 10,000 (the Night Riders) while five of the seven violence recipients are this small. Such growth seems more likely to breed confidence and impatience, not desperation.

I am arguing, then, that it is not the weakness of the user but the weakness of the target that accounts for violence. This is not to say that the weakness of a target is sufficient to produce violence but that, in making it more likely to be profitable, it makes it more likely to occur. As Figure 37.4 showed, many challenging groups are able to gain a positive response without

resorting to violence, and many collapse without the added push of repression. But groups that are failing for other reasons and authorities that are being forced to respond by rising pressures generally do not turn to violence. This is why, in my interpretation, violence is associated with successful change or successful repression: it grows out of confidence and strength and their attendant impatience with the pace of change. It is, in this sense, as much a symptom of success as a cause.

It is worth noting that, with the exception of the Night Riders, none of the groups that used violence made it a primary tactic. Typically it was incidental to the primary means of influence—strikes, bargaining, propaganda, or other nonviolent means. It is the spice, not the meat and potatoes. And, if one considers the Night Riders as merely the striking arm of the respectable Planters Protective Association, even this exception is no exception.

The groups that receive violence, with one exception, are attacked in an atmosphere of countermobilization of which the physical attacks are the cutting edge. They are attacked not merely because they are regarded as threatening—all challenging groups are threatening to some vested interest. They are threatening *and* vulnerable, and most fail to survive the physical attacks to which they are subjected.

OTHER CONSTRAINTS

This argument can be further evaluated by extending it to other constraints in addition to violence. "Constraints are the addition of new disadvantages to the situation or the threat to do so, regardless of the particular resources used" (Gamson, 1968). Violence is a special case of constraints but there are many others.

Twenty-one groups (40 percent) made use of constraints as a means of influence in pursuing their challenge. We have already considered eight of them, those that used violence, and we turn now to the other 13. The most common constraints used by these groups were strikes and boycotts, but they also included such things as efforts to discredit and humiliate individual enemies by personal vituperation. Discrediting efforts directed against "the system" or other more abstract targets are not included, but only individualized, ad

hominem attacks attempting to injure personal reputation.

Included here, for example, is A. Philip Randolph's March on Washington Committee, designed
to push President Roosevelt into a more active role in
ending discrimination in employment. A mass march
in the spring of 1941 to protest racial discrimination
in America would have been a considerable embarrassment to the Roosevelt administration. America
was mobilizing for war behind appeals that contrast-
ed democracy with the racism of the Nazi regime.
Walter White of the NAACP described "the President's skillful attempts to dissuade us" (Quoted in
Garfinkel, 1969). The march was, from the standpoint
of the administration, something to be avoided, a new
disadvantage which the committee was threatening.

William Randolph Heart's Independence League
made liberal use of personal vituperation against
opponents. "Most of Hearst's energy was devoted to
pointing out the personal inequities of boss Charles
F. Murphy. He found himself obliged to go back to
the time of Tweed to discover any parallel in political
corruption. . . . 'Murphy is as evil a specimen of a
criminal boss as we have had since the days of
Tweed'" (Carlson and Bates, 1936, pp. 146–47).

The League of Deliverance made primary use of
the boycott weapon, employing it against businesses
that hired Chinese labor. They threatened worse. The
League's executive committee proposed to notify
offenders of their desires and if not complied with,
"after the expiration of six days it will be the duty of
the Executive Committee to declare the district
dangerous. . . . Should the Chinese remain within the
proclaimed district after the expiration of . . . thirty
days, the general Executive Committee will be
required to abate the danger in whatever manner
seems best to them" (Cross, 1935). The League, however, never had call to go beyond the boycott tactic.

Among the 13 nonviolent constraint users are
three groups that were considered earlier as violence
recipients. Including them makes it more difficult to
interpret the relationship of success to the use of constraints since this is compounded by physical attacks
on the group. Therefore, in Figure 37.5, we include
only those ten groups that employed constraints but

were not involved in violent interactions as either user
or recipient. The advantage again goes to the unruly.
Four-fifths of the constraint users and only two-fifths
of the others are successful.

Constraints other than violence can also be used
as a means of social control. In particular, many
groups experience arrest and imprisonment or depor-
tation of members which can be equally as devastating as physical attack, if not more so. Almost
two-fifths of the sample (20 groups) had members
arrested at some time or another during the period of
challenge. These twenty included all eight of the violence users and four of the seven recipients, leaving
only eight groups that were not involved in violent
interactions but were subjected to arrests.

The Young Peoples Socialist League had people
arrested during both its periods of challenge. "'You're
under arrest'" began an article in *The Challenge*, the
YPSL paper. "This was not the first time members of
the Young Peoples Socialist League had heard this
pronouncement by officers while they were peacefully demonstrating against injustice." During its period of challenge in the World War I era, the national
secretary of the group, William Kruse, was arrested,
tried, convicted, and sentenced to 20 years imprisonment but ultimately won on appeal.

The German-American Bund was subject to
arrests on a number of occasions. Fritz Kuhn, the
group's major leader, was convicted of embezzling
Bund funds, income tax evasion, and forgery. Other
members were indicted on more political charges
such as espionage. Some were tried in New York State
under a rarely invoked statute passed in 1923 as a
measure against the Ku Klux Klan, but Bundists won
on appeal (Rowan, 1939, p. 178).

The American Birth Control League also experienced its share of official harassment. Soon after its
organization, Margaret Sanger arrived at Town Hall
in New York with her featured speaker, Harold Cox,
editor of the *Edinburgh Review*.

> She found a crowd gathered outside. One hundred
> policemen, obviously intending to prevent the meet-
> ing, ringed the locked doors of the hall. When the
> police opened the doors to let people already inside
> exit, those outside rushed in, carrying Mrs. Sanger

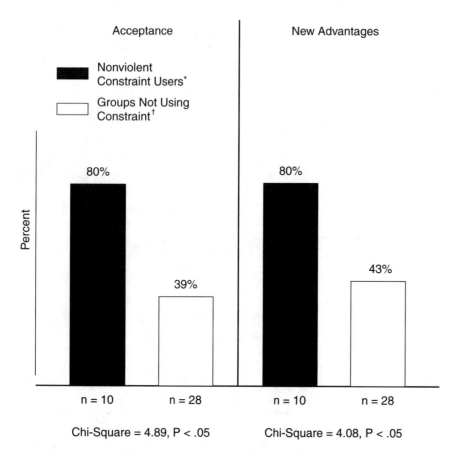

*This includes only those groups making use of constraints as a means of influence that were not involved in violent interactions either as users or recipients.

†This excludes groups that did not use constraints if they were also violence recipients.

FIGURE 37.5   Constraints and Outcome

and Cox before them. Once inside, Mrs. Sanger tried several times to speak, but policemen forcibly removed her from the platform. . . . Cox managed only to blurt, "I have come across the Atlantic to address you," before two policemen hauled him from the stage. The police arrested Mrs. Sanger and led her out of the hall while the audience sang, "My country, 'Tis of Thee."

A few weeks later, with evidence of complicity of the Catholic Church in the raid emerging, Mrs. Juliet Barrett Rublee, a friend of Mrs. Sanger, was arrested "while she was in the act of testifying at an investigation into the charge of church influence behind the [earlier] raid" (Kennedy, 1970, pp. 95–96).

Figure 37.6 considers the eight groups subjected to arrest, again excluding all groups involved in violent interactions.[2] Only two of the eight groups were successful while nearly 60 percent of the remainder were. The results seem even clearer when we examines the two exceptions. Only two of the eight groups made use of nonviolent constraints—the League of Deliverance used the boycott and the United

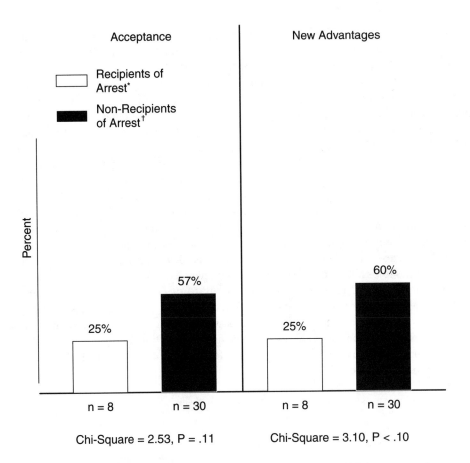

FIGURE 37.6   Arrests and Outcome

Brotherhood of Carpenters and Joiners of America used strikes and boycotts. These two groups were the only successes among the eight groups considered in Figure 37.6. In other words, groups that used neither violence nor any other form of constraint and yet experienced arrest were uniformly unsuccessful. In the absence of offsetting tactics by challenging groups, arrest seems to have the same connection with outcome as receiving violence, both are associated with failure for the receiving group.

There is another interesting fact about the six groups in Figure 37.6 that experience both arrests

and failure. Five out of the six were attempting to displace antagonists as part of their goals, and three of the six advocated violence in principle even though they never actually employed it. Eisinger points out that "as long as protestors do not manipulate the threat of violence explicitly, they enjoy a slim legality, even, occasionally, legitimacy. Once they employ the threat openly, however, they open the way for authorities to suppress their movement or action" (1973, p. 14).

Groups like the Communist Labor Party, the Revolutionary Workers League, and the German-

American Bund put themselves in the position of advocating or accepting violence as a tactic without actually using it. One might call this the strategy of speaking loudly and carrying a small stick. These groups seem to pay the cost of violence without gaining the benefits of employing it. They are both threatening and weak, and their repression becomes a low-cost strategy for those whom they attempt to displace.

SUMMARY

The results on arrests and other constraints seem to parallel those on violence very closely. Unruly groups, those that use violence, strikes, and other constraints, have better than average success. Of the 21 groups that use some form of constraint, fully two-thirds win new advantages and 71 percent win acceptance. Among the ten groups that use no constraints but receive either violence or arrests, none are successful on either criterion. The 22 groups that neither experience nor use constraints fall in the middle, 54 percent (12) win new advantages and half win acceptance.

Virtue, of course, has its own, intrinsic rewards. And a lucky thing it does too, since its instrumental value appears to be dubious. If we cannot say with certainty that violence and other constraints are successful tactics of social influence or social control, we must at least have greater doubt about the proposition that they lead to failure. When used by challenging groups, there is no evidence that they closed doors that are open to those who use only inducements and persuasion. When used against challenging groups, there is no evidence that such tactics bring allies and sympathetic third parties to the effective aid of the beleaguered groups, allowing them to gain what would have been impossible acting alone.

Perhaps it is disconcerting to discover that restraint is not rewarded with success. But those who use more unruly tactics escape misfortune because they are clever enough to use these tactics primarily in situations where public sentiment neutralizes the normal deviance of the action, thus reducing the likelihood and effectiveness of counterattack.

NOTES

1. Hearings before a Subcommittee of the Committee on Education and Labor, United State Senate, 75th Congress (LaFollette Committee). U.S. Government Printing Office, Washington, D.C., 1939.

2. Only three of the 15 groups involved in violent interactions escaped arrests, all violence recipients. The violence in these cases came from hostile third parties—for example, antiabolitionist mobs—and the perpetrators of violence also escaped arrest.

REFERENCES

Billington, Ray Allen. *The Protestant Crusade, 1800–1860.* Gloucester, Mass.: P. Smith, 1963.

Carlson, Oliver and Bates, Ernest S. *Hearst, Lord of San Simeon.* New York: Viking Press, 1936.

Commons, John R. et al., *History of Labor in the United States*, Vol. II. New York: A. M. Kelley, 1966.

Cross, Ira B. *A History of the Labor Movement in California.* Berkeley, California: University of California Press, 1935.

Dahl, Robert *Pluralist Democracy in the United States: Conflicts and Consent.* Chicago: Rand-McNally, 1967.

Eisinger, Peter K. "The Conditions of Protest Behavior in American Cities." *American Political Science Review,* March, 1973, 67:11–28.

Galenson, Walter. *The CIO Challenge to the AFL.* Cambridge, MA: Harvard University Press, 1960.

Gamson, William A. *Power and Discontent.* Homewood, Ill.: Dorsey Press, 1968.

Garfinkel, Herbert. *When Negroes March.* New York: Atheneum, 1969.

Kaplowitz, Stan. "An Experimental Test of a Rationalistic Theory of Deterence." *Journal of Conflict Resolution,* September, 1973, 17:535–72.

Kennedy, David M. *Birth Control in America*. New Haven: Yale University Press, 1970.

Lutz, Alma. *Crusade for Freedom—Women of the Antislavery Movement*. Boston: Beacon Press, 1968.

Nall, J. O. *The Tobacco Night Riders of Kentucky and Tennessee, 1905–1909*. Louisville, Ky.: Standard Press, 1942.

Quint, Howard H. *The Forging of American Socialism: Origins of the Modern Movement*. Indianapolis: Bobbs-Merrill, 1964.

Rowan, Richard W. *Secret Agents against America*. New York: Doubleday, Doran, 1939.

Schattschneider, E. E. *The Semi-Sovereign People*. New York: Holt, Rinehart & Winston, 1960.

Sorin, Gerald. *Abolitionism: A New Perspective*. New York: Praeger, 1972.

Stegner, Wallace. "The Radio Priest and His Flock." Isabell Leighton (ed.), *The Aspirin Age, 1919–1941*. New York: Simon and Schuster, 1949.

Sweeney, Vincent D. *The United Steelworkers of America: Thirty Years Later, 1936–1956* n.p., 1956.

Tull, Charles J. *Father Coughlin and the New Deal*. Syracuse, N.Y.: Syracuse University Press, 1965.

Wechsler, James A. *Revolt on the Campus*. New York: Covici, Friede, 1935.

CHAPTER 38

A CROSS-CULTURAL THEORY OF
POLITICAL CONFLICT AND VIOLENCE

MARC HOWARD ROSS

INTRODUCTION

It is difficult to conceive of a human community where there is no conflict among members, or between persons in the community and outsiders. At the same time, the degree to which conflict is physically violent varies widely. Cases such as the Yanomamo of lowland South America (Chagnon 1967), where feuding and warfare are an ongoing condition of daily life, contrast with the Fore of New Guinea, where open physical expression of differences is rare and strongly discouraged (Sorenson 1978). How can we best understand the variation both in the amount of violence and in the choice of targets?

The research reported here contrasts two explanations for societal variation in conflict behavior. One emphasizes the ways in which the social structure of a society creates divergent interests around which conflicts develop. The other focuses on psychocultural dispositions, explaining violent conflict as a result of culturally learned behaviors and of personality configurations typical in a society. To examine these two different perspectives on violent conflict, hypotheses based on each perspective are tested using data from a world-wide sample of 90 small scale, preindustrial societies.

This [chapter] is a revised and shortened version of Marc Howard Ross, "A Cross-Cultural Theory of Political Conflict and Violence. *Political Psychology*, 1986 (7): 427–469. Reprinted by permission of the author.

The study suggests that psychocultural dispositions rooted in early childhood learning experiences determine a society's overall level of violent conflict. But while psychocultural dispositions affect the propensity to engage in open conflict, they do not determine very precisely who argues, contests, and fights with whom. The structural features of the social, economic, and political system determine whether the people with whom one cooperates and with whom one fights are within one's society, in another society, or both.

The conflict behavior addressed in this article is group behavior, not that of individuals acting alone. It involves efforts of two or more mutually opposed parties to obtain scarce resources at each other's expense through destroying, injuring, thwarting, or otherwise controlling other parties (Mack and Snyder 1957). Societies can differ greatly in their levels of conflict behavior, the ways in which conflicts are played out, and the mechanisms for dispute settlement which are utilized to control or direct conflicts when they occur. My goal is to explain this variation. Why are conflicts in some societies or between members of a society and outsiders violent, while in other cases, where there are clearly disagreements and differences, open violence is rare? Political violence, from this perspective, is not simply present or absent in a society. Rather we need to think about a continuum. At one end violence is common, perhaps endemic; at the midpoint conflict is common but it takes more institutionalized forms: at the low end conflict rarely becomes physically violent.

HYPOTHESES ABOUT CONFLICT AND VIOLENCE

In the extensive literature on violence and conflict there are at least three major explanations of observed variations in violence. Some international relations theorists argue that nations which differ in terms of internal or external conflict are not necessarily very different in terms of their internal characteristics and that conflict is best explained by alliances, constraints in the international system, and status inconsistency, and not by national characteristics (Midlarsky 1975; Zinnes 1980).

In contrast, the two explanations considered in this paper focus on internal characteristics. One framework explains violence and warfare in terms of structural features of society (e.g., Hibbs 1973; Otterbein 1968, 1970), identifying aspects of the social, economic, or political system with patterns of conflict. The other emphasizes psychological factors, or what I call psychocultural dispositions (Montagu 1978). I investigate these two explanations for conflict behavior, first by identifying several major hypotheses from each framework, and then by testing them using data coded from ethnographic reports on a worldwide sample of 90 preindustrial societies. My results suggest that *both* social structural and psychocultural factors are important in understanding differences in the levels and targets of conflict across societies.

Social Structural Hypotheses

Social structural hypotheses see the social, economic, or political structure of a society as crucial in creating interests which shape the organization and level of conflict. Different theories, however, identify a wide range of social structural elements as central. The most common ones are cross-cutting ties, fraternal interest group theory, and socioeconomic complexity. In each the case the structure of society is seen to be related to patterns of conflict within the society and between a society and outside groups.

Cross-Cutting Ties. Cross-cutting ties such as marriage and trading partnerships, connect individuals and communities within a society. The best known structural hypothesis is that these ties limit the severity of overt conflict, and promote the settlement of disputes, by creating shared interests among groups and individuals (Coleman 1957; Colson 1953). For example, marriage can link members of different kinship groups; and religious cults can bring people together form different regions to participate in common ritual activities. One explanation for the relative stability of the American political system is that differences based on religion, age, political ideology and economic interests, for example, create few enduring groups and link different members of a community together in different ways as new issues arise. Divided or multiple loyalties connect diverse and often dispersed members of a society; conversely, the presence of such ties makes it difficult to organize coalitions of persons and factions who will be at odds with others for extended periods of time, for there are primary bonds across social units, producing less suspicion, more trust, and greater cooperation (LeVine and Campbell 1972: 53).

While cross-cutting ties can limit the severity of conflict within a society, they might increase overt conflict between a society and outsiders. By providing a social basis for political unity, they can emphasize the boundaries of a society. The growth of solidarity, of course, might have roots either within the society, or in the actions of outsiders, but for the moment the point is that internal social links, whatever their origin, have important consequences for the stance adopted towards outsiders (LeVine and Campbell 1972).

But what produces cross-cutting ties? Marriage patterns, residence patterns, trade between communities, and groups whose membership cuts across local communities all shape the cross-cutting ties in a society.

a. *Marriage.* Anthropological theory (and sociobiological theory as well) begins, not surprisingly, by looking at kinship and marriage alliances. They are varying viewpoints as to how kinship and marriage influence the expression of conflict. Kinship bonds create mutual obligation and solidarity, while the absence of these ties makes for potentially hostile relationships. In this view a preference for marriage outside the local community inhibits conflict among different communities of the same society because people will not want to fight with those with whom they share kinship and other affective bonds. Of course, internal peace may have a price in terms of external strife as societies with strong bonds among local communities may become more ethnocentric and brazen when facing outsiders. When alliances with neighbors are easily mobilized, attacks against outsiders may be more common. While this view of marriage ties sounds plausible, it has some weaknesses as well. Just because fighting with close kin is potentially disadvantageous does not mean it won't occur. Alliances and exchanges have their own tensions, as the mother-in-law jokes in western society clearly reveal. After all, statistics form our own society show that the vast majority of violent crimes are committed among kin and close friends.

b. *Residence*. Anthropologists pay a good deal of attention to where a new couple resides after marriage. In terms of the impact on violence and conflict, anthropologists have focused particular attention on the dispersion or concentration of related men in a society since they are almost universally dominant in overt fighting and warfare (LeVine and Campbell 1972: 52). Matrilocal or uxorilocal residence (where men live with their wives' kin after marriage) disperses male kin among local communities; some argue this inhibits conflict among communities of the same society while promoting external fighting against external groups (Murphy 1957; LeVine 1965). Data from cross-cultural samples show that matrilocality is associated with external warfare, while patrilocality is more common when internal fighting is high (Ember and Ember 1971; Divale 1974). Exactly why this is the case is the subject of disagreement, however. The Embers, interestingly, hypothesize that warfare patterns shape residence rules. Divale (1974), on the other hand, places a primary role on the effects of migration: patrilocal groups which migrate into previously populated areas adopt matrilocal residence to increase internal peace and to be better united in facing outside enemies (Divale 1974). Some contend

there is less internal conflict in matrilocal societies because organized power groups are not present, while others, in contrast, give a crucial role to psychodynamic, as well as structural, factors in the choice of targets for aggression.

c. *Intercommunity trade*. The functionalist school in international relations advocates the exchange of persons and goods as crucial to inhibiting warfare among nations (Haas 1964). Developing interdependencies among communities will, in this view, inhibit overt fighting between them and encourage the development of peaceful mechanisms for resolving disputes when they do arise.

d. *Cross-community organized groups*. In some societies there are important groups which link members of different residential and kinship units together. For example, among the Ndembu, Turner (1957) describes cult groups which unite individuals who might otherwise be opposed to one another on other structural grounds. Age-sets provide the same kind of cross-cutting linkages in many societies. Where such groups are present, linkages can have political relevance in enhancing the internal unity of society, in inhibiting internal conflict, and in facilitating defense against perceived outside enemies.

Fraternal Interest Group Theory. Fraternal interest groups are power groups made up of male kin who live together and have common interests to protect. Where such fraternal interest groups are present, internal conflict is likely to be high, for it is easy to rapidly mobilize them into collective action which is often violent (van Velzen and van Wetering 1960). In several tests of this hypothesis, Otterbein (1968) and Otterbein and Otterbein (1965) found that in politically uncentralized societies the levels of feuding and internal warfare (armed conflict between different communities of the same society) are related to the presence of fraternal interest groups is not related to external warfare (Otterbein 1970).

Polygynous systems (where men have more than one wife) are commonly viewed as warlike and conflict ridden. One view is that polygyny is usually supported by patrilocality, and conflict is high because related males with common interests are grouped together, as spelled out in fraternal interest group theory. On the other hand, Melvin Ember (1974), in a study of polygyny, argues that warfare and unbalanced sex ratios lead to polygyny, not the other way around, and that polygyny is a response to high male mortality as the community needs to replenish its members (1974: 204).

Socioeconomic Complexity. Despite the popular image of violence and anarchy in the most primitive societies, available studies show that societies at the simplest level of technological complexity are no more prone to violence than highly complex ones. Some of the writing on hunters and gatherers stresses the ways in which coordination and cooperation of the entire community in activities such a hunting are essential for survival, and outbreaks of severe conflict within the community are rare (Marshall 1961; Draper 1978; but also see Knauft 1987). At the same time, some of the most conflict-ridden societies are groups with a similarly low level of complexity such as the Yanomamo in South America or various groups in New Guinea (Chagnon 1967; Meggitt 1977; Koch 1974). Here societies lacking mechanisms of coordination and control also have few means for limiting open conflicts once they break out. The relation between internal conflict and complexity is unclear.

However, external conflict is more prevalent in more complex societies. There is good support for the hypothesis that societies that have been more warlike and more successful in warfare have displaced those that lack such traits (LeVine and Campbell 1972: 72–77). Looking at modern nations there is also a modest tendency for more developed nations to have higher levels of external conflict (Haas 1965).

Political complexity—the rise of a centralized state—has received more attention as a correlate of conflict and warfare than socioeconomic complexity. As the state develops, warfare increases and the type of warfare changes (Wright 1942; Broch and Galtung 1966). Some argue that the development of military leadership produces political leaders and subsequent centralization, while others put the causal arrow in the opposite direction (Service 1975). Materialist interpretations of the rise of the state argue that the

development of stratification and wealth creates the need for a military to protect privileged interests against internal and external predators (Fried 1967). Theories of the state as a mechanism of conquest posit the growth of military sophistication as a way to control neighboring people and resources (Adams 1966).

A somewhat different perspective suggests that even if more centralized systems are more militarily sophisticated, the concentration of political power in a few hands places greater control over the outbreak of violence. This view emphasizes the role of the state as a conflict inhibitor through its control over the instruments of violence (Service 1975). If the state is effective in controlling the overall level of violence as well as its targets, then political centralization will be associated with lower violence both internally and externally.

To summarize, the social structural hypotheses identify different ways in which the organization of a society affects conflict behavior: weak cross-cutting ties and strong fraternal interest groups are expected to raise internal and lower external conflict, while the effects of complexity are more likely to increase the level of both internal and external conflict.

Psychocultural Hypotheses

Early socialization influences adult behavior by shaping the personality of the individual (Harrington and Whiting 1972). Shaping cognition as well as deeper motivations, early learning experiences prepare individuals for patterns of conflict and cooperation in their society. LeVine and Campbell (1972) review psychocultural theories in the area of ethnocentrism and provide three key hypotheses relevant to internal violence and external warfare: harsh socialization, warmth and affection, and male gender identity conflict.

Harsh Socialization. Several psychological approaches associate harsh and severe child training practices with later aggressiveness: psychoanalytic theory (and the authoritarian personality work derived from it), social learning theory, and frustration-aggression theory.

One psychonalytic theory focuses on the development of a superego that monitors behaviors and feelings. As part of psychological maturation, individuals come to repress impulses that are too frightening to be acknowledged at a conscious level. Repression is a normal part of psychological functioning. However, when parents are very hostile and punitive, the child develops an overly harsh superego, leading to severe repression. The repressed, pent up feelings can be highly destructive for either the individual or those around him or her. Identification with aggressive parents and severe repression are the raw material for the expression of violence, according to this psychoanalytic theory. In some cases the feelings are turned inward, while in others they are projected onto others and one's own aggressive feelings are displaced onto available targets (Adorno 1950).

Other theories identify different mechanisms, but the predictions are similar (Zigler and Child 1969). For example, where psychoanalytic and frustration–aggression theory connect severe physical punishment of children with later displacement onto outgroups, social learning theory emphasizes imitation, modeling, and reinforcement. In either case, however, the argument is that children who experience harsh socialization become aggressive adults who engage in overt conflict more readily.

A number of specific cross-cultural studies find a positive association between harsh socialization practices and physical aggression, bellicosity, or warfare (Levinson and Malone 1980: 249). Slater (1968) finds a connection between sexual repression, sadism, and militarism. Others argue that children who are forced to repress their private feelings later identify with aggression by the state. "War," conclude Durbin and Bowlby, "is due to the transformed aggressiveness of individuals" (1939: 41). This is an illustration of the psychoanalytic concept of "identification with the aggressor"; children identify with harsh, punitive parents and become like their parents (Anna Freud 1937).

Warmth and Affection. Affection, warmth, and love-oriented child rearing practices are associated with low violence and conflict. Several studies show that variables measuring harsh socialization practices are *distinct* from indicators of warmth and affection (Ross 1986); these two dimensions are *not* simply opposite poles on the same continuum.

Greater expression of affection toward children, greater emphasis on values such as trust, honesty, and generosity, and closer father-child ties all lead individuals toward cooperation, rather than animosity and aggressiveness. The healthy psychosocial development of the individual in early relationships with parental figures prepares the way for socially cooperative experiences later in life (Winnicott 1965; Greenberg and Mitchell 1983).

Winnicott (1965) uses the term "good enough mother" to refer to the caretaker who provides a child with early experiences resulting in a positive sense of self, and trust and openness toward others. In contrast, if early relationships are highly negative and threatening, psychological growth remains fixated at an early developmental stage, and bonds to others cannot develop. Attachment to others is crucial later in life whether we are speaking about the ability of individuals to form intimate relationships or to join with others in socially cooperative ventures (Bowlby 1969).

The profiles of seven small-scale societies, all low on internal conflict and aggression, present some good examples of this pattern (Montagu 1978). In these societies, great affection is frequently directed toward the child, whose overall feelings of security are high. Overt expression of aggression is discouraged, but not through physical punishment. Finally, these societies lack models of highly aggressive persons whom the child can imitate. Affectionate parent-child relationships are associated with lower conflict, both within one's society and in dealing with outsiders, just as harsh socialization is associated with higher conflict.

Male Gender Identity Conflict. Men who are uncertain about their gender identity tend to be more aggressive, according to several theories. In male dominated cultures, where fathers are distant and aloof from their children, frustration develops when young boys grow up with especially strong bonds to their mothers, anthropologists have theorized (Whiting 1965; Whiting and Whiting 1975a). At adolescence, and sometimes earlier, these bonds may be severed by severe initiation rites or other rituals, so that boys can meet the societal expectations of adult male behavior, but some frustration and insecurity about gender identity remain (Herdt 1987; Munroe, Munroe, and Whiting 1981).

A second source of frustration is maternal ambivalence. Women living in patrilocal, polygynous societies have neither strong ties to their natal families nor strong affective bonds with their husbands. Slater and Slater call this "diluted marriage" (1965). Women in these settings develop strong bonds with their children, but also take out frustration on them, and the male child is "alternatively seduced and rejected" (Slater and Slater, 1965: 242). The result is that males in such cultures develop very ambivalent feelings toward females; narcissistic personalities that are preoccupied with early developmental tasks, pride, and self-enhancement are common, and the males are prone to aggressive actions (Herdt 1987; Huyghe 1986). Despite cultural attempts to deal with male gender ambivalence, the solutions are only partial so that compensatory behaviors seen in bellicosity, aggressive display behavior, and open fighting are common.

Distance father–child ties promote aggressivity, while close, affectionate bonds are associated with low overt conflict according to the male gender identity hypothesis. Many studies support this hypothesis (Ember 1980: 561–62), although several critics have suggested that the same data might be better explained by other theories (e.g., Young 1965; Paige and Paige 1981). A major finding from *The Authoritarian Personality* research was that distant fathers produce children (particularly boys) who are insecure in interpersonal relationships and are more ready to engage in open aggression against outgroups (Adorno et al. 1950).

Detailed observations of children in six cultures show that children are more authoritarian and aggressive in the cultures in which the father is present less, and child–father contact is lower (Whiting and Whit-

ing 1975a). The highest rates of physical assault and homicide occurred in the two cultures in which children spent the least time with adult males, Beatrice Whiting found (1965). She also notes that the absence of fathers is often correlated with juvenile delinquency in industrial societies. Distant fathering is associated with training boys to be warriors, and societies in which fathers are distant are likely to have a high incidence of warfare (Whiting and Whiting 1975b; West and Konner 1976: 203). Among both human and nonhuman primates, close father-child ties are associated with lower aggression and conflict, according to Alcorta (1982). She says that there is noticeably less stress among infants, particularly among males, and lower subsequent aggression, the more that adult males are involved in child rearing.

In summary, the psychocultural hypotheses are: when socialization is harsh and punishing, low in affection and warmth, and when male gender conflict is high, there is a high level of both internal and external conflict.

RESULTS

Procedures

These social structural and psychocultural hypotheses were tested with data obtained from coding ethnographic reports on 90 preindustrial societies located throughout the world. The societies were scored on a number of variables based on reports about politics, socioeconomic organization, and child training. The political codes are described in Ross (1983), while the socioeconomic and child training variables are found in Barry and Schlegel (1980).

Internal violence and conflict was measured by seven variables. Beginning with the most important, they are (1) the severity of conflict between residents of different communities in the same society, (2) the acceptability of using violence against members of the same society but outside the local community, (3) the frequency of internal warfare, (4) the severity of conflict within local communities in the society, (5) the degree to which physical force is used as a mechanism for dispute settlement, (6) the acceptability of violence against members of the community, and (7) the variability of compliance with norms and decisions on the part of members of the local community. Societies on the high end of this scale, such as the Jivaro or Somali, have frequent violent conflict and internal warfare both within and between communities of the same society. Societies at the middle of the scale, such a the Kikuyu or Comanche, have regular conflict, but internal warfare and the use of violence in local disputes is less common. At the low point are societies where conflict itself is milder and physical violence infrequent. The Mbuti Pygmies, Semang, and Papago fall here.

Three variables make up the external warfare and conflict scale: the frequency of external warfare, the degree of hostility expressed to other societies (not just in war), and the acceptability of violence directed to people in other societies. Societies such as the Buganda, Maori, Comanche, and Jivaro are high on this dimension, while low external conflict societies are the !Kung Bushmen, the Lepcha and the Trobriand Islanders.

Findings

[Correlation] results are presented in Table 38.1. They show that both structural and psychocultural variables are significantly related to internal and external conflict and in combination explain conflict better than either set of variables alone. [Multiple regression results not shown].

A closer look shows that low affection, harsh socialization, and male gender identity conflict increase internal *and* external violence and conflict, but the specific structural factors associated with internal and external conflict differ. To explain these results we propose a dispositional basis for aggression and violence rooted in early learning and personality formation, while the targets of aggression are shaped by the structural features of a society. In some cases the targets will be outside one's society, in some they will be inside it, while in many situations both forms of violence will occur. Before elaborating on the general argument, it is useful to first examine the specific results.

Internal Violence and Conflict. Two psychocultural and two structural variables are significantly related to the level of violence and conflict within a society. The more affectionate and warm and the less harsh the socialization in a society, the lower the level of political violence and conflict. This finding suggests that early experiences become critical in establishing an individual's capacity to cooperate with others and provide a framework for interpreting their behavior. Individuals who have experienced early lack of affection and harsh treatment will have much more trouble in establishing warm cooperative bonds with others as adults and will be more prone to view the behavior of others as hostile and threatening. Projecting threat and aggression onto others then provides an easy justification for one's own aggressive actions.

The results concerning structural variables show that the weaker the cross-cutting ties in a society, and the stronger fraternal interest groups are in uncentralized societies, the greater the level of internal violence and conflict. Cross-cutting ties, by providing social and political links among different groups, offer a brake on the expansion of conflict, limit polarization, and lessen the possibility of widespread violence. Fraternal interest groups do the opposite, bringing related males together where it is easy for them to organize violent actions, either defending their own perceived interests or attacking others.

External Warfare and Hostility. The results for external warfare show the same psychocultural basis for external as for internal conflict—lack of affectionate, and presence of harsh, socialization—and there is strong support for the male gender identity hypothesis as a predictor of external violence. Structural factors are important here too, but they are different from those involved in internal violence. Finally, there are some important differences between centralized and uncentralized societies. In uncentralized societies only, external violence is related to a preference for intracommunity marriage and strong cross-cutting ties.

This study of internal and external conflict in 90 preindustrial societies shows *both* psychocultural

TABLE 38.1   Correlations: Internal and external conflict

	PEARSON CORR.
Internal violence and conflict	
Structural variables	
Strength of cross-cutting ties scale	−.24**
Marital endogamy	.04
Fraternal interest group strength in uncentralized societies	.26**
Political power concentration	−.03
Polygyny	.20*
Intercommunity trade	.03
Socioeconomic complexity	.08
Matrilocality #	.05
Psychocultural variables	
Affectionate socialization practices	−.35***
Harsh socialization practices	.33***
Male gender identity conflict	.05

Multiple R = .60 R Square = .36

External violence and conflict	
Structural variables	
Strength of cross-cutting ties in uncentralized societies	.20*
Marital endogamy in uncentralized societies	.28**
Fraternal interest group strength	.24**
Political power concentration	.11
Polygyny	.03
Socioeconomic complexity	.24**
Matrilocality	.14
Psychocultural variables	
Affectionate socialization practices	−.41***
Harsh socialization practices	.30**
Male gender identity conflict	.29**

Multiple R = .69 R Square = .47

Definitions of the variables are provided in the Appendix below.
***statistically significant at the .001 level
**statistically significant at the .01 level
*statistically significant at the .05 level

#results are the same when matrilocality is substituted for patrilocality; but the sign is reversed and structural variables are important. Socialization creates dispositions toward high or low violence in a society. Particular structural conditions then determine the ways in which the violence is directed at others within the society, at outsiders, or in both directions.

The psychocultural argument supported here is rooted in the notion that early relationships provide a template for perceiving the world and for intra- and inter-group cooperation and conflict later in life (Fornari 1975:101). Dispositional patterns emphasize *cultural* constructions and are more than individual personality configurations; they are culturally learned and approved methods for dealing with others. Although participants have little trouble citing "objective" bases for conflict, "She [he] took my toy [land, water, women cows]," what is striking to the outsider is the number of times the same supposedly provocative action occurs and is *not* followed by any overt violence. This is crucial. It means that objective situations alone do not cause conflict; *interpretations* of such situations also play a central role, while the structural features of a society affect who the targets of hostility are likely to be.

Group, and not just individual, processes are especially important as individuals seek to answer difficult questions about the meaning of their lives. Groups, after all, provide social support telling people both that they are not alone and that particular answers are right. Because there cannot be certainty concerning the meaning of many social actions, building social consensus and support becomes crucial. For Whiting (1980) areas such as religion and the interpretation of illness are areas of human behavior producing projective behaviors that are best understood as psychological products. I suggest that conflict and violence should frequently be seen in this same framework as well. Conflict situations are often crucial and very ambiguous. There is great room for individuals to interpret them in terms of their own needs. Conflicts often begin with scanty information concerning a supposedly objective situation, and therefore encourage projective processes.

In this way a full understanding of war and peace within and between societies seems to require an integration of psychocultural and social factors. This should not be very surprising for after all conflict behavior is one of the things that is distinctively human. It is not something we do in a trivial way; it involves and absorbs so much of our emotional energy and resources. Perhaps from looking at the behavior of those human groups who seem most different from ourselves we can learn something about the range of possible human behavior, as well as gain better understanding of ourselves.

APPENDIX: MEASURES AND SOURCES FOR THE INDEPENDENT VARIABLES

In all cases the specific measures used begin with published data for the societies in the Standard Cross-Cultural Sample (Murdock and White 1969). The measurement of the two dependent variables is explained in the text. Included here are brief descriptions of each independent variable; greater detail about the technical aspects of the measures is provided in Ross (1983, 1985). The sources for the nonpolitical variables are found in Barry and Schlegel (1980).

Strength of cross-cutting ties is a scale made up of seven variables including the extent to which individuals living in different communities of the same society are linked together in politically relevant ways, the strength of in-group or we feelings directed toward the wider society—i.e., beyond the local community, the strength of kinship organizations and ritual groups that link different communities, and the extent to which there is intervention in disputes as they develop and community pressures work toward settlement (see Ross 1983).

Intercommunity marriage is a five point measure of the extent to which marriage in a society favors local exogamy vs. endogomy.

Matrilocality and *patrilocality* classifies societies as patrilocal if there is a preference for patrilocal or virilocal residence, otherwise patrilocality is absent; similarly, matrilocality is scored as present if the society is matrilocal or uxorilocal, absent if it is not.

Intercommunity trade is a seven point measure of the extent to which a community in the society trades for foodstuffs.

Fraternal interest group strength is based on Paige and Paige's (1981) measure and includes the presence or absence of brideprice, the presence or absence of patrilineality, and a trichotomized measure of the size of effective kin-based political subunits.

Polygyny is a three point measure—monogamous, less than 20% polygynous marriage, and more than 20% polygynous.

Socioeconomic complexity is a scale made up of eight different highly associated measures: important of agriculture as a contribution to subsistence, importance of animal husbandry, low importance of hunting, low importance of gathering, the degree to which food is stored, the size of the average community in the society, the degree of social stratification, and cultural complexity.

Political complexity is a thirteen variable scale originally called *political power concentration* (Ross, 1983). The crucial variables are: the extent to which leaders act independently in a community, the presence or absence of checks on political leaders, the degree of political role differentiation in a society, the importance of decision making bodies, and the level of taxation.

Harsh socialization is a scale made up of the following socialization measures: severity of pain infliction, extent to which corporal punishment is used, the degree to which children are not indulged, the extent to which children are scolded, the importance of caretakers other than the mother, the degree to which fortitude is stressed as a value, and the degree to which aggressiveness is stressed as a value.

Affectionate socialization is a scale made up of the following socialization measures: the degree to which trust is emphasized as a value during childhood, the degree to which honesty is stressed as a value during childhood, the closeness of the father in childhood, the degree to which generosity is stressed as a value during childhood, the degree to which affection is expressed toward the child, and the extent to which children are valued by the society.

Male gender identity conflict is a seven point measure of the length of abstinence from sexual intercourse by the mother after birth, described as the cultural norm. The seven point measure is from Barry and Paxson (1971). Another measure which Whiting has also used is polygyny (see above).

REFERENCES

Adams, Robert McC. 1966. *The Evolution of Urban Society*. Chicago: Aldine.

Adorno, T. W. et al. 1950. *The Authoritarian Personality*. New York: John Wiley.

Alcorta, Candace Storey. 1982. "Paternal Behavior and Group Competition." *Behavior Science Research* 17:3–23.

Barry, Herbert H. III and Lenora M. Paxson. 1971. "Infancy and Early Childhood: Cross-Cultural Codes 2." *Ethnology* 10:466–508.

Barry, Herbert III and Alice Schlegel (eds.). 1980. *Cross-Cultural Samples and Codes*. Pittsburgh: University of Pittsburgh Press.

Bowlby, John. 1969. *Attachment and Loss*. New York: Basic Books.

Broch, Tom and Johan Galtung. 1966. "Belligerence among the Primitives." *Journal of Peace Research* 3:33–45.

Chagnon, Napoleon. 1967. "Yanomamo Social Organization and Warfare." Pp. 109–159 in *War: The Anthropology of Armed Conflict and Aggression*, edited by Morton Fried, Marvin Harris, and Robert Murphy. Garden City, New York: Natural History Press.

Coleman, James S. 1957. *Community Conflict*. New York: Free Press.

Colson, Elizabeth. 1953. "Social Control and Vengeance in Plateau Tonga Society." *Africa* 23:199–211.

Divale, William T. 1974. "Migration, External Warfare and Matrilocal Residence." *Behavior Science Research* 9:75–133.

Draper, Patricia. 1978. "The Learning Environment for Aggression and Anti-Social Behavior among the Kung." Pp. 31–53 in *Learning Non-Aggression*, edited by Ashley Montagu. New York: Oxford University Press.

Durbin, E. F. M. and John Bowlby. 1939. *Personal Aggressiveness and War.* New York: Columbia University Press.

Ember, Carol R. 1980. "A Cross-Cultural Perspective on Sex Differences." Pp. 531–580 in *Handbook of Cross-Cultural Human Development*, edited by Ruth H. Munroe et al. New York: Garland STPM Press.

Ember, Melvin. 1974. "Warfare, Sex Ratio, and Polygyny." *Ethnology* 13:197–206.

Ember, Melvin and Carol R. Ember. 1971. "The Conditions Favoring Matrilocal Versus Patrilocal Residence." *American Anthropologist* 73:571–594.

Fornari, Franco. 1975. *The Psychoanalysis of War.* Bloomington: Indiana University Press.

Freud, Anna. 1937 [1966]. *The Ego and the Mechanisms of Defense.* New York: International Universities Press.

Fried, Morton H. 1967. *The Evolution of Political Society.* New York: Random House.

Greenberg, Jay R. and Stephen A. Mitchell. 1983. *Object Relations in Psychoanalytic Theory.* Cambridge: Harvard University Press.

Haas, Ernst. 1964. *The Uniting of Europe.* Stanford: Stanford University Press.

Haas, Michael. 1965. "Societal Approaches to the Study of War." *Journal of Peace Research* 4:307–323.

Harrington, Charles and John W. M. Whiting. 1972. "Socialization Processes and Personality." Pp. 469–507 in *Psychological Anthropology*, second ed., edited by Francis L. K. Hsu. Cambridge: Schenkman.

Herdt, Gilbert. 1987. *The Sambia: Ritual and Gender in New Guinea.* New York: Holt, Rinehart & Winston.

Hibbs, Douglas. 1973. *Mass Political Violence: Cross-National Causal Analysis.* New York: John Wiley.

Huyghe, Bernard. 1986. "Toward a Structural Model of Violence: Male Initiation Rituals and Tribal Warfare." Pp. 25–48 in *Peace and War in Cross-Cultural Perspective*, edited by Mary LeCron Foster and Robert A. Rubinstein. New Brunswick: Transaction Books.

Knauft, Bruce. 1987. "Reconsidering Violence in Simple Human Societies: Homicide Among the Gebusi of New Guinea." *Current Anthropology* 28:457–500.

Koch, Klaus Frierich. 1974. *War and Peace in Jalemo.* Cambridge: Harvard University Press.

LeVine, Robert A. 1965. "Socialization, Social Structure and Intersocial Images." Pp. 43–69 in *International Behavior: A Social-Psychological Analysis*, edited by Herbert Kelman. New York: Holt, Rinehart & Winston.

LeVine, Robert A. and Donald Campbell. 1972. *Ethnocentrism: Theories of Conflict, Ethnic Attitudes and Group Behavior.* New York: John Wiley.

Levinson, David and Martin J. Malone. 1980. *Toward Explaining Human Culture: A Critique of the Findings of Worldwide Cross-Cultural Research.* New Haven: HRAF Press.

Mack, Raymond W. and Richard Snyder. 1957. "The Analysis of Social Conflict: Toward an Overview and Synthesis." *Journal of Conflict Resolution* 1:212–248.

Marshall, Lorna. 1961. "Sharing, Talking and Giving: The Relief of Social Tension Among the !Kung Bushmen." *Africa* 31:231–249.

Meggitt, Mervyn. 1977. *Blood Is Their Argument: Warfare among the Mae Enga Tribesmen of the New Guinea Highlands.* Palo Alto: Mayfield.

Midlarsky, Manus. 1975. *On War: Political Violence in the International System.* New York: Free Press.

Montagu, Ashley (ed.). 1978. *Learning Non-Aggression.* New York: Oxford Univ. Press.

Munroe, Robert L., Ruth H. Munroe, and John W. M. Whiting. 1981. "Male Sex-Role Resolutions." Pp. 611–632 in *Handbook of Cross-Cultural Human Development*, edited by Ruth H. Munroe, Robert L. Munroe, and Beatrice B. Whiting. New York and London: Garland STPM Press.

Murdock, George Peter and Douglas R. White. 1969. "Standard Cross-Cultural Sample." *Ethnology* 8:329–369.

Murphy, Robert F. 1957. "Intergroup Hostility and Social Cohesion." *American Anthropologist* 59:1018–1035.

Otterbein, Keith. 1968. "Internal War: A Cross-Cultural Comparison." *American Anthropologist* 70:277–289.

———. 1970. *The Evolution of War.* New Haven: HRAF Press.

Otterbein, Keith F. and Charlotte Swanson Otterbein. 1965. "An Eye for an Eye, a Tooth for a Tooth: A Cross-Cultural Study of Feuding." *American Anthropologist* 67:1470–1482.

Paige, Karen Ericksen and Jeffrey M. Paige. 1981. *The Politics of Reproductive Ritual.* Berkeley: University of California Press.

Ross, Marc Howard. 1983. "Political Decision Making and Conflict: Additional Cross-Cultural Codes and Scales," *Ethnology* 22:169–192.

———. 1985. "Internal and External Violence and Conflict: Cross-Cultural Evidence and a New Analysis." *Journal of Conflict Resolution* 29:547579.

———. 1986. "A Cross-Cultural Theory of Political Conflict and Violence." *Political Psychology.* 7:427–69.

Service, Elman R. 1975. *Origins of the State and Civilization.* New York: Norton.

Slater, Phillip E. 1968. *The Glory of Hera.* Boston: Beacon.

Slater, Phillip E. and Dori A. Slater. 1965. "Maternal Ambivalence and Narcissism: A Cross-Cultural Study." *Merrill-Palmer Quarterly* 11:241–259.

Sorenson, Richard E. 1978. "Cooperation and Freedom among the Fore of New Guinea." In *Learning Non-Aggression,* edited by Ashley Montagu. New York: Oxford.

Turner, Victor. 1957. *Schism and Continuity in an African Society.* Manchester: Manchester University Press.

van Velzen, H. U. E. Thoden and W. van Wetering. 1960. "Residence, Power Groups and Intra-Societal Aggression." *International Archives of Ethnography* 49:169–200.

West, Mary Maxwell and Melvin J. Konner. 1976. "The Role of the Father: An Anthropological Perspective." In *The Role of the Father in Child Development*, edited by Michael E. Lamb. New York: Wiley-Interscience, 185–216.

Whiting, Beatrice B. 1965. "Sex Identity Conflict and Physical Violence: A Comparative Study." *American Anthropologist* 67, part 2:123–140.

———. 1980. "Culture and Social Behavior: A Model for the Development of Social Behavior." *Ethos* 8:95–116.

Whiting, Beatrice B. and John W. M. Whiting. 1975a. *Children of Six Cultures: A Psycho-Cultural Analysis.* Cambridge: Harvard University Press.

Whiting, John W. M. and Beatrice B. Whiting. 1975b. "Aloofness and Intimacy Between Husbands and Wives." *Ethos* 3;183–207.

Winnicott, Donald W. 1965. *The Maturational Process and the Facilitating Environment.* New York: International Universities Press.

Wright, Quincy. 1942. *A Study of War.* 2 vols. Chicago: University of Chicago Press.

Young, Frank. 1965. *Initiation Ceremonies: A Cross-Cultural Study of Status Dramatization.* New York: Bobbs-Merrill.

Zigler, Edward and Irwin L. Child. 1969. "Socialization." In *Handbook of Social Psychology*, second ed., edited by Gardner Lindzey and Elliot Aronson. Reading, Mass.: Addison-Wesley.

Zinnes, Dina A. 1980. "Why War? Evidence on the Outbreak of International Conflict." In *Handbook of Political Conflict*, edited by Ted Robert Gurr. New York: Free Press.

CHAPTER 39

THE GREAT DISRUPTION
HUMAN NATURE AND THE RECONSTITUTION
OF SOCIAL ORDER

FRANCIS FUKUYAMA

A society built around information tends to produce more of the two things people value most in a modern democracy—freedom and equality. Freedom of choice has exploded, in everything from cable channels to low-cost shopping outlets to friends met on the Internet. Hierarchies of all sorts, political and corporate, have come under pressure and begun to crumble.

People associate the information age with the advent of the Internet, in the 1990s, but the shift from the industrial era started more than a generation earlier, with the deindustrialization of the Rust Belt in the United States and comparable movements away from manufacturing in other industrialized countries. This period, roughly the mid-1960s to the early 1990s, was also marked by seriously deteriorating social conditions in most of the industrialized world. Crime and social disorder began to rise, making inner-city areas of the wealthiest societies on earth almost uninhabitable. The decline of kinship as a social institution, which has been going on for more than 200 years, accelerated sharply in the second half of the twentieth century. Marriages and births declined and divorce soared; and one out of every three children in the United States and more than half of all children in Scandinavia were born out of wedlock. Finally, trust and confidence in institutions went into a forty-year decline. Although a majority of people in the United

States and Europe expressed confidence in their governments and fellow citizens during the late 1950s, only a small minority did so by the early 1990s. The nature of people's involvement with one another changed as well—although there is no evidence that people associated with one another less, their ties tended to be less permanent, looser, and with smaller groups of people.

These changes were dramatic; they occurred over a wide range of similar countries; and they all appeared at roughly the same period in history. As such, they constituted a Great Disruption in the social values that had prevailed in the industrial-age society of the mid twentieth century. It is very unusual for social indicators to move together so rapidly; even without knowing why they did so, we have cause to suspect that the reasons might be related. Although William J. Bennett and other conservatives are often attacked for harping on the theme of moral decline, they are essentially correct; the perceived breakdown of social order is not a matter of nostalgia, poor memory, or ignorance about the hypocrises of earlier ages. The decline is readily measurable in statistics in crime, fatherless children, broken trust, reduced opportunities for and outcomes from education, and the like.

Was it simply an accident that these negative social trends, which together reflect a weakening of social bonds and common values in Western societies, occurred just as the economies of those societies were making the transition from the industrial to the information era? The hypothesis of this article is that the

From *The Atlantic Monthly*, pp. 55–80, May 1999. Reprinted by permission of Francis Fukuyama. Graphics have been removed.

two were in fact intimately connected, and that although many blessings have flowed from a more complex, information-based economy, certain bad things also happened to our social and moral life. The connections were technological, economic, and cultural. The changing nature of work tended to substitute mental for physical labor, propelling millions of women into the workplace and undermining the traditional understandings on which the family had been based. Innovations in medical technology leading to the birth-control pill and increasing longevity diminished the role of reproduction and family in people's lives. And the culture of individualism, which in the laboratory and the marketplace leads to innovation and growth, spilled over into the realm of social norms, where it corroded virtually all forms of authority and weakened the bonds holding families, neighborhoods, and nations together. The complete story is, of course, much more complex than this, and differs from one country to another. But broadly speaking, the technological change that brought about what the economist Joseph Schumpeter called "creative destruction" in the marketplace caused similar disruption in the world of social relationships. Indeed, it would be surprising if this were not true.

But there is a bright side, too; social order, once disrupted, tends to get remade, and there are many indications that this is happening today. We can expect a new social order for a simple reason: human beings are *by nature* social creatures, whose most basic drives and instincts lead them to create moral rules that bind them together into communities. They are also by nature rational, and their rationality allows them to spontaneously create ways of cooperating with one another. Religion, though often helpful to this process, is not the *sine qua non* of social order, as many conservatives believe. Neither is a strong and expansive state, as many on the left argue. Man's natural condition is not the war of "every man against every man" envisioned by Thomas Hobbes but rather a civil society made orderly by the presence of a host of moral rules. These assertions, moreover, are empirically supported by a tremendous amount of research coming out of the life sciences in recent years, in fields as diverse as neurophysiology, behavior genet-

ics, evolutionary biology, ethology, and biologically informed approaches to psychology and anthropology. The study of how order arises—not as the result of a top-down mandate by hierarchical authority, whether political or religious, but as the result of self-organization on the part of decentralized individuals—is one of the most interesting and important intellectual developments of our time.

The idea that social order has to come from a centralized, rational, bureaucratic hierarchy was very much associated with the industrial age. The sociologist Max Weber, observing nineteenth-century industrial society, argued that rational bureaucracy was, in fact, the very essence of modern life. We know now, however, that in an information society neither governments nor corporations will rely exclusively on formal bureaucratic rules to organize people. Instead they will decentralize and devolve power, and rely on the people over whom they have nominal authority to be *self-organizing*. The precondition for such self-organization is internalized rules and norms of behavior, a fact that suggests that the world of the twenty-first century will depend heavily on such informal norms. Thus although the transition into an information society has disrupted social norms, a modern, high-tech society cannot get along without them and will face considerable incentives to produce them.

The disruption of social order by the progress of technology is not a new phenomenon. Particularly since the beginning of the Industrial Revolution, human societies have been subject to a relentless process of modernization, as one new production process replaced another. The social disorder of the late eighteenth and early nineteenth centuries in America and Britain can be traced directly to the disruptive effects of the so-called first Industrial Revolution, when steam power and mechanization created new industries in textiles, railroads, and the like. Agricultural societies were transformed into urban industrial societies within the space of perhaps a hundred years, and all the accumulated social norms, habits, and customs that had characterized rural or village life were replaced by the rhythms of the factory and the city.

This shift in norms engendered what is perhaps the most famous concept in modern sociology—the distinction drawn by Ferdinand Tönnies between what he called *Gemeinschaft* ("community") and *Gesellschaft* ("society"). According to Tönnies, the *Gemeinschaft* that characterized a typical pre-modern European peasant society consisted of a dense network of personal relationships based heavily on kinship and on the direct, face-to-face contact that occurs in a small, closed village. Norms were largely unwritten, and individuals were bound to one another in a web of mutual interdependence that touched all aspects of life, from family to work to the few leisure activities that such societies enjoyed. *Gesellschaft*, on the other hand, was the framework of laws and other formal regulations that characterized large, urban industrial societies. Social relationships were more formalized and impersonal; individuals did not depend on one another for support to nearly the same extent, and were therefore much less morally obligated to one another.

Many of the standard sociological texts written in the middle of the twentieth century treated the shift from *Gemeinschaft* to *Gesellschaft* as if it were a one-shot affair; societies were either "traditional" or "modern," and the modern ones somehow constituted the end of the road for social development. But social evolution did not culminate in middle-class American society of the 1950s; industrial societies soon began transforming themselves into what the sociologist Daniel Bell has characterized as post-industrial societies, or what we know as information societies. If this transformation is as momentous as the previous one, we should hardly be surprised that the impact on social values has proved equally great.

Whether information-age democracies can maintain social order in the face of technological and economic change is among their greatest challenges today. From the early 1970s to the early 1990s there was a sudden surge of new democracies in Latin America, Europe, Asia, and the former Communist world. As I argued in *The End of History and the Last Man* (1992), there is a strong logic behind the evolution of political institutions in the direction of modern liberal democracy, based on the correlation between economic development and stable democracy. Political and economic institutions have converged over time in the world's most economically advanced countries, and there are no obvious alternatives to the ones we see before us.

This progressive tendency is not necessarily evident in moral and social development, however. The tendency of contemporary liberal democracies to fall prey to excessive individualism is perhaps their greatest long-term vulnerability, and is particularly visible in the most individualistic of all democracies, the United States. The modern liberal state was premised on the notion that in the interests of political peace, government would not take sides among the differing moral claims made by religion and traditional culture. Church and State were to be kept separate; there would be pluralism in opinions about the most important moral and ethical questions, concerning ultimate ends or the nature of the good. Tolerance would become the cardinal virtue; in place of moral consensus would be a transparent framework of law and institutions that produced political order. Such a political system did not require that people be particularly virtuous; they need only be rational and follow the law in their own self-interest. Similarly, the market-based capitalist economic system that went hand in glove with political liberalism required only that people consult their long-term self-interest to achieve a socially optimal production and distribution of goods.

The societies created on these individualistic premises have worked extraordinarily well, and as the twentieth century comes to a close, there are few real alternatives to liberal democracy and market capitalism as fundamental organizing principles for modern societies. Individual self-interest is a lower but more stable ground than virtue on which to base society. The creation of a rule of law is among the proudest accomplishments of Western civilization—and its benefits become all too obvious when one deals with countries that lack one, such as Russia and China.

But although formal law and strong political and economic institutions are critical, they are not in themselves sufficient to guarantee a successful modern society. To work properly, liberal democracy has always been dependent on certain shared cultural values. This can be seen most clearly in the contrast between the United States and the countries of Latin America. When Argentina, Brazil, Chile, Mexico, and other Latin American countries got their independence, in the nineteenth century, many of them established formal democratic constitutions and legal systems patterned on the presidential system of the United States. Since then not one Latin American country has experienced the political stability, economic growth, or institutional efficacy enjoyed by the United States, though most, fortunately, had returned to democratic government by the end of the 1980s.

There are many complex historical reasons for this, but the most important is a cultural one: the United States was settled primarily by British people and inherited not just British law but British culture as well, whereas Latin America inherited various cultural traditions from the Iberian peninsula. Although the U.S. Constitution enforces a separation between Church and State, American culture was decisively shaped in its formative years by sectarian Protestantism. Sectarian Protestantism reinforced both American individualism and the tendency of the society to be self-organizing in a myriad of voluntary associations and communities. The vitality of American civil society was crucial both for the stability of the country's democratic institutions and for its vibrant economy. The imperial and Latin Catholic traditions of Spain and Portugal, in contrast, reinforced dependence on large, centralized institutions like the State and the Church, weakening an independent civil society. Similarly, the differing abilities of Northern and Southern Europe to make modern institutions work were influenced by religious heritage and cultural tradition.

The problem with most modern liberal democracies is that they cannot take their cultural preconditions for granted. The most successful among them, including the United States, were lucky to have married strong formal institutions to a flexible and supportive informal culture. But nothing in the formal institutions themselves guarantees that the society in which they exist will continue to enjoy the right sort of cultural values and norms under the pressures of technological, economic, and social change. Just the opposite: the individualism, pluralism, and tolerance that are built into the formal institutions tend to encourage cultural diversity, and therefore have the potential to undermine moral values inherited from the past. And a dynamic, technologically innovative economy will by its very nature disrupt existing social relations.

It may be, then, that although large political and economic institutions have long been evolving along a secular path, social life is more cyclical. Social norms that work for one historical period are disrupted by the advances of technology and the economy, and society has to play catch-up in order to establish new norms.

Since the 1960s the West has experienced a series of liberation movements that have sought to free individuals from the constraints of traditional social norms and moral rules. The sexual revolution, the feminist movement, and the 1980s and 1990s movements in favor of gay and lesbian rights have exploded through the Western world. The liberation sought by each of these movements has concerned social rules, norms, and laws that unduly restricted the options and opportunities of individuals—whether they were young people choosing sexual partners, women seeking career opportunities, or gays seeking recognition of their rights. Pop psychology, from the human-potential movement of the 1960s to the self-esteem trend of the 1980s, sought to free individuals from stifling social expectations.

Both the left and the right participated in the effort to free the individual from restrictive rules, but their points of emphasis tended to be different. To put it simply, the left worried about lifestyles and the right worried about money. The left did not want traditional values to unduly constrain women, minorities, gays, the homeless, people accused of crimes, or any number of other groups marginalized by society. The right, on the other hand, did not want communities putting constraints on what people could do with their property—or, in the United States, what they could do with their guns. Left and right each denounced excessive individualism on the part of the other: those who supported reproductive choice tended to oppose choice in buying guns or gas-guzzling cars; those who wanted unlimited consumer choice were appalled when the restraints on criminals were loosened. But neither was willing to give up its preferred sphere of free choice for the sake of constraining the other.

As people soon discovered, there are serious problems with a culture of unbridled individualism, in which the breaking of rules becomes, in a sense, the only remaining rule. The first has to do with the fact that moral values and social rules are not simply arbitrary constraints on individual choice but the precondition for any kind of cooperative enterprise. Indeed, social scientists have recently begun to refer to a society's stock of shared values as "social capital." Like physical capital (land, buildings, machines) and human capital (the skills and knowledge we carry around in our heads), social capital produces wealth and is therefore of economic value to a national economy. But it is also the prerequisite for all forms of group endeavor that take place in a modern society, from running a corner grocery store to lobbying Congress to raising children. Individuals amplify their own power and abilities by following cooperative rules that constrain their freedom of choice, because these also allow them to communicate with others and to coordinate their actions. Social virtues such as honesty, reciprocity, and the keeping of commitments are not worthwhile just as ethical values; they also have a tangible dollar value and help the groups that practice them to achieve shared ends.

The second problem with a culture of individualism is that it ends up being bereft of community. A community is not formed every time a group of people happen to interact with one another; true communities are bound together by the values, norms, and experiences their members share. The deeper and more strongly held those common values the stronger the sense of community. The trade-off between personal freedom and community, however, does not seem obvious or necessary to many. As people have been liberated from their traditional ties to spouses, families, neighborhoods, workplaces, and churches,

they have expected to retain social connectedness. But they have begun to realize that their elective affinities, which they can slide into and out of at will, have left them feeling lonely and disoriented, longing for deeper and more permanent relationships.

A society dedicated to the constant upending of norms and rules in the name of expanding individual freedom of choice will find itself increasingly disorganized, atomized, isolated, and incapable of carrying out common goals and tasks. The same society that wants no limits on its technological innovation also sees no limits on many forms of personal behavior and the consequence is a rise in crime, broken families, parents' failure to fulfill obligations to children, neighbors' refusal to take responsibility for one another, and citizens' opting out of public life.

WHAT HAPPENED

Beginning in about 1965 a large number of indicators that can serve as negative measures of social capital all started moving upward rapidly at the same time. These could be put under three broad headings: crime, family, and trust.

Americans are aware that crime rates began sometime in the 1960s to climb very rapidly—a dramatic change from the early post–Second World War period, when the U.S. murder and robbery rates actually declined. After declining slightly in the mid-1980s, crime rates spurted upward again in the late 1980s and peaked around 1991–1992. The rates for both violent and property crimes have dropped substantially since then. Indeed, they have fallen most dramatically in the areas where they had risen most rapidly—that is, in big cities like New York, Chicago, Detroit, and Los Angeles.

Although the United States is exceptional among developed countries for its high crime rates, crime rose significantly in virtually all other non-Asian developed countries in approximately the same time period. Violent crime rose rapidly in Canada, Finland, Ireland, the Netherlands, New Zealand, Sweden, and the United Kingdom. With regard to crimes against property, a broader measure of disorder, the United States is no longer exceptional: Canada, Denmark, the Netherlands, New Zealand, and Sweden have ended up with theft rates higher than those in the United States over the past generation.

Of the shifts in social norms that constitute the Great Disruption, some of the most dramatic concern those related to reproduction, the family, and relations between the sexes. Divorce rates moved up sharply across the developed world (except in Italy, where divorce was illegal until 1970, and other Catholic countries); by the 1980s half of all American marriages could be expected to end in divorce, and the ratio of divorced to married people had increased fourfold in just thirty years. Births to unmarried women as a proportion of U.S. live births climbed from under five percent to 32 percent from 1940 to 1995. The figure was close to 60 percent in many Scandinavian countries; the United Kingdom, Canada, and France reached levels comparable to that in the United States.

The combined probabilities of single-parent births, divorce, and the dissolution of cohabiting relationships between parents (a situation common in Europe) meant that in most developed countries ever smaller minorities of children would reach the age of eighteen with both parents remaining in the household. The core reproductive function of the family was threatened as well; fertility has dropped so dramatically in Italy, Spain, and Germany that they stand to lose up to 30 percent of their populations each generation, absent new net immigration.

Finally, anyone who has lived through the 1950s to the 1990s in the United States or another Western country can scarcely fail to recognize the widespread changes in values that have taken place over this period in the direction of increasing individualism. Survey data, along with commonsense observation, indicate that people are much less likely to defer to the authority of an ever-broader range of social institutions. Trust in institutions has consequently decreased markedly. In 1958, 73 percent of Americans surveyed said they trusted the federal government to do what is right either "most of the time" or "just about always"; by 1994 the figure had fallen as low as 15 percent. Europeans, although less anti-statist than Americans, have nonetheless seen similar declines in

confidence in such traditional institutions as the Church, the police, and government. Americans trust one another less as well: although 10 percent more Americans evinced more trust than distrust in surveys done in the early 1960s, by the 1990s the distrusters had an almost 30 percent margin over those expressing trust. It is not clear that either the number of groups or group memberships in civil society declined overall in this period, as the political scientist Robert Putnam has suggested. What is clear, however, is that what I call the radius of trust has declined, and social ties have become less binding and long-lasting. (Readers can obtain more detailed statistical information on the Great Disruption at http://mason.gmu.edu/~ffukuyam/.)

SOME PROPOSED CAUSES OF THE DISRUPTION

Changes as great as these will defy attempts to provide simple explanations. However, the fact that many different social indicators moved across a wide group of industrialized countries at roughly the same time simplifies the analytical task somewhat by pointing us toward a more general level of explanation. When the same phenomena occur in a broad range of countries, we can rule out explanations specific to a single country, such as the effects of the Vietnam War or of Watergate.

Several arguments have been put forward to explain why the phenomena we associate with the Great Disruption occurred. Here are three: They were brought on by increasing poverty and income inequality. They were products of the modern welfare state. They were the result of a broad cultural shift that included the decline of religion and the promotion of individualistic self-gratification over community obligation.

The Great Disruption Was Caused by Poverty and Inequality

The idea that such large changes in social norms could be brought on by economic deprivation in countries that are wealthier than any others in human history might give one pause. Poor people in the United

States have higher absolute standards of living than many Americans of past generations, and more per capita wealth than many people in contemporary Third World countries with more-intact family structures. Poverty rates, after coming down dramatically through the 1960s and rebounding slightly thereafter, have not increased in a way that would explain a huge increase in social disorder.

Those favoring the economic hypothesis argue, of course, that it is not absolute levels of poverty that are the source of the problem: modern societies, despite being richer overall, have become more unequal, or else have experienced economic turbulence and job loss that have led to social dysfunction. A casual glance at the comparative data on divorce and illegitimacy rates shows that this correlation cannot possibly be true in the case of family breakdown. If one looks across the Organization for Economic Cooperation and Development, there is no positive correlation between the level of welfare benefits aimed at increasing economic equality and stable families. Indeed, there is a weak positive correlation between high levels of welfare benefits and illegitimacy, tending to support the argument advanced by American conservatives that the welfare state is the cause of and not the cure for family breakdown. The highest rates of illegitimacy are found in Sweden and Denmark, egalitarian countries that cycle upwards of 50 percent of their gross domestic product through the state. The United States cycles less than 30 percent of GDP through the government and has higher levels of inequality, yet it has lower rates of illegitimacy. Japan and Korea, which have minimal welfare-state protections for poor people, also have two of the lowest rates of divorce and illegitimacy in the OECD.

The notion that poverty and inequality beget crime is a commonplace among politicians and voters in democratic societies who seek reasons for justifying welfare and poverty programs. But although there is plenty of evidence of a broad correlation between income inequality and crime, this hardly constitutes a plausible explanation for rapidly rising crime rates in the West. There was no depression in the period from the 1960s to the 1990s to explain the sudden rise in crime; in fact, the great American postwar crime wave began in a period of full employment and general prosperity. (Indeed, the Great Depression of the 1930s saw *decreasing* levels of violent crime in the United States.) Income inequality rose in the United States during the Great Disruption, but crime has also risen in Western developed countries that have remained more egalitarian than the United States. America's greater economic inequality may to some degree explain why its crime rates are higher than, say, Sweden's in any given year, but it does not explain why Swedish rates began to rise in the same period that America's did. Income inequality, moreover, has continued to increase in the United States in the 1990s, while crime rates have fallen; hence the correlation between inequality and crime becomes negative for this period.

The Great Disruption Was Caused by Mistaken Government Policies

The second general explanation for the increase in social disorder is one made by conservatives: it has been primarily associated with Charles Murray's book *Losing Ground*, and before that with the economist Gary Becker. The argument is the mirror image of the left's: it maintains that the perverse incentives created by the welfare state itself explain the rise in family breakdown and crime. The primary American welfare program targeted at poor women, the Depression-era Aid to Families with Dependent Children, provided welfare payments only to single mothers, and thereby penalized women who married the fathers of their children. The United States abolished AFDC in the welfare-reform act of 1996, in part because of arguments concerning its perverse incentives.

There is little doubt that welfare benefits discourage work and create what economists call "moral hazard." What is less clear is their impact on family structure. Welfare benefits in real terms stabilized and then began to decline in the 1980s, whereas the rate of family breakdown continued unabated through the mid-1990s. One analyst suggests that no more than perhaps 15 percent of family breakdown in the United States can be attributed to AFDC and other welfare programs.

The more fundamental weakness of the conservative argument is that illegitimacy is only part of a much larger story of weakening family ties—a story that includes declining fertility, divorce, cohabitation in place of marriage, the separation of cohabiting couples, and the like. Illegitimacy is primarily though not exclusively associated with poverty in the United States and most other countries. Divorce and cohabitation, however, are much more prevalent among the middle and upper classes throughout the West. It is very difficult to lay soaring divorce rates and declining marriage rates at the government's doorstep, except to the extent that the state made divorce legally easier to obtain.

Similarly, rising crime is seen by many conservatives as a result of the weakening of criminal sanctions, which occurred in the same period. Gary Becker has argued that crime can be seen as another form of rational choice: when payoffs from crime go up or costs (in terms of punishment) go down, more crimes will be committed, and vice versa. Many conservatives have argued that crime began to rise in the 1960s because society had grown permissive and the legal system was "coddling criminals." By this reasoning, the tougher enforcement undertaken by communities across the United States in the 1980s—stiffer penalties, more jails, and in some cases more police officers on the streets—was one important reason for falling crime rates in the 1990s.

Although improved policing methods and stronger penalties may well have had a lot to do with declining crime rates in the 1990s, it is hard to argue that the great upsurge in crime in the 1960s was simply the product of police permissiveness. It is true that the United States constrained its police forces and prosecutors in the interests of the rights of criminal defendants through a series of Supreme Court decisions in the 1960s, most notably *Miranda* v. *Arizona*. But police departments quickly learned how to accommodate what were perfectly legitimate concerns over police procedure. A great deal of recent criminological theory ascribes crime to poor socialization and impulse control relatively early in life. It is not that potential criminals do not respond rationally to punishment; rather, the propensity to commit crimes or to respond to given levels of punishment is heavily influenced by upbringing. What may be more relevant to understanding a sudden upsurge in crime is changes in mediating social institutions such as families, neighborhoods, and schools that were taking place in the same period, and changes in the signals that the broader culture was sending to young people.

The Great Disruption Was Caused by a Broad Cultural Shift

This brings us to cultural explanations, which are the most plausible of the three presented here. Increasing individualism and the loosening of communal controls clearly had a huge impact on family life, sexual behavior, and the willingness of people to obey the law. The problem with this line of explanation is not that culture was not a factor but rather that it gives no adequate account of timing: why did culture, which usually evolves extremely slowly, suddenly mutate with extraordinary rapidity after the mid-1960s?

In Britain and the United States the high point of communal social control was the last third of the nineteenth century, when the Victorian ideal of the patriarchal conjugal family was broadly accepted and adolescent sexuality was kept under tight control. The cultural shift that undermined Victorian morality may be thought of as layered: At the top was a realm of abstract ideas promulgated by philosophers, scientists, artists, academics, and the occasional huckster and fraud, who laid the intellectual groundwork for broad-based changes. The second level was one of popular culture, as simpler versions of complex abstract ideas were promulgated through books, newspapers, and other mass media. Finally, there was the layer of actual behavior, as the new norms implicit in the abstract or popularized ideas were embedded in the actions of large populations.

The decline in Victorian morality can be traced to a number of intellectual developments at the end of the nineteenth century and the beginning of the twentieth, and to a second wave that began in the 1940s. At the highest level of thought, Western rationalism began to undermine itself by concluding that no rational grounds supported universal forms of behavior. This was nowhere more evident than in the thought of Friedrich Nietzsche, the father of modern relativism. Nietzsche in effect argued that man, the "beast with red cheeks," was a value-creating animal, and that the manifold "languages of good and evil" spoken by different human cultures were products of the will, rooted nowhere in truth or reason. The Enlightenment had not led to self-evident truths about right or morality; rather, it had exposed the infinite variability of moral arrangements. Attempts to ground values in nature, or in God, were doomed to be exposed as willful acts on the part of the creators of those values. Nietzsche's aphorism "There are no facts, only interpretations" became the watchword for later generations of relativists under the banners of deconstructionism and postmodernism.

In the social sciences undermining of Victorian values was first the work of psychologists. John Dewey, William James, and John Watson, the founder of the behavioralist school of psychology, for differing reasons all contested the Victorian and Christian notion that human nature was innately sinful, and argued that tight social controls over behavior were not necessary for social order. The behavioralists argued that the human mind was a Lockean tabula rasa waiting to be filled with cultural content; the implication was that human beings were far more malleable through social pressure and policy than people had heretofore believed. Sigmund Freud was, of course, enormously influential in promulgating the idea that neurosis originated in the excessive social repression of sexual behavior. Indeed, the spread of psychoanalysis accustomed an entire generation to talking about sex and seeing everyday psychological problems in terms of the libido and its repression.

The cultural historian James Lincoln Collier points to the years on either side of 1912 as critical to the breakdown of Victorian sexual norms in the Unit-

ed States. It was in this period that a series of new dances spread across the nation, along with the opinion that decent women could be seen in dance clubs; the rate of alcohol consumption increased; the feminist movement began in earnest; movies and the technology of modern mass entertainment appeared; literary modernism, whose core was the perpetual delegitimization of established cultural values, moved into high gear; and sexual mores (judging by what little empirical knowledge we have of this period) began to change. Collier argues that the intellectual and cultural grounds for the sexual revolution of the 1960s had already been laid among American elites by the 1920s. Their spread through the rest of the population was delayed, however, by the Depression and the Second World War, which led people to concentrate more on economic survival and domesticity than on self-expression and self-gratification—which most, in any event, could not afford.

The crucial question about the changes in social norms that occurred during the Great Disruption is therefore not whether they had cultural roots, which they obviously did, but how we can explain the timing and speed of the subsequent transformation. We know that culture tends to change very slowly in comparison with other factors, such as economic conditions, public policies, and ideology. In those cases where cultural norms have changed quickly, such as in rapidly modernizing Third World societies, cultural change is clearly being driven by socioeconomic change and is therefore not an autonomous factor.

So with the Great Disruption: the shift away from Victorian values had been occurring gradually for two or three generations by the time the disruption began; than all of a sudden the pace of change sped up enormously. It is hard to believe that people throughout the developed world simply decided to alter their attitudes toward such elemental issues as marriage, divorce, child-rearing, authority, and community so completely in the space of two or three decades without that shift in values being driven by other powerful forces. Those explanations that link changes in cultural variables to specific events in American history, such as Vietnam, Watergate, or the counterculture of the 1960s, betray an even greater provincialism: Why were social norms also disrupted in other societies, from Sweden and Norway to New Zealand and Spain?

If these broad explanations from the Great Disruption are unsatisfactory, we need to look at its different elements more specifically.

WHY RISING CRIME?

Assuming that increases in the crime rate are not simply a statistical artifact of improved police reporting, we need to ask several questions. Why did crime rates increase so dramatically over a relatively short period and in such a wide range of countries? Why are rates beginning to level off or decline in the United States and several other Western countries?

The first and perhaps most straightforward explanation for rising crime rates from the late 1960s to the 1980s, and declining rates thereafter, is a simple demographic one. Crime tends to be committed overwhelmingly by young males aged fifteen to twenty-four. There is doubtless a genetic reason for this, having to do with male propensities for violence and aggression, and it means that when birth rates go up, crime rates will rise fifteen to twenty-four years later. In the United States the number of young people aged fifteen to twenty-four increased by two million from 1950 to 1960, whereas the next decade added 12 million to this age group—an onslaught that has been compared to a barbarian invasion. Not only did greater numbers of young people increase the pool of potential criminals, but their concentration in a "youth culture" may have led to a more-than-proportional increase in efforts to defy authority.

The Baby Boom, however, is only part of the explanation for rising crime rates in the 1960s and 1970s. One criminologist has estimated that the increase in the U.S. murder rate was ten times as great as would be expected from shifts in the demographic structure alone. Other studies have shown that changes in age structure do not correlate well with increases in crime cross-nationally.

A second explanation links crime rates to modernization and related factors such as urbanization, population density, opportunities for crime, and so forth. It is a commonsense proposition that there will be more auto theft and burglary in large cities than in rural areas, because it is easier for criminals to find automobiles and empty homes in the former than in the latter. But urbanization and a changing physical environment are poor explanations for rising crime rates in developed countries after the 1960s. By 1960 the countries under consideration were already industrialized, urbanized societies; no sudden shift from countryside to city began in 1965. In the United States murder rates are much higher in the South than in the North, despite the fact that the latter tends to be more urban and densely populated. Indeed, violence in the South tends to be a rural phenomenon, and most observers who have looked closely into the matter believe that the explanation for high crime rates there is cultural. Japan, Korea, Hong Kong, and Singapore are among the most densely populated, overcrowded urban environments in the world, and yet they did not experience rising crime rates as that urbanization was occurring. This suggests that the human social environment is much more important than the physical one in determining levels of crime.

A third category of explanation is sometimes euphemistically labeled "social heterogeneity." That is, in many societies crime tends to be concentrated among racial or ethnic minorities; to the extent that societies become more ethnically diverse, as virtually all Western developed countries have over the last two generations, crime rates can be expected to rise. The reason that crime rates are frequently higher among minorities is very likely related, as the criminologists Richard Cloward and Lloyd Ohlin have argued, to the fact that minorities are kept from legitimate avenues of social mobility in ways that members of the majority community are not. In other cases the simple fact of heterogeneity may be to blame: neighborhoods that are too diverse culturally, linguistically, religiously, or ethnically never come together as communities to enforce informal norms on their members. But only part of the blame for rising crime rates in the United States can be placed on immigration.

A fourth explanation concerns the more or less contemporaneous changes in the family. The currently dominant school of American criminology holds that early-childhood socialization is one of the most important factors determining the level of subsequent criminality. That is, most people do not make day-to-day choices about whether or not to commit crimes based on the balance of rewards and risks, as the rational-choice school sometimes suggests. The vast majority of people obey the law, particularly with regard to serious offenses, out of habit that was learned relatively early in life. Most crimes are committed by repeat offenders who have failed to learn this basic self-control. In many cases they are acting not rationally but on impulse. Failing to anticipate consequences, they are underterred by the expectation of punishment.

WHY RISING DISTRUST?

In the realm of trust, values, and civil society, we need to explain two things: why there has been a broad-based decline in trust both in institutions and in other people, and how we can reconcile the shift toward fewer shared norms with an apparent growth in groups and in the density of civil society.

The reasons for the decline of trust in an American context have been debated extensively. Robert Putnam argued early on that it might be associated with the rise of television, since the first cohort that grew up watching television was the one that experienced the most precipitous decline in trust levels. Not only does the content of television breed cynicism in its attention to sex and violence, but the fact that Americans spend an average of more than four hours a day watching TV limits their opportunities for face-to-face social activities.

One suspects, however, that a broad phenomenon like the decline of trust has a number of causes, of which television is only one. Tom Smith, of the National Opinion Research Center, performed a statistical analysis of the survey data on trust and found that the lack of it correlates with low socioeconomic status, minority status, traumatic life events, religious polarization, and youth. Poor and uneducated people tend to be more distrustful than the well-to-do or those who have gone to college. Blacks are significantly more distrustful than whites, and there is some correlation between distrust and immigrant status. The traumatic life events affecting trust include, not surprisingly, being a victim of crime and being in poor health. Distrust is associated both with those who do not attend church and with fundamentalists. And younger people are less trusting than older ones.

Which of these factors has changed since the 1960s in a way that could explain the decrease in trust? Income inequality has increased somewhat, and Eric Uslaner, of the University of Maryland, has suggested that this may account for some of the increase in distrust. But poverty rates have fluctuated without increasing overall in this period, and for the vast majority of Americans the so-called "middle-class squeeze" did not represent a drop in real income so much as a stagnation of earnings.

Crime increased dramatically from the mid-sixties to the mid-nineties, and it makes a great deal of sense that someone who has been victimized by crime, or who watches the daily cavalcade of grisly crime stories on the local TV news, would feel distrust not for immediate friends and family but for the larger world. Hence crime would seem to be an important explanation for the increase in distrust after 1965, a conclusion well supported in more-detailed analyses.

The other major social change that has led to traumatic life experiences has been the rise of divorce and family breakdown. Commonsensically, one would think that children who have experienced the divorce of their parents, or have had to deal with a series of boyfriends in a single-parent household, would tend to become cynical about adults in general, and that this might go far toward explaining the increased levels of distrust that show up in survey data.

Despite the apparent decline in trust, there is evidence that groups and group membership are increasing. The most obvious way to reconcile lower levels of trust with greater levels of group membership is to note a reduction in the radius of trust. It is hard to interpret the data either on values or on civil society in any other way than to suggest that the radius of trust is diminishing, not just in the United States but across the developed world. That is, people continue to share norms and values in ways that constitute social capital, and they join groups and organizations in ever larger numbers. But the groups have shifted dramatically in kind. The authority of most large organizations has declined, and the importance in people's lives of a host of smaller associations has grown. Rather than taking pride in being a member of a powerful labor federation or working for a large corporation, or in having served in the military, people identify socially with a local aerobics class, a New Age sect, a co-dependent support group, or an Internet chat room. Rather than seeking authoritative values in a church that once shaped the society's culture, people are picking and choosing their values on an individual basis, in ways that link them with smaller communities of like-minded folk.

The shift to smaller-radius groups is mirrored politically in the almost universal site of interest groups at the expense of broad-based political parties. Parties like the German Christian Democrats and the British Labour Party take a coherent ideological stand on the whole range of issues facing a society, from national defense to social welfare. Though usually based in a particular social class, these parties unite a broad coalition of interests and personalities. Interest groups, on the other hand, focus on single issues such as saving rain forests or promoting poultry farming in the upper Midwest: they may be transnational in scope, but they are much less authoritative, both in the range of issues they deal with and in the numbers of people they bring together.

Contemporary Americans, and contemporary Europeans as well, seek contradictory goals. They are increasingly distrustful of any authority, political or moral, that would constrain their freedom of choice, but they also want a sense of community and the good things that flow from community, such as mutual recognition, participation, belonging, and identity. Community therefore has to be found in smaller, more flexible groups and organizations whose loyalties and membership can overlap, and where entry and exit entail relatively low costs. People may thus be able to reconcile their contradictory desires for autonomy *and* community. But in this bargain the community they get is smaller and weaker

than most of those that have existed in the past. Each community shares less with neighboring ones, and has relatively little hold on its members. The circle that people can trust is necessarily narrower. The essence of the shift in values at the center of the Great Disruption, then, is the rise of moral individualism and the consequent miniaturization of community. These explanations go partway toward explaining why cultural values changed after the 1960s. But at the Great Disruption's core was a shift in values concerning sex and the family—a shift that deserved special emphasis.

MEN BEHAVING BADLY

Although the role of mother can safely be said to be grounded in biology, the role of father is to a great degree socially constructed. In the words of the anthropologist Margaret Mead, "Somewhere at the dawn of human history, some social invention was made under which males started nurturing females and their young." The male role was founded on the provision of resources; "among human beings everywhere [the male] helps provide food for women and children." Being a learned behavior, the male role in nurturing the family is subject to disruption. Mead wrote,

> But the evidence suggests that we should phrase the matter differently for men and women—that men have to learn to want to provide for others, and this behaviour, being learned, is fragile and can disappear rather easily under social conditions that no longer teach it effectively.

The role of fathers, in other words, varies by culture and tradition from intense involvement in the nurturing and education of children to a more distant presence as protector and disciplinarian to the near absence possible for a paycheck provider. It takes a great deal of effort to separate a mother from her newborn infant; in contrast, it often takes a fair amount of effort to involve a father with his.

When we put kinship and family in this context, it is easier to understand why nuclear families have started to break apart at such a rapid rate over the past two generations. The family bond was relatively fragile, based on an exchange of the woman's fertility for the man's resources. Prior to the Great Disruption, all Western societies had in place a complex series of formal and informal laws, rules, norms, and obligations to protect mothers and children by limiting the freedom of fathers to simply ditch one family and start another. Today many people have come to think of marriage as a kind of public celebration of a sexual and emotional union between two adults, which is why gay marriage has become a possibility in the United States and other developed countries. But it is clear that historically the institution of marriage existed to give legal protection to the mother-child unit, and to ensure that adequate economic resources were passed from the father to allow the children to grow up to be viable adults.

What accounts for the breakdown of these norms constraining male behavior, and of the bargain that rested on them? Two very important changes occurred sometime during the early postwar period. The first involved advances in medical technology—that is, birth control and abortion—that permitted women to better control their own reproduction. The second was the movement of women into the paid labor force in most industrialized countries and the steady rise in their incomes—hourly, median, and lifetime—relative to men's over the next thirty years.

The significance of birth control was not simply that it lowered fertility. Indeed, if the effect of birth control is to reduce the number of unwanted pregnancies, it is hard to explain why its advent should have been accompanied by an explosion of illegitimacy and a rise in the abortion rate, or why the use of birth control is positively correlated with illegitimacy across the OECD.

The main impact of the Pill and the sexual revolution that followed it was, as the economists Janet Yellen, George Akerlof, and Michael Katz have shown, to dramatically alter calculations about the risks of sex, and thereby to change *male* behavior. The reason that the rates of birth-control use, abortion, and illegitimacy went up in tandem is that a fourth rate—the number of shotgun marriages—declined substantially at the same time. By these

economists' calculations, in the period 1965–1969 some 59 percent of white brides and 25 percent of black brides were pregnant at the altar. Young people were, evidently, having quite a lot premarital sex in those years, but the social consequences of out-of-wedlock childbearing were mitigated by the norm of male responsibility for the children produced. By the period 1980–1984 the percentages had dropped to 42 and 11, respectively. Because birth control and abortion permitted women for the first time to have sex without worrying about the consequences, men felt liberated from norms requiring them to look after the women they got pregnant.

The second factor altering male behavior was the entry of women into the paid labor force. That female incomes should be related to family breakdown is an argument accepted by many economists, and elaborated most fully by Gary Becker in his work *A Treatise on the Family* (1981). The assumption behind this view is that many marriage contracts are entered into with imperfect information: once married, men and women discover that life is not a perpetual honeymoon, that their spouse's behavior has changed from what it was before marriage, or that their own expectations for partners have changed. Trading in a spouse for someone new, or getting rid of an abusive mate, had been restricted by the fact that many women lacking job skills or experience were dependent on husbands. As female earnings rose, women became better able to support themselves and to raise children without husbands. Rising female incomes also increase the opportunity costs of having children, and therefore lower fertility. Fewer children mean less of what Becker characterizes as the joint capital in the marriage, and hence makes divorce more likely.

A subtler consequence of women's entering the labor force was that the norm of male responsibility was further weakened. In divorcing a dependent wife, a husband would have to face the prospect of either paying alimony or seeing his children slip into poverty. With many wives earning incomes that rivaled those of their husbands, this became less of an issue. The weakening norm of male responsibility, in turn, reinforced the need for women to arm themselves with job skills so as not to be dependent on increasingly unreliable husbands. With a substantial probability that a first marriage will end in divorce, contemporary women would be foolish not to prepare themselves for work.

The decline of nuclear families in the West had strongly negative effects on social capital and was related to an increase in poverty for people at the bottom of the social hierarchy, to increasing levels of crime, and finally to declining trust. But pointing to the negative consequences for social capital of changes in the family is in no way to blame women for these problems. The entry of women into the workplace, the steady closing of the earnings gap with men, and the greater ability of women to control fertility are by and large good things. The most important shift in norms was in the one that dictated male responsibility for wives and children. Even if the shift was triggered by birth control and rising female incomes, men were to blame for the consequences. And it is not as if men always behaved well prior to that: the stability of traditional families was often bought at a high price in terms of emotional and physical distress, and also in lost opportunities—costs that fell disproportionately on the shoulders of women.

On the other hand, these sweeping changes in gender roles have not been the unambiguously good thing that some feminists pretend. Losses have accompanied gains, and those losses have fallen disproportionately on the shoulders of children. This should not surprise anyone: given the fact that female roles have traditionally centered on reproduction and children, we could hardly expect that the movement of women out of the household and into the workplace would have no consequences for families.

Moreover, women themselves have often been the losers in this bargain. Most labor-market gains for women in the 1970s and 1980s were not in glamorous Murphy Brown kinds of jobs but in low-end service-sector jobs. In return for meager financial independence, many women found themselves abandoned by husbands who moved on to younger wives or girlfriends. Because older women are considered less sexually attractive than older men, they had much lower chances of remarrying than did the husbands who left them. The widening of the gap among men between rich and poor had its counterpart among women; educated, ambitious, and talented women broke down barriers, proved they could succeed at male occupations, and saw their incomes rise; but many of their less-educated, less-ambitious, and less-talented sisters saw the floor collapse under them, as they tried to raise children by themselves while in low-paying, dead-end jobs or on welfare. Our consciousness of this process has been distorted by the fact that the women who talk and write and shape the public debate about gender issues come almost exclusively from the former category.

In contrast, men have on balance come out about even. Although many have lost substantial status and income, others (and sometimes the same ones) have quite happily been freed of burdensome responsibilities for wives and children. Hugh Hefner did not invent the Playboy lifestyle in the 1950s; casual access to multiple women has been enjoyed by powerful, wealthy, high-status men throughout history, and has been one of the chief motives for seeking power, wealth, and high status in the first place. What changed after the 1950s was that many rather ordinary men were allowed to live out the fantasy lives of hedonism and serial polygamy formerly reserved to a tiny group at the very top of society. One of the greatest frauds perpetrated during the Great Disruption was the notion that the sexual revolution was gender-neutral, benefiting women and men equally, and that it somehow had a kinship with the feminist revolution. In fact the sexual revolution served the interests of men, and in the end put sharp limits on the gains that women might otherwise have expected from their liberation from traditional roles.

RECONSTRUCTING SOCIAL ORDER

How can we rebuild social capital in the future? The fact that culture and public policy give societies some control over the pace and degree of disruption is not in the long run an answer to how social order will be established at the beginning of the twenty-first century. Japan and some Catholic countries have been able to hold on to traditional family values longer than Scandinavia or the English-speaking world, and this may have saved them some of the social costs experienced by the latter. But it is hard to imagine that they will be able to hold out over the coming generations, much less re-establish anything like the nuclear family of the industrial era, with the father working and the mother staying at home to raise children. Such an outcome would not be desirable, even if it were possible.

We appear to be caught, then, in unpleasant circumstances: going forward seems to promise ever-increasing levels of disorder and social atomization, at the same time that our line of retreat has been cut off. Does this mean that contemporary liberal societies are fated to descend into increasing moral decline and social anarchy, until they somehow implode? Were Edmund Burke and other critics of the Enlightenment right that anarchy was the inevitable product of the effort to replace tradition and religion with reason?

The answer, in my view, is no, for the very simple reason that we human beings are by nature designed to create moral rules and social order for ourselves. The situation of normlessness—what the sociologist Emile Durkheim labeled "anomie"—is intensely uncomfortable for us, and we will seek to create new rules to replace the ones that have been undercut. If technology makes certain old forms of community difficult to sustain, then we will seek out new ones, and we will use our reason to negotiate arrangements to suit our underlying interests, needs, and passions.

To understand why the present situation isn't as hopeless as it may seem, we need to consider the origins of social order per se, on a more abstract level. Many discussions of culture treat social order as if it were a static set of rules handed down from earlier generations. If one was stuck in a low-social-capital or low-trust country, one could do nothing about it. It is true, of course, that public policy is relatively limited in its ability to manipulate culture, and that the best public policies are those shaped by an awareness of cultural constraints. But culture is a dynamic force, one that is constantly being remade—if not by governments then by the interactions of the thousands of decentralized individuals who make up a society.

Although culture tends to evolve more slowly than formal social and political institutions, it nonetheless adapts to changing circumstances.

What we find is that order and social capital have two broad bases of support. The first is biological, and emerges from human nature itself. There is an increasing body of evidence coming out of life sciences that the standard social-science model is inadequate, and that human beings are born with pre-existing cognitive structures and age-specific capabilities for learning that lead them naturally into society. There is, in other words, such a thing as human nature. For the sociologists and anthropologists, the existence of human nature means that cultural relativism needs to be rethought, and that it is possible to discern cultural and moral universals that, if used judiciously, might help to evaluate particular cultural practices. Moreover, human behavior is not nearly as plastic and therefore manipulable as their disciplines have assumed for much of this century. For the economists, human nature implies that the sociological view of human being as inherently social beings is more accurate than their own individualistic model. And for those who are neither sociologists nor economists, an essential humanity confirms a number of commonsense understandings about the way people think and act that have been resolutely denied by earlier generations of social scientists—for example, that men and women are different by nature, that we are political and social creatures with moral instincts, and the like. This insight is extremely important, because it means that social capital will tend to be generated by human beings as a matter of instinct.

The biological revolution that has been under way in the second half of the twentieth century has multiple sources. The most startling advances have been made at the level of molecular biology and biochemistry, where the discovery of the structure of DNA has led to the emergence of an entire industry devoted to genetic manipulation. In neurophysiology great advances have been made in understanding the chemical and physiological bases of psychological phenomena, including an emerging view that the brain is not a general-purpose calculating machine but a highly modular organ with specially adapted capabilities. And finally, on the level of macro behavior, a tremendous amount of new work has been done in animal ethology, behavioral genetics, primatology, and evolutionary psychology and anthropology, suggesting that certain behavioral patterns are much more general than previously believed. For instance, the generalization that females tend to be more selective than males in their choice of mates proves to be true not only across all known human cultures but across virtually all known species that reproduce sexually. It would seem to be only a matter of time before the micro and macro levels of research are connected: with the mapping of complete gene sequences for fruit flies, nematodes, rats, and eventually human beings, it will be possible to turn individual gene sequences on and off and directly observe their effects on behavior.

The second basis of support for social order is human reason, and reason's ability to spontaneously generate solutions to problems of social cooperation. Mankind's natural capabilities for creating social capital do not explain how social capital arises in specific circumstances. The creation of particular rules of behavior is the province of culture rather than nature, and in the cultural realm we find that order is frequently the result of a process of horizontal negotiation, argument, and dialogue among individuals. Order does not need to proceed from the top down—from a lawgiver (or, in contemporary terms, a state) handing down laws or a priest promulgating the word of God.

Neither natural nor spontaneous order is sufficient in itself to produce the totality of rules that constitutes social order per se. Either needs to be supplemented at crucial junctures by hierarchial authority. But when we look back in human history, we see that self-organizing individuals have continuously been creating social capital for themselves, and have managed to adapt to technological and economic changes greater than those faced by Western societies over the past two generations.

Perhaps the easiest way to get a handle on the Great Disruption's future is to look briefly a great disruptions or the past. Indices of social order have increased and decreased over time, suggesting that although social capital may often seem to be in the process of depletion, its stock has increased in certain historical periods. The political scientist Ted Robert Gurr estimates that homicide rates in England were three times as high in the thirteenth century as in the seventeenth, and three times as high in the seventeenth as in the nineteenth; in London they were twice as high in the early nineteenth century as in the 1970s. Both conservatives decrying moral decline and liberals celebrating increased individual choice sometimes talk as if there had been since the early 1600s a steady movement away from Puritan values. But although a secular trend toward greater individualism has been evident over this long time period, many fluctuations in behavior have suggested that societies are perfectly capable of increasing the degree of constraint on individual choice through moral rules.

The Victorian period in Britain and America may seem to many to be the embodiment of traditional values, but Victorianism was in fact a radical movement that emerged in reaction to widespread social disorder at the beginning of the nineteenth century—a movement that deliberately sought to create new social rules and instill virtues in populations that were seen as wallowing in degeneracy.

It would be wrong to assert that the greater social order that came to prevail in Britain and America during the Victorian period was simply the result of changing moral norms. In this period both societies established modern police forces, which replaced the hodgepodge of local agencies and poorly trained deputies that had existed at the beginning of the nineteenth century. In the United States after the Civil War the police focused attention on such minor offenses against public order as public drinking, vagrancy, loitering, and the like, leading to a peak in arrests for this kind of behavior around 1870. Toward the end of the century many states had begun to establish systems of universal education, which sought to put all American children into free public schools—a process that began somewhat later in Britain. But the essential change that took place was a matter of values rather than institutions. At the core of Victorian morality was the inculcation of impulse control in young people—the shaping of what economists today would call their preferences—so that they would not indulge in pleasures like casual sex, alcohol, and gambling.

There are other examples from other cultures of moral renovation. The feudal Tokugawa period in Japan—when power was held by various *daimyo*, or warrior lords—was one of insecurity and frequent violence. The Meiji Restoration, which took place in 1868, established a single centralized state, and stamped out once and for all the kind of banditry that had taken place in feudal Japan. The country developed a new moral system as well. We think of a custom like the lifetime employment that is practiced by large Japanese firms as an ancient cultural tradition, but in fact it dates back only to the late nineteenth century, and was fully implemented among large companies only after the Second World War. Before then there was a high degree of labor mobility; skilled craftsmen in particular were in short supply and constantly on the move from one company to another. Large Japanese companies like Mitsui and Mitsubishi found that they could not attract the skilled labor they needed, and so, with the help of the government, they embarked on a successful campaign to elevate the virtue of loyalty above others.

Could the pattern experienced in the second half of the nineteenth century in Britain and America, or in Japan, repeat itself in the next generation or two? There is growing evidence that the Great Disruption has run its course, and that the process of re-norming has already begun. Growth in the rates of increase in crime, divorce, illegitimacy, and distrust has slowed substantially, and in the 1990s has even reversed in many of the countries that experienced an explosion of disorder over the past two generations. This is particularly true in the United States, where levels of crime are down a good 15 percent from their peaks in the early 1990s. Divorce rates peaked in the early 1980s, and births to single mothers appear to have stopped increasing. Welfare rolls have diminished almost as dramatically as crime rates, in response

both to the 1996 welfare-reform measures and to the opportunities provided by a nearly full-employment economy in the 1990s. Levels of trust in both institutions and individuals have also recovered significantly since the early 1990s.

How far might this re-norming of society go? We are much more likely to see dramatic changes in levels of crime and trust than in norms regarding sex, reproduction, and family life. Indeed, the process of re-norming in the first two spheres is already well under way. With regard to sex and reproduction, however, the technological and economic conditions of our age make it extremely doubtful that anything like a return to Victorian values will take place. Strict rules about sex make sense in a society in which unregulated sex has a high probability of leading to pregnancy and having a child out of wedlock is likely to lead to destitution, if not early death, for both mother and child. The first of these conditions disappeared with birth control; the second was greatly mitigated, though not eliminated, by a combination of female incomes and welfare subsidies. Although the United States has cut back sharply on welfare, no one is about to propose making birth control illegal or reversing the movement of women into the workplace. Nor will the individual pursuit of rational self-interest solve the problems posed by declining fertility: it is precisely the rational interest of parents in their children's long-term life chances that induces them to have fewer children. The importance of kinship as a source of social connectedness will probably continue to decline, and the stability of nuclear families is likely never to fully recover. Those societies, such as Japan and Korea, that have until now bucked this trend more likely to shift toward Western practices than the reverse.

Some religious conservatives hope, and liberals fear, that the problem of moral decline will be resolved by a large-scale return to religious orthodoxy—a Western version of the Ayatollah Khomeini returning to Iran on a jetliner. For a variety of reasons this seems unlikely. Modern societies are so culturally diverse that it is not clear whose version of orthodoxy would prevail. Any true orthodoxy is likely to be seen as a threat to large and important groups in the society, and hence would neither get very far nor serve as a basis for a widening radius of trust. Rather than integrating society, a conservative religious revival might in fact accelerate the movement toward fragmentation and moral miniaturization: the various varieties of Protestant fundamentalism would argue among themselves over doctrine; orthodox Jews would become more orthodox; Muslims and Hindus might start to organize themselves as political-religious communities, and the like.

A return to religiosity is far more likely to take a more benign form, one that in some respects has already started to appear in many parts of the United States. Instead of community arising as a by-product of rigid belief, people will come to religion because of their desire for community. In other words, people will return to religion not necessarily because they accept the truth of revelation but precisely because the absence of community and the transience of social ties in the secular world make them hungry for ritual and cultural tradition. They will help the poor or their neighbors not necessarily because doctrine tells them they must but rather because they want to serve their communities and find that faith-based organizations are the most effective means of doing so. They will repeat ancient prayers and re-enact age-old rituals not because they believe that they were handed down by God but rather because they want their children to have the proper values, and because they want to enjoy the comfort and the sense of shared experience that ritual brings. In this sense they will not be taking religion seriously on its own terms but will use religion as a language with which to express their moral beliefs. Religion becomes a source of ritual in a society that has been stripped bare of ceremony, and thus is a reasonable extension of the natural desire for social relatedness with which all human beings are born. It is something that modern, rational, skeptical

people can take seriously in much the way that they celebrate national independence, dress up in traditional ethnic garb, or read the classics of their own cultural tradition. Understood in these terms, religion loses its hierarchical character and becomes a manifestation of spontaneous order.

Religion is one of the two main sources of an enlarged radius of trust. The other is politics. In the West, Christianity first established the principle of the universality of human dignity, a principle that was brought down from the heavens and turned into a secular doctrine of universal human equality by the Enlightenment. Today we ask politics to bear nearly the entire weight of this enterprise, and it has done a remarkably good job. Those nations built on universal liberal principles have been surprisingly resilient over the past 200 years, despite frequent setbacks and shortcomings. A political order based on Serb ethnic identity or Twelver Shi'ism will never grow beyond the boundaries of some corner of the Balkans or the Middle East, and could certainly never become the governing principle of large, diverse, dynamic, and complex modern societies like those that make up, for example, the Group of Seven.

There seem to be two parallel processes at work. In the political and economic sphere history appears to be progressive and directional, and at the end of the twentieth century has culminated in liberal democracy as the only viable choice for technologically advanced societies. In the social and moral sphere, however, history appears to be cyclical, with social order ebbing and flowing over the course of generations. There is nothing to guarantee upturns in the cycle; our only reason for hope is the very powerful innate human capacity for reconstituting social order. On the success of this process of reconstruction depends the upward direction of the arrow of History.

CHAPTER 40

INSTRUMENTALISM AND THE SOCIAL CONSEQUENCES OF TECHNOLOGICAL CHOICE

WILLIAM GRAVES III

We are deeply implicated in social structures and practices that are, in large part, the consequence of technological choices. Nevertheless, questions regarding such choices are rarely pursued by mainstream sociological analyses. This is generally because the nature of these choices *appears to be* essentially and narrowly instrumental: Particular tools, skills, and techniques are developed and used for the purpose of solving technically defined problems, rather than socially or culturally defined problems. In this way, we are chronically predisposed to focus on the utilitarian means, rather than to contemplate the possible range of social and cultural consequences of particular technological choices.

It is true that instrumentalism has been the target of philosophical critiques of technological conceptions of modern society (Winner 1986; Feeberg 1991; Weizenbaum 1991; Shields 1997a, 1997b), but this does not change the fact that our everyday, taken-for-granted consciousness of technology rests on a fundamentally instrumentalist view of technological choice. It is not at all accidental that we so readily invoke such notions as "productivity," "efficiency," "speed," "ease," "convenience," and, more tellingly, "necessity" when we rationalize our own technological choices. These instrumental notions represent our

---

Original paper written for this volume; some passages have been excerpted from William Graves III, "Ideologies of Computerization," pp. 65–87 in M. A. Shields (ed.), *Work and Technology in Higher Education* (Hillsdale, NJ: Lawrence Erlbaum Associates, 1995).

chronic search for more rational means to ends that we have already accepted as clear and unambiguous.

In one sense, then, an instrumentalist view simply means that we purposely acquire tools to solve predefined problems, not to rethink or redefine them. And this aspect of instrumentalism does serve importantly to reinforce our sense of continuity and mastery of our life world. But closely related to this is another, more troublesome aspect of instrumentalist views of technological choice, which has been called "technocratic consciousness" or "technocratic ideology" (Habermas [1968], 1970a, 1970b): A foundational belief in our ability to transform moral dilemmas, social conflicts and cultural contradictions into purely technical problems that are resolvable *in principle* by concrete technical means. Reinforcing our sense of continuity and mastery, this type of consciousness leads to an uncritical belief in the possibility of total technical control over the entire scope of human problems.

From a sociological point of view, however, all instrumentalist views of technological choice fail to consider that all forms of social action are bound in space and tie both by unacknowledged conditions and unintended consequences (Giddens 1979, 1984). All social actors are knowledgeable, goal-directed agents, but as Karl Marx [1852] 1972, p. 595) compellingly demonstrated, they do not control absolutely either the conditions or the consequences of their own choices. Nevertheless there is no question that both individuals and collectives chronically *do* seek such predictability and control. This, then, leads to key questions in the empirical analysis of the role of technological choice in the production and reproduction of social order—*how much control* do social actors and groups wield over the conditions and consequences of institutionally defined technological choices? And *how* is this control socially articulated and managed?

In this chapter, I will address these questions through discussion and analyses of specific case studies of computerization within formal educational settings. In answer to the second part of the question—*how is control articulated and managed?*—I will attempt to show that a particular kind of instrumentalism I call "ideologies of computerization" establishes the conceptual framework, the fundamental institutional conditions, in terms of which social actors understand, adopt, evaluate, and use computers within formal settings.

In answer to the first part of the question—how much control do social actors and groups wield over the conditions and consequences of institutionally defined technological choices?—I will attempt to show that social actors can and do challenge institutionally defined "ideologies of computerization" (conditions) in ways that open up possibilities for unanticipated social change (consequences). However, I will also attempt to show that such challenges can only be effective when they are informed by a recognizably alternative "ideology of computerization." In a profound sense, I will conclude, our everyday social practices and situated understandings of technology never really escape the basic premises of instrumentalism.

THE ETHNOGRAPHIC APPROACH: SETTINGS, DATA, AND METHODS

From the mid 1980s through the early 1990s, our social science research team at Brown University conducted a series of empirical studies of university efforts to create a comprehensively computerized environment that would integrate all settings, all members, and all activities. We conducted intensive ethnographic studies in a number of different settings undergoing computerization—a university library, six different academic departments at Brown University, two high schools, three clinical departments in the university's teaching hospital, and two undergraduate dormitories (see Shields 1995 for an overview).

Although some survey work was conducted, data collection in all settings relied primarily upon participant observation, informal, unstructured interviews, and formal, structured interviews. The purpose of ethnographic methods is to understand how social actors assign value and significance to their own and others' activities within concrete settings. Of greatest importance, participant observation and on-site informal interviewing allows us to develop an understanding of taken-for-granted concepts, principles, and relationships that are easily overlooked by researchers conducting surveys. In keeping with these basic principles, participant observation, and on-site informal interviewing provided our research team with the preliminary data for designing structured interview schedules and survey questionnaires.

In this chapter, I will draw mainly upon the data collected in two separate studies. The first was an ethnographic study of the computerization of records in the Brown University library system (Graves and Bader 1988). The second was an ethnographic study of the development and use of computers to support curricular development and instruction in two high schools (Graves and Palombo 1989; Nyce and Bader 1995).

TECHNOLOGICAL UTOPIANISM AND IDEOLOGIES OF COMPUTERIZATION

In an amazingly brief period of time, so-called "personal" computers and computer networks have become pervasive features of our everyday lives. In the mid 1980s, however, when we began our Brown University studies, affordable desktop computers with expansive multifunctional capabilities were just beginning to enter the lives of our research subjects. Computer networks were in their infancy. Very few of us had the knowledge or experience that many secondary school students routinely acquire today. A fair number of our research subjects had never used a computer before. Those who did have experience tended to be either computer specialists or people whose knowledge and experience was limited to very specialized, highly structured tasks at the dumb terminals of centralized and invisible mainframe computers. But the situation was quickly changing. We were, it was often claimed, caught up in the sweep of a "computer revolution."

By the end of the decade, John Sculley (1989, p. 1061) of Apple could speak with ringing confidence of unleashing "an avalanche of personal creativity and achievement" and of "thousands of ideas to harvest" that would "represent a rebirth and revival of learning and culture unleashed by new technologies." Although there were notable dissenters, Sculley was evoking the spirit of a pervasive technological utopianism. Only a very few social scientists were interested in the empirical investigation of such widespread claims—asking *how* would the new technologies accomplish all of this, and *why* did such an "avalanche" of creativity and achievement depend on the development and use of "new technologies" in the first place.

Sherry Turkle (1984) provided the most interesting suggestion for an approach to the empirical study of these questions. Users of personal computers, she held, discover such a stunning array of possible functions that they are liberated from the conceptual constraints of a narrow instrumentalism. The personal computer, she convincingly argued, like a "Rorschach ink blot test, is a powerful projective medium" (p. 14 and *passim*). Familiarity with computers, then, could challenge our most basic instrumentalist presuppositions about the nature of technological choice.

In the Brown University studies, we did encounter some empirical support for Turkle's claims. Most dramatically, McQuillan (1995) showed that substantial changes in teaching, learning, and evaluation activities within one university setting were the direct consequence of just such a "projection" of new possibilities *before* computers were actually incorporated into these activities. On the other hand, Anderson, McClard, and Larkin (1995, p. 158) showed that when a networked environment of powerful new desktop computers was introduced into an undergraduate dormitory, students selectively structured their uses of the new resources to reinforce "preestab-

lished routines of student social and academic life." The first study provided empirical support for Turkle's thesis and granted some credence to Sculley's technological utopianism, but the second study did neither. How are we to understand this?

We need to begin by further pursuing Turkle's view. If a computer is a type of "projective medium," then what kinds of understandings and practices do we actually find projected via this medium and what is their origin? Anderson, McClard, and Larkin's ethnographic research documents a nondirective technological intervention into the student life world of the dormitory. The participant–observers play a key role in technical instruction and support within the dorm, but their research requires them to facilitate and document student-defined choices and strategies, not to intervene in the making of those choices. In such a nondirectively defined context, we should not be surprised to see that the understandings and practices actually projected via these media are their "preestablished routines of student social and academic life" (1995, p. 158).

In McQuillan's study, however, we have the case of a professor who was recruited by systems developers, engineers, and technical support staff to assist in the development and incorporation of new computer resources into instructional settings. Actively involved from the early stages of technical development, this professor's academically defined understandings and practices eventually converged with the systems developers' technically defined vision. The instrument for this convergence was the technical architecture of the newly developed "intermedia." This early set of hypertext applications developed at Brown would allow for the creation of an infinite set of cross-referencing links connecting texts, images, student commentary, student-created links, professor's commentary, professor-created links, and, finally, commentaries upon links and upon other commentaries. Instructional activities would be organized to create, analyze, and discuss such cross-referenced corpora of texts and images.

All that the systems developers needed was a technically informed faculty member to redefine pedagogical understandings and practices to conform to the technical logic of this new resource. Professor

Landow accomplished just that. And he himself would later write about the essence of this accomplishment—"Hypertext, by blurring the distinction between author and reader, allows, encourages, even demands new modes of reading, writing, teaching and learning" (Landow 1990, p. 407).

Much more had been blurred in this case than a distinction between author and reader, however. The distinction between software developer and teacher of literature had become blurred in Landow's own academic understandings and instructional practices. What is significant here is that Landow was able to move so easily from "allows" (technological possibilities) to "demands" (technological necessity) in his discussions of a particular form of technology. Such a shift from reflections on technological possibility to assertions of technological necessity is at the very heart of a type of instrumentalism I that call "ideologies of computerization."

An *ideology of computerization* is an imaginatively constituted understanding of the utility of computers that emerges out of reflections on the technical properties of the thing-in-itself. Central to any ideology of computerization is the assumption that the essential properties and capacities of computers direct or determine patterns of thought and action at the individual and collective levels of experience. In their most commonly encountered forms, ideologies of computerization are presented as general assessments of specific computing tools on the basis of technical specifications under imagined and, quite often, unspecified conditions of use.

Since the mid 1980s, an increasing number of faculty, students, and nontechnical staff in schools aggressively promoting academic computing have been dependent on a new cadre of technical support specialists. These specialists have been hired to promote the full range of activities that support instruction and research. For those who are interested in the potential of new technologies but have little experience, the advice, guidance, and support these specialists routinely provide is valuable and often key to the attainment of computing objectives.

At the same time, I and many other technically unsophisticated users periodically become aware of strong expectations that we subordinate our notions of possibility and choice to the presumed logic of particular tools. We become most aware of the normative force of these expectations when we feel we have successfully incorporated a tool into our work routines, but technical support staff advise us that we are "underutilizing" its "capabilities" or using an "inefficient" system, the "wrong" application, or an "inappropriate" technical feature for the particular objectives we seek to attain. In such cases, their ideological message to us is clear—we may *believe* that we have solved our problems, but *until* we have rationally grasped the "intrinsic" connection between the logic of our practices and the logic of our tools, we really have not.

THE CONDITIONS AND CONSEQUENCES OF TECHNOLOGICAL CHOICE

In many settings, although not necessarily in all, administrators and systems developers responsible for computerization will not only present technological choice as technological necessity, but they will also argue that this technological "necessity" must result in a fundamental restructuring of the organization of work. The logic of practices must conform to the logic of these tools.

As the following case study of a university library illustrates, administrators may believe that there are very good grounds for assuming that technological choice must result in the restructuring of the organization of work. At the same time, end users may challenge this technologically mediated interpretation of the "necessary" link between the conditions and consequences of technological choice on equally plausible grounds. They may respond by questioning the legitimacy of the institution's definition of "conditions," "consequences" or the presumed "link" between them.

Case 1: Technological Choice and Routine Record Keeping in a University Library

In an ethnographic study of work and information technologies in the Brown University library system, we found that library administrators had begun instituting organizational changes and restructuring work practices long before "JOSIAH," their new electronic catalog and record-keeping system, had actually entered the workplace. This computing system was still in development and no one could be certain about its direct effects on the character and organization of library work.

Nevertheless, systems developers and library administrators early envisioned the ideal system as a centralized, multifunctional information system that would facilitate the electronic consolidation of all types of paper and electronic records throughout the library system. Behind this vision was a long-range strategic mission shared by many libraries—to provide and gain immediate access to up-to-date library data and information inside or outside the walls of the library (cf. Sack 1986) and to collaborate with other libraries in the development of universal standards for the classification of shared electronic library data (cf. Hass 1980; Jones 1985).

As in many contexts of automation throughout America, this strategic vision was informed by administrative assumptions that a comprehensive, multifunctional computing system would "enhance productivity" and "reduce error" by eliminating redundancies in the traditional library files. This would simplify routine record keeping and eliminate "costly" duplication of effort. In effect, a preconceived understanding of the logic of the computing technology itself would serve as the rationale for redefining institutional structures and practices.

And this dominant ideology of computerization did direct and shape early changes in organizational structure, job definition, and record-keeping practices. In anticipation of future technically defined organizational changes, the position of "Library Systems/Planning Officer," the key administrator responsible for "JOSIAH," was elevated one tier in the institutional hierarchy and now reported directly to the chief executive of the library system, the University Librarian. The University Librarian assigned this position direct responsibility for coordinating several steering and advisory committees composed of the top administrators of the major functional divisions within the library—"Public Services," "Special Collections," and "Technical Services." During the course of our fieldwork, a number of staff librarians reflected on

the future implications of this structural change. As one librarian told us:

> *Library systems positions have really been about technical support. But this change doesn't seem to be about supporting our efforts. It looks to many of us like a major power shift that's going to result in some big changes in the library down the road. . . .*

This was not idle speculation, for the key changes had already begun. The department directly responsible for the library system's card catalog files, the authoritative central source of information on library holdings, had simplified and accelerated its cataloging and maintenance procedures. In the past, professionally trained catalog librarians had painstakingly created a set of original catalog cards for each new acquisition. The goal of this work was to provide staff and patrons with extremely detailed information about each holding, so that patrons could easily locate the *exact* item they wanted and staff could quickly track cross-referenced materials and distinguish between different editions of the same titles in the collections. Creating such original catalog copy was time-consuming and required detailed knowledge of the collections, of the history of changes in cataloging practices, and of current standardized cataloging rules. Since the beginning of the 1980s, however, original cataloging by professional librarians was steadily giving way to "copy cataloging" by nonprofessional library staff. "Copy catalogers" in the Catalog Department are responsible for finding in the RLIN database an existing authoritative full record to match the new item to be cataloged. Unlike catalog librarians, copy catalogers do not create original records, do not make major changes in records, and do not do research on an item to create notes or additional added entries for the files. When a copy cataloger finds a full record already created by the Library of Congress or another authoritative source, that record will be used without major changes. During the year of our study in 1986, approximately 80 percent of all new items cataloged were done by "copy catalogers" working on RLIN, a shared university electronic database of bibliographic records.

During the time of our study, the Catalog department instituted an even more simplified type of copy cataloging called "fast cat." The distinctive feature of this process is that no time is spent before actually ordering catalog cards to check the information on the matched copy against classificatory or descriptive information in the card catalog files. This represented a major change from the recent past when professional catalog librarians routinely changed and expanded the new records to conform to the structures of the library's existing card catalog files and to the specificities of Brown's own collections. The traditional authority of local cataloging and of the library's central card catalog files had finally been subordinated completely to the authority of an electronic database shared by peer research libraries.

Radical changes in cataloging clearly represented the leading edge of a major shift in institutional focus. Collections management throughout the library evolved steadily away from the central card catalog files towards present and future forms of electronic record keeping. Department heads and work-unit supervisors began instituting changes to filing systems and record-keeping practices that would decrease systemic reliance on the card catalog files and simplify record-keeping tasks. In the Serials Department, for example, an abbreviated computer-printed index of all serials called the "Brown University Serials Holding List" began to replace the card catalog files and related serials files as the authoritative information resource. At the time of our study, Serials staff no longer produced or updated detailed holdings records for the central card catalog files. And within a year, Serials catalogers were no longer producing full card catalog records for any new items.

In the Acquisitions Department, an "in-process" filing system was created that incorporated temporary cataloging records and detailed information on monographic series. The purpose of the new file was to centralize all information about the status and location of new acquisitions within the Department itself in order to reduce or eliminate the need for staff to rely upon the central card catalog files or any other files outside of the Department. Thus, Catalog, Acquisitions, and Serials were all beginning to develop new record-keeping systems that relied heavily on information to be found in the RLIN shared electronic database. At the same time, each Department was trying to centralize local files, weed out redundancies within files, close old files, and, in general, simplify all activities involved in the creation of new records and the routine uses of files.

When the long-awaited "JOSIAH" finally arrived, however, it was considerably more limited in scope and functionality than the administration's ideology of computerization had presupposed. Its database did not incorporate all of the most important types of library records; the structure of its applications did not facilitate the routine tasks of most functional areas of the library. And it would take a minimum of three more years of intensive data entry to create a usable database of the library's holdings in the general collections.

Nevertheless, by the time the new computer system was implemented, technologically defined directions of change that were based on the essential concepts of "centralization," "uniformity," and "nonredundancy" were already clearly defined and understood. This was as true for staff who had no direct access to the new technology as it was for those whose work would depend on intensive use of it. A dominant ideology of computerization, rather than any specific properties of the technology itself, had laid the foundation for the formation of a coherent administrative logic that would continue to direct the course of future change in library work.

In the absence of a major implementation of new computing tools, library staff tended to be cautiously optimistic about the future. Nevertheless, there were early indications among nonprofessional support staff, in particular, that this administrative ideology of computerization could and, possibly, would be challenged if and when the proposed multifunctional computer system was fully developed and implemented in all areas of the library. Importantly, the bargaining unit for the nonprofessional staff had already wrested an agreement from the administration that would limit the amount of time staff members spent at computer terminals.

During the course of our participant-observation research with staff prior to implementation of "JOSIAH," we heard a number of challenges to the core notions of "centralization," "uniformity," and "nonredundancy." Often presented to use in the form of critical responses to the kind of organizational changes I have outlined above, staff members in different departments argued that key changes and plans for future change often ignored crucial features of the functional interdependence of departments and work-units:

> Things always fall through the cracks, you know. That's just part of the job. But when we were working with all the different files in the system, it was much easier to catch mistakes and track down the source of problems. There was a lot of overlap, a lot of duplication in different places, but that was very helpful.

Many staff members agreed with this assessment, but others added that quality of working conditions was also an issue:

> I've worked here over seven years. I always loved doing searches before. Checking different files was fun. I didn't have to sit in one place. I was always moving around, checking different files, talking to people in other departments. You really felt a part of it all. You really understood how the whole system works. It wasn't boring. But now I hardly ever leave my work area. I spend too much time on RLIN, but mostly I dread those long hours pawing through that awful new in-process file, frustrated because it's messy.... I always find things misfiled anyway and I just don't trust it.

Of all the library staff interviewed, professional catalog librarians most often endorsed the library's new ideology of computerization.

> We have gotten to the point where our productivity has outstripped our abilities to properly maintain manual filing systems.... The online [JOSIAH] will be a godsend. Authority control will be much simpler and more precise and the total number of access points to a single bibliographic record will be easily increased without having the mess of multiple records.

Significantly, this catalog librarian did not think about the fact that this dramatic increase in "productivity" was driven by organizational changes, such as "fast cat," that had been instituted in early anticipation of a computer system none of the staff had even seen. However, when they reflected upon all of the changes taking place before implementation, even catalog librarians could express deep doubts:

> The issue for catalogers is not online or no online. The issue is will the online allow us the creativity and the intellectual challenges of cataloging we all love or will we just become extremely fast typists in the very end? JOSIAH is not here yet, so we just don't know. However, we have seen many changes in the library that make this a very real concern.

In the Public Services Division, reference staff was most critical of the changes:

> Cataloging is not as rich as it used to be. I don't think catalogers are as detailed as they used to be. Records are just not as complete as they used to be, and for those of us who rely heavily on the card catalog to assist patrons this has become a real problem.
>
> Typical patron requests—"I need a book on porcelain design, but it has to have lots of good color photos"; "I need a good source on the Civil War, but it has to have good maps"; "I need a particular edition of that novel, the one that has John Doe's introductory essay." The card catalog was just the tool that allowed us to respond to such daily requests. We can't count on this anymore and this makes our work here very difficult.

Reference libraries were also the quickest to point to a fundamental flaw in the library's vision and strategic plans for computerization:

> We've always had changes in rules and procedures and this will always be the case. The biggest problem is always the same one—collections grow at tremendous speed and the Library of Congress has to work like the devil to keep up with developments in the fields of knowledge. Contrary to what some people around here suppose, you are never going to get a perfect, completed system. Library work is all about staying on top of the constant changes. It won't be any different with JOSIAH. Everybody has to work under conditions of constant change.

"Centralization" of information and "uniformity" of record-keeping were perceived as threatening to many staff because they identified the traditional information environment with its plurality of standardized and nonstandardized sources of information (both paper and electronic) as facilitating the relative independence and autonomy they had always valued in library work. At the same time, some staff argued that because there were significant differences among libraries in the structure and content of their collections and in the organization of their internal records, centralization and uniformity were very questionable goals for any system of information sharing among libraries.

Because "redundancy" of information was a systematic consequence of the evolution of the library's heterogeneous information environment, many staff members were skeptical of the administrative concept of "nonredundancy." Consonant with the high value they placed on independence and relative autonomy, all staff members saw redundancy as an inevitable consequence of constant change and of the fact that every single staff member maintained his or her own private system for keeping records of daily work-flow. These private records helped them control day-to-day continuity in the face of constant change and prevented them from duplicating their own efforts. Most importantly, almost all staff members were certain that redundancy in record keeping fulfilled the crucial institutional function of guarding against the errors of any single individual.

Building on valued understandings of their work routines, a sophisticated knowledge of the social organization of work within the library and a growing realization of the computing changes taking place in other settings at Brown, a few of the more technologically inclined staff members finally began to raise new kinds of questions:

> Look at what's going on with personal computers right here at Brown. Why can't we have it both ways? Why can't we also have our own personal computers, so each of us can manage our own data and download from JOSIAH only what we need when we need it?
>
> We hear they are passing out computers like candy all over the campus. Everyone is supposed to have a computer on his desk. How about us?

Throughout the library questions about ongoing changes and future plans were beginning to lead in the direction of a challenge to the library's authoritative ideology of computerization. In contrast to the library's own, it was clear than an alternative ideology could emerge, one that envisioned a multifunctional computer system that was "decentralized," "nonuniform," and "redundant." In short, although no consensus had emerged, experienced and knowledgeable members were beginning to formulate coherent challenges to the legitimacy of the institution's claim that a new technology required new patterns of work. Most staff firmly believed that the logic of the system could and should support, not redefine, traditional patterns of library work.

Technological choices are always motivated by a variety of nontechnical concerns and considerations. At the same time, specific technological choices are framed by ideologies of computerization that seek to achieve unchallenged authority by erasing the distinction between technical and nontechnical factors and considerations. When this does happen, technological "possibility" becomes defined as technological "necessity." Conversely, challenges to specific ideologies of computerization can only become effective when they successfully reinstate the distinction between technical and nontechnical considerations. Only in this way can they call attention to a wider range of possible definitions of the relationship between technological choice and patterns of work.

In keeping with the great power of ideologies of computerization, there are logical limits to the types of challenges that end users can effectively issue. These are limits that have been set as a consequence of the institution's initial decision to adopt new technologies. Thus, end-user challenges that insist on absolute distinctions between the logic of computing tools and the logic of work—challenges that, in essence, reject the basis of *all* ideologies of computerization—are not likely to have any impact on the authority of the institution's ideology of computerization. Such ineffective challenges cannot change the prevailing shape or direction of sociotechnical change.

As Bourdieu (1977, 1991) convincingly argued for processes of social change in general, the success of subordinate views ("heterodoxa") in challenging dominant views ("orthodoxa") depends on their recognizability as viable alternatives to the holders of dominant views. In the case of the Brown University Library, for example, staff members were quite capable of arguing that there were important qualitative distinctions that distinguished the logic of electronic record keeping from the routine demands of managing the library collections. Nevertheless, most staff members understood that the only opportunity they would have to effect any institutional reformulation of the nature and direction of technological choice would depend on their ability to redefine the connection between the logic of computing tools and the logic of work. The success of any direct challenge would depend on the staff's ability to convince library administrators that some alternative connection between the logic of technology and the logic of work represented a "better" solution to the fundamental problems of library information management.

Case 2: Technological Choice and Instructional Development in a Secondary School

At a private secondary school embarking upon an experiment in instructional computing, the predevelopment planning stage was quite similar to the earliest stages of the Brown University Library project. Teachers (who were also to be the database developers), school administrators, technical support personnel, and outside consultants began to define and coordinate their diverse responsibilities in support of a single, quite specific ideology of computerization.

Self-consciously based on the computerization ideology of Brown's earlier Intermedia Project (cf. Beeman *et al.* 1988), this experiment was to produce a hypertext database of historical and literary resources that would assist students in understanding the relationship between their studies of American literature and their studies of American history. The teacher responsible for coordinating the project first articulated the problem:

> *This important project just might be the answer to our problems. Even though our students are taking both surveys, one in Literature and one in History, and even while we coordinate the teaching of both of these courses, our students* still *do not develop any interesting ideas about the relationship between history and*

literature. Literature is about writing; History is about events. No connection; End of story.

Central to the ideology of computerization defining this project was the presupposition that the logical architecture of hypertext, with its "nonhierarchical webs" of "electronic links" connecting diverse textual and graphic materials, would facilitate an analogous form of integrated understanding in student-users. The project team envisioned as an outcome a "seamless web" of historical-literary knowledge in the minds of high school students.

Although this ideology of computerization provide the impetus and direction for the overall design and organization of activities, some project members were cautiously skeptical of this particular ideology from the very beginning. And in marked contrast to the Brown University Library project, the actual process of developing the new American history/ literature database eventually resulted in the emergence of *two* radically different challenges to the dominant ideology of computerization. A different definition of the form and function of the new computing technology characterized each challenge.

On the one hand, the history teacher/developer gradually came to perceive the computing technology as little more than a medium for electronic storage. At the end of the first year, he and the literature teacher/developer had entered a significant amount of textual, graphic, and audio materials into the computers. But when we questioned him about different strategies for creating electronic links, he redirected our questions:

> *I am not primarily concerned about linkages here and I actually care very little about when, where and how they get created. I think it is far more important that we get a broad range of historical and literary materials into the database for students to use. I don't mean to say that linkages are not important, just secondary.*

This teacher clearly came to see the new technology as a medium for the provision of information. He was most concerned to provide students with independent and immediate access outside of class to the diverse types of materials he had traditionally employed as illustrations and examples to support his lectures and class discussions. During one interview, he told us:

My private files are stuffed with years of accumulated teaching materials. Now I finally have a way of delivering all of that directly into the hands of my students. This is wonderful!

This basic understanding was central to the ways he developed the database and the ways he directed students to make use of the new technology. In his role as developer, he devoted an immense amount of time and effort to scanning pictures, charts, and maps and digitizing audiotapes. Having entered these into the database, he would subgroup them chronologically, using the same historical time-line that defined both the history and the literature courses.

In his role as teacher, he would direct students to prepare for or follow up specific lectures and discussions by reviewing all materials in the database grouped under a specific chronological period of American history. Sometimes he gave them very little direction; at other times he gave them a very specific request for information they could find only in the database. In effect, the database became a basic reference tool for his students.

As he gradually came to articulate it, the computing technology was analogous in form and function to the school's library:

Because of the way we have grouped and sub-grouped both historical and literary materials according to a common time-line, this is much more convenient for our students. Still I think this is just a logical extension of the library.

By the end of the first year of the project, the history teacher had come to view the logic of hypertext with its nonhierarchical webs and linkages as largely irrelevant to his pedagogical goals. In one memorable interview, he told us:

Let's not talk about learning and computers. Let's talk about the relationship between teachers and students because this is at the heart of the matter. It is what we do in the classroom that develops student understanding. The computer lab is just a resource we use to support what goes on in the classroom.

Involved in the same activities and developing the same database, the literature teacher/developer gradually came to perceive the same technology very

differently. She came to see hypertext as a very good medium for the creative exploration of intertexuality and for the rich historical contextualization of literary works. Her academically defined interest in "contextualizing literary texts" inspired her to devote an immense amount of time and effort to the development of a rich hypertext corpus of diverse literary and historical texts and images. She did not agree at all with the history teacher that linkages and webs were secondary:

Doing this work is so exciting. As I discover new materials to enter into the database, and as I study the materials he [the history teacher] has put in, I do find myself thinking very carefully about links and connections. It's quite stimulating, actually, because now I find myself creating new materials to go back and recontextualize what I had done earlier. It's just like doing research and you just can't imagine how much I am enjoying this.

In the second semester of the project, she began directing her students to work intensively with the new hypertext corpora. In preparation for class discussions of specific literary texts, she would give them very broad, sensitizing questions designed to encourage them to think about the relationship between the texts and their historical contexts. Then she would send the students to the computer lab to prepare for the next class discussion.

But she was never completely satisfied with the results of these computer-mediated assignments. At the end of the first year of the project, she concluded unhappily that the electronic corpus was a "lifeless product":

I myself learned a lot doing this, but I don't think the same can be said for my students. I have often devised questions for them to guide them in their use of the computer. I usually did this to set up the next class discussion of a particular assigned text. I just have to say that I have been disappointed by how little this has improved class discussion.

She finally decided that involving students in the active process of "creative research" and "serendipitous discovery" should constitute the desired learning goals, not the careful study of the constructed hypertext corpora themselves. In fact, she finally refused to believe that systematic study of the corpora the teacher/developers had constructed could lead students to an integrated understanding of history and literature.

Our findings at the end of the first year supported her viewpoint. We conducted structured interviews and also "talk aloud" sessions at the computer with each of the students. During these sessions, the student was given the general task of introducing the system to an interviewer, after which the interviewer would instruct her to "show me something interesting that you think you learned while using this system." We found no evidence that any of the students had achieved any integrated understanding of history and literature as a result of working with this new technology (see Graves and Palombo 1989).

Although for very different reasons, the literature teacher would agree with the history teacher that the logic of student learning and understanding was still the logic of the teacher–student relationships, regardless of the technology employed. However, she would not agree with him that the new technology was a "reference" or "a logical extension of the library." She came to see the new technology as analogous in form and function to a tool for the creative inscription, recording, and organization of materials. However, the students, not the teachers, would have to create the databases themselves in order to gain any understanding of the conceptual relevance of webs and linkages.

At the beginning of this experiment, both teachers were quite intrigued by the apparently revolutionary potential of hypertext. Within a year, however, neither teacher believed that there was any necessary connection between the logic of hypertext and the logic of either teaching or learning. For the history teacher, hypertext was little more than a convenient storehouse for his traditional assortment of illustrative and supplementary instructional materials. For the literature teacher, hypertext was a novel and interesting tool students could be taught to employ in the service of a fairly traditional academic process of research and discovery. However, it was decidedly not the logic of hypertext that absorbed her attention. It was the explorative nature of the research process

as she had always known it that she kept in constant focus. She needed to teach them what she herself knew about this process. Hypertext could provide an interesting and convenient tool that "allowed" for this, but there was nothing essential about hypertext that would, as Landow (1990, p. 407) had described it, "encourage" or "demand" new modes of reading, writing, teaching or learning."

Each teacher's understanding and use of this new technology called into question the presupposed intrinsic connection between the logic of hypertext and the logic of student learning and understanding. Nevertheless, neither one of these actual challenges had weakened in the least the legitimacy of that authoritative ideology of computerization that had provided the framework and rationale for this development project. This was because these project members, as developers and as teachers, could not reach consensus on an alternative ideology that could provide a new definition of the technological choice. If they had done so, they could have challenged the legitimacy of the dominant ideology of computerization, thus paving the way for a transformation of strategies for future development, implementation, and use.

The fact that they did not formulate an effective challenge meant that the first year ended as it had begun: Teachers, school administrators, technical support personnel and outside consultants continued to define and coordinate their diverse responsibilities in support of the same ideology of computerization.

Furthermore, by the second year of this project, the scope of the development-implementation effort had been broadened to include the American history and literature teachers and students at a neighboring public high school. As the number of different views proliferated, the possibility of achieving consensus about materials, links, pedagogical strategies, and uses became increasingly remote. As a result, in the second year open discussions about the content and evaluative uses of materials became recast as monolithic, technically defined problems. Fundamental questions about and challenges to the project's ideology of computerization were thus avoided:

[P]roject meetings became arenas in which technical issues like how HyperCard stack icons should be represented were discussed. Issues about which materials should be in the ACCESS corpus and which links should be made there for the most part never became project issues. Instead, when questions of this order arose, they were either masked or reworked into technical idioms (Nyce and Bader 1995, p. 139).

In such cases, the limits of possibility for sociotechnical change continue to be defined and directed entirely by the specific ideology of computerization that framed the institutions' initial technological choices. In such cases, neither Sculley's "avalanche of personal creativity" nor the liberating promise of Turkle's "projective medium" have much to do with the actual consequences of these institutionally defined choices.

THE TECHNO-LOGIC AND SOCIO-LOGIC OF AN INFORMATION SOCIETY

The sheer ubiquity of computing tools and the accelerating interest in taking full advantage of those tools in every domain of contemporary social life could mean that we are well on the way to taking the computer for granted as an essential and unproblematic tool. In a limited sense we already do. For most of us, the "computer revolution" is over.

Government, industry, and education continue to invest heavily in new computing technologies on the basis of explicit claims that computerization entails positive, qualitative changes in productivity, efficiency, and communication. It is this accelerating commitment that Daniel Bell very early identified as one of the defining characteristics that our steady march toward a "post-industrial society" (Bell 1973).

At the same time, a growing number of published case studies of computerization in government, industry, and education demonstrate that the qualitative changes envisioned by designers, developers, and administrators do not necessarily follow from institutional decisions to automate work processes or to adopt new informational technologies. Computers, as the technological utopians, argue, may very well provide limitless technological possibilities. Never-

theless, these are *logical* possibilities, not *socially constituted* possibilities. As I have tried to show in this chapter, although institutions do make and rationalize technological choices in conformity with quite specifically defined ideologies of computerization, end users of new technologies do not necessarily come to understand or to use new computing tools in conformity with those same ideologies.

The case studies presented here show that end users are certainly being socialized into institutionally defined and structured understandings and uses of computing tools. However, they come to subordinate these new technical definitions and expectations to a much broader range of motives, interests, understandings, and experiences than any designer, developer, or administrator could ever technologically encompass. As we have seen, designers, developers, computing administrators, and technical support staff do not pay close attention to the diverse ways in which end users come to understand technological possibilities and limits. If they were to make a commitment to doing so, they would recognize that the fundamental engine for sociotechnical change is neither technical nor economic. It is social, it is conceptual and it is grounded in the practical experiences and understandings of end users. At the same time, we can see how institutional technological choices establish expectations that guide, channel, and limit the realization of end users' motives, interests, understandings, and experiences.

At the level of macroanalysis, these cases show that institutional ideologies of computerization define and objectify the rationale, conditions, opportunities, and limits of sociotechnical change. At the level of microanalysis, however, we have seen that it is the character of end-user response that serves either to reinforce that ideology or to challenge it. End-user challenges, although not limitless, create new possibilities for transforming the rationale, conditions, opportunities, and limits of sociotechnical change.

By proposing a determinate, intrinsic connection between the logic of computing tools and the logic of computing uses, ideologies of computerization promote visions of technologically shaped or driven change. This is a powerful force in our new contemporary society. Ideologies of computerization continue to inform public and scholarly debate over the implications of "an information technology revolution." The media, popular literature, computing journals, grant proposals, and development plans do not reject in toto ideologies of computerization. They only reject specific ideologies of computerization in favor of some alternative ideological formulation of the tool–work relationship.

What seems to characterize our contemporary information society is a continuous contest among diverse ideologies of computerization. This contest is crucial because it prevents us from taking computer technologies totally for granted; it chronically rein-vigorates skeptical denials that there is anything intrinsic to computing tools that channels, shapes, or necessarily facilitates any specific pattern of understanding or use. Ultimately, it is this contest rather than the belief in any specific ideology of computerization that ensures long-term continuous change in technical development, marketing, patterns of use, and end-user knowledge and belief. Our new information society is based on a never-ending search for the perfect fit between technically defined means and socially defined ends. It is nothing other than the search to secure the unfulfilled promises of *all* ideologies of computerization.

REFERENCES

Anderson, K., McClard, A., and Larkin, J. 1995. "The Social Ecology of Student Life: The Integration of Technological Innovation in a Residence Hall." Pp. 141–159 in M. A. Shields (ed.), *Work and Technology in Higher Education*. Hillsdale, NJ: Lawrence Erlbaum Associates.

Beeman, W., Anderson, K., Bader, G., Larkin, J., McClard, A., McQuillan, P., and M. Shields. 1988. *Intermedia: A Case Study of Innovation in Higher Education*. Unpublished report to the Annenberg/CPB Project. Providence, RI: Brown University.

Bell, D. 1973. *The Coming of Post-Industrial Society: A Venture in Social Forecasting*. New York: Basic Books.

Bourdieu, P. 1977. *Outline of a Theory of Practice*. Cambridge: Cambridge University Press.

———. 1991. *Language and Symbolic Power*. Cambridge: Polity Press.

Feenberg, A. 1991. *Critical Theory of Technology*. New York: Oxford University Press.

Giddens, A. 1979. *Central Problems in Social Theory*. Berkeley: University of California Press.

———. 1984. *The Constitution of Society: Outline of the Theory of Structuration*. Berkeley: University of California Press.

Graves, W. III, and Bader, G. 1988. *The Library as Information System: Aspects of Continuity and Change in the Staff's World*. IRIS Technical Report 87-3. Providence, RI: Brown University.

———, and Palombo, M. 1989. *Project Access—Ethnographic Report for Year One*. Unpublished report to McDonnell Foundation and Apple Computer. Providence, RI: Brown University.

———. 1995. "Ideologies of Computerization." Pp. 65–87 in M. A. Shields (ed.), *Work and Technology in Higher Education*. Hillsdale, NJ: Lawrence Erlbaum Associates.

Haas, W. 1980. "Research Libraries and the Dynamics of Change." *Scholarly Publishing*, 11:195–202.

Habermas, J. [1968] 1970a "Technical Progress and the Social Life-World." Pp. 50–80 in *Toward a Rational Society*. Boston: Beacon Press.

———. [1968] 1970b. "Technology and Science as 'Ideology'." Pp. 81–122 in *Toward a Rational Society*. Boston: Beacon Press.

Jones, C. 1985. "Academic Libraries and Computing: A Time of Change." *EDUCOM Bulletin*, 20:9–12.

Landow, G. 1990. "Hypertext and Collaborative Work: The Examples of Intermedia." Pp. 407–428 in J. Galegher, R. Kraut, and C. Egido (eds.), *Intellectual Teamwork: Social and Technological Foundations of Cooperative Work*. Hillsdale, NJ: Lawrence Erlbaum Associates.

Marx, Karl. [1852] 1972. "The Eighteenth Brumaire of Louis Bonaparte." Pp. 594–617 in R. C. Tucker (ed.), *The Marx-Engels Reader*. New York: W. W. Norton & Company.

McQuillan, P. 1995. "Computers and Pedagogy: The Invisible Presence," Pp. 103–129 in M. A. Shields (ed.), *Work and Technology in Higher Education*. Hillsdale, NJ: Lawrence Erlbaum Associates.

Nyce, J., and Bader, G. 1995. "To Move Away from Meaning: Collaboration, Consensus and Work in a Hypermedia Project." Pp. 131–139 in M. A. Shields (ed.), *Work and Technology in Higher Education*. Hillsdale, NJ: Lawrence Erlbaum Associates.

Sack, J. 1986. "Open Systems for Open Minds: Building the Library Without Walls." *College and Research Libraries* 47(6):535–544.

Sculley, J. 1989. "The Relationship Between Business and Higher Education: A Perspective on the 21st Century." *Communications of the ACM*, 32(9):1056–1061.

Shields, M. A. (ed.). 1995. *Work and Technology in Higher Education*. Hillsdale, NJ: Lawrence Erlbaum Associates.

———. 1997a. "Reinventing Technology in Social Theory." Pp. 187–216 in J. Lehmann (ed.), *Current Perspectives in Social Theory*, v. 17. Greenwich, CT: JAI Press.

———. 1997b. "The Invisible Presence: Revealing a Theory of Technology in Habermas' Later Work." Paper presented at the annual meeting of the American Sociological Association, Toronto, August 11.

Turkle, S. 1984. The Second Self: Computers and the Human Spirit. New York: Simon and Schuster.

Weizenbaum, J. 1991. "Against the Imperialism of Instrumental Reason." Pp. 728–742 in C. Dunlop and R. Kling (eds.), *Computerization and Controversy: Value Conflicts and Social Choices*. San Diego: Academic Press.

Winner, L. 1986. *The Whale and the Reactor: A Search for Limits in an Age of High Technology*. Chicago: University of Chicago Press.